Harcourt
Language

W9-CQJ-249

Harcourt

Orlando   Boston   Dallas   Chicago   San Diego

Copyright © 2002 by Harcourt, Inc.

All rights reserved. No part of this publication may be reproduced or transmitted in any form or by any means, electronic or mechanical, including photocopy, recording, or any information storage and retrieval system, without permission in writing from the publisher.

Teachers using HARCOURT LANGUAGE may photocopy Copying Masters in complete pages in sufficient quantities for classroom use only and not for resale.

HARCOURT and the Harcourt Logo are trademarks of Harcourt, Inc.

Acknowledgments appear in the back of this book.

Printed in the United States of America

ISBN 0-15-317841-8

8 9 10 11 12 13 14 15   030   2008 2007 2006 2005

Harcourt
Language

Teacher's Edition

SENIOR AUTHORS
Roger C. Farr ◆ Dorothy S. Strickland

AUTHORS
Helen Brown ◆ Karen S. Kutiper ◆ Hallie Kay Yopp

SENIOR CONSULTANT
Asa G. Hilliard III

CONSULTANT
Diane L. Lowe

Harcourt

Orlando   Boston   Dallas   Chicago   San Diego

Visit *The Learning Site!*
www.harcourtschool.com

Harcourt Language

AUTHORS

Senior Authors

DR. ROGER C. FARR

Chancellor's Professor and Director of the Center for Innovation in Assessment, Indiana University

RESEARCH CONTRIBUTIONS:
Assessment, Portfolios,
Reading-Writing Strategies,
Staff Development

DR. DOROTHY S. STRICKLAND

The State of New Jersey Professor of Reading, Rutgers University

RESEARCH CONTRIBUTIONS:
Emergent Literacy,
Linguistic and Cultural Diversity,
Intervention,
Integrated Language Arts,
Writing

Authors

DR. HELEN BROWN
Assistant Superintendent for Metropolitan
Nashville Schools, Tennessee
RESEARCH CONTRIBUTIONS: Classroom Management,
Listening and Speaking, Staff Development, Curriculum Design

DR. KAREN KUTIPER
English/Language Arts Consultant,
Harris County Department of Education, Texas
RESEARCH CONTRIBUTIONS: Classroom Management,
Listening and Speaking, Staff Development, Early Literacy

DR. HALLIE KAY YOPP
Professor, Department of Elementary Bilingual and
Reading Education, California State University, Fullerton
RESEARCH CONTRIBUTIONS: Emergent Literacy,
Word/Vocabulary Development, Kindergarten Assessment

Senior Consultant

DR. ASA G. HILLIARD III
Fuller E. Callaway Professor of Urban Education,
Department of Educational Foundations,
Georgia State University, Atlanta
RESEARCH CONTRIBUTIONS: Multicultural Literature
and Education

Consultant

DR. DIANE L. LOWE
Professor, Education Department, and Advisor to
the Master of Education in Literacy and Language
Program, Framingham State College, Massachusetts
RESEARCH CONTRIBUTIONS: Literature-based Instruction,
Reading Comprehension, Reading and Writing Connections,
Reader Response

Contents

Unit 1

Social Studies

Grammar: All About Sentences
Writing: Sentences About a Picture
Personal Story

CHAPTER 1   Sentences

CHAPTER 2   Parts of a Sentence

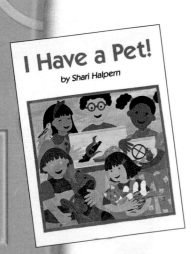

CHAPTER 3   Writer's Craft: Developing Ideas and Topics

Unit 2

Social Studies

Grammar: All About Nouns
Writing: Thank-You Note
Friendly Letter

CHAPTER 7   Nouns

CHAPTER 8   Plural Nouns

CHAPTER 9   Writer's Craft: Adding Details

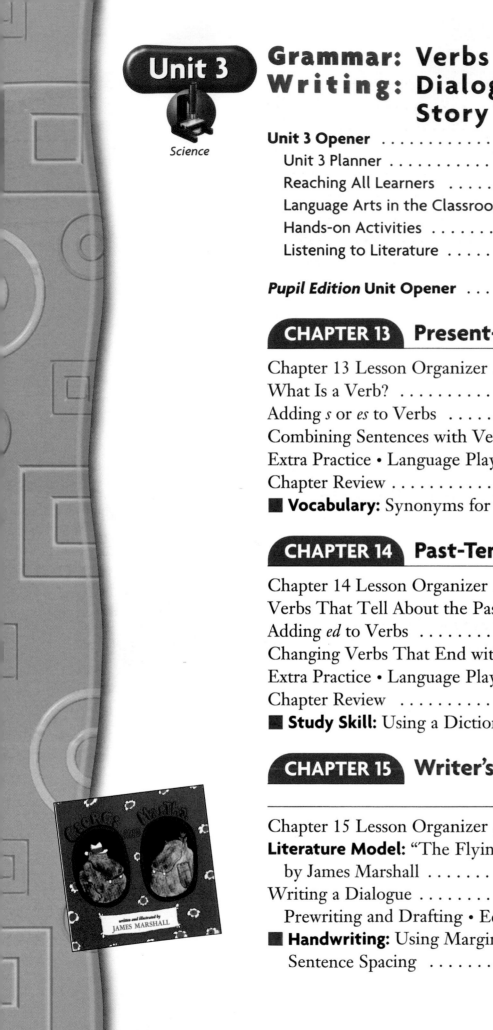

Unit 3

Science

Grammar: Verbs
Writing: Dialogue
Story

CHAPTER 13   Present-Tense Verbs

CHAPTER 14   Past-Tense Verbs

CHAPTER 15   Writer's Craft: Using Quotations to Show Feelings

Unit 4

Science and Math

Grammar: All About Adjectives
Writing: Poem
Expository/Paragraph That Describes

CHAPTER 19   Adjectives

CHAPTER 20   More Adjectives

CHAPTER 21   Writer's Craft: Using Colorful Words

CHAPTER 28　Helping Verbs

CHAPTER 29　Adverbs

CHAPTER 30　Writing Workshop: How-to Paragraph

Unit 6
Science

Grammar: Usage Wrap-Up
Writing: Book Report
Expository/Research Report

CHAPTER 31   Using Nouns and Pronouns Correctly

CHAPTER 32   Using Verbs Correctly

CHAPTER 33   Writer's Craft: Using Examples

Resources

Customizing Instruction

DETERMINING YOUR INSTRUCTIONAL FOCUS

You can use your children's writing to help plan your instruction. First, provide a prompt such as the one at the right to determine children's strengths and weaknesses as writers.

INITIAL WRITING PROMPT What is your favorite season? Write a composition for your teacher. Explain which season is your favorite, and tell why. Be sure to support your ideas with facts and details.

Assess whether children:

- ☑ focus on their purpose and audience for writing
- ☑ use an organization that makes sense
- ☑ express their ideas freely and confidently
- ☑ choose effective words and sentence types
- ☑ support their ideas with facts and details
- ☑ use conventions of standard English, including complete sentences, subject-verb agreement, and appropriate verb tenses
- ☑ use capitalization and end punctuation appropriately

Use the At a Glance section of the *Pupil Edition* table of contents to identify chapters that cover the skills children need.

UNIT-LEVEL PROMPTS A more specific prompt for each unit is provided in the Reaching All Learners section of this *Teacher's Edition*. You can use these prompts to tailor your instruction for individuals or groups. The Reaching All Learners section also provides classroom management suggestions.

Harcourt *Language*

makes it easy to fit thorough, child-centered language arts instruction into your day. You can follow the sequence of the program as it is, or you can use these strategies to suit your individual teaching style.

Assessment Resources

- Student Record Forms — R65–R68
- How to Score Writing and The Traits of Good Writing — R69–R70
- Reproducible Rubrics for Writing — R71–R76
- Student Self-Assessment Checklists — R77–R79
- Formal and Informal Assessment Tools — end of unit
- Language Skills and Writing Assessment including model papers

To adapt rubrics to a 5-6-point scoring system, see How to Score Writing, pages R69–R70 in this *Teacher's Edition*.

TEACHING WRITING WITH *HARCOURT LANGUAGE*

Harcourt Language gives you the instructional tools you need to develop fluent, confident writers.

Build Fluency and Apply Grammar Skills

DAILY LANGUAGE PRACTICE

BRIDGE TO WRITING
Language instruction should build standard usage to help children become effective communicators. In every grammar chapter, Bridge to Writing applies previously learned grammar skills in a sentence-completion activity.

Writing Connection
Harcourt Language provides a wide variety of brief activities that build creativity, confidence, and fluency. The Writing Connections in every grammar chapter apply the grammar skills in fictional, functional, and cross-curricular writing and to pieces in children's Writing Portfolios.

Learn the Strategies Good Writers Use

Writer's Craft In every unit, this chapter teaches the strategies that help children polish their writing—and achieve their highest possible scores—the strategies that make "competent" papers into "outstanding" papers:

- Developing Ideas and Topics
- Adding Details
- Using Quotations to Show Feelings
- Using Colorful Words
- Using Exact Words
- Giving Examples

Children apply writer's craft strategies in fluency-building activities as well as in the context of writing a composition. This experience prepares children for the Writing Workshop chapter.

STANDARDIZED TEST PREP

Harcourt Language makes preparing children for future high-stakes tests a top priority. In addition to a Standardized Test Prep page in every grammar chapter, *Harcourt Language* prepares children for writing tests with instruction in Writer's Craft as well as the most commonly tested writing forms.

Apply Writer's Craft to Longer Writing Forms

Writing Workshop In every unit, this chapter develops a solid foundation in the writing forms that children will encounter most frequently on state and standardized tests:

- Expressive Writing (personal story, friendly letter, story)
- Informative/Expository Writing (paragraph that describes, how-to paragraph, research report)

SENIOR AUTHORS
Roger C. Farr • Dorothy S. Strickland

AUTHORS
Helen Brown • Karen S. Kutiper • Hallie Kay Yopp

SENIOR CONSULTANT
Asa G. Hilliard III

CONSULTANT
Diane L. Lowe

Harcourt

Orlando   Boston   Dallas   Chicago   San Diego

Visit *The Learning Site!*
www.harcourtschool.com

Copyright © 2002 by Harcourt, Inc.

All rights reserved. No part of this publication may be reproduced or transmitted in any form or by any means, electronic or mechanical, including photocopy, recording, or any information storage and retrieval system, without permission in writing from the publisher.

Requests for permission to make copies of any part of the work should be mailed to the following address: School Permissions, Harcourt, Inc., 6277 Sea Harbor Drive, Orlando, Florida 32887-6777.

HARCOURT and the Harcourt Logo are trademarks of Harcourt, Inc.

Acknowledgments appear in the back of this work.

Printed in the United States of America.

ISBN 0-15-319094-9

1 2 3 4 5 6 7 8 9 10 032 2003 2002 2001 2000

Contents

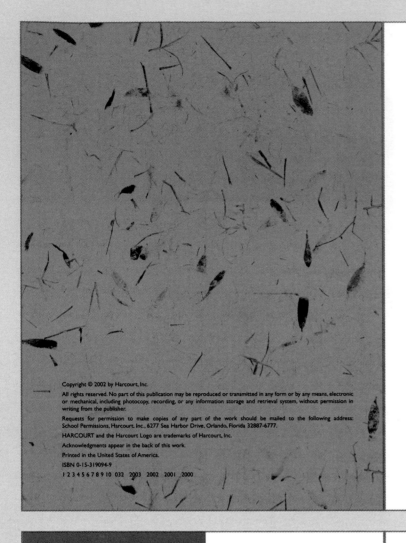

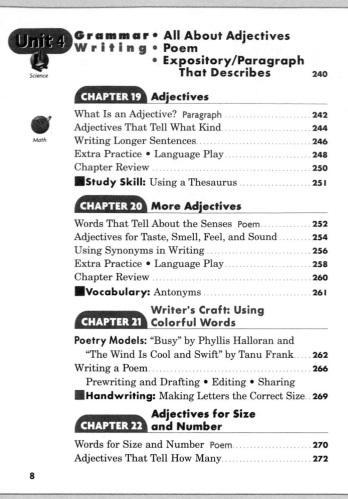

8

9

10

11

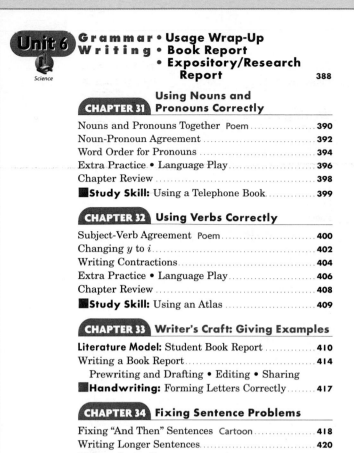

Handbook

Ben Bradshaw
2 Denton Road
Spring Lake, NJ 07762

Tanya Jackson
111 Hicks Street
Brooklyn, NY 11201

14

15

At a Glance

Listening and Speaking

Grammar, Usage, and Mechanics

Writing Forms

Introducing the Book

Preview the Book

Before children read pages 18-21, invite them to comment on the cover and then to preview the book by looking through the table of contents. Point out that a table of contents shows everything in a book in order. This book has six units plus a Handbook at the back. Explain that the Handbook is a reference source that will help children in their writing. The At a Glance section of the table of contents provides a quick way to find specific grammar, writing, and listening and speaking skills.

Grammar

HOW LANGUAGE WORKS

Have children read page 18 silently, including the words on the colored blocks. Then ask a volunteer to read the text aloud. Discuss the answers to the questions, and talk about how our language builds from letters to words and on up to paragraphs and beyond. Then have volunteers give examples for each block.

Writing

THE WRITING PROCESS

Read aloud the introduction to the writing process on page 19, and have volunteers read the information about each stage aloud. Call on children to paraphrase the information in their own words.

Strategies for Writing

What Good Writers Do Read page 20 with children and have them tell how and when they use the strategies. Explain that using writing strategies will help them become better writers and will also help them do their best on writing tests. You may want to have volunteers copy the strategy list onto chart paper to display in the classroom.

Keeping a Journal and a Portfolio

Have children read each section of page 21 and then discuss it. If children do not have notebooks, they can make journals using cardboard, a hole punch, yarn, and paper. Explain that they should write in their journals frequently to record their ideas and reflections. They can also use their journals as a source of ideas that they can discover, develop and refine for longer pieces. Have them reserve a section in the back of their journals for a word bank of interesting words to use in their writing.

You may want to use expandable file folders for portfolios. Keep the portfolios in a special area of the classroom where children can access them easily. In your own records, keep a copy of the Writing Conference Checklist (page R67) for each child. Annotate the form during portfolio conferences to monitor individual children's growth as writers.

The Building Blocks of Language

The language that you read, speak, and write is made up of different parts that work together. Some of these parts you already know. Others you will learn about and use as you read this book. Which of these parts do you already know? Which parts help make up other parts?

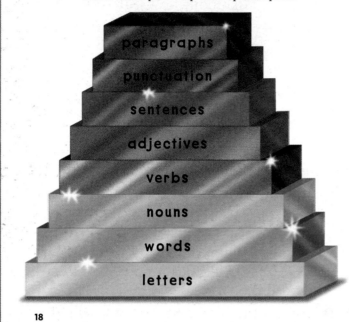

paragraphs

punctuation

sentences

adjectives

verbs

nouns

words

letters

18

The Writing Process

When you write, use a plan to help you. Think about *what* you want to write, for *whom* you are writing, and *why* you are writing. Then use these stages to help you. You can move back and forth between the stages of the writing process at any time.

Prewrite
Plan your writing. Brainstorm ideas. Find information about the idea you choose.

Publish
Decide how you want to publish your writing. Share your writing with others.

Draft
Use your prewriting ideas to write a first draft. Do not worry about making mistakes.

Proofread
Check your writing for mistakes. Correct mistakes in capital letters, end marks, and spelling.

Revise
Read your first draft. Talk about it with others. Change parts to make your writing better.

19

Use these strategies to help you write. Look for What Good Writers Do in every writing chapter.

What Good Writers Do

 List or draw your ideas before you write.

 Remember for whom you are writing and why.

 Use your own words.

 Use an order that makes sense.

 Use different kinds of sentences to make your writing interesting.

 Use exact words.

 Give examples.

 Revise your writing to make it better.

Proofread for grammar, spelling, capitalization, and punctuation.

20

Keeping a Journal

Many writers keep a journal. A **journal** is a place to write down thoughts and record ideas for writing. A journal is also a good place to help you keep a record of interesting things that happen.

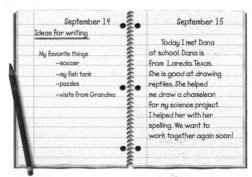

September 14
Ideas for writing

My favorite things
—soccer
—my fish tank
—puzzles
—visits from Grandma

September 15

Today I met Dana at school. Dana is from Laredo, Texas. She is good at drawing reptiles. She helped me draw a chameleon for my science project. I helped her with her spelling. We want to work together again soon!

Vocabulary Power

You may also want to keep a word bank of new words in your journal to use for writing. Look for a new Vocabulary Power word in every chapter of this book.

Keeping a Portfolio

A **portfolio** is a place such as a folder where you keep writing pieces, pictures, and other work. A portfolio helps you see how your work changes over time. Make a portfolio. Keep your work in it. Look at your work over time to see how it gets better.

21

Unit 1

Grammar
- All About Sentences

Writing
- Sentences About a Picture
- Personal Story

September 9

My first day back at school was Wednesday. I met my new teacher, Mr. Connor. He is very nice. I saw most of my friends, too. Timmy sits next to me.

Unit 1

Grammar • Sentences
Writing • Sentences About a Picture
• Personal Story

Chapters	Grammar	Writing	Listening/ Speaking/Viewing
1			
Sentences pp. 24–33	**Sentences** Usage and Mechanics: Word Order in a Sentence, Beginning and Ending a Sentence Extra Practice Chapter Review Daily Language Practice	**Writing Connections** Complete Sentences Proofreading For Sale Sign	**"The Little Turtle"** **Activities** Animal Clues Language Play **Use Prior Knowledge**
2			
Parts of a Sentence pp. 34–43	**Parts of a Sentence** Usage and Mechanics: Naming and Telling Parts, Combining Parts of Sentences Extra Practice Chapter Review Daily Language Practice	**Writing Connections** Revising Drafting Sentence About a Picture	**"April Rain Song"** **Activities** Talk About Something You Like Language Play **Use Prior Knowledge**
3			
Short Process Writing: Sentences About a Picture pp. 44–51	Daily Language Practice	**Sentences About a Picture** Prewriting and Drafting Editing Writer's Craft: Developing Ideas and Topics **Writing and Thinking:** Reflect	**"I Have a Pet!"** **Sharing Sentences About a Picture** **Activities** Read and Respond to the Model Reflect **Use Prior Knowledge**
4			
Statements and Questions pp. 52–61	**Statements and Questions** Usage and Mechanics: Different Kinds of Sentences, Using Statements and Questions Extra Practice Chapter Review Daily Language Practice	**Writing Connections** Sentence Variety Keeping to Main Idea Interview **Activity** Sentences About Color	**"What Is Pink?"** **Activities** Interview a Classmate Language Play **Use Prior Knowledge** Play a Game Mother, May I?
5			
Exclamations and Commands pp. 62–71	**Exclamations and Commands** Usage and Mechanics: Exclamations and Commands, Using Different Kinds of Sentences Extra Practice Chapter Review Daily Language Practice	**Writing Connections** Recipe Revising Directions	**"Hurry!"** **Activities** Share Commands Language Play **Use Prior Knowledge** Simon Says
6			
Long Process Writing: Personal Story pp. 72–89	Daily Language Practice	**Personal Story** Prewriting Drafting Revising Proofreading Publishing **Reading-Writing Connection:** Parts of a Personal Story	Read and Respond to the Model Generate Questions Sharing Your Writing Speaking Tips Listening Tips

Unit Wrap-Up Writing Across the Curriculum: Social Studies, pp. 92–93

Vocabulary/Study Skills/ Technology/ Handwriting

Vocabulary Power

Words of the week: *capture, clutch, grab, grasp,* **seize**
Study Skill: Using the Parts of Your Book

Vocabulary Power

Words of the week: *anthem, folk song, jingle,* **lullaby**, *serenade*
Study Skill: Using Alphabetical Order

Vocabulary Power

Words of the week: **burrow**, *cave, lair, lodge, roost*
Handwriting: Using Correct Position When Writing
Hands-on Activities, pp. 21I–21J

Vocabulary Power

Words of the week: *entirely, mostly, partly, totally,* **wholly**
Vocabulary: Homophones

Vocabulary Power

Words of the week: *agreement, disagreement, disharmory,* **harmony**, *togetherness*
Technology: Using a Computer
Challenge: Computer Time

Vocabulary Power

Words of the week: *brightest,* **glossiest**, *shiniest, sleekest, smoothest*

Language Minutes

- **Begin** a sentence by telling a naming part to a partner. Have your partner add a telling part then begin a new sentence for you to complete. SPEAKING/LISTENING

- **Write** and illustrate a silly sentence using homophones. Some of the words you may want to use are: *see/sea; hear/here; ate/eight.* WRITING

- **Give** a partner directions to find something. Use commands such as: "Turn right," or "Walk to the desk." SPEAKING/LISTENING

- **Create** a story with a partner. Pick a topic you both like. Make sure all your sentences go together. VIEWING/WRITING

- **Make up** sentences about a picture you find in the sports pages of a newspaper. Use different kinds of sentences. SPEAKING/VIEWING

- **Role-Play** an interview with a partner. Take turns playing a famous author and the interviewer. SPEAKING/LISTENING

Technology Resources

Grammar Jingles™ **CD, Primary**
Grammar Practice and Assessment **CD-ROM**
Writing Express **CD-ROM**
Media Literacy and Communication Skills **Package**
 Visit *The Learning Site!*
www.harcourtschool.com

Reaching All Learners

Intervention

SUPPORT ACTIVITIES To help you meet the needs of children who require extra support, use the following activities with individual children or small groups.

- Write sentences by writing the individual words on word cards. Then show the cards to children in scrambled order. Have them put the sentences in the correct order.

- Show children pictures that might represent naming and telling parts of sentences and have them use the pictures to help them form sentences.

- Write a period, a question mark, and an exclamation mark on three large cards. Have children sit in a circle. Say a sentence in a level tone of voice and without expression. Then hold up a chosen end mark for the sentence and have a volunteer repeat the sentence using an appropriate tone of voice.

INTERACTIVE WRITING Use interactive writing as a collaborative event in which you and the children participate in constructing a written message. Throughout the process, your goal is to support children as they build an understanding of how language works. Use these basic tips as you involve children in interactive writing activities:

- Always have children "share the pen," or share the physical act of writing words and sentences with you. This can be done on chart paper, at the board, or on a wipe-off board.

- Carry on a running conversation during interactive writing so that you and your children think aloud as you are composing.

- Use prompts to encourage children to participate actively as well as solve problems. For example, ask, "What kind of sentence might go here?"

Challenge

Some children require more challenging activities. To help you meet the needs of these children, use these suggestions.

- **ILLUSTRATE A SCENE** Have children illustrate a scene from a favorite story. Then have them write complete sentences about the characters and their actions.

- **WRITE SECRET MESSAGES** Have children prepare "secret messages" by substituting symbols or numbers for words or letters. Have children create their own code and write statements, questions, exclamations, or commands using the code, which other children can, in turn, decode.

- **MAKE A POSTER** Have children make a poster that explains what makes a good sentence. Tell them to include information on beginning and ending sentences as well as tell about the parts of sentences.

Inclusion

LEARNING DIFFICULTIES Some children may have difficulty following directions for practice activities. For each activity, provide small-group or one-to-one instruction.

VISUALLY IMPAIRED To help visually-impaired children, use oral-language activities to spark the learning. You may tape-record the four types of sentences, stressing intonation so children can hear the differences.

HEARING IMPAIRED Use graphic aids such as picture/word cards, sentence charts, and webs. Create a bulletin board of sentence types.

Teaching Grammar from Writing

PRETEST
Use the following prompt as a pretest to assess children's ability to write complete sentences, to use different sentence types, and to punctuate sentences.

WRITING PROMPT
Think about something you like to do. Draw a picture. Write two sentences that tell about your picture.

EVALUATE AND PLAN
Analyze children's writing to determine how you can best meet their individual needs for instruction. Use the chart below to identify and remedy problems.

COMMON PROBLEMS	CHAPTERS TO USE
Writes words out of order in sentences.	Chapter 1: Sentences
Does not capitalize the beginning of sentences.	Chapter 1: Sentences
Does not use end punctuation with sentences.	Chapter 1: Sentences
Repeats the subject of sentences instead of combining sentences.	Chapter 2: Parts of a Sentence
Uses only one kind of sentence in writing.	Chapter 4: Statements and Questions
Writes sentences that are unrelated to each other or the topic.	Chapter 4: Statements and Questions

Classroom Management

DURING...	SOME CHILDREN CAN...
Grammar Reteaching	Work on the Writing Across the Curriculum project.
Independent Practice	Begin the Writing Connection. Participate in Language Centers.
Portfolio Conferences	Complete Self-Evaluation forms. (See pages R78–R79 in this *Teacher's Edition*.) Participate in peer conferences.

Approaches to Writing Instruction

LANGUAGE ARTS IN THE CLASSROOM

A variety of approaches to writing instruction may happen in the classroom at any given time. Emergent and early writers will benefit from the language experience approach, shared writing, and interactive writing. Each of these approaches may be used with the writing process.

The following presents information about each kind of writing approach that you may use with your children.

LANGUAGE EXPERIENCE APPROACH The teacher acts as a scribe and records children's ideas in a group setting. This approach allows children to openly express themselves through oral language and not feel threatened because they do not yet possess the mechanics of written language.

SHARED WRITING The teacher works with a small group of children, placing the emphasis on the composing process. The teacher and children work together to plan the text, and then the teacher acts as a facilitator to help children develop and organize ideas.

INTERACTIVE WRITING Shared writing and interactive writing are similar processes except that in interactive writing, the teacher and the children "share the pen." The teacher determines when to involve children in the writing based on the focus of instruction. The teacher models the writing form and shapes children's language through prompts that help them write words and phrases.

GUIDED WRITING The teacher offers assistance by guiding students' writing, responding to it, and extending children's thinking in the composing process. Guided writing may happen during whole class, small group, or one-to-one instruction as part of the Writing Workshop. The teacher's role is one of facilitator helping children discover what they want to say and how to express it in writing with clarity.

Interactive Writing

Interactive writing is a form of assisted writing or scaffolded instruction. Interactive writing is a process in which the teacher and children compose and construct a written message. The teacher acts as a model, demonstrating the writing process of composing texts while both the teacher and children scribe.

Interactive writing includes these stages.

CONSTRUCT THE TEXT After the teacher and children determine the purpose and the audience they are writing for, they "share the pen," writing the text together letter by letter or word by word. This allows the children to think about how they are using language to communicate meaning. The teacher or the children direct attention to particular features of words and talk about them.

REREAD, REVISE, AND PROOFREAD These steps serve as an opportunity to clarify and enhance the meaning of texts. They also teach children to

- check their work as they write
- recognize the importance of conventions
- check the meaning of the text.

REVISIT THE TEXT It is important to revisit the text to focus on concepts related to word solving. Word solving helps children figure out unfamiliar words as they read and spell words as they write. The teacher should help children

- notice that some words look like other words
- recognize word parts
- connect words by how they look.

Hands-on Activities

Word-Order Fun

MATERIALS: tagboard strips

DIRECTIONS:

1. Write the words to well-known nursery rhymes on tagboard strips, one word per strip.

2. Have children form small groups. Give each group the words for one rhyme.

3. Have children reconstruct the rhymes by putting the words in order. Then have them read the rhymes aloud.

Mary had a little lamb.

Discovery Sentences

MATERIALS: old newspapers, magazines

DIRECTIONS:

1. Have children cut out pictures from newspapers or magazines showing different events, such as a sports game, a parade, or people doing things together.

2. Ask children to write different sentences about their pictures to help them discover ideas about what they see.

3. After they are finished, tell children to circle one main idea about the pictures and share that sentence with classmates.

Sentence-Part Salad

MATERIALS: tagboard, colored markers, tape or glue

DIRECTIONS:

1. Write sentences on tagboard strips. Cut the strips in half so that one half has the naming part of the sentence and one half has the telling part.

2. Shuffle the strips and place in a pile.

3. Have children take turns choosing strips from the pile until everyone has a whole sentence that makes sense.

4. Children can read their sentences aloud. Then have them make a chart with the headings Naming Part and Telling Part and tape their sentence parts on the chart for other children to read and share.

Naming Part	Telling Part
The children	ate lunch.
The rangers	keep the park clean.

Question-and-Answer Speech Balloons

MATERIALS: white paper, scissors, glue or tape, pictures of people talking, old magazines

DIRECTIONS:

1. Gather or cut out pictures of people who are speaking to other people.

2. Children work in pairs. Have them select a picture and write a statement or question for each person pictured.

3. Have children cut out their questions or statements in the shape of speech balloons. Children can tape their speech balloons above the pictures and then share them with other pairs.

Sentence Shuffle

MATERIALS: 3 boxes, markers, paper

DIRECTIONS:

1. Write the words *commands, exclamations,* and *questions* on three different boxes.

2. Have children work in small groups to write several commands, exclamations, and questions.

3. Then have children shuffle their sentences and place them face down in a pile.

4. Children take turns selecting a sentence, reading it aloud using the appropriate expression, and then placing it in the correct box.

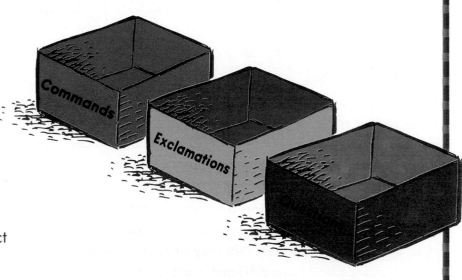

THE PERFECT SPOT

BY ROBERT J. BLAKE

WHEN DAD GOES INTO THE WOODS, he brings his paints, his easel, and a big canvas. When I go into the woods with him, I bring a net, a jar, and some shortbread. We share the shortbread.

My dad has been all over the woods looking for just the right scene to make just the right painting. He likes oak trees, shadows, rocks, and water.

I have been all over the woods looking for a unicorn beetle, a sphinx caterpillar, and a green cricket frog.

I found a red salamander under a rock.

"Look, Dad," I said. But he was busy. I found an ambush bug and a unicorn beetle, and dropped them into my jar together. "Don't fight, you guys," I told them.

We hurried on. We hadn't found the right spot yet.

"This looks like a good place," I said. There were lots of trees.

"Too gray."

"How about over here?" The shadows were great.

"We did that yesterday."

"Do you like this old stump?"

"I'm not in a stump mood," Dad grumbled. So we kept walking. A good spot can be hard to find.

We hiked on the trail and off the trail. We climbed up the hill, down through the glen, and over the footbridge. My legs were getting tired.

"Can we stop and look for a frog?"

"Not now!" Dad said.

Then I saw the waterfall.

"How about that?" I asked.

There were trees, rocks, and shadows. Even Dad seemed interested. And on the other side of the water, under a big tree root, was a green cricket frog! I snuck up on it as quietly as I could.

Just as I was about to catch it Dad yelled, "COME ON! LET'S MOVE ON!"

Building Background

Author Robert J. Blake is a painter as well as a writer. He often takes his own son, Christian, on outings into the woods to find scenes to paint. Blake lives in New Jersey. He has illustrated other books, such as *Riptide* by Frances Ward Weller and *Finding Foxes* by Allison Blyler.

INTRODUCE THE LISTENING SELECTION You may wish to tell children that this personal story is told from the point of view of a young boy who accompanies his father in the woods. Suggest that they think about how the man and the boy have different plans as the story unfolds.

Determine a Purpose for Listening

Tell children that this selection is a personal story that describes an adventure in the woods shared by a painter and his son. Ask children to decide whether their purpose for listening is

- to gain information
- to solve problems
- to enjoy and appreciate. (to enjoy and appreciate)

The frog jumped. I jumped. I tried to grab it but I missed. I slipped and fell and I wound up in the stream.

Dad dropped his painting gear, and crossed from rock to rock. He hit one that I had gotten all wet, slipped, his foot went in, and he got a soaker.

I sat still and tried to be small. I was sure he was going to yell at me.

But he didn't. He just started laughing.

He bumped me with his shoulder and I bumped him back. He splashed me and I splashed him back. For a while we ran around and bumped and splashed and laughed.

Then for a while we said nothing.

"Should we move on now?" I asked.

"Why?" he said. "We've found the perfect spot!"

Dad hummed as he set up his easel and began to paint.

I poked around the rocks, and before long, out came the green cricket frog. We sat and blinked at each other.

I didn't try to catch him this time.

Listening Comprehension

LISTEN FOR TOPIC, MAIN IDEAS, AND DETAILS Explain to children that in this passage, the narrator tells how two characters have different thoughts about how to spend their time in the woods and what makes the perfect spot. You may want to pause after the beginning to allow children to discuss what they think are the topic and main ideas of the story. Invite children to listen for details that support the main ideas.

```
TOPIC

   MAIN IDEA

          DETAILS

   MAIN IDEA

          DETAILS
```

PERSONAL RESPONSE *How does the writer develop the main idea about what the man and boy each wanted to do?* (Possible responses: The writer develops the main idea by giving examples and details, such as the insects and frogs that the boy wants to catch, or the tree stumps the father might want to paint.) INFERENTIAL: AUTHOR'S CRAFT

Unit 1

Grammar
- Sentences

Writing
- Sentences About a Picture
- Personal Story

Introducing the Unit

ORAL LANGUAGE/VIEWING

DISCUSS THE IMAGES. Tap children's prior knowledge by inviting them to name and then to tell about using the items they see on these two pages. Then have children look at and read the journal entry. Guide them to notice that the writer included thoughts and feelings as well as told what happened. Then ask questions such as these:

- **Which item in the photograph is your favorite? Why?** (Responses will vary.)
- **How do you think the journal writer felt about the first day of school?** (Responses will vary.)
- **Does anyone here keep a journal at home? What kinds of things do you write or draw in it?** (Responses will vary.)

ENCOURAGE CHILDREN'S QUESTIONS. List children's responses on the board. Encourage children to ask about how others use their personal journals. Then have children write journal entries that tell about something that happened at school.

Unit 1

Grammar
- All About Sentences

Writing
- Sentences About a Picture
- Personal Story

22

Viewing and Representing

• • • • • • • • • • • • • • • • • • • •

COMPARE/CONTRAST PRINT AND VISUAL MEDIA Have children find photographs or draw pictures that illustrate their journal entries. Invite children to share their pictures and journal entries with the class and to explain how the information in the pictures is similar to and different from the information in the journal entries.

MEDIA LITERACY AND COMMUNICATION SKILLS PACKAGE Use the video to extend children's oral and visual literacy. See pages 6–7 of the *Teacher's Guide*.

September 9

My first day back at school was Wednesday. I met my new teacher, Mr. Connor. He is very nice. I saw most of my friends, too. Timmy sits next to me.

23

Previewing the Unit

Read and discuss the unit contents list with children. Ask them to explain in their own words the terms they already recognize, such as *sentence*, *statement*, *question*, *exclamation*, and *command*. Tell them that in this unit they will learn more about sentences and the parts of a sentence. Point out the two writing chapters in this unit. Explain that they will learn how to write different kinds of sentences to make their writing better when they write about a picture and write a personal story.

SOCIAL STUDIES CONNECTIONS Children will be exposed to a variety of social studies topics in this unit:

- Teamwork
- Sports
- Pets
- Activities
- Cooking

School-Home Connection

You may want to use Home Letter 1, page R94.

LESSON ORGANIZER	DAY 1 	DAY 2
DAILY LANGUAGE PRACTICE TRANSPARENCIES 1, 2	1. Stan haz many stamps. (has) 2. He keps them in a big book. (keeps) **Bridge to Writing** Stan ___ (form of like) to collect stamps.	1. the girl singh a song. (The; sings) 2. The children keep teh beat (the; .) **Bridge to Writing** Mom listens to our song ___ (punctuation mark)
ORAL WARM-UP Listening/Speaking	Use Sentences to Describe p. 24	Sentence Completion p. 26 *Grammar Jingles™* CD Track 1
TEACH/MODEL GRAMMAR **KEY** ✔ = tested skill	✔ **WHAT IS A SENTENCE?** pp. 24–25 • To listen critically to interpret and evaluate a poem • To understand that a sentence is a group of words that tells a complete thought	✔ **WORD ORDER IN A SENTENCE** pp. 26–27 • To understand that the words in a sentence should be in an order that makes sense • To use words in an order that makes sense when writing sentences
Reaching All Learners	**Challenge:** Activity Card 1 p. R41 *Practice Book* p. 1 **ESL:** *ESL Manual* pp. 8, 9 **Reteach:** *Reteach Activities Copying Masters* p. R17	**Modified Instruction** Below-Level: Write and Order Sentences Above-Level: Write Additional Sentences **ESL:** Word Order p. 26 *ESL Manual* pp. 8, 10 **Reteach:** *Reteach Activities Copying Masters* p. R17
WRITING	Writing Complete Sentences p. 25 Summarize/Reflect	Writing Connection p. 27 Writing Complete Sentences Summarize/Reflect
CROSS-CURRICULAR/ ENRICHMENT	**Vocabulary Power** Word Meaning p. 24 **seize**, capture, clutch, grab, grasp See *Vocabulary Power* book.	**Vocabulary Power** Synonyms p. 24 *Vocabulary Power* book p. 1 **Vocabulary activity**

UNIT 1

DAY 3	DAY 4	DAY 5
1. Ruby teh crayon uses. (uses the crayon)	**1.** mary has a new book (Mary; .)	**1.** vicky likes to .draw (Vicky; draw.)
2. She an apple. draws (She draws an apple.)	**2.** it Is about animals. (It; is)	**2.** She Drew the Garden. (drew; garden)
Bridge to Writing I have a (describing word) sweater.	**Bridge to Writing** She loves books about animals (end punctuation)	**Bridge to Writing** The flowers are pretty (punctuation mark)
Write Complete Sentences p. 28 *Grammar Jingles*™ CD Track 1	Describe Objects p. 30	
✔ **BEGINNING AND ENDING A SENTENCE** pp. 28–29 • To understand that a sentence begins with a capital letter and ends with an end mark • To write sentences using correct capitalization and end punctuation	**EXTRA PRACTICE** p. 30 • To understand the correct word order, capitalization, and punctuation in a sentence • To use sentences in writing 🏆 **Practice and Assessment**	**TEST PREP CHAPTER REVIEW** p. 32 • To review word order, capitalization, and punctuation • To identify parts of a book 🏆 **Test Preparation**
Modified Instruction Below-Level: Underline First and Last Words Above-Level: Write Additional Sentences **ESL:** *ESL Manual* pp. 8, 11 **Reteach:** *Reteach Activities Copying Masters* p. R17 **Challenge:** *Changing Sentences* p. 29	**Challenge:** Catalogs p. 31 *Practice Book* p. 4 **ESL:** Write About a Toy p. 30 *ESL Manual* pp. 8, 12	**Challenge:** Finding the Parts of a Book p. 33 *ESL Manual* pp. 8, 13 *Practice Book* p. 5
Writing Connection p. 29 Proofreading Summarize	Writing Connection p. 31 For Sale Sign	Study Skill p. 33 Using the Parts of Your Book
Vocabulary Power Word Families p. 24 *Vocabulary Power* book p. 2	**Vocabulary Power** Figurative Language p. 24 *Vocabulary Power* book p. 3 🏆 **Vocabulary activity**	**Vocabulary Power** Graphics/Art p. 24

What Is a Sentence?

OBJECTIVES
- To listen critically to interpret and evaluate a poem
- To understand that a sentence is a group of words that tells a complete thought

SPIRAL REVIEW

DAILY LANGUAGE PRACTICE

TRANSPARENCY I

① Stan haz many stamps. (has)

② He keps them in a big book. (keeps)

BRIDGE TO WRITING Stan ___ (form of *like*) to collect stamps.

ORAL WARM-UP

USE PRIOR KNOWLEDGE Show children a picture of a turtle. Ask volunteers to describe what they see and to imagine or show how a turtle might act. Encourage children to say complete sentences by beginning each response with the words "A turtle . . ." Write some of the sentences on chart paper.

TEACH/MODEL

Call on a volunteer to read the title of the poem. Have children discuss what they think they will read in the poem. Read the poem aloud, pausing at the end of each sentence. Then reread the poem, asking children to join you. Remind them to adapt their volume as they read chorally.

DEVELOP ORAL LANGUAGE Have children share their favorite lines from the poem. Explain that each line of the first verse of the poem is a sentence. Ask volunteers to demonstrate or say other sentences that might describe the turtle in the poem. Add their sentences to the list on chart paper.

What Is a Sentence?

Read the poem.

The Little Turtle

There was a little turtle.
He lived in a box.
He swam in a puddle.
He climbed on the rocks.

He snapped at a mosquito,
He snapped at a flea,
He snapped at a minnow.
And he snapped at me.

He caught the mosquito,
He caught the flea,
He caught the minnow.
But he didn't catch me.

Vachel Lindsay

24

Vocabulary Power

DAY ① WORD MEANING Introduce and define *seize* (to take, to grab onto). Have volunteers demonstrate the meaning by seizing various classroom items.

DAY ② SYNONYMS Write: *seize, bring, grab*. **Which of the words have the same meaning?** (See also *Vocabulary Power*, page 1.)

DAY ③ WORD FAMILIES List: *seize, seizes, seized*. **What other endings can be added to *seize*?** (See also *Vocabulary Power*, page 2.)

DAY ④ FIGURATIVE LANGUAGE Write: *I was seized by a need for ice cream.* **What does this sentence mean?** (See also *Vocabulary Power*, page 3.)

DAY ⑤ GRAPHICS/ART Invite children to make posters to illustrate the saying "Seize the Day!"

Say clues for your classmates about an animal and what it does, but do not tell its name. Make your clues sound like the lines in "The Little Turtle."

> A **sentence** is a group of words that tells a complete thought. It begins with a capital letter and ends with an end mark.
>
> **T**he turtle swims in the pond**.**

Work with a partner. Add a word to each group of words to make a sentence. Possible responses are given.

There was a little ____boy____.

He lived in a ____house____.

He ____fell____ in a puddle.

He ____climbed____ on the rocks.

He caught a ____turtle____.

He ____caught____ a flea.

He caught a ____bug____.

But he didn't catch ____me____.

25

WRITE Write children's clue sentences on the board. Have children practice reading them. Then read the definition and example on page 25 with children. Call on volunteers to point to the beginning and end of each sentence on the board.

Read the first item at the bottom of page 25 with children. Have them work in pairs to complete the sentences and share them with the class. Have volunteers read their sentences aloud.

WRAP-UP/ASSESS

SUMMARIZE Reread the poem with children. Then have them summarize and reflect on what they learned about sentences. You may want to have children write their reflections in their journals, or to record sentences they made while completing the page. **REFLECTION**

REACHING ALL LEARNERS RETEACH

INTERVENTION Lessons in **visual**, **auditory**, and **kinesthetic** modalities: p. R17 and *Reteach Activities Copying Masters*, p. 1.

page 1

What Is a Sentence?

Read each group of words aloud. Circle the sentence in each pair.

1. (Becky kicks the ball.)   3. The ball
   Becky kicks the   (The ball is in the goal.)

2. gives it a hard   4. (Becky scores a point.)
   (She gives it a hard kick.)   scores a point.

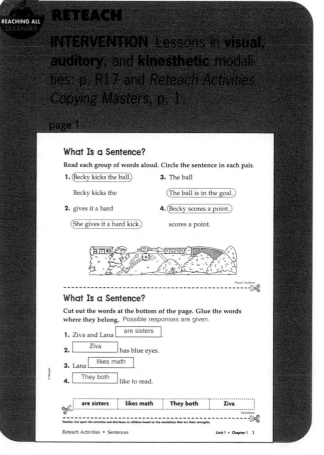

What Is a Sentence?

Cut out the words at the bottom of the page. Glue the words where they belong. Possible responses are given.

1. Ziva and Lana | are sisters |

2. | Ziva | has blue eyes.

3. Lana | likes math |

4. | They both | like to read.

| are sisters | likes math | They both | Ziva |

Reteach Activities • Sentences   Unit 1 • Chapter 1 1

REACHING ALL LEARNERS PRACTICE page 1

Name _____

What Is a Sentence?

A. Draw a line under each sentence.

1. The family is building a treehouse.
2. Mandy hammers the nails.
3. paints the wood.
4. Dad sews drapes.
5. The little sister

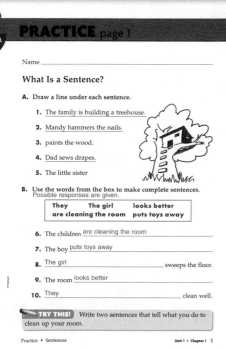

B. Use the words from the box to make complete sentences. Possible responses are given.

| They | The girl | looks better |
| are cleaning the room | puts toys away | |

6. The children are cleaning the room

7. The boy puts toys away

8. The girl _____ sweeps the floor.

9. The room looks better

10. They _____ clean well.

> **TRY THIS!** Write two sentences that tell what you do to clean up your room.

Practice • Sentences   Unit 1 • Chapter 1 1

REACHING ALL LEARNERS CHALLENGE

MAKE A TURTLE BOX Have children use **Challenge Activity Card 1** (page R41) to make the box where the turtle lives. Invite groups of children to use their clay models to act out the poem. Children can store their models in the box.

Challenge Activity Card 1

Make a Turtle Box

Word Order in a Sentence

OBJECTIVES
- To understand that the words in a sentence should be in an order that makes sense
- To use words in an order that makes sense when writing sentences

DAILY LANGUAGE PRACTICE

TRANSPARENCY 1

1. the girl singh a song. (The; sings)
2. The children keep teh beat (the; .)

BRIDGE TO WRITING Mom listens to our song (punctuation mark)

ORAL WARM-UP

AROUND THE ROOM Say the beginning of a sentence and ask a volunteer to complete it. Continue around the classroom with one child beginning a sentence and another child completing it.

Grammar Jingles™ **CD, Primary** Use Track 1 for review and reinforcement of sentences.

TEACH/MODEL

Write each word of the example sentence on a separate word card. Place the cards in random order and have children read the sentence you've formed. Discuss whether the sentence makes sense or not. Keep shifting the order of the words until children think the sentence makes sense. Then read and discuss the explanation and examples on page 26. Have children point to the beginning and end of the sentence.

GUIDED PRACTICE Work with children to complete each sentence. Encourage children to read each sentence aloud to decide whether it makes sense or not.

Word Order in a Sentence

The words in a sentence should be in an order that makes sense. If the words are mixed up, the sentence does not make sense.

Sentence	The boy plays a trumpet.
Not a Sentence	The plays trumpet boy a.

Guided Practice

Write each group of words in an order that makes sense.

1. Sol plays piano the.
   Sol plays the piano.
2. Fern the beats drum loudly.
   Fern beats the drum loudly.
3. blows clearly horn He the.
   He blows the horn clearly.
4. Mona guitar the strums.
   Mona strums the guitar.
5. the Everyone to listens band.
   Everyone listens to the band.

26

Vocabulary Power page 1

Name _____ Synonyms

Synonyms are words that have similar meanings.

small–little–tiny   jump–leap–hop   cry–sob–weep

The word *seize* has many synonyms. Read the words in the box. Circle the four words that mean the same or almost the same as *seize*.

(grab)	forget	drop	(capture)
lose	(clutch)	(grasp)	shout

Draw a picture to show the meaning of each action.

grab	capture
Pictures will vary.	
clutch	grasp

Vocabulary Power   Unit 1 • Chapter 1   1

REACHING ALL LEARNERS   **ESL**

WORD ORDER Some children may have trouble with word order in English, such as where to place subjects or adjectives. Write on a strip of paper, a short sentence such as *I have a blue cap*. Read it aloud with children. Then cut out and mix up the words. Have volunteers put the words back in order. Repeat with another sentence, without showing the correct word order first.

Remember The words in a sentence should be in an order that makes sense.

Independent Practice

Write each group of words in an order that makes sense.

6. Tony likes to hats wear.
   Tony likes to wear hats.
7. are dresses pretty Purple.
   Purple dresses are pretty.
8. Mary sneakers buys red.
   Mary buys red sneakers.
9. Cara running has shoes.
   Cara has running shoes.
10. wears José boots cowboy.
    José wears cowboy boots.
11. has Lucy pretty sweaters.
    Lucy has pretty sweaters.
12. Pablo wear vests likes to.
    Pablo likes to wear vests.
13. Some baseball children collect caps.
    Some children collect baseball caps.
14. wears Wally striped socks.
    Wally wears striped socks.
15. closet in Red the dresses hang.
    Red dresses hang in the closet.

Writing Connection

Writing Complete Sentences What kinds of clothes do you like? Write sentences that tell about their color and style. Then draw pictures to go with the sentences. Put the sentences and the pictures together to make a catalog.

27

Independent Practice

Have children complete the Independent Practice, or modify it by using the following suggestions:

MODIFIED INSTRUCTIONS

BELOW-LEVEL STUDENTS Suggest children write on a separate piece of paper each word of a sentence and order the words until the sentence makes sense.

ABOVE-LEVEL STUDENTS After children are finished, have them choose words from different sentences in the activity to write at least three more sentences.

Writing Connection

Writing Complete Sentences Remind children that the words in a sentence should be in an order that makes sense.

Sharing Basket As children generate their catalogs and other writing, encourage them to place pieces in the Sharing Basket. Allow time for children to read aloud their writing from the Author's Chair.

WRAP-UP/ASSESS

SUMMARIZE Ask children to reflect on what they know about sentences and summarize their learning. **REFLECTION**

REACHING ALL LEARNERS — RETEACH

INTERVENTION Lessons in **visual, auditory,** and **kinesthetic** modalities, p. R17 and *Reteach Activities Copying Masters*, p. 2,

page 2

REACHING ALL LEARNERS

PRACTICE page 2

Name _____

Word Order in a Sentence

A. Read the groups of words. Underline the sentences that are in the correct order.

1. Gloria likes oranges.
2. apple juice always drinks Jem.
3. favorite her drink It is.
4. Bananas are tasty.
5. Luis likes grapes best.

B. Write each group of words in an order that makes sense.

6. food. Bob likes spicy

   Bob likes spicy food.

7. lots of Sue eats fruit.

   Sue eats lots of fruit.

8. Jake to drink wants milk.

   Jake wants to drink milk.

TRY THIS! Think about a healthful food that you like to eat. Write sentences to tell about the food.

2 Unit 1 • Chapter 1   Practice • Sentences

REACHING ALL LEARNERS

CHALLENGE

PAPER BAG SENTENCES Fill paper bags with word strips cut out from different sentences, such as the sentences on pages 26–27. In teams, have children use the words to make as many sentences as possible. Make a class list of sentences by asking volunteers to record the group sentences on chart paper.

Word Order in a Sentence

Read each group of words in Column A aloud. Draw a line to the sentence in Column B that shows the words in the correct order.

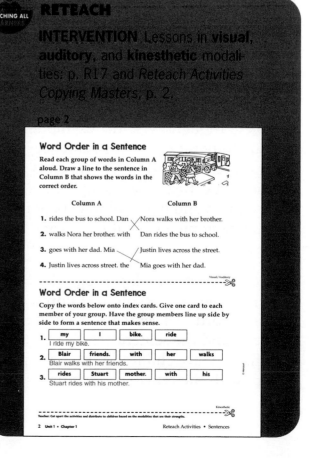

Column A	Column B
1. rides the bus to school. Dan	Nora walks with her brother.
2. walks Nora her brother. with	Dan rides the bus to school.
3. goes with her dad. Mia	Justin lives across the street.
4. Justin lives across street. the	Mia goes with her dad.

Visual/Auditory

Word Order in a Sentence

Copy the words below onto index cards. Give one card to each member of your group. Have the group members line up side by side to form a sentence that makes sense.

1. | my | I | bike. | ride |
   I ride my bike.

2. | Blair | friends. | with | her | walks |
   Blair walks with her friends.

3. | rides | Stuart | mother. | with | his |
   Stuart rides with his mother.

Kinesthetic

Teacher: Cut apart the activities and distribute to children based on the modalities that are their strengths.

2 Unit 1 • Chapter 1   Reteach Activities • Sentences

Beginning and Ending a Sentence

OBJECTIVES

- To understand that a sentence begins with a capital letter and ends with an end mark
- To write sentences using correct capitalization and end punctuation

DAILY LANGUAGE PRACTICE

TRANSPARENCY I

1 Ruby teh crayon uses. (uses the crayon.)

2 She an apple. draws (She draws an apple.)

BRIDGE TO WRITING I have a (describing word) sweater.

ORAL WARM-UP

USE PRIOR KNOWLEDGE Invite volunteers to say sentences about themselves. Write the sentences on chart paper. Then ask children to come forward and underline the first letter of a sentence and circle the end mark.

Grammar Jingles™ **CD, Primary** Use Track 1 for review and reinforcement of sentences.

TEACH/MODEL

Remind children that a sentence tells a complete thought. Use the examples in the box to point out that a sentence begins with a capital letter and ends with an end mark. Read the example sentences aloud and have volunteers point out the beginning capital letters and end marks.

GUIDED PRACTICE Work through the first sentence together. Remind children that the first word of a sentence needs a capital letter and the sentence ends with an end mark. Have children repeat the procedure with the remaining sentences.

Beginning and Ending a Sentence

> A sentence begins with a capital letter and ends with an end mark.
>
> **J**immy likes to draw.
> **H**is sister likes to paint.

Guided Practice

Write each sentence correctly.

1. caleb mixes the paints
   Caleb mixes the paints.
2. i always draw flowers
   I always draw flowers.
3. my mom likes to use crayons
   My mom likes to use crayons.
4. dad enjoys cutting out pictures
   Dad enjoys cutting out pictures.
5. my grandpa paints a picture
   My grandpa paints a picture.

28

Vocabulary Power page 2

Name _____

Endings can be added to base words to make new words.

| help | pitch | stop | like | run | make |
| helps | pitches | stopped | liked | running | making |

Fill in the chart to make new words.

Base Word	Add s or es	Add ed	Add ing
grasp	grasps	grasped	grasping
clutch	clutches	clutched	clutching
grab	grabs	grabbed	grabbing
seize	seizes	seized	seizing
capture	captures	captured	capturing

Choose one of the words you wrote in the chart. Draw a picture and write a sentence using the word.

2   Unit 1 • Chapter 1   Vocabulary Power

REACHING ALL LEARNERS · ESL

DESCRIPTIONS Display an object such as a toy or a fruit from a foreign country. Invite children to describe the object, using complete sentences. Write some of the sentences on the board. Then call on volunteers to underline the capital letter at the beginning of each sentence or the end mark.

Remember A sentence begins with a capital letter and ends with an end mark.

Independent Practice

Write each sentence correctly.

6. we can make a picture together
   We can make a picture together.
7. i want to draw the animals
   I want to draw the animals.
8. you can draw the sky
   You can draw the sky.
9. megan can help
   Megan can help.
10. she is a good artist
    She is a good artist.
11. we can cut out shapes
    We can cut out shapes.
12. my little brother likes to use glue
    My little brother likes to use glue.
13. he will glue the shapes
    He will glue the shapes.
14. he can add glitter
    He can add glitter.
15. we made a beautiful picture
    We made a beautiful picture.

Writing Connection

Proofreading Look through your Writing Portfolio. Choose a piece of writing. Check to see that each sentence begins with a capital letter and ends with an end mark. Fix any mistakes.

Hold down the *shift* key and press the letter key to make a capital letter.

29

Independent Practice

Have children complete the Independent Practice, or modify it by using the following suggestions:

MODIFIED INSTRUCTION

BELOW-LEVEL STUDENTS Have children underline the first and last words in each item. They can then rewrite the item, beginning the first word with a capital letter and adding an end mark after the last word.

ABOVE-LEVEL STUDENTS After children are finished, have them write additional sentences. They can then share them with a partner to make sure they used the correct capitalization and end punctuation.

Writing Connection

Proofreading Help children select an appropriate piece of writing to proofread. Suggest that they underline the first letter at the beginning of each sentence and circle the end mark.

WRAP-UP/ASSESS

SUMMARIZE Ask children to summarize and reflect about what they have learned about sentences. **REFLECTION**

RETEACH

INTERVENTION Lessons in **visual, auditory,** and **kinesthetic** modalities: p. R17 and *Reteach Activities Copying Masters*, p. 3.

REACHING ALL LEARNERS

PRACTICE page 3

Name _____

Beginning and Ending a Sentence

A. Read each pair of sentences. Circle the sentence that begins and ends correctly.

1. (The girl picks red and yellow flowers.)
   the girl picks red and yellow flowers.
2. she wants to give them to her mom
   (She wants to give them to her mom.)
3. (The flowers smell sweet.)
   The flowers smell sweet

B. Write each sentence correctly.

4. the baby can clap
   The baby can clap.
5. the boy knows how to walk
   The boy knows how to walk.
6. my big sister writes her name
   My big sister writes her name.

TRY THIS! Draw pictures of three people you know. Write a sentence about each person.

Practice • Sentences   Unit 1 • Chapter 1 3

CHALLENGE

CHANGING SENTENCES Prepare and give children several unfinished sentences such as these:

____ wants a new ____

____ likes ____

____ is ____

____ has ____

Have partners take turns filling in the blanks and writing the completed sentences.

---

page 3

Beginning and Ending a Sentence

Read each sentence aloud. Circle the capital letter at the beginning of each sentence and the end mark at the end of each sentence.

EXAMPLE: (M)y mom sings a song(.)

1. (J)im's dad stands on his head(.)
2. (B)en's brother can juggle(.)
3. (O)ur dad whistles well(.)
4. (I) like to dance(.)
5. (K)ate plays the piano(.)

Visual/Auditory

Beginning and Ending a Sentence

Cut out the words and end marks at the bottom of the page. Glue them in the correct place. Possible responses are given.

1. Mr. Snell   is a teacher .
2. Staci   takes care of animals .
3. The   man owns a bookstore .

| Mr. Snell | Staci | The | . | . | . |

Kinesthetic

Teacher: Cut apart the activities and distribute to children based on the modalities that are their strengths.

Reteach Activities • Sentences   Unit 1 • Chapter 1 3

Extra Practice

OBJECTIVES
- To understand the correct word order, capitalization, and punctuation in a sentence
- To use sentences in writing

DAILY LANGUAGE PRACTICE

TRANSPARENCY 2

1 mary has a new book (Mary; .)

2 it Is about animals. (It; is)

BRIDGE TO WRITING She loves books about animals (end punctuation)

ORAL WARM-UP

USE PRIOR KNOWLEDGE Display several objects, such as a stuffed animal, a crayon, a book, a building block, and a ball. Have a volunteer choose an object in secret and tell sentences about it. The first child who guesses the object then chooses and describes an object.

TEACH/MODEL

Read each set of directions to help children understand how to complete each section. Have children share their answers in small groups before you read aloud the answers to them.

WRAP-UP/ASSESS

SUMMARIZE Ask children to reflect on and discuss any special problems they had in completing the practice before you have them summarize what they have learned about sentences. You may want children to write their reflections in their journals.

ADDITIONAL PRACTICE Additional items of Extra Practice are provided on pages 466-467 of the *Pupil Edition*.

TECHNOLOGY

Grammar Practice and Assessment CD-ROM

Writing Express CD-ROM

INTERNET Visit *The Learning Site!*
www.harcourtschool.com

Extra Practice

Write each group of words that is a sentence.

1. Steven is a fast reader.
   Steven is a fast reader.
2. He likes to read true stories.
   He likes to read true stories.
3. The story he likes best

Write each group of words in an order that makes sense.

4. Lori good artist is a.
   Lori is a good artist.
5. She also funny writes stories.
   She also writes funny stories.
6. Many about animals are stories.
   Many stories are about animals.

Write each sentence correctly. Use capital letters and end marks.

7. tami tells jokes
   Tami tells jokes.
8. everyone laughs at her jokes
   Everyone laughs at her jokes.
9. she likes to be silly
   She likes to be silly.
10. tami makes people smile
    Tami makes people smile.

30

Vocabulary Power page 3

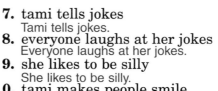 **ESL**

Name _____

What does this saying mean? Put on your thinking cap.

You can't wear a "thinking cap." The saying means to think hard about something.

What does this saying mean? Seize the day!

When you "seize the day," you use the day to do many different things.

It's time to put on your thinking cap. Draw a picture to show the meaning of the underlined words.	It's lunchtime. Let's grab a bite.
I'm learning how to use a map. I can grasp the idea.	I'm in a play. My character is sad. I have to capture the feeling.

Vocabulary Power   Unit 1 • Chapter 1   3

REACHING ALL LEARNERS

WRITE ABOUT A TOY Ask children to draw their favorite toys. Then pair children with more fluent English speakers to help them tell and write sentences about the toy.

Language Play

Make a Sentence
- Take turns with a partner.
- Choose an item from each column.
- Put the words together and write a sentence.
- Score one point for each sentence.
- See who can get 5 points first.

the boy	has	a big sandwich
she	likes	very loudly
Jack	is	on the chalkboard
the girl	sings	a green sweater
the teacher	writes	always late

Writing Connection

Functional Writing: For Sale Sign Think about something you could sell. Make a sign that tells others about it. Write sentences for the sign. Use this sign as a model.

For Sale
I have a red bike for sale.
It costs only ten dollars.
Stop by if you want to see it.

31

Language Play

Have children play "Make a Sentence" in pairs. Model how to choose an item from each column to make a sentence. Point out that they must decrease the space between the words in each column to make their sentences readable. Remind children to use a capital letter at the beginning and an end mark at the end of each sentence they write.

Writing Connection

For Sale Sign Check to see that children have successfully written sentences for a sign by using the criteria below.

CRITERIA
- ☑ Tells a complete thought in each sentence.
- ☑ Writes sentences in which the word order makes sense.
- ☑ Begins each sentence with a capital letter.
- ☑ Ends each sentence with an end mark.

 You may want to have children place their writing in their portfolios or take it home to share with family members.

PRACTICE page 4

Name _____

Extra Practice

A. Underline each group of words that is a sentence.

1. <u>I am the oldest child.</u>
   am the oldest child.

2. The tallest in the family
   <u>Jack is the tallest in the family.</u>

B. Write the words in an order that makes sense.

3. fix Mom can anything.
   Mom can fix anything.

4. cooks Dad dinner night. each
   Dad cooks dinner each night.

C. Write each sentence correctly.

5. the boys want to build a ship
   The boys want to build a ship.

6. they ask Grandma to help them
   They ask Grandma to help them.

4 Unit 1 • Chapter 1   Practice • Sentences

CHALLENGE

CATALOGS Have children cut out magazine pictures of objects that interest them. Have them glue each picture to a sheet of paper and write sentences to describe it. Invite children to add a title page, and then bind the pages with string to make a catalog.

Chapter Review

OBJECTIVES
- To review word order, capitalization, and punctuation in sentences
- To identify and use the different parts of a book

DAILY LANGUAGE PRACTICE

TRANSPARENCY 2

1 vicky likes to .draw (Vicky; draw.)

2 She Drew the Garden. (drew; garden)

BRIDGE TO WRITING The flowers are pretty (punctuation mark)

STANDARDIZED TEST PREP

Read each set of directions with children to make sure they understand how to complete each section. You may wish to have children complete this page independently and use it as an assessment.

TEST PREPARATION TIP
Item Type: Multiple Choice

TIP

Model this strategy to help children determine the correct answer:

I know that the words in a sentence should be in an order that makes sense. I also know that a sentence begins with a capital letter and ends with an end mark.

The order of the words in the first sentence makes sense, but it doesn't start with a capital letter or end with an end mark. Choice _b_ has a beginning capital and a period. I choose _b_.

Sentences

Chapter Review

Read each sentence. Is it written correctly? Choose the best answer.

1. brooke wants a cat
   - **a.** Brooke wants a cat
   - **b.** Brooke wants a cat.
   - **c.** correct as is

2. tim has a big dog.
   - **a.** Tim has a big dog.
   - **b.** Tim has a big dog
   - **c.** correct as is

3. The boy finds a turtle.
   - **a.** The boy finds a turtle
   - **b.** the boy finds a turtle
   - **c.** correct as is

4. A black horse Zack has.
   - **a.** Zack has a black horse.
   - **b.** zack has a black horse.
   - **c.** correct as is

5. My dad keeps bees
   - **a.** my dad keeps bees.
   - **b.** My dad keeps bees.
   - **c.** correct as is

6. has two Tia rabbits
   - **a.** tia has two rabbits.
   - **b.** Tia has two rabbits.
   - **c.** correct as is

7. Simone fish likes.
   - **a.** simone likes fish
   - **b.** Simone likes fish.
   - **c.** correct as is

8. Lee has an ant farm.
   - **a.** Lee has an ant farm
   - **b.** Lee farm has an ant
   - **c.** correct as is

Visit our website for more activities with sentences:
www.harcourtschool.com

32

Language Skills Assessment

PORTFOLIO ASSESSMENT
Have children select their best work from the following activities:

- **Writing Connection**, *pages 27, 31*; TE activities, *pages 27, 29, 30 and 31.*

ONGOING ASSESSMENT
Evaluate the performance of 4-6 students using appropriate checklists and record forms from pages R65–R68 and R77–R79.

INTERNET Activities and exercises to help students prepare for state and standardized assessments appear on *The Learning Site:*

www.harcourtschool.com

■ Study Skills ■

Using the Parts of Your Book

Most books have special pages that give information about what is inside the book. There is a **table of contents** in the front of your book. It shows the chapters, or parts of the book. It shows the page number of the beginning of each chapter.

There is a **glossary** at the back of the book. It tells the meanings of important words in the book. It is like a dictionary. Your book also has a thesaurus in the back. A **thesaurus** gives synonyms for words. **Synonyms** are words that mean almost the same.

Practice

Use the example page to answer the questions.

1. What is the title of Chapter 2? Parts of a Sentence

2. On what page does Chapter 1 begin? page 24

3. How many chapters are in this table of contents? 3

Answer these questions.

4. Where is the glossary of a book? at the back

5. What can you find in a thesaurus? synonyms for words

TABLE OF CONTENTS

Chapter	Page
1 Sentences	24
2 Parts of a Sentence	34
3 Writing Sentences About a Picture	44

33

■ Study Skills ■

Using the Parts of Your Book

TEACH/MODEL

Read through each explanation and the examples on page 33 together. As you read through the table of contents, show children how to use a finger to run across a line. You may want to show children various books, such as a science book, a catalog, or a storybook and point to their different parts, asking children to name and talk about them. You may want to ask questions to review the information, such as *What is a glossary? Why would you use a table of contents? Why would you use a glossary?*

PRACTICE Have children use the example page to complete the questions.

WRAP-UP/ASSESS

SUMMARIZE Ask children to tell what they have learned about the different parts of some books.

PRACTICE page 5

Name _____

Using the Parts of Your Book

Contents

Chapter	page
1 Here Comes Buster	3
2 Missing Slippers	9
3 Off to School	14
4 Buster Saves the Day	18

Use the table of contents to answer each question.

1. How many chapters does the book have? 4

2. What is the name of the first chapter?
Here Comes Buster

3. On what page does Chapter 2 begin? 9

4. What is the name of Chapter 3?
Off to School

5. What chapter is called "Buster Saves the Day"? 4

▶ **TRY THIS!** Think about a book you might like to write. Make up a title page and table of contents for it.

Practice • Sentences   Unit 1 • Chapter 1 5

CHALLENGE

FINDING THE PARTS OF A BOOK Have small groups select books from the classroom library, and ask them to locate the table of contents and the glossary. Each group can then make a short presentation to explain what readers will find in each part of the book.

LESSON ORGANIZER	DAY 1	DAY 2
 **DAILY LANGUAGE PRACTICE**  TRANSPARENCIES 3, 4	1. walk I to the store (I walk; .) 2. my friend goes with Me. (My; me) **Bridge to Writing** Alice likes to hike (punctuation mark)	1. IT is rainning today. (It; raining) 2. We can't go .Outside (outside.) **Bridge to Writing** I (telling part) .
ORAL WARM-UP Listening/Speaking	Listening/Speaking Talk About Rain p. 34	Talk about a classmate p. 36 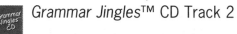 *Grammar Jingles™* CD Track 2
TEACH/MODEL GRAMMAR **KEY** ✔ = tested skill	✔ **WHAT ARE THE PARTS OF A SENTENCE?** pp. 34–35 • To listen critically to interpret and evaluate a poem • To understand that a sentence has a naming part and a telling part	✔ **NAMING PARTS AND TELLING PARTS** pp. 36–37 • To identify the naming and telling parts of sentences • To recognize that the naming and telling parts of a sentence work together
Reaching All Learners	**Challenge:** Make a Sentence Umbrella p. 35 Activity Card 2, p. R42 **ESL:** *ESL Manual* pp. 14-15 *Practice Book* p. 6 **Reteach:** *Reteach Activities Copying Masters* p. 4	**Modified Instruction** Below-Level: Find naming parts Above-Level: Write and identify naming parts **Challenge:** Event Report p. 37 **ESL:** Make up Sentences p. 36 *ESL Manual* pp. 14, 16 *Practice Book* p. 7 **Reteach:** *Reteach Activities Copying Masters* p. 5

WRITING	Complete Sentences p. 35
	
	  Summarize/Reflect
		Writing Connection p. 37
		 Revising
		  Summarize/Reflect

CROSS-CURRICULAR/ ENRICHMENT	**Vocabulary Power** Word Meaning p. 34 **lullaby,** anthem, folk song, jingle, serenade See *Vocabulary Power* book.	**Vocabulary Power** Context Clues p. 34 *Vocabulary Power* book p. 4 🖳 **Vocabulary activity**

DAY 3

1. jessie an apple picks. (Jessie picks; an apple.)
2. Wayne its a red apple, (eats; .)

Bridge to Writing (naming part) likes carrots.

Name and recall things people like
 p. 38
Grammar Jingles™ CD Track 2

✔ **COMBINING PARTS OF SENTENCES** pp. 38–39
• To understand that two naming parts can be joined
• To join the naming parts of sentences

Modified Instruction
  Below-Level: Identify naming and telling parts
  Above-Level: Write Additional Sentences
Challenge: Make a Web p. 39
ESL: Use a Chart p. 38
  ESL Manual pp. 14, 17
Practice Book p. 8
Reteach: *Reteach Activities Copying Masters* p. 6

Writing Connection p. 39
  Drafting
 Summarize/Reflect

Vocabulary Power
  Classify/Categorize p. 34
  Vocabulary Power book p.5
 Vocabulary activity

DAY 4

1. Morgan adn shane eat lunch. (and; Shane)
2. carlos Maria and drink milk. (Carlos and Maria)

Bridge to Writing (combine naming parts with and) love warm milk.

Tell about a favorite story character
  p. 40

EXTRA PRACTICE p. 40
• To review the different parts of a sentence
• To write sentences and combine their naming parts using the word *and*
 Practice Assessment

Challenge: My Best Friend p. 41
ESL: Shared Writing p. 40
  ESL Manual pp. 14, 18
Practice Book p. 9

Writing Connection p. 41
  Sentence About a Picture

Vocabulary Power
  Compare/Contrast p. 34
  Vocabulary Power book p.6
Vocabulary activity

DAY 5

1. Eric and. fred love science. (and Fred)
2. Fred and Nora likes books (like; .)

Bridge to Writing Jose (combining word) Lucia are my friends.

TEST PREP **Chapter Review** p. 42
• To review and identify the parts of a sentence
• To alphabetize words to the first and second letter
Test Preparation

Challenge: Make a People Box p. 43
Practice Book p. 10
ESL: *ESL Manual* pp. 14, 19

Study Skill p. 43
  Using ABC Order

Vocabulary Power
  Perform p. 34
Technology p. 42

What Are the Parts of a Sentence?

OBJECTIVES
- To listen critically to interpret and evaluate a poem
- To understand that a sentence has a naming part and a telling part

DAILY LANGUAGE PRACTICE

TRANSPARENCY 3

1 walk I to the store (I walk; .)

2 my friend goes with Me. (My; me)

BRIDGE TO WRITING Alice likes to hike (punctuation mark)

ORAL WARM-UP

USE PRIOR KNOWLEDGE Ask children to tell what they know about rain. Discuss with them what they like and don't like about rain. Write their responses as sentences in two columns.

TEACH/MODEL

Tell children to open their books to page 34. Have them use the illustration to predict what the poem will be about. Then have them read the title and use it to refine their predictions. As you read the second stanza of the poem aloud, say the naming part of each sentence in a different way from the telling part to show the two parts of each sentence. Have volunteers read the poem, using the same emphasis.

DEVELOP ORAL LANGUAGE Ask children to discuss what happens when it rains and why some people love rain. Be sure children use complete sentences.

What Are the Parts of a Sentence?

Read the poem.

April Rain Song

Let the rain kiss you.
Let the rain beat upon your head
  with silver liquid drops.
Let the rain sing you a lullaby.

The rain makes still pools
  on the sidewalk.
The rain makes running pools
  in the gutter.
The rain plays a little sleep-song
  on our roof at night—

And I love the rain.

Langston Hughes

34

Vocabulary Power

DAY 1 WORD MEANING Introduce and define *lullaby* (a kind of song). Ask: **When does a mother sing a lullaby?** Invite volunteers to sing a lullaby such as "Rock-a-by-Baby."

DAY 2 CONTEXT CLUES Write: The <u>lullaby</u> made me feel sleepy. **What words help you understand *lullaby*?** (See also *Vocabulary Power*, page 4.)

DAY 3 CLASSIFY AND CATEGORIZE Write *song* and *dance*. **Which word tells what a lullaby is?** (See also *Vocabulary Power*, page 5.)

DAY 4 COMPARE/CONTRAST Write *lullaby* and *anthem*. **How are they alike? Different?** (See also *Vocabulary Power*, page 6.)

DAY 5 PERFORM Invite groups of volunteers to sing a favorite song. Discuss the various kinds of songs performed.

Talk with a group about something you like. Use complete sentences to tell what it does and why you like it.

A sentence has two parts.

- The **naming part** names who or what the sentence is about.

 Felipe likes the rain.
 The rain makes pools on the ground.

- The **telling part** tells what someone or something is or does.

 The rain **falls from a silver sky.**
 Felipe **walks in the rain.**

Write a naming part to complete each sentence. Responses will vary.

_____ plays in puddles.

_____ looks like silver.

_____ dances on the sidewalk.

Write a telling part to complete each sentence. Responses will vary.

The rain _____.

The rain _____.

The rain _____.

35

WRITE Use children's responses about the rain to start a conversation about things they like. Encourage children to use complete sentences. Then read the explanations and talk about the example sentences in the box. You may then want to have children identify the parts of the sentences you wrote for the Warm-Up activity and then label them.

Then read the first item at the bottom of page 35 together. Point out that there is more than one correct response. Have children work with partners to complete the items and then share them with classmates.

WRAP-UP/ASSESS

SUMMARIZE Reread the poem with children. Then have children summarize and reflect on what they have learned about the parts of a sentence. You may want children to write their reflections in their journals. **REFLECTION**

RETEACH

INTERVENTION Lessons in **visual, auditory,** and **kinesthetic** modalities: p. R18 and *Reteach Activities Copying Masters,* page 4.

page 4

What Are the Parts of a Sentence?

Write words from the box to complete each sentence.

| Sally | hits the ball | Charlie | catches the ball |

1. _____ Charlie _____ throws the ball.

2. Sally _____ hits the ball _____.

3. Charlie _____ catches the ball _____.

4. _____ Sally _____ is on first base.

What Are the Parts of a Sentence?

Cut out the sentence parts below. Glue them in place to finish the sentences.

1. Sally likes to plant flowers.

2. Charlie likes to help.

3. Flower seeds are brown.

4. The flowers will be blue.

| likes to help. | are brown. | Sally | The flowers |

Teacher: Cut apart the sentence activities and distribute to children based on their modalities that are their strengths.

4 **Unit 1 • Chapter 2** Reteach Activities • Parts of a Sentence

---

REACHING ALL LEARNERS

PRACTICE page 6

Name _____

What Are the Parts of a Sentence?

A. Write a naming part to complete each sentence.
Responses will vary.

1. _____ go to school every day.

2. _____ is my friend.

3. _____ have fun on the playground.

4. _____ line up for lunch.

5. _____ has a tasty lunch.

B. Write a telling part to complete each sentence.
Responses will vary.

6. My teacher _____

7. My friend _____

8. The school _____

9. My class _____

10. The playground _____

TRY THIS! Think about three classmates. Write a sentence about each one. Make sure each sentence has a naming part and a telling part.

6 **Unit 1 • Chapter 2**   Practice • Parts of a Sentence

CHALLENGE

MAKE A SENTENCE UMBRELLA Have children use **Challenge Activity Card 2** (page R42) to write sentences about the rain. Make sure they write complete sentences. Invite children to display and share their umbrellas.

Challenge Activity Card 2

Make a Sentence Umbrella

1. Cut out a large shape of an umbrella.
2. Find pictures of things you use or see when it rains. Glue them on your umbrella.
3. Write a sentence by each picture.
4. Tape your umbrella to a cardboard handle and display it.

You need:
- colored paper
- old magazines
- scissors, glue
- crayons or markers
- cardboard strip
- tape

Naming Parts and Telling Parts

OBJECTIVES
* To identify the naming and telling parts of sentences
* To recognize that the naming and telling parts of a sentence work together to tell a complete thought in writing

DAILY LANGUAGE PRACTICE

TRANSPARENCY 3

1 IT is rainning today. (It; raining)

2 We can't go .Outside (outside.)

BRIDGE TO WRITING I (telling part).

ORAL WARM-UP

USE PRIOR KNOWLEDGE Ask a volunteer to say his or her name. Then tell something about him or her, such as *Lucy has brown hair*. Ask other volunteers to say their names. Then have other children tell something about them.

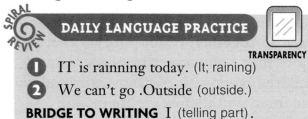

***Grammar Jingles*™ CD, Primary** Use Track 2 for review and reinforcement of sentence parts.

TEACH/MODEL

Have children recall what they learned about sentences in Chapter 1. Read aloud the sentences in the instruction box. Point out that the naming part of each sentence is set off from the telling part. Have two volunteers read each sentence, one reading the naming part and the other reading the telling part.

GUIDED PRACTICE Tell children to first find who or what the sentence is about. This will help them identify the naming part. Next they identify the telling part, which tells what someone or something does.

Naming Parts and Telling Parts

In a sentence, the naming part works with the telling part to tell a complete thought.

naming part	telling part
Jeff	kicks the ball.
The ball	rolls into the goal.

Guided Practice

Write each sentence. Circle the naming part. Underline the telling part.

1. (Jeff) plays soccer.
2. (Pat) kicks the ball far.
3. (The ball) rolls across the grass.
4. (Jeff) joins a team.
5. (The team) wins many games.

36

Vocabulary Power page 4

Name _____   Context Clues

Context clues can help you understand the meaning of new words.

Grandpa sang a <u>lullaby</u> to the baby. The baby <u>soon</u> fell asleep.

What kind of song is a *lullaby*? Fast and loud or slow and soothing? Underline the words that help you understand that a *lullaby* is slow and soothing.

Use the clues to help you understand the meaning of the underlined words. Circle the letter beside the correct meaning.

1. When we sing our country's <u>anthem</u>, we stand up.
   An anthem is a song _____.
   Ⓐ of praise
   B that is slow and sad
   C with a good beat

2. My mom wrote a <u>jingle</u> for Poppy Popcorn.
   A jingle is a song _____.
   A for bells
   B for dancing
   Ⓒ to sell something

3. My grandmother learned this <u>folk song</u> from her grandmother.
   A folk song is _____.
   A about grandparents
   B about folks
   Ⓒ very old

4. On Valentine's Day, Dad stood outside and sang a <u>serenade</u> to Mom.
   A serenade is a song _____.
   A about hearts
   Ⓑ sung to someone
   C that only fathers can sing

4   Unit 1 • Chapter 2   Vocabulary Power

REACHING ALL
ESL

MAKE UP SENTENCES Write *naming part* on five index cards and *telling part* on five others. Place them in a bag. Have children work in pairs. Partners each pick a card and then talk about and decide whether they have the parts needed to make a complete sentence. If so, they make up a sentence, each providing the part he or she picked. If they picked the same part, they both pick again.

Remember The naming part and the telling part of a sentence work together. They make a complete thought.

Independent Practice

Write each sentence. Circle the naming part. Underline the telling part.

6. (Jeff) goes to the first practice.
7. (Dave and Maria) are on the team.
8. (Dave) runs and kicks well.
9. (Maria) stops the ball at the net.
10. (Jeff) worries about his playing.
11. (The coach) helps him.
12. (Dave) helps Jeff kick better.
13. (Maria) helps Jeff stop the ball.
14. (Jeff) practices every day.
15. (Jeff) plays better now.

Writing Connection

Revising Choose a piece of your writing. Make sure your sentences are complete thoughts. Find the naming part and the telling part In each sentence. Add words if you need to do so.

 Use your computer to help you fix your sentences.

37

Independent Practice

Have children complete the Independent Practice, or modify it by using the following suggestions:

MODIFIED INSTRUCTION

BELOW-LEVEL STUDENTS Have children ask themselves *Who?* or *What?* to find the naming part.

ABOVE-LEVEL STUDENTS Have children write sentences that have two naming parts and one telling part as in item 7. They can swap sentences with a partner and circle the naming parts.

Writing Connection

Revising Help children select a piece of writing to revise. They can work with partners to identify the sentence parts. Have volunteers place their sentences in the Sharing Basket to share with classmates.

WRAP-UP/ASSESS

 SUMMARIZE Invite children to reflect on what they have learned about the different parts of a sentence. After they write their thoughts on what they learned, have them share their ideas in a small group.

REFLECTION

RETEACH

INTERVENTION Lessons in **visual**, **auditory**, and **kinesthetic** modalities, p. R18 and *Reteach Activities Copying Masters*, page 5.

page 5

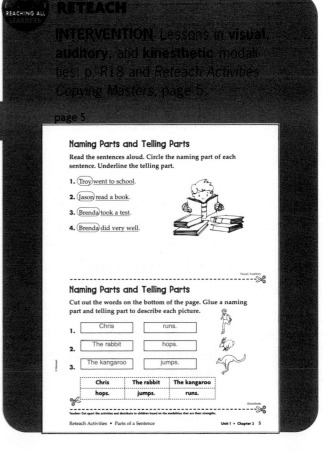

PRACTICE page 7

Name _____

Naming Parts and Telling Parts

A. Read each sentence. Circle the naming part of each sentence. Underline the telling part.

1. (School) is open five days a week.
2. (My teacher) checks who is here.
3. (I) read books.
4. (My class) learns new things each day.
5. (We) eat lunch at noon.

B. Use a naming part or telling part from the box to complete each sentence.

| The children | help after school | |
| Robert | has a good class | Jane |

6. Ms. Smith ___ has a good class ___
7. ___ Robert ___ always comes to school on time.
8. ___ Jane ___ does her homework neatly.
9. The boys ___ help after school ___
10. ___ The children ___ walk in a straight line.

TRY THIS! Write a note to a friend. Tell about something you did. Be sure to write at least two sentences.

Practice • Parts of a Sentence   Unit 1 • Chapter 2   7

CHALLENGE

EVENT REPORT Suggest children think of an event at which they saw many people do something. Invite children to write sentences about the event, using different colored pencils for the naming and telling parts.

Sam ran after the ball.
Lucy got the ball.
Lucy tossed it to Peter.

Naming Parts and Telling Parts

Read the sentences aloud. Circle the naming part of each sentence. Underline the telling part.

1. (Troy) went to school.
2. (Jason) read a book.
3. (Brenda) took a test.
4. (Brenda) did very well.

Naming Parts and Telling Parts

Cut out the words on the bottom of the page. Glue a naming part and telling part to describe each picture.

1. Chris | runs.
2. The rabbit | hops.
3. The kangaroo | jumps.

| Chris | The rabbit | The kangaroo |
| hops. | jumps. | runs. |

Reteach Activities • Parts of a Sentence   Unit 1 • Chapter 2   5

Combining Parts of Sentences

OBJECTIVES
• To understand that two naming parts can be joined with the word *and* when the telling parts are the same
• To join the naming parts of sentences with the same telling parts using the word *and*

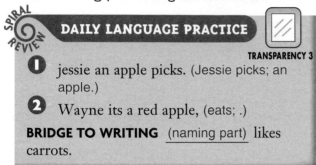

DAILY LANGUAGE PRACTICE

TRANSPARENCY 3

❶ jessie an apple picks. (Jessie picks; an apple.)

❷ Wayne its a red apple, (eats; .)

BRIDGE TO WRITING (naming part) likes carrots.

ORAL WARM-UP

USE PRIOR KNOWLEDGE Invite children to name things they like. Then have volunteers recall two children who liked the same thing. Have them say a complete sentence about the children, such as *Nora and Kim like snow.*

Grammar Jingles™ **CD, Primary** Use Track 2 for review and reinforcement of sentences.

TEACH/MODEL

Have children orally define what the naming and telling parts of a sentence are. Ask them to think of instances when they have used the word *and*. Then introduce the concept by reading the instruction box aloud. Point out that when two naming parts are combined in some sentences, the verb must be changed to tell about more than one.

GUIDED PRACTICE Work through the first item together. Have children identify the parts of the sentences that are the same. Show children how to combine the naming parts using *and*. Repeat with the remaining items.

Combining Parts of Sentences

Sometimes the telling parts of two sentences are the same. You can join the two naming parts using **and**.

> Girls enjoy reading books.
> Boys enjoy reading books.
> Girls **and** boys enjoy reading books.

Guided Practice

Use *and* to join each pair of sentences. Write the new sentence.

1. Danny liked books about sports.
   Clare liked books about sports.
   Danny and Clare liked books about sports.
2. Mom read the newspaper.
   My teacher read the newspaper.
   Mom and my teacher read the newspaper.
3. Beth found animal books.
   Joey found animal books.
   Beth and Joey found animal books.
4. Trisha got pop-up books.
   Tony got pop-up books.
   Trisha and Tony got pop-up books.
5. Pam waited in line.
   Luis waited in line.
   Pam and Luis waited in line.

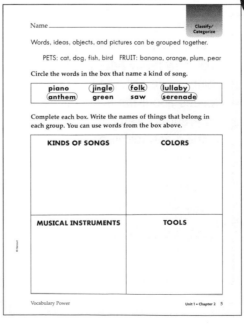

38

Vocabulary Power page 5

Name _____

Classify/Categorize

Words, ideas, objects, and pictures can be grouped together.

PETS: cat, dog, fish, bird   FRUIT: banana, orange, plum, pear

Circle the words in the box that name a kind of song.

piano	jingle	folk	lullaby
anthem	green	saw	serenade

Complete each box. Write the names of things that belong in each group. You can use words from the box above.

KINDS OF SONGS	COLORS
MUSICAL INSTRUMENTS	TOOLS

Vocabulary Power   Unit 1 • Chapter 2   5

REACHING ALL LEARNERS   **ESL**

USE A CHART On the board, draw a two-column chart with the headings *Naming Part* and *Telling Part*. Then ask children to tell what they like to do. Write their names in the first column and their activities in the second. Call on volunteers to draw lines to link two naming parts that have the same telling part. Then ask questions such as *Who likes soccer?* Model an answer, such as *Julio and Mark like soccer.*

Independent Practice

Use *and* to join each pair of sentences. Write the new sentence.

6. My friends read.

   I read.
   My friends and I read.

7. Gina loved the new book.

   Linda loved the new book.
   Gina and Linda loved the new book.

8. John couldn't find a book to buy.

   Eric couldn't find a book to buy.
   John and Eric couldn't find a book to buy.

9. Kim looked on the joke book shelf.

   Eric looked on the joke book shelf.
   Kim and Eric looked on the joke book shelf.

10. Shana wanted to buy magazines.

    Lin wanted to buy magazines.
    Shana and Lin wanted to buy magazines.

Writing Connection

Drafting Think about a fun place. Write sentences about it, like these:

  Tina went to the park.

  Maria went to the park.

  Tina and Maria went to the park.

Share your sentences with a partner.

You can use your computer to write and join the sentences.

39

Independent Practice

Have children complete the Independent Practice, or modify it by using the following suggestions:

MODIFIED INSTRUCTION

BELOW-LEVEL STUDENTS Have children work in pairs to circle the naming part and underline the telling part in each sentence. Have one child read a pair of sentences and the other combine the naming parts using *and*.

ABOVE-LEVEL STUDENTS After children are finished, invite them to write a sentence that has a combined naming part. Have them swap papers with a partner and write two new sentences with only one naming part.

Writing Connection

Drafting As children develop their drafts, remind them to compose sentences with elaborated subjects by joining naming parts with *and*.

WRAP-UP/ASSESS

SUMMARIZE Have children summarize what they know about combining parts of sentences.

RETEACH

INTERVENTION Lessons in **visual, auditory,** and **kinesthetic** modalities: p. R18 and *Reteach Activities Copying Masters,* page 6.

PRACTICE page 8

Name _____

Combining Parts of Sentences

Use *and* to join each pair of sentences. Write the new sentence.

1. Pumpkins are ripe. Apples are ripe.
   Pumpkins and apples are ripe.

2. Farms sell pumpkins. Stores sell pumpkins.
   Farms and stores sell pumpkins.

3. My friends pick apples. I pick apples.
   My friends and I pick apples.

4. Dad can make a pie. Mom can make a pie.
   Dad and Mom can make a pie.

5. Apples taste sweet. Pumpkins taste sweet.
   Apples and pumpkins taste sweet.

6. The boys eat pie. The girls eat pie.
   The boys and girls eat pie.

TRY THIS! Think about two friends. What can they both do? What do they both have? Write one sentence telling about both friends. Use *and* to combine the naming parts.

8 Unit 1 • Chapter 2   Practice • Parts of a Sentence

CHALLENGE

MAKE A WEB Ask children to think about what they like about a toy store. Have them create simple webs. In the middle they write their name. In the outer circles they write what they like. Then have children share their webs. Have each child write a sentence combining naming parts using *and*.

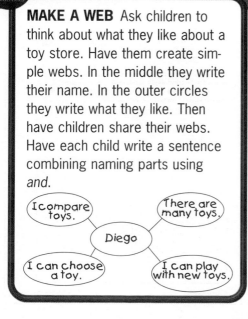

page 6

Combining Parts of Sentences

Read aloud each group of sentences. Underline the telling part in each sentence. Circle the word that joins the sentences.

1. The frogs swim in the pond.
   The fish swim in the pond.

   The frogs (and) the fish swim in the pond.

2. The goats climb the mountain.
   The deer climb the mountain.

   The goats (and) the deer climb the mountain.

Combining Parts of Sentences

Read each pair of sentences. Then cut out the sentence strips on the bottom of the page. Glue them in the boxes to join the sentences.

1. Mom loved to fish. The children loved to fish.

   | Mom | and | the children loved to fish |

2. Doug caught fish. Jean caught fish.

   | Doug | and | Jean caught fish |

   | Jean caught fish | Mom |
   | Doug | the children loved to fish |

Teacher: Cut apart the activities and distribute to children based on the modalities that are their strengths.

6 Unit 1 • Chapter 2   Reteach Activities • Parts of a Sentence

Extra Practice

OBJECTIVES
- To review the different parts of a sentence
- To write sentences and combine their naming parts using the word *and*

DAILY LANGUAGE PRACTICE

TRANSPARENCY 4

1 Morgan adn shane eat lunch. (and; Shane)

2 carlos Maria and drink milk. (Carlos and Maria)

BRIDGE TO WRITING (combining naming parts with *and*) love warm milk.

ORAL WARM-UP

USE PRIOR KNOWLEDGE Have volunteers take turns to tell a sentence about a character from a favorite story. Repeat each sentence or write it on the board. Invite children to identify the naming and telling parts.

TEACH/MODEL

Read each set of directions with children. Be sure they understand how to complete each section. Explain to children that they can fill the items in the first activity with the naming parts of their choice.

WRAP-UP/ASSESS

SUMMARIZE Ask children to reflect on and discuss any special problems they had in completing the practice. Then have them summarize what they have learned about the different parts of sentences and how they can combine sentence parts.

ADDITIONAL PRACTICE Additional items of Extra Practice are provided on page 466 of the *Pupil Edition.*

TECHNOLOGY

Grammar Practice and Assessment CD-ROM

Writing Express CD-ROM

INTERNET Visit *The Learning Site!*
www.harcourtschool.com

Extra Practice

Write a naming part for each sentence. Answers will vary.

1. _____ calls upstairs.
2. _____ comes downstairs.
3. _____ sings "Happy Birthday."
4. _____ is surprised.
5. _____ remembers what day it is.

Write the telling part of each sentence.

6. The children go to a birthday party.
7. They eat birthday cake.
8. Everyone brings presents.

Use *and* to join the naming parts from each sentence pair. Write the new sentence.

9. Grandma sang "Happy Birthday."
   Mom sang "Happy Birthday."
   Grandma and Mom sang "Happy Birthday."
10. Jane played a game.
   Tommy played a game.
   Jane and Tommy played a game.

40

Vocabulary Power page 6

Name _____

The words in the box are related because they name kinds of songs—but each kind of song is different from the others.

lullaby	jingle
serenade	anthem
folk song	

Draw pictures about different kinds of songs. For example, a picture for "lullaby" would not show people dancing and clapping their hands. Choose songs from the box above or think of other kinds of songs. Label each picture.

6 Unit 1 • Chapter 2   Vocabulary Power

REACHING ALL LEARNERS **ESL**

SHARED WRITING Pair children with different levels of proficiency. Have partners discuss their favorite activities and draw one thing they both like to do. Have one child dictate and the other write a sentence that uses *and* to combine the naming parts.

Mario and Yoko play baseball.

Language Play

Heads or Tails?
- Take turns with a partner.
- Choose a sentence from a book.
- Flip a coin or two-sided chip. If it is heads, say the naming part. If it is tails, say the telling part.
- You get one point for each sentence part you say correctly. The first player with 10 points wins.

Writing Connection

Sentence About a Picture Draw a picture that shows something you and a friend like to do. Then write a sentence about it. Make sure that your name and your friend's name are both in the naming part. Use this picture and sentence as a model.

Dennis and Tommy ride bikes.

41

Language Play

Have pairs of children play "Heads or Tails." Provide children with books. Invite them to pick a sentence they like or to pick one at random by opening the book and pointing to a sentence. Model how to play the game and keep score.

Writing Connection

Sentence About a Picture Check to see that children have successfully written sentences and combined naming parts by using the criteria below.

CRITERIA
- ☑ Begins own name and friend's name with a capital letter.
- ☑ Uses *and* to combine the naming parts of the sentence.
- ☑ Writes a telling part to the sentence.
- ☑ Ends the sentence with an end mark.

Portfolio Opportunity You may want to have children place their writing in their portfolios or take it home to share with family members.

PRACTICE page 9

Name _____

Extra Practice

A. Circle the naming part in each sentence.

1. (Board games) are fun.
2. (You) have to play with friends.
3. (Each game) is different.
4. (I) win sometimes.

B. Circle the telling part in each sentence.

5. My friends (win other times)
6. I (like other games, too)
7. Tag (is fun.)
8. My friends (can not catch me!)

C. Use *and* to join each pair of sentences. Write the new sentence.

9. Joe can play checkers. Tina can play checkers.
   Joe and Tina can play checkers.

10. My sisters play ball. I play ball.
   My sisters and I play ball.

Practice • Parts of a Sentence   Unit 1 • Chapter 2   9

CHALLENGE

MY BEST FRIEND Have children write a story to tell about something they have done or seen with their best friend. When they are finished, have them circle the naming parts and underline the telling parts of their sentences. Invite them to look for sentences whose naming parts they can combine and revise accordingly.

Chapter Review

OBJECTIVES

- To review and identify the parts of a sentence
- To alphabetize words to the first and second letter

DAILY LANGUAGE PRACTICE

TRANSPARENCY 5

1 Eric and. fred love science. (and Fred)

2 Fred and Nora likes books (like; .)

BRIDGE TO WRITING Jose (combining word) Lucia are my friends.

STANDARDIZED TEST PREP

Read the directions with children to make sure they understand how to complete page 42. You may wish to have children complete this page independently and use it as an assessment.

TEST PREPARATION TIP
Item Type: Multiple Choice

TIP

Model this strategy to help children determine the correct answer.

First, I read the directions and make sure I understand what I need to do. Then I read the first sentence and the three answer choices. I see that only a part of the first sentence is underlined, so I know that _c_ is not the correct answer. *Some people* tells me who the sentence is about. It is the naming part of the sentence. So I choose _a_.

Chapter Review — STANDARDIZED TEST PREP

Choose the answer that best tells about the underlined words.

1. <u>Some people</u> have brown hair.
   a. <u>naming part</u>
   b. telling part
   c. complete sentence

2. <u>My Uncle Bill combs his hair.</u>
   a. naming part
   b. telling part
   c. <u>complete sentence</u>

3. <u>Tony</u> reaches the tallest shelf in the classroom.
   a. <u>naming part</u>
   b. telling part
   c. complete sentence

4. Mr. Thomas <u>reaches the tallest shelf in the school.</u>
   a. naming part
   b. <u>telling part</u>
   c. complete sentence

5. <u>Connie runs the fastest.</u>
   a. naming part
   b. telling part
   c. <u>complete sentence</u>

6. Steve <u>wears blue sneakers.</u>
   a. naming part
   b. <u>telling part</u>
   c. complete sentence

Visit our website for more activities with parts of sentences:
www.harcourtschool.com

42

Language Skills Assessment

PORTFOLIO ASSESSMENT
Have children select their best work from the following activities:

- **Writing Connection,** *pages 37, 39, and 41; TE activities, pages 35, 37, and 41.*

ONGOING ASSESSMENT
Evaluate the performance of 4-6 students using appropriate checklists and record forms from pages R65–R68 and R77–R79.

INTERNET Activities and exercises to help students prepare for state and standardized assessments appear on *The Learning Site:*
www.harcourtschool.com

■ Study Skills ■

Using ABC Order

The letters of the alphabet are in a special order called **ABC order**, or alphabetical order.

a b c d e f g h i j k l m n o p q r s t u v w x y z

Words can be put in ABC order so that they are easier to find in long lists. Your book's glossary and thesaurus are in ABC order. Dictionaries are also in ABC order. Use the first letters of words to put them in ABC order. These words are in ABC order.

    cook   **f**riend   **j**elly

When words begin with the same first letter, use the second letter to put them in ABC order.

    d**a**rk   d**i**sh   d**o**g

Practice

Write the words in ABC order.

1. for, igloo, goat   for, goat, igloo

2. meal, maybe, mother   maybe, meal, mother

3. star, sandwich, space   sandwich, space, star

Answer these questions.

4. To find the word *sentence* in your glossary, would you look near the beginning, middle, or end? near the end

5. On what page is *sentence* in your glossary?   page 504

43

REACHING ALL LEARNERS

PRACTICE page 10

Name _____

Using ABC Order

Use the thesaurus page to answer each question.

afraid filled with fear
   frightened scared
cry to shed tears
   sob weep
eat to take food into the body
   gobble taste
pretty nice-looking or beautiful
   beautiful lovely
take to move or carry something
   bring carry
walk to move by using the feet
   step stroll

1. Which word comes before *take*?
   pretty

2. What is the first word on this list?
   afraid

3. Where would you find the word *sad*?
between pretty and take

4. Would the word *clear* come before or after *cry*?
   before

5. Name a word that would come after *eat* but before *pretty*.
Answers will vary. Accept all reasonable responses.

6. What word comes after *cry*? _____ eat

TRY THIS! Make your own thesaurus. List ten words and their synonyms. Put them in alphabetical order.

10 Unit 1 • Chapter 3   Practice • Parts of a Sentence

REACHING ALL LEARNERS

CHALLENGE

MAKE A PEOPLE BOX Have children write the names of their friends and family members on separate index cards. Ask them to use alphabetical order to sort the cards. Children can add the address, birthday, or other information about each person. Have children store their cards in boxes.

Heidi Thomas		Molly Miller	

■ Study Skills ■

Using ABC Order

TEACH/MODEL

Explain to children that they will learn how to put words in ABC order. Read the definition on top of page 43. Then read the alphabet across the page with children. Use it as a reference point when discussing that the letter *c* comes before the letter *f* and that the letter *j* follows both. It can get trickier when children have to use the second letter to put the words in order. You may want to suggest that they pretend the first letter isn't even there.

PRACTICE You may want to complete the first item with children. Remind children to use the first or second letter to put the words in ABC order. When children are finished, have volunteers share their answers.

WRAP-UP/ASSESS

SUMMARIZE Ask children to tell what they have learned about ABC order and summarize how it can help them look for words in glossaries and dictionaries.

Writing Sentences About a Picture
pages 44–51

LESSON ORGANIZER	DAY 1	DAY 2
DAILY LANGUAGE PRACTICE TRANSPARENCY 5	1. lizards have scales (Lizards; scales.) 2. they sit on rocks (They; rocks.)	1. raymond is a good friend (Raymond; .) 2. he likes to eat bugs (He; .)
ORAL WARM-UP Listening/Speaking	Talk About Pictures and Sentences p. 44	Describe an Animal p. 46
TEACH/MODEL WRITING 	✔ **WRITING SENTENCES ABOUT A PICTURE** **Literature Model:** "I Have a Pet!" pp. 44–45 **WRITER'S CRAFT** • To read and respond to sentences about a picture as a model for writing • To develop ideas and topics **Think About It** p. 45	**GUIDED WRITING** **Developing Ideas and Topics** pp. 46–47 • To use brainstorming to develop ideas and topics • To write a list of details about an animal **Writing and Thinking:** Reflect p. 47
Reaching All Learners	**ESL:** Building Vocabulary p. 45 *ESL Manual* pp. 20–21	**Challenge:** Add Interesting Details p. 47 **ESL:** *ESL Manual* p. 20
GRAMMAR	**Unit 1 Review** pp. 90-91	**Unit 1 Review** pp. 90-91
CROSS-CURRICULAR/ ENRICHMENT	**Science Connection:** Food Chain p. 45 **Vocabulary Power** Word Meaning p. 44 ┌─────────────────────────────┐ **burrow**, cave, lair, lodge, roost See **Vocabulary Power** book. └─────────────────────────────┘ **Self-Initiated Writing** p. 45	**School-Home Connection:** Riddle Game p. 46 **Math Connection:** Animal Word Problems p. 47 **Vocabulary Power** Context Clues p. 44 *Vocabulary Power* book, p. 7 **Vocabulary Activity**

KEY
✔ = tested writing form/skill

UNIT 1

DAY 3

1. what is your favorite game (What; game?)
2. i like to play checkers (I; checkers.)

Tell About Making Lists p. 48

GUIDED WRITING
✔ **Applying the Craft** pp. 48–49
• To use sentences about a picture as a model for writing
• To prewrite and draft original sentences
Read and Respond to the Model p. 48

Interactive Writing: p. 49
ESL:
Choosing Topics p. 49
ESL Manual p. 20

Unit 1 Review pp. 90–91

Vocabulary Power

Multi-meaning Words p. 44
Vocabulary Power book, p. 8

DAY 4

1. kim drew a tree house (Kim; .)
2. she wrote about her picture (She; .)

Discuss Sentences That Tell About Pictures p. 50

GUIDED WRITING
EDITING YOUR SENTENCES
p. 50
• To peer conference in editing sentences about a picture
• To edit sentences and share them aloud

Peer Conferencing p. 50
ESL:
ESL Manual p. 20

Unit 1 Review pp. 90–91

LISTENING AND SPEAKING:
Using Props p. 50
Vocabulary Power

Content-Area Words p. 44
Vocabulary Power book, p.9
Vocabulary Activity

DAY 5

1. He sentence wrote a. (He wrote a sentence.)
2. picture She a drew. (She drew a picture.)

Discuss Writing Positions p. 51

HANDWRITING
USING CORRECT POSITION WHEN WRITING p. 51
• To use correct positions when writing
• To use correct stroke when forming letters

Writing Resource:
Paper Position p. 51
ESL:
ESL Manual p. 20

Unit 1 Review pp. 90–91

Vocabulary Power

Graphics/Art p. 44

Writer's Craft
Developing Ideas and Topics

OBJECTIVES
- To read and respond to sentences about a picture as a model for writing
- To develop ideas and topics

DAILY LANGUAGE PRACTICE

TRANSPARENCY 5

1 lizards have scales (Lizards; scales.)

2 they sit on rocks (They; rocks.)

ORAL WARM-UP

USE PRIOR KNOWLEDGE Invite children to tell about pictures they have seen that have sentences to describe them. These might include newspaper photos with captions or magazine articles.

TEACH/MODEL

Read and discuss the introduction on page 44 with children. You may want to demonstrate brainstorming a short list of ideas about a topic. Then have them read the sentences from "I Have a Pet" and discuss the illustrations.

ANALYZE THE LITERATURE Use these questions for discussing the sentences and pictures.

1. **Which details tell about the jobs that Sophie's owner does?** (She gives the hamster food and water and cleans the cage.) **LITERAL: NOTE DETAILS**

2. **How is Raymond's cage different from Sophie's?** (Possible response: Sophie's cage is filled with wood chips. Raymond has a rock and a branch in his cage.) **INFERENTIAL: COMPARE AND CONTRAST**

Developing Ideas and Topics

Writers can find **topics**, or ideas, for writing in many ways. One way is to **brainstorm** ideas. When you brainstorm, you make a list of all the ideas that come to your mind. Then you can look at the list and choose the best topics for writing.

Read these sentences and look at the pictures about pets. How do you think the writers chose what to write about?

I Have a Pet!
by Shari Halpern

Sophie is my hamster. I give her food and water, and I clean out her cage. I take out the old, dirty wood chips and put in new, clean ones. Sophie likes to burrow under them and make a soft bed to sleep in.

44

Vocabulary Power

DAY 1 WORD MEANING Introduce and define **burrow** (home dug in the ground by an animal). **Name some animals that dig burrows** (rabbit, mole).

DAY 2 CONTEXT CLUES Write: *The mole is safe and snug in its burrow.* **What words help you understand burrow?** (See also *Vocabulary Power*, page 7.)

DAY 3 MULTI-MEANING WORDS Write: *Do you burrow under the covers on cold nights?* **What does burrow mean?** (See also *Vocabulary Power*, page 8.)

DAY 4 CONTENT-AREA WORDS Write: *Science, Math, Gym.* **In which class would you learn about burrows?** (See also *Vocabulary Power*, page 9.)

DAY 5 GRAPHICS/ART Have children make a book about animal homes, illustrating and labeling the animal homes, such as a burrow.

This is my pet lizard. His name is Raymond. He lives in a glass cage with a rock and a branch that he likes to sit on. I make sure Raymond gets fresh water and crickets to eat.

Think About It

1. What were the most interesting things you learned about Sophie and Raymond?

2. Why do you think the two children wrote about their pets? How do they feel about their pets?

45

ANALYZE SENTENCES ABOUT A PICTURE

Explain that writers develop topics and ideas by giving details to interest readers and help them learn new things about the subject. Sentences that tell about a picture should tell the main idea of the picture and also tell about some of the details shown in the picture.

Have children tell what each picture is mainly about and share some of the sentence details that support the illustrations.

Think About It

1. Ask volunteers to tell what information they found most interesting. **CRITICAL:** EXPRESS PERSONAL OPINIONS

2. Children may observe that the children in the examples chose these subjects because they are fond of their pets and they thought others would be interested in reading about them. **CRITICAL:** RECOGNIZE AUTHOR'S PURPOSE

SELF-INITIATED WRITING Have children respond to the sentences they just read through self-initiated writing, which might include writing original sentences about the pictures or generating ideas for writing by using prewriting techniques such as listing key thoughts or drawing. Children could also respond by other methods, such as through drama.

WRAP-UP/ASSESS

SUMMARIZE Have children consider how they can develop topics and ideas through brainstorming and drawing pictures, and writing sentences. Children can record their reflections in their journals. **REFLECTION**

Science Connection

FOOD CHAIN Children can explore a food chain and determine where lizards, hamsters, and other pets would be on the chain if they lived only in the wild. Children can then record what they have learned by drawing a picture of a food chain and labeling the animals that appear on it.

REACHING ALL ESL

BUILDING VOCABULARY If possible, display real objects such as a hamster cage, wood chips, and other details from the sentences. Add labels and have children read them aloud.

Writer's Craft
Developing Ideas and Topics

OBJECTIVES
- To use brainstorming to develop ideas and topics
- To write a list of details about an animal

DAILY LANGUAGE PRACTICE

TRANSPARENCY 5

1. raymond is a good friend (Raymond; .)
2. he likes to eat bugs (He; .)

ORAL WARM-UP

USE PRIOR KNOWLEDGE Display a classroom pet or a stuffed toy animal. Ask children to brainstorm words and phrases that tell about it. Make a list and read it with children.

GUIDED WRITING

BRAINSTORM IDEAS AND TOPICS Read and discuss the introductory material with children. Explain that they will brainstorm a list of ideas about an animal and use the Idea Bank to help them. Then guide them in making choices about which ideas they would include in writing sentences. Discuss the reasons for their choices.

Sentences About a Picture

Writer's Craft
Developing Ideas and Topics

When you brainstorm, you think of many ideas for your writing before you start. Raymond's owner brainstormed this list of topics for his sentences.

> Topics for Writing
> My fishing trip
> (My pet lizard)
> My best friend

He chose to write about his pet lizard, Raymond. He thought that Raymond would be the most interesting topic. He also thought his classmates would like to know about Raymond.

Then he drew a picture of Raymond.

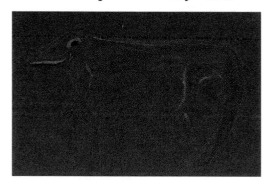

46

Vocabulary Power page 7

Name _____ Context Clues

Context means "the way in which a word is used." What context clues help you understand the meaning of the underlined word?

Some animals dig underground homes called burrows.

The words animals, dig, and underground homes help you understand that burrows are "underground homes."

Answer each question by circling the letter beside the best answer.

1. The mother fox takes food to her babies in their safe lair. What clues help you understand that a lair is a home?
   A the, to, her   **B** food, babies, safe

2. All those birds have a roost in that little birdhouse. What clues help you understand that birds perch in a roost?
   A all, that, little   **B** birds, birdhouse

3. The beavers used sticks, twigs, and leaves to build their lodge. What clues help you understand how beavers make a lodge?
   A sticks, twigs, leaves, build   B used, and, leaves

4. The opening in the side of the hill leads to a bear's cave. What clues help you understand that a cave is underground?
   A opening, side of the hill   B side, leads to a

Vocabulary Power   Unit 1 • Chapter 3   7

School-Home Connection

RIDDLE GAME Children can play a riddle game with family members by describing details about people, pets, or household objects and having others identify the subject based on the clues.

A. Brainstorm a list of ideas for writing about an animal. Then decide which idea would be the most interesting to you and your classmates. Use the Idea Bank if you need help getting started.

Idea Bank

What is my favorite animal?
   Where does the animal live?
   What color is it?
   Does the animal have fur?
What pet do I have?
   How do I help take care of it?
   What does it eat?

B. Draw a picture of your animal.

Writing and Thinking

Reflect Tell what helped you choose ideas from your brainstorming list. Write your ideas. Share your ideas in a small group.

47

DEVELOP IDEAS AND TOPICS Have children draw a picture of their animal. Ask them to refer to their list of ideas and to include some of the ideas in the picture.

Writing and Thinking

Reflect Read the text and discuss children's ideas before they write them. Encourage children to share in small groups what helped them choose ideas from their list. Children can record their ideas in their journals and then share them with the group.

WRAP-UP/ASSESS

SUMMARIZE Ask volunteers to summarize why brainstorming a list and drawing a picture are useful ways for coming up with interesting writing ideas.

Math Connection

• • • • • • • • • • • • • • • •

ANIMAL WORD PROBLEMS
Children can make up word problems about the animals pictured on the page. For example: *If 1 hippo weighs 2,000 pounds, how much do 3 hippos weigh?* (6,000 pounds) *If a spider catches 1 fly a day, how many will it catch in 2 weeks?* (14 flies) Children can present the problems they write for classmates to solve.

CHALLENGE
REACHING ALL LEARNERS

ADD INTERESTING DETAILS
Encourage children to add interesting details to their animal pictures such as colors, shapes, and textures. Then they should add words to their brainstorming list to tell about these details and other details such as sizes and sounds. Explain that these ideas will help them write clearer, more interesting sentences.

Writer's Craft
Applying the Craft

Applying the Craft

OBJECTIVES
- To use sentences about a picture as a model for writing
- To prewrite and draft original sentences

DAILY LANGUAGE PRACTICE

TRANSPARENCY 5

1 what is your favorite game (What; game?)

2 i like to play checkers (I; checkers.)

ORAL WARM-UP

USE PRIOR KNOWLEDGE Invite children to tell about times they have made lists to remember details.

GUIDED WRITING

READ AND RESPOND TO THE MODEL Have children look at John's picture, and ask a volunteer to read the sentences aloud as others read silently.

FOCUS ON ORGANIZATION Have children reread John's sentences and look again at his picture. Ask volunteers to tell how the picture and sentences go together.

Looking at the Model

1. Possible response: John likes to play checkers. **INFERENTIAL: MAIN IDEA**
2. Children may suggest that John's sentences may not have told the main idea or that his writing and picture might not have had as many interesting details. **CRITICAL: MAKE JUDGMENTS**

Read these sentences about a picture that a student named John wrote. Think about the main idea of the picture and John's sentences.

main idea sentence

I love to play checkers. My dad often plays with me. Sometimes I win!

Looking at the Model

1. What is the main idea of John's sentences?

2. How would John's writing have been different if he had not brainstormed ideas for writing or drawn a picture before he wrote sentences?

48

Vocabulary Power page 8

Name _____   Multi-Meaning Words

Many words have more than one meaning.

An animal's underground home is called a burrow.
I'm going to burrow under the blanket to get warm.

All of the underlined words can name animal homes. Draw a picture to show another meaning for each underlined word.

1. I'm so tired! Let's stop and roost on this bench.	2. Joe cleared the snow off the roof. He was afraid the roof might cave in.
3. The pirates hid the stolen treasure in their secret lair. No one could find it.	4. When we went to the beach, we stayed at the Seaside Lodge.

8 Unit 1 • Chapter 3   Vocabulary Power

EVALUATION CRITERIA

SENTENCES ABOUT A PICTURE Review the criteria that make up good sentences about a picture:

- The sentences tell the main idea of the picture.
- Each sentence tells a complete thought, begins with a capital letter, and ends with an end mark.

Work with children to establish additional criteria. List their ideas.

Your Turn

Draw a picture that tells about you and a pet or something you like to do. Then write sentences that tell about your picture.

Prewriting and Drafting

STEP 1 **Pick a topic.**

Brainstorm a list of ideas. Choose the most interesting idea. Circle it.

> Things I Like to Do
> 1.
> 2.
> 3.

STEP 2 **Draw a picture.**

Your picture should show something about your topic. Add information you want your classmates to know.

STEP 3 **Write your sentences.**

Use your picture and What Good Writers Do to write a draft of your sentences. Make sure your first sentence tells the main idea of your picture.

What Good Writers Do

 Remember for whom you are writing.

 Don't worry about mistakes. You can fix them later.

49

Your Turn Explain to children they will use the prewriting and drafting steps and What Good Writers Do to draw a picture and write about it.

Prewriting and Drafting Read the directions with children. Encourage volunteers to suggest some topics they might write their sentences about. Demonstrate how to list topics and choose the best one. Have children do the same with their own lists. Read What Good Writers Do aloud, and remind children to think about these tips as they prepare their drafts.

 Children can use word-processing software to compose their drafts.

 PORTFOLIO Remind children to place their first drafts in their Writing Portfolios.

WRAP-UP/ASSESS

SUMMARIZE Ask volunteers to review the steps they followed in writing a first draft. You may want to have children reflect on what they learned and record their thoughts in their journal. **REFLECTION**

INTERACTIVE WRITING

MODEL DRAFTING Guide children in selecting ideas from a brainstormed list and expanding them into complete sentences. Elicit children's ideas, and have them help you write sentences or parts of sentences as you move through the drafting process.

REACHING ALL LEARNERS **ESL**

CHOOSING TOPICS Children can dictate their topics. Work with them to choose a topic. Encourage them to draw a detailed picture. Then ask them to talk about their picture and to say their sentences before writing them down.

Writer's Craft
Editing Your Sentences

OBJECTIVES
- To peer conference in editing sentences about a picture
- To edit sentences and share them aloud

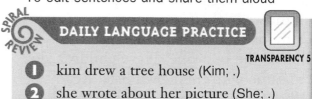

DAILY LANGUAGE PRACTICE

TRANSPARENCY 5

1. kim drew a tree house (Kim; .)
2. she wrote about her picture (She; .)

ORAL WARM-UP

Review the features sentences about a picture should have, and discuss what children expect when they read sentences like these.

GUIDED WRITING

EDITING YOUR SENTENCES ABOUT A PICTURE
Explain that the next step in writing is to edit the draft. Model for children how to use the Editor's Marks.

PEER CONFERENCING Have children use the checklist and the Editor's Marks as they work with peers to improve their work.

SHARING WITH OTHERS Have volunteers share their revised pictures and sentences in small groups. They can take turns telling what they like about others' sentences about a picture and what they like about creating their own.

WRAP-UP/ASSESS

SUMMARIZE Have volunteers summarize the steps they followed. Children can reflect on their own work and rate the results on a scale of 1–4. Ask children to hold up fingers to show their scores, attach their scores to their writing, and place it in their Writing Portfolio. Over time, have children review their portfolio to see how their writing improves.

Sentences About a Picture **Writer's Craft**

Editing Your Sentences

Share your sentences about a picture with a few classmates. Together think about how you can make your sentences better. Use the checklist and the Editor's Marks to help you revise your sentences.

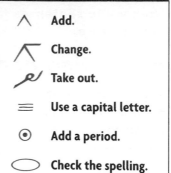

	Editor's Marks
∧	Add.
⋀	Change.
ℰ	Take out.
=	Use a capital letter.
⊙	Add a period.
⬯	Check the spelling.

✓ My sentences tell about the main idea of my picture.

✓ Each sentence tells a complete thought.

Sharing with Others

Meet with a partner or in a small group. Show your picture. Read your sentences aloud.

50

Vocabulary Power page 9

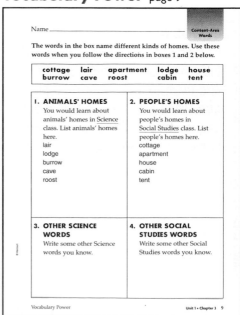

Name _____

Content-Area Words

The words in the box name different kinds of homes. Use these words when you follow the directions in boxes 1 and 2 below.

cottage	lair	apartment	lodge	house
burrow	cave	roost	cabin	tent

1. ANIMALS' HOMES
You would learn about animals' homes in Science class. List animals' homes here.
lair
lodge
burrow
cave
roost

2. PEOPLE'S HOMES
You would learn about people's homes in Social Studies class. List people's homes here.
cottage
apartment
house
cabin
tent

3. OTHER SCIENCE WORDS
Write some other Science words you know.

4. OTHER SOCIAL STUDIES WORDS
Write some other Social Studies words you know.

Vocabulary Power   Unit 1 • Chapter 1   9

LISTENING AND SPEAKING

USING PROPS As children read their sentences aloud, remind them to display their picture so that the audience can see and hear easily.

•Handwriting•

Using Correct Position When Writing

> **Follow these tips for better writing.**
>
> **Pencil Grip and Paper Position**
> ✓ Hold your pencil and place your paper as shown.
>
>
> right hand
>
> **Posture**
> ✓ Sit up straight. Face your desk, and place both feet on the floor.
>
> left hand
>
> **Stroke**
> ✓ Make your letters smooth and even.
>
> | Pet | Pet |
> |-----|-----|
> | **smooth and even** | **too shaky** |
> | Pet | Pet |
> | **too heavy** | **too light** |

Write these words. Follow the tips.

1. sentence
2. capital letter
3. end mark

51

Writing Resource
• • • • • • • • • • • • • •

For children who need additional help, you can use tape to outline corners on their desktops to mark where to position their paper. Also, for children who grip the pencil too tightly, you might provide soft rubber pencil grips.

EVALUATION CRITERIA

SELF-EVALUATION Have children revisit the evaluation criteria you helped them establish earlier and informally rate their writing of sentences about a picture by writing their score (on a 1–4 scale) on the corner of their papers or by raising their fingers.

•Handwriting•

Using Correct Position When Writing

OBJECTIVE
- To use correct positions when writing
- To use correct stroke when forming letters

SPIRAL REVIEW

DAILY LANGUAGE PRACTICE

TRANSPARENCY 5

❶ He sentence wrote a. (He wrote a sentence.)

❷ picture She a drew. (She drew a picture.)

TEACH/MODEL

Have all children practice using the correct pencil and paper positions and the correct posture for writing. Suggest corrections where needed. Guide any left-handed students to adapt positions as appropriate.

Discuss using correct stroke when writing, and talk about the model word *Pet* with children. Then have children write *Pet* and the words in items 1-3. Refer them to the handwriting models on pages 490-493 (R11) in their handbooks for help. (See also R92-93)

Have children compare their writing with the positive and negative models on the page in their book.

CURSIVE WRITING Have children who write in cursive apply the concepts in this lesson to their writing.

WRAP-UP/ASSESS

SUMMARIZE Ask volunteers to summarize the writing tips. You may want to have children recopy a piece of their writing and evaluate how the tips improve their writing. **REFLECTION**

LESSON ORGANIZER	DAY 1	DAY 2
DAILY LANGUAGE PRACTICE	1. sky The is blue (The sky; .) 2. the sun Is shiny. (The; is) **Bridge to Writing** <u>(naming part)</u> paints a yellow sun.	1. what is redd? (What; red) 2. Teh flower is Red. (The; red) **Bridge to Writing** What color is <u>(name of object)</u> ?
ORAL WARM-UP Listening/Speaking	Talk About Your Favorite Colors p. 52	Play a Game p. 54  *Grammar Jingles™* CD Track 3
TEACH/MODEL GRAMMAR **KEY** ✔ = tested skill	✔ **DIFFERENT KINDS OF SENTENCES** pp. 52-53 • To listen critically to interpret and evaluate a poem • To recognize that a statement is a sentence that tells something and a question asks something	✔ **USING STATEMENTS AND QUESTIONS** pp. 54-55 • To use correct capitalization and punctuation in statements and questions • To use statements and questions in writing
Reaching All Learners	*Practice Book* p. 11 **Challenge:** Make a City Quilt p. 53 Activity Card 3, p. R43 **ESL:** *ESL Manual* pp. 22-23 **Reteach:** *Reteach Activities Copying Masters* p. 7	**Modified Instruction** Below-Level: Underline Words Above-Level: Write and Answer Questions **Challenge:** Joke Book p. 55 **ESL:** Hold Your Cards p. 54 *ESL Manual* pp. 22, 24 *Practice Book* p. 12 **Reteach:** *Reteach Activities Copying Masters* p. 8
WRITING	Complete Sentences p. 53 Summarize/Reflect	Writing Connection p. 55 Sentence Variety Summarize/Reflect
CROSS-CURRICULAR/ ENRICHMENT	 **Vocabulary Power** Word Meaning, p. 52 **wholly,** entirely, mostly, partly, totally See **Vocabulary Power** book.	**Vocabulary Power** Related Words, p. 52 *Vocabulary Power* book p. 10 **Vocabulary activity**

Visit *The Learning Site!*
www.harcourtschool.com

WRITING ACTIVITIES
Writing Express CD-ROM

DAY 3

1. do you want to dig in the sand (Do; ?)

2. wE go to the beach every year? (We; .)

Bridge to Writing Where do you swim <u>(punctuation mark)</u>

 Tell sentences that go along with a
topic p. 56
Grammar Jingles™ CD Track 3

✔ **SENTENCES THAT GO
TOGETHER** pp. 56-57
- To understand that a group of
sentences can tell about the
same idea
- To revise writing so that sentences tell about the same idea

Modified Instruction
Below-Level: Finding the Sentence
that doesn't fit
Above-Level: Write Additional
Sentences
Challenge: Chain Stories p. 57
ESL: One Topic p. 56
ESL Manual pp. 22, 25
Practice Book p. 13
Reteach: *Reteach Activities
Copying Masters* p. 9

Writing Connection p. 57
Keeping to the Main Idea
Summarize/Reflect

Vocabulary Power
Word Families, p. 52
Vocabulary Power book
p. 11
Vocabulary activity

DAY 4

1. mike likes to go to the beach (Mike; .)

2. did you watch the diver. (Did; ?)

Bridge to Writing We built a sand
castle <u>(punctuation mark)</u>

Play Mother May I p. 58

EXTRA PRACTICE p. 58
- To identify and punctuate correctly statements and questions
- To use statements and questions in writing

Practice and Assessment

Challenge: Write a Scene p. 59
ESL: Poster Talk p. 58
ESL Manual pp. 22, 26
Practice Book p. 14

Writing Connection p. 59
Paragraph

Vocabulary Power
Homophones, p. 52
Vocabulary Power book
p. 12
Vocabulary activity

DAY 5

1. do you know where the beach is (Do; ?)

2. my parents like to play in the sand,
too? (My; .)

Bridge to Writing I like the beach
<u>(punctuation mark)</u>

TEST PREP CHAPTER REVIEW p. 60
- To review statements and
questions and to recognize that
groups of sentences should tell
about one subject
- To identify homophones

Test Preparation

Challenge: Homophone Rhymes
p. 61
Practice Book p. 15
ESL: *ESL Manual* pp. 22, 27

Summarize

Vocabulary
Homophones p. 61

Vocabulary Power

Rhyming Words, p. 52

Different Kinds of Sentences

OBJECTIVES
- To listen critically to interpret and evaluate a poem
- To recognize that a statement is a sentence that tells something and that a question is a sentence that asks something

SPIRAL REVIEW

DAILY LANGUAGE PRACTICE

TRANSPARENCY 6

1 sky The is blue (The sky; .)

2 the sun Is shiny. (The; is)

BRIDGE TO WRITING (naming part) paints a yellow sun.

ORAL WARM-UP

USE PRIOR KNOWLEDGE Have children name their favorite colors. Write the colors on the board and then ask for examples of things that are each color. Write the questions and answers on chart paper.

TEACH/MODEL

Have a volunteer read aloud the title of the poem on page 52. Ask children to predict the answer to the question. Then start reading the poem aloud. Pause after each question and have children discuss the possible answers. Then reread the poem, having volunteers take turns reading the questions and answers.

DEVELOP ORAL LANGUAGE Prompt children to describe examples from the poem in complete sentences, such as *What is red? A poppy is red.* Invite volunteers to compare objects and their colors by asking and answering questions. Add their questions to the list on chart paper.

Different Kinds of Sentences

Read the poem.

What Is Pink?

What is pink? A rose is pink
By the fountain's brink.

What is red? A poppy's red
In its barley bed.

What is blue? The sky is blue
Where the clouds float through.

What is white? A swan is white
Sailing in the light.

What is yellow? Pears are yellow,
Rich and ripe and mellow.

What is green? The grass is green,
With small flowers between.

What is violet? Clouds are violet
In the summer twilight.

What is orange? Why, an orange,
Just an orange!

Christina Rossetti

52

Vocabulary Power

DAY 1 WORD MEANINGS Introduce and define *wholly* (totally, completely). Ask children if the sky is wholly, or totally, blue.

DAY 2 RELATED WORDS Write: *wholly, happy, totally.* **Which two words have the same meaning?** (See also *Vocabulary Power,* page 10.)

DAY 3 WORD FAMILIES Write *wholly.* **What is the base word? What ending has been added to *whole* to make *wholly?*** (See also *Vocabulary Power,* page 11.)

DAY 4 HOMOPHONES Write: *This book is ___wholly___ new.* Swiss cheese is ___holey___. Discuss how the underlined words are alike and different. (See also *Vocabulary Power,* page 12.)

DAY 5 RHYMING WORDS Write: *Humpty-Dumpty was wholly roly-poly.* **Which words rhyme?** Interested children can illustrate the sentence. Others can make a list of rhyming words.

Talk with a partner about colors you like best and why. Then use a crayon to write sentences about your favorite color.

A **statement** is a sentence that tells something.

The apple is red.

A **question** is a sentence that asks something.

What else is red?

Write words to complete each question and statement. Add new lines to the poem. Responses will vary.

What is white? _A cloud_ is white.

What is yellow? _____ is yellow.

What is red? _____ is red.

What is _____? _____ is _____ .

What is _____? _____ is _____ .

53

WRITE Have small groups brainstorm objects that are each of the colors mentioned in the poem. Then ask, *What is pink?* Have volunteers read aloud the words they wrote. Explain that when you ask *What is pink?* you ask a question. When you say *My dress is pink*, you make a statement. Read the definitions in the box and talk about the example sentences.

Then read the first item at the bottom of page 53 together. Point out the pattern from the poem. Have children fill in the last two items with colors they like. Invite them to share their lines with a partner.

WRAP-UP/ASSESS

SUMMARIZE Reread the poem with children. Then have children summarize and reflect on what they have learned about statements and questions. You may want children to write their reflections in their journals. **REFLECTION**

RETEACH

REACHING ALL LEARNERS

INTERVENTION Lessons in **visual**, **auditory**, and **kinesthetic** modalities: p. R19 and *Reteach Activities Copying Masters*, page 7.

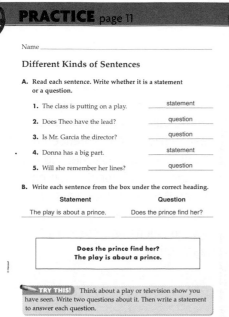

PRACTICE page 11

Name _____

Different Kinds of Sentences

A. Read each sentence. Write whether it is a statement or a question.

1. The class is putting on a play. _____statement_____
2. Does Theo have the lead? _____question_____
3. Is Mr. Garcia the director? _____question_____
4. Donna has a big part. _____statement_____
5. Will she remember her lines? _____question_____

B. Write each sentence from the box under the correct heading.

Statement	Question
The play is about a prince.	Does the prince find her?

Does the prince find her?
The play is about a prince.

TRY THIS! Think about a play or television show you have seen. Write two questions about it. Then write a statement to answer each question.

Practice • Statements and Questions   Unit 1 • Chapter 4   11

CHALLENGE

REACHING ALL LEARNERS

MAKE A CITY QUILT Have children use **Challenge Activity Card 3** (page R43) to make a quilt about their community. Encourage them to pick various places and to think of what they might want to show about them. Paste all the cards on one large piece of felt. You can add a title and a border before displaying the quilt.

Challenge Activity Card 3
Make a City Quilt

page 7

Different Kinds of Sentences

Circle the capital letter at the beginning of each sentence. Talk about and underline each end mark.

EXAMPLE: My grandma makes fancy quilts.

1. She cuts and sews the fabric.
2. What colors does she use?
3. How many quilts has she made?
4. Which one is your favorite?
5. Grandma made this one for me.

Visual/Auditory

Different Kinds of Sentences

Cut an index card in half. Write a period on one half and a question mark on the other. Have a partner read the sentences aloud. Hold up the period when you hear a statement. Hold up the question mark when you hear a question.

1. Eddie picks a red balloon.
2. What is his favorite color?
3. Karen wants a green one.
4. Is the balloon going to pop?

Add an end mark to the end of each sentence.

Kinesthetic

Teacher: Cut apart the activities and distribute to children based on the modalities that are their strengths.

Reteach Activities • Statements and Questions   Unit 1 • Chapter 4   7

Using Statements and Questions

OBJECTIVES
- To use correct capitalization and punctuation in statements and questions
- To use statements and questions in writing

DAILY LANGUAGE PRACTICE

TRANSPARENCY 6

1 what is redd? (What; red)

2 Teh flower is Red. (The; red)

BRIDGE TO WRITING What color is (name of object) ?

ORAL WARM-UP

PLAY A GAME Have children sit in a circle. One child begins with a question, such as *Who wears red today?* The next child answers, *(Name) wears red today* and then asks another question. Keep playing until each child has asked and answered a question.

Grammar Jingles™ **CD, Primary** Use Track 3 for review and reinforcement of sentences.

TEACH/MODEL

Use the examples to explain the punctuation marks used in statements and questions. Point out to children that questions may begin with words such as *who, what, where, when, why, how, can, are,* and *do.* Have children discuss what each sentence tells about.

GUIDED PRACTICE Help children write each sentence. Tell them to decide whether each sentence tells about something or asks something. Ask them to read each sentence aloud to help them decide.

Using Statements and Questions

> A statement begins with a capital letter and ends with a **period (.)**.
>
> **J**osé likes to swim.
>
> A question begins with a capital letter and ends with a **question mark (?)**.
>
> **D**o you like to swim, too?

Guided Practice

Write each sentence correctly.

1. the boys live by the beach
   The boys live by the beach.
2. do they like to swim
   Do they like to swim?
3. they swim when the water
   is warm
   They swim when the water is warm.
4. can they swim far
   Can they swim far?
5. they swim with their families
   They swim with their families.

54

Vocabulary Power page 10

Name_____ Related Words

Related Words are alike in some way. The words *whole* and *wholly* are related because of the base word *whole*.	whole + -ly = wholly The *whole* sky is not blue. The sky is not *wholly* blue.
Words can also be related by meaning. Draw a circle around the two words that mean the same as *wholly*. Draw a box around the two words that describe parts of a whole.	(totally) (entirely) [mostly] [partly]

Draw pictures to show the meaning of the underlined words:

mostly red	totally yellow
entirely green	partly pink

10 Unit 1 • Chapter 4 Vocabulary Power

ESL REACHING ALL LEARNERS

HOLD YOUR CARDS Some children may have trouble knowing when to use a period or a question mark. Prepare a period card and a question mark card for each child. Read sentences aloud to children and ask them to hold up the correct punctuation card when they hear each sentence. Then ask children to practice saying questions and statements for each other.

Remember A statement ends with a *period*.
A question ends with a *question mark*.

Independent Practice

Write each sentence correctly.

6. Zora swims well
   Zora swims well.
7. when did she learn to swim
   When did she learn to swim?
8. would you like to take lessons
   Would you like to take lessons?
9. you need a swimsuit
   You need a swimsuit.
10. where can you get one
    Where can you get one?
11. is Joe a good diver
    Is Joe a good diver?
12. Joe learned to dive last year
    Joe learned to dive last year.
13. the girls swim very fast
    The girls swim very fast.
14. did you see their flippers
    Did you see their flippers?
15. flippers help them swim faster
    Flippers help them swim faster.

Writing Connection

Asking Questions Write a question to ask classmates what sport they like best. Ask your question. Then write statements to tell their answers. Share your information with your classmates.

To type a question mark (?), hold down the shift key when you press ? .

55

Independent Practice

Have children complete the Independent Practice, or modify it by using the following suggestions:

MODIFIED INSTRUCTION

BELOW-LEVEL STUDENTS Suggest children read each sentence aloud to a partner. They may want to underline words that signal questions to help them *(when, would, where, is, did)*.

ABOVE-LEVEL STUDENTS Have children write their own questions, exchange papers with a partner, and answer each other's questions with statements.

Writing Connection

Asking Questions Remind children to write a question when they want to find out something and to write a statement when they want to tell something. Have volunteers place their questions and answers in the Sharing Basket to share with others.

WRAP-UP/ASSESS

SUMMARIZE Invite children to summarize and reflect on what they have learned about statements and questions. **REFLECTION**

RETEACH

INTERVENTION Lessons in **visual**, **auditory**, and **kinesthetic** modalities: p. R19 and *Reteach Activities Copying Masters*, page 8.

PRACTICE page 12

Name _____

Using Statements and Questions

A. Write an *S* beside each statement. Write a *Q* beside each question.

1. Who is playing the piano? Q
2. Kareem is playing the piano. S
3. What is the name of the song? Q
4. I wish I could play like that. S
5. Have you ever taken lessons? Q

B. Write each sentence correctly.

6. Max drew this flower
   Max drew this flower.
7. is it a rose
   Is it a rose?
8. how did he draw it
   How did he draw it?

TRY THIS! Write two questions to ask a partner. Then trade papers. Write answers to your partner's questions.

12 Unit 1 • Chapter 4   Practice • Statements and Questions

CHALLENGE

JOKE BOOK Have children write and illustrate a class joke book. Provide joke books for reference. Suggest children recall or write original jokes that begin with questions. Then have them write the jokes on paper and illustrate them. Combine the jokes to form a book.

Ms. Warren's Class Joke Book

---

page 8

Using Statements and Questions

Read each pair of sentences aloud. Circle the question.

1. Who is sitting in the chair?
   Geri is sitting in the chair.
2. She is listening to music.
   What is she doing?
3. Is it loud music?
   She does not like loud music.
4. The music is soft.
   Did Geri turn the music down?

- -

Using Statements and Questions

Cut out the words and end marks on the bottom of the page. Glue them where they belong.

1. Who   has new sneakers   ?
2. The   new sneakers belong to you   .
3. Were   your old shoes too small   ?
4. Why   did you pick blue sneakers   ?

| Were | Why | ? | ? |
| Who | The | . | . |

Teacher: Cut apart the activities and distribute to children based on the modalities that are their strengths.

8 Unit 1 • Chapter 4   Reteach Activities • Statements and Questions

Sentences That Go Together

OBJECTIVES

- To understand that a group of sentences can tell about the same idea
- To revise writing to leave out sentences that do not tell about the same idea

DAILY LANGUAGE PRACTICE

TRANSPARENCY 6

1 do you want to dig in the sand (Do; ?)

2 wE go to the beach every year? (We; .)

BRIDGE TO WRITING Where do you swim (punctuation mark)

ORAL WARM-UP

USE PRIOR KNOWLEDGE Read the following sentence to children: *It was the best trip we ever had.* Invite volunteers to tell sentences that might go along with this topic. Discuss with children that the topic is the best trip so all the sentences should tell about that topic.

Grammar Jingles™ **CD, Primary** Use Track 3 for review and reinforcement of sentences.

TEACH/MODEL

Introduce the concept by using the explanation and example. Reread the sample paragraph. Ask children what the main idea is and discuss how the sentences tell about that idea.

GUIDED PRACTICE Work through the first paragraph together. Have children decide the topic. (The pool is fun.) Then call on a volunteer to tell which sentence does not belong. Repeat the procedure with the second paragraph.

Sentences That Go Together

> Sentences that go together tell about one idea.
>
>   Jesse is a good swimmer. He can swim for a long time without getting tired. He can even do the backstroke.
>
> A group of sentences that tells about one main idea is called a **paragraph**. The first line of a paragraph is indented, or written a little to the right.

Guided Practice

Write the paragraph. Leave out the sentence that does not belong.

1. The pool is fun. We float on our backs. ~~We pet the pony at the zoo.~~ The lifeguard shows us games. The fastest swimmers get prizes.

2. Which animals live in the water? ~~Cats climb trees.~~ Dolphins live in water but breathe air. Frogs need to stay wet. Turtles can swim well and spend part of the time in water.

56

Vocabulary Power page 11

Name _____

Words that have the same base word are part of the same word family.

| whole |
| wholly |

whole + ly = wholly

Add -ly to the these words:

entire + ly = _____   total + ly = _____

most + ly = _____   part + ly = _____

Draw a picture to show the meaning of the underlined word.

full + ly = <u>fully</u>	entire + ly = <u>entirely</u>
one + ly = <u>only</u>	part + ly = <u>partly</u>

Vocabulary Power   Unit 1 • Chapter 4   11

REACHING ALL LEARNERS   ESL

ONE TOPIC Some children may have difficulty writing sentences that keep to one topic. To help them, display their favorite book or fairy tale and have them talk about the story. Write some of their sentences on the board, including some that do not belong. Read aloud the sentences with children and discuss why some sentences do not belong.

Independent Practice

Write each paragraph. Leave out the one sentence that does not belong.

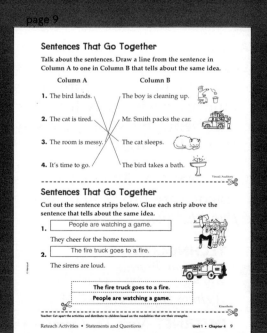

3. What can we do at the beach? We can build sandcastles. Later, we can float on tubes. We can pick up shells, too. ~~We can make snowballs.~~

4. Fish make great pets. Goldfish are pretty and come in many colors. ~~Dogs are fun pets.~~ Most fish are quiet. Most fish don't eat much either.

5. How do my friends learn to swim? Carla takes swim lessons. Ming practices every day at the pool. ~~Roberto rides the bus to school.~~ Alex uses a kickboard.

Writing Connection

Keeping to the Main Idea Read the paragraph. There is a line under the main idea. Write a sentence to add to the paragraph. Be sure it tells about the main idea.

<u>Whales are interesting animals.</u> They live in the ocean. They come up to breathe air. Whales have strong tails for swimming.

57

Independent Practice

Have children complete the Independent Practice, or modify it by using the following suggestions:

MODIFIED INSTRUCTION

BELOW-LEVEL STUDENTS To help children find which sentence doesn't belong, suggest that they circle the sentence that tells what the topic is and underline the sentences that tell more about the topic.

ABOVE-LEVEL STUDENTS After children are finished, invite them to think of a topic and then write three sentences that tell about the topic and one sentence that does not. They can then trade with a partner and find the sentence that does not belong.

Writing Connection

Keeping to the Main Idea Have children work in pairs to determine how well their sentences keep to the main idea. They can ask questions such as *Does this sentence tell why whales are interesting?*

WRAP-UP/ASSESS

My Journal

SUMMARIZE Ask children to summarize and reflect on what they have learned about writing a group of sentences about a topic. **REFLECTION**

REACHING ALL LEARNERS

RETEACH

INTERVENTION Lessons in **visual**, **auditory**, and **kinesthetic** modalities: p. R19 and *Reteach Activities Copying Masters*, page 9.

page 9

REACHING ALL LEARNERS

PRACTICE page 13

Name _____

Sentences That Go Together

A. Read each paragraph. Cross out the sentence that doesn't belong.

1. We learned about paintbrushes in art class. People use one kind of brush for oil paint. ~~I read about plants in my science book.~~ They use another kind for watercolor paint.

2. Nia is a good artist. She draws neat pictures. ~~Nia lives on Lake Street.~~ Then she colors the pictures with crayons. Sometimes she even paints them.

B. Write the sentence from the box that belongs in the paragraph.

3. Maria is in the school play. She wants to play her part well. _____She practices her lines often._____ Her brother helps her remember the lines.

> The costume is yellow.
> Jeff plays the piano.
> **She practices her lines often.**

TRY THIS! Write a paragraph about something you do well. Then read the sentences to make sure they all go together.

Practice • Statements and Questions   Unit 1 • Chapter 4 **13**

CHALLENGE

CHAIN STORIES Have groups create chain stories. Provide each group with a topic and tell children to take turns adding one sentence at a time to their story. One child may write down the sentences and then read them back to the group. Tell children to discuss whether each sentence matches the topic.

Sentences That Go Together

Talk about the sentences. Draw a line from the sentence in Column A to one in Column B that tells about the same idea.

Column A	Column B
1. The bird lands.	The boy is cleaning up.
2. The cat is tired.	Mr. Smith packs the car.
3. The room is messy.	The cat sleeps.
4. It's time to go.	The bird takes a bath.

Sentences That Go Together

Cut out the sentence strips below. Glue each strip above the sentence that tells about the same idea.

1. | People are watching a game. |
   They cheer for the home team.

2. | The fire truck goes to a fire. |
   The sirens are loud.

> **The fire truck goes to a fire.**
> **People are watching a game.**

Teacher: Cut apart the activities and distribute to children based on the modalities that are their strengths.

Reteach Activities • Statements and Questions   Unit 1 • Chapter 4 **9**

Extra Practice

OBJECTIVES

- To identify and punctuate correctly statements and questions
- To use statements and questions in writing

DAILY LANGUAGE PRACTICE

TRANSPARENCY 7

1 mike likes to go to the beach (Mike; .)

2 did you watch the diver. (Did; ?)

BRIDGE TO WRITING We built a sand castle (punctuation mark)

ORAL WARM-UP

PLAY MOTHER, MAY I? Play a short game of "Mother, May I?" with children. Ask them to use statements to describe the actions they see and do. Have them rephrase the statements as questions. Try to work a Vocabulary Power word into the game.

TEACH/MODEL

Read each set of directions to help children understand how to complete each section. Have children share their answers in small groups before you read aloud the answers to them.

WRAP-UP/ASSESS

SUMMARIZE Ask children to reflect on and discuss any special problems they had in completing the practice before you have them summarize what they have learned about statements, questions, and sentences that belong together.

ADDITIONAL PRACTICE Additional items for Extra Practice are provided on page 467 of the *Pupil Edition.*

TECHNOLOGY

Grammar Practice and Assessment CD-ROM

Writing Express CD-ROM

INTERNET Visit *The Learning Site!* www.harcourtschool.com

Statements and Questions

Extra Practice

Read the sentences. Write only the statements.

1. Can you jump off the diving board?
2. <u>Mara likes to play tag.</u>
3. <u>Erik climbs the stairs to the slide.</u>
4. Do you like the slide?

Write each sentence correctly. Use capital letters and end marks.

5. the sand is not very hot
   The sand is not very hot.
6. may I help make the castle
   May I help make the castle?
7. do you want the shovel
   Do you want the shovel?

Write the paragraph. Leave out the sentence that does not belong.

8. The children worked together to make a sandcastle. Tasha put sand in a bucket. Then her sister added water. ~~David did his homework.~~ Kevin shaped the sand into a castle.

58

Vocabulary Power page 12

Name _____

Homophones are words that sound the same.

   The words whole and hole sound the same.

Are the words whole and hole spelled the same? (NO)
Do the words whole and hole have the same meaning? (NO)

What about the following underlined words? Write YES or NO.

   The sky is not <u>wholly</u> blue.   Swiss Cheese is <u>holey.</u>

Do <u>wholly</u> and <u>holey</u> sound the same? _____

Are <u>wholly</u> and <u>holey</u> spelled the same? _____

Do <u>wholly</u> and <u>holey</u> mean the same? _____

The following words are homophones. Circle one of the words. Draw a picture to show the meaning of the word you circled.

pair-pear	to-too-two
ate-eight	red-read

12   Unit 1 • Chapter 4   Vocabulary Power

REACHING ALL LEARNERS — ESL

POSTER TALK Some children may have trouble with questions and statements. Display a poster showing various activities. Ask questions as you point to different parts of the poster. Invite volunteers to answer in complete sentences. Then make statements and have volunteers ask questions, such as *The boy walks on the beach. Who walks on the beach? Why does he walk on the beach?*

Language Play

Riddles
- Take turns with a partner.
- Find an object in the room. Don't tell your partner what it is.
- Make up clues to help your partner guess the object. Use statements and questions.
- Write a few riddles like this one.

> I am yellow. I am made out of wood. I get shorter each time I am used. What am I?
>
> A pencil

Writing Connection

Paragraph Remember that a **paragraph** is a group of sentences that tells about one main idea. One sentence tells the main idea. The other sentences are **details**. They tell more about the main idea.

> I like to go to Green Park with my family. ⎤— main idea
> We hike through the woods. We play on the
> swings or play tag in the big field. Then we
> usually fish in the lake and cook out. It's fun! ⎦— details

Write a paragraph about a place you like to visit.
Write a sentence to tell the main idea. Indent the first line.
Write detail sentences to tell why you like the place.

59

Language Play

Read the example riddle aloud with children. Suggest they select interesting and colorful objects for their riddles. Remind them to speak at an appropriate rate and volume for telling riddles to one person.

Writing Connection

Paragraph Check to see that children have successfully written a paragraph by using the criteria below.

CRITERIA
- ☑ Indents the first line.
- ☑ Begins each sentence with a capital letter.
- ☑ Includes one sentence that tells the main idea.
- ☑ Includes sentences that go together to tell about the main idea.

Sharing Basket You may want to have children place their writing in the Sharing Basket to share with classmates.

PRACTICE page 14

REACHING ALL LEARNERS

Name _____

Extra Practice

A. Write the correct word to fill in each blank. Then write the word in the puzzle.

	1.		2.
	p		a
3. t	e	l	l	s
	r		k
	i		s
	o		
	d		

1. A statement ends with a ___period___.

2. A question is a sentence that ___asks___ something.

3. A statement is a sentence that ___tells___ something.

B. Write each sentence correctly.

4. sami likes to play tennis
   Sami likes to play tennis.

5. she plays each Saturday
   She plays each Saturday.

6. is she going to play today
   Is she going to play today?

C. Underline the sentence that belongs with the group of sentences from Part B.

7. Sami's game is not far from here.
   Sami used to play soccer.

14 Unit 1 • Chapter 4   Practice • Statements and Questions

CHALLENGE

REACHING ALL LEARNERS

WRITE A SCENE Have pairs of children role-play a scene in which one child can speak only in questions and the other can speak only in statements. Suggest children plan their scenes and jot down a list of questions and answers. Then have them present their scene to the class.

Chapter Review

OBJECTIVES

- To review statements and questions and to recognize that groups of sentences should tell about one topic
- To identify homophones and recognize that they sound alike but have different spellings and meanings

DAILY LANGUAGE PRACTICE

TRANSPARENCY 7

1 do you know where the beach is (Do; ?)

2 my parents like to play in the sand, too? (My; .)

BRIDGE TO WRITING I like the beach ___ (punctuation mark)

STANDARDIZED TEST PREP

Read the directions for each section with children to make sure they understand what they need to do. You may wish to have children complete this page independently and use it as an assessment.

TEST PREPARATION TIP

Item Type: Multiple Choice

TIP

Model this strategy to help children insure that they understand the directions.

I listened to the directions being read aloud, but I'm still not sure I know what to do. I'll read the directions slowly to myself. I think the directions mean that one of the statements or questions is written correctly and I just have to choose the answer that shows this. I'll do the first one and if I still do not understand what to do I will ask for help.

Chapter Review

Choose the answer that shows the statement or question written correctly.

1. We have jobs at home.
   - **a.** we have jobs at home.
   - **b.** We have jobs at home?
   - **c.** correct as is

2. my sister clears the table
   - **a.** My sister clears the table.
   - **b.** My sister clears the table?
   - **c.** correct as is

3. does Dad wash the dishes
   - **a.** Does Dad wash the dishes.
   - **b.** Does Dad wash the dishes?
   - **c.** correct as is

4. Lee takes out the trash
   - **a.** Lee takes out the trash?
   - **b.** Lee takes out the trash.
   - **c.** correct as is

Write the paragraph. Leave out the sentence that does not belong.

5. I keep my room clean. ~~I leave my socks on the floor.~~ I put my toys away. I fold my shirts and make my bed.

 Visit our website for more activities with statements and questions: www.harcourtschool.com

60

Language Assessment

PORTFOLIO ASSESSMENT
Have children select their best work from the following activities:

- **Writing Connection**, pages 55, 57, 59; TE activities, pages 53 and 57.

ONGOING ASSESSMENT
Evaluate the performance of 4-6 children using appropriate checklists and record forms from pages R65–R68 and R77-79.

INTERNET Activities and exercises to help children prepare for state and standardized assessments appear on *The Learning Site:*
www.harcourtschool.com

■ Vocabulary ■

Homophones

Homophones are words that sound alike but have different spellings and meanings. Knowing homophones and their meanings will help you spell words correctly.

I **see** the boat on the **sea**.

Practice

Write the two words that sound alike in each pair of sentences. Tell how they are different.

1. Did you <u>hear</u> the news?

   The baseball player will be <u>here</u> soon.

2. I like to <u>write</u> stories.

   Do you want to read one <u>right</u> now?

3. <u>Where</u> are you going?

   Will you <u>wear</u> your new shoes?

4. Malik <u>ate</u> a plum.

   Yoko will eat <u>eight</u> grapes.

5. Maria <u>won</u> the race.

   Was she in <u>one</u> race or two?

61

■ Vocabulary ■

Homophones

TEACH/MODEL

Say the following words aloud: *right, by,* and *flour*. Ask children to use each word in a sentence. Then write the words on the board and point out sentences in which homophones were used instead. Write the homophone next to its sound-alike partner. Explain that words that sound alike but have different meanings and spellings are called *homophones*.

PRACTICE After children are finished, have them share their answers. Then ask them to make up their own sentences using homophones.

WRAP-UP/ASSESS

SUMMARIZE Ask children to tell what they have learned about homophones and how recognizing which homophone to use will make their writing more accurate. Some children may want to make a Homophone Wall on a classroom bulletin board or wall.

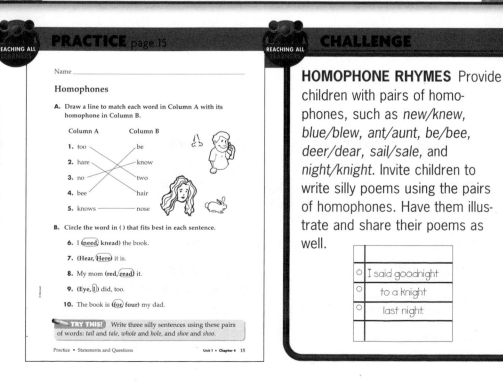

PRACTICE page 15

Name _____

Homophones

A. Draw a line to match each word in Column A with its homophone in Column B.

Column A   Column B

1. too   be
2. hare   know
3. no   two
4. bee   hair
5. knows   nose

B. Circle the word in ( ) that fits best in each sentence.

6. I (need, knead) the book.
7. (Hear, Here) it is.
8. My mom (red, read) it.
9. (Eye, I) did, too.
10. The book is (for, four) my dad.

TRY THIS! Write three silly sentences using these pairs of words: *tail* and *tale*, *whole* and *hole*, and *shoe* and *shoo*.

Practice • Statements and Questions   Unit 1 • Chapter 4   15

CHALLENGE

HOMOPHONE RHYMES Provide children with pairs of homophones, such as *new/knew, blue/blew, ant/aunt, be/bee, deer/dear, sail/sale,* and *night/knight*. Invite children to write silly poems using the pairs of homophones. Have them illustrate and share their poems as well.

I said goodnight
to a knight
last night.

LESSON ORGANIZER	**DAY 1**	**DAY 2**
DAILY LANGUAGE PRACTICE TRANSPARENCY 8, 9	1. we like watermelon (We; .) 2. Wat do you like (What; ?) **Bridge to Writing** Do you like kiwi fruit (punctuation mark)	1. eat this apple (Eat; .) 2. Watt a great sandwich that is (What; !) **Bridge to Writing** That mustard is so spicy (punctuation mark)
ORAL WARM-UP Listening/Speaking	Make up Exclamations and Commands p. 62	Play Simon Says p. 64 *Grammar Jingles™* CD Track 3
TEACH/MODEL GRAMMAR **KEY** ✔ = tested skill	✔ **MORE KINDS OF SENTENCES** pp. 62-63 • To listen critically to interpret and evaluate a poem • To identify exclamations and commands	✔ **EXCLAMATIONS AND COMMANDS** pp. 64-65 • To understand and punctuate correctly exclamations and commands • To use commands in writing
Reaching All Learners	**Challenge:** Make a Robot p. 63 Activity Card, p. R44 **ESL:** *ESL Manual* pp. 28-29 *Practice Book* p. 16 **Reteach:** *Reteach Activities Copying Masters* p. 10	**Modified Instruction** Below-Level: Say Sentences Aloud Above-Level: Write Sentences **Challenge:** Write a Poem p. 65 **ESL:** Say the Verb p. 64 *ESL Manual* pp. 28, 30 *Practice Book* p. 17 **Reteach:** *Reteach Activities Copying Masters* p. 11

WRITING	Write exclamations and commands p. 63
	  Summarize/Reflect
		Writing Connection p. 65
		 Writing a Recipe
		  Summarize/Reflect

CROSS-CURRICULAR/ ENRICHMENT	**Vocabulary Power** Word Meaning, p. 62 harmony, agreement, disagreement, disharmony, togetherness See *Vocabulary Power* book.	**Vocabulary Power** Synonyms/Antonyms, p. 62 *Vocabulary Power* book p. 13 **Vocabulary activity**

Visit _The Learning Site!_
www.harcourtschool.com
WRITING ACTIVITIES
Writing Express CD-ROM

DAY 3	DAY 4	DAY 5
1. what a strong hit that is. (What; !)	**1.** Who kickt the ball (kicked; ?)	**1.** Is which your favorite book (Which is; ?)
2. Givve me the ball! (Give; .)	**2.** what a strong kick that was? (What; !)	**2.** Show! it to me (Show; .)
Bridge to Writing Hit it with the bat (punctuation mark)	**Bridge to Writing** Kick the ball hard (punctuation mark)	**Bridge to Writing** What a funny title (punctuation mark)
Act out and Describe An Action p. 66 _Grammar Jingles_™ CD Track 3	Discuss a Picture p. 68	
✔ **USING DIFFERENT KINDS OF SENTENCES** pp. 66-67 • To identify different kinds of sentences • To use different kinds of sentences in writing and to punctuate them	**EXTRA PRACTICE** p. 68 • To recognize, write, and punctuate statements, questions, exclamations, and commands **Practice and Assessment**	**TEST PREP CHAPTER REVIEW** p. 70 • To review exclamations and commands • To use a word processing program to input and add text **Test Preparation**
Modified Instruction Below-Level: Say Changes Aloud Above-Level: Change Statements **Challenge:** Rewriting p. 67 **ESL:** Punctuation p. 66 _ESL Manual_ pp. 28, 31 _Practice Book_ p. 18 **Reteach:** _Reteach Activities Copying Masters_ p. 12	**Challenge:** Make a Map p. 69 **ESL:** Shared Writing p. 68 _ESL Manual_ pp. 28, 32 _Practice Book_ p. 19	**Challenge:** Computer Time p. 71 _ESL Manual_ pp. 28, 33 _Practice Book_ p. 20
Writing Connection p. 67 Revising Summarize/Reflect	Writing Connection p. 69 Directions	Technology p. 71 Using a Computer
 **Vocabulary Power** Prefixes/Suffixes p. 62 _Vocabulary Power_ book p. 14 **Vocabulary activity**	**Vocabulary Power** Related Words p. 62 _Vocabulary Power_ book p. 15 Language Play p. 69 **Vocabulary activity**	**Vocabulary Power** Comparison p. 62

More Kinds of Sentences

OBJECTIVES

- To listen critically to interpret and evaluate a poem
- To identify exclamations and commands

DAILY LANGUAGE PRACTICE

TRANSPARENCY 8

1 we like watermelon (We; .)

2 Wat do you like (What; ?)

BRIDGE TO WRITING Do you like kiwi fruit (punctuation mark)

ORAL WARM-UP

USE PRIOR KNOWLEDGE Ask children what they might say on different occasions, such as while playing with a puppy, asking someone to hurry up, getting a gift, or being surprised. Begin a list of exclamations and commands on chart paper.

TEACH/MODEL

Have children open to page 62 and describe the illustration. Have them use the title and the illustration to predict what the poem will be about. Read the poem aloud, asking children to listen to the way you say the sentences. Then reread the poem, having children join in with you. Remind them to speak in an appropriate volume.

DEVELOP ORAL LANGUAGE Ask children to recall some of the exclamations and commands from the poem. Invite volunteers to demonstrate or describe other words or sentences that tell someone to do something in a hurry. Add exclamations to the list on chart paper.

More Kinds of Sentences

Read the poem.

Hurry!

Hurry! says the morning,
Don't be late for school!

Hurry! says the teacher,
Hand in papers now!

Hurry! says the mother,
Supper's getting cold!

Hurry! says the father,
Time to go to bed!

slowly, says the darkness,
you can talk to me . . .

Eve Merriam

62

Vocabulary Power

DAY 1 WORD MEANING Write: *When we work together we are in* harmony. Discuss specific times when children have worked in harmony.

DAY 2 SYNONYMS/ANTONYMS Write: *harmony, together, apart.* **Which two words have similar meanings? Which are opposites?** (See also *Vocabulary Power*, page 13.)

DAY 3 PREFIXES/SUFFIXES Write: *harmony, disharmony.* **How does adding *dis-* to the beginning of harmony change the meaning?** (See also *Vocabulary Power*, page 14.)

DAY 4 RELATED WORDS Write: *The four singers sang in harmony.* **What does *harmony* have to do with singing and music?** (See also *Vocabulary Power*, page 15.)

DAY 5 COMPARISON **Would you rather sing in harmony or work in harmony with classmates? Why?**

What are some things you say when you are in a hurry? What do you say when you want someone to do something? Say them to a classmate. Act them out.

An **exclamation** is a sentence that shows strong feeling.

Bill's drawing is super! It is great!

A **command** is a sentence that tells someone to do something.

Show me the drawing. Please give it to me.

What do you think the two characters in the picture are saying? Write one exclamation and one command for each bubble.

63

WRITE Copy children's sentences on the board or on chart paper. Have children practice reading the sentences using appropriate rate and volume for the occasion. Read aloud the definitions in the box, and talk about the example sentences.

Then look at the illustration at the bottom of page 63 together. Have children write dialogue and then share their work with a partner.

WRAP-UP/ASSESS

SUMMARIZE Reread the poem with children. Then have them summarize what they have learned about exclamations and commands. You may want children to write their summaries in their journals as well as record exclamations they thought of while completing the page.

RETEACH

INTERVENTION Lessons in **visual**, **auditory**, and **kinesthetic** modalities: p. R20 and *Reteach Activities Copying Masters*, p. 10.

page 10

More Kinds of Sentences

Read the sentences aloud. Draw a line under each exclamation. Circle each command.

1. Ingrid likes to jump.
2. How high she jumps!
3. Look at her.
4. Would you like to try?
5. I can jump high, too!
6. Watch me jump.

More Kinds of Sentences

Cut out the cards. Read one set of sentences to a partner. Tell your partner to follow the commands, but to "freeze" if you read an exclamation or a question. Then have your partner read the other set of sentences to you.

1. Stand up.	1. Pick up a book.
2. Jump one time.	2. Open the book.
3. What a great jump!	3. You're a good listener!
4. Can you jump higher?	4. Turn the page.
5. Sit down.	5. Can you read this?

10   Unit 1 • Chapter 5   Reteach Activities • Exclamations and Commands

PRACTICE page 16

Name _____

More Kinds of Sentences

A. Read each sentence. Write the exclamations.

1. Do you hear the drum?
_____

2. Bill plays so loudly!
Bill plays so loudly!

3. The band is great!
The band is great!

B. Read each pair of sentences. Write the command.

4. My father is in a band.
Hand the CD to me.
Hand the CD to me.

5. Listen to this.
Is that your father playing?
Listen to this.

TRY THIS! Think about the type of music you like best. Write an exclamation that shows how you feel about the music.

16   Unit 1 • Chapter 5   Practice • Exclamations and Commands

CHALLENGE

MAKE A ROBOT Have children use **Challenge Activity Card 4** (page R44) to make a robot. Tell them that the note cards are their robots' programs. Then have a volunteer pick a card and act out the command as a robot would. Ask the class to guess the command.

Challenge Activity Card 4

Make a Robot

Exclamations and Commands

OBJECTIVES
• To understand and punctuate correctly exclamations and commands
• To use commands in writing

DAILY LANGUAGE PRACTICE
TRANSPARENCY 8

1 eat this apple (Eat; .)

2 Watt a great sandwich that is (What; !)

BRIDGE TO WRITING That mustard is so spicy (punctuation mark)

ORAL WARM-UP

PLAY SIMON SAYS Have volunteers take turns giving commands to the class, such as "Put your hands on your head." Children should speak at a rate that allows the class time to follow each command.

Grammar Jingles™ **CD, Primary** Use Track 3 for reinforcement and review of exclamations and commands

TEACH/MODEL

Use the explanation and examples to explain the difference between an exclamation and a command. Point out the correct punctuation, and then illustrate it by saying each sentence with appropriate feeling.

GUIDED PRACTICE Work with children to complete each sentence. Have them read each sentence aloud to decide whether it shows strong emotion or gives a command.

Exclamations and Commands

An exclamation is a sentence that shows strong feeling. It ends with an **exclamation point (!)**.

Making salad is a great idea!

A command is an order. It usually ends with a **period (.)**.

Mix the fruit together.

Guided Practice

Write the exclamations and the commands. Use the correct end marks.

1. What a good cook Tom is!
2. Get Tom's cookbook.
3. Open the book, please.
4. Turn to the first recipe.
5. That fruit salad looks great!

64

Vocabulary Power page 13

Name _____ Synonyms/Antonyms

Some words have the same or almost the same meanings. Other words have opposite meanings.

same meanings: little, small
opposite meanings: small, large

Which words mean the same as the word in dark print? Which mean the opposite? Write the words in the correct box.

harmony agreement disagreement
disharmony togetherness

Same meaning as harmony	Opposite of harmony
agreement	disagreement
togetherness	disharmony

Draw a picture to show the meaning of the sentences.

We are working together. We're in agreement. We are in harmony.	We are working together. We're having a disagreement. We are in disharmony.

Vocabulary Power   Unit 1 • Chapter 5   13

REACHING ALL LEARNERS   **ESL**

SAY THE VERB Some children may have difficulty differentiating between exclamations and commands. To help clarify, ask a volunteer to say an exclamation or give a command. Then ask the other children to act out what they heard. Point out that if they can act it out, then it is a command.

Remember An exclamation ends with an exclamation point. A command usually ends with a period.

Independent Practice

Write the exclamations and the commands. Use the correct end marks.

6. I just love strawberries!

7. Taste a cherry, Tracy.

8. Get Ricardo a bowl of peaches.

9. Do not give me any bananas.

10. Cream with fruit is great!

11. What a yummy treat this is!

12. Cody, have some fresh fruit.

13. Give Pat a spoon.

14. Sit down and eat.

15. What different tastes we all have!

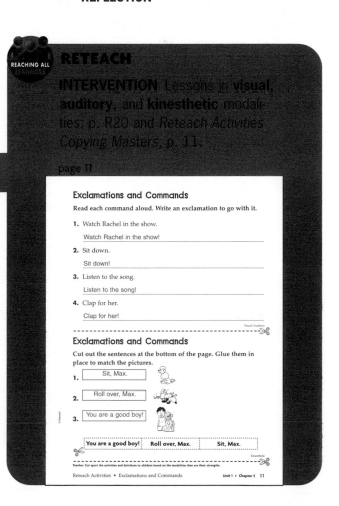

Writing Connection

Writing a Recipe Draw your favorite fruit. Write sentences that tell someone how to fix the fruit the way you like to eat it. Make each sentence a command.

To type an exclamation point hold down the shift key while you press the ! key.

65

Independent Practice

Have children complete the Independent Practice, or modify it by using the following suggestions:

MODIFIED INSTRUCTION

BELOW-LEVEL STUDENTS Have partners read a sentence aloud, and decide whether it gives a command or tells about a strong feeling.

ABOVE-LEVEL STUDENTS After children are finished, have them write at least two more exclamations and two more commands.

Writing Connection

Writing a Recipe Tell children that a recipe explains how to fix something to eat. Remind them that commands are used in writing to tell someone to do something and should end with periods. Have volunteers place their recipes in the Sharing Basket.

WRAP-UP/ASSESS

SUMMARIZE Ask children to reflect on and summarize what they have learned about exclamations and commands.

REFLECTION

RETEACH

INTERVENTION Lessons in **visual**, **auditory**, and **kinesthetic** modalities: p. R20 and *Reteach Activities Copying Masters*, p. 11.

page 11

PRACTICE page 17

Name _____

Exclamations and Commands

A. Write whether each sentence is an exclamation or a command.

1. Hurry to the table. — command

2. What a yummy meal! — exclamation

3. Look at the pizza. — command

4. This is great! — exclamation

B. Write the exclamations and the commands. Use the correct end marks.

5. Pass the carrots to me
   Pass the carrots to me.

6. The cheese is hot
   The cheese is hot!

7. Pizza is my favorite
   Pizza is my favorite!

TRY THIS! Draw a picture of something that could happen at school. Write a command and an exclamation about your picture.

Practice • Exclamations and Commands   Unit 1 • Chapter 5   17

CHALLENGE

WRITE A POEM Have children write and illustrate their own poems using exclamations and commands. Encourage them to think about the people who might ask them to do something during the day and why they might ask this. Ask volunteers to read their poems aloud.

---

page 11

Exclamations and Commands

Read each command aloud. Write an exclamation to go with it.

1. Watch Rachel in the show.
   Watch Rachel in the show!

2. Sit down.
   Sit down!

3. Listen to the song.
   Listen to the song!

4. Clap for her.
   Clap for her!

Exclamations and Commands

Cut out the sentences at the bottom of the page. Glue them in place to match the pictures.

1. Sit, Max.

2. Roll over, Max.

3. You are a good boy!

| You are a good boy! | Roll over, Max. | Sit, Max. |

Teacher: Cut apart the activities and distribute to children based on the modalities that are their strengths.

Reteach Activities • Exclamations and Commands   Unit 1 • Chapter 5   11

Using Different Kinds of Sentences

OBJECTIVES
- To identify different kinds of sentences
- To use different kinds of sentences in writing and to punctuate them

1 what a strong hit that was. (What; !)

2 Givve me the ball! (Give; .)

BRIDGE TO WRITING Hit it with the bat (punctuation mark)

ORAL WARM-UP

USE PRIOR KNOWLEDGE Have volunteers act out a sports-related activity, such as throwing a ball. Have children think of exclamations or commands to say about the action.

Grammar Jingles™ **CD, Primary** Use Track 3 for reinforcement and review of different kinds of sentences.

TEACH/MODEL

Introduce the concept by using the explanation and the examples. Read each sentence aloud with the appropriate tone of voice. Ask children to discuss the difference between a question (it asks something), a statement (it tells something), an exclamation (it shows a strong feeling), and a command (it tells someone to do something). Review the punctuation at the end of each sentence.

GUIDED PRACTICE Show children how to reorder the words in the first two sentences. Remind them to put the correct punctuation at the end of the sentence. Work through the remaining sentences together.

Exclamations and Commands   **Grammar-Writing Connection**

Using Different Kinds of Sentences

There are four kinds of sentences. Using different kinds of sentences makes your writing more interesting.

Stan is a good catcher.	**statement**
Is Stan a good catcher?	**question**
What a good catcher he is!	**exclamation**
Catch the ball.	**command**

Guided Practice

Change each statement into the kind of sentence shown in ( ). Write the new sentence.

1. Molly can hit the ball hard. (question)
   Can Molly hit the ball hard?
2. She has a great arm. (exclamation)
   What a great arm she has!
3. Tennis is her favorite sport. (question)
   Is tennis her favorite sport?
4. Can you ask Molly yourself? (command)
   Ask Molly yourself.
5. Molly won the game. (exclamation)
   Molly won the game!

66

Vocabulary Power page 14

Name _____   Prefixes/ Suffixes

Adding a beginning or an ending to a base word can change the meaning.

dis + harmony = disharmony
together + ness = togetherness

Add dis- to the beginning of these words to make new words.	Choose one word and draw a picture to show its meaning.
agreement ____ disagreement	
please ____ displease	
appear ____ disappear	
color ____ discolor	
continue ____ discontinue	

Add -ness to the end of these words to make new words.	Choose one word and draw a picture to show its meaning.
together ____ togetherness	
bright ____ brightness	
silly ____ silliness	
dark ____ darkness	
fresh ____ freshness	

14   Unit 1 • Chapter 5   Vocabulary Power

REACHING ALL LEARNERS   **ESL**

PUNCTUATION Place word cards with the words *question, statement, exclamation,* and *command* in a basket. Hand out punctuation cards, one per child, with either a period, an exclamation mark, or a question mark. Call on a volunteer to pick a word card. If the word card matches the volunteer's punctuation card, she or he says and acts out a sentence. If not, call on the next volunteer.

Remember Use different kinds of sentences to make your writing more interesting.

Independent Practice

Change each statement into the kind of sentence shown in ( ). Write the new sentence.

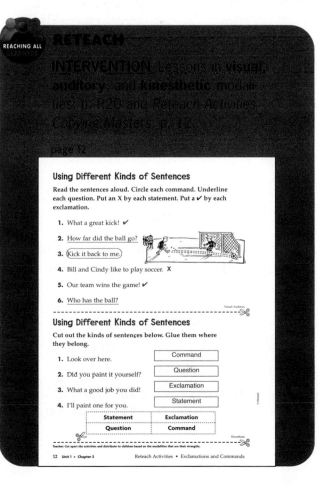

6. The play starts at eight. (question)
   Does the play start at eight?
7. Someone is in my seat. (question)
   Is someone in my seat?
8. Should you ask her to move? (command)
   Ask her to move.
9. Anna has the lead in the play. (question)
   Does Anna have the lead in the play?
10. She is a good actress. (exclamation)
    What a good actress she is!
11. Do you want to look at the costumes? (command)
    Look at the costumes.
12. Teddy's mom made them. (question)
    Did Teddy's mom make them?
13. They are beautiful. (exclamation)
    How beautiful they are!
14. Do you want to listen to the band? (command)
    Listen to the band.
15. The music is nice. (question)
    Is the music nice?

Writing Connection

Revising Look through your Writing Portfolio. Choose one piece of writing. Look at the kinds of sentences you used. Could you change any sentences to different kinds of sentences? Revise your writing.

Use Editor's Marks to make changes. Then copy the changes onto the document on the computer.

67

Independent Practice

Have children complete the Independent Practice, or modify it by using the following suggestions:

MODIFIED INSTRUCTION

BELOW-LEVEL STUDENTS Suggest that children think about what each kind of sentence tells about before they make any changes. Then suggest they say their changes aloud first to see if they make sense.

ABOVE-LEVEL STUDENTS After children are finished, have them change the statements into other kinds of sentences.

Writing Connection

Revising Help children select an appropriate piece of writing to revise. Suggest that they underline the sentences they want to change. After children revise their sentences, have them edit for appropriate punctuation.

WRAP-UP/ASSESS

SUMMARIZE Have children summarize and reflect about what they know about different kinds of sentences. **REFLECTION**

RETEACH

INTERVENTION Lessons in visual, auditory, and kinesthetic modalities, p. R20 and Reteach Activities Copying Masters, p. 12

page 12

Using Different Kinds of Sentences

Read the sentences aloud. Circle each command. Underline each question. Put an X by each statement. Put a ✔ by each exclamation.

1. What a great kick! ✔
2. How far did the ball go?
3. Kick it back to me.
4. Bill and Cindy like to play soccer. X
5. Our team wins the game! ✔
6. Who has the ball?

Using Different Kinds of Sentences

Cut out the kinds of sentences below. Glue them where they belong.

1. Look over here.   Command
2. Did you paint it yourself?   Question
3. What a good job you did!   Exclamation
4. I'll paint one for you.   Statement

Statement	Exclamation
Question	Command

12 Unit 1 • Chapter 5   Reteach Activities • Exclamations and Commands

---

PRACTICE page 18

Name _____

Using Different Kinds of Sentences

A. Draw a line from each sentence in Column A to the word in Column B that tells what kind of sentence it is.

Column A	Column B
1. Feed the dog.	question
2. Is it Kara's pet?	statement
3. What a beautiful animal!	command
4. Kara loves Fido.	exclamation

B. Finish each sentence. Use the word in ( ) to tell you what type of sentence to write. Use the correct end marks. Possible responses are given.

5. (statement) Pat and her dog ___are in the park.___
6. (question) When ___did they arrive?___
7. (exclamation) What a ___pretty dog!___
8. (exclamation) It's such a ___sunny day!___
9. (command) ___Finish___ the game.

TRY THIS! Make a poster that tells about the students in your class. Include statements, questions, exclamations, and commands on your poster.

18 Unit 1 • Chapter 5   Practice • Exclamations and Commands

CHALLENGE

REWRITING Have children find and cut out different kinds of sentences in old newspapers. Have them paste each sentence on a separate sheet of paper. Then ask them to rewrite the sentences, changing them into other kinds of sentences.

JOE WON THE RACE.

Who won the race?
Joe won the race!
Win the race, Joe.

Extra Practice

OBJECTIVES

- To recognize, write, and punctuate statements, questions, exclamations, and commands

DAILY LANGUAGE PRACTICE

TRANSPARENCY 9

① Who kickt the ball (kicked; ?)

② what a strong kick that was? (What; !)

BRIDGE TO WRITING Kick the ball hard (punctuation mark)

ORAL WARM-UP

USE PRIOR KNOWLEDGE Show children a picture of a race or other activity. Ask volunteers to discuss the picture, using different kinds of sentences. Try to work a Vocabulary Power word into the activity.

TEACH/MODEL

Read each set of directions aloud to help children understand how to complete each section. Have children share their answers in small groups before you read aloud the answers to them.

WRAP-UP/ASSESS

SUMMARIZE Ask children to reflect on and discuss any special problems they had in completing the practice. Then have them summarize what they have learned about exclamations, commands, statements, and questions.

ADDITIONAL PRACTICE Additional items of Extra Practice are provided on page 467 of the *Pupil Edition.*

TECHNOLOGY

Grammar Practice and Assessment CD-ROM

Writing Express CD-ROM

INTERNET Visit *The Learning Site!*
www.harcourtschool.com

Exclamations and Commands

Extra Practice

Write only the exclamations and the commands. Use the correct end marks.

1. What an exciting race
   What an exciting race!
2. Who do you think is fastest

3. I don't know who will win

4. Get ready for the race to start
   Get ready for the race to start.
5. Watch Tama go
   Watch Tama go.
6. Look how fast Brian runs
   Look how fast Brian runs!
7. Is that Wong in front

8. Wong is the winner
   Wong is the winner!

Change each statement into the kind of sentence shown in ( ). Write the new sentence.

9. We can find out who is tallest. (question)
   Can we find out who is tallest?
10. Should you get a yardstick? (command)
    Get a yardstick.
11. Is it in the drawer? (statement)
    It is in the drawer.
12. You are really funny. (exclamation)
    You are really funny!
13. Kevin is the tallest. (question)
    Is Kevin the tallest?
14. I think I am taller than he is. (question)
    Am I taller than he is?
15. Will you measure Jeannie next? (command)
    Measure Jeannie next.

68

Vocabulary Power page 15

Name_____ Related Words

Some words are related by meaning. The following words are related because they all have something to do with music.

sing   harmony   melody

Circle the words in the box that are related to music.

(band) (singer)   garden (lyrics) (piano)
boat   telephone (tune)   (dance) lunchbox

These words are related because they all have something to do with friendship.

togetherness   talk   play   understanding

Write some other related words. Draw a picture about friendship.

Vocabulary Power   Unit 1 • Chapter 5   15

REACHING ALL LEARNERS   **ESL**

SHARED WRITING You may wish to have children write the directions on page 69 as a shared writing activity. Work with small groups. Have children act out and say what they do to walk over to their desks. Then write what they say as commands. Have a volunteer read the directions aloud and act them out to make sure they work. Have children revise the directions if they do not work.

Language Play

Command Tic-Tac-Toe
- Take turns with a partner. You are X. Your partner is O.
- Pick a box. Use the word to give a command.
- If you give a command correctly, put a marker on the box.
- The first player to get three in a row wins.
- When you are finished, say an exclamation to show how you feel.

come	read	it
jump	talk	leave
throw	walk	run

Have children play "Command Tic-Tac-Toe" in pairs. Model how to pick a box and use the word in a command. Children can also write their commands and exclamations.

Writing Connection

Directions Have children identify the effective features of their written directions by using the criteria below.

CRITERIA
- ☑ Writes sentences that are short and clear.
- ☑ All sentences are commands.
- ☑ Begins each sentence with a capital letter.
- ☑ Ends each sentence with a period.

PORTFOLIO OPPORTUNITY You may want to have children place their writing in their portfolios or take it home to share with family members.

Writing Connection

Directions Directions can help you find your way. Write directions that will help others find their way to your desk at school. Write each sentence as a command. Draw a map to explain the directions.

Directions to my desk

1. Walk to the row of desks next to the windows.
2. Turn left.
3. Stop at the last desk.

69

REACHING ALL LEARNERS

PRACTICE page 19

Name _____

Extra Practice

A. Circle the commands. Underline the exclamations.
1. (Look at the dancers.)
2. They jump so high!
3. The dance is beautiful!

B. Write each exclamation and command correctly.
4. lily dances well
   Lily dances well!
5. watch her turn
   Watch her turn.

C. Change each statement into a new kind of sentence shown in ( ). Write the new sentence. Possible responses are given.
6. Lily loves to dance. **(question)**
   Does Lily love to dance?
7. She does a graceful turn. **(exclamation)**
   What a graceful turn she does!

Practice • Exclamations and Commands   Unit 1 • Chapter 5 19

REACHING ALL LEARNERS

CHALLENGE

MAKE A MAP Have children work in small groups to write directions for getting from their classroom to the library, cafeteria, or school office. Invite children to draw a map to accompany their directions.

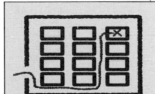

Chapter Review

STANDARDIZED TEST PREP

OBJECTIVES

- To review exclamations and commands
- To use a word processing program to input and add text

DAILY LANGUAGE PRACTICE

TRANSPARENCY 9

1 Is which your favorite book (Which is; ?)

2 Show! it to me (Show; .)

BRIDGE TO WRITING What a funny title (punctuation mark)

STANDARDIZED TEST PREP

Read the directions with children to make sure they understand how to complete the page. You may wish to have children complete this page independently and use it as an assessment.

TEST PREPARATION TIP

Item Type: Multiple Choice

TIP

Model this strategy to help children determine the correct answer:

First I read the sentence aloud to decide what kind of sentence it is. The first sentence tells someone to do something, so it is a command. I know that a command begins with a capital letter and ends with a period. Answer _a_ does not begin with a capital letter, so it is not correct. Answer _b_ begins with a capital letter but does not end with a period, so _b_ is not correct. Item _c_ is the right answer.

Chapter Review

STANDARDIZED TEST PREP

Read each sentence. Choose the answer that shows it written correctly.

1. Let's write our own books.
   - **a.** let's write our own books.
   - **b.** Let's write our own books
   - **c.** correct as is

2. How I love to draw
   - **a.** How I love to draw!
   - **b.** how I love to draw
   - **c.** correct as is

3. Write the sentences here.
   - **a.** Write the sentences here
   - **b.** write the sentences here
   - **c.** correct as is

4. What great pages these are
   - **a.** what great pages these are
   - **b.** What great pages these are!
   - **c.** correct as is

5. Finish your work
   - **a.** finish your work.
   - **b.** Finish your work.
   - **c.** correct as is

6. How well we work together
   - **a.** How well we work together!
   - **b.** how well we work together
   - **c.** correct as is

 Visit our website for more activities with exclamations and commands:
www.harcourtschool.com

70

Language Skills Assessment

· ·

PORTFOLIO ASSESSMENT
Have children select their best work from the following activities:

- **Writing Connection**, pages 65, 67, 69; TE activities, pages 63, 65, 67, 68, 69

ONGOING ASSESSMENT
Evaluate the performance of 4-6 students using appropriate checklists and record forms from pages R65–R68 and R77–R79.

 INTERNET Activities and exercises to help students prepare for state and standardized assessments appear on *The Learning Site:*
www.harcourtschool.com

■ Technology ■

Using a Computer

A computer can help you prewrite, write, revise, proofread, and publish your writing.

monitor ——
CPU ——
keyboard ——
—— printer
—— mouse

A **word processing program** helps you write on your computer. The letters and words you write are called **text**. All the text in one piece of writing is called a **document**.

How to Type Text	Open a document. Press the keys on the keyboard.
How to Add Text	Move the cursor to where you want the new text. Type the text.

Practice

Type the riddle on your computer. Look at the Editor's Marks. Use your computer to make the changes.

What kind of fish can ‸see at night‸(a starfish)
                  you   ?

71

■ Technology ■

Using a Computer

TEACH/MODEL

Show a computer to children and ask them to identify the different components. Then model writing on the computer by opening a document and typing a sentence. As you add to the sentence, explain aloud what you are doing. Use the directions in the chart to explain the different steps as you demonstrate the tasks.

PRACTICE Have students type the riddle and use their computer to make changes.

WRAP-UP/ASSESS

SUMMARIZE Ask children to tell what they have learned about using a computer and explain how using a computer can help make their writing more interesting.

REACHING ALL LEARNERS

PRACTICE page 20

Name_____

Using a Computer

A. Use the words in the box to label the parts of the computer.

| keyboard   monitor   printer   mouse   hard drive |

monitor
keyboard
hard drive
mouse
printer

B. Type each sentence on your computer. Follow the proofreading marks to make changes to the text.

       cute
1. I have two ‸cats.
   Their
2. ~~There~~ names are Haley and Leo.
      soft
3. Haley has ‸white fur.

4. ‸leo looks like a tiger.

TRY THIS! Use the computer to write a sentence about yourself. Then go back and correct the sentence by using the cursor, keyboard, and Delete key.

20 Unit 1 • Chapter 5   Practice • Exclamations and Commands

REACHING ALL LEARNERS

CHALLENGE

COMPUTER TIME Have children select and type on the computer a piece of writing from their writing portfolios or the poem they wrote for the Challenge activity on page 65. Encourage them to use the computer to edit their writing. If possible, have them print out and illustrate their work.

Writing a Personal Story

pages 72–89

LESSON ORGANIZER	DAY 1	DAY 2
 **DAILY LANGUAGE PRACTICE** TRANSPARENCY 10	1. she had shinnee red shoes (She; shiny; shoes.) 2. they were a preshant from Grandmama (They; present; Grandmama.)	1. oh, no She fell. (Oh; no!) 2. can you cleen my muddy dress. (Can; clean; dress?)
ORAL WARM-UP Listening/Speaking	Discuss Special Events p. 72	Talk About Sequence Charts p. 82
TEACH/MODEL WRITING 	**Literature Model:** "Red Dancing Shoes," pp. 72–78 • To read and respond to a personal story as a model for writing • To identify the elements of a story map **Reading-Writing Connection:** Parts of a Personal Story p. 79 **A Student Model** p. 80	**GUIDED WRITING** ✔ **Prewriting** pp 82–83 • To brainstorm and select a writing topic • To use a sequence chart to plan a personal story **Transparency 11**
Reaching All Learners	**Options for Reading** p. 73 ESL Manual pp. 34–35 **ESL:** Words With *ed* or *ing* Endings p. 75	**Interactive Writing** p. 83 **Challenge:** Writing Prompt p. 83 **ESL:** *ESL Manual* p. 34
GRAMMAR	**Unit 1 Review** pp. 90–91	**Unit 1 Review** pp. 90–91
CROSS-CURRICULAR/ ENRICHMENT	**Music Connection:** Dance Music p. 74 **Social Studies Connection:** Dance p. 76 **School-Home Connection:** p. 77	**Vocabulary Power** **Word Families** p. 72 *Vocabulary Power* book, p. 16 Vocabulary activity

KEY
✔ = tested writing form/skill

Vocabulary Power

glossiest, brightest, shiniest, sleekest, smoothest
See **Vocabulary Power** book.

DAY **3**	DAY **4**	DAY **5**

1. is Grandmama hoam (Is; home?)	1. is it yer birthday (Is; your; birthday?)	1. watch out for that pudel! (Watch; puddle!)
2. let's go vizett her. (Let's; visit; her.)	2. what a saprize (What; surprise!)	2. why are yu muddy. (Why; you; muddy?)

Identify Story Sequence p. 84	Review Story Elements p. 86	Sharing Stories p. 88

GUIDED WRITING ✔ **Drafting** pp. 84–85 • To draft a personal story that tells what happens first, next, last • To write about a problem they experienced and how it was solved **Transparency 12**	**GUIDED WRITING** ✔ **Revising and Proofreading** p. 86–87 • To revise a personal story • To proofread writing for capitalization, punctuation, grammar, and spelling • To use Editor's Marks to make revisions and corrections **Transparencies 12, 12a, 12b**	**GUIDED WRITING** ✔ **Publishing** p. 88 • To make final copies of revised personal stories • To share personal stories with others **Scoring Rubric** p. 88 **Handwriting** p. 89 **Practice and Assessment**
Interactive Writing p. 85 **ESL:** *ESL Manual* p. 34	**Proofreading Practice** **ESL:** *ESL Manual* p. 34	**ESL:** Using Notes p.89 *ESL Manual* p. 34

Unit 1 Review pp. 90–91	**Unit 1 Review** pp. 90–91	**Unit 1 Review** pp. 90–91

Writer's Craft: Point of View p. 85 **Vocabulary Power** Compare/Contrast p. 72 *Vocabulary Power* book p. 17	**Spelling Connection:** Spelling Strategies p. 87 **Vocabulary activity** **Vocabulary Power** Expand Word Meaning p. 72 *Vocabulary Power* book p. 18	**LISTENING AND SPEAKING:** Sharing Your Writing p. 89 **Vocabulary Power** **Antonyms** p. 72

Read the Literature

OBJECTIVES
- To read and respond to a personal story as a model for writing
- To identify the elements of a story map

SPIRAL REVIEW

DAILY LANGUAGE PRACTICE

TRANSPARENCY 10

1 she had shinnee red shoes (She; shiny; shoes.)

2 they were a preshant from Grand-mama (They; present; Grandmama.)

ORAL WARM-UP

USE PRIOR KNOWLEDGE Tell children that they will read a personal story, a story about the person who wrote it, to prepare for their own writing.

Read the introduction on page 72 with children. Invite them to tell about special things that have happened to them.

PREREADING STRATEGIES

VOCABULARY Have children read the story title. Ask children what they have received as presents. Ask children what was special about the present they received and to whom they might have wanted to show it. Make a chart of children's ideas.

Present	Show It To	How It Is Special
doll truck baseball glove	Uncle Harry Grandma my sister	

PREVIEW/SET PURPOSE Have children preview the pictures in the selection. Encourage them to predict what they think the story will be about.

In a personal story, a writer tells about something that happened in his or her life. As you read "Red Dancing Shoes," think about what happened to this girl and how she felt.

RED DANCING SHOES

by Denise Lewis Patrick   paintings by James E. Ransome

Grandmama went on a trip. When she came back, she brought everybody presents.

My present was the most special. It was a pair of the finest, reddest, shiniest shoes that anyone had ever seen.

"Thank you, Grandmama," I whispered.

72

Vocabulary Power

DAY 1 WORD MEANINGS Introduce and define the word <u>glossiest</u> (most shiny). Write: *The red dancing shoes were the <u>glossiest</u> of all.* **How would you draw these dancing shoes?**

DAY 2 WORD FAMILIES List: *glossy, glossier, glossiest.* **What is the base word? What endings were added to the base word?** (See also *Vocabulary Power,* page 16.)

DAY 3 COMPARE/CONTRAST Discuss: **What animal has the glossiest fur? Why do you think that?** (See also *Vocabulary Power,* page 17.)

DAY 4 EXPAND WORD MEANING Write: *Mom painted the walls with <u>gloss</u> paint.* **Why would she do that? What is gloss paint?** (See also *Vocabulary Power,* page 18.)

DAY 5 ANTONYMS **Make a list of words that mean the opposite of glossy, bright, shiny, sleek, smooth.**

"They're dancing shoes!" Grandmama told me. "Why don't you try them out?" she said.

Big Sister guessed just what I was thinking. "If you want to show off your shoes," she said, "come with me."

Big Sister walked out the door. I danced. Then I stopped and peeked down at my feet. My red dancing shoes smiled up at me!

"Can we stop at Nen's?" I asked. "I want to show her my dancing shoes."

Nen is Grandmama's sister. She's my favorite aunt. She always lets me swing in the big wooden swing on her front porch.

73

OPTIONS FOR READING

DIRECTED READING Use the questions.

PARTNER READING Pair readers to take turns reading alternate paragraphs.

INDEPENDENT READING Have children read the story silently and then together in small groups. Children can share ideas about what they like about the girl's shoes.

READING LIKE A WRITER

Pages 72–73 Tell children that in this story the main character gets a present. Have them preview the pictures to predict what she gets and how she feels about her present.

1. **What is the present?** (a pair of shiny red shoes) **LITERAL: NOTE DETAILS**

2. **What does the girl think of her present? How can you tell?** (She loves the shoes. She looks very pleased in the picture and she uses words like *most special* and *finest* to describe the shoes.) **CRITICAL: IDENTIFY WITH CHARACTERS**

3. **What do you think the author means when she says her "shoes smiled up at me?"** (Responses may include the girl saw her smiling reflection in the shiny shoes, or the shoes just felt good to wear and made her feel happy.) **CRITICAL: AUTHOR'S CRAFT/INTERPRET IMAGERY**

SELECTION SUMMARY

FICTION: STORY A girl gets a wonderful present from her grandmother—a shiny new pair of red dancing shoes. As she heads off to show them to her aunt, she trips and gets the shoes all muddy. The girl fears that her shoes are ruined, yet Nen makes them as good as new.

ABOUT THE AUTHOR

Denise Lewis Patrick has written numerous children's books, includ- ing *Shaina's Garden*, that feature African American characters. Slightly older readers will enjoy *The Adventures of Midnight Son* and *The Longest Ride*.

Illustrator **James E. Ransome**, who studied at Pratt Institute, tries to portray characters with unique qualities. He also has written and illustrated his own books.

Pages 74–75 Have children examine the pictures and discuss what will happen on the way to visit Nen. Then have them read to confirm their predictions.

1. **Why does the girl want to show Nen her new shoes?** (She's very excited about her new shoes. Nen is her favorite aunt, so she wants to share her excitement with Nen.) **INFERENTIAL: DRAW CONCLUSIONS**

2. **What happens as the girl is running to show Nen her shoes?** (She falls in the dirt and gets her shoes muddy.) **INFERENTIAL: IMPORTANT DETAILS**

3. **Why does the girl think the shoes won't "dance" anymore?** (They're not pretty and new; they're no longer fun to wear.) **CRITICAL: INTERPRET STORY EVENTS/IDENTIFY WITH CHARACTER**

We turned the corner. I could see Nen sitting in her swing. I wanted her to see my red dancing shoes *now*. Suddenly those shoes started running. I was running too.

"Nen! Look!" I shouted.

"Be careful," Big Sister said.

Just as Nen looked up at me, I tripped on a rock. "WOOF!" I fell onto the dusty path, making a smoky brown cloud all around me.

74

Music Connection

• • • • • • • • • • • • • • •

DANCE MUSIC Collect recordings of various dance music, including the Twist if possible. Play the music for children, encouraging them to tap their toes with the music.

Nen was off the swing in a second, picking me up. Big Sister was dusting off my clothes. I looked down at my feet. The beautiful, shiny, wonderful, red dancing shoes were sticky and blotchy and muddy.

"M-My dancing shoes!" I cried. I couldn't take my eyes off my shoes. They didn't look new anymore. They didn't look pretty anymore. I bet they couldn't even dance anymore.

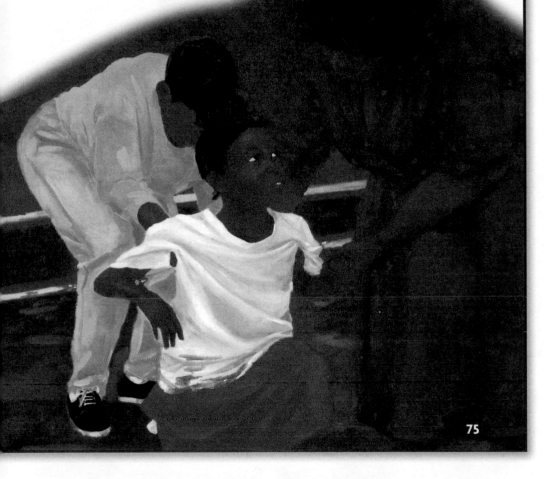

75

CREATE MENTAL IMAGES Explain to children that imagining themselves in a scene in a story can help them better understand and appreciate the story events.

Suggest that they close their eyes and picture themselves as the girl, running excitedly to show off her new shoes. Then have them imagine themselves falling in the dirt. What sounds do they hear? Can they smell the choking dust? How do their hands and knees feel? What do they feel like altogether, especially when they see that the shiny red shoes are muddy?

Explain that by creating mental images of scenes described in a story, readers have a much better idea of what is happening.

Pages 76–77 Have children preview the pages and discuss what they think will happen next.

1. **Why do you think the girl can't dance in her shoes now?** (Responses may include: She doesn't think her shoes are pretty or new now, so she is not as excited about them. She is sad and doesn't feel like dancing.) **CRITICAL: IDENTIFY WITH CHARACTERS**

2. **What does Nen do next?** (She takes the girl into the kitchen and sits her on a chair. Nen unbuckles the girl's shoes. She wets a cloth and rubs the cloth over each shoe.) **INFERENTIAL: SUMMARIZE**

"Let's sit down," Nen said. She went inside and brought us glasses of cool lemonade. "Do you feel better?" she asked.

"No," I said.

"I see you have pretty new shoes," she said.

"Not anymore," I said.

"Those are her dancing shoes," said Big Sister.

"I can't dance in them now," I told Nen.

"Are you sure?" she asked me.

I turned my toes in. Then I turned my toes out. My littlest toes started feeling funny.

"It's not the same," I sighed. "They used to be shiny and red and new."

"Let's go into the kitchen," Nen said.

76

Social Studies Connection

• • • • • • • • • • • • • •

DANCE Explain that different dances have been popular at different times. Tell children that the Twist was a dance craze popular in the early 1960s. Have children ask friends and family members to teach them steps from other popular dances. Children can demonstrate for classmates what they learn.

REACHING ALL LEARNERS   ESL

WORDS WITH *ED* OR *ING* ENDINGS Have children page through the story to find words ending with *ed*, such as *stopped*, *danced*, and *peeked*. Explain that the *ed* shows that an action happened in the past. Have children act out the meaning of each word. Then have them look for words ending with *ing*. Explain that the *ing* ending shows that the action is happening now. Have children act out the words.

She took my hand and smiled her secret smile. Then she sat me on a chair and unbuckled my shoes. She took a cloth and ran some water over it.

Nen pulled one of my feet onto her lap. The she held the cloth tight and rubbed it back and forth over my shoe. She did the same thing to the other one.

77

School-Home Connection

Ask children to share with family members personal stories of times when things went wrong but someone in the family made things better.

Page 78 Ask children to predict how the story will end. Then have them read to check their predictions.

1. **How does the story end?** (The girl sees her shoes looking like new. She is so happy, she dances the twist.) **INFERENTIAL: SUMMARIZE**

2. **Why does the girl walk home?** (She does not want to trip and fall. Her shoes might really be ruined.) **INFERENTIAL: DRAW CONCLUSIONS**

Think About It

Ask volunteers to retell what happened first, next, and last in the story.

1. The girl with the red dancing shoes is telling the story. She uses the words *I* and *me* to tell about what happened. **CRITICAL:** INTERPRET TEXT STRUCTURE

2. She is very excited; her present is the "most special." When the shoes get dirty, she is very upset; she thinks her shoes won't dance anymore. **INFERENTIAL:** DETERMINE CHARACTERS' EMOTIONS

"All right," she smiled. "How do you like your dancing shoes now?"

I looked. I blinked. I looked again.

"MY SHINY, RED DANCING SHOES ARE BACK!" I shouted. I jumped off the chair and danced the Twist.

"I love my clean, shiny, red dancing shoes," I giggled, spinning around and around.

Big Sister looked at Nen's big kitchen clock and said, "We'd better get on home."

This time, I walked—I did not run. I looked down at my shiny red dancing shoes. They smiled at me ... again.

Think About It

1. Who is telling the story about the red dancing shoes? How do you know?

2. How does the girl feel when she first gets her new shoes? How does she feel when she thinks they are ruined?

78

Response to Literature

WRITING PROMPT You may want to have children write in response to "Red Dancing Shoes." Use the writing prompt below, or another you choose. Before children begin, you may want to review what qualities a sentence about a picture should have.

Imagine that you are the girl telling the story. Draw a picture of you in your new red shoes. Write one or more sentences about your picture.

Informal Assessment You can use children's writing to assess informally their understanding of the story and their ability to write a cohesive piece. Note areas where children might benefit from instruction in writing and grammar.

Parts of a Personal Story

In "Red Dancing Shoes," the writer tells about something special that happened to her. Because she is telling about herself, she uses words such as *I*, *me*, and *my* in her story. She also uses time-order words, such as *then* and *now*, to show the order in which things happened.

On a sheet of paper, complete the sequence chart for "Red Dancing Shoes."

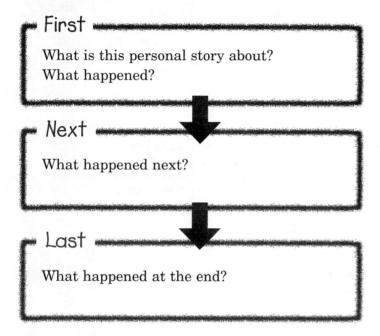

First
What is this personal story about?
What happened?

Next
What happened next?

Last
What happened at the end?

79

Parts of a Personal Story

ANALYZE THE LITERATURE Discuss the elements of a personal story. Explain that a good personal story tells something interesting that happened to the writer. Tell children that the writer uses words like *I* and *me* to describe himself or herself. Explain that the story usually tells about something that happened first, what happened next, and what happened last. Guide children in completing the beginning of the story map by eliciting their ideas about what to write in the box. Have children complete the remaining parts of the story map on their own.

Informal Assessment

• • • • • • • • • • • • • • • • •

You can informally assess children's **comprehension** of the selection and their knowledge of the **structure of a personal story** by encouraging them to retell the events of "Red Dancing Shoes." Note how well children sequence story events.

A Student Model

READ AND RESPOND TO THE MODEL Explain that you will read a personal story as children set a purpose for listening. Then read "My Purple Glasses" aloud as children listen. Ask them how they liked hearing a story about something that happened to the writer. Tell children that they can use this published student piece as a model for their own writing.

FOCUS ON ORGANIZATION Ask children to read the story to themselves and to focus on the sidenotes as they read. Then have volunteers summarize what happens in each part of the story and tell how each part helps to develop the story.

FOCUS ON WRITER'S CRAFT Have children find and read the time-order words that Cara uses in her story. Help them recognize that these time-order words help readers understand the order of events in the story.

A Student Model

Cara liked reading about what happened to the girl with the red shoes. She wrote a story about what happened when she got glasses. Read her story and think about what happens.

My Purple Glasses

This year when I started school, I could not read the board well. The words looked fuzzy. I told my mom about this. She thought I might need glasses. I was upset. How would I look in glasses?

Soon my mom took me to the eye doctor. First I tried on some big glasses. They looked bad. Then I found some purple glasses. I liked them. The next week I wore my glasses to school. Everyone said I looked cool! In class, I could read all the words on the board, too.

A good beginning helps get readers interested.

Time-order words help show the order in which things happen.

80

LISTENING AND SPEAKING

GENERATE QUESTIONS Have children work in small groups to compare "Red Dancing Shoes" and "My Purple Glasses" and discuss questions such as these:
- What happens first, next, and last in the story?
- What clue words show the order that things happen?

Instruct children to ask their own questions as well and contribute ideas within their groups.

EVALUATION CRITERIA

ESTABLISH CRITERIA FOR WRITING Have children locate the rubric on writing personal stories in their handbooks on page 482. Tell them that they will know they have done a good job if the personal stories they write follow each item on the list. Add others you may generate together. Remind children to refer to this rubric as they write. (See also page 88 and R71 in this *Teacher's Edition.*)

Looking at the Model

1. Who tells the story? How do you know?
2. What is the story about?
3. What happens first? What happens next?
4. How does Cara feel at the end? Why?

Writer's Craft

Find the different kinds of sentences Cara used in her story. How do they help make the story better?

Time-Order Words

Cara used the words *this year*, *soon*, *first*, *then*, and *the next week*. How do they help you know the order in which things happened?

81

Looking at the Model

1. **Who tells the story?** (Cara tells the story.) **How do you know?** (She uses words like *I* and *me*.)
2. **What is the story about?** (Cara tells what happened when she first got glasses.)
3. **What happens first?** (At first, Cara can't see the board at school. Her mom takes her to the eye doctor.) **What happens next?** (She didn't want any of the glasses. She thought she would look bad.)
4. **How does Cara feel at the end?** (She is happy with her purple glasses.) **Why?** (Everyone thinks she looks cool, and she can see the board.)

SELF-INITIATED WRITING Have children choose a way to respond to the models they just read, which may include self-initiated writing or another method such as art or dance. For example, children may choose to write to discover ideas, list key thoughts, or draw and label pictures.

WRAP-UP/ASSESS

Have children share their story maps from page 79. Ask whether they like what happens first, next, or last in "Red Dancing Shoes" best and why they liked the part. Then ask them to tell about their favorite parts of "My Purple Glasses."

TAKE-HOME BOOK 1 provides an additional model of a personal story and home activities. See *Practice Book* pages 121–122.

Prewriting

OBJECTIVES
- To brainstorm and select a writing topic
- To use a graphic organizer to plan a personal story

DAILY LANGUAGE PRACTICE

1 oh, no She fell. (Oh; no!)
                                 TRANSPARENCY 10

2 can you cleen my muddy dress.
   (Can; clean; dress?)

ORAL WARM-UP

USE PRIOR KNOWLEDGE Have children discuss stories they have heard about things that happened to the person telling the story. Talk about some of the reasons children like to hear and read these kinds of stories.

GUIDED WRITING

TALK ABOUT A STORY MAP Explain to children that a sequence chart is useful for organizing information to write a personal story. Have children talk about what Cara did in the prewriting stage. Discuss the following questions in the group.

1. **What might Cara have done before she started her sequence chart?** (She probably made a list of things that had happened to her that might make a good story and decided on the most interesting thing.)

2. **How did it help Cara to complete a sequence chart before she started writing a draft?** (It helped her organize her ideas so that the events would be in order.)

 Use **Transparency 11** for an additional way to model the prewriting stage.

Prewriting

Before Cara wrote her personal story, she drew pictures and made a list of ideas for her story. Then Cara thought about her classmates who would read her story. She thought they would like to hear about the time she got glasses.

Cara used this sequence chart to write the events in the order they happened.

First
What is this personal story about? What happened?
This year I could not read the board well. My mom took me to the eye doctor for glasses.

Next
What happened next?
I didn't want any of the glasses. I thought they would look bad.

Last
What happened at the end?
I found some purple glasses. I wore them to school. Everyone said I looked cool. I could see well.

82

TRANSPARENCY 11

PREWRITING: PERSONAL STORY

First
What is this personal story about? What happened?

Next
What happened next?

Last
What happened at the end?

Vocabulary Power page 16

Name _____   Word Families

Words that have the same base word are in the same word family.

glossy   glossier   glossiest

Add -er and -est to these words to make word families.

bright	shiny
brighter	shinier
brightest	shiniest
sleek	**smooth**
sleeker	smoother
sleekest	smoothest

Draw pictures to show the meaning of the underlined words.

the brightest object in the sky	the sleekest fur of all
the shiniest shoes in the store	the smoothest ice cream ever

Your Turn

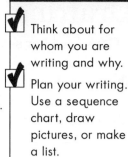

STEP 1 Think of ideas.

Make a list of things that have happened to you. Draw or write your ideas.

STEP 2 Choose an idea.

Think about who will read your personal story. Choose an idea that you and your readers will like.

STEP 3 Complete a plan.

List the events in the order they happened.

What Good Writers Do

☑ Think about for whom you are writing and why.

☑ Plan your writing. Use a sequence chart, draw pictures, or make a list.

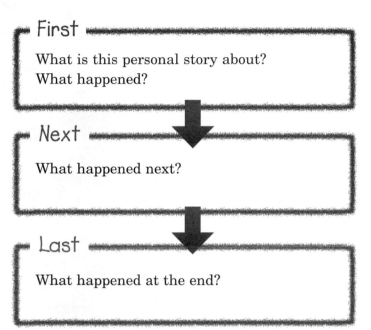

First

What is this personal story about?
What happened?

Next

What happened next?

Last

What happened at the end?

83

Your Turn Review the prewriting steps to help children plan for their personal stories. Have them begin by brainstorming possible story ideas and selecting one. Then have them complete the sequence chart.

WRAP-UP/ASSESS

SUMMARIZE Invite volunteers to summarize the steps they used to complete their sequence charts. Encourage children to reflect on how brainstorming ideas and filling in a sequence chart help them plan their writing. Have them think about how they might work differently the next time they fill in a sequence chart.

 You may want to have children write in their journals their reflections about prewriting. After they write, have small groups discuss their ideas about what worked best for them. **REFLECTION**

INTERACTIVE WRITING

SHARE THE PEN You may want to work through the writing process together to write a group story. To plan the story, use **Transparency 11** or a group story map recorded on chart paper. Model how to brainstorm and organize ideas. Encourage children to share the pen as you write their ideas.

REACHING ALL LEARNERS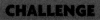

CHALLENGE

WRITING PROMPT Children who demonstrate proficiency in writing can write a story in response to the prompt below.

Write a story about yourself for your classmates. Tell about something that happened to you.

Drafting

OBJECTIVES
- To draft a personal story that tells what happens first, next, and last
- To write about a problem they experienced and how it was solved

DAILY LANGUAGE PRACTICE

TRANSPARENCY 10

1. is Grandmama hoam (Is; home?)
2. let's go vizett her. (Let's; visit; her.)

ORAL WARM-UP

USE PRIOR KNOWLEDGE Invite volunteers to tell brief stories about something interesting that happened to them recently, or tell one yourself. Have the group identify what happened first, next, and last in the story.

GUIDED WRITING

DISCUSS FIRST DRAFTS Explain to children that a first draft is not final and does not need to be perfect. Use the writing model to discuss writing a first draft. Ask questions such as the following about Cara's draft.

- **In which part of the story does Cara let the reader know who the story is about and when it happened? Does it match the her prewriting plan?** (in the beginning; yes)
- **What are some ways to make this personal story better?** (Accept reasonable responses.)

Tell children that spelling and punctuation errors will be addressed later in the proofreading stage.

12 Use **Transparency 12** for an additional teaching model.

Drafting

Cara used her sequence chart to write a draft of her personal story on her computer. She worked quickly because she knew a draft is just a first try. She did not worry about making mistakes. She knew she could fix them later.

DRAFT My Purple Glasses

This year when I started school, I could not read the board well. The words looked bad and fuzzy. I told my mom about this. She thought I might need glasses. I was upset.

Soon my mom took me to the eye doctor. First I tried on some big glasses. They looked bad. I found some purple glasses. I liked them. I wore my glasses to school. Everyone said I looked cool!

84

TRANSPARENCY 12

DRAFT My Purple Glasses

This year when I started school, I could not read the board well. The words looked bad and fuzzy. I told my mom about this. She thought I might need glasses. I was upset.

Soon my mom took me to the eye doctor. First I tried on some big glasses. They looked bad. I found some purple glasses. I liked them. I wore my glasses to school. Everyone said I looked cool!

Vocabulary Power page 17

Name _____

Compare/Contrast

The words glossier and glossiest can be used to compare things.

   My cat has glossier fur than your cat.
   My cat has the glossiest fur of all the cats.

Add -er or -est to the word in dark print. Write the word that best completes the sentence.

shiny 1. That star is the ___shiniest___ star in the sky.

smooth 2. Apples feel ___smoother___ than oranges.

sleek 3. Cheetahs are ___sleeker___ than hippos.

bumpy 4. This is the ___bumpiest___ road in town.

funny 5. Barb's joke was ___funnier___ than mine.

tasty 6. I think popcorn is the ___tastiest___ treat.

Complete and draw a picture for each sentence.

___ is brighter than ___	___ is the brightest.

Vocabulary Power   Unit 1 • Chapter 6   17

Read Cara's first draft. See how it follows her sequence chart. What might she write next?

First

What is this personal story about? What happened?

This year I could not read the board well. My mom took me to the eye doctor for glasses.

Next

What happened next?

I didn't want any of the glasses. I thought they would look bad.

Last

What happened at the end?

I found some purple glasses. I wore them to school. Everyone said I looked cool. I could see well.

Your Turn

Use your sequence chart and What Good Writers Do to write a draft of your personal story.

What Good Writers Do

☑ Remember why you are writing and who will read your personal story.

☑ Be sure all your sentences tell about your personal story.

☑ Tell what happened in order.

☑ Use different kinds of sentences.

You can write your draft quickly on a computer.

85

Your Turn Tell children that they will use their story maps and What Good Writers Do to work on their first drafts. Read over What Good Writers Do with children. Remind them to use information from their sequence charts as they write their drafts. Suggest that they write quickly, focusing on their ideas. Later they will have a chance to fix any mistakes or make other changes.

 Show children how to label their drafts so they can find their files again. Suggest that they use key words from their story title and the word *draft*.

PORTFOLIO Remind children to put their drafts in their Writing Portfolios.

WRAP-UP/ASSESS

SUMMARIZE Invite volunteers to tell what elements should be included in a first draft.

 You may wish to have children record in their journals their thoughts on writing a draft.
REFLECTION

INTERACTIVE WRITING

SHARE THE PEN Display the sequence chart you made on chart paper during prewriting. Write a first draft as a group, referring to the sequence chart as you write. Encourage children's suggestions and comments. You could also use **Transparency 12** to show how to create a draft.

Writer's Craft

POINT OF VIEW Ask children how they knew who was telling the story in "Red Dancing Shoes." Write the words *I, me, my, we, us,* and *our* on the board. Ask volunteers to use the words in sentences in which they tell about something that happened to them. Explain that when they write a personal story they are telling about events that happened to them. So, we use these pronouns to describe ourselves. Tell children that they will use pronouns such as these as they write a personal story.

Revising

OBJECTIVES
- To revise a personal story
- To proofread writing for capitalization, punctuation, grammar, and spelling
- To use Editor's Marks to make revisions and corrections

DAILY LANGUAGE PRACTICE

TRANSPARENCY 10

❶ is it yer birthday (Is; your; birthday?)

❷ what a saprize (What; surprise!)

ORAL WARM-UP

Review with children the elements they should include in a personal story.

GUIDED WRITING

DISCUSS REVISING Have a volunteer read aloud the Editor's Marks. Other children can form the add and delete symbols in the air. Then have children read Cara's revision. Talk about how Cara's revisions improve her draft. Discuss any other changes that would improve the story.

 Use **Transparencies 12** and **12a** to model how to revise.

Your Turn Role-play with a volunteer how to offer constructive feedback in discussing revisions. Comment first on something you like about the draft and then specific suggestions about something that could be improved.

REVISIT THE EVALUATION CRITERIA Have children use the rubric for writing a personal story as well as the evaluation criteria they established earlier in responding constructively to their own and each other's writing.

Writing a Personal Story

Revising

Cara shared her draft with some classmates. They had some ideas about how to make it better. Read to see how Cara **revised** her personal story.

> **DRAFT**
>
> My Purple Glasses
>
> This year when I started school, I could not read the board well. The words looked ~~bad and~~ fuzzy. I told my mom about this. She thought I might need glasses. I was upset. ∧ *How would I look with glasses?*
>
> Soon my mom took me to the eye doctor. First I tried on some big glasses. They looked bad. ∧ *Then* I found some purple glasses. I liked them. ∧ *The next week* I wore my glasses to school. Everyone said I looked cool! In class, i could read all the words on the bord, too

86

What Good Writers Do

✓ Did you tell what happened in order?

✓ Did you use different kinds of sentences?

✓ Do you need to give more information?

Editor's Marks

∧ Add.

 Take out.

╱╲ Change.

Your Turn

Now share your personal story with some partners. Ask them how to make it better. Use What Good Writers Do and the Editor's Marks to make changes.

TRANSPARENCIES 12, 12a

> **DRAFT**
>
> My Purple Glasses
>
> This year when I started school, I could not read the board well. The words looked ~~bad and~~ fuzzy. I told my mom about this. She thought I might need glasses. I was upset. ∧ *How would I look with glasses?*
>
> Soon my mom took me to the eye doctor. First I tried on some big glasses. They looked bad. ∧ *Then* I found some purple glasses. I liked them. ∧ *The next week* I wore my glasses to school. Everyone said I looked cool! In class, i could read all the words on the bord, too

---

Vocabulary Power page 18

Name _____

Expand Word Meanings

Some words can be used in many different ways. Read these sentences. Think about the meanings of the underlined words.

> The glossiest shoes are the shiniest of all.
> We are going to paint the room with gloss paint.

Gloss paint is a kind of paint that is shiny when it dries.

Circle the meaning of each underlined word.

1. Raj is the brightest boy in math class.
   shiniest
   sunniest
   (smartest)

2. Bonnie has the smoothest manners of anyone I know.
   (most polite)
   least lumpy
   flattest

3. Ali shines in art class.
   sparks
   (does well)
   becomes glossy

4. Tom has a bright smile.
   sleek
   (happy)
   sun-shaped

Lights can shine, beam, glow, or sparkle. Draw a picture to show how people can do the same.

18 Unit 1 • Chapter 6   Vocabulary Power

Proofreading

Cara read her story one more time. She looked for mistakes. Think about why she made the changes in red.

 DRAFT   My Purple Glasses

This year when I started school, I could not read the board well. The words looked ~~bad and~~ fuzzy. I told my mom about this. She thought I might need glasses. I was upset. ∧ How would I look with glasses?

Soon my mom took me to the eye doctor. First I tried on some big glasses. They looked bad. ∧ Then I found some purple glasses. I liked them. ∧ The next week I wore my glasses to school. Everyone said I looked cool! In class, i̲ could read all the words on the bⓞrd, too⊙ board

Y☺ur Turn

Read your personal story again. Use What Good Writers Do and the Editor's Marks to fix any mistakes.

What Good Writers Do

☑ Make sure each sentence begins with a capital letter.

☑ Be sure each kind of sentence has the correct end mark.

☑ Check your spelling.

Editor's Marks

≡ **Use a capital letter.**

⊙ **Add a period.**

◯ **Check the spelling.**

You can add new sentences on a computer without rewriting the story.

87

Proofreading

MODEL PROOFREADING On the board, write a sentence with a spelling error, such as this: *These are dansing shoes.* Invite children to discuss the sentence in small groups to identify the error. Show how to correct the sentence using the Editing Mark.

REVIEW THE EDITOR'S MARKS Have children read Cara's revision. Discuss the reasons for any proofreading corrections that are shown.

12b Display **Transparencies 12, 12a, and 12b** to model how to proofread a story. Talk about each change that was made.

Y☺ur Turn Suggest that children review their work against each point in What Good Writers Do.

 Demonstrate for children how to return to an existing computer file to add details or revise sentences.

WRAP-UP/ASSESS

SUMMARIZE Have children reflect on and summarize what they have learned about proofreading their personal stories.

REFLECTION

Visit *The Learning Site!*
www.harcourtschool.com

TRANSPARENCIES 12, 12a, 12b

 DRAFT   My Purple Glasses

This year when I started school, I could not read the board well. The words looked ~~bad and~~ fuzzy. I told my mom about this. She thought I might need glasses. I was upset. ∧ How would I look with glasses?

Soon my mom took me to the eye doctor. First I tried on some big glasses. They looked bad. ∧ Then I found some purple glasses. I liked them. ∧ The next week I wore my glasses to school. Everyone said I looked cool! In class, i̲ could read all the words on the bⓞrd, too⊙ board

---

Spelling Connection

SPELLING STRATEGIES Suggest that children try different strategies such as these to check the spelling.

• Look it up in a dictionary.
• Use a computer spell checker.
• Ask a good speller.

Publishing

OBJECTIVES
- To make final copies of revised personal stories
- To share personal stories with others

DAILY LANGUAGE PRACTICE

TRANSPARENCY 10

1 watch out for that pudel! (Watch; puddle!)

2 why are yu muddy. (Why; you; muddy?)

ORAL WARM-UP

Review with children some ways they have observed others sharing personal stories. (TV interviews, magazine stories, books) Discuss some of the features of these different ways of sharing stories.

GUIDED WRITING

Discuss how Cara shared her personal story with others.

Your Turn Have children make a clean copy of their personal story by hand or on a computer. Then they can choose a way to publish their story.

- **Make a comic strip.** Prepare an outline of cartoon frames for children. Have them draft in pencil and then go over the pencil with a marker.
- **Make a flip book.** Explain that small changes in drawings from one page to the next will be most effective.

WRAP-UP/ASSESS

SHARE Invite volunteers to share their personal stories. Remind children to put their finished pieces in their Writing Portfolios.

☑ **Writing Conference Checklist,** page R67.

Activities and exercises to help students prepare for state and standardized assessments appear on *The Learning Site:* www.harcourtschool.com

---

Publishing

Cara copied some photos of herself. Then she cut them out and glued them onto a copy of her personal story to share with her friends.

Your Turn

Make a clean copy of your story. You can use your computer, if you like. Here are some other ideas for publishing your story in a special way.

- **Turn your story into a comic strip.** Draw pictures to show the beginning, the middle, and the end of your personal story. Add speech bubbles to show what different people say in each part of the story.

- **Make a flip book.** Draw a picture for each event. Attach the flip book to a clean copy of your story.

Add your finished personal story to your Writing Portfolio.

88

SCORING RUBRIC

4 ADVANCED
Planning: Discusses, uses a plan to write.
Content: Responds to complete task, including using first-person point of view.
Organization: Events are described in order.
Mechanics: Few or no errors in punctuation, capitalization, and grammar.

3 PROFICIENT
Planning: Listens and uses a plan to write.
Content: Responds to task.
Organization: Events are in logical order.
Mechanics: Some errors in punctuation, capitalization, and grammar.

2 BASIC
Planning: Makes limited use of planning resources.
Content: Does not completely respond to task.
Organization: Some events are confusing or out of logical order.
Mechanics: Several errors in punctuation, capitalization, and grammar.

1 LIMITED
Planning: Fails to make use of planning resources.
Content: Does not respond to task.
Organization: Little attempt to tell a complete personal story in logical order.
Mechanics: Lacks meaningful use of punctuation, capitalization, and grammar.

For information on adapting this rubric to 5- or 6-point scales, see pages R69–70.

Listening and Speaking

Sharing Your Writing

> **You can share something that happened to you by reading your personal story aloud. Think about how to keep your listeners' interest. Practice these tips.**
>
> ### Speaking Tips
>
> - Hold your paper low. This way your listeners can see your face and hear you better.
> - Use your voice to show funny, sad, or exciting parts of your story.
> - Your listeners should be able to hear statements, questions, commands, and exclamations by the way you use your voice.
> - Speak loudly and clearly enough to be heard.

> ### Listening Tips
>
> - Listen to find out what event the person is telling about. What is the story's main idea?
> - What happens first, next, and last?
> - How does the story end? Does the ending surprise you?

89

ESL

USING NOTES Have children draw simple outline faces with smiles, frowns, and so on, on self-stick notes. Have children place the notes in the margins in the appropriate places on their personal story. As volunteers read their stories, the faces can remind them of how they should look and sound.

Handwriting
• • • • • • • • • • • •

USING PROPER POSTURE
Remind children that proper posture and pencil grip will improve their handwriting. If needed, review correct letter formation.

Listening and Speaking

Sharing Your Writing

OBJECTIVES
- To use spoken language appropriately in sharing a personal story
- To listen attentively and ask relevant questions as others present personal stories

ORAL WARM-UP

Ask children to think about times they have listened to others tell personal stories. Discuss how good storytellers use their voices to make the stories interesting, funny, scary, or exciting.

TEACH/MODEL

REVIEW THE TIPS Have volunteers read aloud the tips. Invite volunteers to demonstrate how to use the tips by repeating a simple statement in several ways for different emphasis and meanings, for example: *You were really scared.* Tell children that a good audience listens politely and carefully. Children may ask questions of the speaker or make related comments when the story is finished.

CONSIDER AUDIENCE Have children think about and discuss how they might adjust their speaking rate and volume when reading aloud their writing before different audiences such as (a) a large crowd or (b) a class guest who is sitting next to them.

WRAP-UP/ASSESS

SUMMARIZE Have children summarize what they learned about sharing their writing and listening to others.

☑ **Listening and Speaking Evaluation Forms,** pages R65 and R77.

Unit 1

OBJECTIVES
- To identify and write complete sentences
- To order the words in a sentence so they make sense
- To identify the naming parts and telling parts of sentences
- To use *and* to combine parts of sentences

Unit Review
Have children complete the exercises, or modify them using these suggestions:

MODIFIED INSTRUCTION

BELOW-LEVEL STUDENTS For items 1-4, write *who* or *what* and *what happens* on the board. Remind children that if they can't find both of these things, the group of words isn't a sentence.

Write the words for items 5-8 on separate strips of paper. Have children arrange the strips in an order that makes sense.

Have children underline the first word in each sentence of items 9-10 and draw a circle after the last word.

For items 11-14, ask children where the naming part usually comes in the sentence. Point out that the rest of the sentence is the telling part.

Have children underline the sentence parts that are the same in items 15 and 16.

ABOVE-LEVEL STUDENTS For items 1-4, challenge children to write each group of words that is not a sentence as a complete sentence. Then have them circle the naming part and underline the telling part.

After children have completed items 15–17, have them identify the naming parts of the sentences.

Unit 1

What Is a Sentence? pages 24–25
Write each group of words that is a sentence.

1. School starts today.
   School starts today.
2. gets up early
3. Mai eats breakfast.
   Mai eats breakfast.
4. the school bus

Word Order in a Sentence pages 26–27
Write each group of words in an order that makes sense.

5. Lee ahead of us runs.
   Lee runs ahead of us.
6. Amy with me walks.
   Amy walks with me.
7. to us waves Sal.
   Sal waves to us.
8. the bus Max sees.
   Max sees the bus.

Beginning and Ending a Sentence pages 28–29
Write each sentence correctly.

9. the bus stops here
   The bus stops here.
10. we get in a line
    We get in a line.

Naming Parts and Telling Parts pages 36–37
Write each sentence. Circle the naming part. Underline the telling part.

11. (Tomas) gets on the bus.
12. (He) helps his friend.
13. (Sue and Mai) sit together.
14. (Our driver) shuts the door.

Combining Parts of Sentences pages 38–39
Use *and* to join each pair of sentences. Write the new sentence.

15. Todd sat behind us.
    Sam sat behind us.
    Todd and Sam sat behind us.
16. Amy talked.
    I talked.
    Amy and I talked.
17. Matt waved.
    Jim waved.
    Matt and Jim waved.

90

TEST PREP

TIP

Remind children that a sentence must tell a complete thought. A sentence begins with a capital letter and ends with an end mark.

HANDS ON Activity

Provide a topic for children, such as doing something fun or describing a favorite sport. Have each child write the words to a sentence that relates to the topic on separate slips of paper. Then have children work in groups and use the slips of words to make up new sentences.

Using Statements and Questions pages 54–55

Write each sentence correctly.

18. what is your name
What is your name?

19. you can sit with us
You can sit with us.

20. are you in second grade
Are you in second grade?

21. we just moved here
We just moved here.

Sentences That Go Together pages 56–57

Write the paragraph. Leave out the sentence that does not belong.

22.   I really like my new school. Most of the kids are friendly. My teacher is so nice. I get to use a computer every day too. ~~I like baseball.~~

Exclamations and Commands pages 64–65

Write each sentence correctly.

23. computers are great
Computers are great!

24. Look at this game
Look at this game.

25. teach us how to play
Teach us how to play.

26. what fun this game is
What fun this game is!

Using Different Kinds of Sentences pages 66–67

Change each sentence into the kind of sentence shown in ( ). Write the new sentence.

27. You eat lunch at noon. (question) Do you eat lunch at noon?

28. You should get in line. (command) Get in line.

29. This is the cafeteria. (question) Is this the cafeteria?

30. You should try this soup. (command) Try this soup.

31. Watch out for the desserts. (exclamation) Watch out for the desserts!

32. Are the peaches and plums delicious? (statement)
The peaches and plums are delicious.

91

OBJECTIVES

- To begin statements, questions, exclamations, and commands with capital letters and end them with correct punctuation
- To identify sentences that do not belong with other sentences
- To write different kinds of sentences

Unit Review

Have children complete the exercises, or modify them using these suggestions:

MODIFIED INSTRUCTION

BELOW-LEVEL STUDENTS For items 18–21, write a period and a question mark on the board. Ask children when they should use each mark. Remind them to use a question mark if the sentence can be answered.

For items 23–26, ask children if the sentence shows strong feelings or tells someone what to do.

Write the words *statement*, *question*, *exclamation*, and *command* on the board. Have children discuss the purpose of each type of sentence before they complete items 27–30.

ABOVE-LEVEL STUDENTS For items 18–21, challenge children to rewrite each sentence so that it answers the question or asks a question.

Ask children to write another sentence that belongs with the other sentences in item 22.

TEST PREP

Activities and exercises to help children prepare for state and standardized assessments appear on our website.

 Visit The Learning Site!
www.harcourtschool.com

Assessment

SKILLS ASSESSMENT

Use the **Language and Writing Skills Tests** to assess the grammar and writing skills taught in this unit. Model papers are included.

PORTFOLIO ASSESSMENT

Schedule portfolio conferences with individual students while others are completing the Unit Review exercises. Have each child complete the Self-Evaluation Checklist on pages R78–R79 and place it with the unit's writing in their Portfolios.

Who's Who

OBJECTIVES

- To write questions for investigating and to take notes from relevant sources
- To publish a school Who's Who book

INTRODUCE THE PROJECT

USE PRIOR KNOWLEDGE Read the introduction aloud with children. Have them discuss what different school workers do. If possible, share a Who's Who book with children.

GENERATE QUESTIONS Ask children to generate questions about how and why a Who's Who book is made. Encourage children to answer each other's questions.

Make a Plan

Have children list people to be included in the book and the questions to ask. Tell children to use separate sheets of paper for each person so they can record responses and make illustrations. Then have them select which people they want to talk to.

Get and Record Information

Demonstrate how to use a tape recorder or other media equipment children need. Children can make a chart about what they need to record, such as names, addresses, and jobs.

Put the Information Together

Ask children to write a sentence that tells the main idea about the person they interviewed and one or two sentences that give details about the person.

Social Studies

Who's Who

A Who's Who is a book that tells who people are and what they do. Work together with classmates to make a School Who's Who.

Make a Plan

- List the people who will be in your book. Include your classmates, your teacher, and school workers.
- Decide what you want to find out about each person. Make a list of questions to ask.
- Decide who will talk to each person. Decide who will write and draw each book page.

Get and Record Information

- Talk to the people. Ask them your questions. Write or tape-record the answers.
- Invite the people to speak to the class. Take notes. Videotape the speaker, if you can.
- Draw pictures of the people. Show what they like to do or how they do their jobs. If you have a camera, take photos, too.

Put the Information Together

- Use your notes to write a few sentences about each person. Use your computer if you want.
- Add your pictures and photos.

92

Technology

USE A WORD PROCESSOR
Review with children how to use word processing software. Point out the features of your program. Have children choose different fonts for headings, questions, and answers. Demonstrate how bold face and italics make text stand out. Review the insert and delete functions of your program, so children can edit their work as needed.

School-Home Connection

HOME WHO'S WHO Children can work with family members to make a list of people in their family. Together, they find out more about the people listed then record and illustrate the answers in a Who's Who book. They can add family pictures or memorabilia, such as old report cards or certificates.

Publishing

- Make a clean copy of each page.

- Put all the pages and pictures together into a book.

- Ask your teacher to help you make copies of your book. Make one for everybody in the book and everybody who helped make it.

- Share your book. Take turns reading pages from it to the class or to other classes.

- Put your Who's Who on your school's website.

Books to Read

Who's Who in My Family?
by Loreen Leedy
Nonfiction
Students in Ms. Fox's class learn where they fit in their family trees. See how every family is special.
Award-Winning Author

Wilson Sat Alone
by Debra Hess
Realistic Fiction
A new girl in the class helps Wilson find out who's who at school.

93

Publishing

Children may want to make a display in the media center. They may want to display their lists of questions and notes to show how they created the book. They may also want to invite family members to share a reading and signing of the school Who's Who.

WRITING You may want to have children write about their experiences making the book, reflecting on what they liked best and what they found difficult. Children can post their article on the school bulletin board or e-mail it to friends and family members.

STUDENT SELF-ASSESSMENT

Ask children to read the Who's Who book and determine whether it explains who each person is and what each person does. Ask children to discuss what they would do differently and why.

Books to Read
Children can use these books to extend their learning about or understanding of family trees and meeting new people. Discuss additional questions children have and how reading these books may help them find the answers.

REACHING ALL **CHALLENGE**

COME READ! Ask children to create an ad to encourage people in the school to come and read the Who's Who. Invite children to use different kinds of sentences and colorful words and pictures in their ads. Have them give a reason in the ad for why people should read their book.

Assessment Strategies and Resources

FORMAL ASSESSMENT

If you want to know more about a child's mastery of the language and writing skills taught in Unit 1, **then** administer the first *Language Skills and Writing Assessment* for Unit 1. The test consists of two parts:

Language Skills: **sentences, parts of sentences, statements and questions, exclamations and commands,** and **sentences about a picture**

Writing Task: Write a **personal story.** Scoring guidelines and model papers are included.

INFORMAL ASSESSMENT TOOLS

 Using Portfolios

During a conference with children, discuss their personal stories and what they chose to include in their **writing portfolios.** You may want to use the Writing Conference Checklist on p. R67 as well as other checklists. Ask the following types of questions about their personal story:

• How did you plan your story?
• What kinds of problems did you have in writing your personal story?
• What did you do well?
• Which part do you like the best?

You can check children's understanding of **grammar** by evaluating it in their writing as well. Look for these points:

• Does each sentence begin with a capital letter and end with the correct punctuation?
• Does each sentence tell a complete thought?
• Are different kinds of sentences used?

Oral Language Assessment

Use these guidelines to evaluate oral language:

Listening and Speaking

• Listens politely and carefully
• Listens to obtain information
• Speaks clearly and uses eye contact
• Provides support for ideas
• Uses gestures and facial expressions
• Adjusts rate and volume to the topic and audience

Informal Assessment Reminder

If you used the pre-instruction writing prompt suggested in Teaching Grammar from Writing, **then** remember to compare the results with the writing done by children after the grammar and writing instruction.

Unit 2

Grammar
- All About Nouns

Writing
- Thank-You Note
- Friendly Letter

Nove[...]

Dear Vicky,
   Thank you for the great pie you and your mother made for my family. It made our Thanksgiving dinner extra special! We are glad to have such nice new neighbors.

Your friend,

Ying

Reaching All Learners

Intervention

SUPPORT ACTIVITIES To help you meet the needs of children who require extra support, use the following activities with individual children or small groups.

- Write the headings *People*, *Places*, and *Things* on chart paper. Have children name words for each category. Include plural nouns and proper nouns as well. Then ask children to illustrate the words on separate sheets of paper and write the matching word under each picture.

INTERACTIVE WRITING Draw a picture of a box on the board. Write the word *surprises* above the box. Have children name things that could be surprises and write the words on the box or around it. Then have children work in small groups to write about different surprises. Remind them to use nouns.

Challenge

Some children require more challenging activities. To help you meet the needs of these children, use these suggestions.

- **WRITE/ACT OUT AN ADVERTISEMENT** Have children work in pairs to write an advertisement for a product. Have them use pronouns, plural nouns, and proper nouns. Then have them act out or present the ads. Listeners can write down the nouns and pronouns they hear.

- **MAKE A POSTER** Invite groups of children to make holiday posters. Have each group choose a holiday and draw pictures of ways to celebrate it. Then ask each group to label the poster with the holiday's name, its date, and the month in which it is celebrated. Children can write captions for their illustrations.

English as a Second Language

ESL STRATEGIES Use these strategies with children who find the chapters on plural nouns and pronouns very challenging.

- Do the practice exercises together orally, using pantomime, pictures, and realia.

- Make pairs of word cards for plural nouns, having the plural on one side and the singular on the other. Children can use the words in sentences to learn the differences.

- For pronouns, have volunteers make up sentences about themselves or class members and share them orally.

Inclusion

LEARNING DIFFICULTIES Many children will benefit from extra help with pronouns.

- Have pairs copy two sentences with nouns from a magazine. Have them rewrite the sentences by substituting pronouns for the nouns. Have them share their sentences.

- For practice activities throughout the unit, provide small-group or one-to-one instruction.

VISUALLY IMPAIRED Have children listen as you say the endings of plural nouns such as *girls* and *toys*. Write the words on the board in large print, read them with children, and point out the *s* endings.

Teaching Grammar from Writing

PRETEST

Use the following prompt as a pretest to assess children's ability to use nouns to name people, places, and things in writing and to use plural nouns, proper nouns, possessives, and pronouns in writing.

WRITING PROMPT

Write sentences that tell about a person and place you like to visit. Draw a picture, if you like, to go with your sentences.

EVALUATE AND PLAN

Analyze children's writing to determine how you can best meet their individual needs for instruction. Use the chart below to identify and remedy problems.

COMMON PROBLEMS	CHAPTERS TO USE
Incorrectly writes possessive nouns.	Chapter 7: Nouns
Does not correctly write plural nouns.	Chapter 8: Plural Nouns
Does not capitalize proper nouns.	Chapter 10: Proper Nouns
Does not capitalize the names of days, months, and holidays.	Chapter 10: Proper Nouns
Uses incorrect pronouns to take the place of nouns.	Chapter 11: Pronouns
Incorrectly uses *I* and *me*.	Chapter 11: Pronouns

Classroom Management

DURING...	SOME CHILDREN CAN...
Grammar Reteaching	Work on the Writing Across the Curriculum project.
Independent Practice	Begin the Writing Connection. Participate in Language Centers.
Portfolio Conferences	Complete Self-Evaluation forms. (See pages R78–R79 in this *Teacher's Edition*.) Participate in peer conferences.

The Writing Center

LANGUAGE ARTS IN THE CLASSROOM

AUTHOR'S CHAIR Place a chair in a prominent place for a child to sit in as writing is shared. Make available a rug or cushions for the audience to sit on.

SHARING BASKET Provide a basket in which children can place a piece of writing that they are willing to share at some point during the day.

PORTFOLIOS Store children's portfolios in boxes or crates. Organize in alphabetical order by first name. Each individual portfolio should be expandable. Some examples are:

- accordion folders
- pocket folders
- manila folders with yarn extenders attached to each side

PICTURE BOX Pictures cut from magazines, brochures, ad circulars, and coloring books can be organized in folders by topic. Children can help themselves to the pictures for their writing and publishing.

WORD WALL It is also beneficial to have your classroom Word Wall located in a strategic place so children have access to it, not only during vocabulary and phonics instruction, but also while writing.

WORK TABLE A large table with labeled bins and work space is ideal. Bins are needed to contain materials to write on, to write with, and to use for bookmaking. Consider the following materials:

- white and colored paper
- stationery, cards, self-stick labels
- blank books
- regular and colored pencils
- pens, markers, crayons
- glue sticks, tape, stapler, rulers
- yarn, brass fasteners
- hole punch, pencil sharpeners
- date stamp, rubber stamps, and ink pads

Class Names
Adam
Beth
Carlos
Danielle
Emilea
Hideo
Jordan
Kayla
Kimiko
Luke
Mateo
Nickie
Rachel
Sarah
Thomas
Willy

Our Writing Spot

Our ABCs
Aa Bb Cc Dd Ee Ff Gg Hh Ii
Jj Kk Ll Mm Nn Oo Pp Qq Rr Ss
Tt Uu Vv Ww Xx Yy Zz

white
colors
cards
labels
Blank Books
yarn
Picture Box

portfolios A-L
portfolios M-Z

Hands-on Activities

Classroom Nouns

MATERIALS: chart paper divided into three columns with the headings *People, Places, Things*; other paper; markers

DIRECTIONS:

1. Divide the class into three groups. Each group represents either people, places, or things.

2. Have each group make a list of all the nouns in their category that they can see represented in their classroom.

3. Invite groups to share their lists. Make sure there are no duplicates.

4. Have children from each group record their words under the proper category on the large chart.

People	Places	Things
Mrs. Andrews	classroom	computer
Aza	reading center	bookcase
Erin	science center	paper
Carlos	math table	crayons
Jessica	computer area	desk

Plural Pictures

MATERIALS: old magazines, scissors, index cards, glue, markers

DIRECTIONS:

1. Write the following word pairs on the board: *foot/feet, child/children, man/men, woman/women, tooth/teeth.*

2. Provide partners with magazines. Tell them to find pictures for the word pairs. Children glue each picture on a separate index card.

3. Have children place the cards face down and then take turns choosing a card.

4. One partner says the word that best describes the picture, tells if it is singular or plural, and uses it in a sentence.

Singular-Noun Portraits

MATERIALS: paper plates or large paper circles, markers or crayons

DIRECTIONS:

1. Provide each child with four paper plates. Tell them to label the plates *Animal, Person, Place,* and *Thing.*

2. Read sentences aloud to children that contain nouns for people, places, animals, and things. All the nouns should be regular singular nouns, such as *The cat purrs. See the nurse.*

3. Children write the nouns they hear on the appropriate plate.

4. Children can illustrate the nouns they wrote on the other side of the plates and use them in sentences.

5. Display children's plates.

Proper Nouns Match

MATERIALS: index cards, markers

DIRECTIONS:

1. Write these nouns on index cards: *city, park, river, lake, person, animal.*

2. On other index cards write several proper nouns for each of the common nouns listed. For example: *Dallas, Brentwood Park, Mississippi River, Lake Tahoe, Michael Jordan, Lassie.*

3. Distribute the proper noun cards randomly to children.

4. Hold up a common noun card and read it aloud. Children who have a proper noun in that category should stand, hold up their card, and one at a time say the nouns aloud.

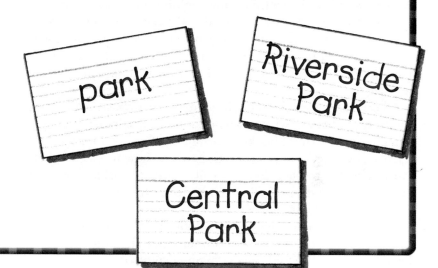

Pronoun Tic-Tac-Toe

MATERIALS: large tagboard sheet divided with lines to look like a Tic-Tac-Toe board, two colors of tagboard, markers, scissors

DIRECTIONS:

1. Write the following sentences in the squares of the board: *Jan and Lee play. The flowers grow. My picture is pretty. The girl dances. My friend plays with ____. The boy sings. ____ like my friends. Jonathan runs. My house is big.*

2. Make two sets of different-colored tagboard cards with these pronouns: *he* (2 cards), *she, it* (2 cards), *they* (2 cards), *I, me.*

3. Have children work in teams. Give each team a set of cards.

4. Taking turns, each team places a pronoun card on the appropriate square of the board and reads the sentence with the pronoun.

5. The next team does the same. The first team to get three cards in a row wins.

Jan ... ee *they*	The flowers grow.	My picture is pretty.
Th... d... *she*	My f... plays w... ___. *me*	T...y *he*
___ like my friends.	Jonathan runs.	My h... is *it*

WANDA'S ROSES

BY PAT BRISSON

ONE MORNING IN MAY on the way to school, Wanda noticed a bush growing in the empty corner lot at Fillmore and Hudson streets. It must have been growing for a while because it was about two feet tall, and Wanda was surprised she hadn't noticed it before. But there it was — bare and thorny — and Wanda, who loved beautiful things, felt her heart beat faster.

"A rosebush!" she said to herself. "My very own rosebush!"

Now, the rosebush didn't really belong to Wanda, but since nobody seemed to own the lot or the heaps of junk that were piled there, she decided she would care for this bush and make it her own.

All during school she thought about her rosebush. During Art she drew pictures of what it would look like in bloom. During Library she borrowed books on arranging flowers. During Science she asked so many questions about how to take care of it that finally her teacher said she really must stop asking questions about roses and start thinking about electricity, which was what the lesson was about.

After school she rushed to the rosebush. It was still bare and thorny. Maybe it needs some more sun, thought Wanda. She put down her schoolbag and began dragging some of the nearby trash out to the curb. Mrs. Turner, who was on her way to the store, stopped to help her with a broken chair.

"Cleaning up the neighborhood, Wanda?" Mrs. Turner asked. "That's a nice project for you."

"Oh, I'm not just cleaning," Wanda told her. "I'm helping my rosebush to get more sun so it will bloom."

"Your rosebush?" Mrs. Turner asked. "Where is your rosebush?"

"Over there," Wanda said, pointing proudly to the bare, thorny bush.

Mr. Claudel was on his way home from work, saw Wanda trying to drag an old door, and stopped to help.

"Cleaning up the neighborhood, are you, Wanda?" he asked.

"Not just cleaning, Mr. Claudel," Wanda told him. "I'm getting rid of this trash so my rosebush will get more air."

"A rosebush? Here?" Mr. Claudel asked. Wanda showed him the rosebush.

"I don't know much about gardening, Wanda," Mr. Claudel said, frowning, "but I don't think that's a rosebush."

"Sure it is," said Wanda, "and in a few weeks this lot will be filled with the sweetest-smelling roses you ever saw." She thanked Mr. Claudel for his help and went off to drag away some more trash.

Mr. Claudel shook his head. "If that's a rosebush," he said to himself, "then I'm the king of France."

Every day after school that week and the next, Wanda worked in the empty lot. Mrs. Giamoni, who lived in an apartment next door, gave Wanda trash bags for the old shoes, bottles, and broken toys that she was picking up.

"You've done a great job cleaning up this lot, Wanda," Mrs. Giamoni told her.

"Oh, I'm not just cleaning," Wanda said. "I have to get rid of all this trash so my rosebush will get enough sun and fresh air to bloom."

"Where is your rosebush?" Mrs. Giamoni asked. Wanda showed her.

Mrs. Giamoni put her hand on Wanda's shoulder and spoke softly to her. "Wanda," she said, "this is not a rosebush."

"Oh, but it is," said Wanda. "In a few weeks this lot will be filled with the most beautiful roses you ever saw."

Building Background

Author Pat Brisson has penned many books including *Your Best Friend, Kate; Kate Heads West; The Magic Carpet;* and *Benny's Pennies.* An avid gardener, Pat Brisson grows roses.

INTRODUCE THE LISTENING SELECTION As you read the story, prompt children to listen for details that help them visualize what the "garden" looks like. Make sure they understand what a thornbush and a rosebush are. Suggest children also listen for details to support the main idea of the story.

Determine a Purpose for Listening

Tell children that this is a story about a girl who believes that a thornbush is a rosebush and that roses will grow from it. It has many details that tell how things look in the garden. These details provide more information about what Wanda does. There is also an invitation in the story. Ask children to decide whether their purpose for listening is

• to gain information

• to solve problems

• to enjoy and appreciate. (to enjoy and appreciate)

"That would be nice," said Mrs. Giamoni, "but I don't want you to be disappointed if this bush doesn't bloom."

"Don't worry, Mrs. Giamoni," Wanda answered. "I won't be disappointed."

Mrs. Giamoni sighed. That is not a rosebush and will never be one, she thought to herself.

The next week, when the rosebush still wasn't blooming, Wanda talked to her school librarian. "I need some books about getting roses to bloom," she told Ms. Jones.

"Oh, do you have a rosebush, Wanda?" Ms. Jones asked.

"Yes, but it doesn't have flowers yet, and I know it has enough sun and fresh air."

"Does it have enough water?" Ms. Jones asked.

"Water!" Wanda said. "Of course! That will make it bloom."

That afternoon she hurried to the rosebush. It was still bare and thorny. She looked at the dry ground and smiled.

"Don't worry, little bush," she said out loud. "I'll get you some water, and then you'll be able to grow flowers."

Wanda went to the butcher shop across the street.

"Mr. Sanchez, would you please give me some water for my rosebush?"

"Rosebush? Is that what I see you taking care of and talking to every day over there? Are you sure that's a rosebush, Wanda?" Mr. Sanchez asked.

"Oh, yes, I'm sure," Wanda said. "But it can't bloom because it needs water." Mr. Sanchez gave her water in a plastic bucket.

"I hope that really is a rosebush, Wanda," he said, looking at her doubtfully.

"You'll see," Wanda told him. "In a few weeks that whole lot will be full of roses."

As Wanda carried the water to her rosebush Mr. Sanchez muttered, "In a few weeks that thornbush will still be a thornbush."

Every day Wanda ran to her rosebush after school, but every day it was still bare and thorny. She watered it and sang to it and checked its bare branches for roses.

Then one day in June, Wanda had an idea. Looking at the bare, thorny bush, she said, "If my rosebush won't give roses to me, I'll just have to give roses to my rosebush." When she saw Mrs. Turner, Mr. Claudel, Mrs. Giamoni, Ms. Jones, and Mr. Sanchez, she gave each of them an invitation that said:

Please come for tea and muffins in Wanda's rose garden Saturday morning at 9.

"Oh, dear," said Mrs. Turner. "Is she still expecting to get roses from that bush?"

"Oh, no," said Mr. Claudel. "And she's worked so hard, too...."

"Oh, my," said Mrs. Giamoni. She'll be so disappointed...."

"Oh, darn," said Mr. Sanchez. "There must be something I can do...."

"Oh, good," said Ms. Jones, who had only heard about the bush from Wanda and hadn't seen it for herself. "I'll bring the muffins."

The night before the tea party everyone was very busy. The next morning at nine, everyone was surprised to see Wanda's rosebush covered with roses—paper roses that Wanda had made herself and carefully tied to each bare, thorny branch.

But more surprising yet, everyone who came to the party had brought along a rosebush to plant near Wanda's (except Ms. Jones, who had brought delicious blueberry muffins).

After they had eaten their muffins and drunk their tea, they all got busy planting rosebushes. Mr. Claudel and Mrs. Turner dug the holes, Mrs. Giamoni held the bushes in place while Wanda and Ms. Jones filled in around the roots with soil, and Mr. Sanchez brought water from his shop and watered them all thoroughly.

When the work was finished, Mr. Claudel said, "Wanda, this is going to be a rose garden fit for a king!"

"Or a queen!" said Mrs. Turner. Wanda and the others smiled.

Later that summer the whole lot was filled with the biggest, most beautiful, sweetest-smelling roses that anyone had ever seen—just as Wanda had always said it would be.

Listening Comprehension

LISTEN FOR DETAILS Explain to children that in this story, the writer uses details to help the reader visualize what the empty lot and the "rosebush" are like. She also provides details to support the main idea by giving information about how Wanda cleans up the lot and how the neighbors support her efforts.

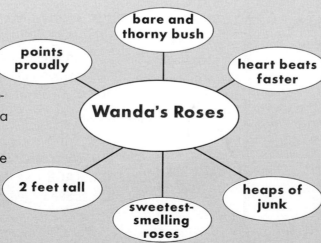

bare and thorny bush

points proudly

heart beats faster

Wanda's Roses

2 feet tall

sweetest-smelling roses

heaps of junk

PERSONAL RESPONSE *How does Wanda feel when she first sees the bush in the empty lot? What words help you know that?* (Possible responses: excited—felt her heart beat faster; surprised— she hadn't noticed it before; thrilled—my very own rosebush.) INFERENTIAL: IMPORTANT DETAILS

Unit 2

Grammar
● All About Nouns

Writing
● Thank-You Note
● Friendly Letter

Introducing the Unit

ORAL LANGUAGE/VIEWING

DISCUSS THE IMAGES. Invite children to tell the most important things they see on these two pages (mailboxes, thank-you note). Have them discuss the purpose of mailboxes and where they see mailboxes. Then ask children about letters they have written and received. Ask questions such as these:

* **What kind of note do you see here? What information does it tell?** (It is a thank-you note. It thanks the neighbors for making a pie for Thanksgiving.)
* **Whom have you written letters or notes to? Why?** (Responses will vary.)
* **What kinds of notes and letters have you received? What kinds of letters and notes have you written?** (Responses will vary.)

 ENCOURAGE CHILDREN'S QUESTIONS. List children's questions about letter writing on the board. Then discuss different kinds of notes and letters and the information that is found in each kind. Encourage children to talk about why people write letters. Then have children write in their journals lists of people they might like to write letters to.

Unit 2

Grammar
● All About Nouns

Writing
● Thank-You Note
● Friendly Letter

94

Viewing and Representing

● ● ● ● ● ● ● ● ● ● ● ● ● ● ● ● ● ●

COMPARE/CONTRAST PRINT AND VISUAL MEDIA Provide children with an assortment of greeting cards. Have them discuss ways the cards are alike and different. Then suggest that children make their own greeting cards, using construction paper and crayons or markers. When they have finished, invite them to explain for whom the card was made and how the pictures and words go together to give a message.

 MEDIA LITERACY AND COMMUNICATION SKILLS PACKAGE Use the video to extend children's oral and visual literacy. See pages 6–7 of the *Teacher's Guide*.

Dear Vicky,

Thank you for the great pie you and your mother made for my family. It made our Thanksgiving dinner extra special! We are glad to have such nice new neighbors.

Your friend,

Ying

Previewing the Unit

Read and discuss the unit contents list with children. Ask them to give examples of nouns and pronouns and any other terms they may already know. Tell them that in this unit they will learn about different kinds of nouns and pronouns. They will also learn how to write nouns that name more than one. Point out the two writing chapters. Explain that learning more about nouns and pronouns will help them write better notes and letters.

SOCIAL STUDIES CONNECTIONS Children will be exposed to a variety of social studies topics in this unit:

- Moving
- Gardening
- Class trip
- Environment
- Helping others
- Music
- Sports

School-Home Connection

You may want to use Home Letter 2, page R95.

LESSON ORGANIZER	DAY 1	DAY 2
DAILY LANGUAGE PRACTICE TRANSPARENCIES 13, 14	1. what a great poem. (What; !) 2. Read it too me now? (to; .) **Bridge to Writing** Write a poem now (punctuation mark)	1. My sisster plays in the Garden. (sister; garden) 2. She likes the new swign? (swing.) **Bridge to Writing** I like to play with (noun).
ORAL WARM-UP Listening/Speaking	Talk About People, Places, and Things p. 96	Play I Spy p. 98 *Grammar Jingles*™ CD, Primary, Track 4
TEACH/MODEL GRAMMAR **KEY** ✔ = tested skill	✔ **WHAT IS A NOUN?** pp. 96-97 • To listen critically to interpret and evaluate a poem • To recognize that a noun names a person, a place, an animal, or a thing	✔ **NOUNS FOR PEOPLE, PLACES, AND THINGS** pp. 98-99 • To understand that a noun can name a person, a place, an animal, or a thing • To use nouns that name people, places, animals, and things in writing

 **Reaching All Learners**	**Challenge:** Make a House of Nouns, p. 97
	 Activity Card 5, p. R45
	 ESL: *ESL Manual* pp. 36, 37
	 Practice Book p. 21
	 Reteach: *Reteach Activities Copying Masters* book p. 13
		Modified Instruction
		   Below-Level: Circle Words
		   Above-Level: Write Sentences
		 Challenge: Make a Mural p. 99
		 ESL: Play Charades p. 98
		 ESL Manual pp. 36, 38
		 Practice Book p. 22
		 Reteach: *Reteach Activities Copying Masters* p. 14

WRITING	Write Nouns p. 97 Summarize	Writing Connection p. 99 Diary Entry Summarize/Reflect
CROSS-CURRICULAR/ ENRICHMENT	**Vocabulary Power** Word Meaning p. 96 **countryside,** farmland, field, meadow, pasture See ***Vocabulary Power*** book.	**Vocabulary Power** Content-Area Words p. 96 *Vocabulary Power* book p. 19 **Vocabulary activity**

Visit *The Learning Site!*
www.harcourtschool.com

WRITING ACTIVITIES
Writing Express CD-ROM

DAY 3

1. My ant Nelly Is kind. (aunt; is)
2. i went to the zo with her. (I; zoo)

Bridge to Writing I have a green (noun).

Talk About Things People Own p. 100
 Grammar Jingles™ CD, Primary, Track 4

✔ **USING POSSESSIVE NOUNS** pp. 100-101
• To understand how to add an apostrophe and the letter *s* to a noun to show ownership
• To use possessive nouns in writing

Modified Instruction
Below-Level: Circle the Owner
Above-Level: Write Additional Sentences With Possessive Nouns
Challenge: What Is It? p. 101
ESL: Whose Is It? p. 100
ESL Manual pp. 36, 39
Practice Book p. 23
Reteach: *Reteach Activities Copying Masters* p. 15

Writing Connection p. 101
Adding Possessive Nouns
Summarize/Reflect

Vocabulary Power
Compound Words p. 96
Vocabulary Power book p. 20
Vocabulary activity

DAY 4

1. that is my uncles book. (That; uncle's)
2. You can pet Peter dog's. (Peter's; dog)

Bridge to Writing This is my (possessive noun) computer.

Telling a Story p. 102

EXTRA PRACTICE p. 102
• To identify and write nouns
• To use possessive nouns in writing

 Practice and Assessment

Challenge: Where I Go p. 103
ESL: From Home p. 102
ESL Manual pp. 36, 40
Practice Book p. 24

Writing Connection p. 103
Labels

Vocabulary Power
Analogies p. 96
Vocabulary Power book p. 21
Vocabulary activity

DAY 5

1. Diegos' bike are broken. (Diego's; is)
2. Can I take care of Grandpas dog. (Grandpa's; ?)

Bridge to Writing Juan's (noun) is six years old.

TEST PREP **CHAPTER REVIEW** p. 104
• To review nouns for people, places, animals, and things and to identify possessive nouns
• To identify and write compound nouns

 Test preparation

Challenge: Make a Compound Noun Machine p. 105
Practice Book p. 25
ESL: *ESL Manual* pp. 36, 41

Writing Application p. 105
Sentences with compound nouns
Summarize

Vocabulary
Compound Nouns p. 105
Vocabulary Power
Graphics/Art p. 96

What Is a Noun?

OBJECTIVES

- To listen critically to interpret and evaluate a poem
- To recognize that a noun names a person, a place, an animal, or a thing

SPIRAL REVIEW

DAILY LANGUAGE PRACTICE

TRANSPARENCY 13

1 what a great poem. (What; !)

2 Read it too me now? (to; .)

BRIDGE TO WRITING Write a poem now (punctuation mark)

ORAL WARM-UP

USE PRIOR KNOWLEDGE Ask children to talk about the people, places, and things they might see in the park. Ask them to name things with which they play. Write the nouns they use to set up a **Noun Word Wall.**

TEACH/MODEL

Have children read the title and the first two lines of the poem on page 96. Invite them to answer the question and predict what the rest of the poem will be about. Then read the poem aloud, asking children to notice the things the person sees. Have children join in as you reread the poem.

DEVELOP ORAL LANGUAGE Ask children to recall the things the child in the poem sees. Prompt children with questions such as these:

- **What is seen when the swing goes up?**
- **What is seen when the swing goes down?**

Ask volunteers to pantomime swinging and tell what they see. Add the nouns to the **Noun Word Wall.**

What Is a Noun?

Read the poem.

The Swing

How do you like to go up in a swing,
  Up in the air so blue?
Oh, I do think it the pleasantest thing
  Ever a child can do!

Up in the air and over the wall,
  Till I can see so wide,
Rivers and trees and cattle and all
  Over the countryside —

Till I look down on the garden green,
  Down on the roof so brown —
Up in the air I go flying again,
  Up in the air and down!

  Robert Louis Stevenson

96

Vocabulary Power

DAY 1 WORD MEANING Write: *countryside.* **Find the word in the poem "The Swing." What might you see in the countryside?**

DAY 2 CONTENT-AREA WORDS Write: *Farms, Cities, Numbers.* **Which topic would include the countryside? Why?** (See also *Vocabulary Power,* page 19.)

DAY 3 COMPOUND WORDS Write: *countryside.* **What two words make up this compound word?** (See also *Vocabulary Power,* page 20.)

DAY 4 ANALOGIES Write: *field–country, sidewalk– _____* **You can see a field in the country. Where can you see a sidewalk?** (See also *Vocabulary Power,* page 21.)

DAY 5 GRAPHICS/ART **Draw a mural of a countryside. Attach labels to various features in your mural.**

What things does the person in the poem see while swinging? What things do you see when you swing? Make a list.

Naming words name people, places, animals, or things. A naming word is also called a **noun**.

My **brother** likes the **playground**.

Sometimes he sees **squirrels** there.

He likes to go on the **swings**.

Add new lines to the poem. Write nouns to complete the sentence. Responses will vary.

Up in the air and over the wall,

Till I can see so wide,

_____ and _____ and _____ and _____

Over the countryside.

97

WRITE Have children list things they can see when playing on a swing. Ask them to share their lists, and add the nouns to the **Noun Word Wall**. Explain that a noun is a word that names a person, a place, an animal, or a thing. Read the example sentences in the box. Have children identify the noun for a person, a place, an animal, and a thing.

Then go over the directions at the bottom of page 97. Encourage children to be creative. Remind them that all their answers must be nouns. Have children share their work with a partner.

WRAP-UP/ASSESS

SUMMARIZE Reread the poem with children. Then have them summarize what they learned about nouns. Ask them to write in their journals what they learned about nouns as well as examples for each type of noun.

RETEACH

REACHING ALL LEARNERS

INTERVENTION Lessons in **visual**, **auditory**, and **kinesthetic** modalities: p. R21 and *Reteach Activities Copying Masters*, p. 13.

page 13

CHING ALL LEARNERS

PRACTICE page 21

Name_____

What Is a Noun?

A. Circle the noun in each group. Write it on the line.

1. ask (book) on   book
2. (school) over tell   school
3. with sad (girl)   girl
4. happy (desk) under   desk
5. (teacher) glad say   teacher

B. Write a noun from the box to complete each sentence. Possible responses are given.

brother	bucket	beach	castle	sand

6. The ___beach___ is fun.
7. We play in the ___sand___
8. I use a ___bucket___
9. My ___brother___ shapes the sand.
10. Our ___castle___ is nice.

TRY THIS! Write three sentences to tell about the people, places, and things you see on your way to school.

Practice • Nouns   Unit 2 • Chapter 7   21

REACHING ALL LEARNERS

CHALLENGE

MAKE A HOUSE OF NOUNS

Have children use **Challenge Activity Card 5** (page R45) to write nouns for people who live in or often visit their homes and for things they have at home. Place the houses on a wall to make a Noun Town.

Challenge Activity Card 5

Make a House of Nouns

You need:
• paper
• crayons or markers
• scissors

1. Draw your house. Show the different rooms.
2. Label the rooms. Write nouns to name the people and things in each room. You can also add pictures.
3. Cut out your house. Write your name on it. Share your house with classmates.

What Is a Noun?

Look at and talk about each picture. Write the noun from the box to complete each sentence.

bookstore	baby	button	blanket

1. Jake goes to the ___bookstore___
2. My coat has one ___button___
3. Put the ___blanket___ on the bed.
4. The ___baby___ takes a nap.

Visual / Auditory

- -

What Is a Noun?

Cut out the nouns at the bottom of the page. Glue the word that best fits each sentence.

1. The children get on the [bus]
2. The bus goes to the [park]
3. There are many [kites] in the park.
4. The [children] learn to fly kites.

bus	park	kites	children

Kinesthetic

Teacher: Cut apart the activities and distribute to children based on the modalities that are their strength.

Reteach Activities • Nouns   Unit 2 • Chapter 7   13

Nouns for People, Places, Animals, and Things

OBJECTIVES
- To understand that a noun can name a person, a place, an animal, or a thing
- To use nouns that name people, places, animals, and things in writing

SPIRAL REVIEW

DAILY LANGUAGE PRACTICE

TRANSPARENCY 13

1 My sisster plays in the Garden.

(sister; garden)

2 She likes the new swign? (swing.)

BRIDGE TO WRITING I like to play with __(noun)__ .

ORAL WARM-UP

PLAY "I SPY" Ask a volunteer to describe something in the classroom, and have children guess what it is. The first child who guesses right becomes the leader.

Grammar Jingles™ **CD, Primary** Use Track 4 for review and reinforcement of nouns.

TEACH/MODEL

Talk about how important nouns are when we speak or write. Ask a child to try to say a sentence, first without using nouns and then using nouns. Write the sentence on the board, and have a volunteer circle the nouns. Read the explanation and examples on page 98. Have children identify the nouns. Encourage them to think of other nouns that name people, places, animals, and things, and add them to the **Noun Word Wall**.

GUIDED PRACTICE Work with children to complete each sentence. Model how to use the clue in parentheses and the words in the box. Tell children that more than one word may make sense.

Nouns for People, Places, Animals, and Things

> A noun can name a person, a place, an animal, or a thing.
>
> My **uncle** is moving.
> He is going to a new **town**.
> He will buy a **dog** when he gets there.
> He will need a **truck**.

Guided Practice

Choose a noun from the chart to finish each sentence. Use the clue in ( ). Possible responses are given.

People	Places	Animals	Things
aunt	house	dog	boxes
brother	park	cat	books

1. My ___aunt___ is moving. (person)
2. She packs many ___boxes___. (things)
3. I help carry out her ___cat___. (animal)
4. I like her new ___house___. (place)
5. It is next to the ___park___. (place)

98

Vocabulary Power page 19

Name_____ Content-Area Words

You would probably find all of these words in a book about the sea.

salt   water   fish   waves   tides   shells   shore

Think about the words you might find in a book about farms. Fill in the word web below. Use words from the box. Add other words.

| field | sidewalk | pasture | farmland | skyscraper |
| desk | airport | meadow | gym | countryside |

field
pasture
FARMS
farmland
meadow
countryside

Vocabulary Power   Unit 2 • Chapter 7   19

ESL

REACHING ALL LEARNERS

PLAY CHARADES Provide cards with simple pictures of animals and tools on them. Ask a child to pick a card and act out clues for classmates to guess the picture. (The child can make sounds but cannot say any words.)

Remember Nouns name people, places, animals, and things.

Independent Practice

Choose a noun from the chart to finish each sentence. Use the clue in ( ). Possible responses are given.

People	Places	Animals	Things
movers	kitchen	parrot	books
brother	dining room	dog	dishes
aunt	bedroom	squirrel	pans

6. The ___movers___ are here. (people)

7. They unpack the ___books___. (things)

8. My ___aunt___ unpacks them, too. (person)

9. I take the ___dishes___ out of a box. (things)

10. I put them in the ___kitchen___. (place)

11. Next door, a ___dog___ barks. (animal)

12. I look out a window and see a ___squirrel___. (animal)

Writing Connection

Diary Entry Think about what you did yesterday. Write sentences to tell about the people, places, animals, and things you saw.

Use **Search** and **Find** to find a word on your computer quickly.

99

Independent Practice

Have children complete the Independent Practice, or modify it by using the following suggestions:

MODIFIED INSTRUCTION

BELOW-LEVEL STUDENTS Ask children to circle the word in parentheses. Point out that they should choose their answer from the column with the matching heading. Have children try the word in the sentence before writing it.

ABOVE-LEVEL STUDENTS After they have finished, ask children to write three new sentences, using as many nouns from the box as they can.

Writing Connection

Diary Entry Remind children to name the people, places, animals, and things they saw. Have volunteers place their sentences in the Sharing Basket to share with others.

WRAP-UP/ASSESS

SUMMARIZE Ask children to summarize what they have learned about nouns. Have them reflect on what they have learned in their journals.

REFLECTION

RETEACH

INTERVENTION Lessons in **visual, auditory,** and **kinesthetic** modalities: p. R21 and *Reteach Activities Copying Masters*, p. 14.

page 14

Nouns for People, Places, Animals, and Things

Talk about and use the nouns from the box to label the picture.

hat   brush
painter   can
ladder

| ladder |
| brush |
| painter |
| can |
| hat |

Complete the picture. Show where the painter is and label the place. Add an animal to the picture and label it.

- -

Nouns for People, Places, Animals, and Things

Divide a paper plate into four parts. Label the parts *People, Places, Animals,* and *Things.* Find the nouns in the sentences below. Write each noun on the plate.

1. My dad went to school.

2. He painted the walls.

3. He saw a lizard.

4. My mom painted the fence.

People   Places

Animals   Things

Cut out pictures of nouns in magazines. Glue them where they belong on the plate.

14 Unit 2 • Chapter 7   Reteach Activities • Nouns

PRACTICE page 22

Name _____

Nouns for People, Places, Animals, and Things

A. Underline the noun in each sentence. Write it on the line.

1. The boy wanted to paint.   boy
2. He took some paper.   paper
3. He used gray paint.   paint
4. He painted a whale.   whale
5. It was swimming in the ocean.   ocean

B. Write the noun from the box that best fits in each sentence.

| picture | parents | students | paper | sea |

6. Mrs. Jackson's ___students___ went to the art room.
7. They put a sheet of ___paper___ on the wall.
8. They painted a large ___picture___.
9. It showed fish swimming in the ___sea___.
10. The children showed it to their ___parents___.

TRY THIS! Look around the room. Write three sentences about things you see. You may draw a picture of each thing.

22 Unit 2 • Chapter 7   Practice • Nouns

CHALLENGE

MAKE A MURAL Have children work in groups to create a mural of their school. Have them think of the people, places, and things they see at school and draw them on the mural. Then have children color and label people, places, and things on the mural.

Library
Miss Luz   Computer   Books

Using Possessive Nouns

OBJECTIVES
- To understand how to add an apostrophe and the letter *s* to a noun to show ownership
- To use possessive nouns in writing

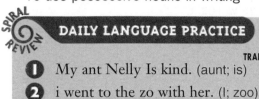

DAILY LANGUAGE PRACTICE

TRANSPARENCY 13

❶ My ant Nelly Is kind. (aunt; is)

❷ i went to the zo with her. (I; zoo)

BRIDGE TO WRITING I have a green (noun).

ORAL WARM-UP

USE PRIOR KNOWLEDGE Ask children to talk about things that belong to various class-mates. You may want to model a sentence, such as *Jack's shirt is red.* Tell children to listen to how the noun ends.

 Grammar Jingles™ **CD, Primary** Use Track 4 for review and reinforcement of nouns.

TEACH/MODEL

Read the explanation and examples in the box. Point out that an apostrophe and an *s* at the end of a noun means the noun is possessive. Explain that the apostrophe and the *s* follow the name of the owner.

GUIDED PRACTICE Work through the first item together. First ask a volunteer to read the underlined words. Ask who the owner is. (my aunt) Next ask the child to say what *my aunt* owns. (a garden) Ask how you can rewrite the phrase with an apostrophe and an *s*. (My aunt's garden) Repeat the procedure with the remaining items.

Using Possessive Nouns

A **possessive noun** shows ownership. It tells what someone or something owns or has.

the **cat's** dish   my **dad's** hat

Add an **apostrophe (')** and the letter **s** to show ownership by one person or thing.

The truck of my uncle is red.
My **uncle's** truck is red.

Guided Practice

Use 's to rewrite the underlined words in each sentence.

1. The garden of my aunt is big. My aunt's garden
2. The friend of my brother is working in it. My brother's friend
3. The friend of my sister helps, too. My sister's friend
4. The chair of my uncle should be put away. My uncle's chair
5. The toy of the dog is on the grass. The dog's toy

100

Vocabulary Power page 20

Name Raven   Compound Words

A compound word is made by putting two words together.

country + side = countryside

Join the word in dark print with the other words. In the last box, draw and label a picture for one of the words you wrote.

side	in out walk	yard	back farm stick
	inside		backyard
	outside		farmyard
	sidewalk		yardstick
land	grass dream mark	house	hen farm boat
	grassland		henhouse
	dreamland		farmhouse
	landmark		houseboat/boathouse
field	corn ball work		
	cornfield		
	ballfield		
	fieldwork		

20   Unit 2 • Chapter 7   Vocabulary Power

ESL

REACHING ALL LEARNERS

WHOSE IS IT? Help children understand word order when using possessive nouns. Make, cut apart, and mix strips with names of people, places, animals, or things; the names of things each can own; and the letter *s* and an apostrophe. Say a sentence, such as *Mara has a book.* Invite children to pick and place the matching strips to form the possessive. (Mara's book)

Remember Add an *apostrophe (')* and the letter *s* after a noun to show ownership.

Independent Practice

Use 's to rewrite the underlined words in each sentence.

6. Tom fixes <u>the fence of the neighbor</u>. the neighbor's fence

7. My brother trims <u>the rose bushes of my cousin</u>. my cousin's rose bushes

8. Leaves fall in <u>the hair of my brother</u>. my brother's hair

9. <u>The sister of Diego</u> brings us lemonade. Diego's sister

10. We all drink <u>the lemonade of Nina</u>. Nina's lemonade

11. A <u>nest of a bird</u> is on the ground. bird's nest

12. I put it back in <u>the branches of the oak tree</u>. the oak tree's branches

13. Later Pam cleans <u>the rake of her father</u>. her father's rake

14. Dave and I put away <u>tools of my aunt</u>. my aunt's tools

15. <u>The neighbor of my aunt</u> asks us to work in her garden. My aunt's neighbor

Writing Connection

Adding Possessive Nouns Look over a piece of writing in your Writing Portfolio. Find places where you could add possessive nouns to show what someone or something owns. Then check to be sure you used 's correctly.

To add an apostrophe ('), press **"** . Do not add a space between the apostrophe and the next letter.

101

Independent Practice

Have children complete the Independent Practice, or modify it by using the following suggestions:

MODIFIED INSTRUCTION

BELOW-LEVEL STUDENTS Suggest that children circle the owner and draw an arrow to the object that is owned to help them see the pattern.

ABOVE-LEVEL STUDENTS After they have finished, ask children to write two sentences using possessive nouns. Have a partner rewrite the sentences without using the possessive.

Writing Connection

Adding Possessive Nouns Help children identify ownership in their pieces of writing. Ask them to circle the owner and underline what is owned.

WRAP-UP/ASSESS

SUMMARIZE Have children summarize and reflect on what they know about using possessive nouns. Ask them to record their thoughts in their journals. **REFLECTION**

RETEACH

INTERVENTION Lessons in **visual, auditory,** and **kinesthetic** modalities: p. R21 and *Reteach Activities Copying Masters,* p. 15.

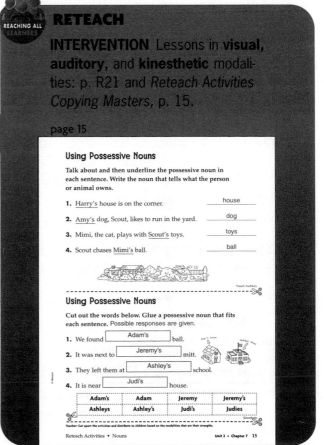

PRACTICE page 23

REACHING ALL LEARNERS

Name _____

Using Possessive Nouns

A. Add 's to each word in ( ) to show ownership. Write the new word on the line.

1. We went to my (grandmother) grandmother's house.

2. We sat in my (grandfather) grandfather's chair.

3. It was my (aunt) aunt's birthday.

4. I took my (uncle) uncle's hat.

5. It looked silly on the (baby) baby's head.

B. Use 's to rewrite the underlined words in each sentence.

6. My family put the food in the truck of my dad. my dad's truck

7. I borrowed the book of José. José's book

8. I put it in the bag of my mother. my mother's bag

9. The dog of the neighbor came, too. neighbor's dog

10. Jeff put the snack of the dog in his pocket. dog's snack

TRY THIS! Write a list of things to take on a picnic. Make sure to use possessive nouns. Draw a picture of each thing.

Practice • Nouns   Unit 2 • Chapter 7 23

CHALLENGE

REACHING ALL LEARNERS

WHAT IS IT? Have children write poems about things their family members own. Have children use the computer to type and edit their writing. Have them print their writing and illustrate it.

I like my aunt's car.
The car's seats are blue.
My dad's car has
blue seats, too.

---

page 15

Using Possessive Nouns

Talk about and then underline the possessive noun in each sentence. Write the noun that tells what the person or animal owns.

1. Harry's house is on the corner. house

2. Amy's dog, Scout, likes to run in the yard. dog

3. Mimi, the cat, plays with Scout's toys. toys

4. Scout chases Mimi's ball. ball

Using Possessive Nouns

Cut out the words below. Glue a possessive noun that fits each sentence. Possible responses are given.

1. We found Adam's ball.

2. It was next to Jeremy's mitt.

3. They left them at Ashley's school.

4. It is near Judi's house.

Adam's	Adam	Jeremy	Jeremy's
Ashleys	Ashley's	Judi's	Judies

Teacher: Cut apart the activities and distribute to children based on the modalities that are their strengths.

Reteach Activities • Nouns   Unit 2 • Chapter 7 15

Extra Practice

OBJECTIVES
- To identify and write nouns
- To use possessive nouns in writing

1 that is my uncles book. (That; uncle's)

2 You can pet Peter dog's. (Peter's; dog)

BRIDGE TO WRITING This is my _____ computer.
(possessive noun)

ORAL WARM-UP

TELLING A STORY Ask a volunteer to retell a story he or she likes. Have children raise one hand whenever they hear a noun, and raise both hands if they hear a possessive noun. Encourage the story-teller to use possessive nouns. Try to work a Vocabulary Power word into the activity.

TEACH/MODEL

Read each set of directions to help children understand how to complete the section. Have children share their answers in small groups before you read aloud the answers to them.

WRAP-UP/ASSESS

SUMMARIZE Ask children to reflect on and discuss any special problems they had in completing the practice. Have them summarize what they have learned about nouns.

ADDITIONAL PRACTICE Extra practice items are provided on page 468 of the *Pupil Edition.*

TECHNOLOGY

Grammar Practice and Assessment CD-ROM

Writing Express CD-ROM

INTERNET Visit *The Learning Site!*
www.harcourtschool.com

Extra Practice

Write the noun in each sentence.

1. My <u>family</u> likes to work hard.
2. We rake <u>leaves</u>.
3. Will we clean the <u>house</u>?
4. Soon we will work in the <u>garden</u>.

Choose the best noun from the box to complete each sentence.

ladder	shed	bush	brother

5. My dad trims the big rose ___bush___.
6. Be careful on that high ___ladder___!
7. Please get the rake from the ___shed___.
8. My ___brother___ plants some flowers.

Rewrite each sentence. Use 's to rewrite the underlined words.

9. Hang on to the <u>leash of the dog</u>. Hang on to the dog's leash.
10. We do not want him to play in <u>the flowers of my brother</u>. We do not want him to play in my brother's flowers.

102

Vocabulary Power page 21

Name _____   Analogies

Look at each word puzzle. Think about why the words go together.

big—large	up—down	round—ball
hot—warm	city—country	square—box

Big and large have similar meanings. Why does warm belong with hot?
Up and down are opposites. Why does country belong with city?
A ball is round. Why does box belong with square?

Complete the word puzzles. Think about why the first two words go together. Write a word that goes with the third word in the same way. Use the words in the box to help you.

gardener	cow	sad	small	bird	sand

1. shiny — bright
   little — small

2. no — yes
   happy — sad

3. kitten — cat
   calf — cow

4. farm — farmer
   garden — gardener

5. pasture — grass
   desert — sand

6. gallop — horse
   fly — bird

Vocabulary Power   Unit 2 • Chapter 7   21

REACHING ALL ... ESL

FROM HOME Ask children to bring (with permission) or draw something from home that belongs to a family member or a friend. Have children tell a partner what the object is and to whom it belongs; then ask them to act out its use. Have the partner say something to respond.

This is my sister's doll. The doll's dress is called a kimono.

Your sister's doll is pretty.

Language Play

I'm Going on a Trip
Play this game with a group.
- The first player begins by saying, "I'm going on a trip and bringing an _____." He or she adds a noun that begins with the letter *A*.
- The second player repeats what the first player said. Then he or she adds a noun that begins with the letter *B*.
- Play goes on in the same way through the alphabet. See how long your list can get!

Language Play

Have children play "I'm Going on a Trip" in groups. Remind them to listen carefully to remember what has been said before. If you wish, ask groups to record the nouns they use. You may add these words to the **Noun Word Wall.**

Writing Connection

Functional Writing: Labels Check to see that children have successfully written labels by using the criteria below.

CRITERIA
- ☑ Begins each label with a proper noun.
- ☑ Writes an apostrophe and an *s* after the owner's name.
- ☑ Writes the object owned after the *'s.*
- ☑ Spaces words and letters correctly.

📁 **PORTFOLIO OPPORTUNITY** You may want to have children place their writing in their portfolios or in the Sharing Basket.

Writing Connection

Functional Writing: Labels A label can show who owns something. Make labels for your things. Write them on self-stick notes if you want to do so. Then stick them onto your things.

PRACTICE page 24
REACHING ALL LEARNERS

Name _____

Extra Practice

A. Find the noun in each sentence. Write it on the line.

1. She likes her colorful bird. _____ bird
2. He never even says a word. _____ word
3. I have a small stuffed bear. _____ bear
4. He has a lot of brown hair. _____ hair

B. Write a noun from the box to finish each sentence.

| cat | dog | hat | log |

5. Mark has a puppy _____ dog
6. It likes to hide in a _____ log
7. Cathy has a furry _____ cat
8. It likes to play with her brother's _____ hat

C. Add *'s* to make each noun in ( ) possessive. Write the sentence.

9. Have you seen my (brother) snake?
   Have you seen my brother's snake?
10. He tried to eat (Charlie) cake.
    He tried to eat Charlie's cake.

24 Unit 2 • Chapter 7   Practice • Nouns

CHALLENGE
REACHING ALL LEARNERS

WHERE I GO Have children list the places they would like to visit. Places can be real or imaginary. Then children pick one place and write about what they would see and whom they would meet there. Then children can draw a picture to illustrate their work.

I go under the sea. I swim with divers. I see a shark.

Chapter Review

OBJECTIVES

- To review nouns for people, places, animals, and things and to identify possessive nouns
- To identify and write compound nouns

DAILY LANGUAGE PRACTICE

TRANSPARENCY 14

1 Diegos' bike are broken. (Diego's; is)

2 Can I take care of Grandpas dog. (Grandpa's; ?)

BRIDGE TO WRITING Juan's (noun) is six years old.

STANDARDIZED TEST PREP

Read the directions with children. Make sure they understand what they have to do. You may wish to use this page as an assessment after children have completed it independently.

TEST PREPARATION TIP

Item Type: Multiple Choice

TIP

Model this strategy to help children determine the correct answer:

First I read the entire sentence. Then I look carefully at the underlined word. The underlined word is a noun followed by an apostrophe and an *s*. I read the four answer choices. The noun *girl* names a person, so the answer could be *a*. The apostrophe and *s* after *girl* are underlined, too. That tells me *girl's* is a possessive noun. I choose *d, possessive noun*. It is the best answer because it describes *girl's* better than *a* does.

Chapter Review

Choose the best answer for each underlined word or words.

1. The girl's dog was lost.
  - **a.** person
  - **b.** place
  - **c.** thing
  - **d. possessive noun**

2. The neighbors helped her.
  - **a. people**
  - **b.** place
  - **c.** thing
  - **d.** possessive noun

3. Mrs. Jackson looked in the park.
  - **a.** person
  - **b. place**
  - **c.** thing
  - **d.** possessive noun

4. Mr. Gomez found the dog's toy.
  - **a.** person
  - **b.** place
  - **c.** thing
  - **d. possessive noun**

5. A little boy found the dog.
  - **a. person**
  - **b.** place
  - **c.** thing
  - **d.** possessive noun

6. The dog was in the yard.
  - **a.** person
  - **b. place**
  - **c.** thing
  - **d.** possessive noun

 Visit our website for more activities with possessives:
www.harcourtschool.com

104

Language Skills Assessment

• •

PORTFOLIO ASSESSMENT
Have children select their best work from the following activities:

- **Writing Connection** pages 99, 101, and 103; TE activities, pages 101 and 103

ONGOING ASSESSMENT
Evaluate the performance of 4-6 children using appropriate checklists and record forms from pages R65–R68 and R77-R79.

INTERNET Activities and exercises to help children prepare for state and standardized assessments appear on *The Learning Site:*
www.harcourtschool.com

■ Vocabulary ■

Compound Nouns

> A **compound noun** is made up of two nouns. The two nouns together make a new noun.
>
> gold + fish = goldfish
> base + ball = baseball

Practice

Look at each picture. Put together one word from each box to write a compound noun that names the picture.

| door | dog | suit |
| star | foot | grass |

| house | ball | fish |
| case | hopper | bell |

1. doghouse

2. suitcase

3. starfish

4. football

5. doorbell

6. grasshopper

105

■ Vocabulary ■

Compound Nouns

TEACH/MODEL

Write the word *doorbell* on the board. Ask a volunteer to circle the two nouns in the word. Discuss the meaning of the word with children. Then read the explanation and examples in the box. Ask children to say the two nouns separately and then together as a compound word. Ask them to brainstorm other compound nouns. Add these words to the **Noun Word Wall**.

PRACTICE When children have finished, invite volunteers to make up sentences using some of the compound nouns they wrote. Have them share their sentences, and ask the group to identify the compound words.

WRAP-UP/ASSESS

SUMMARIZE Ask children to tell what they have learned about compound nouns. Discuss how using compound nouns can make their writing more exact and more interesting.

PRACTICE page 25

Name _____

Compound Nouns

A. Underline the compound noun in each sentence. Write the two nouns that make it up.

1. My uncle lives on a <u>houseboat</u>. _____ house boat

2. He has a small <u>bedroom</u>. _____ bed room

3. There is a short <u>footstool</u>. _____ foot stool

4. There is a warm <u>bedspread</u>. _____ bed spread

5. His books are in the <u>bookcase</u>. _____ book case

B. Match a word in Column A with one in Column B to make a compound noun. Write the compound nouns.

	Column A	Column B
6. fireplace	fire	bone
7. backbone	back	plane
8. airplane	air	nail
9. drumstick	drum	place
10. fingernail	finger	stick

TRY THIS! Look around the classroom to find objects that are compound nouns. Write sentences using the words. Draw pictures to go with the sentences.

Practice • Nouns   Unit 2 • Chapter 7 25

CHALLENGE

MAKE A COMPOUND NOUN MACHINE Have children decorate a box and label it "Compound Noun Machine." Ask small groups to think of at least ten nouns that could be part of a compound noun. Write each noun on a separate card. Place the cards in the box. Have volunteers pull out two cards, read them in order, and decide whether the compound noun makes sense.

LESSON ORGANIZER	DAY 1	DAY 2
 **DAILY LANGUAGE PRACTICE** TRANSPARENCIES T5–T6	1. My brohter has a new houss. (brother; house) 2. My sisters' name is sue. (sister's; Sue) **Bridge to Writing** I like to go to (noun for a place) .	1. silk worms makes silk. (Silk; make) 2. This is Lucys' silk scarf (Lucy's; .) **Bridge to Writing** I like (possessive noun) new bike.
ORAL WARM-UP Listening/Speaking	Talk About Clothes p. 106	Name Classroom Objects p. 108 Grammar Jingles™ CD, Primary, Track 5
TEACH/MODEL GRAMMAR **KEY** ✔ = tested skill	✔ **NOUNS THAT NAME MORE THAN ONE** 106-107 • To listen critically to interpret and evaluate a poem • To recognize that some nouns name more than one	✔ **MAKING NOUNS PLURAL** 108-109 • To recognize that the letter s can be added to most nouns to name more than one • To recognize that for nouns ending in s, ch, sh, or x, es must be added to the noun to name more than one
 **Reaching All Learners**	**Challenge:** All About Silk Worms p. 107 Activity Card 6, p. R46 **ESL:** ESL Manual pp. 42–43 Practice Book p. 26 **Reteach:** Reteach Activities Copying Masters p. 16	**Modified Instruction** Below-Level: Recite Both Answers Above-Level: Write Sentences Using Plural Nouns **Challenge:** More Than One p. 109 **ESL:** Plural Nouns Pick p. 108 ESL Manual pp. 42, 44 Practice Book p. 27 **Reteach:** Reteach Activities Copying Masters p. 17

WRITING	Write About Pictures p. 107
	
	  Summarize/Reflect
		Writing Connection p. 109
		 Revising
		  Summarize

CROSS-CURRICULAR/ ENRICHMENT	**Vocabulary Power** Word Meaning p. 106 adult, **cocoons**, cycle, larvae, pupa See **Vocabulary Power** book.	**Vocabulary Power** Content-Area Words p. 106 Vocabulary Power book p. 22 **Vocabulary activity**

DAY 3

1. Three piges played in the muds. (pigs; mud)

2. Did you eat two peachs. (peaches; ?)

Bridge to Writing She has three (plural of *watch*).

Talk About How Many p. 110

 Grammar Jingles™ CD, Primary, Track 5

✔ **PLURAL NOUNS THAT CHANGE SPELLING** 110-111
  • To recognize that some nouns change spelling to name more than one
  • To use nouns that name more than one in writing

Modified Instruction
  Below-Level: Make Up Rhymes
  Above-Level: Write Sentences
Challenge: What Happened?
  p. 111
ESL: Play Cards p. 110
  ESL Manual pp. 42, 45
Practice Book p. 28
Reteach: *Reteach Activities Copying Masters* p. 18

Writing Connection p. 111
  Giving Reasons
 Summarize/Reflect

Vocabulary Power
  Related Words p. 106
  Vocabulary Power book p. 23
Vocabulary Activity

DAY 4

1. Four man watched the two wolf. (men; wolves)

2. Three child saw two mouses. (children; mice)

Bridge to Writing An elephant has four big (plural of *foot*).

Play Riddles p. 112

EXTRA PRACTICE 112
  • To identify nouns that name more than one
  • To write and spell nouns that name more than one, including nouns that change spelling to name more than one
  Practice and Assessment

Challenge: Funny Picnic p. 113
ESL: Finding Nouns p. 112
  ESL Manual pp. 42, 46
Practice Book p. 29

Writing Connection p. 113
  Shopping List

Vocabulary Power
  Word Families p. 106
  Vocabulary Power book p. 24
  Language Play p. 113
Vocabulary activity

DAY 5

1. Two woman sang four song. (women; songs)

2. Tina dropped twoo dishs (two; dishes.)

Bridge to Writing Four young (plural of *man*) built the science museum.

TEST PREP CHAPTER REVIEW 114
  • To review nouns that name more than one
  • To locate words in a dictionary using alphabetical order and guide words
  Test Preparation

Challenge:
  Dictionary Practice p. 115
ESL: *ESL Manual* pp. 42, 47
Practice Book p. 30

Writing Application p. 115
  Find Dictionary Words

Study Skill
  Finding Words in a Dictonary
  p. 115
Vocabulary Power

Exemplification p. 106

Nouns That Name More Than One

OBJECTIVES
- To listen critically to interpret and evaluate a poem
- To recognize that some nouns name more than one

DAILY LANGUAGE PRACTICE

TRANSPARENCY 15

1 My brohter has a new houss. (brother; house)

2 My sisters' name is sue. (sister's; Sue)

BRIDGE TO WRITING I like to go to (noun for a place) .

ORAL WARM-UP

USE PRIOR KNOWLEDGE Show several pictures of different types of clothing. Ask children to name the articles they see, using plural words such as *dresses, shirts,* and *shoes.* Begin a list of plural nouns on chart paper, or add these nouns to your **Word Wall.**

TEACH/MODEL

Ask children to open their books to page 106. Read the poem aloud, asking them to listen for the nouns. Discuss the meanings of the words *mulberry, cocoon,* and *silk.* Then reread the poem, having children join in with you.

DEVELOP ORAL LANGUAGE Ask children to recall the nouns from the poem. If necessary, ask questions about the animals in the poem and what they eat.

Record their responses on the board and read the nouns aloud. Ask children to use them in sentences of their own. Add nouns to the list on chart paper or to the **Word Wall.**

Nouns That Name More Than One

Read the poem.

Little Silk Worms

Little silk worms, if you please,
Eat up all the mulberry leaves.
Make cocoons as white as milk,
And we'll make clothes of purest silk.

Demi

106

Vocabulary Power

DAY 1 WORD MEANING Write: *cocoons.* **Find the word in the poem "Little Silk Worms."** *Cocoons* are wrappings that keep baby silkworms safe. **Find a cocoon in the picture.**

DAY 2 CONTENT-AREA WORDS Write: *Math, Science, Music.* **In which class might you learn about cocoons?** (See also *Vocabulary Power,* page 22.)

DAY 3 RELATED WORDS Write: *cocoon, shelter.* **Why do these words go together? Name some other shelters.** (See also *Vocabulary Power,* page 23.)

DAY 4 WORD FAMILIES List: *cocoon, cocoons; larva, larvae.* **Which words mean one? Which words mean more than one?** (See also *Vocabulary Power,* page 24.)

DAY 5 EXEMPLIFICATION Have children draw pictures of the stages in the life of a butterfly and label the stages.

Read the poem again with a partner. Tell in your own words what the silk worms are doing. Then talk about what is happening in the other pictures.

> Some nouns name more than one.
>
> Little silk **worms** make **cocoons**.

In a small group, play a game using nouns that name more than one.

- The first player says, "On my trip, I saw one (<u>noun</u>)."

- The next player repeats the sentence and then adds words to tell about two people or things.

- Keep going until each player has had a few turns.

- How many things did your group see?

107

WRITE Invite volunteers to share their responses about the pictures. Explain that nouns that name more than one person, place, animal, or thing are **plural nouns**. Read the definition in the box, and talk about the example sentence.

Read the game directions at the bottom of page 107 together. Be sure that children understand how to play. You may suggest that they record the nouns they use. Have groups play the game and then share their responses.

WRAP-UP/ASSESS

SUMMARIZE Reread the poem with children. Then have children reflect on what they have learned about nouns. You may want children to write their reflections in their journals. **REFLECTION**

REACHING ALL
LEARNERS
RETEACH

INTERVENTION Use visual, auditory, and kinesthetic modalities, p. R28 and Reteach Activities Copying Masters, p. 16.

page 16

Nouns That Name More Than One

Talk about the pictures. Write a word from the box to tell what each picture shows.

| stars | glasses | benches | trees |

1. glasses   2. stars
3. benches   4. trees

Nouns That Name More Than One

Circle the nouns that name more than one.

(pencils)   book   (crayons)

Count each item below that is in your desk. If you have more than one, write the number on the line.
Responses will vary.

_____ pencils   _____ books   _____ crayons

16 Unit 2 • Chapter 8   Reteach Activities • Plural Nouns

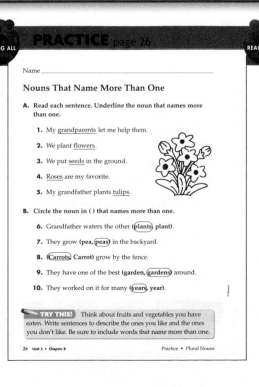

REACHING ALL
LEARNERS
PRACTICE page 26

Name _____

Nouns That Name More Than One

A. Read each sentence. Underline the noun that names more than one.

1. My <u>grandparents</u> let me help them.
2. We plant <u>flowers</u>.
3. We put <u>seeds</u> in the ground.
4. <u>Roses</u> are my favorite.
5. My grandfather plants <u>tulips</u>.

B. Circle the noun in ( ) that names more than one.

6. Grandfather waters the other (plants, plant).
7. They grow (pea, peas) in the backyard.
8. (Carrots, Carrot) grow by the fence.
9. They have one of the best (garden, gardens) around.
10. They worked on it for many (years, year).

TRY THIS! Think about fruits and vegetables you have eaten. Write sentences to describe the ones you like and the ones you don't like. Be sure to include words that name more than one.

26 Unit 2 • Chapter 8   Practice • Plural Nouns

REACHING ALL
LEARNERS
CHALLENGE

ALL ABOUT SILK WORMS Have children use **Challenge Activity Card 6** (page R46) to find out more about silk and silk worms and then present the information to the class. Children can draw their own pictures from the poem to support their explanation about silk making.

Challenge Activity Card 6
Find Out About Silkworms

Making Nouns Plural

OBJECTIVES
- To recognize that the letter *s* can be added to most nouns to name more than one
- To recognize that for nouns ending in *s*, *ch*, *sh*, or *x*, *es* must be added to the noun to name more than one

DAILY LANGUAGE PRACTICE

TRANSPARENCY 15

1 silk worms makes silk. (Silk; make)

2 This is Lucys' silk scarf (Lucy's; .)

BRIDGE TO WRITING I like _____ (possessive noun) new bike.

ORAL WARM-UP

USE PRIOR KNOWLEDGE Have children name groups of things they see in the classroom, such as books, pens, or toys. Add some of their suggestions to the **Word Wall.**

Grammar Jingles™ **CD Primary** Use Track 5 for review and reinforcement of plural nouns.

TEACH/MODEL

Read aloud the first explanation and the example. Ask questions such as these: *Which noun names more than one?* (gifts) *How do you know?* (There are two gifts. The word ends with an *s*.) Then read the second explanation and sentence. Ask children which is the plural noun and why they think it ends in *es*.

GUIDED PRACTICE Work with children to complete each sentence. Have them identify the last letter of each noun to help them decide whether to add *s* or *es*.

Making Nouns Plural

Some nouns name more than one. Add **s** to most nouns to name more than one.

　Tim received two **gifts**.

Add **es** if the noun ends with **s**, **ch**, **sh**, or **x** to name more than one.

　Sue has three **dresses**.

Guided Practice

Write the correct noun in ( ) to finish each sentence.

1. On our class trip, I had lunch with my two (friends, friendes).

2. First we sat on three (chairs, chaires).

3. We put three (sandwichs, sandwiches) on the picnic table.

4. We also got out three (pears, peares).

5. Then we shared our three (lunchs, lunches).

108

Vocabulary Power page 22

Name _____

Content-Area Words

Read the following science article. Think about the meaning of the underlined words.

The Life of the Butterfly

Butterflies start out as eggs. The eggs hatch into caterpillars, or larvae. Caterpillars eat and grow quickly. Then they make shells, or cocoons.

Inside its cocoon, the caterpillar is called a pupa. The pupa grows, changes, and becomes an adult.

When the cocoon cracks open, out comes a butterfly! The butterfly lays eggs, and the cycle begins again.

Moths have a life cycle similar to butterflies. Use what you learned about butterflies to tell about moths.

Moth eggs hatch into caterpillars, or ___larvae___.

The caterpillars wrap themselves in ___cocoons___.

Inside a cocoon, a caterpillar is called a ___pupa___.

The pupa grows into an ___adult___.

When the cocoon cracks open, out comes a moth.

The moth lays eggs, and the ___cycle___ begins again.

22　Unit 2 • Chapter 8　　Vocabulary Power

PLURAL NOUN PICK Provide each child with two cards, one with the letter *s* and one with *es*. Write words such as *beach, cloud, color, class, bush, fox, animal, lunch, box, book, dog, bench,* and *dish* on slips of paper. Have children pick a word slip and add *s* or *es* to make the noun name more than one. Then ask children to use the words in sentences.

Remember Add *s* to most nouns to name more than one. Add *es* to nouns that end with *s*, *ch*, *sh*, or *x* to name more than one.

Independent Practice

Write the correct noun in ( ) to finish each sentence.

6. My class went on a trip with two other (classs, <u>classes</u>).

7. We took two (buss, <u>buses</u>) to get to the park.

8. There we met with three park (<u>rangers</u>, rangeres).

9. They showed us many different (<u>plants</u>, plantes).

10. They told us about the (<u>animals</u>, animales).

11. We saw something move in the (bushs, <u>bushes</u>).

12. It was a family of (foxs, <u>foxes</u>).

13. At lunchtime we sat on (benchs, <u>benches</u>) to eat.

14. We shared our bread with some (<u>birds</u>, birdes).

15. After lunch we planted (<u>flowers</u>, floweres).

Writing Connection

Revising Look through your Writing Portfolio. Choose one piece of writing. Find nouns that name more than one. Check to see if you added *s* or *es* correctly. Revise your writing.

Use a computer to revise. Place the cursor at the end of the word. Type the letters you need to add.

109

Independent Practice

Have children complete the Independent Practice, or modify it by using the following suggestions:

MODIFIED INSTRUCTION

BELOW-LEVEL STUDENTS Suggest that children say aloud both answer choices to help them decide whether the plural noun should end with an *s* or *es*.

ABOVE-LEVEL STUDENTS After children are finished, suggest they list four animals or plants they might see at a park. Then have them write sentences using nouns that name more than one.

Writing Connection

Revising Help children select appropriate pieces of writing to revise. Suggest they underline nouns that name more than one and circle the endings.

WRAP-UP/ASSESS

SUMMARIZE Ask children to summarize what they have learned about nouns that name more than one.

RETEACH

INTERVENTION Lessons in **visual**, **auditory**, and **kinesthetic** modalities: p. R22 and *Reteach Activities Copying Masters*, p. 17.

page 17

PRACTICE page 27

Name _Raven_

Making Nouns Plural

A. Write the word that names more than one.

1. one plum   two   plums
2. one grape   five   grapes
3. one peach   three peaches
4. one apple   four   apples
5. one melon   two   melons

B. Add *s* or *es* to make the word in ( ) mean more than one. Write the word on the line.

6. Nancy saw a pile of (dish) _dishes_ in the store.

7. They had pretty (flower) _flowers_ painted on them.

8. Then she saw some (glass) _glasses_

9. They had cute (animal) _animals_ painted on them.

10. The salesman packed them in (box) _boxes_

TRY THIS! Make a list of things you see more than one of in the classroom. Then illustrate the list.

Practice • Plural Nouns   Unit 2 • Chapter 8 27

CHALLENGE

MORE THAN ONE Use picture cards of things whose plural names end with *s* or *es*, such as *books, benches, dresses,* and *dogs*. Have children work in pairs. One child picks a card, says the noun in the plural form, and writes it. The partner then uses this plural noun in a sentence.

dogs

Making Nouns Plural

Read each sentence aloud. Underline the noun that names more than one. Circle the letter or letters that were added to name more than one.

1. The boy(s) went to the park.
2. They saw the girl(s).
3. They all raced around the bush(es).
4. They played with ball(s).
5. They had a picnic under the tree(s).
6. They ate sandwich(es).

Visual/Auditory

Making Nouns Plural

Cut out the letters on the bottom of the page. Glue *s* or *es* where it belongs in each sentence.

1. The children put the ball [s] away.
2. They sat down on the bench [es].
3. Their lunch [es] were on the table.
4. For dessert, they had apple [s] and peach [es].

es es es s s

Kinesthetic

Teacher: Cut apart the activities and distribute to children based on the modalities that are their strengths.

Reteach Activities • Plural Nouns   Unit 2 • Chapter 8 17

Plural Nouns That Change Spelling

OBJECTIVES
- To recognize that some nouns change spelling to name more than one
- To use nouns that name more than one in writing

DAILY LANGUAGE PRACTICE

TRANSPARENCY 15

1 Three piges played in the muds. (pigs; mud)

2 Did you eat two peachs. (peaches; ?)

BRIDGE TO WRITING She has three ___ (plural of *watch*).

ORAL WARM-UP

USE PRIOR KNOWLEDGE Ask children how many feet or teeth they have, and how many children are in the classroom. Write their answers on the board, and then write each noun in the singular. Invite a volunteer to draw a line between the singular and plural nouns. Discuss how the plural was formed for these nouns.

Grammar Jingles™ **CD Primary** Use Track 5 for reinforcement and review of plural nouns.

TEACH/MODEL

Read the explanation in the box. Call on volunteers to read the examples and identify the singular and plural nouns. Ask them how these plural nouns are different from other nouns that name more than one. (These nouns don't end with *s* or *es*.)

GUIDED PRACTICE Work through the first item together. Have children read the sentence aloud and say the correct plural. Encourage children to note how each plural is spelled. Repeat the procedure with the remaining items.

Plural Nouns That Change Spelling

Some nouns change spelling to name more than one.

One	More Than One	One	More Than One
child →	children	foot →	feet
man →	men	tooth →	teeth
woman →	women	mouse →	mice
wife →	wives	wolf →	wolves

Guided Practice

Write the noun in ( ) to mean more than one.

1. Evan brought two pictures of (mouse) to class.   mice

2. Latasha showed a painting of three (wolf).   wolves

3. Antonio shared a book about many famous (man) and (woman).   men, women

4. Holly showed two (leaf) that she found on a class trip to the park.   leaves

5. All the (child) enjoyed this show-and-tell day.   children

110

Vocabulary Power page 23

Name _____

Words can be related in many different ways.

These are stages in the life of a moth: <u>cocoon</u>, <u>pupa</u>, <u>adult</u>. These are different kinds of birds: <u>robin</u>, <u>cardinal</u>, <u>woodpecker</u>. These are games you play with a ball: <u>football</u>, <u>basketball</u>, <u>baseball</u>.

Brainstorm words that are related in some way to the words in dark print. Tell how your words are related.

baby	shell
These words are related because	These words are related because
cycle	butterfly
These words are related because	These words are related because

Vocabulary Power   Unit 2 • Chapter 8   23

ESL

REACHING ALL LEARNERS

PLAY CARDS Provide pairs of children with a set of word cards for singular and plural nouns on the chart on page 110. Children put the cards face down and take turns picking one. If the card they pick shows the plural or singular of a word they already hold, they put the pair down. If the stack is empty, children pick a card from the partner. Partners should continue until all the words have been paired.

Remember Some nouns change spelling to name more than one.

Independent Practice

Write the noun in ( ) to mean more than one.

6. Mrs. Min took the (child) to the zoo.   children

7. Two (man) passed out maps.   men

8. Their (wife) were the tour guides.   wives

9. The (woman) took the class to see the lions.   women

10. Jasmine liked watching all the (wolf).   wolves

11. The gorilla scratched his ears with both his (foot).   feet

12. The guides showed them some special (mouse).   mice

13. The biggest mouse had very large (tooth).   teeth

14. The class thanked the two (woman) for the tour.   women

15. All the (child) had a good time.   children

Writing Connection

Giving Reasons Think about a trip you have taken and what you liked about it. Then write a paragraph to tell friends why they should take the trip, too. Include plural nouns as you tell about details you think others would like.

Use a computer to write your paragraph. Save your writing. Add more details later.

111

Independent Practice

Have children complete the Independent Practice, or modify it by using the following suggestions:

MODIFIED INSTRUCTION

BELOW-LEVEL STUDENTS Suggest that children make up rhymes to help them remember the spellings of the plural nouns on page 110.

ABOVE-LEVEL STUDENTS After children have finished, tell them to write additional sentences using singular nouns. Then have them trade sentences with a partner, and rewrite the sentences making the nouns plural.

Writing Connection

Giving Reasons Remind children that one way to get people to do something is to give reasons why. Have children give their reasons and add details. Remind them to check that the plural nouns are spelled correctly.

WRAP-UP/ASSESS

SUMMARIZE In their journals, have children summarize and reflect on writing plural nouns that change spelling. **REFLECTION**

RETEACH

INTERVENTION Lessons in **visual**, **auditory**, and **kinesthetic** modalities: p. R22 and *Reteach Activities Copying Masters*, p. 18.

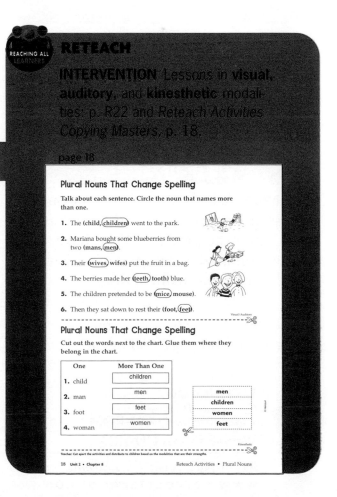

PRACTICE page 28

Name _____

Plural Nouns That Change Spelling

A. Draw a line from each noun that names one to the form of that noun that names more than one.

1. mouse — teeth
2. woman — men
3. tooth — women
4. child — mice
5. man — children

B. Change the spelling to make each noun in ( ) mean more than one. Write the new sentence.

6. The (child) went to the pet store.
   The children went to the pet store.

7. The (man) in the store were nice.
   The men in the store were nice.

8. They had white (mouse).
   Thy had white mice.

TRY THIS! Write a note to a friend about an animal. Talk about parts of the animal's body. Use as many plural nouns that change spelling as you can.

28 Unit 2 • Chapter 8   Practice • Plural Nouns

CHALLENGE

WHAT HAPPENED? Ask children to recall a school or community event they were part of. Have them write a news story about the event. Encourage them to use plural nouns such as *children, men,* and *women* in their descriptions. Have children publish their work as a newspaper article, including illustrations. Have them share their work with a partner.

page 18

Plural Nouns That Change Spelling

Talk about each sentence. Circle the noun that names more than one.

1. The (child, children) went to the park.
2. Mariana bought some blueberries from two (mans, men).
3. Their (wives, wifes) put the fruit in a bag.
4. The berries made her (teeth, tooth) blue.
5. The children pretended to be (mice, mouse).
6. Then they sat down to rest their (foot, feet).

Plural Nouns That Change Spelling

Cut out the words next to the chart. Glue them where they belong in the chart.

One	More Than One
1. child	children
2. man	men
3. foot	feet
4. woman	women

men
children
women
feet

18 Unit 2 • Chapter 8   Reteach Activities • Plural Nouns

Extra Practice

OBJECTIVES
- To identify nouns that name more than one
- To write and spell nouns that name more than one, including nouns that change spelling to name more than one

DAILY LANGUAGE PRACTICE

TRANSPARENCY 16

1 Four man watched the two wolf. (men; wolves)

2 Three child saw two mouses. (children; mice)

BRIDGE TO WRITING An elephant has four big (plural of *foot*).

ORAL WARM-UP

PLAY RIDDLES Tell children clues to plural nouns, such as: *We grow and become loose in your mouth.* (teeth) *We rest under you.* (feet) *We are on each side of your head.* (ears) *We wait in the park for you to sit on us.* (benches)

TEACH/MODEL

Read each set of directions aloud. Be sure that children understand how to complete each section. Have children share their answers in small groups before you read aloud the answers to them.

WRAP-UP/ASSESS

SUMMARIZE Ask children to reflect on and discuss any special problems they had in completing the practice. Then have them summarize what they have learned about nouns that name more than one.

ADDITIONAL PRACTICE Extra practice items are provided on page 468 of the *Pupil Edition*.

TECHNOLOGY
Grammar Practice and Assessment CD-ROM
Writing Express CD-ROM

INTERNET Visit *The Learning Site!*
www.harcourtschool.com

Extra Practice

Write the noun in ( ) to mean more than one.

1. Barry, Carlos, and their class slept under the (star). stars

2. They slept in sleeping (bag). bags

3. They told each other silly (joke). jokes

4. The next day they made (sandwich) for lunch. sandwiches

5. They also ate ripe (peach). peaches

6. After lunch the class washed their (dish). dishes

7. That was when Carlos broke two (glass). glasses

Choose a noun from the box to finish each sentence. Change the noun to mean more than one.

wolf	tooth	child

8. All the ___children___ had a contest.

9. They wanted to see who had lost the most ___teeth___.

10. The winner got a poster of a family of ___wolves___.

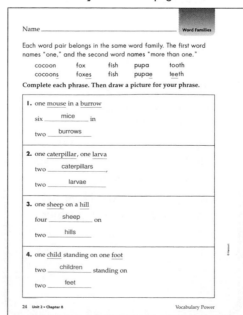

112

Vocabulary Power page 24

Name _____ Word Families

Each word pair belongs in the same word family. The first word names "one," and the second word names "more than one."

cocoon	fox	fish	pupa	tooth
cocoons	foxes	fish	pupae	teeth

Complete each phrase. Then draw a picture for your phrase.

1. one mouse in a burrow
   six ___mice___ in
   two ___burrows___

2. one caterpillar, one larva
   two ___caterpillars___
   two ___larvae___

3. one sheep on a hill
   four ___sheep___ on
   two ___hills___

4. one child standing on one foot
   two ___children___ standing on
   two ___feet___

24 Unit 2 • Chapter 8   Vocabulary Power

 ESL

FINDING NOUNS Some children may mistake singular nouns that end with *s* as being plural nouns. Give them a list of 20 words that end with *s*. Some of these words should be plural nouns, and some should be singular nouns that end with *s*, such as *dress* and *bus*. Have children circle the nouns that name more than one and cross out those that do not.

Plural Race

- Take turns with a partner.
- Roll a number cube.
  Move that many spaces.
- Spell the plural of the word on which you land. Use the word in a sentence. If you are not correct, go back 2.
- The first one to the end wins.

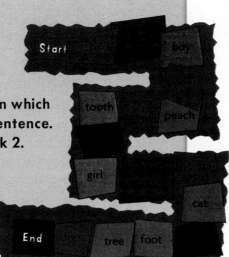

Writing Connection

Shopping List A shopping list can help you remember what to buy. Make a list of things you might buy at a store. Be sure to include the number of each thing you must buy.

Shopping List

5 pencils

2 notebooks

3 folders

4 paintbrushes

113

Have children play "Plural Race" in pairs. Model how to roll and read the number cube and how to move the correct number of spaces. After children spell the plural word, encourage them to write it in a sentence.

Writing Connection

Shopping List Check to see that children have successfully written a list by using the criteria below.

CRITERIA
- ✔ Writes one item per line.
- ✔ Correctly spells nouns that name more than one.
- ✔ Writes the number of each item needed.

 PORTFOLIO OPPORTUNITY You may want to have children place their writing in their portfolios or take it home to share with family members.

REACHING ALL PRACTICE page 29

Name _____

Extra Practice

A. Add *s* or *es* to make the word in ( ) mean more than one.

1. I am 45 (inch) _____inches_____ tall.
2. I have two older (sister) _____sisters_____.
3. A pair of (glass) _____glasses_____ help me see.
4. I have two (dog) _____dogs_____.

B. Change the spelling to make each underlined word mean more than one. Write the new sentence.

5. Tara drew two woman.
   Tara drew two women.

6. Anton traced his foot.
   Anton traced his feet.

7. They both drew wolf.
   They both drew wolves.

8. The child like to draw.
   The children like to draw.

Practice • Plural Nouns   Unit 2 • Chapter 8   29

REACHING ALL CHALLENGE

FUNNY PICNIC Have children write sentences about a funny picnic, using as many of the plural nouns as possible from the game path for "Plural Race" on page 113. Children can share their writing with a group.

Chapter Review

OBJECTIVES

- To review nouns that name more than one
- To locate words in a dictionary using alphabetical order and guide words

DAILY LANGUAGE PRACTICE

TRANSPARENCY 16

1 Two woman sang four song. (women; songs)

2 Tina dropped twoo dishs (two; dishes.)

BRIDGE TO WRITING Four young _____ (plural of *man*) built the science museum.

STANDARDIZED TEST PREP

Read the directions with children to make sure they understand how to complete each section. You may wish to have children complete this page independently and use it as an assessment.

TEST PREPARATION TIP
Item Type: Multiple Choice

TIP

Model this strategy to help children determine the correct answer:

As *peach* is written in the first sentence, I see that it names one. The last two letters of *peach* are *ch*, so I know I need to add *es* to make it name more than one. I look at the three answer choices and find *b, peaches.* Then I reread the sentence with the answer to be sure I have selected the correct answer.

Plural Nouns

Chapter Review STANDARDIZED TEST PREP

Choose the best answer for each underlined word.

1. My brother and I like to pick fuzzy <u>peach</u>.
   - **a.** peachs
   - **b. peaches**
   - **c.** correct as is

2. They grow on <u>trees</u> near our house.
   - **a.** tree
   - **b.** treees
   - **c. correct as is**

3. We keep the peaches in <u>baskets</u>.
   - **a.** basket
   - **b.** basketes
   - **c. correct as is**

4. My brother and I put two peaches in our lunch <u>boxs</u>.
   - **a.** box
   - **b. boxes**
   - **c.** correct as is

5. I shared my fruit with <u>friendes</u> at school.
   - **a. friends**
   - **b.** friend
   - **c.** correct as is

6. We bit into the fruit with our <u>toothes</u>.
   - **a. teeth**
   - **b.** tooths
   - **c.** correct as is

 Visit our website for more activities with plural nouns:
www.harcourtschool.com

114

Language Skills Assessment

PORTFOLIO ASSESSMENT
Have children select their best work from the following activities:

- **Writing Connection,** *pages 111 and 113;* TE activities, pages *107, 111, and 113.*

ONGOING ASSESSMENT
Evaluate the performance of 4-6 students using appropriate checklists and record forms from pages R65–R68 and R77–R79.

For activities and exercises to help children prepare for state and standardized assessments, visit our website:
www.harcourtschool.com

■ Study Skills ■

Finding Words in a Dictionary

A **dictionary** is a book that gives the meanings of words. The words are in alphabetical order. To find a word, first look at the two **guide words** at the top of each page. The first guide word tells the first word on the page. The second guide word tells the last word on the page.

rabbit	rate
rab•bit [rab′ ət] A small animal with long ears, a short tail, and soft fur. **The *rabbit* lives in a hole.**	**rack•et** [rak′ ət] A loud or confusing noise. **The rain made a *racket*.**
race [rās] A contest to find out who is fastest. **They had a *race* to the finish line.**	**raft** [raft] A flat boat made of logs or boards tied together. **They floated down the river on a *raft*.**

Practice

Write the words that would be found on the dictionary page. Use the guide words to help you.

1. <u>rack</u>   2. swim   3. <u>ramp</u>   4. <u>rain</u>   5. rose

115

■ Study Skills ■

Finding Words in a Dictionary

TEACH/MODEL

Write these words on the board: *telephone, apple, water, basket.* Ask children where they could look to find the meaning of each word (in a dictionary). Then have volunteers list the steps they would take to find the words. Have children recall what they know about alphabetical order. Point out the guide words on dictionary pages and on the sample page.

PRACTICE After children are finished, have them share their answers. Then tell them to use a dictionary to look up words of interest to them.

WRAP-UP/ASSESS

SUMMARIZE Have volunteers tell what they have learned about finding words in a dictionary. Ask them how they could use a dictionary to make their writing more precise and interesting. Some children may want to make a dictionary-use poster for a classroom bulletin board or wall.

PRACTICE page 30

Name _____

Finding Words in a Dictionary

A. Look at each set of guide words. Write a word from the box that could be on that dictionary page.

free	cent	bone	leaf	hen

1.	big	burn	bone
2.	card	cook	cent
3.	late	line	leaf
4.	happy	hurry	hen
5.	face	fun	free

B. Circle the word in each group that could be on a dictionary page with the guide words *lad* and *land.*

6. map, (lamp,) lend
7. (lame,) limp, boy
8. lost, left, (ladder)
9. learn, (lady,) lose
10. (lake,) light, luck

TRY THIS! Look at a dictionary. Write the guide words for three pages. Use some of the words to write two sentences.

30 Unit 2 • Chapter 8   Practice • Plural Nouns

CHALLENGE

DICTIONARY PRACTICE Have children work in pairs. Each partner writes three to five words on a sheet of paper. Partners then exchange papers, put the words in alphabetical order, and look up the words in a dictionary. For each word, children write the definition and the guide words that were on the dictionary page.

CHAPTER **8** 115

Writing a Thank-You Note

pages 116–123

LESSON ORGANIZER	DAY 1	DAY 2
 **DAILY LANGUAGE PRACTICE** 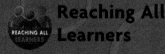 TRANSPARENCY 17	1. have you been to Mexico (Have; Mexico?) 2. my family is from there (My; there.)	1. my uncles are cowboy. (My; cowboys) 2. They have two horse named Bud and sue (horses; Sue.)
ORAL WARM-UP **Listening/Speaking**	Talk About Thank-You Notes p. 116	Discuss What Details Add to Writing p. 118
TEACH/MODEL WRITING 	✔ **WRITING A THANK-YOU NOTE** **Literature Model:** "Kate Heads West" p. 117 **WRITER'S CRAFT** • To read and respond to a thank-you note as a model for writing • To add details **Think About It** p. 117	**GUIDED WRITING** **Adding Details** pp. 118–119 • To write details to develop sentences • To add details to a letter **Writing and Thinking:** Reflect p. 119
Reaching All Learners	**ESL:** Building Vocabulary p. 117 *ESL Manual* pp. 48–49	**ESL:** Idea Bank Partners p. 118 *ESL Manual* p. 48 **Challenge:** Comical Cloze p. 119
GRAMMAR	**Unit 2 Review** pp. 162–163	**Unit 2 Review** pp. 162–163
CROSS-CURRICULAR/ ENRICHMENT	**Social Studies Connection:** Using a Map p. 117 **Vocabulary Power** Word Meaning p. 116 Self-Initiated Writing p. 117 bronco, lasso, **rodeo**, saddle, steer See *Vocabulary Power* book.	**Vocabulary Power** Context Clues p. 116 *Vocabulary Power* book, *p. 25* **Vocabulary activity** **Art Connection:** Art Fair p. 119

KEY
✔ = tested writing form/skill

DAY 3

1. we had cookouts last weekend
   (We; weekend.)

2. the kids played game like Capture
   the Flag. (The; games)

Talk About Sending Thank-You Notes
   p. 120

GUIDED WRITING
✔ **Applying the Craft**
   pp. 120–121
   • To use a thank-you note with
     details as a model for writing
   • To prewrite and draft an origi-
     nal thank-you note

**Read and Respond to the
Model** p. 120

Interactive Writing: Model
Drafting p. 121
ESL:
ESL Manual p. 48

Unit 2 Review pp. 162–163

School-Home Connection:
Thanks, Mom p. 121

Vocabulary Power

Vocabulary Power book, p. 26
Word Origins p. 116

🖥 **Vocabulary activity**

DAY 4

1. have you gotten many letter?
   (Have; letters)

2. Thos letters have pretty stamp.
   (Those; stamps)

Discuss Revising p. 122

GUIDED WRITING
Editing Your Thank-You Note
   p. 122
   • To edit sentences and share
     them aloud
   • To share writing with others

Peer Conferencing p. 122
ESL:
ESL Manual p. 48

Unit 2 Review pp. 162–163

LISTENING AND SPEAKING:
   Thank-You Notes p. 122

Vocabulary Power

Classify/Categorize p. 116
Vocabulary Power book, p. 27

🖥 **Vocabulary activity**

DAY 5

1. i wrote a thank-you note today
   (I; today.)

2. Hav you read the two note.
   (Have; notes?)

HANDWRITING
**Using Correct Letter
Spacing** p. 123
   • To use appropriate letter
     spacing when writing

Writing Resource:
   Letter Spacing p. 123
ESL:
ESL Manual p. 48

Unit 2 Review pp. 162–163

Vocabulary Power

Multiple-Meaning Words
   p. 116

Writer's Craft
Adding Details

OBJECTIVES
- To read and respond to a thank-you note as a model for writing
- To add details

SPIRAL REVIEW

DAILY LANGUAGE PRACTICE

TRANSPARENCY 17

1 have you been to Mexico (Have; Mexico?)

2 my family is from there (My; there.)

ORAL WARM-UP

USE PRIOR KNOWLEDGE Invite children to tell about times they have written, read, or received thank-you notes.

TEACH/MODEL

Read the introduction on page 116 and discuss it with children. Have them read the model letter and talk about the elements it includes.

ANALYZE THE LITERATURE Use these questions for discussing the sentences.

1. **Why is Kate sending the letter?** (She wants to thank the Toopers for taking her on a trip.) **LITERAL: NOTE DETAILS**

2. **Why did Kate get to go on the trip?** (Possible response: She is Lucy's best friend.) **INFERENTIAL: DRAW CONCLUSIONS**

Adding Details

In a **thank-you note**, a writer thanks someone for a gift or for doing something nice. A thank-you note has five parts. The **heading** tells the writer's address and the date. The **greeting** says "hello." The **body** tells why the writer is thanking the person. The **closing** says "good-bye." Finally the **signature** tells who wrote the note.

A good writer adds **details**, or exact information, about a gift to the body of a thank-you note. Details show the reader that the writer really liked the gift.

Read the thank-you note on the next page. Look at how the writer adds details to show her thanks.

116

Vocabulary Power

DAY 1 WORD MEANING Write: *rodeo*. **Find *rodeo* in the thank-you note on page 117. What do you think a rodeo is?** (a kind of show)

DAY 2 CONTEXT CLUES Write: *My dad won the bull-riding contest at the rodeo .* **What clues help you understand what a *rodeo* is?** (See also *Vocabulary Power*, page 25.)

DAY 3 WORD ORIGINS Write: *rodeo*. **The word *rodeo* is a Spanish word that comes from Mexico. What other Spanish words do you know?** (See also *Vocabulary Power*, page 26.)

DAY 4 CLASSIFY/CATEGORIZE Write *Toys, Sports, Cities*. **In which category does *rodeo* belong? Why?** (See also *Vocabulary Power*, page 27.)

DAY 5 MULIPLE-MEANING WORDS Have children illustrate the following phrases: a steer, to steer; a saddle, to saddle; a lasso, to lasso.

B. Ac

from

Kate Heads West

by Pat Brisson ◆ *illustrated by Rick Brown*

25 Abbot St.
Phillipsburg, New Jersey 08865
September 4, 2001

Dear Mr. and Mrs. Tooper,

   Thanks for taking me on vacation with you. I had a great time. The things I liked best were walking to Mexico and the raft ride down the Colorado River. I also liked the cowgirls at the rodeo.

   I learned a lot about Oklahoma cowboys, Texas deserts, New Mexico bats, and Arizona Indians. The best thing I learned was how lucky Lucy is to have you for parents and how lucky I am to be

                  Lucy's best friend,

                  Kate

P.S. I want you to know I wrote this thank-you note even before my mother told me to do so.

Think About It

1. Find the five parts in Kate's thank-you note.
2. What details has Kate added to show that she is truly thankful?

117

ADDING DETAILS Explain that writers add details in thank-you notes to help their readers know how much they truly appreciate a gift or a special act.

Have children discuss the details in the letter that help achieve this purpose.

Think About It

1. Have volunteers identify each specific part of the note. Children may note an additional part — the P.S. at the end. **CRITICAL:** INTERPRET TEXT STRUCTURE
2. Have children discuss which details show Kate's gratitude and how they think the Toopers will respond. **CRITICAL:** RECOGNIZE AUTHOR'S PURPOSE

SELF-INITIATED WRITING Have children respond to the letter they just read through self-initiated writing, which might include writing additional details or drawing. Children could also respond through other methods, such as drama.

WRAP-UP/ASSESS

SUMMARIZE Have children talk about how details can help a writer express thoughts in a thank-you note. They can record their personal reflections in their journals. **REFLECTION**

Re
add
ab

ART
plete
illustr
liked

Social Studies Connection

• • • • • • • • • • • •

USING A MAP Children can use a map to locate the places named in the letter and then use an encyclopedia to learn more about each one.

REACHING ALL   ESL

BUILDING VOCABULARY
Display labeled pictures of the nouns named in the letter including *raft ride* and *rodeo* or help children make their own picture dictionary of these terms. Have children use the labeled pictures to help them talk about the different details in the note.

Writer's Craft
Applying the Craft

OBJECTIVES
- To use a thank-you note with details as a model for writing
- To prewrite and draft an original thank-you note

DAILY LANGUAGE PRACTICE

TRANSPARENCY 17

1. we had cookouts last weekend (We; weekend.)
2. the kids played game like Capture the Flag. (The; games)

ORAL WARM-UP

USE PRIOR KNOWLEDGE Ask children to tell about reasons they might have wanted to write someone a thank-you note, such as when they received a special gift or when someone did something special for them.

GUIDED WRITING

READ AND RESPOND TO THE MODEL Have volunteers read the page aloud, including the model sentences, as others follow silently. Tell children to use this published student model as a model for their own writing.

Looking at the Model

1. Children may note that some of the more effective details engage readers' senses. **CRITICAL:** INTERPRET TEXT STRUCTURE
2. Children may suggest that the details Tanya adds will help Ben feel that she sincerely enjoyed her visit. **CRITICAL:** EXPRESS PERSONAL OPINIONS

 Writing a Thank-You Note

Writer's Craft

Applying the Craft

Read this student thank-you note. Think about how the underlined words add details.

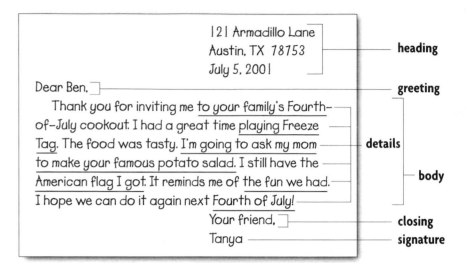

Looking at the Model

1. Which parts of this note help make good word pictures? Why?
2. Does Tanya sound thankful? Why? How do you think Ben will feel when he reads this note? Why?

120

Vocabulary Power page 26

Name _____ Word Origins

Many English words come from words in other languages. These words come from the Spanish language of Mexico. Which word names a snack you might have at a rodeo? Circle the word.

rodeo   bronco   lasso   (nachos)

The names of many foods come from other languages. Circle the names of the foods you have eaten.

bagel	taco	pizza
baklava	goulash	ravioli
burrito	knish	spaghetti
chili	mousse	succotash
chow mein	pierogi	tortilla

Draw and label some of your favorite foods. Use a dictionary to find out if the names come from a language other than English.

26   Unit 2 • Chapter 9   Vocabulary Power

EVALUATION CRITERIA

THANK-YOU NOTE Review the criteria that make up a good thank-you note which children should apply to their writing.

- The letter should include a heading, a greeting, a body, a closing, and a signature.
- The body of the letter should include details that help make good word pictures.

Encourage children to establish additional criteria. List their ideas.

Your Turn

Write a thank-you note. Add details that show why you are thankful and how you feel.

Prewriting and Drafting

STEP 1 **Develop your ideas.**

Ask yourself these questions.

• Whom should I thank? Why am I thankful?

• What details can I add?

STEP 2 **Brainstorm details.**

Make a chart. Tell why you are thankful.

> **Whom I Want to Thank**
>
> **Why I Am Thankful**
>
> **Details About Why I Am Thankful**

STEP 3 **Write your draft.**

Use your chart and What Good Writers Do to write a draft of your thank-you note. Use words to let your personality show.

What Good Writers Do

✓ Plan your ideas.

✓ Remember to add details that show your reader why you are thankful.

✓ Add details that let your voice and personality show.

Student Handbook

Use the friendly letter checklist on page 483 to make sure you have all the parts of a good letter.

121

Your Turn Explain to children they will use the prewriting and drafting steps and What Good Writers Do to prewrite and draft a thank-you letter.

Prewriting and Drafting Read the directions with children. Encourage volunteers to suggest some topics they might use in their sentences. Elicit ideas on details that they could add to some of these topics. Record the ideas in a chart.

Read aloud What Good Writers Do, and remind children to think about these tips and the handbook checklist as they prepare their drafts.

 You may wish to have children use word-processing software to compose their drafts.

 PORTFOLIO Remind children to place their first drafts in their Working Portfolios.

 SUMMARIZE Ask volunteers to review the steps they followed in writing a first draft. You may want to have children reflect on what they learned about prewriting and drafting a thank-you note and record their thoughts in their journal. **REFLECTION**

INTERACTIVE WRITING

MODEL DRAFTING Model how to chart details to develop a topic. Then think aloud as you expand these details into complete sentences. Incorporate children's ideas as you model the drafting process. Have children participate in the drafting process by writing additional words and sentences.

 School-Home Connection

THANKS, MOM Children can write and illustrate thank-you notes to show their appreciation to family members for special family outings, such as dining out and attending movies or sporting events, or even for everyday events, such as cooking meals and doing laundry.

Writer's Craft
Editing Your Thank-You Note

OBJECTIVES
- To edit sentences and share them aloud
- To share writing with others.

DAILY LANGUAGE PRACTICE

TRANSPARENCY 17

1. have you gotten many letter? (Have; letters)
2. Thos letters have pretty stamp. (Those; stamps)

ORAL WARM-UP

Discuss with children some ways they might improve their letters such as to include details or use words that sound natural or appropriate for their audience.

GUIDED WRITING

EDITING YOUR THANK-YOU NOTE Remind children that the next step in writing is to edit the draft. Model for them how to use the Editor's Marks. Review the parts of a letter that should be included.

PEER CONFERENCING Have children use the checklist and the Editor's Marks as they confer with classmates on improving their letters.

SHARING WITH OTHERS Have volunteers share their edited thank-you notes in small groups and then write a final draft to mail or e-mail. Remind children to use their best handwriting if they choose to write the notes by hand.

WRAP-UP/ASSESS

SUMMARIZE Have volunteers summarize the steps they followed in writing and editing their letters. Children can reflect on their work and rate their effort on a scale of 1–4 on a self-stick note. Children can attach their ratings to their writing and place it in their writing portfolio.

Writer's Craft

Editing Your Thank-You Note

Share your draft with a few classmates. Talk about ways to make your thank-you note better. Use the checklist and the Editor's Marks to help you revise your writing.

- ✓ My thank-you note tells why I am thankful. I give details that explain why I am thankful.
- ✓ My thank-you note has a heading, a greeting, a body, a closing, and a signature.

Editor's Marks

∧	Add.
⋀	Change.
ℯ	Take out.
=	Use a capital letter.
⊙	Add a period.
◯	Check the spelling.

Sharing with Others

Meet with a partner or a small group. Share your thank-you note. Read it aloud. Then you may want to mail your thank-you note.

122

Vocabulary Power page 27

Name _____

Classify/Categorize

Words can be grouped together because they name things that belong in the same category.

COLORS: red, gray, green   EXERCISES: push-ups, jumping-jacks

Write words from the box under RODEO or CIRCUS.

bronco-riding	tumblers	steer-roping
tightrope walkers	lasso tricks	juggling

RODEO	CIRCUS
bronco-riding	tumblers
steer-roping	tightrope walkers
lasso tricks	juggling

Write the names of things that belong in these categories.

TELEVISION SHOWS	ANIMAL SOUNDS

Vocabulary Power   Unit 2 • Chapter 9   27

LISTENING AND SPEAKING

THANK-YOU NOTES As children share their sentences, have them display a clean copy so that group members can help check that the parts of the letter are arranged correctly.

•Handwriting•

Using Correct Letter Spacing

> It is important to write neatly so that others can read your writing. Follow this tip to make sure your letters are spaced correctly.
>
> ✔ Make sure letters are not too close together or too far apart.
>
> | correct | too close | too far apart |
> |---------|-----------|---------------|
> | thank | thank | t h a n k |

Write these sentences. Use your best handwriting. Remember to space your letters correctly.

Thanks! I like the shirt.

It matches my jeans.

I will wear it all the time.

123

Writing Resource
• • • • • • • • • • • • • •

LETTER SPACING For children who need additional help, suggest that they make sure that their letters don't touch each other. Also have them make sure that a reader can tell where each word begins and ends.

EVALUATION CRITERIA

SELF-EVALUATION Have children revisit the evaluation criteria they established earlier and informally rate their writing of a thank-you note by writing their score (on a 1-4 scale) on the corner of their papers or by raising their fingers.

•Handwriting•

Using Correct Letter Spacing

OBJECTIVE
• To use appropriate letter spacing when writing

 SPIRAL REVIEW

DAILY LANGUAGE PRACTICE

TRANSPARENCY 17

1 i wrote a thank-you note today (I; today.)

2 Hav you read the two note. (Have; notes?)

TEACH/MODEL

Ask children to take a good look at the white spaces between the letters in the words *correct*, *too close*, and *too far apart* on page 123. Explain that the correct amount of spacing makes it easier for readers to read what you write.

Have volunteers read the tips aloud. Then have all children practice using the tips as they write the sentences shown at the bottom of their page. Provide feedback on the handwriting exercise.

You may wish to have children refer to the handwriting models on pages 490–493 in their handbooks. (see also R92–R93)

CURSIVE WRITING Have children who write in cursive apply the concepts in this lesson to their writing.

WRAP-UP/ASSESS

 SUMMARIZE Ask volunteers to restate the writing tips in their own words. You may want to have children recopy a piece of their writing and evaluate how the tips improve their writing. **REFLECTION**

LESSON ORGANIZER	DAY **1**	DAY **2**
DAILY LANGUAGE PRACTICE	**1.** We had three box and many book. (boxes; books) **2.** These two child got two dress. (children; dresses) **Bridge to Writing** We saw two wild ___ (plural of *wolf*) on TV.	**1.** linda lives in dallas. (Linda; Dallas) **2.** My dog rocky is fun? (Rocky; .) **Bridge to Writing** I live in ___ (name for a place) .
ORAL WARM-UP Listening/Speaking	Look for Nouns p. 124	Talk About Your Pet p. 126  *Grammar Jingles*™ CD, Primary, Track 6
TEACH/MODEL GRAMMAR **KEY** ✔ = tested skill	✔ **WHAT IS A PROPER NOUN?** pp. 124-125 • To listen critically to interpret and evaluate a rhyme • To recognize that a proper noun can name a person, a place, or an animal and begins with a capital letter	✔ **PEOPLE, PLACES, AND ANIMALS** pp. 126-127 • To identify proper nouns that name people, places, and animals • To use proper nouns in writing and begin proper nouns with capital letters
Reaching All Learners	**Challenge:** Atlas Research p. 125 *Practice Book* p. 31 **ESL:** *ESL Manual* pp. 50-51 **Reteach:** *Reteach Activities Copying Masters* p. 19	**Modified Instruction** Below-Level: Circle Letters Above-Level: Add Proper Nouns to Sentences **Challenge:** Make a Class Book p. 127 **ESL:** Write Nouns p. 126 *ESL Manual* p. 50, p. 52 *Practice Book* p. 32 **Reteach:** *Reteach Activities Copying Masters* p. 20
WRITING	Write Proper Nouns p. 125 Summarize/Reflect	Writing Connection p. 127 Writing Information Summarize/Reflect
CROSS-CURRICULAR/ ENRICHMENT	**Vocabulary Power** Word Meaning, p. 124 **ambassador,** chairperson, mayor, officer, president See **Vocabulary Power** book.	**Vocabulary Power** Titles for People p. 124 *Vocabulary Power* book p. 28 **Vocabulary activity**

DAY 3

1. Carol miller lives in florida. (Miller; Florida)
2. Fluffy is todd's Cat. (Todd's; cat)

Bridge to Writing My teacher's name is (name for a person) .

Talk About Dates p. 128

 Grammar Jingles™ CD, Primary, Track 6

✔ **DAYS, MONTHS, AND HOLIDAYS** pp. 128-129
- To identify proper nouns that name days, months, and holidays
- To use proper nouns for days, months, and holidays in writing

Modified Instruction
Below-Level: Answer When
Above-Level: Write Sentences About a Holiday
Challenge: Activity Card 7, p. R47
ESL: Sharing Holidays p. 128
ESL Manual p. 50, p. 53
Practice Book p. 33
Reteach: *Reteach Activities Copying Masters* p. 21

Writing Connection p. 129
Elaboration
 Summarize/Reflect

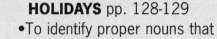

Abbreviations p. 124
Vocabulary Power book p. 29
Vocabulary activity

DAY 4

1. Next monday is labor Day. (Monday; Labor)
2. Mother's day is in may. (Day; May)

Bridge to Writing (name for a month) is my favorite month.

Play Charades p. 130

EXTRA PRACTICE p. 130
- To recognize that proper nouns begin with capital letters
- To use proper nouns in writing
Practice and Assessment

Challenge: Calendar of Events p. 131
ESL: Weekly Big Book p. 130
ESL Manual p. 50, p. 54
Practice Book p. 34

Writing Connection p. 131
Help Certificate

Vocabulary Power

Expand Word Meaning p. 124
Vocabulary Power book p. 30
Language Play p. 131
Vocabulary activity

DAY 5

1. Is thanksgiving always on a thursday? (Thanksgiving; Thursday)
2. yoshi lives in utah. (Yoshi; Utah)

Bridge to Writing On (day of the week) we go to school.

TEST PREP CHAPTER REVIEW p. 132
- To review proper nouns and recognize that they begin with capital letters
- To understand an abbreviation and to capitalize and punctuate it correctly
Test Preparation

Challenge: Write an Invitation p. 133
ESL Manual p. 50, p. 55
Practice Book p. 35

Writing Application p. 133
Abbreviations and Titles

Vocabulary Power

Perform p. 124
Vocabulary
Abbreviations and Titles

What Is a Proper Noun?

OBJECTIVES

- To listen critically to interpret and evaluate a rhyme
- To recognize that a proper noun can name a person, a place, or an animal and begins with a capital letter

SPIRAL REVIEW

DAILY LANGUAGE PRACTICE

TRANSPARENCY 18

1 We had three box and many book.
(boxes; books)

2 These two child got two dress.
(children; dresses)

BRIDGE TO WRITING We saw two wild (plural of *wolf*) on TV.

ORAL WARM-UP

LOOK FOR NOUNS Ask children to look through a magazine or newspaper for nouns that start with capital letters. Invite children to reflect on what these nouns have in common. Begin a list of these nouns on chart paper, or set up a **Noun Word Wall**.

TEACH/MODEL

Have children look at the poem on page 124. Read the poem aloud, asking children to listen to the patterns. Then tell children to find nouns in the poem and say whether they name a person, place, or thing. Ask children what they notice about the names of people and places.

DEVELOP ORAL LANGUAGE Have children think of different people, places, and things. Ask questions such as: *What is your name? Where do you come from? What things do you like?* Add the proper nouns to the **Word Wall**.

What Is a Proper Noun?

Read the rhyme.

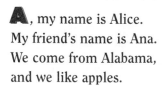

A, my name is Alice.
My friend's name is Ana.
We come from Alabama,
and we like apples.

B, my name is Bob.
My sister's name is Barbara.
We come from Boston,
and we like bread.

C, my name is Conchita.
My friend's name is Carl.
We come from California,
and we like cars.

124

Vocabulary Power

DAY 1 WORD MEANING Introduce and define *ambassador* (a messenger). Ask volunteers to act as ambassadors to other classrooms. Have them deliver messages.

DAY 2 TITLES FOR PEOPLE Write: *Jane Starr is an ambassador to another country. I think Ambassador Starr works hard.* **What do these sentences tell you about the meaning of ambassador?** (See also *Vocabulary Power*, page 28.)

DAY 3 ABBREVIATIONS List: *Ambassador Starr, Amb. Starr.* **What are the first three letters in Ambassador? What does Amb. mean?** (See also *Vocabulary Power*, page 29.)

DAY 4 EXPAND WORD MEANING Write: *Bob is an ambassador for kindness.* **What does this sentence mean?** (See also *Vocabulary Power*, page 30.)

DAY 5 PERFORM Provide opportunities for children to act as group leaders. Encourage them to give themselves titles such as "Mayor of Math City."

Choose something you like. Then name places or people whose names begin with the same letter.

Some nouns begin with capital letters. These nouns are called **proper nouns**.

Special names of people, places, and animals are proper nouns.

> **Barbara** likes books.
> She comes from **Boston**.
> She has a dog named **Buddy**.

Finish the rhyme by writing proper nouns. Possible responses are given.

D, my name is ___David___.
My friend's name is ___Doug___.
We come from ___Dallas___,
and we like dinosaurs.

E, my name is ___Eric___.
My friend's name is ___Eva___.
We come from ___El Paso___,
and we like eggs.

125

WRITE Ask children to name cities or towns they have visited. Write the names on the board and point out that they start with capital letters. Explain that these are **proper nouns**. Read the definition in the box and talk about the example sentences. Have children add names of people, places and animals they know.

Then read the first item at the bottom on page 125 together. Remind children that proper nouns begin with capital letters. Have children complete the items and then share their work with a partner.

WRAP-UP/ASSESS

SUMMARIZE Have children summarize and reflect on what they have learned about proper nouns. Ask them to write their reflections in their journals and begin a list of proper nouns. **REFLECTION**

INTERVENTION Lessons in **visual, auditory,** and **kinesthetic** modalities: p. R23 and *Reteach Activities Copying Masters* p. 19.

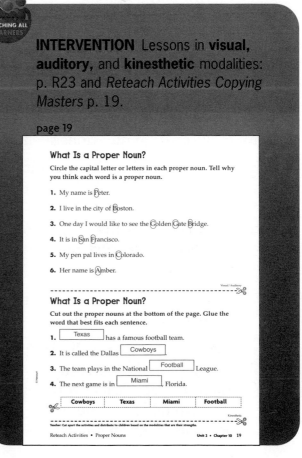

PRACTICE page 31

Name _____

What Is a Proper Noun?

A. Underline the proper noun in each sentence.

1. My name is Angela.
2. I live in New York City.
3. My friend Sara is on a trip.
4. She will be in Texas for a week.
5. I'm taking care of her cat Sage.

B. Write a proper noun to finish each sentence.
Responses will vary. Possible responses are given.

6. My favorite cousin is ___Jake___
7. He lives in the state of ___Oregon___
8. The name of his town is ___Oakmont___
9. My teacher is ___James Smith___
10. If I had a pet bird, I would name it ___Bebe___

TRY THIS! Plan a story. Write sentences to tell about the two main characters. What are their names? Where do they live? Use proper nouns.

Practice • Proper Nouns   Unit 2 • Chapter 10 31

CHALLENGE

ATLAS RESEARCH Have groups of children use an atlas to write new verses for the rhyme. Ask them to list places that begin with each letter of the alphabet. Then have them follow the pattern and complete their verses. Encourage them to illustrate and share their verses.

> *H, my name is Henri.*
> *My friend's name is Harry.*
> *We come from Haiti,*
> *and we like ham.*

page 19

What Is a Proper Noun?

Circle the capital letter or letters in each proper noun. Tell why you think each word is a proper noun.

1. My name is Peter.
2. I live in the city of Boston.
3. One day I would like to see the Golden Gate Bridge.
4. It is in San Francisco.
5. My pen pal lives in Colorado.
6. Her name is Amber.

Visual/Auditory

What Is a Proper Noun?

Cut out the proper nouns at the bottom of the page. Glue the word that best fits each sentence.

1. [Texas] has a famous football team.
2. It is called the Dallas [Cowboys]
3. The team plays in the National [Football] League.
4. The next game is in [Miami], Florida.

| Cowboys | Texas | Miami | Football |

Kinesthetic

Teacher: Cut apart the activities and distribute to children based on the modalities that are their strength.

Reteach Activities • Proper Nouns   Unit 2 • Chapter 10 19

People, Places, and Animals

OBJECTIVES
- To identify proper nouns that name people, places, and animals
- To use proper nouns in writing and to begin proper nouns with capital letters

DAILY LANGUAGE PRACTICE

TRANSPARENCY 18

1 linda lives in dallas. (Linda; Dallas)

2 My dog rocky is fun? (Rocky; .)

BRIDGE TO WRITING I live in (name for a place).

ORAL WARM-UP

USE PRIOR KNOWLEDGE Have volunteers talk about their pets. Invite them to share information about the pets and who takes care of them. Have the class clap each time they hear a proper noun. Add the proper nouns to the **Word Wall.**

Grammar Jingles™ **CD, Primary** Use Track 6 for review and reinforcement of proper nouns.

TEACH/MODEL

Talk about the example sentences. Prompt children with questions such as:

- **Which names begin with a capital letter?** (Linda Miller, West Side School, Fuzz)
- **Why does** *Linda Miller* **begin with a capital letter but** *teacher* **does not?** (*Linda Miller* is a special name.)

Point out that every word of a proper noun is capitalized, not just the first word.

GUIDED PRACTICE Work with children to complete each sentence correctly. Remind them to begin each word in the name with a capital letter and to say if it is a person, a place, or an animal.

People, Places, and Animals

The special names of people, places, and animals are proper nouns. Proper nouns begin with capital letters.

> **Linda Miller** is my favorite teacher.
> My school is called **West Side School.**
> Our class pet is a hamster named **Fuzz.**

Guided Practice

Write the proper noun in ( ) correctly. Then tell if it is a person, a place, or an animal.

1. Today my sister and I went to help (emma jones).
   Emma Jones; person
2. First we gave a bath to her dog (rocky).
   Rocky; animal
3. Next we walked it down (fernwood street).
   Fernwood Street; place
4. Then her daughter (kim) drove us to town.
   Kim; person
5. She took us to (ray's pizza) for lunch.
   Ray's Pizza; place

126

Vocabulary Power page 28

Name _____

Titles for People

Many people work for the government. These workers often have special titles. Being an <u>ambassador</u> is an important job.

One country sends an <u>ambassador</u> to another country. The <u>ambassador</u> helps the two countries exchange ideas.

Match these titles with the jobs.

officer	president	chairperson	mayor

1. The leader of a city is a ___mayor___.
2. A member of the police force is a police ___officer___.
3. The leader of a country is a ___president___.
4. Someone in charge of a meeting is a ___chairperson___.

Which job would you like to have? Draw a picture and write about why you would like the job.

28   Unit 2 • Chapter 10   Vocabulary Power

REACHING ALL LEARNERS   ESL

WRITE NOUNS Write the words *went to* on the board. Ask children to make up sentences that begin with a name of a person they know and end with a place they know. Encourage volunteers to name places from their native countries. Invite children to share and discuss the sentences they wrote and the proper nouns they used to complete them.

Felipe went to San Juan.

Remember The special names of people, places, and animals are proper nouns.

Independent Practice

Write the proper noun in ( ) correctly. Then tell if it is a person, a place, or an animal.

6. Last month my class cleaned (maple park).
   Maple Park; place
7. My friend (carl) picked up some paper.
   Carl; person
8. He found a postcard from (los angeles).
   Los Angeles; place
9. He also saw a ticket for a game at (ashley field).
   Ashley Field; place
10. (ana alonso) raked the leaves.
    Ana Alonso; person
11. We washed benches by (sun lake).
    Sun Lake; place
12. (latisha) and I planted some flowers.
    Latisha; person
13. A man walked by with his dog, (rex).
    Rex; animal
14. The man's name was (alex king).
    Alex King; person
15. He went to (south school) fifty years ago!
    South School; place

Writing Connection

Writing Information Write important information about yourself. Write your name, the street and city where you live, the name of your school, and the name of your pet, if you have one.

To make a capital letter on the computer, hold the **shift** key and type the letter you need.

127

Independent Practice

Have children complete the Independent Practice, or modify it by using the following suggestions:

MODIFIED INSTRUCTION

BELOW-LEVEL STUDENTS Ask children to circle the letters that need to be capitalized.

ABOVE-LEVEL STUDENTS After they are finished, ask children to add proper nouns for people, places, or animals to some of the sentences.

Writing Connection

Writing Information Have children begin proper nouns with capital letters. You may want to have them record the information on cards and place the cards in the Sharing Basket.

WRAP-UP/ASSESS

SUMMARIZE Invite children to summarize what they have learned about proper nouns.

RETEACH

INTERVENTION Lessons in **visual**, **auditory**, and **kinesthetic** modalities: p. R23 and *Reteach Activities Copying Masters*, page 20.

page 20

PRACTICE page 32

Name _____

People, Places, and Animals

A. Write the proper noun in ( ) correctly.

1. My friend, **(dan thorpe)**, needed help. — Dan Thorpe
2. His dog, **(buster)**, ran off after a squirrel. — Buster
3. My brother, **(ed)**, came with us. — Ed
4. We ran to **(oak park)**. — Oak Park
5. We found the dog at **(spring pond)**! — Spring Pond

B. Write a proper noun to complete each sentence. Possible responses are given.

6. My name is ___ Annie Smith
7. I live in the town of ___ Ames
8. That's in the state of ___ Idaho

TRY THIS! Write sentences about a time you helped a friend or a family member. Use proper nouns.

32 Unit 2 • Chapter 10   Practice • Proper Nouns

CHALLENGE

MAKE A CLASS BOOK Ask each child to record the name, address, and birthday of a partner on an index card. Have volunteers sort the cards in alphabetical order before binding them into a class book. Children may want to add information, such as pet names or favorite book characters.

---

page 20

People, Places, and Animals

Underline the proper noun in each sentence. Circle the first letter of each proper noun. Then tell whether the noun is a person, a place, or an animal.

1. My friend Melanie Jones has a horse. — person
2. She named the horse White Star. — animal
3. Her parents bought the horse in Ohio. — place
4. They keep the horse at Spring Stables. — place
5. It is on Mountain Road. — place

People, Places, and Animals

Cut out the letters below. Glue them in place to write the special names correctly. Then tell whether each proper noun names a person, place, or an animal.

1. [S]eth drove me to the stables. — person
2. I helped [K]im [L]ee feed the horses. — person
3. We stopped at [M]el's [M]art for carrots. — place
4. It's on [A]pple [A]venue. — place

| A | A | K | L | S | M | M |

Teacher: Cut apart the activities and distribute to children based on the modalities that are their strengths.

20 Unit 2 • Chapter 10   Reteach Activities • Proper Nouns

Days, Months, and Holidays

OBJECTIVES

- To identify proper nouns that name days, months, and holidays and recognize that they begin with capital letters
- To use proper nouns for days, months, and holidays in writing

DAILY LANGUAGE PRACTICE

TRANSPARENCY 18

1 Carol miller lives in florida. (Miller; Florida)

2 Fluffy is todd's Cat. (Todd's; cat)

BRIDGE TO WRITING My teacher's name is (name for a person).

ORAL WARM-UP

USE PRIOR KNOWLEDGE Call on a volunteer to name today's date. Ask children to name holidays and birthdays that occur during the current month. Add the names of holidays to the **Word Wall.**

Grammar Jingles™ **CD, Primary** Use Track 6 for review and reinforcement of proper nouns.

TEACH/MODEL

Read the explanations in the box. Write the example sentences on the board. Ask children to read aloud all the words that begin with capital letters. Then call on volunteers to circle the names of days, months, and holidays.

GUIDED PRACTICE Work through the first item together. Have children identify the proper nouns. Call on volunteers to say how and why they should be capitalized. Repeat the procedure with the remaining items.

Days, Months, and Holidays

The names of days, months, and holidays are proper nouns. The names of days and months begin with capital letters.

The first **Monday** in **September** is next week.

All important words in the names of holidays begin with capital letters.

Thanksgiving and **Labor Day** are my dad's favorite holidays.

Guided Practice

Find proper nouns that should be capitalized. Write each one correctly.

1. This year I helped my family from january to december.
January, December
2. I helped Mom plan the new year's day party.
New Year's Day
3. Then in february, I helped Dad shovel snow.
February
4. I did some spring cleaning in march.
March
5. I cleaned my room every saturday.
Saturday

128

Vocabulary Power page 29

Name _____ Abbreviations

An abbreviation is a short form of a word. It usually begins with a capital letter and ends with a period. An abbreviation comes from letters in the word.

Ambassador Ying lives on Spencer Avenue.
Amb.   Ying lives on Spencer Ave.

Complete each person's name by writing an abbreviation. Use the underlined letters in the word in dark print. (Don't forget the capital letter and the period.)

president 1. Here's a picture of ___Pres.___ Grant.

officer 2. I think ___Off.___ Jake is in charge of traffic.

captain 3. The owner of the boat is ___Capt.___ Hakel.

general 4. My aunt is in the army. She is ___Gen.___ Beller.

professor 5. In college, my history teacher was ___Prof.___ Gomez.

Complete each place name by writing an abbreviation. Use the underlined letters in the word in dark print.

university 6. My mom works at the ___Univ.___ of Texas.

saint 7. That huge building is ___St.___ Mary's Hospital.

route 8. This highway is called ___Rte.___ 95.

Vocabulary Power   Unit 2 • Chapter 10   29

REACHING ALL LEARNERS | **ESL**

SHARING HOLIDAYS Ask children to talk about holidays they celebrate at home. You may want to have them bring in related objects or pictures. Have them answer questions, such as: *When is the holiday? Who celebrates it? Why? Do you wear special clothes? What makes the holiday special?* Ask volunteers to share information with the class.

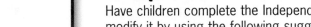

Remember Begin the names of days, months, and holidays with capital letters.

Independent Practice

Find proper nouns that should be capitalized. Write each one correctly.

6. In april I dug the garden with Grandpa.
   April
7. I grew flowers for mother's day.
   Mother's Day
8. Finally school was out in june.
   June
9. I got to wash the car every tuesday.
   Tuesday
10. I made salad for the fourth of july picnic.
    Fourth of July
11. In august I went to the beach.
    August
12. By labor day I was ready for school.
    Labor Day
13. I helped Dad rake leaves in october.
    October
14. I set the table on thanksgiving.
    Thanksgiving
15. In december I decorated the house.
    December

Writing Connection

Elaboration Draw a picture of yourself helping your family at a special time during the year. Write a caption for the picture. Use proper nouns to tell what you do, when you do it, and how doing it helps.

 Use your computer's spell-check to help you make sure you capitalized all the proper nouns.

129

Independent Practice

Have children complete the Independent Practice or modify it by using the following suggestions:

MODIFIED INSTRUCTION

BELOW-LEVEL STUDENTS Suggest that children answer the question *when* and then circle the words that need to be capitalized.

ABOVE-LEVEL STUDENTS After they are finished, ask children to choose a holiday or a date from the activity and write two sentences about it.

Writing Connection

Elaboration Help children think of a holiday. Then have them use their drawings to generate ideas. Suggest that they write all the proper nouns with different colored pencils.

WRAP-UP/ASSESS

SUMMARIZE Have children summarize and reflect on what they know about special names.

REFLECTION

RETEACH

INTERVENTION Lessons in **visual**, **auditory**, and **kinesthetic** modalities: p. R23 and *Reteach Activities Copying Masters*, p. 21.

page 21

PRACTICE page 33

Name _____

Days, Months, and Holidays

A. Underline the names of days, months, and holidays in the sentences.

1. Today is the last day of June.
2. Jimmy and I can't wait for Fourth of July.
3. Our picnic is on Sunday at Oak Park.
4. Our last picnic was on Memorial Day.
5. We are baking cookies on Saturday.

B. Write each day, month, or holiday correctly.

6. This is the last week of november. _____ November
7. My mom's favorite holiday is on thursday. _____ Thursday
8. Do you like thanksgiving, too? _____ Thanksgiving
9. My favorite holiday is in december. _____ December
10. We will start decorating next friday. _____ Friday

TRY THIS! Write sentences about your favorite month. Why is it your favorite? What special days do you enjoy during that month? How do you help make them special?

Practice • Proper Nouns   Unit 2 • Chapter 10   **33**

CHALLENGE

MAKE A HOLIDAY CHART

Have children use **Challenge Activity Card 7** (page R47) to make a monthly holiday calendar. You may want to have children work in pairs or small groups. Have children put their pages in order, and then paste the pages on a large sheet of paper to make a class calendar.

Challenge Activity Card 7
Make a Holiday Chart

Days, Months, and Holidays

Write the first letter of each day, month, or holiday.

J D M T W

1. M onday
2. J une
3. T hanksgiving
4. D ecember
5. W ednesday

Days, Months, and Holidays

Cut out the nouns below. Glue them in place to correctly answer the questions.

1. What holiday is in February? Valentine's Day
2. What day comes before Friday? Thursday
3. What is the first month of the year? January
4. On what holiday can you trick people? April Fools Day

Thursday	April Fools Day
January	Valentine's Day

Teacher: Cut apart the activities and distribute to children based on the modalities that are their strengths.

Reteach Activities • Proper Nouns   Unit 2 • Chapter 10   **21**

Extra Practice

OBJECTIVES
- To recognize that proper nouns begin with capital letters
- To use proper nouns in writing

DAILY LANGUAGE PRACTICE

TRANSPARENCY 19

1 Next monday is labor Day. (Monday; Labor)

2 Mother's day is in may. (Day; May)

BRIDGE TO WRITING ___(name for a month)___ is my favorite month.

ORAL WARM-UP

PLAY CHARADES Ask volunteers to act out something they do on a holiday. Have other children guess what they are doing and the names of the holidays. Try to work a Vocabulary Power word into the game.

TEACH/MODEL

Read each set of directions to help children understand how to complete each section. Have children share their answers in small groups before you read aloud the correct answers to them.

WRAP-UP/ASSESS

SUMMARIZE Ask children to reflect on and discuss any special problems they had in completing the practice pages before you have them summarize what they have learned about proper nouns.

ADDITIONAL PRACTICE Additional items of Extra Practice are provided on page 469 of the *Pupil Edition.*

TECHNOLOGY
Grammar Practice and Assessment CD-ROM
Writing Express CD-ROM

INTERNET Visit *The Learning Site!*
www.harcourtschool.com

Proper Nouns

Extra Practice

Write each proper noun correctly.

1. The jackson family has many pets.
   Jackson
2. stan takes care of them.
   Stan
3. He feeds millie the goldfish every day.
   Millie
4. In the morning, he walks his dog foxy.
   Foxy
5. He buys dog toys in a store called doggy's.
   Doggy's
6. That store is in mapletown.
   Mapletown

Write the names of days, months, and holidays correctly.

7. Stan gave a treat to his dog last november.
   November
8. One thursday he gave it some turkey.
   Thursday
9. The next friday he gave it some more.
   Friday
10. Now his dog loves thanksgiving!
    Thanksgiving

130

Vocabulary Power page 30

Name _____

You don't have to work for the government to be an <u>ambassador</u>. These sentences tell about another kind of <u>ambassador</u>.

Erin is an <u>ambassador</u> for the local animal shelter.
Donald is an <u>ambassador</u> for healthy eating.

What kind of <u>ambassador</u> would you like to be? Think about something that is important to you. Draw and write about your ideas.

You can also be a <u>president</u>. Start a club. You can be <u>president</u> of your club. Draw and write about your ideas.

You can be a <u>chairperson</u>. Hold a meeting. Lead the meeting. Draw and write about yourself being a <u>chairperson</u>.

30 Unit 2 • Chapter 10   Vocabulary Power

ESL

WEEKLY BIG BOOK Pair children with different levels of proficiency. Invite pairs to make a big book. Have children write a day of the week on each page and then fill the page with the names of the people they met that day, what they did, and any other information they may want to add. Have children illustrate and talk about their big books.

Language Play

Tic-Tac-Toe
- Each player needs 6 markers. Take turns choosing a square.
- Tell if the words are written correctly. If they are not, tell how to fix them.
- Put a marker on the square if you are right.
- The first player to get three in a row across, down, or on a slant wins.

Texas	October	sunday
Rover	Emma Hong	chicago
peter wolf	Labor Day	may

Writing Connection

Help Certificate Make a promise to do an extra chore. Put your promise in writing. Give it to a family member as a gift. Include your name and the month when you will do the chore.

> I, Lisa Lynch, promise to clear the table every night for one week. I will do this chore in November. I'll even clean up after Thanksgiving dinner next Thursday.

131

Language Play

Have children play "Tic-Tac-Toe" in pairs. Read aloud the instructions with children. Model how to choose a square, how to tell if the words are written correctly, and how to correct them. Show children how to put the markers on the squares. Be sure they understand the different ways they can win: across, down, or diagonally.

Writing Connection

Help Certificate Check to see that children have successfully written a Help Certificate by using the criteria below.

CRITERIA
- ☑ Writes his or her name.
- ☑ Describes the chore.
- ☑ Writes the month during which he or she will do the chore.
- ☑ Begins each proper noun with a capital letter.

📁 **Portfolio Opportunity** You may want to have children take the certificate home, e-mail it to friends or family members, or put it in their portfolio.

PRACTICE page 34

Name _____

Extra Practice

A. Use proper nouns from the box to complete the sentences.

The girl	Rover	the dog
Pet Palace	the store	Jennifer

1. _____Jennifer_____ has a huge dog.
2. She walks _____Rover_____ twice a day.
3. Today she went to _____Pet Palace_____ for a new leash.

B. Underline each letter that should be a capital letter. Then write the proper nouns correctly.

4. Her brother b̲en drove her. _____Ben_____
5. They drove down p̲ine r̲oad. _____Pine Road_____

C. Circle each day, month, and holiday that is not correct. Write it correctly on the line.

6. Jen goes to camp in (july). _____July_____
7. She will be back before (labor day). _____Labor Day_____
8. I'll walk Fritz each (monday). _____Monday_____

34 Unit 2 • Chapter 10   Practice • Proper Nouns

CHALLENGE

CALENDAR OF EVENTS Ask children to make a calendar of upcoming events in the community. Suggest that they use local newspapers to do their research. Have them write the title of each event, where and when it will take place, who will participate, and what will happen. Invite children to illustrate and post their calendars on a bulletin board.

Chapter Review

OBJECTIVES
- To review proper nouns and recognize that they begin with capital letters
- To understand that an abbreviation is a short way to write a word and to capitalize and punctuate an abbreviation correctly

DAILY LANGUAGE PRACTICE

TRANSPARENCY 19

1 Is thanksgiving always on a thursday? (Thanksgiving; Thursday)

2 yoshi lives in utah. (Yoshi; Utah)

BRIDGE TO WRITING On <u>(day of the week)</u> we go to school.

STANDARDIZED TEST PREP

Read the directions with children to make sure they understand how to complete each section. You may wish to use this page as an assessment after children have completed it independently.

TEST PREPARATION TIP
Item Type: Multiple Choice

 TIP

Model this strategy to help children determine the correct answer:

What kind of word is *August*? It's a proper noun. I know that proper nouns begin with capital letters. *August* begins with a capital letter in the sentence. I look at the three answer choices; *a* and *b* are not correct. I choose *c. correct as is* because *August* is correct in the sentence.

Chapter Review
STANDARDIZED TEST PREP

Choose the best answer for each underlined word or words.

1. The Jones family moved last <u>August</u>.
   - **a.** august
   - **b.** AugusT
   - **c. correct as is**

2. They moved to <u>Houston, texas</u>.
   - **a.** houston, texas
   - **b.** <u>Houston, Texas</u>
   - **c.** correct as is

3. Even little <u>ashley Jones</u> helped unpack.
   - **a.** ashley jones
   - **b.** <u>Ashley Jones</u>
   - **c.** correct as is

4. They started unpacking on a <u>thursDay</u>.
   - **a.** <u>Thursday</u>
   - **b.** thursday
   - **c.** correct as is

5. Their pet dog <u>Roxy</u> slept in an empty box.
   - **a.** roxy
   - **b.** ROxy
   - **c. correct as is**

6. By <u>labor Day</u>, the family was moved in.
   - **a.** <u>Labor Day</u>
   - **b.** labor day
   - **c.** correct as is

 Visit our website for more activities with proper nouns:
www.harcourtschool.com

132

Language Skills Assessment

. . . .

PORTFOLIO ASSESSMENT
Have children select their best work from the following activities:

- **Writing Connection,** *pages 127, 129, and 131;* TE activities, *pages 125, 127, 129, 130, 131 and 133.*

ONGOING ASSESSMENT
Evaluate the performance of 4-6 students using appropriate checklists and record forms from pages R65–R68 and R77–R79.

INTERNET Activities and exercises to help students prepare for state and standardized assessments appear on *The Learning Site:*
www.harcourtschool.com

■ Vocabulary ■

Abbreviations and Titles

An **abbreviation** is a short way to write a word. It begins with a capital letter and ends with a period.

Titles	Days		Months	
Mister **Mr.**	Sunday	**Sun.**	January	**Jan.**
Mr. Gomez	Monday	**Mon.**	February	**Feb.**
Missus **Mrs.**	Tuesday	**Tues.**	March	**Mar.**
Mrs. Reed	Wednesday	**Wed.**	April	**Apr.**
	Thursday	**Thurs.**	May	—
Doctor **Dr.**	Friday	**Fri.**	June	—
Dr. Choi	Saturday	**Sat.**	July	—
			August	**Aug.**
			September	**Sept.**
			October	**Oct.**
			November	**Nov.**
			December	**Dec.**

Practice

Write the abbreviation for each noun.

1. Doctor
   Dr.
2. Missus
   Mrs.
3. Saturday
   Sat.
4. Friday
   Fri.
5. December
   Dec.
6. February
   Feb.

Mr. Gomez
Manager

133

■ Vocabulary ■

Abbreviations and Titles

TEACH/MODEL

On the board, write the titles *Mister*, *Missus*, and *Doctor*. Also write the days of the week and the months of the year. Ask volunteers if they know any short ways to write any of these words. Have volunteers write the abbreviations they know on the board. Read the explanation in the box. Explain that the abbreviations in the chart are shorter ways to write these words. Write abbreviations on the board, and then have children say the full words.

PRACTICE When children are finished, have them compose original sentences using the abbreviations and share the sentences with classmates.

WRAP-UP/ASSESS

SUMMARIZE Ask children to tell what they have learned about abbreviations. You may wish to point out that only the abbreviations for titles are used in formal writing.

PRACTICE page 35

REACHING ALL LEARNERS

Name_____

Abbreviations and Titles

A. Write the abbreviation for each day or month.

1. September _____ Sept.
2. Thursday _____ Thurs.
3. Tuesday _____ Tues.
4. December _____ Dec.
5. August _____ Aug.
6. Sunday _____ Sun.

B. Underline each title that should have a capital letter and end with a period. Write each title and name correctly.

7. mr and mrs Lee took Bootsy to the vet.
   Mr. and Mrs. Lee

8. Bootsy's vet is dr Anderson.
   Dr. Anderson

TRY THIS! Plan your week. List the abbreviations for the days of the week. Next to each abbreviation, write what you would like to do that day.

Practice • Proper Nouns   Unit 2 • Chapter 10 35

CHALLENGE

REACHING ALL LEARNERS

WRITE AN INVITATION Have children write and decorate invitations to holiday events of their choice. Have them use abbreviations in dates, names, and addresses. They may want to create stationery for their invitations, by hand or on the computer. Invite children to share their invitations.

Mr. Carlos DaSilva
invites you to a party
on Sat. Dec. 12.

LESSON ORGANIZER	DAY 1	DAY 2
DAILY LANGUAGE PRACTICE TRANSPARENCIES 20, 21	1. My teacher is Mrs jones. (Mrs.; Jones) 2. She has a Cat named sam. (cat; Sam) **Bridge to Writing** I live in the state of __(name of state)__ .	1. Do thay like thanksgiving? (they; Thanksgiving) 2. she had dinner with sally. (She; Sally) **Bridge to Writing** __(pronoun)__ is very smart.
ORAL WARM-UP **Listening/Speaking**	Talk About People p. 134	Play "I Spy" p. 136 *Grammar Jingles™* CD, Primary, Track 7
TEACH/MODEL **GRAMMAR** **KEY** ✔ = tested skill	✔ **WHAT IS A PRONOUN?** pp. 134-135 **Literature:** "Something Big Has Been Here" by Jack Prelutsky • To interpret a poem • To understand that a pronoun takes the place of a noun	✔ *HE, SHE, IT,* AND *THEY* pp. 136-137 • To recognize that *he, she, it,* and *they* are pronouns • To use pronouns in writing
Reaching All Learners	**Challenge:** Make a Pronoun Wheel p. 135 Activity Card 8, p. R48 *Practice Book* p. 36 **ESL:** *ESL Manual* pp. 56-57 **Reteach:** *Reteach Activities Copying Masters* p. 22	**Modified Instruction** Below-Level: Identify Who or What Above-Level: Sentence Pairs **Challenge:** Write a Dialogue p. 137 **ESL:** Use Pronouns p. 136 *ESL Manual* pp. 56, 58 *Practice Book* p. 37 **Reteach:** *Reteach Activities Copying Masters* p. 23
WRITING	Write a Riddle p. 135 Summarize/Reflect	Writing Connection p. 137 Revising Summarize/Reflect
CROSS-CURRICULAR/ ENRICHMENT	**Vocabulary Power** Word Meaning p. 134 **rattlesnake,** cattail, cowhand, pigtail, turtleneck See ***Vocabulary Power*** book.	**Vocabulary Power** Compound Words p. 134 *Vocabulary Power* book p. 31 💻 **Vocabulary activity**

Visit *The Learning Site!*
www.harcourtschool.com

WRITING ACTIVITIES
Writing Express CD-ROM

DAY 3

1. Mrs. luz is my teacher. He teaches me many things. (Luz; She or Mr.)

2. He is a picture of chicago. (It; Chicago)

Bridge to Writing (pronoun) are very happy to go on a trip.

Talk About Yourself p. 138
 Grammar Jingles™ CD, Primary, Track 7

I AND ME pp. 138-139
• To understand that *I* and *me* take the place of a speaker's name
• To write *I* in the naming part of a sentence and *me* in the telling part of a sentence

Modified Instruction
Below-Level: Sentence Parts
Above-Level: Using *I* and *Me*
Challenge: Personal Stories p. 139
ESL: I Give You, You Give Me p. 138; *ESL Manual* pp. 56, 59
Practice Book p. 38
Reteach: *Reteach Activities Copying Masters* p. 24

Writing Connection p. 139
Personal Story
 Summarize/Reflect

Vocabulary Power

Word Families p. 134
Vocabulary Power book p. 32
Vocabulary activity

DAY 4

1. mikio took it from I. (Mikio; me)

2. Will you watch I play soccer. (me; ?)

Bridge to Writing (pronoun) am a good reader.

Say Sentences With Pronouns p. 140

EXTRA PRACTICE p. 140
• To identify pronouns and understand that they take the place of nouns
• To use pronouns in writing
Practice and Assessment

Challenge: What Do They Do? p. 141
ESL: Neighborhood Workers p. 140
ESL Manual pp. 56, 60
Practice Book p. 39

Writing Connection p. 141
Postcard

Vocabulary Power

Onomatopoeia p. 134
Vocabulary Power book p. 33
Language Play p. 141
Vocabulary activity

DAY 5

1. she often plays with I. (She; me)

2. Me like to play with herr. (I; her)

Bridge to Writing Maria tells (pronoun) a story.

TEST PREP **CHAPTER REVIEW** p. 142
• To review pronouns *he, she, it, they, I,* and *me*
• To use a computer to send and receive e-mail messages
Test Preparation

Challenge: Make an E-mail Address Book p. 143
Practice Book p. 40
ESL: *ESL Manual* pp. 56, 61

Technology p. 143
Sending E-mail

Vocabulary Power

Compound Words p. 134

What Is a Pronoun?

OBJECTIVES

- To listen critically to interpret a poem
- To understand that a pronoun is a word that takes the place of a noun

---

DAILY LANGUAGE PRACTICE

TRANSPARENCY 20

1 My teacher is Mrs jones. (Mrs.; Jones)

2 She has a Cat named sam. (cat; Sam)

BRIDGE TO WRITING I live in the state of (name of state) .

ORAL WARM-UP

USE PRIOR KNOWLEDGE Discuss with children the evidence people leave behind that tells you that someone has been in a place. For example, the person might leave books, clothes, or food. He or she might remove something or make a mess. Write children's sentences on the board. Point to pronouns they used, and set up a **Pronoun Word Wall**.

TEACH/MODEL

Have children turn to page 134. Ask them to use the title and the illustration to predict what the poem will be about. Then read the poem aloud, asking children to listen to the words that refer to "something big." Reread the poem, having children join in with you.

DEVELOP ORAL LANGUAGE Ask children what they think the word *it* refers to in the poem. Then discuss the poem. You may want to ask questions such as these:

- **How do you know *it* is big?**
- **Do you think *it* is friendly?**
- **What might happen if you met *it*?**

What Is a Pronoun?

Read the poem.

Something BIG Has Been Here

Something big has been here,
what it was, I do not know,
for I did not see it coming,
and I did not see it go,
but I hope I never meet it,
if I do, I'm in a fix,
for it left behind its footprints,
they are size nine-fifty-six.

Jack Prelutsky

134

Vocabulary Power

DAY 1 WORD MEANING Write: *rattlesnake*. **How do you think this snake got his name?**

DAY 2 COMPOUND WORDS Write: *rattlesnake*. **What two words are combined to form this word?** (See also *Vocabulary Power*, page 31.)

DAY 3 WORD FAMILIES List: *rattlesnake, snakeskin, blacksnake*. **Why do we say that these words are in the same word family?** (See also *Vocabulary Power*, page 32.)

DAY 4 ONOMATOPOEIA Write: *moo, meow, oink*. **Which word tells the sound a cat makes? A pig? A cow?** (See also *Vocabulary Power*, page 33.)

DAY 5 COMPOUND WORDS List: *cat, tail, house, fly, stick, jump, cow, snow, rain*. **Make a list of compound words. Here are some words you might use.**

Talk about what the big thing in the poem could be. Then describe something to your classmates, but do not name it. Can they guess what it is?

A **pronoun** is a word that takes the place of a noun. The words *he*, *she*, *it*, and *they* are pronouns.

A **tyrannosaurus** was very big. **It** was more than 45 feet long.

Write a riddle like the one below. Use pronouns. Then read it to a partner. Can your partner guess the answer?

It is large and gray.

It has a long trunk and big white tusks.

You may see it in a zoo or a circus.

What is it?

Answer: It is an elephant.

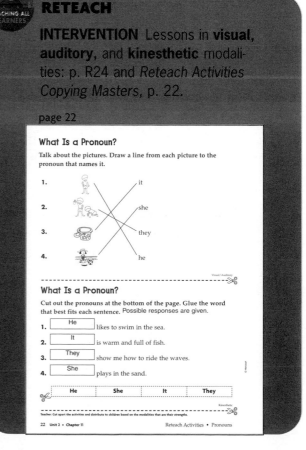

135

WRITE Encourage children to use complete sentences as they tell what the big thing in the poem is. Suggest that children think about the color, size, and unique characteristics of their animal as they offer clues. Read aloud the definition and the example sentences. Have a volunteer name the noun in the first sentence and the pronoun that replaces it in the second sentence. Then have children make up sentences using the pronouns in the box. Add the pronouns to the **Word Wall**.

Encourage children to be creative as they write their riddles.

WRAP-UP/ASSESS

SUMMARIZE Reread the poem with children. Then have them summarize and reflect on what they learned about pronouns.
REFLECTION

RETEACH

INTERVENTION Lessons in **visual, auditory,** and **kinesthetic** modalities: p. R24 and *Reteach Activities Copying Masters,* p. 22.

PRACTICE page 36

Name _____

What Is a Pronoun?

A. Underline the pronoun in each sentence.

1. They pick up trash in the park.
2. She holds the bag for Carlos.
3. He places the trash in the bag.
4. When it gets heavy, Sara uses a new bag.
5. They are working hard.

B. Write a pronoun from the box to complete each sentence.
Possible responses are given.

They	He	It	She

6. She likes helping Carlos.
7. He asked her to be his partner.
8. They offered to clean the park.
9. It is a project for their school.
10. She hopes the park will stay clean.

TRY THIS! Write two sentences about ways you and your classmates could help at school. Use pronouns in your sentences.

36 Unit 2 • Chapter 11   Practice • Pronouns

CHALLENGE

MAKE A PRONOUN WHEEL
Have children use **Challenge Activity Card 8** (page R48) to make a pronoun wheel. Model how to fold the plate in half three times to divide it into six parts. Display the completed wheels. Allow time for volunteers to choose wheels and read some of the sections.

Challenge Activity Card 8
Make a Pronoun Wheel

page 22

What Is a Pronoun?

Talk about the pictures. Draw a line from each picture to the pronoun that names it.

1. ———— it
2. ———— she
3. ———— they
4. ———— he

Visual/Auditory

What Is a Pronoun?

Cut out the pronouns at the bottom of the page. Glue the word that best fits each sentence. Possible responses are given.

1. He likes to swim in the sea.
2. It is warm and full of fish.
3. They show me how to ride the waves.
4. She plays in the sand.

He	She	It	They

Kinesthetic

Teacher: Cut apart the activities and distribute to children based on the modalities that are their strengths.

22 Unit 2 • Chapter 11   Reteach Activities • Pronouns

He, She, It, and *They*

OBJECTIVES
- To recognize that *he, she, it,* and *they* are pronouns
- To use pronouns in writing

DAILY LANGUAGE PRACTICE

TRANSPARENCY 20

1 Do thay like thanksgiving? (they; Thanksgiving)

2 she had dinner with sally. (She; Sally)

BRIDGE TO WRITING (pronoun) is very smart.

ORAL WARM-UP

PLAY "I SPY" Describe something in the classroom, and ask children to guess what it is. Then invite children to offer clues for classmates.

 *Grammar Jingles*™ **CD, Primary** Use Track 7 for review and reinforcement of pronouns.

TEACH/MODEL

Read aloud the explanation and sentences on page 136. Ask children why each pronoun is used. Explain that pronouns make writing more interesting by adding variety. Say two sentences, such as *The children play at the park. The children ride on the swings.* Ask children how they could change the second sentence to make it sound better. (Change *The children* to *They.*)

GUIDED PRACTICE Have them tell whether each noun in parentheses tells about a boy or a girl, about more than one, or about an animal or thing before they decide which pronoun is correct.

He, She, It, and *They*

> *He*, *she*, *it*, and **they** are pronouns. *He* and *she* tell about other people. *It* tells about an animal or thing. *They* tells about more than one.
>
> | noun | **Matt** likes to sing. |
> | pronoun | **He** likes to sing. |
> | nouns | **Ken** and **Amy** practice at school. |
> | pronoun | **They** practice at school. |

Guided Practice

Write a pronoun for the word or words in ( ).

1. (The game) will be on Monday. It
2. (Maria) will play catcher. She
3. Can (Philip) bat first? he
4. (Julia and Daniel) will play on the same team. They
5. Does (Carla) want to pitch? she

136

Vocabulary Power page 31

Name _____

Compound Words

A compound word is made by joining two words together. Some compound words mean exactly what they say.

    rattle + snake = rattlesnake
    A *rattlesnake* is a snake that makes a rattling sound.

Some compound words can fool you. Join these words together to make compound words.

1. cat + tail = _____ cattail
2. cow + hand = _____ cowhand
3. pig + tail = _____ pigtail
4. turtle + neck = _____ turtleneck

Circle the meaning of each compound word.

5. What is a pigtail?   a pig's curly tail   (braided hair)
6. What is a cowhand?   a cow-shaped hand   (someone who works with cattle)
7. What is a turtleneck?   a collar decorated with turtles   (a high collar)
8. What is a cattail?   a cat's long, fluffy tail   (a plant whose flowers look like a cat's tail)

Vocabulary Power   Unit 2 • Chapter 11   31

ESL

REACHING ALL LEARNERS

USE PRONOUNS Provide children with word cards for the pronouns *it, he, she,* and *they.* Display pictures of animals and people, such as a girl, two boys, a firefighter, and a dinosaur. Have children hold up the card with the pronoun that would take the place of the noun pictured. Invite children to say the pronoun and to use it in a sentence about the picture.

> **Remember** Use the pronouns *he, she, it,* and *they* to take the place of nouns.

Independent Practice

Write a pronoun for the word or words in ( ).

6. (Christina) played first base. She

7. (Tom) ran quickly. He

8. (Rosa, Marta, and Tina) scored home runs. They

9. At the end, (the children) ran around the bases. they

10. (The parents) cheered loudly. They

11. Everyone enjoyed (the game). it

12. (Ms. Ortiz) was very proud of us. She

13. (Jonah and Carol) want to play soccer next week. They

14. (Lee) said that is a great idea. He

15. (The soccer game) will be very exciting. It

Writing Connection

Revising Look at a piece of your writing. Find places where you have used the same noun in two sentences in a row. Change the noun in the second sentence to a pronoun. This will make your writing smoother.

Highlight a word you want to change. Type the new word. The old word will be deleted when you type the new one.

137

Independent Practice

Have children complete the Independent Practice, or modify it by using the following suggestions:

MODIFIED INSTRUCTION

BELOW-LEVEL STUDENTS Have children tell whether the word in parentheses tells about a person, an animal, or a thing. Then have them decide whether it tells about one or more than one.

ABOVE-LEVEL STUDENTS After they have finished, ask children to write two pairs of sentences. In the first item they write a noun; in the second item they replace it with a pronoun.

Writing Connection

Revising Have children underline the nouns they want to replace. Remind them that *he, she,* and *it* tell about one and that *they* tells about more than one. Have children check to be sure verbs match pronouns in number.

WRAP-UP/ASSESS

SUMMARIZE Ask children to reflect on what they have learned about pronouns.

REFLECTION

REACHING ALL LEARNERS

RETEACH

INTERVENTION Lessons in **visual, auditory,** and **kinesthetic** modalities: p. R24 and *Reteach Activities Copying Masters,* p. 23.

page 23

REACHING ALL LEARNERS

PRACTICE page 37

Name _____

He, She, It, and *They*

A. Draw a line from the word or words in column A to the correct pronoun in column B.

Column A	Column B
1. Pedro and Miguel	it
2. Mark	they
3. the table	she
4. my mother	he

B. Write a pronoun for the word or words in ( ).

5. (My grandmother) had a birthday party. She

6. (My aunts and uncles) surprised her with a cake. They

7. Then (my father) sang a song for her. he

8. (My cousins) played the music. They

9. (My grandmother) danced with me. She

10. (The party) was wonderful! It

TRY THIS! Write two sentences about your classmates. Then change all the nouns to pronouns, and write the sentences again.

Practice • Pronouns   Unit 2 • Chapter 11 37

CHALLENGE

REACHING ALL LEARNERS

WRITE A DIALOGUE Have children work in pairs with one child writing what the other says about what he or she likes in the town or school. Tell them to begin each sentence with: *She said* or *he said.* Then have partners trade roles and the other writes what the partner says. Allow time for partners to read their dialogues aloud to the group.

He said, "The firefighters work hard."

She said, "They help many people."

He, She, It and *They*

Circle the pronoun in each sentence.

1. (It) is a beautiful day.

2. (They) went swimming.

3. (He) jumped into the lake.

4. (She) swam to the dock.

Visual/Auditory

He, She, It and *They*

Cut out the pronouns at the bottom of the page. Glue a word that fits each sentence. Possible responses are given.

1. They played catch.

2. It was a good game.

3. She ran very fast.

4. He threw his ball.

| She | It | He | They |

Kinesthetic

Teacher: Cut apart the activities and distribute to children based on the modalities that are their strength.

Reteach Activities • Pronouns   Unit 2 • Chapter 11 23

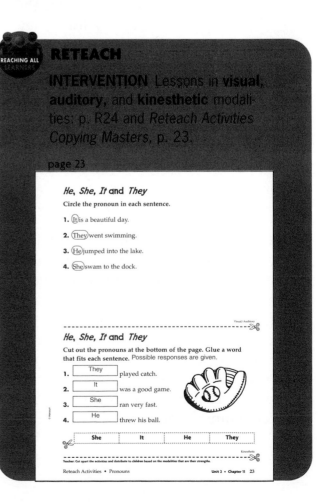

I and *Me*

OBJECTIVES
- To understand that the pronouns *I* and *me* take the place of the speaker's name
- To write *I* in the naming part of a sentence and *me* in the telling part of a sentence

DAILY LANGUAGE PRACTICE
TRANSPARENCY 20

1 Mrs. luz is my teacher. He teaches me many things. (Luz; She or Mr.)

2 He is a picture of chicago. (It; Chicago)

BRIDGE TO WRITING (pronoun) are very happy to go on a trip.

ORAL WARM-UP

USE PRIOR KNOWLEDGE Ask volunteers to talk about themselves and then to talk about people they know. Discuss with children how the sentences differ. Write some on the board. Add the pronouns to the **Pronoun Word Wall**.

Grammar Jingles™ **CD, Primary** Use Track 7 for review and reinforcement of pronouns.

TEACH/MODEL

Read the explanation and the examples in the box. Point out that *I* and *me* are used differently even though they both refer to the same person. Act out different sentences, such as *I give John the book. John gives the book back to **me**.*

GUIDED PRACTICE Work through the first item together. Ask whether the answer choices are in the naming part or the telling part of the sentence. Next ask what pronoun we use instead of our name for the naming part. Then ask a volunteer to read the sentence with *I* and again with *me* to confirm that *I* is correct. (*I*) Repeat the procedure with the remaining items.

I and *Me*

You can use the pronouns **I** and **me** to take the place of your name when you tell about yourself. Use **I** in the naming part of a sentence. Use **me** in the telling part of a sentence.

naming part	**I** play ball with Sue.
telling part	Sue throws the ball to **me**.

Guided Practice

Write the correct word to complete each sentence.

1. (I, Me) play baseball with Dad.
2. Dad pitches the ball to (I, me).
3. (I, Me) hit the ball.
4. Dad shows (I, me) how to throw.
5. Dad and (I, me) like baseball.

138

Vocabulary Power page 32

Name _____ **Word Families**

These compound words belong to the same word family. Underline the word that appears in each compound word.

rattlesnake   snakeweed   snakebite   blacksnake

Make compound words. The word in dark print should be in each compound word.

1. **cat** nip fish bear	2. **tail** pig gate spin
catnip	pigtail
catfish	tailgate
bearcat	tailspin
3. **hand** cow shake book	4. **neck** turtle band tie
cowhand	turtleneck
handshake	neckband
handbook	necktie
5. **bird** yellow call seed	6. **house** tree fly plant
yellowbird	treehouse
birdcall	housefly
birdseed	houseplant

32   Unit 2 • Chapter 11   Vocabulary Power

REACHING ALL LEARNERS   **ESL**

I GIVE YOU, YOU GIVE ME

Have children sit in a circle. One child starts by saying, "I give you (name of an object)." The next child says, "He/She gives me (name of the object)," turns to the next child and adds, "I give you (name of another object)." Keep going around until all children have said the sentences.

Remember
Use *I* in the naming part of a sentence. Use *me* in the telling part of a sentence.

Independent Practice

Write the correct word to complete each sentence.

6. My aunt and (<u>I</u>, me) went to a baseball game.

7. My aunt gave (I, <u>me</u>) the tickets to hold.

8. (<u>I</u>, me) gave the tickets to the man.

9. My aunt and (<u>I</u>, me) went inside.

10. (<u>I</u>, me) sat next to my aunt.

11. (<u>I</u>, me) cheered for our team.

12. A player gave a ball to (I, <u>me</u>).

13. The player told my aunt and (I, <u>me</u>) his name, too.

14. (<u>I</u>, me) showed the ball to my aunt.

15. (<u>I</u>, me) was very happy.

Writing Connection

Story About Me Think of something fun that you did. Write sentences that tell about it. Use *I* or *me* in each sentence. You may draw a picture if you want.

139

Independent Practice
Have children complete the Independent Practice, or modify it by using the following suggestions:

MODIFIED INSTRUCTION

BELOW-LEVEL STUDENTS Suggest that children divide each sentence into naming and telling parts to help them choose the correct pronoun.

ABOVE-LEVEL STUDENTS After they have finished, ask children to write a sentence using *I* and a sentence using *me*.

Writing Connection

Story About Me Invite children to use their drawings to help them think of additional ideas. Remind them of when to use *I* and *me* and to write complete sentences.

WRAP-UP/ASSESS

SUMMARIZE Have children reflect on and summarize what they know about using *I* and *me*. **REFLECTION**

RETEACH

INTERVENTION Lessons in **visual, auditory,** and **kinesthetic** modalities: p. R24 and *Reteach Activities Copying Masters,* p. 24.

page 24

I and *Me*

Work with a partner to circle the pronoun *I* or *me* in each sentence.

EXAMPLE: Melissa and (I) are playing hide-and-seek.

1. Melissa looks for (me).
2. (I) look for her.
3. Tim wants to play with Melissa and (me).
4. Tim chases (me).
5. Melissa and (I) chase Tim.

I and *Me*

Cut out and glue the finger puppets below. Draw a picture of yourself above each word. Read the sentences aloud to a partner. Use the *I* puppet if *I* belongs in the sentence. Use the *me* puppet if *me* belongs.

1. Tim and ___I___ look for Mia. Then Tim and Mia look for ___me___.
2. ___I___ ask them to play. They play with ___me___ all day.

24 Unit 2 • Chapter 11   Reteach Activities • Pronouns

PRACTICE page 38

Name _____

I and *Me*

A. Write *I* or *me* to complete each sentence.

1. My mom had a surprise for ___me___.
2. My mom and ___I___ went to the circus.
3. ___I___ brought Mikio, too.
4. Mikio and ___I___ saw the tumbling clowns.
5. The circus made ___me___ very happy.

B. Choose *I* or *me* to complete each sentence. Write the new sentence.

6. Mikio and (**I**, me) went to the zoo.
Mikio and I went to the zoo.

7. (**I**, Me) liked the penguins.
I liked the penguins.

8. They made (I, **me**) laugh.
They made me laugh.

TRY THIS! Write three sentences about a school trip you took. Be sure to use pronouns. Draw a picture if you want.

38 Unit 2 • Chapter 11   Practice • Pronouns

CHALLENGE

PERSONAL STORIES Have children write stories about themselves. Encourage them to list first activities they like and then to add lines about who helps them or teaches them. Have them present their work to the class.

I play soccer.
My dad plays with me.
Mr. Rendon is my coach.
He teaches me how to kick the ball.

Extra Practice

OBJECTIVES
- To identify pronouns and understand that they take the place of nouns
- To use pronouns in writing

DAILY LANGUAGE PRACTICE

TRANSPARENCY 21

1 mikio took it from I. (Mikio; me)

2 Will you watch I play soccer. (me; ?)

BRIDGE TO WRITING (pronoun) am a good reader.

ORAL WARM-UP

USE PRIOR KNOWLEDGE Ask a volunteer to say a sentence that includes a pronoun. Have another child change the pronoun to a noun and say a sentence. Then reverse the process having a volunteer start with a pronoun. Try to work a Vocabulary Power word into the game.

TEACH/MODEL

Read aloud each set of directions to help children understand how to complete each section. Have children share their answers in small groups before you read aloud the correct answers to them.

WRAP-UP/ASSESS

SUMMARIZE Ask children to reflect on and discuss any special problems they had in completing the practice before they summarize what they have learned about pronouns.

ADDITIONAL PRACTICE Extra practice items are provided on page 469 of the *Pupil Edition*.

TECHNOLOGY
Grammar Practice and Assessment CD-ROM

Writing Express CD-ROM

INTERNET Visit *The Learning Site!*
www.harcourtschool.com

Extra Practice

Write the pronoun in each sentence.

1. I like books about animals.
2. They like stories about children.
3. Which story does she like best?
4. He likes books about sports.

Write a pronoun for the word or words in ( ).

5. (My sister) wants to write her own book. She
6. (My parents) are both writers. They
7. Did (your father) write a book for children? he
8. Is (the book) at the library? it
9. (My cousin Stella) found the book on the shelf. She
10. (The girls) read it at home. They

Write *I* or *me* to complete each sentence.

11. My mother gave (I, me) a new book.
12. (I, me) read it to my brother.
13. My brother and (I, me) like the book very much.
14. (I, me) show it to my friend.
15. My friend tells (I, me) he likes it, too.

140

Vocabulary Power page 33

Name _____

Some words describe sounds. A rattlesnake got its name because of the sound it makes when it's getting ready to strike.

Read the sound word. Write the name of an animal that makes the sound.

1. mew _____   2. hoot _____

3. cluck _____   4. roar _____

5. growl _____   6. croak _____

7. squeal _____   8. buzz _____

Other words name sounds in nature. Draw pictures to show what could make the following sounds. In the last two boxes, draw about and write some other sound words.

drip-drip-drop	whoosh
crack! boom!	ker-plop!

Vocabulary Power   Unit 2 • Chapter 11   33

ESL

NEIGHBORHOOD WORKERS
Have children draw a picture of a person who works in their neighborhood. Ask them to write or say a sentence about the worker. Display the pictures, and have children share their sentences.

Language Play

Pronoun Play
- Play this game with a partner.
- Make game cards like the ones here.
- Put the cards in a pile. Take turns picking a card.
- Say a pronoun for the word or words on the card. Then use the pronoun in a sentence.
- Score one point for each correct sentence you say. The first one to get five points wins.

girl

coach

game

shoes

Ramon and Joe

players

ball

Anita and Molly

goal

boys

Writing Connection

Postcard Make a postcard to send to a friend. On the front, draw a picture of something you did. On the back, write a note telling about what you did. Be sure to use pronouns correctly.

Dear Tony,
I had a great soccer game yesterday. It was a lot of fun. Tommy and I made two goals each. This picture shows me kicking a goal!
   Your friend,
   Pete

Tony De Luna
200 Elm Street
Brooklyn, NY 11201

141

Language Play

Have children play "Pronoun Play" in pairs. Remind them to use what they have learned about pronouns. Ask children to listen carefully to their partner's sentence so they can be sure it is correct.

Writing Connection

Postcard Check to see that children have successfully written a postcard by using the criteria below.

CRITERIA
- ☑ Describes a personal experience.
- ☑ Writes complete sentences.
- ☑ Begins proper names with capital letters.
- ☑ Uses pronouns correctly.

☐ **PORTFOLIO OPPORTUNITY** You may want to have children share their postcard with family members, mail it to the addressee, or place it in their portfolio.

PRACTICE page 39

REACHING ALL LEARNERS

Name **Raven**

Extra Practice

A. Write a pronoun to replace the underlined word or words in each sentence. Then write the pronoun in the puzzle.

1. My dad brought in my birthday gift.
   He
2. The gift was in a big box. It
3. My mom placed it in the living room. She
4. Mom and Dad told me it was a surprise. They

B. Change the underlined word or words in each sentence to a pronoun. Rewrite the sentence.

5. My friends all came. They all came.
6. Bob came, too. He came, too.
7. A new bike was in the box! A new bike was in it!

C. Write the correct word to complete each sentence.

8. My sister gave (I, me) me a present.
9. (I, Me) I gave her a hug.
10. My sister and (I, me) I are good friends.

Practice • Pronouns   Unit 2 • Chapter 11   39

CHALLENGE

REACHING ALL LEARNERS

WHAT DO THEY DO? Have children work in pairs or small groups to find out what various people in the school do. They might interview the principal, the music teacher, a cafeteria worker, and so on. Have children take notes and then write a paragraph about the person. Encourage them to use pronouns. They may wish to draw a picture of the person.

Chapter Review

OBJECTIVES

- To review pronouns *he, she, it, they, I* and *me*
- To use a computer to send and receive e-mail messages

  DAILY LANGUAGE PRACTICE

TRANSPARENCY 21

1 she often plays with I. (She; me)

2 Me like to play with herr. (I; her)

BRIDGE TO WRITING Maria tells (pronoun) a story.

STANDARDIZED TEST PREP

Read aloud the directions to make sure children understand how to complete the activity. You may wish to have children complete this page independently before you use it as an assessment.

TEST PREPARATION TIP
Item Type: Multiple Choice

TIP

Model this strategy to help children determine the correct answer:

I look at the underlined words and see that they name one person. It is the naming part of the sentence. I look at the answer choices. I know that *they* is a pronoun that tells about more than one, so *a. They* is not the right answer. I know that *it* is used to replace a thing, so it cannot replace *The pilot. She* tells about one person. So I choose *c. She.*

Chapter Review

Choose the best answer for each underlined word or words.

1. The <u>pilot</u> flies the plane.

   a. They   **b.** It   **c. She**

2. The <u>plane</u> goes up high.

   a. It   **b.** He   **c.** She

3. Are <u>Carol and Bob</u> flying to Texas?

   a. they   **b.** she   **c.** he

4. On Monday <u>Bob</u> is going to Dallas.

   a. she   **b.** it   **c. he**

5. Then <u>Carol and Bob</u> are going to San Antonio.

   a. he   **b. they**   **c.** it

6. <u>My mom and I</u> flew on an airplane.

   a. Me and my mom   **b.** My mom and me   **c. correct as is**

7. She likes to travel with <u>I and my brother</u>.

   a. my brother and I   **b. my brother and me**   **c.** correct as is

 Visit our website for more activities with pronouns:
www.harcourtschool.com

142

Language Skills Assessment

• •

PORTFOLIO ASSESSMENT
Have children select their best work from the following activities:

- **Writing Connection**, *pages 137, 139, and 141;* TE activities, *pages 135, 137, 139, and 141.*

ONGOING ASSESSMENT
Evaluate the performance of 4-6 children using appropriate checklists and record forms from pages R65–R68 and R77–R79.

 INTERNET Activities and exercises to help children prepare for state and standardized assessments appear on *The Learning Site:*

www.harcourtschool.com

■ Technology ■

Sending E-mail

You can use your computer to get and send e-mail messages. If your computer has a modem, you can send e-mail to other people who have modems.

Send
Click on this to send your e-mail.

Address
Type the person's e-mail address here.

Subject
Type a few words to tell what the e-mail is about.

Message
Type your note.

To: danblanco@net.com   Send   Close

Subject: Weather for my school play

Message Box:
Dear Uncle Dan,
    My school play will be outdoors tomorrow. I watched the weather on the news today. It is going to be sunny tomorrow. There is only a small chance of rain.
    I hope you can make it if the weather is nice. Write back if you can come.
                    Love,
                    Patty

Practice

Before you start an e-mail, ask your teacher or parent if it is all right. Remember to think about whom you would like to e-mail and what you want to say. Send an e-mail message to someone you know.

143

■ Technology ■
Sending E-mail

TEACH/MODEL

Read aloud the explanation in the box. Explain that e-mail is a very quick way to send messages by using a computer and a modem. You may want to explain that a modem sends information between computers by using telephone lines. Explain that for people to send and receive e-mail, they must have an e-mail address. Discuss different kinds of e-mail people send. Encourage children to think about to whom they would send an e-mail and what they would say.

PRACTICE When children have finished, remind them to reread their messages before they send them. They should check for spelling and grammatical errors. They should also make sure they have the correct e-mail address of the recipient. Have them print their messages and share them with the class.

WRAP-UP/ASSESS

SUMMARIZE Ask children to tell what they have learned about sending e-mail. Ask them to discuss how e-mail is different from regular mail.

REACHING ALL LEARNERS
PRACTICE page 40

Name _____

Sending E-mail

Answer the questions about the e-mail message.

To: stephanie@email.com
From: beth@email.com
Subject: My new puppy

Dear Stephanie,
    I am so excited! I just got a new puppy. Her name is Bailey. Right now she is very small, but she will get a little bigger before long. She has white fur with colored spots on it.
    I hope you can come and meet her soon!
Love,
Beth

1. Who is the writer of this message?   Beth
2. What is Beth's address?   beth@email.com
3. What is the subject?   My new puppy
4. Who is getting this message?   Stephanie
5. What is Beth's e-mail about?   her puppy, Bailey

TRY THIS! Write an e-mail message that you would like to send to someone. Then ask your teacher or parent if you can send it. Type your message on the computer, and send it to a friend.

40   Unit 2 • Chapter 11   Practice • Pronouns

REACHING ALL LEARNERS
CHALLENGE

MAKE AN E-MAIL ADDRESS BOOK Invite children to collect e-mail addresses from friends, family members, and businesses. Ask them to compare the addresses. Have them write what they have discovered. Then have them rewrite the e-mail addresses in alphabetical order by name of individual or business on separate sheets of paper. (Suggest they put three letters on a page.) Then help them staple the pages together to form a directory.

Writing a Friendly Letter

pages 144-161

LESSON ORGANIZER	DAY 1	DAY 2
DAILY LANGUAGE PRACTICE TRANSPARENCY 22.	1. Jans mother got three letter from her (Jan's; letters; her.) 2. she wrote about the hens new chickes. (She; hen's; chicks)	1. my uncle dennis lives in utah. (My; Dennis; Utah) 2. I am going to see him on saturday, June 20? (Saturday, June 20.)
ORAL WARM-UP **Listening/Speaking**	Talk About Reading and Writing Letters p. 144	Talk About Information in Letters p. 154
TEACH/MODEL WRITING 	**Literature Model:** "Don't Forget to Write," pp. 144–150 • To read and respond to a story written as a friendly letter as a model for writing • To identify the parts of a friendly letter **Reading-Writing Connection:** Parts of a Letter p. 151 **A Student Model** pp.152–153	**GUIDED WRITING** ✔ **Prewriting** pp. 154–155 • To brainstorm and select a writing topic • To use a web to plan topics to include in a letter **Transparency** 23
Reaching All Learners	**Options for Reading** p. 145 **ESL:** The Big Picture p. 148 *ESL Manual* pp. 62–63	**Interactive Writing** p. 155 **CHALLENGE:** Friendly Letter p. 155 **ESL:** *ESL Manual* p. 62
GRAMMAR	**Unit 2 Review** pp. 162–163	**Unit 2 Review** pp. 162-163
CROSS-CURRICULAR/ ENRICHMENT	**Math Connection:** Missing Teeth p. 146 **Music Connection:** Old MacDonald p. 148 **School-Home Connection:** Illustrating Family Stories p. 149 **WRITER'S CRAFT:** Figurative Language p. 149 ▶ Vocabulary Power Word Meanings p. 144	▶ Vocabulary Power Related Words p. 144 *Vocabulary Power* book p. 34 🏆 **Vocabulary activity**

KEY
✔ = tested /skill

explored, delve, inquire, observe, quest
See *Vocabulary Power* book.

DAY 3	DAY 4	DAY 5
1. Me got these kitens from jeff (I; kittens; Jeff.)	1. give I Grandads extra hat, please. (Give; me; Grandad's)	1. we will be in vermont for seven day. (We; Vermont; days)
2. i remember kerry because her has red hair. (I; Kerry; she)	2. Moms sister and me made cookies (Mom's; I; cookies.)	2. Bee buzz around parker Farm (Bees; Parker; Farm.)
Talk About Sending and Receiving Letters p. 156	Review the Elements of a Friendly Letter p. 158	Discuss Different Types of Letters p. 160
GUIDED WRITING ✔ **Drafting** pp. 156–157 • To draft a friendly letter • To write a friendly letter with a heading, greeting, body, closing, and signature **Transparency** 24 **Proofreading practice**	**GUIDED WRITING** ✔ **Revising and Proofreading** pp. 158–159 • To revise a friendly letter • To proofread a letter for capitalization, punctuation, grammar, and spelling • To use Editor's Marks to make revisions and corrections **Transparencies** 24, 24a, 24b **Proofreading practice**	**GUIDED WRITING** ✔ **Publishing** p. 160 • To make final copies of revised friendly letters • To share letters **Scoring Rubric** p. 160 **Handwriting** Word and Letter Spacing p. 161 **Practice and assessment**
Interactive Writing p. 157 **ESL:** *ESL Manual* p. 62	**ESL:** *ESL Manual* p. 62	**ESL:** Making Introductions p. 161 *ESL Manual* p. 62
Unit 2 Review pp. 162–163	**Unit 2 Review** pp. 162–163 Summarize/Reflect	**Unit 2 Review** pp. 162–163
WRITER'S CRAFT: Pronouns p. 157 **Vocabulary Power** Word Families p. 144 *Vocabulary Power* book p. 35	**Spelling Connection:** Spelling Strategies p. 159 **Vocabulary Power** Expand Word Meaning p. 144 *Vocabulary Power* book p. 36 **Vocabulary activity**	**LISTENING AND SPEAKING:** Making Introductions p. 161 **Vocabulary Power** Comparison p. 144

Assessment Strategies and Resources

FORMAL ASSESSMENT

If you want to know more about a child's mastery of the language and writing skills taught in Unit 2, **then** administer the first *Language Skills and Writing Assessment* for Unit 2. The test consists of two parts:

Language Skills: **nouns, plural nouns, proper nouns, pronouns,** and **thank-you note**

Writing Task: Write a **friendly letter.** Scoring guidelines and model papers are included.

INFORMAL ASSESSMENT TOOLS

 Using Portfolios

During a conference with children, discuss their friendly letters and other writing they chose to include in their **writing portfolios.** You may want to use the Writing Conference Checklist on p. R67 as well as other checklists. Ask the following types of questions about their friendly letters:

- To whom did you write your friendly letter?
- What are the different parts of your letter?
- What did you write in each part?
- How did you plan your letter?
- What kinds of revisions did you make? Why?
- What is your favorite part?

You can check children's understanding of **grammar** by evaluating it in their writing as well. Look for these points:

- Does each proper noun begin with a capital letter?

- Do plural nouns have the correct plural endings?
- Is the spelling of nouns changed in the plural when needed?
- Are the pronouns *I, me, he, she, it,* and *they* used appropriately?

Oral Language Assessment

Use these guidelines to evaluate oral language:

Listening and Speaking
- Listens and speaks courteously during oral introductions
- Uses nonverbal communication effectively when making introductions
- Chooses appropriate spoken language, including rate and volume

Informal Assessment Reminder

If you used the pre-instruction writing prompt suggested in Teaching Grammar from Writing, **then** remember to compare the results with the writing done by children after the grammar and writing instruction.

Unit 3

Grammar
- Verbs

Writing
- Dialogue
- Story

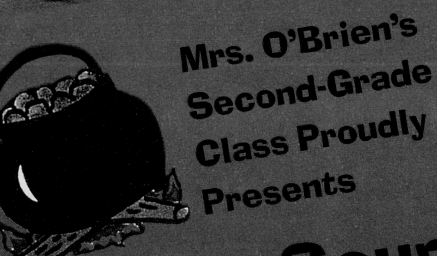

Mrs. O'Brien's Second-Grade Class Proudly Presents

"Stone Soup"

December 15

Greenville Elementary School

Auditorium

7:30 P.M.

Unit 3

Grammar • Verbs
Writing • Dialogue
• Story

Chapters	Grammar	Writing	Listening/ Speaking/Viewing
13 **Present-Tense Verbs** pp. 170–179	**What Is a Verb?** Usage and Mechanics: Adding *s* or *es* to Verbs, Combining Sentences with Verbs Extra Practice Chapter Review Daily Language Practice	**Writing Connections** Using Exact Words Revising Functional Writing: To-Do List	**"On Our Way"** **Activities** Tell Ways You Can Walk Language Play **Use Prior Knowledge** Play Simon Says
14 **Past-Tense Verbs** pp. 180–189	**Verbs That Tell About the Past** Usage and Mechanics: Adding *ed* to Verbs, Changing Verbs That End with *e* Extra Practice Chapter Review Daily Language Practice	**Writing Connections** Writing a Journal Entry Revising A Friendly Letter	**"Tommy"** **Activities** Tell About Something You Did Language Play **Use Prior Knowledge** Word Association Memory Game
15 **Short Process Writing: Dialogue** pp. 190–197	Daily Language Practice	**Dialogue** Prewriting and Drafting Editing Writer's Craft: Using Quotations to Show Feeling Writing and Thinking: Reflect	**"The Flying Machine" from "George and Martha"** **Sharing with Others** Read and Respond to the Model Reflect **Use Prior Knowledge**
16 **Forms of *Be*** pp. 198–207	**The Verbs *Am*, *Is*, and *Are*** Usage and Mechanics: Using *Am*, *Is*, and *Are*; Using *Was* and *Were* Extra Practice Chapter Review Daily Language Practice	**Writing Connections** Write About Yourself Using the Right Verbs Write a Description	**"I Am Running in a Circle"** **Activities** Talk About the Poem Language Play **Use Prior Knowledge** Talk About a Picture
17 **Forms of *Have*** pp. 208–217	**The Verbs *Has*, *Have*, and *Had*** Usage and Mechanics: Using *Has*, *Have*, and *Had*; Agreement with *Has*, *Have*, and *Had* Extra Practice Chapter Review Daily Language Practice	**Writing Connections** Recording Information Revising Time Line	**"What If?"** **Activities** Talk About an Animal You Like Language Play **Use Prior Knowledge** Play What Comes Next?
18 **Long Process Writing: Story** pp. 218–235	Daily Language Practice	**Story** Prewriting Drafting Revising Proofreading Publishing **Reading-Writing Connections:** Parts of a Story	Reading Like a Writer Read and Respond to the Model Telling a Story **Use Prior Knowledge**

Unit Wrap-Up **Writing Across the Curriculum: Science, pp. 238–239**

Vocabulary/Study Skills/ Technology/ Handwriting

Vocabulary Power

Words of the week: *flicker, **flutter**, quiver, shiver, sputter*
Vocabulary: Synonyms for Verbs
Technology: Writing Connection

Vocabulary Power

Words of the week: *communicate, confer, **consulting**, converse, recommend*
Study Skill: Using a Dictionary Entry
Technology: Writing Connection

Vocabulary Power

Words of the week: *category, family, similar, **species**, specimen*
Handwriting: Using Margins and Correct Word and Sentence Spacing
Hands-on Activities, pp. 167I–167J

Vocabulary Power

Words of the week: *circular, orbit, **revolving**, spinning, spiral*
Study Skill: Taking a Test
Technology: Writing Connection

Vocabulary Power

Words of the week: *anchored, attached, connected, **fastened**, united*
Technology: Editing on a Computer
Writing Connection
Challenge: Computer Revision

Vocabulary Power

Words of the week: *beasts, beings, **creatures**, critters, varmints*

Language Minutes

- **Act Out** an activity, such as dancing or hopping for your partner to guess. Have your partner **tell** others what you are doing. SPEAKING/VIEWING

- **Tell** what the weather **was** like yesterday. Your partner will tell you what it was like the day before that. Keep going back and forth until you don't remember anymore. SPEAKING/LISTENING

- **Make Up** a dialogue between two animals you like. Remember to use **quotations** when you write it. **Act out** the dialogue with a partner. WRITING/SPEAKING

- **Describe** how you **are** today and how you **were** yesterday. SPEAKING

- **Change** desks with a partner. Then **describe** what he or she has on the desk. Remember to use the correct forms of *have*. VIEWING/SPEAKING

- **Say** a sentence to **start a story** that happened in the **past**. Have partners take turns to add to the story. Then add an ending to the story. SPEAKING/LISTENING

Technology Resources

Grammar Jingles™ CD, **Primary**

Grammar Practice and Assessment **CD-ROM**

Writing Express **CD-ROM**

Media Literacy and Communication Skills **Package**

Visit *The Learning Site!*
www.harcourtschool.com

Reaching All Learners

Intervention

SUPPORT ACTIVITIES To help you meet the needs of children who require extra support, use the following activities with individual children or small groups.

- Write the headings *Yesterday* and *Today* on chart paper. Have children name activities for each category using present- and past-tense action verbs. Then ask volunteers to recall who does/did which activity written on the chart.

- Show a poster or pictures of people engaged in several activities. Ask children to use verbs to tell what the people are doing. Then ask them to change their sentences to tell what the people did yesterday.

INTERACTIVE WRITING Draw a flow chart on the board. Have the class use the flow chart to retell the beginning, middle, and ending of a familiar story. Children should use action verbs in their retelling.

Challenge

Some children require more challenging activities. To help you meet the needs of these children, use these suggestions.

- **SEARCH FOR VERBS** Have children look for different kinds of verbs in printed sources such as textbooks, chapter books, newspapers, and so on. Have children write each verb and the sentence in which it was found.

- **TELL ABOUT YOURSELF** Invite children to draw a picture of themselves as they are now and a picture showing them when they were younger. Have children share their pictures and tell sentences to describe how they are/were, what they do/did, and what they have/had.

- **WRITE DIALOGUES** Tell children to select a topic they like, such as a favorite book, movie, or sport. Then have them work in pairs to write a dialogue about it. Children can act out their dialogues for the class and publish them in a class book.

English as a Second Language

ESL STRATEGIES Pair more fluent English speakers with second-language learners. Have pairs write and act out sentences.

- One child uses pictures or props to create the naming part. The other acts out an activity to create the verb and telling part.

- Have other children guess the sentence and say it aloud.

- Have the class repeat the sentence aloud. Invite pairs to write their sentences.

Multi-Age Classroom

Pair younger and older children to write silly sentences using *is*, *am*, and *are*.

- Write the words *is*, *am*, and *are* on cards as well as other words children can use to form sentences.

- Invite pairs to write silly sentences and illustrate them.

- Older partners can write while younger children illustrate and read aloud the sentences.

- Have children share their silly sentences.

Teaching Grammar from Writing

PRETEST
Use the following prompt as a pretest to assess children's ability to use present- and past-tense verbs correctly in writing, and to use forms of *be* and *have* in writing.

WRITING PROMPT
Think about a television program or play you really enjoyed. Write a paragraph for your teacher that tells what happened in that program or play and why you enjoyed it.

EVALUATE AND PLAN
Analyze children's writing to determine how you can best meet their individual needs for instruction. Use the chart below to identify and remedy problems.

COMMON PROBLEMS	CHAPTERS TO USE
Is unsure whether to add *s* or *es* to present-tense verbs.	Chapter 13: Present-Tense Verbs
Does not correctly add *ed* to verbs to form past-tense verbs.	Chapter 13: Past-Tense Verbs
Does not know how to write correctly the past-tense form of verbs that end in *e*.	Chapter 14: Past-Tense Verbs
Does not write dialogue correctly.	Chapter 15: Dialogue/ Quotations
Incorrectly use forms of *Be*.	Chapter 16: Forms of *Be*
Incorrectly use forms of *Have*.	Chapter 17: Forms of *Have*

Classroom Management

DURING...	SOME CHILDREN CAN...
Grammar Reteaching	Work on the Writing Across the Curriculum project.
Independent Practice	Begin the Writing Connection. Participate in Language Centers.
Portfolio Conferences	Complete Self-Evaluation forms. (See pages R78–R79 in this *Teacher's Edition*.) Participate in peer conferences.

Sharing Time

LANGUAGE ARTS IN THE CLASSROOM

Sharing Time can be one of the most effective oral language experiences in the class day.

THAT SPECIAL PLACE FOR SHARING Have a special area in the classroom where children can gather around the presenter such as a large carpeted area. Allow children to ask questions. Always ask the presenter permission to allow children to touch or hold the object. If feasible, have the objects on display in a safe place for the remainder of the day.

DO IT IN SMALL GROUPS Those who want to share can be distributed around the room with their items or stories. Children are organized into small groups, sharing with one of the sharers at a time. After some time has passed, the children move to another sharer. Think of it as Centers for Sharing!

CHILDREN WHO ARE RELUCTANT TO SHARE Because there are many children who never seem to share, try having a day when everyone shares their favorite song, their favorite book, or their favorite food. This type of inventory will allow for everyone to speak without fear.

LET THEM GUESS A twist on Sharing Time is letting the sharer present the item to be shared as a mystery. The audience tries to guess while the sharer provides hints.

DON'T FORGET YOURSELF Children love to hear what you have to share. Sharing shows that you care enough to want to share a little bit about you.

ASK MEANINGFUL QUESTIONS Provide a model for children's questions by asking interesting, relevant, and clearly stated questions for the presenter to answer. Include questions that will guide the presenter as he or she shares an item with the group.

- **Why did you choose to share the _____ with our class?**
- **Who can add any ideas to what (name of presenter) has told us?**
- **Are the items that were shared today alike in any way? How?**

Hands-on Activities

Verb Fun

MATERIALS: sheet of chart paper, number cube, playing chips

DIRECTIONS:

1. Make a border of boxes on a large sheet of chart paper to form a game board. Label one corner box *Start*. Label the last box *End*.

2. Have children find magazine pictures showing one or several people doing an action. Have them glue a picture in each box of the board.

3. The first player rolls the number cube and moves the correct number of spaces from the Start box. The player then names the verb that describes the action pictured and uses it in a present-tense sentence.

4. Keep playing until one player gets to the End box.

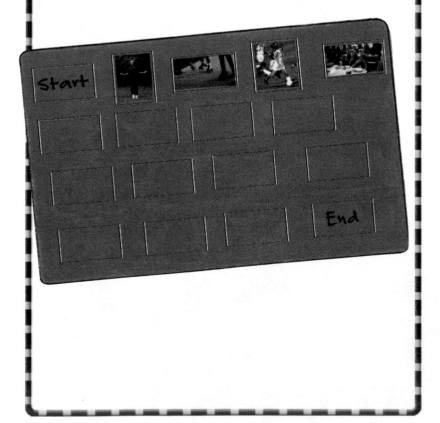

Sentence Completion

MATERIALS: sentence strips

DIRECTIONS:

1. Write past-tense sentences on sentence strips, but leave out the verbs.

2. Write the missing verbs in the present tense on the chalkboard or on chart paper.

3. Have children pick a present-tense verb and write it in the past tense to complete the sentences.

It rained hard last night.

Dictionary Fun

MATERIALS: dictionaries, paper and pencils, box

DIRECTIONS:

1. In a box, place paper strips with a different action verb written on each one.

2. Have children work in pairs. Each pair picks a strip.

3. Invite children to look up the meaning of the verb in the dictionary and then write it down in their own words.

4. Have children read aloud their dictionary entries. Remind them to speak clearly and slowly. Based on the definition given, another pair composes a sample sentence using the defined verb.

Which Verb Is Needed?

MATERIALS: index cards, markers

DIRECTIONS:

1. Write the verbs *is, am, are, was,* and *were* on index cards and give them to five children to hold.

2. Say or write sentences such as the following, leaving out the verbs in parentheses: *Nick (is) home today. Mrs. Wang (was) at the library yesterday. They (are) in the garden now. The children (were) busy last night. I (am) happy to be with my friend this afternoon.*

3. Ask children to identify which child holding a verb should come forward to complete each sentence.

4. Have children read the completed sentences aloud.

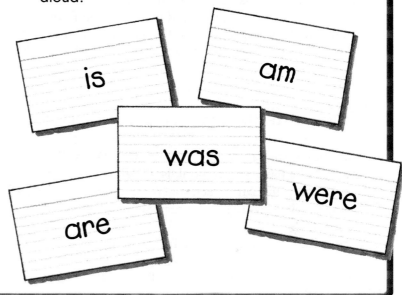

Has, Have, Had Hot Potato

MATERIALS: construction paper, tape player, cassette

DIRECTIONS:

1. Cut three potato shapes from construction paper. Write *has* on one potato, *had* on the second, and *have* on the third.

2. Have children sit in a circle. Each child takes a potato.

3. Play music. Tell children to pass the potato to their right while the music is playing. When the music ends or stops, the children holding potatoes say a sentence using the words they are holding.

4. Keep playing until each child has had three turns.

Note: As an alternate, you may want to use the *Grammar Jingles*™ CD for the music.

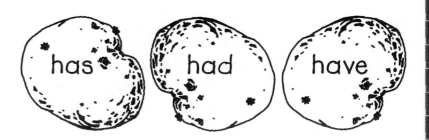

Listening to Literature

Author's Day

BY DANIEL PINKWATER

A RUSTY GREEN CAR came into the parking lot. Driving the car was a man drinking coffee out of a plastic foam cup. Empty plastic foam cups rattled and rolled on the floor of the car. The car had a noisy motor, and made a lot of smoke. It had a bumper sticker that said: I'D RATHER BE WRITING.

The car came to a stop, and Bramwell Wink-Porter, the famous author, got out. He looked up at the banner over the door of the school. It said

WELCOME MR. BRAMWELL WINK-PORTER
AUTHOR OF THE FUZZY BUNNY

"I did not write *The Fuzzy Bunny*," Bramwell Wink-Porter said to himself. "The name of my book is *The Bunny Brothers*."

Mr. Carramba and Mrs. Feenbogen came out of the school. "Welcome to Melvinville Elementary School," Mrs. Feenbogen said.

"All the children are excited," Mr. Carramba said. "They have all read your book, *The Fuzzy Bunny*."

"I did not write *The Fuzzy Bunny*," Bramwell Wink-Porter said.

"Such modesty!" Mrs. Feenbogen said.

"*The Fuzzy Bunny* was written by Abigail Finkdotter," Bramwell Wink-Porter said. "Not me."

"I have never met a famous author," said Mr. Carramba. "This is the most exciting thing that has ever happened to me."

"My book is called *The Bunny Brothers*," Bramwell Wink-Porter said.

"I am so thrilled that you are here," said Mr. Carramba.

"Yes," said Mrs. Feenbogen. "So am I. And perhaps you could talk about *The Fuzzy Bunny*, even though you did not write it."

"Come to the library," Mr. Carramba said. "We have just gotten a box of your books. This is so exciting!"

In the library, Mr. Carramba opened a large box. "This just came," he said. "Here are many copies of your book."

"This book is *Bunnies for Breakfast* by Lemuel Crankstarter," Bramwell Wink-Porter said. "I did not write this. My book is called *The Bunny Brothers*."

"Well, it is time to get started," Mr. Carramba said. "You will begin with a visit to the kindergarten class. But first . . . I am so excited . . . I think I am going to faint."

Mr. Carramba threw himself to the floor.

"Oh! Mr. Carramba has fainted!" Mrs. Feenbogen said. "Send for Howard the janitor!"

"Wouldn't it be better to send for the nurse?" Bramwell Wink-Porter asked.

"Howard is also a nurse," Mrs. Feenbogen said. "He will take care of Mr. Carramba."

Mrs. Feenbogen stepped over Mr. Carramba, and took Bramwell Wink-Porter to the kindergarten. "The kindergarten teacher's name is Mrs. Neatfeet," she told him.

The kindergarten class had made pancakes for a treat. The pancakes were lumpy and dirty. Some of the pancakes had pieces of crayon in them. The children were having fun playing with syrup.

"Look, class!" Mrs. Neatfeet said. "It is Mr. Bramwell Wink-Porter, author of *The Fuzzy Bunny*!"

"*The Bunny Brothers*," Bramwell Wink-Porter said.

"Shall we give Mr. Bramwell Wink-Porter a hug?" Mrs. Neatfeet asked the kindergarten class.

Building Background

Born in Tennessee, Daniel Pinkwater has written and illustrated more than 25 children's book including *I Was a Second Grade Werewolf*, *Second-Grape Ape*, *Doodle Flute*, and *Guys from Space*. In addition to writing and illustrating, Daniel Pinkwater is well-known for his commentaries given on National Public Radio's "All Things Considered."

INTRODUCE THE LISTENING SELECTION Before you read the story, tell children to listen critically to decide what the words spoken by the visiting author, the teachers, and the students tell about their feelings. Emphasize that they should think about the words and try to determine how they would feel in the same situation.

Determine a Purpose for Listening

Tell children that this is a story about an author's visit to an elementary school. There are some problems because everyone thinks he wrote a book that he did not write. It has dialogue that helps the reader understand how the author in the story is feeling as well as how thrilled the teachers and students are. Ask children to describe whether their purpose for listening is

- to gain information
- to solve problems (to solve problems)
- to enjoy and appreciate.

The kindergartners crowded around Bramwell Wink-Porter, and hugged him.

"They are very sticky children," Bramwell Wink-Porter said.

"They are not usually this sticky," Mrs. Neatfeet told him. "It is the syrup."

"Yes," said Bramwell Wink-Porter.

After being made to eat a cold, lumpy pancake with a piece of green crayon in it, Bramwell Wink-Porter was taken to meet the first graders.

"Don't come in yet!" said Mrs. Fleetstreet, the first grade teacher. "We have a surprise for you."

The surprise was that all the first graders had Fuzzy Bunny masks, and Fuzzy Bunny hats with ears. They had made the masks and hats themselves.

"What a surprise," said Bramwell Wink-Porter.

"We love *The Fuzzy Bunny*!" the first graders all said at the same time.

"Thank you," said Bramwell Wink-Porter.

Wearing the adult-size Fuzzy Bunny hat with ears the first grade had given him, Bramwell Wink-Porter was taken to the gym to talk with the second and third grades.

The second and third graders had prepared questions to ask the famous author.

"Was it hard to write *The Fuzzy Bunny*?" they asked him.

"No, it was not very hard...I suppose," Bramwell Wink-Porter said.

"What is your favorite book?" another child asked.

"My favorite book is *Moby Dick* by Herman Melville," Bramwell Wink-Porter answered.

"No—I mean your favorite book that you wrote."

"Oh. Well, I'd have to say *The Bunny Brothers*," Bramwell Wink-Porter said.

The second and third graders looked at one another.

"You haven't read that one, have you?" Bramwell Wink-Porter said. "Well, I hope you will."

"What is your favorite rodent?"

"That's easy—a bunny," said Bramwell Wink-Porter.

"A bunny isn't properly a rodent. Bunnies belong to the order Lagomorpha."

"In that case, I'd say gerbils are my favorite rodents. Gerbils are rodents, aren't they?"

"What is your shoe size?"

"Ten."

"Do you have a favorite kind of toast?"

"Yes, raisin."

"Have you ever been to South America?"

"No."

"Would you like to go there?"

"Yes."

"Which is better, grape soda or ginger ale?"

"Grape soda."

"Have you ever been bitten by a horse?"

"Yes."

"That's all the time we have, children," Mrs. Feenbogen said. "Let's give Mr. Bramwell Wink-Porter a big hand."

The second and third grades applauded, and Mrs. Feenbogen led Bramwell Wink-Porter out of the gym.

"Now you have met some of the children in our school," Mrs. Feenbogen said. "It was very kind of you to visit us."

"Thank you," Bramwell Wink-Porter said. "I enjoyed my visit."

"Now I will escort you to your car," Mrs. Feenbogen said.

In the hall, they met a second grader, wearing a Fuzzy Bunny mask and hat. "Mr. Wink-Porter," the second grader said. "I have one last question to ask you."

"What is your question?" Bramwell Wink-Porter asked.

The second grader asked, "Do you think you might ever write a book about us?"

Listening Comprehension

LISTEN FOR QUOTATIONS TO SHOW FEELINGS Explain to children that in this story, the writer uses dialogue to describe the feelings of the characters. Listening for who is speaking and what they express will help children determine the way the characters feel about each other and the visiting author.

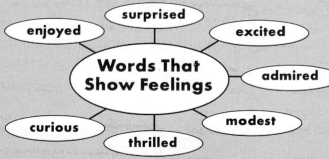

surprised
enjoyed
excited
Words That Show Feelings
admired
curious
thrilled
modest

PERSONAL RESPONSE *What feelings did the other characters have toward Bramwell Wink-Porter? How do you know this?* (Possible responses: They enjoy his visit. A character says he is excited and faints. He also says he is thrilled. Another character tells him that everyone enjoyed his visit. The children ask a lot of questions.)

INFERENTIAL: DETERMINE CHARACTERS' EMOTIONS

Unit 3

Grammar
- Verbs

Writing
- Dialogue
- Story

Introducing the Unit

ORAL LANGUAGE/VIEWING

DISCUSS THE IMAGES Tap children's prior knowledge by inviting them to describe what they see on these two pages (children's stage, program for a play). Have children tell about experiences they have had on a stage or in front of an audience. Elicit from them how the stage was set up, what they wore, what they felt like, and what they had to say and do. Discuss good behaviors expected from their audiences as well. Ask questions such as these:

- **What did you perform?** (Responses will vary.)
- **If it was a play, what did some of the characters say and do?** (Responses will vary.)
- **How did you feel when you were performing?** (Responses will vary.)
- **If you could be any character in a play, who would you be? Why?** (Responses will vary.)

ENCOURAGE CHILDREN'S QUESTIONS Encourage children's questions about performances and discuss their responses. Then have children write/draw in their journals about plays and performances.

Unit 3

Grammar
- Verbs

Writing
- Dialogue
- Story

168

Viewing and Representing

COMPARE/CONTRAST PRINT AND VISUAL MEDIA Have small groups of children decide which characters they would include in a play. Then have them plan what the characters might say and do. Children can share their ideas with classmates through a story board, pictures, or a comic strip. Have children share which characters they like best and why.

For evaluation criteria, see the checklist on page R77.

MEDIA LITERACY AND COMMUNICATION

SKILLS PACKAGE Use the video to extend children's oral and visual literacy. See pages 6–7 of the *Teacher's Guide*.

Mrs. O'Brien's
Second-Grade
Class Proudly
Presents

"Stone Soup"

December 15
Greenville Elementary School
Auditorium
7:30 P.M.

Previewing the Unit

Read and discuss the unit contents list with children. Ask what a verb might be. Then tell them that in this unit they will learn how and when to use different verb forms in their writing. Encourage children to talk about the term *dialogue*. Discuss how writing a dialogue might make a story better.

SCIENCE CONNECTION Children will be exposed to a variety of science topics in this unit:

- Pets and wild animals
- Nature
- Aquatic animals
- Reptiles

School-Home Connection

You may want to use Home Letter 3, page R96.

LESSON ORGANIZER 	DAY 1	DAY 2
DAILY LANGUAGE PRACTICE TRANSPARENCIES 25, 26	**1.** i lik my painting. (I; like) **2.** Does Ellen like the drawing Ellen made (she; made?) **Bridge to Writing** Ellen says she likes (pronoun) own painting best of all.	**1.** the dog licks I. (The; me) **2.** me leep lik a frog. (I leap like) **Bridge to Writing** (pronoun) like to (verb) like a (noun).
ORAL WARM-UP Listening/Speaking	Pantomime Animals' Movements p. 170	Act Out School Activities p. 172 *Grammar Jingles™* CD, Primary, Track 8
TEACH/MODEL GRAMMAR **KEY** ✔ = tested skill	✔ **WHAT IS A VERB?** pp. 170-171 • To interpret and dramatize a poem • To recognize that a verb can tell about an action	✔ **ADDING S OR ES TO VERBS** pp. 172-173 • To recognize that s is added to most verbs that tell what one person or thing does • To recognize that es is added to verbs that end in ss, ch, sh, and x
Reaching All Learners	**Challenge:** Activity Card 9, p. R49 *Practice Book* p. 41 **ESL:** *ESL Manual* pp. 64, 65 **Reteach:** *Reteach Activities Copying Masters* p. 25	**Modified Instruction** Below-Level: Circle Naming Parts Above-Level: Write Additional Verbs **Challenge:** Animal Riddles p. 173 **ESL:** Act Out Sentences p. 172 *ESL Manual* pp. 64, 66 *Practice Book* p. 42 **Reteach:** *Reteach Activities Copying Masters* p. 26
WRITING	Write Patterned Sentences p. 171 Summarize/Reflect	Writing Connection p. 173 Using Exact Words Summarize/Reflect
CROSS-CURRICULAR/ ENRICHMENT	**Vocabulary Power** Word Meaning p. 170 flutter, flicker, quiver, shiver, sputter See **Vocabulary Power** book.	**Vocabulary Power** Related Words p. 170 *Vocabulary Power* book p. 37 **Vocabulary activity**

Visit *The Learning Site!*
www.harcourtschool.com
WRITING ACTIVITIES
Writing Express CD-ROM

DAY 3

1. jim catch the ball. (Jim catches)
2. Lin creaps like a snak. (creeps; snake)

Bridge to Writing Bonnie <u>(verb)</u> like a <u>(noun)</u>.

Perform Actions p. 174
 Grammar Jingles™ CD, Primary, Track 8

✔ **COMBINING SENTENCES WITH VERBS** pp. 174-175
- To use *and* to combine verbs in sentences
- To use combined sentences in writing

Modified Instruction
Below-Level: Circle Parts
Above-Level: Sentences
Challenge: Verb Search p. 175
ESL: Joining Sentences p. 174
ESL Manual pp. 64, 67
Practice Book p. 43
Reteach: *Reteach Activities Copying Masters* p. 27

Writing Connection p. 175
Revising
Summarize/Reflect

Vocabulary Power
Multi-Meaning Words p. 170
Vocabulary Power book p.38
Vocabulary activity

DAY 4

1. Aisha reeds the book and Aisha takes nots. (reads; and takes notes)
2. The cats watches the read bird. (watch; red)

Bridge to Writing Bob opens the door <u>(and)</u> lets the cats out.

Play Simon Says p. 176

✔ **EXTRA PRACTICE** p. 176
- To recognize when to add *s* or *es* to a present-tense verb
- To use *and* to combine verbs in sentences

 Practice and Assessment

Challenge: Pet Sentences p. 177
ESL: Interactive Writing p. 176
ESL Manual pp. 64, 68
Practice Book p. 44

Writing Connection p. 177
To-Do List

Vocabulary Power
Rhyming Words p. 170
Vocabulary Power book p.39
Vocabulary activity

DAY 5

1. Do you know why Jane brush the horse. (brushes; horse?)
2. marco fix the door. (Marco; fixes)

Bridge to Writing The horse <u>(verb)</u> over the hill.

TEST PREP CHAPTER REVIEW p. 178
- To review present-tense verbs; review combining verbs
- Use synonyms for commonly used verbs in writing

Test Preparation

Challenge: Revise Your Writing p. 179
Practice Book p. 45
ESL: *ESL Manual* pp. 64, 69

Writing Application p. 179
Sentences with Synonyms

VOCABULARY
Synonyms for Verbs p. 179
Vocabulary Power
Alliteration p. 170

What Is a Verb?

OBJECTIVES
- To interpret and dramatize a poem
- To recognize that a verb can tell about an action

DAILY LANGUAGE PRACTICE

TRANSPARENCY 25

1 i lik my painting. (I; like)

2 Does Ellen like the drawing Ellen made (she; made?)

BRIDGE TO WRITING Ellen says she likes _____ (pronoun) own painting best of all.

ORAL WARM-UP

USE PRIOR KNOWLEDGE Ask volunteers to think of animals they know and pantomime the animals' movements. Have others guess each animal and tell how it moves, using words such as *hop*, *trot*, and *crawl*. Begin a list of these words on chart paper or set up a **Verb Word Wall.**

TEACH/MODEL

Have children open to page 170 and describe the illustration. Have them use the title and the illustration to predict what the poem will be about. Read the poem aloud. Then reread the poem, having children join in with you.

DEVELOP ORAL LANGUAGE Ask children to recall some of the actions from the poem. Prompt them to act out the actions by asking questions such as these:

- **How would a frog leap?**
- **How does a butterfly flutter?**

Ask volunteers to demonstrate or describe other ways to move. Add verbs to the list on chart paper or to the **Word Wall.**

What Is a Verb?

Read the poem.

~On Our Way~

What kind of walk shall we take today?
Leap like a frog? Creep like a snail?
Scamper like a squirrel with a funny tail?

Flutter like a butterfly? Chicken peck?
Stretch like a turtle with a poking out neck?

Trot like a pony, clip clop clop?
Swing like a monkey in a treetop?

Scuttle like a crab? Kangaroo jump?
Plod like a camel with an up and down hump?

We could even try a brand-new way—
walking down the street
on our own two feet.

Eve Merriam

170

Vocabulary Power

DAY 1 WORD MEANING Write: *flutter*. **Find *flutter* in the poem "On Our Way."** **How does a butterfly flutter?** (by flapping its wings)

DAY 2 RELATED WORDS Write: *flow, flutter, flap*. **Which two words describe the same kind of movement?** (See also *Vocabulary Power*, page 37.)

DAY 3 MULTI-MEANING WORDS Write: *I'm in a flutter when I'm late for school.* **What does *being in a flutter* mean?** (See also *Vocabulary Power*, page 38.)

DAY 4 RHYMING WORDS Write: *flutter, sputter.* **How are these words alike? Name another word that rhymes.** (See also *Vocabulary Power*, page 39.)

DAY 5 ALLITERATION Write: *Butterflies flit, flap, flitter, and flutter in a flurry.* Discuss which words have similar meanings. Invite children to say the tongue twister faster and faster. **Make a list of words that begin like *sputter*. Write your own tongue twister.**

Show or tell about ways you can walk. Then write words that tell about other ways you can move.

A **verb** can tell about an action that happens now.

I **leap** like a frog.
I **creep** like a snail.

Write a verb and an animal name in each item to add new lines for the poem. Responses will vary.

Gallop like a horse ?

_____ like a _____ ?

_____ like a _____ ?

_____ like a _____ ?

_____ like a _____ ?

_____ like a _____ ?

171

WRITE Use the children's demonstrations of other ways they might move to help them generate action words. Invite volunteers to read their lists of words aloud. Explain that words that tell how they move or what they do are **verbs.** Read the definition in the box and talk about the example sentences.

Then read the first item at the bottom of page 171 together. Point out the pattern from the poem: ____ like a ____? Have children complete the items and then share them with a partner.

WRAP-UP/ASSESS

SUMMARIZE Reread the poem with children. Then have them reflect on what they have learned about verbs. You may want children to write their reflections in their journals, as well as record action verbs they brainstormed while completing the page. **REFLECTION**

REACHING ALL
RETEACH

INTERVENTION Lessons in visual, auditory, and kinesthetic modalities, p. R25 and *Reteach Activities Copying Masters*, p. 25

page 25

What Is a Verb?
Talk about each picture. Write a verb from the box to complete each sentence.

| runs | swim | fly | jumps |

1. Fish _____swim_____.   2. Many birds _____fly_____.

3. This cat _____runs_____ fast.   4. The frog _____jumps_____ far.

What Is a Verb?
Color each box that has a verb.

| walk | digs | tall | he |
| skips | four | runs | crawl |

Work with a partner to write sentences using the verbs. Then act out the sentences. Responses will vary.

_____

_____

_____

Reteach Activities • Present-Tense Verbs   Unit 3 • Chapter 13 25

PRACTICE page 41

REACHING ALL LEARNERS

Name _____

What Is a Verb?

A. Underline the verb in each sentence.

1. The park rangers <u>hike</u> to the lake.
2. One ranger <u>points</u> to some raccoons.
3. One raccoon <u>takes</u> some food.
4. It <u>washes</u> the food in the water.
5. The raccoons <u>eat</u> the food.

B. Write the verb from the box that best completes each sentence.

| pet | find | sleeps | name | drinks |

6. The firefighters _____find_____ a tiny, lost kitten.

7. The kitten _____drinks_____ a whole bowl of milk.

8. The firefighters _____pet_____ the kitten's fur.

9. They _____name_____ the kitten Sparky.

10. Sparky _____sleeps_____ in a firefighter's hat!

TRY THIS! Write four sentences about the things a kitten may do. Underline the verbs.

Practice • Present-Tense Verbs   Unit 3 • Chapter 13 41

CHALLENGE

REACHING ALL LEARNERS

MAKE AN ANIMAL MASK Have children use **Challenge Activity Card 9** (page R49) to make masks of their favorite animals in the poem. Then reread the poem and have children act it out. Ask volunteers to say more sentences about animals.

Challenge Activity Card 9

Make an Animal Mask

Materials:
• paper plate
• crayons or markers
• paper scraps
• glue

1. Choose an animal from the poem.
2. Draw the animal's face.
3. Add eyes, ears, and other details.
4. Use your mask to act out the poem.

CHAPTER 13 171

Adding *s* or *es* to Verbs

OBJECTIVES
- To recognize that *s* is added to most verbs that tell what one person or thing does
- To recognize that *es* is added to verbs that end in *ss*, *ch*, *sh*, and *x*

SPIRAL REVIEW

DAILY LANGUAGE PRACTICE

TRANSPARENCY 25

1 the dog licks I. (The; me)

2 me leep lik a frog. (I leap like)

BRIDGE TO WRITING (pronoun) like to (verb) like a (noun) .

ORAL WARM-UP

USE PRIOR KNOWLEDGE Have volunteers act out some of the things they do during the school day. Ask other children to give an oral description of each action and identify the verb in each sentence.

***Grammar Jingles*™ CD, Primary** Use Track 8 for review and reinforcement of present-tense verbs.

TEACH/MODEL

Introduce the concept of present-tense verbs and when to add *s* or *es* by using the explanation and the examples.

- **Which word is the verb in the first sentence?** (feeds)
- **When is the action taking place?** (now)
- **Who is doing the action?** (Mr. Bing)

Write sentences like the following on the board: *Tom and Kate walk the dog. The books go on the shelf.* Point out that when the naming part of a sentence includes more than one person or thing, the verb does not have *s* or *es* added to it.

GUIDED PRACTICE Work with children to complete each sentence. Encourage children to listen for the difference between verbs to which *s* is added and those to which *es* is added.

172 **UNIT 3**

Adding *s* or *es* to Verbs

Add *s* to most verbs to tell what one person or thing does now.

Mr. Bing **feeds** the animals in the pet shop.

Add *es* if the verb ends in *ss*, *ch*, *sh*, or *x*.

Mrs. Bing **brushes** the dogs.

Guided Practice

Write the correct verb to finish each sentence.

1. The Bings (<u>bring</u>, brings) pets to the park.
2. One rabbit (eat, <u>eats</u>) food.
3. Then it (hop, <u>hops</u>) out of its cage.
4. Nina and Jean (<u>spot</u>, spots) the rabbit.
5. Nina (catch, <u>catches</u>) it.

172

Vocabulary Power page 37

Name _____

These words are related because they describe ways to move.

   swim   float   dive

The words in dark print describe other ways to move. Draw pictures to show the word meanings. For number 6, write and draw about your own word.

1. flutter	2. flicker
3. shiver	4. quiver
5. sputter	6. _____

Vocabulary Power   Unit 3 • Chapter 13   37

REACHING ALL LEARNERS   **ESL**

ACT OUT SENTENCES Some children may think that adding *s* or *es* to a verb indicates the plural as with nouns. To help clarify, have volunteers act out actions while other children say each volunteer's name and movements, such as *Tim runs.* Repeat the sentence each time to emphasize the ending sound.

Remember Add *s* to most verbs to tell what one person or thing does now. Add *es* if the verb ends in *ss*, *ch*, *sh*, or *x*.

Independent Practice

Write the correct verb to finish each sentence.

6. Mr. and Mrs. Bing (<u>train</u>, trains) animals.

7. Mrs. Bing (give, <u>gives</u>) a rabbit to the girls.

8. The girls (<u>thank</u>, thanks) Mrs. Bing.

9. Animals (<u>help</u>, helps) people in different ways.

10. Coco (open, <u>opens</u>) doors for Jim.

11. Rover (fetch, <u>fetches</u>) things for Claire.

12. He (kiss, <u>kisses</u>) Claire with a big lick.

13. The guide dog (lead, <u>leads</u>) a girl.

14. The girl and the dog (<u>walk</u>, walks) across the street.

15. Animals and people (<u>work</u>, works) as a team.

Writing Connection

Using Exact Words Draw a picture of animals at a pet store. Write sentences. Use verbs to tell exactly what the animals are doing.

Use your computer to write and print out your sentences.

173

Independent Practice

Have children complete the Independent Practice, or modify it by using the following suggestions:

MODIFIED INSTRUCTION

BELOW-LEVEL STUDENTS Suggest children circle the naming part of each sentence to help them decide which word is the verb.

ABOVE-LEVEL STUDENTS After children have finished, invite them to write at least two additional verbs that would fit in each sentence.

Writing Connection

Using Exact Words Remind children that using exact words helps make their writing better. Have volunteers place their sentences in the Sharing Basket to share with others.

WRAP-UP/ASSESS

SUMMARIZE Have children reflect on what they have learned about verbs that tell what one person or thing is doing now. Have them summarize what they have learned.

REFLECTION

RETEACH

INTERVENTION Lessons in **visual**, **auditory**, and **kinesthetic** modalities: p. R25 and *Reteach Activities Copying Masters*, p. 26.

PRACTICE page 42

Name _____

Adding *s* or *es* to Verbs

Write the verb from the box that best completes each sentence. Add *s* or *es* if you need to do so.

sleep	roll	eat	brush	feed
close	drive	kiss	watch	toss

1. She ___drives___ the tractor to the field.

2. Nancy ___kisses___ the kitten.

3. Martin ___watches___ the ducks in the pond.

4. The pig ___rolls___ in the mud.

5. Jim ___tosses___ hay to the cows.

6. The man ___brushes___ the horse.

7. The cows ___eat___ hay.

8. The dog ___sleeps___ near the cow.

9. Mary ___feeds___ the hens.

10. She ___closes___ the barn door.

TRY THIS! Write three sentences about things that happen on a farm. Use some verbs from the box above.

42 Unit 3 • Chapter 13   Practice • Present-Tense Verbs

CHALLENGE

ANIMAL RIDDLES Have children choose some of the verbs from pages 172-173 and write a riddle for each one. Then partners can read their riddles to one another, solve them, and spell the answers.

Someone does this to clean a pet's fur. The word has seven letters.

What is it? (**brushes**)

Adding *s* or *es* to Verbs

Talk about each picture. Read each sentence aloud. Circle the letter or letters that were added to the verb to show that one person is doing something.

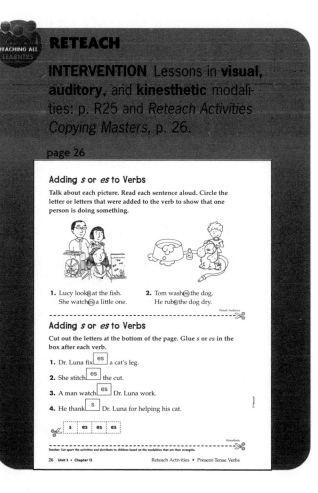

1. Lucy looks at the fish. She watches a little one.

2. Tom washes the dog. He rubs the dog dry.

Adding *s* or *es* to Verbs

Cut out the letters at the bottom of the page. Glue *s* or *es* in the box after each verb.

1. Dr. Luna fix [es] a cat's leg.

2. She stitch [es] the cut.

3. A man watch [es] Dr. Luna work.

4. He thank [s] Dr. Luna for helping his cat.

| s | es | es | es |

26 Unit 3 • Chapter 13   Reteach Activities • Present-Tense Verbs

Combining Sentences with Verbs

OBJECTIVES
- To use *and* to combine verbs in sentences
- To use combined sentences in writing

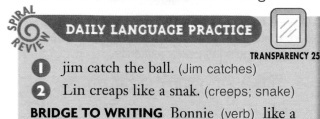

DAILY LANGUAGE PRACTICE

TRANSPARENCY 25

1 jim catch the ball. (Jim catches)

2 Lin creaps like a snak. (creeps; snake)

BRIDGE TO WRITING Bonnie (verb) like a (noun) .

ORAL WARM-UP

USE PRIOR KNOWLEDGE Ask volunteers to perform two different actions. As each volunteer does the actions, have children say two sentences about them, such as *Dan smiles* and *Dan hops*. Explain to children that they can say the same thing in an easier, clearer way by putting the two sentences together, such as *Dan smiles and hops*.

***Grammar Jingles*™ CD, Primary** Use Track 8 for review and reinforcement of present-tense verbs.

TEACH/MODEL

Introduce the concept by using the explanation and the examples. Reread the last sample sentence aloud. Point out that this sentence is clearer because it does not repeat the naming part.

GUIDED PRACTICE Work through the first item together. Have children identify the parts in both sentences that are the same (The ranger) and then decide where to place the word *and*. Call on a volunteer to combine the sentences. Repeat the procedure with the remaining items.

Combining Sentences with Verbs

The naming parts of two sentences are sometimes the same. You can join the sentences by using **and**. This can make your writing easier to read and understand.

Molly looks in the bush.
Molly sees a bird.

Molly looks in the bush **and** sees a bird.

Guided Practice

Use *and* to join each pair of sentences. Write the new sentence.

1. The ranger drives the jeep.
   The ranger watches for animals.
   The ranger drives the jeep and watches for animals.
2. We go on a tour.
   We see many squirrels.
   We go on a tour and see many squirrels.
3. The squirrels carry nuts.
   The squirrels climb trees.
   The squirrels carry nuts and climb trees.
4. We find deer tracks.
   We spot two deer.
   We find deer tracks and spot two deer.

174

Vocabulary Power page 38

Name _____

Multi-Meaning Words

Many words have more than one meaning. Read these sentences.

A. The lightning bolts <u>flash</u>.   **B.** I'll be back in a <u>flash</u>.
In **A** <u>flash</u> means "to blaze quickly." In **B** <u>flash</u> means "a very short amount of time."

Read the sentence pairs. Draw a picture of yourself to show the meaning of the sentence in dark print.

1. The candlelight can <u>flicker</u>. I just felt a <u>flicker</u> of a chill.	**2.** Butterflies <u>flutter</u> to and fro. My stomach is starting to <u>flutter</u>.
3. The leaves <u>shiver</u> in the breeze. **Cold weather makes me <u>shiver</u>.**	**4.** The fire will soon <u>sputter</u> and die. **I'm so happy, I'm starting to <u>sputter</u>.**

38   Unit 3 • Chapter 13   Vocabulary Power

REACHING ALL LEARNERS   **ESL**

JOINING SENTENCES Provide children with a word card for *and* and pairs of sentence strips with sentences that have the same subject, such as the following: *Ming runs. Ming catches the ball.* Have children cut apart the sentence strips, combine the verb parts of the two sentences by using the word card *and*, and read aloud the sentence.

Ming runs   and   catches the ball

Remember
When the naming parts of two sentences are the same, you can join the sentences by using *and*.

Independent Practice

Use *and* to join each pair of sentences. Write the new sentence.

5. Chris brushes the horses.
   Chris cleans the stable.
   Chris brushes the horses and cleans the stable.

6. Von washes dogs.
   Von clips their nails.
   Von washes dogs and clips their nails.

7. Vets help sick animals.
   Vets check healthy animals.
   Vets help sick animals and check healthy animals.

8. Tanya cares for bees.
   Tanya collects honey.
   Tanya cares for bees and collects honey.

9. Rangers help wild animals.
   Rangers teach about animals.
   Rangers help wild animals and teach about animals.

10. Some scientists study the ocean.
    Some scientists learn about fish.
    Some scientists study the ocean and learn about fish.

Writing Connection
Revising Look through your Writing Portfolio. Choose one piece of writing. Find the naming parts in your sentences. Which sentences could you combine? Revise your writing.

 Use your computer to help you combine sentences.

175

Independent Practice
Have children complete the Independent Practice, or modify it by using the following suggestions:

MODIFIED INSTRUCTION

BELOW-LEVEL STUDENTS Suggest that children circle the part of each sentence that is the same to help them figure out how to combine the verbs.

ABOVE-LEVEL STUDENTS After children are finished, invite them to write additional sentence pairs in which the naming parts are the same. Then have them trade sentences with a partner and combine each other's sentence pairs.

Writing Connection
Revising Help children to select appropriate pieces of writing to revise, as needed. Suggest they underline the sentences they will combine.

WRAP-UP/ASSESS

SUMMARIZE Have children summarize and reflect about what they know about combining sentences that have the same naming parts. **REFLECTION**

RETEACH

INTERVENTION Lessons in **visual**, **auditory**, and **kinesthetic** modalities: p. R25 and *Reteach Activities Copying Masters*, p. 27.

page 27

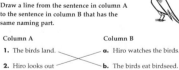

PRACTICE page 43

Name _____

Combining Sentences with Verbs

A. Draw a line from the sentence in column A to the sentence in column B that has the same naming part.

Column A | Column B
1. The birds land. | a. Hiro watches the birds.
2. Hiro looks out the window. | b. The birds eat birdseed.
3. A cat sees the birds. | c. A cat chases them away.

B. Use *and* to join each sentence pair above that has the same naming part. Write the new sentences on the lines.

4. The birds land and eat birdseed.
5. Hiro looks out the window and watches the birds.
6. A cat sees the birds and chases them away.

TRY THIS! Write two sentences about an animal. Make sure the sentences have the same naming part. Then trade papers with a classmate. Join the sentences by using *and*.

Practice • Present-Tense Verbs   Unit 3 • Chapter 13 43

CHALLENGE

VERB SEARCH Provide children with old newspapers, and invite them to find and cut out examples of sentences in which two telling parts have been combined. Have them glue their examples on paper, discuss them, and then display them on a bulletin board titled "Writers Combine Sentences."

---

page 27

Combining Sentences with Verbs

Read each group of sentences. Circle the naming part in each sentence. Underline the word that joins the sentences.

1. Min runs. Min jumps.
   Min runs and jumps.

2. The frog leaps. The frog hops.
   The frog leaps and hops.

Combining Sentences with Verbs

Read each pair of sentences. Then cut apart the matching sentence strips. Glue them in the boxes to join the sentences. Cut off the parts you don't need.

1. The cats cuddle. The cats purr.
   The cats cuddle | and | purr

2. The rabbit looks in the garden. The rabbit finds lettuce.
   The rabbit looks in the garden | and | finds lettuce

   The cats cuddle. | The cats purr.
   The rabbit looks in the garden. | The rabbit finds lettuce.

Reteach Activities • Present-Tense Verbs   Unit 3 • Chapter 13 27

Extra Practice

OBJECTIVES

- To recognize when to add *s* or *es* to a present-tense verb
- To use *and* to combine verbs in sentences

DAILY LANGUAGE PRACTICE
TRANSPARENCY 26

1 Aisha reeds the book and Aisha takes nots. (reads; and takes notes)

2 The cats watches the read bird. (watch; red)

BRIDGE TO WRITING Bob opens the door (and) lets the cats out.

ORAL WARM-UP

PLAY SIMON SAYS Play a short game of "Simon Says" with children. Then ask them to use complete sentences to describe the different actions they see. Try to work *scamper*, a Vocabulary Power word, into the game.

TEACH/MODEL

Read each set of directions to help children understand how to complete each section. Have children share their answers in small groups before you read aloud the correct answers.

WRAP-UP/ASSESS

SUMMARIZE Ask children to reflect on and discuss any special problems they had in completing the practice before you have them summarize what they have learned about verbs.

ADDITIONAL PRACTICE Extra practice items are provided on page 470 of the *Pupil Edition* (R4 *Teacher's Edition*).

TECHNOLOGY

Grammar Practice and Assessment CD-ROM

Writing Express CD-ROM

INTERNET Visit *The Learning Site!*
www.harcourtschool.com

Extra Practice

Write the verb in each sentence.

1. Mia <u>calls</u> her cats Fred and Barney.
2. Fred <u>eats</u> all the time.
3. Barney <u>sleeps</u> most of the day.
4. The two cats <u>race</u> all around the house.

Write the verb in ( ) to finish each sentence. Add *s* or *es* if you need to.

5. Mia and little Paco (play) with the cats.
   play
6. Mia (tell) Paco to be careful.
   tells
7. Paco (touch) the cats gently.
   touches
8. Fred and Barney (purr) happily.
   purr

Read each pair of sentences. Use *and* to join them. Write the new sentence.

9. The cat meows.
   The cat jumps on Mia's lap.
   The cat meows and jumps on Mia's lap.
10. Barney jumps up.
    Barney knocks over a cup.
    Barney jumps up and knocks over a cup.

176

Vocabulary Power page 39

Name _____   Rhyming Words

Some rhyming words have similar meanings. Most don't. Circle the words that rhyme and have a similar meaning.

float—coat   (shake—quake)   tickle—pickle

Write rhyming words for the word in dark print. Draw and label a picture for one of the rhyming words.

Possible responses include:

| flutter | butter | flicker | quicker |
| clutter | mutter | slicker | wicker |

| quiver | liver | flash | dash |
| sliver | giver | mash | clash |

Vocabulary Power   Unit 3 • Chapter 13   39

REACHING ALL LEARNERS **ESL**

INTERACTIVE WRITING You may wish to have children write the to-do list on page 177 as an interactive writing activity. Work with small groups to brainstorm a list of things that the class has to do during the course of the school day. Record the list on chart paper, inviting children to "share the pen." Then have children edit the list to conform to the criteria on *Teacher's Edition* page 177.

Language Play

Roll a Verb
- Take turns with a partner. Roll two number cubes. Add up the numbers.
- Use the verb in a sentence. You get one point for each verb used correctly.
- The first player with five points wins.

brush 2	
hug 3	watch 4
feed 5	teach 6
comb 7	wash 8
hold 9	train 10
bark 11	climb 12

Writing Connection

Functional Writing: To-Do List A to-do list can help you remember what you have to do. Make your own to-do list. Begin each sentence in the list with an action verb.

> To Do
> • See Mrs. Ralph about the art show.
> • Play soccer at 3:30.
> • Meet Mom at her office at 5:00.
> • Write spelling words before dinner.

177

Language Play

Have children play "Roll a Verb" in pairs. Model how to roll two number cubes and find the corresponding verb. After children roll for a verb, they can either write a sentence or say one, adding *s* or *es* as needed.

Writing Connection

Functional Writing: To-Do List Check to see that children have successfully written a to-do list by using the criteria below.

CRITERIA
- ☑ Writes sentences that are short.
- ☑ Begins each sentence with an action verb.
- ☑ Begins each sentence with a capital letter.
- ☑ Punctuates the sentences correctly.

PORTFOLIO OPPORTUNITY You may want to have children place their writing in their portfolios or take it home to share with family members.

PRACTICE page 44

Name_____

Extra Practice

A. Underline the verb in each sentence. Then write it in the puzzle.

1. Patrick <u>plays</u> with his dog, Rex.
2. They <u>tease</u> each other.
3. Patrick <u>hides</u> Rex's toy.

(crossword puzzle: 1. p l a y s; 2. t e a s e; 3. h i d e s)

B. Write the verb from the box that best completes each sentence. Add *s* or *es* if you need to do so.

put	get	rush

4. The dog ___gets___ the toy from its hiding place.
5. The dog ___puts___ the toy near Patrick.

C. Use *and* to join the sentences. Write the new sentence.

6. The dog watches Patrick. The dog grabs the toy.
   The dog watches Patrick and grabs the toy.

7. Dad smiles. Dad gives Patrick another toy.
   Dad smiles and gives Patrick another toy.

44 Unit 3 • Chapter 13   Practice • Present-Tense Verbs

CHALLENGE

PET SENTENCES Ask children to write sentences about taking care of a real or imaginary pet, using as many verbs as they can from the verb boxes in Language Play. Children can share their writing in small groups.

Chapter Review

OBJECTIVES

- To review present-tense verbs and when to add the endings *s* or *es*; review combining verbs in sentences
- To use synonyms for commonly used verbs to make writing more interesting

DAILY LANGUAGE PRACTICE

TRANSPARENCY 26

1 Do you know why Jane brush the horse. (brushes; horse?)

2 marco fix the door. (Marco; fixes)

BRIDGE TO WRITING The horse (verb) over the hill.

STANDARDIZED TEST PREP

Read each set of directions with children to make sure they understand how to complete each section. You may wish to have children complete this page independently and use it as an assessment.

TEST PREPARATION TIP
Item Type: Multiple Choice

 TIP

Model this strategy to help children determine the correct answer:

How many people or animals are in the naming part of the sentence? I see one: Dr. Jackson. Does the verb end with *ss*, *ch*, *sh*, or *x*? No, so I know that the verb needs to end with *s*. *Works* already ends with *s*. I look at the three answer choices and find *c. correct as is*. Then I reread the sentence to check that it makes sense.

Present-Tense Verbs

Chapter Review

Choose the correct answer for each underlined word.

1. Dr. Jackson <u>works</u> in an animal hospital.

   a. work

   b. workes

   <u>c. correct as is</u>

2. Maria <u>tell</u> the vet that Gus cut his leg.

   <u>a. tells</u>

   b. telles

   c. correct as is

3. She and the nurse <u>wash</u> Gus's cut.

   a. washs

   b. washes

   <u>c. correct as is</u>

4. Then Dr. Jackson <u>stitch</u> the cut.

   a. stitchs

   <u>b. stitches</u>

   c. correct as is

Use *and* to join the pair of sentences. Write the new sentence.

5. Maria gives Gus a treat. Maria takes him home.

   Maria gives Gus a treat and takes him home.

6. Gus feels better now. Gus wags his tail.

   Gus feels better now and wags his tail.

 Visit our website for more activities with verbs:
www.harcourtschool.com

178

Language Skills Assessment

PORTFOLIO ASSESSMENT
Have children select their best work from the following activities:

- **Writing Connection** *pages 173, 175, 177;* TE activities, *pages 171, 175, 177.*

ONGOING ASSESSMENT
Evaluate the performance of 4-6 children using the appropriate checklists and record forms on pages R65–R68 and R77–R79.

INTERNET Activities and exercises to help children prepare for state and standardized assessments appear on *The Learning Site:*
www.harcourtschool.com

■ Vocabulary ■

Synonyms for Verbs

A **synonym** is a word that means the same or almost the same as another word. Using synonyms for some verbs can make your writing more interesting.

They **walk** to the lake.
They **march** to the lake.
They **stroll** to the lake.

Practice

Write two synonyms for each underlined verb. Then choose one synonym, and rewrite the sentence. Possible responses are given.

1. A bear and her cubs <u>run</u> to the lake. race   dash

2. The bear <u>gets</u> some fish. catches   grabs

3. The cubs <u>look</u> at her. stare   gaze

4. The bears <u>jump</u> on a rock. hop   leap

5. Then they all <u>eat</u> the fish. gobble   taste

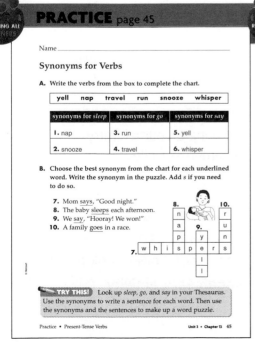

179

■ Vocabulary ■

Synonyms for Verbs

TEACH/MODEL

On the board write the following verbs.

hop	crawl
run	jump
creep	race
rush	jog

Ask volunteers to draw lines between the verb pairs that mean the same or almost the same and then read them aloud. Explain that words that mean the same or almost the same are called *synonyms*.

PRACTICE When children are finished, have volunteers share their sentences with classmates.

WRAP-UP/ASSESS

SUMMARIZE Ask children to tell what they have learned about synonyms for verbs and explain how using synonyms of verbs might make their writing more interesting.

PRACTICE page 45

Name _____

Synonyms for Verbs

A. Write the verbs from the box to complete the chart.

yell	nap	travel	run	snooze	whisper

synonyms for *sleep*	synonyms for *go*	synonyms for *say*
1. nap	3. run	5. yell
2. snooze	4. travel	6. whisper

B. Choose the best synonym from the chart for each underlined word. Write the synonym in the puzzle. Add *s* if you need to do so.

7. Mom <u>says</u>, "Good night."
8. The baby <u>sleeps</u> each afternoon.
9. We <u>say</u>, "Hooray! We won!"
10. A family <u>goes</u> in a race.

TRY THIS! Look up *sleep*, *go*, and *say* in your Thesaurus. Use the synonyms to write a sentence for each word. Then use the synonyms and the sentences to make up a word puzzle.

Practice • Present-Tense Verbs   Unit 1 • Chapter 13   45

CHALLENGE

REVISE YOUR WRITING Suggest that children select a piece of writing from their Writing Portfolios and replace some of the verbs they used with more exact synonyms. Encourage them to use the thesaurus at the back of their books.

speak   talk   say   tell

LESSON ORGANIZER	DAY 1	DAY 2
DAILY LANGUAGE PRACTICE 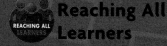 TRANSPARENCIES 27, 28	1. The child watchs and water the plants. (watches; waters) 2. She walk in the garden. She sees the flowers. (walks; and sees) **Bridge to Writing** Sue _(present-tense verb)_ the flowers.	1. Now I walked to the store (walk; .) 2. Mom cooked the eggs and, served themm. (and served; them) **Bridge to Writing** Dad _(past-tense verb)_ by the pond yesterday.
ORAL WARM-UP **Listening/Speaking**	Act Out a Plant Growing p. 180	Word Association p. 182 *Grammar Jingles*™ CD, Primary, Track
TEACH/MODEL GRAMMAR **KEY** ✔ = tested skill	✔ **VERBS THAT TELL ABOUT THE PAST** pp. 180-181 • To listen critically to interpret and dramatize a poem • To recognize that a verb can tell about an action that happened in the past	✔ **ADDING *ED* TO VERBS** pp. 182-183 • To recognize that most verbs that tell about the past end in *ed* • To use past-tense verbs in writing
Reaching All Learners	*Practice Book* p. 46 **Challenge:** Activity Card 10, p. R50 **ESL:** *ESL Manual* pp. 70–71 **Reteach:** *Reteach Activities Copying Masters* p. 28	**Modified Instruction** Below-Level: Add Yesterday to the Sentence Above-Level: Write Sentences **Challenge:** Silly Sentences p. 183 **ESL:** Say the Verb p. 182 *ESL Manual* p. 70, p. 72 *Practice Book* p. 47 **Reteach:** *Reteach Activities Copying Masters* p. 29
WRITING	Write Verbs In the Past p. 181 Summarize/Reflect	Writing Connection p. 183 Writing a Journal Entry Summarize/Reflect
CROSS-CURRICULAR/ ENRICHMENT	**Vocabulary Power** Word Meaning p. 180 **consulting,** communicate, confer, converse, recommend See *Vocabulary Power* book.	**Vocabulary Power** Synonyms p. 180 *Vocabulary Power* book p. 40 **Vocabulary activity**

DAY 3

1. they look at the stars last night. (They; looked)

2. It rain yesterday? (rained; .)

Bridge to Writing Ramon (past-tense verb) a cake last week.

Act Out Action Verbs p. 184
 Grammar Jingles™ CD, Primary, Track 9

✔ **CHANGING VERBS THAT END WITH *E*** pp. 184-185
  • To understand that when a verb ends with *e*, the letter *e* is dropped before adding *ed*
  • To revise writing to include correct past-tense verb forms

- - - - - - - - - - - - - - - - - -

Modified Instruction
  Below-Level: Cross Out Final *e*
  Above-Level: Write Verbs
Challenge: Rhyming Verbs
  p. 185
ESL: Adding *ed* p. 184
  ESL Manual pp. 70, 73
  Practice Book p. 48
Reteach: *Reteach Activities Copying Masters* p. 30

- - - - - - - - - - - - - - - - - -

Writing Connection p. 185
  Revising
  Summarize/Reflect

Vocabulary Power
  Word Families p. 180
  Vocabulary Power book p. 41
  Vocabulary activity

DAY 4

1. sue race to the show yesterday. (Sue; raced)

2. Max danceed with Nadia Last week. (danced; last)

Bridge to Writing Jill (past-tense verb) with Tim yesterday.

Memory Game p. 186

EXTRA PRACTICE p. 186
  • To understand and write the correct past-tense form of verbs that end in *e*
  • To use verbs that tell about the past in writing
Practice and Assessment

- - - - - - - - - - - - - - - - - -

Challenge: Plant Poems p. 187
ESL: What Did You Do? p. 186
  ESL Manual pp. 70, 74
  Practice Book p. 49

- - - - - - - - - - - - - - - - - -

Writing Connection p. 187
  A Friendly Letter

Vocabulary Power
  Abbreviations p. 180
  Vocabulary Power book p. 42
  Language Play p. 187
  Vocabulary activity

DAY 5

1. Who watch the show last night. (watched; ?)

2. i likeed the show last night. (I; liked)

Bridge to Writing They (past-tense verb) with friends yesterday.

TEST PREP **CHAPTER REVIEW** p. 188
  • To review past-tense verbs and how to form them
  • To locate entry words in a dictionary
Test Preparation

- - - - - - - - - - - - - - - - - -

Practice Book p. 50
Challenge: Make a Poster p. 189
ESL Manual p. 70, p. 75

- - - - - - - - - - - - - - - - - -

Study Skills p. 189
  Using a Dictionary Entry

Vocabulary Power
  Classify/Categorize p. 180

Verbs That Tell About the Past

CHAPTER 14

Past-Tense Verbs

OBJECTIVES

- To listen critically to interpret and dramatize a poem
- To recognize that a verb can tell about an action that happened in the past

SPIRAL REVIEW

DAILY LANGUAGE PRACTICE

TRANSPARENCY 27

1 The child watchs and water the plants. (watches; waters)

2 She walk in the garden. She sees the flowers. (walks; and sees)

BRIDGE TO WRITING Sue (present-tense verb) the flowers.

ORAL WARM-UP

USE PRIOR KNOWLEDGE Ask children to act out a plant growing from a seed and then tell about the actions using past-tense verbs. Begin a list of past-tense verbs on chart paper or add the words to your **Verb Word Wall.**

TEACH/MODEL

Have children open to page 180. Read aloud the first line, and then ask children to predict what happens next. Finish reading the poem. Ask children to listen for words that tell about past actions.

DEVELOP ORAL LANGUAGE Reread the poem with children. Ask children to name the actions in the poem. Invite volunteers to think about other actions and to pantomime them. Add past-tense verbs they think of to the list on chart paper or to the **Word Wall.**

Verbs That Tell About the Past

Read the poem.

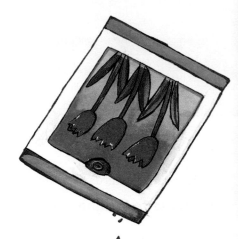

Tommy

I put a seed into the ground
And said, "I'll watch it grow."
I watered it and cared for it
As well as I could know.

One day I walked in my backyard,
And oh, what did I see!
My seed had popped itself right out,
Without consulting me.

Gwendolyn Brooks

180

Vocabulary Power

DAY 1 WORD MEANING Write: *consulting.* **Find this word in the poem "Tommy." What does it mean?** (asking, exchanging ideas with)

DAY 2 SYNONYMS Write *consulting, asking, forgetting.* **Which two words have similar meanings?** (See also *Vocabulary Power,* page 40.)

DAY 3 WORD FAMILIES List: *consulted, consulting.* **How are these words alike? Different?** (See also *Vocabulary Power,* page 41.)

DAY 4 ABBREVIATIONS Write: *Let's consult Dr. Appleton.* **What does the underlined word mean? Why would you consult a doctor?** (See also *Vocabulary Power,* page 42.)

DAY 5 CLASSIFY/CATEGORIZE List children's interests, such as animals or stars. **Whom would you consult to learn more about your interest?** Use the following during discussion: *communicate, confer, converse, recommend.*

Think about something you did.
Maybe you planted a seed or made a
craft. Show or tell about what happened.
Then write verbs that tell what happened.

> A **verb** can tell about an action that
> happened in the past.
>
> Last week I **played** in my backyard.
>
> I **watered** the plant yesterday.

**Write a verb that tells about the past in
each sentence.**

Last spring I _____ seeds.

I _____ the dirt.

I _____ all the weeds.

Every day I _____ the seeds.

At last a plant _____ up.

181

WRITE Ask volunteers to read their verbs
aloud. Explain that they have told about
something that was done or that has
already happened. In their sentences,
they used **past-tense verbs** to tell about
the past. Have children identify the past-
tense verbs in the example. Ask them
how they know the action happened in
the past. (because of the words *last week*
and *yesterday*)

Organize children into pairs. Direct
them to the first item at the bottom of
page 181. Explain that they should work
with their partners to fill in the blank
with a verb that tells what happened in
the past.

WRAP-UP/ASSESS

SUMMARIZE Have children summarize and reflect on what they
have learned about past-tense
verbs. Ask children to write
their reflections in their journals.

REFLECTION

RETEACH

INTERVENTION Lessons in **visual,
auditory,** and **kinesthetic** modalities: p. R26 and *Reteach Activities
Copying Masters*, p. 28.

PRACTICE page 46

Name _____

Verbs That Tell About the Past

A. Underline the verb in each sentence that
tells about the past. Write it on the line.

1. The bird landed on the grass. _____ landed
2. It picked up a worm. _____ picked
3. Two squirrels climbed up a tree. _____ climbed
4. They stuffed their cheeks with acorns. _____ stuffed
5. The squirrels played in the tree. _____ played

B. Use a word from the box to complete each sentence.
Possible responses are given.

watched	jumped	buzzed	leaped	crawled

6. A rabbit _____ leaped _____ on the grass.
7. A snake _____ crawled _____ near the rabbit.
8. Some bees _____ buzzed _____ around.
9. Frogs _____ jumped _____ by the pond.
10. The children _____ watched _____ the animals.

TRY THIS! Write two sentences about animals you have
seen outside your home or school. Use verbs that tell about the past.

46   Unit 3 • Chapter 14   Practice • Past-Tense Verbs

CHALLENGE

YESTERDAY Have children use
Challenge Activity Card 10
(page R50) to record what they
did yesterday. Then have children
display their plates and talk about
what they did. Call on volunteers
to act out some of the actions.

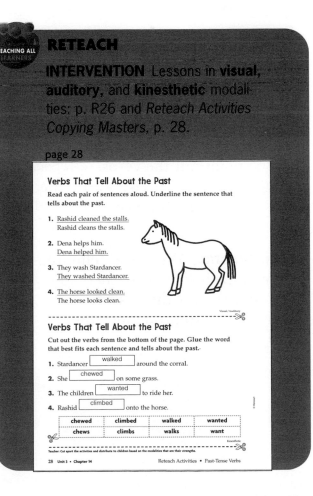

Challenge Activity Card 10

Yesterday

You need:
• paper plate
• crayons or markers

1. Draw lines to make four parts on a paper plate.
2. Write a word in each part: morning, afternoon, evening, and night.
3. In each part, write things you did yesterday at that time.

page 28

Verbs That Tell About the Past

Read each pair of sentences aloud. Underline the sentence that
tells about the past.

1. Rashid cleaned the stalls.
   Rashid cleans the stalls.

2. Dena helps him.
   Dena helped him.

3. They wash Stardancer.
   They washed Stardancer.

4. The horse looked clean.
   The horse looks clean.

Verbs That Tell About the Past

Cut out the verbs from the bottom of the page. Glue the word
that best fits each sentence and tells about the past.

1. Stardancer _____ walked _____ around the corral.
2. She _____ chewed _____ on some grass.
3. The children _____ wanted _____ to ride her.
4. Rashid _____ climbed _____ onto the horse.

chewed	climbed	walked	wanted
chews	climbs	walks	want

28   Unit 3 • Chapter 14   Reteach Activities • Past-Tense Verbs

Adding *ed* to Verbs

OBJECTIVES
- To recognize that most verbs that tell about the past end in *ed*
- To use past-tense verbs in writing

DAILY LANGUAGE PRACTICE

TRANSPARENCY 27

1 Now I walked to the store (walk; .)

2 Mom cooked the eggs and, served themm. (and served them)

BRIDGE TO WRITING Dad _____ (past-tense verb by the pond yesterday.

ORAL WARM-UP

WORD ASSOCIATION Say a past-tense verb related to the outdoors. Ask a volunteer to say another past-tense verb he or she associates with the verb you said. Continue with each child, in turn.

***Grammar Jingles*™ CD, Primary** Use Track 9 for review and reinforcement of past-tense verbs.

TEACH/MODEL

Introduce the concept of verbs that tell about the past by using the explanation and the examples. Have children identify the words that tell when each action took place. (*last night, yesterday*) Then ask them to point out the verbs. (*cleaned, fished*) Ask: **How do you know the verbs tell about the past?** (They end in *ed*.)

GUIDED PRACTICE Work with children to complete each sentence. Encourage them to listen for the *ed* endings. Remind them to pronounce the *ed* clearly.

Adding *ed* to Verbs

> Many verbs end with **ed** to tell about something that happened in the past.
>
> Last night I **cleaned** my tent.
>
> Yesterday I **fished** in the river.

Guided Practice

Write the verb that tells about the past.

1. Yesterday we (<u>walked</u>, walk) up a steep mountain.

2. In the morning I (pack, <u>packed</u>) my backpack.

3. I (<u>stuffed</u>, stuff) a sweater into the backpack.

4. I (<u>added</u>, add) a bottle of water.

5. We (climb, <u>climbed</u>) all afternoon.

182

Vocabulary Power page 40

Name _____   Synonyms

Synonyms have similar meanings. The following words are synonyms.

talk—speak   trade—exchange   send—transmit

Think about the meaning of the underlined word. Choose and write the word that has a similar meaning.

1. The nurse is <u>consulting</u> the doctor.
   agreeing   asking   writing   _asking_
2. My friend and I <u>converse</u> by phone.
   speak   giggle   explore   _speak_
3. My parents <u>confer</u> with my teacher.
   travel   instruct   meet   _meet_
4. I <u>recommend</u> that you read this book.
   advise   order   understand   _advise_
5. Writing is one way to <u>communicate</u> ideas.
   forget   observe   express   _express_

Draw pictures to show different ways to <u>communicate</u>.

40 Unit 3 • Chapter 14   Vocabulary Power

ESL

REACHING ALL LEARNERS

SAY THE VERB Help children hear the difference in pronunciation between a present- and past-tense verb. Say and act out sentences, such as: *Now I walk. Yesterday I walked.* Repeat the first sentence. Then say *Yesterday I . . .* and have children complete it. Repeat the answer (*I walked*). Repeat with other verbs, such as *dance, jump,* and *rest.*

Remember Many verbs end with *ed* to tell about something that happened in the past.

Independent Practice

Write the verb that tells about the past.

6. Ned (leaps, <u>leaped</u>) over logs.

7. Sara (<u>gathered</u>, gathers) acorns.

8. Everyone (collects, <u>collected</u>) leaves from the ground.

9. We (<u>jumped</u>, jump) on rocks near the river.

10. We (rest, <u>rested</u>) for an hour.

11. Ned (<u>fished</u>, fishes) in the river.

12. He (pulls, <u>pulled</u>) out a little fish.

13. Ned (<u>tossed</u>, toss) it back into the water.

14. Then the wind (turns, <u>turned</u>) cold.

15. We (walk, <u>walked</u>) back down the mountain.

Writing Connection

Writing a Journal Entry Think about a walk you have taken. Draw pictures that show things you did. Write a sentence about each picture. Use verbs that show that the actions happened in the past.

Save your work on your computer. You can add more details later.

183

Independent Practice

Have children complete the Independent Practice, or modify it by using the following suggestions:

MODIFIED INSTRUCTION

BELOW-LEVEL STUDENTS Have children circle the verbs and underline their endings. Suggest they add the word *yesterday* to the sentence to help them decide which verb to choose.

ABOVE-LEVEL STUDENTS After children are finished, invite them to write two sentences of their own that tell about what someone might have done when he or she camped.

Writing Connection

Writing a Journal Entry Remind children to use past-tense verbs that tell what they saw, heard, smelled, and felt on their walk. Have volunteers place their sentences in the Sharing Basket to share with others.

WRAP-UP/ASSESS

SUMMARIZE Ask children to write a brief summary of what they have learned about past-tense verbs in their journals.

REFLECTION

RETEACH

INTERVENTION Lessons in **visual, auditory,** and **kinesthetic** modalities: p. R26 and *Reteach Activities Copying Masters*, p. 29.

PRACTICE page 47

Name _____

Adding *ed* to Verbs

A. Circle the ending that was added to each verb to tell about the past.

1. Kate milk(ed) the cows.
2. The cow push(ed) the calf gently.
3. Joshua lift(ed) the bucket.
4. He dump(ed) the hay on the ground.
5. The cows chew(ed) on the food.

B. Change the verb in ( ) to tell about the past.

6. Kate (pour) _____poured_____ water in a bucket.
7. Joshua (fill) _____filled_____ another one.
8. The animals (enjoy) _____enjoyed_____ the cool water.
9. The cows (rest) _____rested_____ .
10. The children (finish) _____finished_____ their chores.

TRY THIS! Write two sentences that tell about chores you have done. Use verbs that tell about the past in your sentences.

Practice • Past-Tense Verbs   Unit 3 • Chapter 14   47

CHALLENGE

SILLY SENTENCES Have children work in pairs. Each child writes two sentences that tell about the past but leaves out the past-tense verbs. Then, without hearing the sentences, have each partner supply two past-tense verbs that end in *ed* for his or her partner's sentences. Partners write, and then share and revise the completed sentences.

I <u>opened</u> the brown bag.
I <u>watched</u> the brown bear.

page 29

Adding *ed* to Verbs

Read each sentence aloud. Circle the ending that was added to each verb to make it tell about the past.

EXAMPLE: The eggshells crack(ed)

1. The ducklings hatch(ed)
2. They stretch(ed) their wings.
3. The mother duck quack(ed) proudly.
4. She walk(ed) to the pond.
5. The ducklings follow(ed) her.

- -

Adding *ed* to Verbs

Cut out the verbs at the bottom of the page. Glue the word that best fits each sentence. Circle the part of each verb that makes it tell about the past.

1. A duckling ___splashed___ in the pond.
2. It ___opened___ its bill.
3. Ross ___tossed___ bread into the pond.
4. The duckling ___snatched___ the food.

| snatched | opened | splashed | tossed |

Teacher: Cut apart the activities and distribute to children based on the modalities that are their strengths.

Reteach Activities • Past-Tense Verbs   Unit 3 • Chapter 14   29

Changing Verbs That End with *e*

OBJECTIVES
- To understand that when a verb ends with *e*, the letter *e* is dropped before adding *ed*
- To revise a selected piece of writing to include correct past-tense verb forms

DAILY LANGUAGE PRACTICE

TRANSPARENCY 27

1 they look at the stars last night.
(They; looked)

2 It rain yesterday? (rained; .)

BRIDGE TO WRITING Ramon _____ (past-tense verb) a cake last week.

ORAL WARM-UP

USE PRIOR KNOWLEDGE Write the verbs *wave*, *race*, and *dance* on the board and have volunteers act them out. Then ask other children to use the past tense of these verbs to tell what the volunteers did. Write each past-tense verb on the board under its present-tense form. Have volunteers point out how the past-tense verbs were formed.

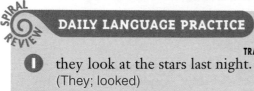

***Grammar Jingles*™ CD, Primary** Use Track 9 for review and reinforcement of past-tense verbs.

TEACH/MODEL

Introduce the concept by using the explanation and the examples. Write the first verb on the board. Discuss what word you get when you add *ed*. (*likeed*) Explain that the *e* needs to be removed before the *ed* is added.

GUIDED PRACTICE Work through the first item together. Have children say the past-tense verb and then decide how to spell it. Call on a volunteer to supply the answer. Repeat for the remaining items.

Changing Verbs That End with *e*

> If a verb ends with the letter **e**, drop the **e** before adding **ed**.
>
> They **like** red leaves.
> Last fall they **liked** red leaves.
>
> I **rake** the leaves.
> Last week I **raked** the leaves.

Guided Practice

Write the verb in ( ) to tell about the past.

1. The hikers (hope) for a sunny day. hoped
2. Mom (pile) wood on the fire. piled
3. Dad (place) a pan of water on the fire. placed
4. Karen (share) her bread with the birds. shared
5. They (hike) all day. hiked

184

Vocabulary Power page 41

Name _____   Word Families

The following words belong to the same word family. Underline the base word in each.

consulting   consultant   consultation

1. Write the base word at the top of each word ladder.

confer	converse
conferred	converses
conferring	conversing
conference	conversation
recommend	communicate
recommended	communicates
recommending	communicating
recommendation	communication

2. Get together with some classmates. Have a conference. Converse about your favorite books. Ask each other to make recommendations. Draw a picture to show how you and your friends communicated.

Vocabulary Power   Unit 3 • Chapter 14   41

REACHING ALL LEARNERS   **ESL**

ADDING *ed* Provide children with two letter cards—*e* and *d* and word cards for verbs ending in *e*, such as *hike*, *hope*, *race*, and *face*. Have children talk with each other to form the past-tense of the verbs by putting the letter cards in the correct place.

Remember If a verb ends with the letter *e*, drop the *e* before adding *ed*.

Independent Practice

Write the verb in ( ) to tell about the past.

6. The family (like) to hike early. liked

7. They (line) up to walk on the trail. lined

8. Mark (time) the hike with his watch. timed

9. Mom saw a nest where a bird (live). lived

10. Karen (love) the birds. loved

11. She (surprise) the bird with a piece of bread. surprised

12. She (save) the bread from breakfast. saved

13. The family (arrive) at the tent on time. arrived

14. Mark (dance) because he was glad. danced

15. Everyone (celebrate). celebrated

Writing Connection

Revising Look through your Writing Portfolio. Choose a story. Check the past-tense verbs to make sure you wrote them correctly.

You can highlight incorrect past-tense verbs with your mouse and then type in the correct verb.

185

Independent Practice

Have children complete the Independent Practice, or modify it by using the following suggestions:

MODIFIED INSTRUCTION

BELOW-LEVEL STUDENTS Suggest that children cross out the final *e* in each word before adding *ed*.

ABOVE-LEVEL STUDENTS After children have finished, have them write additional verbs that end in *e* that would fit some of the sentences.

Writing Connection

Revising Help children select appropriate pieces of writing to revise as needed. Suggest that they use colored pencils to circle past-tense verbs that need to be corrected.

WRAP-UP/ASSESS

SUMMARIZE Ask children to summarize and reflect on what they know about changing verbs that end in *e*. After children write their thoughts in their journals, have them share their ideas with a partner. **REFLECTION**

RETEACH

INTERVENTION Lessons in **visual**, **auditory**, and **kinesthetic** modalities: p. R26 and *Reteach Activities Copying Masters*, p. 30.

PRACTICE page 48

Name _____

Changing Verbs That End with *e*

A. Change the verb in ( ) to tell about the past.

1. The goat (poke) the fence. poked

2. It (move) quickly. moved

3. Gina (close) the gate. closed

4. The children (tease) the animal. teased

5. The goat (chase) after them. chased

B. Change the verb in each sentence to tell about the past. Write the new sentence.

6. Mom races outside.
   Mom raced outside.

7. She places the goat in the pen.
   She placed the goat in the pen.

8. Mom saves the day.
   Mom saved the day.

TRY THIS! Write two sentences about a pet you own or an animal you have seen. Describe things the animal did. Use verbs that tell about the past in your sentences.

48 Unit 3 • Chapter 14   Practice • Past-Tense Verbs

CHALLENGE

RHYMING VERBS Have children write some of the past-tense verbs that end in *e* from pages 184–185. Then have them list rhyming words under each verb. Children can share their lists and create poems using the rhyming words.

saved   paved   waved

---

page 30

Changing Verbs That End with *e*

Talk about the verbs. Draw a line from the verb in Column A to the form of that verb that tells about the past in Column B.

Column A	Column B
1. hike	raked
2. arrive	arrived
3. rake	hiked
4. share _____	shared

Changing Verbs That End with *e*

Cut out the letters below. Glue an ending to each verb. Put an X through the letter in each verb that should be dropped.

1. Mom hir**x** ed Cassie to work for her.

2. Cassie lin**x** ed the bird cage with newspaper.

3. Cassie plac**x** ed the bird inside.

4. Mom prais**x** ed Cassie for her hard work.

ed ed ed ed

30 Unit 3 • Chapter 14   Reteach Activities • Past-Tense Verbs

Extra Practice

OBJECTIVES
- To understand and write the correct past-tense form of verbs that end in *e*
- To use verbs that tell about the past in writing

DAILY LANGUAGE PRACTICE
TRANSPARENCY 28

1 sue race to the show yesterday.
(Sue; raced)

2 Max danceed with Nadia Last week.
(danced; last)

BRIDGE TO WRITING Jill past-tense verb
with Tim yesterday.

ORAL WARM-UP

MEMORY GAME Show a few pictures of children playing or doing other actions. Turn one of the pictures over. Have a volunteer recall what the child did on it. Repeat with the other pictures.

TEACH/MODEL

Read each set of directions to help children understand how to complete each section. Have children share their answers in small groups before you read aloud the answers.

WRAP-UP/ASSESS

SUMMARIZE Ask children to reflect on and discuss any special problems they had in completing the practice before you have them summarize what they have learned about verbs that tell about the past.

ADDITIONAL PRACTICE Additional items of Extra Practice are provided on page 470 of the *Pupil Edition* (R4 *Teachers Edition*).

TECHNOLOGY
Grammar Practice and Assessment CD-ROM
Writing Express CD-ROM

INTERNET Visit *The Learning Site!*
www.harcourtschool.com

Past-Tense Verbs

Extra Practice

Read each sentence. Write the verb that tells about the past.

1. It <u>snowed</u> outside last night.

2. We <u>picked</u> up our backpacks.

3. Dad <u>opened</u> the cabin door.

Write the verb in ( ) that tells about the past.

4. Ted (watches, <u>watched</u>) the snowflakes.

5. Mom (mixes, <u>mixed</u>) the hot chocolate.

6. We (<u>listened</u>, listens) to stories.

Write the verb in ( ) to tell about the past.

7. Kendra (tape) the stories. taped

8. She (invite) Ted to help. invited

9. Ted (hope) to hike in the snow. hoped

10. Kendra (promise) to go with him. promised

186

Vocabulary Power page 42

Name_____
Abbreviations

An abbreviation is a short way to write a word.

Street—St.   August—Aug.   President—Pres.

Write the abbreviations. Then answer the questions. Write or draw or do both. Share your ideas with classmates.

1. _Prof._ Ed James is an expert on space and space travel.
Professor
If you could confer with an expert on space, what would you ask?

2. _Pres._ George Washington was born in 1732.
President
If you could have a conversation with George Washington, what would you talk about?

3. _Dr._ Fritz works at _Mt._ J. Animal Hospital.
Doctor   Mount
How do you think an animal doctor communicates with animals?

42   Unit 3 • Chapter 14
Vocabulary Power

ESL
REACHING ALL LEARNERS

WHAT DID YOU DO? Place word cards with the verbs *dance, play, listen, walk, jump, climb,* and *rest* in a paper bag. Have a volunteer choose a verb and pantomime it to answer the question "What did you do yesterday?" The first child who guesses the action is the next leader. Write each past-tense answer on the board and say it aloud. Have children act it out as they repeat it after you.

Language Play

Act Out the Past
- Think of something you did in the past week.
- Act it out for a classmate.
- Have the classmate guess what you did. Tell about it, using past-tense verbs.
- Then have your classmate act out something for you to guess.

Writing Connection

A Friendly Letter Write a letter to a friend. Tell your friend what you did this past weekend. Remember to write your verbs in the past tense. Use the following letter as a model.

> 62 Sea Drive
>
> Orlando, Florida 32887
>
> March 5, 200–
>
> Dear Sal,
>
> On Saturday I cleaned my room. Then I helped my dad fix my bike. I played in a basketball game, too. Later my whole family watched a great movie. What did you do over the weekend?
>
> Your friend,
>
> Pete

187

Language Play

Have children play "Act Out the Past" in pairs. Model how to do this and emphasize that children should not use words while they are acting out their actions. After partners have acted out, they can write or tell about what each other did.

Writing Connection

A Friendly Letter Check to see that children have successfully written a friendly letter by using the criteria below. See also the rubric copying master on page R72, which may be adapted for this use and distributed to children for self-assessment.

CRITERIA
- ☑ Writes a heading and a greeting.
- ☑ Writes complete sentences that begin with capital letters and have correct end punctuation.
- ☑ Includes past-tense verbs in the appropriate sentences.
- ☑ Writes a closing and adds a signature.

> You may want to have children place their writing in their portfolios or e-mail it to friends or family members.

PRACTICE page 49

Name _____

Extra Practice

A. Underline the verb in each sentence that tells about the past.

1. Lou visited the zoo.

2. The lions roared.

3. They stayed in their cage.

B. Circle the verb that tells about the past. Write it on the line.

4. The tigers (walk, walked) __walked__ around.

5. A giraffe (stretch, stretched) __stretched__ its neck.

6. The seals (barked, bark) __barked__

C. Change the verb in ( ) to tell about the past. Write the new sentence.

7. Dylan (face) the monkey.

   Dylan faced the monkey.

8. He (smile) at the monkey.

   He smiled at the monkey.

Practice • Past-Tense Verbs   Unit 3 • Chapter 14   49

CHALLENGE

PLANT POEMS Have children choose a plant they would like to be. Then ask them to imagine they are that plant and write a poem about how they grew from a seed, using past-tense verbs. Have children illustrate the poem and then share it with a partner.

Chapter Review

OBJECTIVES

- To review past-tense verbs and how to form them by adding *ed* or dropping the *e* before adding *ed*
- To locate entry words in a dictionary and to recognize that some entry words have more than one meaning

DAILY LANGUAGE PRACTICE

TRANSPARENCY 28

1 Who watch the show last night. (watched; ?)

2 i likeed the show last night. (I; liked)

BRIDGE TO WRITING They _____ (past-tense verb) with friends yesterday.

STANDARDIZED TEST PREP

Read the directions with children to make sure they understand what they have to do. You may wish to have children complete this page independently and use it as an assessment.

TEST PREPARATION TIP
Item Type: Multiple Choice

 TIP

Model this strategy to help children determine the correct answer:

First I look for the verb in the sentence. I know that *enjoy* is a verb.

I know that many verbs that tell about the past end with *ed*. I look at the three answer choices. Item *c* is not the answer because the verb in the sentence does not end with *ed*. Item *b* does not work because the verb in *b* does not end with *ed*. The verb in *a* ends with *ed*, so it tells about the past. I choose *a*.

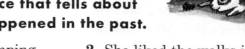

Chapter Review   STANDARDIZED TEST PREP

Choose the sentence that tells about something that happened in the past.

1. Jane enjoy her camping trip.
   a. Jane enjoyed her camping trip.
   b. Jane enjoys her camping trip.
   c. correct as is

2. She liked the walks in the woods.
   a. She likes the walks in the woods.
   b. She like the walks in the woods.
   c. correct as is

3. Jane watch a deer.
   a. Jane watches a deer.
   b. Jane watched a deer.
   c. correct as is

4. She followed a rabbit.
   a. She following a rabbit.
   b. She follows a rabbit.
   c. correct as is

5. Her friends walk with her.
   a. Her friends walked with her.
   b. Her friends walking with her.
   c. correct as is

6. They prepare sandwiches for lunch.
   a. They prepares sandwiches for lunch.
   b. They prepared sandwiches for lunch.
   c. correct as is

Visit our website for more activities with past-tense verbs:
www.harcourtschool.com

188

Language Skills Assessment

PORTFOLIO ASSESSMENT
Have children select their best work from the following activities:

- **Writing Connection**, *pages 183, 185, 187;* TE activities, *pages 181 and 187.*

ONGOING ASSESSMENT
Evaluate the performance of 4-6 students using appropriate checklists and record forms from pages R65–R68 and R77–R79.

INTERNET Activities and exercises to help students prepare for state and standardized assessments appear on *The Learning Site:*

www.harcourtschool.com

■Study Skills■

Using a Dictionary Entry

The words in dark print in a dictionary are called **entry words**. The entry words are listed in alphabetical order. If a word has more than one meaning, the meanings are numbered. Sometimes an example sentence is given to make a meaning clearer.

entry word → **pick** [pik] **1.** To choose: **We pick a movie we like. 2.** To eat without being hungry: **Sometimes I pick at my supper.**

meaning

example sentence

Practice

Use the dictionary entry to answer the questions.

1. What is the first meaning of the verb *pick*?
   to choose
2. What is the second meaning of *pick*?
   to eat without being hungry
3. Which entry word would come after *pick—pen*, *pie*, or *paddle*? pie

4. What is the example sentence for the first meaning of *pick*? We pick a movie we like.

5. Write your own example sentence for the second meaning of *pick*. Responses will vary.

189

■ Study Skills ■

Using a Dictionary Entry

TEACH/MODEL

Write these words on the board in alphabetical order: *liked, listened, lived, looked,* and *loved.* Ask children how the words are arranged. (in ABC order) Then ask them in which type of book they would see words in this kind of order. (in a dictionary) Explain that knowing how to find words in a dictionary will help them learn the meanings of new words and how to say them.

PRACTICE To help children complete the questions, you may want to model a response to the first item, such as *First, I look at the dictionary page to find the word* pick. *I see the number 1 and read the meaning. The first meaning is* "to choose." After children have finished, ask volunteers to share their answers.

WRAP-UP/ASSESS

SUMMARIZE Ask children to tell what they have learned about dictionary entries and to explain how the different parts of an entry can help them when reading and writing.

PRACTICE page 50

Name _____

Using a Dictionary Entry

bat 1. a wooden stick: *Bill hit the ball with the bat.* **2.** a kind of flying mammal that comes out at night: *Jill saw the bat fly down from the roof.*
beat 1. to hit: *I beat the drum.* **2.** to win: *I beat him in the race.*
bed 1. furniture made for sleeping: *Pascal rested on his*

bed. **2.** bottom layer: *The beans were on a bed of lettuce.*
begin to start: *The alphabet begins with the letter A.*
best 1. better than anything else: *Rosa is the best athlete.*
bold 1. very brave or confident: *The king was a bold leader.*
2. bright, like a color: *She wore a bold blue dress.*

A. Use the dictionary entries to answer the questions.

1. What entry word comes after the word *beat*? ___ bed

2. How many definitions are given for the word *bat*? ___ two

3. What is the meaning of the word *begin*? ___ to start

4. What does the word *beat* mean in this sentence? Gina beat Tim at checkers. ___ to win

TRY THIS! Choose four words from the sample dictionary page. Use each word in a sentence.

50 Unit 3 • Chapter 14   Practice • Past-Tense Verbs

CHALLENGE

MAKE A POSTER Have children work in groups to make a poster illustrating the parts of a dictionary entry. Invite them to use a word from the Word Wall or from a dictionary. Encourage children to use different colors for each part and to label their examples. Children can draw or cut out magazine pictures to illustrate their entries.

Writing Dialogue
pages 190–197

LESSON ORGANIZER	DAY 1	DAY 2
DAILY LANGUAGE PRACTICE	1. martha wave to George from the ground. (Martha waved) 2. george smiled down at her (George; her.)	1. clyde meow for help when his tail got stuck yesterday. (Clyde meowed) 2. midge open the door for him. (Midge opened)
ORAL WARM-UP Listening/Speaking	Ask and Answer Questions p. 190	Create Dialogue p. 192
TEACH/MODEL WRITING 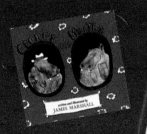	✔ **WRITING DIALOGUE** **Literature Model:** "The Flying Machine" from *George and Martha* pp. 190–191 **WRITER'S CRAFT** • To read and respond to dialogue as a model for writing • To read dialogue in a way that shows feelings **Think About It** p. 191	**GUIDED WRITING** **Using Quotations to Show Feeling** pp. 192–193 • To write sentences to show feeling • To write sentences as quotations using exact verbs • To rewrite sentences as dialogue **Writing and Thinking:** Reflect p. 193
Reaching All Learners	**ESL:** *ESL Manual* pp. 76–77	**ESL:** Correct Style p. 192 *ESL Manual* p. 76 **Challenge:** Skits and Quotes p. 193
GRAMMAR	**Unit 3 Review** pp. 236–237	**Unit 3 Review** pp. 236–237
CROSS-CURRICULAR/ ENRICHMENT **KEY** ✔ = tested writing form/skill	**Social Studies Connection:** Flight Firsts p. 191 **School-Home Connection:** More by Marshall p. 191 **Self-Initiated Writing** p. 191 **Vocabulary Power** **Word Meaning** p. 190 category, family, similar, **species**, specimen See *Vocabulary Power* book.	**Art Connection:** Illustrate the Story p. 193 **Vocabulary Power** **Content-Area Words** p. 190 *Vocabulary Power* book, p. 43 **Vocabulary activity**

DAY 3	DAY 4	DAY 5
1. We baked many cookie Yesterday. (cookies; yesterday) **2.** We sold tehm at the fair" (them; .)	**1.** me write like I speak (I; speak.) **2.** jerry listen to a funny joke now. (Jerry; listens)	**1.** Who's there" asked Jean. ("Who's there?") **2.** "it's Henry," sayed Lucile. (It's; said)
Compare Dialogue Formats p. 194	Discuss Elements of Dialogue p. 196	Discuss Word and Sentence Spacing p. 197
GUIDED WRITING ✔ **Applying the Craft** pp. 194–195 • To use a dialogue as a model for writing • To prewrite and draft an original dialogue **Read and Respond to the Model** p. 194	**GUIDED WRITING** **Editing Your Dialogue** p. 196 • To peer conference in editing dialogues • To edit dialogues and share them aloud	**HANDWRITING** **Using Margins and Correct Word and Sentence Spacing** p. 197 • To use margins and correct word and sentence spacing when writing
Interactive Writing: Model Drafting p. 195 **ESL:** *ESL Manual* p. 76	**Peer Conferencing** p. 196 **ESL:** *ESL Manual* p. 76	**Writing Resource:** Using a Template p. 197 **ESL:** *ESL Manual* p. 76
Unit 3 Review pp. 236–237	**Unit 3 Review** pp. 236–237	**Unit 3 Review** pp. 236–237
Vocabulary Power Multi-Meaning Words p. 190 *Vocabulary Power* book, p. 44 🖥 **Vocabulary activity**	**LISTENING AND SPEAKING:** Create Mental Images p. 196 **Vocabulary Power** Analogies p. 190 *Vocabulary Power* book, p. 45 🖥 **Vocabulary activity**	**Vocabulary Power** Classify/Categorize p. 190

Writer's Craft:
Using Quotations to Show Feeling

OBJECTIVES

- To read and respond to dialogue as a model for writing
- To read dialogue in a way that shows feelings

DAILY LANGUAGE PRACTICE

TRANSPARENCY 29

1 martha wave to George from the ground. (Martha waved)

2 george smiled down at her (George;.)

ORAL WARM-UP

USE PRIOR KNOWLEDGE Ask a few volunteers simple questions such as *How are you?* or *What is the weather like today?* Write their complete responses as quotations, using quotation marks and dialogue words such as *said Kelly*. Tell children that in this chapter they will be learning how to write speaker's words.

TEACH/MODEL

Read and discuss the introductory text on page 190. Have children read the dialogue.

ANALYZE THE LITERATURE Use these questions for discussing the dialogue.

1. **What is George trying to do?** (He wants to be the first of his species to fly.)
   LITERAL: IMPORTANT DETAILS

2. **What makes the story funny?** (Possible response: The way the characters talk to each other and the fact that George doesn't realize that if he gets out of the basket to make it lighter, he will no longer be in it to fly.) **INFERENTIAL: DRAW CONCLUSIONS**

Using Quotations to Show Feeling

Many stories have dialogue. In **dialogue**, a writer tells the exact words that characters say to each other. Dialogue helps readers better understand what the characters are like.

In dialogue, a character's exact words are placed inside **quotation marks** (" "). A word such as *said* or *cried* is in the sentence to tell how the character said the words.

Read this dialogue. How do the characters' words help you know what they are like?

from *George and Martha*
by James Marshall

"I'm going to be the first of my species to fly!" said George.

"Then why aren't you flying?" asked Martha. "It seems to me that you are still on the ground."

"You are right," said George. "I don't seem to be going anywhere at all."

190

Vocabulary Power

DAY 1 WORD MEANING Introduce and define *species* (group, category). Point out the first sentence in the story "The Flying Machine." Discuss what George means.

DAY 2 CONTENT-AREA WORDS Write: *There are many __species__ of animals and plants.* **In which class would you learn about species: math, art, or science?** (See also *Vocabulary Power*, page 43.)

DAY 3 MULTI-MEANING WORDS Write: *A tiger is a species of the cat __family__ . I am the oldest child in my __family__ .* Discuss the different meanings of *family*. (See also *Vocabulary Power*, page 44.)

DAY 4 ANALOGIES List: *tiger-cat, rose-_____.* **A tiger is a kind of cat. A rose is a kind of . . .** (flower) (See also *Vocabulary Power*, page 45.)

DAY 5 CLASSIFY/CATEGORIZE Write: *Animal, Plant, Family Members, Toy.* **Write or draw three or more things that belong in each category.**

"Maybe the basket is too heavy," said Martha.

"Yes," said George, "I think you are right again. Maybe if I climb out, the basket will be lighter."

"Oh dear!" cried George. "Now what have I done? There goes my flying machine!"

"That's all right," said Martha. "I would rather have you down here with me."

With a partner, read the dialogue aloud as if you were George and Martha talking to each other. Read only the character's exact words.

Think About It

1. How do Martha and George feel about each other? How do you know?

2. How could you tell who was talking in this dialogue?

191

Social Studies Connection

. . . .

FLIGHT FIRSTS Children may be interested in learning more about famous firsts in balloon flight. Have them write questions for investigation and conduct research to find the answers. Suggest that they check the following web site: *www.didyouknow .com/balloons.htm*

School-Home Connection

. . . .

MORE BY MARSHALL You might want to send home a list of other humorous James Marshall books for families to borrow from the library and read together, including numerous George and Martha books, as well as *Fox All Week* and *Miss Nelson Is Missing*.

USING QUOTATIONS Explain that writers use characters' exact words to help readers know more about the characters. They use verbs such as *cried*, *said*, and *asked*, to help readers understand characters' feelings and the way the words are said.

Discuss some of the dialogue in the story that helps achieve this purpose.

Think About It

1. Have children note how they can tell the characters' feelings for each other, using details such as Martha's statement at the end. **CRITICAL:** EXPRESS PERSONAL OPINIONS

2. Have children point out dialogue words such as *said* and *asked* that indicate which character is speaking. **LITERAL:** IMPORTANT DETAILS

SELF-INITIATED WRITING Have children respond to the story they just read through self-initiated writing, which might include writing a summary, a list of dialogue words from the story, or an original dialogue that quotes a friend. You might also want the children to respond by other methods, such as through drama or art.

WRAP-UP/ASSESS

SUMMARIZE Have children discuss how and why writers use quotations to show characters' feelings. They can record their personal reflections in their journals. **REFLECTION**

Writer's Craft:
Using Quotations to Show Feeling

OBJECTIVES
- To write sentences to show feeling
- To write sentences as quotations using exact verbs
- To rewrite sentences as dialogue

SPIRAL REVIEW

DAILY LANGUAGE PRACTICE

TRANSPARENCY 29

1. clyde meow for help when his tail got stuck yesterday. (Clyde; meowed)
2. midge open the door for him. (Midge; opened)

ORAL WARM-UP

USE PRIOR KNOWLEDGE Ask volunteers to make up sentences with everyday language, such as what they might say if they were hungry. Write the responses on the board, and ask how to change them into quotations by adding quotation marks and dialogue words.

GUIDED WRITING

COMPARE SENTENCES Read and discuss the introductory material. Read the directions and the first example in exercise A and have children complete the rest on their own or with partners.

USE THE WORD BANK Have children complete exercise B by expanding their sentences into dialogue using verbs such as those in the Word Bank. They can also use these verbs as they complete exercise C.

Using Quotations to Show Feeling

Dialogue helps readers know what characters are like and what they feel. Quotation marks show where each speaker's exact words begin and end. Writers try to make characters sound like real people talking by using everyday language. Exact verbs such as *cried* give clues about how characters feel.

"Oh dear!" cried George. "Now what have I done? There goes my flying machine!"

"That's all right," said Martha.

A. What words could you say for each of these feelings? Write a sentence to tell your exact words.

1. hurt *"Ouch! That stings."*
2. happy
3. sad
4. angry
5. surprised
6. scared

B. Write an exact verb for each sentence in Part A to tell how you would say it. Use the Word Bank or your thesaurus.

"Ouch! That stings," I yelled.

Word Bank	
asked	whispered
screamed	cried
yelled	shouted
called	whined

Vocabulary Power page 43

Name _____

The following words have special meanings in science. The words are used to group all living things.

category   family   similar   species   specimen

This chart shows how scientists use these words. What animal is the chart about? Fill in the last box.

KINGDOM	Animal
CLASS	Mammal (warm-blooded, has hair or fur)
ORDER	Carnivore (eats meat)
FAMILY	Cat (includes cats of all sizes)
SPECIES	Tiger

- Each category in the chart tells about the tiger.
- The tiger is similar to other animals in many ways.
- The cat family is very large. The tiger is one species of cat.
- To see a specimen, you have to visit a zoo. A specimen is "one."

What other species do you think belong to the cat family? Draw and label a specimen. How is your cat similar to a tiger?

Vocabulary Power   Unit 3 • Chapter 15   43

REACHING ALL LEARNERS | **ESL**

CORRECT STYLE Children from different language backgrounds may not be familiar with the conventions of using quotation marks and capital letters as commonly done in English. Provide additional practice for these students, including examples showing where the conventions may differ from their home language.

C. Read the paragraph below. Then write sentences for it as dialogue. A sample dialogue has been started for you.

Clyde's tail was stuck in the door. He asked Midge for help. She thought that maybe opening the door would help. Clyde thought that was a good idea. Midge opened the door so Clyde could get his tail out. Then she asked if his tail felt better. Clyde said it did and thanked Midge for her help.

"Ow!" yelled Clyde.
"What's wrong?" asked Midge.

Writing and Thinking

Reflect Tell what helped you write the paragraph as dialogue. Write your ideas. Share your ideas in a small group.

193

WRITING DIALOGUE Read the directions for exercise C. Discuss the paragraph, leading children to understand that without dialogue, the story isn't very exciting. Have children work with partners to rewrite the story of Clyde and Midge. Provide time for children to show their work and compare their ideas.

Writing and Thinking

Children can discuss ideas with group members and then record in their journals any new reflections on writing dialogue. **REFLECTION**

WRAP-UP/ASSESS

SUMMARIZE Ask volunteers to summarize ways to write dialogue that expresses feelings.

Art Connection

ILLUSTRATE THE STORY Some children might enjoy drawing pictures to go with the dialogue. They can combine the pictures and dialogue to make a picture book.

CHALLENGE
REACHING ALL LEARNERS

SKITS AND QUOTES Children can practice and present skits using the dialogue they wrote for exercise C or other original sentences they create.

Writer's Craft
Applying the Craft

OBJECTIVES
- To use a dialogue as a model for writing
- To prewrite and draft an original dialogue

DAILY LANGUAGE PRACTICE

TRANSPARENCY 29

❶ We baked many cookie Yesterday.
(cookies; yesterday)

❷ We sold tehm at the fair" (them; .)

ORAL WARM-UP

USE PRIOR KNOWLEDGE Have volunteers compare dialogue in a comic strip with that in a story format. Discuss how a story provides additional information about a character's feelings.

GUIDED WRITING

READ AND RESPOND TO THE MODEL Read and discuss the model, using the questions on page 194.

Looking at the Model

1. Children should recognize that words such as *smiling*, *groaned*, and *chuckled* provide clues to characters' changing feelings. **INFERENTIAL: INTERPRET CHARACTERS**
2. Children may suggest that they felt the same way when they told or listened to a joke. **CRITICAL: EXPRESS PERSONAL OPINIONS**

Writing Dialogue **Writer's Craft**

Applying the Craft

Read this dialogue a second grader wrote. Think about how the dialogue shows the characters' feelings.

The Riddle

"What a great day this is!" Chris said smiling.

"The sun is out. The birds are singing."

"That makes me think of a riddle," said Mike.

"Oh, no," Chris groaned. "Not one of your riddles again!"

"Three birds sat on the fence," Mike said. "Now what is the difference between *here* and *there?*"

here

there

Looking at the Model

1. How do Chris and Mike feel at different parts of the dialogue? How do you know? Which words give clues about how the characters feel?

2. When have you felt the way the characters do? Do you think the writer has felt the same way, too? Why or why not?

194

Vocabulary Power page 44

Name _____

Some words have special scientific meanings, but they also have everyday meanings.

My kitten Jingles is a member of the cat <u>family</u>.
Jingles is also a member of my <u>family</u>!

Complete the sentences. Share your ideas with classmates.

1. My friend and I have <u>similar</u> _____

2. That _____ is a sad <u>specimen</u>!

3. These things belong in the "_____" <u>category</u>.

4. The _____ is so good that it must be a special <u>species</u>!

Draw pictures for two of the sentences above. Label your pictures.

44   Unit 3 • Chapter 15   Vocabulary Power

SELF-INITIATED WRITING

EVALUATION CRITERIA Work with children to establish criteria for what makes good dialogue. Encourage children to add additional criteria. Children should apply the criteria to their writing.

- Dialogue helps readers know what characters are like.
- Dialogue lets readers know how characters are feeling.
- Dialogue is natural—it sounds the way people sound when they talk.

Your Turn

Write a dialogue for your classmates about two characters and something funny that happened to them.

Prewriting and Drafting

STEP 1 **Develop your ideas.**
Think of two interesting characters. What are they like? What problem might they have?

STEP 2 **Brainstorm what your characters would say to each other.**
Draw pictures of your characters. Think about how they feel. Write words they would say.

STEP 3 **Write a draft of your dialogue.**
Use What Good Writers Do to help you. Include dialogue that helps the reader understand what each character is like.

What Good Writers Do

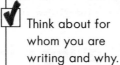 Think about for whom you are writing and why.

Student Handbook

Use your Thesaurus to help you find just the right words to use in your dialogue.

195

Your Turn Explain to children they will use the prewriting and drafting steps and What Good Writers Do to write a dialogue between two characters.

Prewriting and Drafting Read the directions and the steps with children. Encourage volunteers to share some ideas they might use in their drawings. Remind children that they already know how to turn their ideas into sentences with dialogue.

Read What Good Writers Do and suggest that children keep these tips in mind as they work on their drafts.

You may wish to have children use word-processing software to compose their drafts.

Have children place their first drafts in their Writing Portfolios.

WRAP-UP/ASSESS

SUMMARIZE Ask volunteers to summarize the steps they followed in prewriting and drafting. You may want to have children record in their journal their reflections on writing a dialogue.
REFLECTION

INTERACTIVE WRITING

MODEL DRAFTING Elicit from children one or more ideas for a dialogue between two characters. Incorporate their suggestions as well as have them "share the pen" and write some of the dialogue themselves as together you draft a conversation using speech balloons.

Editing Your Dialogue

OBJECTIVES
- To peer conference in editing dialogues.
- To edit dialogues and share them aloud

DAILY LANGUAGE PRACTICE

TRANSPARENCY 29

1 me write like I speak (I; speak.)

2 jerry listen to a funny joke now. (Jerry; listens)

ORAL WARM-UP

Discuss some of the elements a good written dialogue should include. Ask children to predict the next writing step.

GUIDED WRITING

EDITING YOUR DIALOGUE Read the directions and the checklist, and then model how to use the Editor's Marks.

PEER CONFERENCING Have children use the checklist and the Editor's Marks in their conference on improving their dialogues. Remind children to edit their writing for correct grammar and usage in particular, checking that their verb tenses are correct.

SHARING WITH OTHERS Have volunteers share their final dialogues in small groups.

WRAP-UP/ASSESS

SUMMARIZE Volunteers can summarize the process they used to draft and edit their dialogues. Have children evaluate their final product using a scale of 1–4 on a self-stick note. Children can attach their ratings to their writing and place it in their Writing Portfolio.

 Writing Dialogue

Writer's Craft

Editing Your Dialogue

Read your dialogue with a partner or a group of classmates. Talk about ways to make it better. Use the checklist and the Editor's Marks to help you revise it.

Editor's Marks

∧	Change.
ℯ	Take out.
≡	Use a capital letter.
∧	Add a comma.
∨	Add quotation marks.

✓ My dialogue uses everyday language and tells what the characters are feeling.

✓ My dialogue uses quotation marks around the speakers' exact words.

✓ The quotations are written correctly.

Sharing with Others

Meet with a partner or small group. Share your dialogue. Read it aloud. Use your voice to show how each speaker would say the quotations.

196

Vocabulary Power page 45

Name _____   Analogies

Look at the following word puzzles. Think about how the first two words go together. What one word completes each puzzle? cat

roar–tiger	puppy–dog	birds–bird
meow– cat	kitten– cat	cats– cat

Complete these word puzzles. Remember to think about how the first two words go together.

1. moon–night	**2.** mittens–hands
sun– day	boots– feet
3. similar–different	**4.** doctor–Dr.
down– up	street– St.
5. mouse–mice	**6.** category–group
tooth– teeth	glad– happy
7. nose–smell	**8.** hard–soft
eyes– see	rough– smooth
9. prince–princess	**10.** fish–scales
king– queen	bear– fur

Make up two word puzzles on another sheet of paper. Ask a classmate to complete them.

Vocabulary Power   Unit 3 • Chapter 15   45

LISTENING AND SPEAKING

CREATE MENTAL IMAGES Suggest that listeners try to picture the different speakers as readers vary their voices in reading their dialogues. Have children also think about and use a volume and rate appropriate to reading before a partner or before a small group.

•Handwriting•

Using Margins and Correct Word and Sentence Spacing

> Make sure you put enough space along the side of your paper and between words and sentences. Follow these tips.
>
> - Begin writing to the right of the red line. Leave a pencil space.
> - The space between words and sentences should be as wide as a pencil.
>
>
> He ran. Then he jumped.

Write these sentences. Use your best handwriting. Follow the tips to leave enough space.

Kim talked.
She told a story.
Dad liked it.

197

Writing Resource
. . . .

USING A TEMPLATE For children who need additional help, cut out a cardboard template the width of a pencil. They can use the template to measure the space between words and sentences until they feel confident in writing without this guide.

EVALUATION CRITERIA

Have children revisit the evaluation criteria they established earlier and informally rate their writing of dialogue by writing their score (on a 1–4 scale) on the corner of their papers or by raising their fingers. Encourage their efforts but briefly discuss things that they can do to help continue to do better and better.

•Handwriting•

Using Margins and Correct Word and Sentence Spacing

OBJECTIVE
- To use margins and correct word and sentence spacing when writing

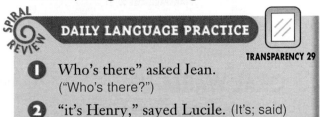

SPIRAL REVIEW **DAILY LANGUAGE PRACTICE**

TRANSPARENCY 29

❶ Who's there" asked Jean. ("Who's there?")

❷ "it's Henry," sayed Lucile. (It's; said)

TEACH/MODEL

Explain that the correct spacing between words and sentences helps readers more easily read your writing.

Have volunteers read the tips aloud. Then have all children use a pencil and lined paper to copy the practice sentences, measuring the spaces between words and sentences with a pencil width. Provide feedback on the handwriting exercise.

You may wish to have children refer to the handwriting models on pages 490–493 in their handbooks (see also R92-R93).

CURSIVE WRITING Have children who write in cursive apply the concepts in this lesson to their writing.

WRAP-UP/ASSESS

SUMMARIZE Ask volunteers to summarize the handwriting tips in their own words. Children may recopy a favorite piece of their writing including their dialogues, paying special attention to the word and sentence spacing.

LESSON ORGANIZER	DAY 1	DAY 2
DAILY LANGUAGE PRACTICE TRANSPARENCIES 30, 31	1. Jim lookd in the water" (looked; .) 2. he watcheed a starfish. (He watched) **Bridge to Writing** He (past tense of like) the boat trip.	1. i ham tired. (I; am) 2. Dad iss Sleepy, too. (is; sleepy) **Bridge to Writing** I am (describing word) .
ORAL WARM-UP **Listening/Speaking**	Complete and Act Out a Sentence p. 198	Talk About a Picture p. 200 *Grammar Jingles™* CD, Primary, Track 10
TEACH/MODEL **GRAMMAR** **KEY** ✔ = tested skill	✔ **THE VERBS *AM*, *IS*, AND *ARE*** pp. 198-199 •To listen critically to interpret a poem •To understand that *am*, *is*, and *are* tell what someone or something is like	✔ **USING *AM*, *IS*, AND *ARE*** pp. 200-201 •To understand that *am*, *is*, and *are* tell about now and tell what someone or something is like •To use the verbs *am*, *is*, and *are* in writing
 **Reaching All Learners**	*Practice Book* p. 51 **Challenge:** Activity Card 11, p. R51 **ESL:** *ESL Manual* pp. 78, 79 **Reteach:** *Reteach Activities Copying Masters* p. 31	**Modified Instruction** Below-Level: Say Nouns Aloud Above-Level: Write Sentences **Challenge:** Play Cards p. 201 **ESL:** Pair Up p. 200 *ESL Manual*, pp. 78, 80 *Practice Book* p. 52 **Reteach:** *Reteach Activities Copying Masters* p. 32

WRITING	Write About Feelings p. 199
	
	  Summarize/Reflect
		Writing Connection p. 201
		 Write About Yourself
		  Summarize/Reflect

CROSS-CURRICULAR/ ENRICHMENT	**Vocabulary Power** Word Meaning p. 198 circular, orbit, **revolving**, spinning, spiral See ***Vocabulary Power*** book	**Vocabulary Power** Context Clues p. 198 *Vocabulary Power* book, p. 46 **Vocabulary activity**

DAY 3

1. Dad am in the kar. (is; car)
2. Mom and Dad is late? for the movie. (are; late for)

Bridge to Writing I <u>(form of be)</u> a good writer.

Compare Things That Have Grown
 p. 202
Grammar Jingles™ CD, Primary, Track 10

✔ **USING *WAS* AND *WERE***
pp. 202–203
• To understand that the verbs *was* and *were* tell what someone or something was like in the past
• To use the verbs *was* and *were* in writing

Modified Instruction
Below-Level: Find Nouns
Above-Level: Write Sentences
Challenge: Poetry Booklets
p. 203
ESL: I Was... p. 202
ESL Manual, pp. 78, 81
Practice Book p. 53
Reteach: *Reteach Activities Copying Masters* p. 33

Writing Connection p. 203
Using the Right Verbs
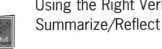 Summarize/Reflect

 Vocabulary Power
Word Families p. 198
Vocabulary Power book, p. 47
Vocabulary activity

DAY 4

1. Breakfast were tasty yesterday Morning. (was; morning)
2. The cereals was hott. (were; hot)

Bridge to Writing The orange juice <u>(form of be)</u> fresh yesterday morning.

Classify Sentences p. 204

EXTRA PRACTICE p. 204
• To understand when to use the verbs *am, is, are, was,* and *were*
• To use the verbs *am, is, are, was,* and *were* in writing
 Practice and Assessment

Challenge: People Pictures
p. 205
ESL: Find Sentences p. 204
ESL Manual pp. 78, 82
Practice Book p. 54

Writing Connection p. 205
Write a Description

Vocabulary Power
Multi-Meaning Words p. 198
Vocabulary Power book, p. 48
Vocabulary activity

DAY 5

1. Two chairs was broken, (were; .)
2. One table were very olde. (was; old)

Bridge to Writing Two years ago, my clothes <u>(form of be)</u> smaller.

Discuss Test Directions p. 206

TEST PREP **CHAPTER REVIEW** p. 206
• To review the verbs *am, is, are, was,* and *were*
• To recognize the different parts of a test and understand how to take a test
Test Preparation

Challenge: Test Review p. 207
Practice Book p. 55
ESL: *ESL Manual* pp. 78, 83

Study Skills p. 207
Taking a Test

Vocabulary Power
Synonyms p. 198

The Verbs *Am, Is,* and *Are*

OBJECTIVES
- To listen critically to interpret a poem
- To understand that *am, is,* and *are* tell what someone or something is like

SPIRAL REVIEW

DAILY LANGUAGE PRACTICE

TRANSPARENCY 30

1 Jim lookd in the water" (looked; .)

2 he watcheed a starfish. (He watched)

BRIDGE TO WRITING He _____ (past tense of *like*) the boat trip.

ORAL WARM-UP

USE PRIOR KNOWLEDGE Ask volunteers to think of a word to complete the sentence *I am* ____ and act out the sentence. Then have other children guess the word and say *You are* ____ or *He/She is* ____. Begin a list of sentences that use the verbs *am, is,* or *are* on chart paper or add these words to your **Verb Word Wall**.

TEACH/MODEL

Have children open to page 198. Have them use the title to predict what the poem will be about. Read the poem aloud, asking children to listen to what is happening in the poem. Then have volunteers read aloud the poem.

DEVELOP ORAL LANGUAGE Prompt children to say complete sentences by saying part of a sentence about the poem and having them add the rest. Remind children that the poem uses words to describe what someone is feeling. Ask volunteers to demonstrate or suggest other sentences that tell what someone is like. Add the sentences to the list on chart paper.

The Verbs *Am, Is,* and *Are*

Read the poem.

I Am Running in a Circle

I am running in a circle
and my feet are getting sore,
and my head is
spinning
spinning
as it's never spun before.
I am
dizzy
dizzy
dizzy.
Oh! I cannot bear much more.
I am trapped in a
revolving
. . . volving
. . . volving
. . . volving door!

Jack Prelutsky

198

Vocabulary Power

DAY 1 WORD MEANINGS Introduce and define *revolving*. Have children act out the meaning by moving in a circle around their chairs.

DAY 2 CONTEXT CLUES Write: *The planets are revolving around the sun.* **What word or words help you understand the meaning of *revolving*?** (See also *Vocabulary Power,* page 46.)

DAY 3 WORD FAMILIES List: *revolve, revolving.* **What is the base word? What other endings can you add to *revolve*?** (See also *Vocabulary Power,* page 47.)

DAY 4 MULTI-MEANING WORDS Write: *My interests revolve around sports.* **What does this sentence mean?** (See also *Vocabulary Power,* page 48.)

DAY 5 SYNONYMS Have children make a word web for *revolve* by writing words with similar meanings.

Use the words *am*, *is*, and *are* to tell about the poem and about what might happen next.

Some verbs do not show action. They tell what someone or something is like.

I **am** very dizzy.
She **is** tired of spinning.
My feet **are** sore.

Write about how you would feel if you were going around and around in a circle.

I am _upset from going around_

around

around

around.

I am _____

_____

_____

_____.

I am _____

_____

_____

_____!

199

WRITE Write volunteers' sentences on the board or on chart paper. Have children read them as you underline the verbs *am*, *is*, or *are*. Explain that some verbs do not show action. They tell what someone or something is like. Read the definitions in the box, and talk about the example sentences.

Then read the first item at the bottom of page 199 together. Point out the pattern from the poem. Have children complete the items and then share them with a partner.

WRAP-UP/ASSESS

SUMMARIZE Reread the poem with children. Then have them summarize and reflect on what they have learned about *is*, *am*, and *are*. Ask children to write their reflections in their journals as well as to record sentences they brainstormed while completing the page. REFLECTION

RETEACH

INTERVENTION Lessons in **visual**, **auditory**, and **kinesthetic** modalities: p. R27 and *Reteach Activities Copying Masters*, p. 31.

page 31

The Verbs *Am*, *Is*, and *Are*
Read each sentence aloud. Circle the verb.

EXAMPLE: One leaf (is) yellow.

1. Two leaves (are) red.
2. I (am) cold.
3. The trees (are) tall.
4. The branches (are) thick.
5. The wind (is) loud.

Visual / Auditory

The Verbs *Am*, *Is*, and *Are*
Cut out the verbs at the bottom of the page. Glue them where they belong.

1. The bags of leaves [are] almost full.
2. One [is] open.
3. I [am] tired.
4. Kevin [is] tired, too.

| is | is | am | are |

Kinesthetic

Teacher: Cut apart the activities and distribute to children based on the modalities that are their strengths.

Reteach Activities • Forms of *Be*   Unit 3 • Chapter 16   31

PRACTICE page 51

Name _____

The Verbs *Am*, *Is*, and *Are*

A. Read each sentence. Draw a line under the verb.

1. I <u>am</u> busy.
2. The telescope <u>is</u> on the tripod.
3. All of the clouds <u>are</u> gone.
4. The stars <u>are</u> bright.
5. The night <u>is</u> pretty.

B. Write a word from the box to complete each sentence.

| are | is | am |

6. The sky __is__ black.
7. Mom and I __are__ outside.
8. The telescope __is__ mine.
9. I __am__ proud.
10. We __are__ excited.

▶ **TRY THIS!** Write three sentences that tell about the sky at night or during the day. Use the verbs *am*, *is*, and *are*.

Practice • Forms of *Be*   Unit 3 • Chapter 16   51

CHALLENGE

THEN AND NOW Have children use **Challenge Activity Card 11** (page R51) to write about what they were like in the past and how they are now. Encourage them to add details. Display the albums and have children talk about the pictures.

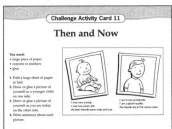

Challenge Activity Card 11
Then and Now

Using *Am*, *Is*, and *Are*

OBJECTIVES

- To understand that the verbs *am*, *is*, and *are* tell about now and tell what someone or something is like
- To use the verbs *am*, *is*, and *are* in writing

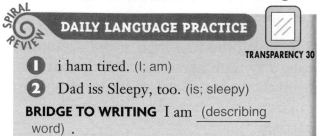

DAILY LANGUAGE PRACTICE

TRANSPARENCY 30

1 i ham tired. (I; am)

2 Dad iss Sleepy, too. (is; sleepy)

BRIDGE TO WRITING I am ___(describing word)___ .

ORAL WARM-UP

TALK ABOUT A PICTURE Have children work in small groups. Give each group a picture of people enjoying an outdoor activity. Have group members discuss the picture, using the verbs *am*, *is*, and *are*. Then ask follow-up questions that prompt children to use the pictures to support their spoken messages.

Grammar Jingles™ **CD, Primary** Use Track 10 for review and reinforcement of the forms of *be*.

TEACH/MODEL

Use the explanation and examples to explain when to use *am*, *is*, and *are*. You may want to explain that *you* is followed by *are*, even when *you* names one. Tell children that *am* is used only after *I*.

GUIDED PRACTICE Work with children to complete each sentence. Encourage them to read each sentence aloud to decide whether to use the verb *am*, *is*, or *are* to complete it. Children can also refer to the chart at the top of page 200.

Using *Am*, *Is*, and *Are*

Some verbs do not show action. They tell what someone or something is like. The verbs **am**, **is**, and **are** tell about now.

I **am** seven years old.

Use	With	Example
am	I	I **am** tall.
is	nouns that name one	The bird **is** yellow.
are	nouns that name more than one	Many birds **are** brown.

Guided Practice

Choose the correct verb to finish each sentence.

1. I (<u>am</u>, is, are) outside with my Aunt Sue.

2. The weather (am, <u>is</u>, are) warm.

3. We (am, is, <u>are</u>) by the pond.

4. Aunt Sue (am, <u>is</u>, are) glad the sky is sunny.

5. I (<u>am</u>, is, are) happy to be with her.

200

Vocabulary Power page 46

Name _____

What word in the sentence helps you understand the meaning of <u>revolving</u>?

> The Earth is <u>revolving</u> around the sun.

The word <u>around</u> helps you understand that <u>revolving</u> means "going around."

The word <u>around</u> can help you understand the meaning of other words. Read each sentence. Draw a picture to show the meaning of the underlined word.

1. The moon's path around the Earth is called an <u>orbit</u>.	2. The dancer is <u>spinning</u> around on one foot!
3. We walked around in a <u>circular</u> path.	4. If I twist a string around my finger, I can make a <u>spiral</u>.

46 Unit 3 • Chapter 16   Vocabulary Power

REACHING ALL LEARNERS

ESL

PAIR UP Some children may have difficulty choosing the correct form of *be*. Divide the class into two groups. Hand out cards with various nouns or pronouns to one group, and cards with *am*, *is*, and *are* to the other. Have children pair up, matching a noun and a verb form, and then work together to make up a sentence to share with the group.

Remember The verbs *am*, *is*, and *are* tell what someone or something is like. They tell about now.

Independent Practice

Choose the correct verb to finish each sentence.

6. Two frogs (am, is, <u>are</u>) by the pond.

7. One frog (am, <u>is</u>, are) green.

8. Many fish (am, is, <u>are</u>) in the water.

9. They (am, is, <u>are</u>) brown and red.

10. I (<u>am</u>, is, are) in a boat with Aunt Sue.

11. Aunt Sue (am, <u>is</u>, are) a teacher.

12. Today I (<u>am</u>, is, are) Aunt Sue's student.

13. She (am, <u>is</u>, are) here to teach me about pond animals.

14. Some ducks (am, is, <u>are</u>) near the boat now.

15. I (<u>am</u>, is, are) happy to learn about ducks.

Writing Connection

Write About Yourself Draw a picture of yourself and some classmates. Then write sentences that tell what you are like. Check to see if you used *am*, *is*, and *are* correctly.

You can choose different fonts, or letter styles, to write and print out your sentences.

201

Independent Practice

Have children complete the Independent Practice, or modify it by using the following suggestions:

MODIFIED INSTRUCTION

BELOW-LEVEL STUDENTS Suggest that children underline the noun and say it aloud to decide whether it names one or more than one. They can also use the chart at the top of page 200.

ABOVE-LEVEL STUDENTS After children have finished, have them write at least three more sentences using the verbs *am*, *is*, and *are*.

Writing Connection

Write About Yourself Remind children that each sentence should tell about themselves. Suggest that children place their pictures and sentences in the Sharing Basket to share with others.

WRAP-UP/ASSESS

SUMMARIZE Ask children to reflect on what they have learned about the verbs *am*, *is*, and *are*. Have them summarize what they have learned. **REFLECTION**

RETEACH

INTERVENTION Lessons in **visual**, **auditory**, and **kinesthetic** modalities: p. R27 and *Reteach Activities Copying Masters*, p. 32.

page 32

Using *Am, Is,* and *Are*

Look at the picture. Use a verb from the box to complete each sentence.

is	are	am

1. The baby __is__ small.

2. I __am__ older than the baby.

3. Cara __is__ older than I am.

4. The baby and I __are__ younger than Cara.

Visual/Auditory

Using *Am, Is,* and *Are*

1. Make a verb cube.
   - Cut along the dotted lines.
   - Fold on the solid lines.
   - Tape the sides together.

   are
   is   is
   am
   are

2. Play a game with a partner.
   - Take turns. Roll the cube.
   - Read the verb on the top.
   - Say a sentence using the verb.

   Kinesthetic

Teacher: Cut apart the activities and distribute to children based on the modalities that are their strengths.

32   Unit 3 • Chapter 16   Reteach Activities • Forms of *Be*

PRACTICE page 52

Name _____

Using *Am, Is,* and *Are*

A. Circle the correct verb to finish each sentence.

1. I (**am**, is, are) in the park.
2. The birds (am, is, **are**) in the trees.
3. They (am, is, **are**) loud.
4. A squirrel (am, **is**, are) on the bench.
5. It (am, **is**, are) brown.

B. Write *am*, *is*, or *are* to complete each sentence.

6. Two rabbits __are__ near.
7. The squirrel __is__ quiet.
8. I __am__ quiet, too.
9. The squirrel __is__ very still.
10. Then the rabbits __are__ gone.

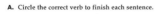

TRY THIS! Write sentences about a park that you have visited. Tell about the people or animals you saw. Use the verbs *am*, *is*, and *are* in your sentences.

52   Unit 3 • Chapter 16   Practice • Forms of *Be*

CHALLENGE

PLAY CARDS Write the words *am*, *is*, and *are* on three sets of index cards. (There should be nine cards.) Have children put the cards face down on a table. Have them take turns choosing a card and using the verb in a sentence. Once all the cards have been chosen, shuffle them and try again so that children can create different sentences.

Using *Was* and *Were*

OBJECTIVES

- To understand that the verbs *was* and *were* tell what someone or something was like in the past
- To use the verbs *was* and *were* in writing

DAILY LANGUAGE PRACTICE

TRANSPARENCY 30

1 Dad am in the kar. (is; car)

2 Mom and Dad is late? for the movie. (are; late for)

BRIDGE TO WRITING I _____ (form of *be*) a good writer.

ORAL WARM-UP

USE PRIOR KNOWLEDGE Show children pictures of seedlings and grown plants, butterflies and caterpillars, puppies and adult dogs. Invite children to compare the plants or animals when young and when grown. Write sentences with *was* and *were* on the board.

Grammar Jingles™ **CD, Primary** Use Track 10 for review and reinforcement of the forms of *be*.

TEACH/MODEL

Have children read the explanation and the example sentences. Ask them to identify the noun in the naming part of each sentence and tell whether it names one or more than one. You may want to have children make up sentences using *was* and *were*. You can also discuss the sentences from the Oral Warm-Up.

GUIDED PRACTICE Ask volunteers to read each sentence and identify the noun or nouns in the naming part. Have them decide whether it names one or more than one before writing the answer.

Forms of *Be*   **Grammar-Writing Connection**

Using *Was* and *Were*

The verbs **was** and **were** tell what someone or something was like. They tell about the past.

Use **was** with nouns that name one.

Yesterday the girl **was** happy.

Use **were** with nouns that name more than one.

Last night the girls **were** tired.

Guided Practice

Write *was* or *were* to complete each sentence.

1. My parents and I __were__ at the beach last Saturday.

2. My towel __was__ warm.

3. The waves __were__ low.

4. The water __was__ cool.

5. I __was__ glad to find shells.

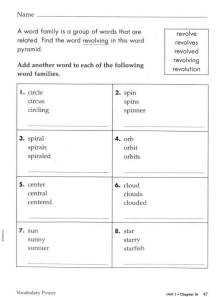

202

Vocabulary Power page 47

Name _____

A word family is a group of words that are related. Find the word revolving in this word pyramid.

| revolve |
| revolves |
| revolved |
| revolving |
| revolution |

Add another word to each of the following word families.

1. circle circus circling	2. spin spins spinner
3. spiral spirals spiraled	4. orb orbit orbits
5. center central centered	6. cloud clouds clouded
7. sun sunny sunnier	8. star starry starfish

Vocabulary Power   Unit 3 • Chapter 16   47

REACHING ALL LEARNERS   **ESL**

I WAS. . . Have pairs of children act out together how they both felt or what they were like in the past. Ask the class to guess the answer. (You/They were little.) Ask one of the partners to confirm. (Yes, I was little; We were little.) Write some of the sentences on the board, and have children discuss why they chose to use *was* and *were*.

Independent Practice

Write *was* or *were* to complete each sentence.

6. Yesterday the beach __was__ clean.

7. The ocean __was__ blue.

8. My parents __were__ with me.

9. We __were__ happy to be outside.

10. I __was__ interested in the animals on the sand.

11. Some shells __were__ white.

12. A crab __was__ next to the shells.

13. The crab's two front claws __were__ big.

14. Many birds __were__ on the beach, too.

15. The beach __was__ full of life!

Writing Connection

Using the Right Verbs Imagine you went to the beach or a lake last summer. Write sentences to tell about what you saw there. Be sure to use *was* and *were* correctly.

Change *Is* to *was* by going to the **Edit** menu and clicking on **Replace**.

203

Independent Practice

Have children complete the Independent Practice, or modify it by using the following suggestions:

MODIFIED INSTRUCTION

BELOW-LEVEL STUDENTS Suggest that children find the noun and decide whether it names one or more than one before they write their answers.

ABOVE-LEVEL STUDENTS After children have finished, have them write four sentences using the verbs *was* and *were*.

Writing Connection

Using the Right Verbs Have children edit their completed sentences toward standard grammar by confirming that the verb *to be* is in the past tense and agrees with the subject in number.

WRAP-UP/ASSESS

SUMMARIZE Ask children to reflect on what they have learned about the verbs *was* and *were*.

REACHING ALL LEARNERS — RETEACH

INTERVENTION Lessons in **visual**, **auditory**, and **kinesthetic** modalities: p. R27 and *Reteach Activities Copying Masters*, p. 33.

page 33

PRACTICE page 53

Name_____

Using *Was* and *Were*

A. Circle the correct verb to finish each sentence.

1. Grace (**was**, were) on the boat.
2. Her parents (was, **were**) with her.
3. Many fish (was, **were**) in the water.
4. A seagull (**was**, were) overhead.
5. The sky (**was**, were) clear.

B. Write *was* or *were* to complete each sentence.

6. The weather __was__ hot.
7. Soon Grace and her parents __were__ on the shore.
8. Shells __were__ everywhere.
9. Grace __was__ happy.
10. Pretty shells __were__ easy to find.

TRY THIS! Write two sentences about the last time you had time off from school. How did you feel? Where did you go? Use the verbs *was* and *were* in your sentences.

Practice • Forms of Be   Unit 3 • Chapter 16 53

CHALLENGE

POETRY BOOKLETS Have children reread the poem on page 198. Then have them choose an action, such as dancing, using a swing, climbing, going down a slide, or jumping. Have them write how they felt when doing the activity, using *was* and *were* with the format of the poem. Children can illustrate the lines. Allow time for volunteers to read their poems aloud. Then collect the poems and put them together in a booklet in the class library.

Using *Was* and *Were*

Read aloud each sentence. Circle the verb.

EXAMPLE: The children (were) hungry.

1. The grapefruit (was) sour.
2. The grapes (were) sweet.
3. The cracker (was) salty.
4. The apples (were) juicy.
5. The bread (was) soft.

- - - - - - - - - - - - - - - -

Using *Was* and *Were*

Cut out the verbs at the bottom of the page. Glue them where they belong.

1. The glasses [were] full.
2. The food [was] ready.
3. The table [was] set.
4. The children [were] happy.

| was | was | were | were |

Teacher: Cut apart the activities and distribute to children based on the modalities that are their strength.

Reteach Activities • Forms of Be   Unit 3 • Chapter 16 33

Extra Practice

OBJECTIVES

• To understand when to use the verbs *am*, *is*, *are*, *was*, and *were*

• To use the verbs *am*, *is*, *are*, *was*, and *were* in writing

DAILY LANGUAGE PRACTICE

TRANSPARENCY 31

1 Breakfast were tasty yesterday Morning. (was; morning)

2 The cereals was hott. (were; hot)

BRIDGE TO WRITING The orange juice ___(form of be)___ fresh yesterday morning.

ORAL WARM-UP

USE PRIOR KNOWLEDGE Say a sentence, such as *I am happy.* Have children say if the sentence tells about today or yesterday. Invite children to change the sentence to tell about the other day. (*I was happy.*) Repeat with other sentences.

TEACH/MODEL

Read each set of directions with children. Have them share their answers in small groups before you read aloud the answers.

WRAP-UP/ASSESS

SUMMARIZE Ask children to reflect on and discuss any special problems they had in completing the practice before you have them summarize what they have learned about the different forms of *be*. You may want children to write their reflections in their journals.

ADDITIONAL PRACTICE Extra practice items are on page 471 of the *Pupil Edition* (R4 *Teacher's Edition*).

TECHNOLOGY

Grammar Practice and Assessment CD-ROM

Writing Express CD-ROM

INTERNET Visit *The Learning Site!* www.harcourtschool.com

Forms of *Be*

Extra Practice

Write *am*, *is*, or *are* to finish each sentence.

1. The birds ___are___ very loud.

2. They ___are___ on the beach.

3. This bird ___is___ hungry.

4. I ___am___ hungry, too!

Write *was* or *were* to finish each sentence.

5. My parents ___were___ on the beach blanket.

6. Mom ___was___ reading a book.

7. A crab ___was___ next to her foot.

Read each sentence. Write the correct verb to complete it.

is	am	are	was	were

8. I ___am___ tired now.

9. Last week the beach ___was___ quiet.

10. Now we ___are___ back home.

204

Vocabulary Power page 48

Name _____

Multi-Meaning Words

Many words have several different meanings.

The planets are revolving around the sun.
Be careful when you walk through a revolving door.

Read each pair of sentences. Think about the meaning of the underlined word or words. Circle the letter beside the meaning.

1. Sandy fixed her hair in spiral curls.	Don't let the noise spiral out of control!
(A) a circular shape	F spin in circles
B a square shape	G turn into a circular shape
C a triangle shape	(H) grow too loud

2. The toy top is spinning faster and faster.	It's fun to listen when Gramps starts spinning a story.
A flying	F twirling a book
(B) turning	G turning the pages in a book
C jumping	(H) making up a story

3. To write an *o*, you make a circle.	Robert and I have the same circle of friends.
(A) round shape	F friends who stand in a circle
B square shape	(G) group of friends
C straight line	H round-shaped friends

Write two sentences. Use two different meanings for star.

_____

_____

48 Unit 3 • Chapter 16   Vocabulary Power

ESL

REACHING ALL LEARNERS

FIND SENTENCES Have children work with English-proficient peers. Invite them to look in newspapers for sentences that include various forms of *be*. Then have children cut out sentences and decide whether each one tells about now or about the past. Have them change the sentence so it tells about the other time.

THE RACE WAS FUN

The race is fun

Language Play

Picture Talk

- Bring in or draw two pictures of yourself. One should show you as you are now. The other should show you as a baby.
- Show one picture and tell about yourself. Then tell about the other picture.
- Be sure to use *is*, *am*, *are*, *was*, and *were* correctly.

Writing Connection

Write a Description Think about a person or animal you know well. Write sentences that tell about what he or she is like. Check to be sure you used the verbs *am*, *is*, *are*, *was*, and *were* correctly.

My Cat Tiger

My cat's name is Tiger. Tiger is black and white. His eyes are yellow, and his nose is pink. His claws are sharp. Tiger was funny when he was a kitten. He still likes to play.

205

Language Play

Have children take turns showing their pictures. Children can share in pairs. If children are reluctant to share or do not have any pictures, invite them to talk about someone they know or about a pet.

Writing Connection

Write a Description Have children identify the most effective features of their description by using the criteria below.

CRITERIA
- ☑ Writes details that tell about the topic.
- ☑ Writes the verbs *am*, *is*, *are*, *was*, and *were* correctly.
- ☑ Begins proper names with capital letters.

📁 **PORTFOLIO OPPORTUNITY** You may want to have children place their descriptions in their portfolios or share them with family members.

PRACTICE page 54

Name _____

Extra Practice

A. Circle the verb in each sentence.

1. The snow (is) deep.
2. The trees (are) bare.
3. I (am) wet.

B. Write the correct verb to finish each sentence.

4. I (am, is, are) __am__ cold.
5. A deer (am, is, are) __is__ close.
6. Bushes (am, is, are) __are__ between us.

C. Choose the verb that completes each sentence correctly. Write the new sentence.

7. The deer's eyes (was, were) bright. The deer's eyes were bright.
8. Its fur (was, were) brown. Its fur was brown.
9. Then the deer (was, were) gone. Then the deer was gone.
10. I (was, were) sad. I was sad.

54 Unit 3 • Chapter 16   Practice • Forms of *Be*

CHALLENGE

PEOPLE PICTURES Children can draw people they like, such as friends, family members, story characters, or celebrities, and write sentences to go with the pictures. Suggest that children count the number of times they use the words *am*, *is*, *are*, *was*, and *were* in their sentences. Hang the pictures and sentences in a picture gallery.

My grandpa is very kind. He was a rancher.

Chapter Review

OBJECTIVES

- To review the verbs *am*, *is*, *are*, *was*, and *were*
- To recognize the different parts of a test and understand how to take a test

DAILY LANGUAGE PRACTICE

TRANSPARENCY 31

1 Two chairs was broken, (were; .)

2 One table were very olde. (was; old)

BRIDGE TO WRITING Two years ago, my clothes (form of *be*) smaller.

STANDARDIZED TEST PREP

Read each set of directions with children to make sure they understand how to complete each section. You may wish to have children complete this page independently and use it as an assessment.

TEST PREPARATION TIP
Item Type: Multiple Choice

TIP

Model this strategy to help children determine the correct answer:

I read the sentence. I look at the naming part. Does the noun tell about one or about more than one?

In the first sentence, *bag* tells about one. I know that *is* is used with a noun that names one. I look at the verb. The verb is *are*, so the sentence is not correct. I read the answer choices. I know that *a* is not correct because you use *am* after *I*. So I choose *b* because *is* tells about one. I read the sentence again with my answer choice to make sure it makes sense.

Forms of *Be*

Chapter Review   STANDARDIZED TEST PREP

Choose the best answer for each underlined word.

1. My red bag <u>are</u> packed.
   - **a.** am
   - **b.** <u>is</u>
   - **c.** correct as is

2. I <u>am</u> ready to go.
   - **a.** is
   - **b.** are
   - **c.** <u>correct as is</u>

3. My two brothers <u>is</u> ready.
   - **a.** <u>are</u>
   - **b.** am
   - **c.** correct as is

4. Last year we <u>are</u> not ready.
   - **a.** was
   - **b.** <u>were</u>
   - **c.** correct as is

5. My father <u>are</u> upset with us.
   - **a.** <u>was</u>
   - **b.** were
   - **c.** correct as is

6. We missed the train because we <u>were</u> late.
   - **a.** was
   - **b.** is
   - **c.** <u>correct as is</u>

7. We <u>is</u> not late today.
   - **a.** was
   - **b.** <u>are</u>
   - **c.** correct as is

8. We <u>was</u> on the train!
   - **a.** <u>are</u>
   - **b.** is
   - **c.** correct as is

Visit our website for more activities with verbs:
www.harcourtschool.com

206

Language Skills Assessment

PORTFOLIO ASSESSMENT
Have children select their best work from the following activities:

- **Writing Connection,** *pages 199, 201, 203, 205;* TE activities, *pages 199, 203, 205*

ONGOING ASSESSMENT
Evaluate the performance of 4-6 children using appropriate checklists and record forms from pages R65–R68 and R77–R79.

INTERNET Activities and exercises to help children prepare for state and standardized assessments appear on *The Learning Site:*
www.harcourtschool.com

■ Study Skills ■

Taking a Test

Many schools give language tests. Here are the parts of one kind of test.

directions → **Choose the best answer for each underlined word.**

item → **1.** Many shells <u>was</u> pink.
   a. is   **b.** were   **c.** correct as is

important word

answer choices

Follow these tips when you take a test.

- Read or listen to all the directions.
- Plan your time. Answer the easy items first. Then go back and do the hard ones.
- Find the important word or words in the item. This will help you choose the right answer.
- Read all the answer choices. Then you can choose the best one.

Practice

Read each sentence. Write *True* if it is true. Write *False* if it is not true.

1. Before you start a test, read all the directions. True

2. The directions tell how to do the test. True

3. You should answer the hard questions first. False

4. You should read all the answers before you choose one. True

207

■ Study Skills ■

Taking a Test

TEACH/MODEL

Read the introduction with children. Then discuss the labeled parts of the sample before reading the directions with children. Discuss why *was* is the important word. Explain that *was* is not correct, so *c. correct as is* cannot be the best answer. Discuss how *is* is not correct in the sentence, so *a. is* cannot be the best answer. Ask children to try *were* in the sentence to confirm that *b. were* is the best answer. Then read and discuss the tips. You may want to make a chart of the tips.

PRACTICE You may want to do the practice part together as a group. Then invite volunteers to read and answer each example.

WRAP-UP/ASSESS

SUMMARIZE Ask children to summarize what they have learned about taking a test and how it will help them next time they need to take a test.

PRACTICE page 55

REACHING ALL LEARNERS

Name _____

Taking A Test

A. Fill in the circle next to the correct answer.

1. Which answer choices should you read?
   ○ only the correct choice
   ○ half of the choices
   ● all of the choices

2. When should you read the directions?
   ○ after the test
   ● before the test
   ○ during the test

3. How should you plan your time on a test?
   ○ You should work very quickly.
   ● You should do the easy items first.
   ○ You should spend time on the hard items first.

B. Fill in the circle that finishes the sentence correctly.

4. When you read an item, _____.
   ○ you should read quickly.
   ○ you should guess the answer right away.
   ● you should find the important word or words.

TRY THIS! Work with a partner. Write short, fun quizzes for each other. Then do each other's quizzes. Did you follow the directions?

Practice • Forms of Be   Unit 3 • Chapter 16 **55**

CHALLENGE

REACHING ALL LEARNERS

TEST REVIEW Have children work in groups to write additional test-taking tips. Encourage them to think of all they need to have and do when taking a test. Have them list materials (pencil, paper), and strategies. Invite children to post their tips on a bulletin board or a wall.

LESSON ORGANIZER	DAY 1	DAY 2
DAILY LANGUAGE PRACTICE TRANSPARENCIES 32, 33	1. the boy be happy today. (The; is) 2. Now we is on hte train. (are; the) **Bridge to Writing** Yesterday I <u>(form of be)</u> at Aunt Claire's house.	1. We hadd a teacher named mr. Jones. (had; Mr.) 2. I hav Mrs. smith as my teacher. (have; Smith) **Bridge to Writing** The children <u>(verb that does not show action)</u> a new music teacher today.
ORAL WARM-UP Listening/Speaking	Discuss Animals' Bodies p. 208	Describe Things p. 210  *Grammar Jingles*™ CD, Primary, Track 11
TEACH/MODEL GRAMMAR **KEY** ✔ = tested skill	✔ **THE VERBS *HAS*, *HAVE*, AND *HAD*** pp. 208–209 • To interpret and dramatize a poem • To recognize that some verbs show that something belongs to someone	✔ **USING *HAS*, *HAVE*, AND *HAD*** pp. 210–211 • To recognize that *has* and *have* tell about now and that *had* tells about the past • To use the verbs *has*, *have*, and *had* in writing
Reaching All Learners	*Practice Book* p. 56 **Challenge:** Activity Card 12, p. R52 **ESL:** *ESL Manual* pp. 84, 85 **Reteach:** *Reteach Activities Copying Masters* p. 34	**Modified Instruction** Below-Level: Circle the Naming Part Above-Level: Rewrite Sentences **Challenge:** Write Riddles p. 211 **ESL:** Name the Object p. 210 *ESL Manual* pp. 84, 86 *Practice Book* p. 57 **Reteach:** *Reteach Activities Copying Masters* p. 35

WRITING	Complete Sentences p. 209
	
	  Summarize/Reflect
		Writing Connection p. 211
		 Recording Information
		  Summarize/Reflect

CROSS-CURRICULAR/ ENRICHMENT	**Vocabulary Power** Word Meaning, p. 208 anchored, attached, connected, **fastened**, untied See ***Vocabulary Power*** book.	**Vocabulary Power** Synonyms, p. 208 *Vocabulary Power* book, p. 49 **Vocabulary activity**

DAY 3

1. we has a new dog. (We; have)

2. Yesterday we have two friend at our house. (had; friends)

Bridge to Writing They <u>(form of have)</u> two games to play today.

Talk About Yesterday and Today p. 212
Grammar Jingles™ CD, Primary, Track 11

✔ **AGREEMENT WITH *HAS, HAVE, AND HAD*** pp. 212-213
• To understand that *has, have,* and *had* agree with the naming part of a sentence
• To revise a piece of writing to use *has, have,* and *had* correctly

Modified Instruction
Below-Level: Say Naming Parts
Above-Level: Write Sentences
Challenge: Inventions p. 213
ESL: Memory Game p. 212
ESL Manual pp. 84, 87
Practice Book p. 58
Reteach: *Reteach Activities Copying Masters* p. 36

Writing Connection p. 213
Revising
Summarize/Reflect

Vocabulary Power
Prefixes, p. 208
Vocabulary Power book, p. 50
Vocabulary activity

DAY 4

1. The library have a book about Horses. (has; horses)

2. My horse has a carrot yesterday? (had; yesterday.)

Bridge to Writing Now the horse <u>(form of have)</u> a blanket on its back.

Play "What Comes Next?" p. 214

EXTRA PRACTICE p. 214
• To understand how to use *has* and *have* to tell about now and *had* to tell about the past
• To use *has, have,* and *had* in writing
Practice and Assessment

Challenge: Tell About a Trip p. 215
ESL: Role Play p. 214
ESL Manual, pp. 84, 88
Practice Book p. 59

Writing Connection p. 215
Time Line

Vocabulary Power
Expand Word Meaning, p. 208
Vocabulary Power book, p. 51
Vocabulary activity

DAY 5

1. Did you had a good time at the play last week. (have; week?)

2. Jane and yoshi has a cousin in New York. (Yoshi; have)

Bridge to Writing Peter <u>(form of have)</u> three dogs now.

TEST PREP **Chapter Review** p. 216
• To review when to use *has, have,* and *had*
• To use available technology such as word processing to revise pieces of writing
Test Preparation

Practice Book p. 60
Challenge: Computer Revision p. 217
ESL: *ESL Manual* pp. 84, 89

Technology p. 217
Editing on a Computer

Vocabulary Power
Related Words. p. 208

The Verbs *Has*, *Have*, and *Had*

OBJECTIVES
- To interpret and dramatize a poem
- To recognize that some verbs show that something belongs to someone

DAILY LANGUAGE PRACTICE

TRANSPARENCY 32

1 the boy be happy today. (The; is)

2 Now we is on hte train. (are; the)

BRIDGE TO WRITING Yesterday I ___ (form of *be*) at Aunt Claire's house.

ORAL WARM-UP

USE PRIOR KNOWLEDGE Ask children to point to their legs, arms, and nose. Then briefly discuss whether all animals have these same parts and how these parts differ. List their ideas on the board.

TEACH/MODEL

Have children turn to the poem on page 208, read the title, and look at the illustration. Read the poem aloud. Help children notice how some lines begin with the same words. Then reread the poem, having children join in and act out the lines.

DEVELOP ORAL LANGUAGE Prompt children to think about the poem by asking questions such as these:

- **How does a snake move?**
- **Would you like to have wings and fly?**

Encourage children to respond in complete sentences using *has*, *have*, and *had*. Add the forms of the verb *have* to the **Word Wall**.

The Verbs *Has*, *Have*, and *Had*

Read the poem.

What If?

A cat has four.
A bird has two.
If snakes had these,
What could they do?

A worm has none.
A bee has two.
If you had these,
What could you do?

Dolphins have them.
Whales do, too.
If we had these,
What could we do?

Kathryn Corbett

208

Vocabulary Power

DAY 1 WORD MEANINGS Introduce and define *fastened* (joined, connected). **Why is it important to have your seatbelt fastened?**

DAY 2 SYNONYMS Write: *fastened*. **Name words that have a similar meaning.** (See also *Vocabulary Power*, page 49.)

DAY 3 PREFIXES List: *fastened*, *unfastened*, *refastened*. Have children use paper clips and papers to show word meaning. (See also *Vocabulary Power*, page 50.)

DAY 4 EXPAND WORD MEANING Listen: **Josie fastened her eyes on the TV. What does this sentence mean? Describe or tell what Josie did.** (See also *Vocabulary Power*, page 51.)

DAY 5 RELATED WORDS **Make a list of items that could be used as fasteners** (paper clips, buttons, snaps, zipper, . . .).

Talk with a partner about the answers to the poem's riddles. Then talk about things animals have that you do not have. What do those things help animals do?

> Some verbs do not show action. They show that something belongs to someone.
>
> I **have** a book about elephants.
> The book **has** many pictures.
> I **had** a toy elephant once.

Work in a group to finish these sentences. Try to write a different thing for each animal.

A rabbit has _____.

A dog has _____.

A frog has _____.

A fish has _____.

Seals have _____.

Chickens have _____.

Porcupines have _____.

209

WRITE Use children's discussions about animals to generate animal parts to add beside the list on the board begun in Warm-Up. Then read the definition in the box and talk about the example sentences. Remind children that every sentence needs a verb.

Read the items at the bottom of page 209 together. Point out that there are many choices for most of the blanks but that children should think of what is unique to each animal. Work with children to complete the items.

WRAP-UP/ASSESS

SUMMARIZE Reread the poem with children. Then have them summarize and reflect on what they learned about the forms of verbs that do not show action. Ask them to write their reflections in their journals as well as sentences they thought of while completing this page.
REFLECTION

REACHING ALL LEARNERS

RETEACH

INTERVENTION Lessons in **visual, auditory,** and **kinesthetic** modalities: p. R28 and *Reteach Activities Copying Masters*, p. 34.

page 34

The Verbs *Has, Have,* and *Had*
Read aloud each sentence. Circle the verb.

EXAMPLE: Pine trees (have) pinecones.

1. An oak tree (has) acorns.
2. Last fall, this apple tree (had) apples.
3. I (have) an orange tree in my yard.
4. It (has) many oranges.
5. I (had) a pear tree last year.

The Verbs *Has, Have,* and *Had*

Make this chart on a sheet of paper.

has	have	had

Cut out the sentences below. Glue each sentence under the verb that best completes it.

A pine tree ___ sharp needles.	Some gardens _have_ many flowers.
Last month that tree _had_ many flowers.	Apples _have_ seeds.
Pam _has_ a pinecone now.	Our garden _had_ roses last spring.

34 Unit 3 • Chapter 17   Reteach Activities • Forms of *Have*

REACHING ALL LEARNERS

PRACTICE page 56

Name _____

The Verbs *Has, Have,* and *Had*

A. Read each sentence. Underline the verb.

1. The plant has leaves.
2. Flowers have stems.
3. Last summer, I had a bunch of roses.
4. We had a flower garden.
5. Now we have a vegetable garden.

B. Write *has, have,* or *had* to complete each sentence.

6. The carrots __have__ green tops now.
7. Yesterday, the garden __had__ bugs.
8. Last spring, I __had__ a watering can.
9. Today, I __have__ a new can.
10. My brother __has__ a new can, too.

TRY THIS! Write one sentence about something you have now. Write another sentence about something you had before. Use *have* and *had* in your sentences.

56 Unit 3 • Chapter 17   Practice • Forms of *Have*

REACHING ALL

CHALLENGE

MAKE YOUR CLASSROOM
Have children use **Challenge Activity Card 12** (page R52) to write about what they have now and what they had last year in their classroom. Display the cutouts, and have children compare their classrooms.

Challenge Activity Card 12

Make Your Classroom

Using *Has*, *Have*, and *Had*

OBJECTIVES
• To recognize that *has* and *have* tell about now and that *had* tells about the past
• To use the verbs *has, have,* and *had* in writing

DAILY LANGUAGE PRACTICE

TRANSPARENCY 32

1 We hadd a teacher named mr. Jones. (had; Mr.)

2 I hav Mrs. smith as my teacher. (have; Smith)

BRIDGE TO WRITING The children ___(verb that does not show action)___ a new music teacher today.

ORAL WARM-UP

USE PRIOR KNOWLEDGE Ask children to describe some of the things they have at home. Write some of their sentences on the board.

Grammar Jingles™ **CD, Primary** Use Track 11 for review and reinforcement of the forms of *have*.

TEACH/MODEL

Read the explanation and examples with children. Explain that *had* is used to tell about one and about more than one. Ask children to alter when something happened by changing the verb in these examples, such as: *Last week we had soup for lunch. Today we have soup for lunch.* Point out the use of *has, have,* or *had* in the sentences from Oral Warm-Up.

GUIDED PRACTICE Work with children to complete each sentence. Remind them to notice when things happen to choose the correct form of *have.*

Using *Has*, *Have*, and *Had*

> The verbs **has** and **have** tell about now.
> Use **has** to tell about one.
>
> The snake **has** smooth skin.
>
> Use **have** to tell about more than one.
>
> Snakes **have** long bodies.
>
> The verb **had** tells about the past.
>
> Weeks ago the snake **had** green skin.
> The snakes **had** a smaller cage last year.

Guided Practice

Write *has*, *have*, or *had* to complete each sentence.

1. Today we ___have___ a snake.
2. Pat ___has___ a box for the snake now.
3. Most snakes ___have___ thin, pointy tongues.
4. Last week we ___had___ a turtle in the box.
5. Yesterday the turtle ___had___ a good meal.

210

Vocabulary Power page 49

Name _____   Synonyms

These words are synonyms. They have similar meanings.

anchored   attached   connected   fastened   united

Draw a picture for each word. Label each picture with a short sentence. For example: My hand is <u>connected</u> to my arm.

1.	2.
3.	4.
5.	

Vocabulary Power   Unit 3 • Chapter 17   49

REACHING ALL LEARNERS   **ESL**

NAME THE OBJECT Have each child select an object and hide it (or a picture of it) behind his or her back. Ask the group to guess what it is by asking questions. Encourage them to ask what the object has.

Does it have pages? Do they have numbers?

Remember The verbs *has* and *have* tell about now. The verb *had* tells about the past.

Independent Practice

Write *has*, *have*, or *had* to complete each sentence.

6. Martha now ___has___ many pets.

7. Her birds ___have___ colorful feathers.

8. The rabbits ___have___ white fur.

9. Each pet ___has___ its own food today.

10. The animals now ___have___ cages.

11. Martha ___has___ a lot of work each day.

12. She ___had___ a busy day yesterday.

13. Yesterday the rabbits ___had___ a messy cage.

14. Today they ___have___ a clean cage.

15. Now the rabbits ___have___ a nice home.

Writing Connection

Recording Information Draw an animal you have or would like to have as a pet. Write a list of what you know about the animal. Tell what it looks like. Tell about its home. Use *has*, *have*, and *had* correctly.

You can use a computer drawing program to make a picture of the pet.

211

Independent Practice

Have children complete the Independent Practice, or modify it by using the following suggestions:

MODIFIED INSTRUCTION

BELOW-LEVEL STUDENTS Ask children to use their fingers to circle the naming part of each sentence. Then ask them to use their fingers to underline any time words.

ABOVE-LEVEL STUDENTS After they have finished, ask children to rewrite two sentences, changing the time.

Writing Connection

Recording Information Remind children to think about when to use *has*, *have*, and *had*. Have volunteers place their pictures and lists in the Sharing Basket to share with others.

WRAP-UP/ASSESS

SUMMARIZE Ask children to summarize what they have learned about *has*, *have*, and *had*.

RETEACH

INTERVENTION Lessons in **visual, auditory,** and **kinesthetic** modalities: p. R28 and *Reteach Activities Copying Masters*, p.35.

PRACTICE page 57

Name _____

Using *Has*, *Have*, and *Had*

A. Circle the verb that correctly completes each sentence.

1. Animals (**has**, have) different body parts.

2. A giraffe (**has**, have) a long neck.

3. Elephants (has, **have**) trunks.

4. A zebra (**has**, have) stripes.

5. Last week, I saw a horse that (have, **had**) a mane.

B. Write *has*, *have*, or *had* to complete each sentence.

6. Turtles ___have___ shells.

7. A lion ___has___ sharp teeth.

8. A parrot ___has___ colorful feathers.

9. Last winter, I ___had___ a gerbil with a long tail.

10. Now I ___have___ a furry hamster.

TRY THIS! Think about three animals. Write a sentence about each animal that tells how it is different from the other two. Use the verbs *has*, *have*, and *had* in your sentences.

Practice • Forms of *Have*   Unit 3 • Chapter 17   57

CHALLENGE

WRITE RIDDLES Have children write riddles on index cards to describe themselves. Have them write three or four clues, using *have*, *has*, or *had* in each. Put the riddles in a box. As time permits, select a riddle and read it to the group to solve.

I have brown hair.
My bag has two
pockets.
I had an old red bike

---

page 35

Using *Has*, *Have*, and *Had*

Use a verb from the box to complete each sentence.

has	have	had

1. The twins ___have___ many crayons.

2. Today the gold crayon ___has___ a sharp tip.

3. It ___had___ a dull tip yesterday.

4. Now Ned ___has___ a good sharpener.

Using *Has*, *Have*, and *Had*

Cut out the verbs at the bottom of the page. Glue them where they belong.

1. Ned and Nora ___have___ white paper today.

2. The paper ___has___ lines.

3. Today Nora ___has___ homework.

4. Yesterday she ___had___ homework, too.

has	has	have	had

Teacher: Cut apart the activities and distribute to children based on the modalities that are their strengths.

Reteach Activities • Forms of *Have*   Unit 3 • Chapter 17   35

Agreement with *Has*, *Have*, and *Had*

OBJECTIVES

- To understand that *has*, *have*, and *had* agree with the naming part of a sentence
- To revise a piece of writing to make sure the verb *has*, *have*, and *had* agree with the naming part

 DAILY LANGUAGE PRACTICE

TRANSPARENCY 32

1 we has a new dog. (We; have)

2 Yesterday we have two friend at our house. (had; friends)

BRIDGE TO WRITING They _____ (form of have) two games to play today.

ORAL WARM-UP

USE PRIOR KNOWLEDGE Have children compare what they have for lunch today with what they had yesterday.

 ***Grammar Jingles*™ CD, Primary** Use Track 11 for review and reinforcement of forms of *have*.

TEACH/MODEL

Read aloud the explanation in the box. Then draw children's attention to the chart. Have volunteers create an example sentence for each pronoun.

GUIDED PRACTICE Read aloud the first item at the bottom of page 212. Ask a volunteer to identify the time word (*Yesterday*) and to tell whether the sentence takes place now or in the past. (past) Then ask children to say the naming part of the sentence (*Tami*). Ask if *has* goes with the telling part (yes) and the time word (no). Ask how children could change the sentence so it is correct. (change *has* to *had*) Repeat with the remaining items.

Agreement with *Has*, *Have*, and *Had*

Choose the form of *have* that agrees with, or goes with, the naming part of a sentence.

Pronoun	Now	The Past
I, you, we, they	have	had
he, she, it	has	had

Use *has* when the naming part tells about one. Use *have* with *I* and *you* and to tell about more than one. Use *had* to tell about the past.

Guided Practice

Decide if *have*, *has*, or *had* is used correctly. Write the incorrect sentences correctly.

1. Yesterday Tami has plans to go swimming.
   Yesterday Tami had plans to go swimming.
2. Yesterday she had her swimsuit on.
3. Yesterday her friends had flippers.
4. Today Tami had a mask.
   Today Tami has a mask.
5. Now her friends had snorkels, too.
   Now her friends have snorkels, too.

212

Vocabulary Power page 50

Name _____   Prefixes

Adding a prefix to a base word changes the meaning.

The string is tied. The string is untied. I have retied the string.

1. Add un- and re- to attached and fastened. Write the new words.

   unattached   unfastened

   reattached   refastened

2. Add un-, dis-, and re- to connected. Write the new words.

   unconnected   disconnected

   reconnected

3. Add un- to anchored. Add re- to united. Write the new words.

   unanchored   reunited

4. Draw and label pictures about two words you wrote.

50 Unit 3 • Chapter 17   Vocabulary Power

ESL

MEMORY GAME Ask each child to draw a picture of something he or she owns. Each child then shows the picture to the class and says, "I have a …" After everyone has shown his or her picture, take turns going around the room and seeing who can remember what the other children have. Encourage children to say complete sentences, such as "Peter has a bike."

Remember Choose the form of *have* that agrees with, or goes with, the naming part of the sentence.

Independent Practice

Decide if *have*, *has*, or *had* is used correctly. Write the incorrect sentences correctly.

6. The ocean has many animals.

7. Now I had pictures of the ocean.
   Now I have pictures of the ocean.

8. You had time to look at them now.
   You have time to look at them now.

9. The dolphin in the picture has little teeth.

10. That fish has stripes.

11. I had a fish tank now.
    I have a fish tank now.

12. Last year it has five fish in it.
    Last year it had five fish in it.

13. Now the tank has only three fish.

14. That starfish has five arms.

15. Last summer I have a starfish, too.
    Last summer I had a starfish, too.

Writing Connection

Revising Choose a piece of writing from your Writing Portfolio. Check to see whether you have used *have*, *has*, and *had* correctly. Revise any sentences that need changing.

Use your computer's grammar checker to look for sentences in which *have*, *has*, or *had* is used incorrectly.

213

Independent Practice

Have children complete the Independent Practice, or modify it by using the following suggestions:

MODIFIED INSTRUCTION

BELOW-LEVEL STUDENTS Suggest that children say the naming part and time word in each sentence to help them choose the correct verb in the chart.

ABOVE-LEVEL STUDENTS After they have finished, ask children to write two sentences about fish, using the verbs *has*, *have*, or *had*.

Writing Connection

Revising Help children select appropriate pieces of writing to revise. Have them focus on editing their writing for subject-verb agreement and appropriate verb tense.

WRAP-UP/ASSESS

SUMMARIZE Have children summarize and reflect on what they know about *has*, *have* and *had*.

REFLECTION

RETEACH

INTERVENTION Lessons in **visual**, **auditory**, and **kinesthetic** modalities: p. R28 and *Reteach Activities Copying Masters*, p. 36.

page 36

Agreement with *Has, Have,* and *Had*

Read each pair of sentences aloud. Underline the sentence that uses *has, have,* or *had* correctly.

1. Tess have a brown shirt.
   <u>Tess has a brown shirt.</u>

2. <u>Bill and Jeff have new shoes.</u>
   Bill and Jeff has new shoes.

3. Yesterday Angie have a blue skirt.
   <u>Yesterday Angie had a blue skirt.</u>

4. <u>Sonya and Rob have jeans.</u>
   Sonya and Rob has jeans.

Visual/Auditory

Agreement with *Has, Have,* and *Had*

Cut out the verbs below. Glue the word that best fits each sentence.

1. Jason [has] freckles.

2. Linda and Jess [have] black hair.

3. Will [has] long legs.

4. Last year our class [had] a pet hamster.

| have | has | had | has |

Kinesthetic

36 Unit 3 • Chapter 17   Reteach Activities • Forms of *Have*

PRACTICE page 58

Name _____

Agreement with *Has, Have,* and *Had*

A. Use the verbs from the box to complete the sentences.

| had | has | have |

1. I __have__ my new bathing suit on today.

2. Mom __has__ one on now, too.

3. Yesterday I __had__ fun in the pool.

B. Decide if *has, have,* or *had* is used correctly in each sentence. Write the incorrect sentences correctly.

4. We has a big pool.
   We have a big pool.

5. We have races there each summer.
   _____

6. Now I had three ribbons.
   Now I have three ribbons.

TRY THIS! Write two sentences about something you own. Use *has, have,* and *had.*

58 Unit 3 • Chapter 17   Practice • Forms of *Have*

CHALLENGE

INVENTIONS Have children use encyclopedias or computer software to find out about an invention they like to use, such as a computer, a radio, or a video game. Ask them to write a paragraph about it, listing its features and describing it, but not naming it. Ask them to illustrate their work. Invite children to read their descriptions aloud. Have the group guess the invention. Children should include forms of *has*, *have*, and *had* in their descriptions.

Extra Practice

OBJECTIVES
- To understand how to use *has* and *have* to tell about now and *had* to tell about the past
- To use *has*, *have*, and *had* in writing

DAILY LANGUAGE PRACTICE

TRANSPARENCY 33

1 The library have a book about Horses. (has; horses)

2 My horse has a carrot yesterday? (had; yesterday.)

BRIDGE TO WRITING Now the horse _(form of have)_ a blanket on its back.

ORAL WARM-UP

PLAY "WHAT COMES NEXT?" Start by saying, *First I had one chair.* Have a child add another piece of furniture to your sentence. (Next I had a chair and a table.) The next child adds on. Tell children that they must try to remember and say all the things that came before.

TEACH/MODEL

Read each set of directions to help children understand how to complete each section. You may want to have children share their answers in small groups before you read aloud the answers.

WRAP-UP/ASSESS

SUMMARIZE Ask children to reflect on and discuss any problems they had in completing the practice before they summarize what they have learned about the verbs *has*, *have*, and *had*.

ADDITIONAL PRACTICE Extra practice items are provided on page 471 of the *Pupil Edition* (R4 *Teacher's Edition*).

TECHNOLOGY
Grammar Practice and Assessment CD-ROM

Writing Express CD-ROM

INTERNET Visit *The Learning Site!*
www.harcourtschool.com

Forms of *Have*

Extra Practice

Write *has*, *have*, or *had* to complete each sentence.

1. We ___have___ a pond near our house.

2. Today the pond ___has___ frogs in it.

3. A frog ___has___ four legs.

4. Frogs ___have___ lungs for breathing air.

5. Two months ago, the pond ___had___ tadpoles in it.

6. Those tadpoles ___had___ tiny legs.

Decide if *have*, *has*, or *had* is used correctly. Write the incorrect sentences correctly.

7. Now the pond near our house had rocks by it.
Now the pond near our house has rocks by it.

8. Last night the rocks have salamanders on them.
Last night the rocks had salamanders on them.

9. I saw a salamander that have spots.
I saw a salamander that had spots.

10. The pond always has many animals near it.

214

Vocabulary Power page 51

Name _____

Expand Word Meaning

The following words have similar meanings. Their meanings are similar to "joined together" or "combined together."

anchored   attached   connected   fastened   united

The words have other meanings as well. Read the numbered sentences. Write the letter of the sentence that comes next. The first is done for you.

__C__ 1. I'm not moving.

__D__ 2. I'm very fond of my sister.

__E__ 3. My friend and I agree.

__B__ 4. The cat spies a bird.

__A__ 5. Apples and oranges are fruit.

A. They are connected.

B. Her eyes are fastened on it.

C. I'm staying anchored to my desk!

D. We're very attached to each other.

E. We are united!

Choose one of the sentence pairs. Draw a picture to show what the sentences mean.

Vocabulary Power   Unit 3 • Chapter 17   51

ESL
REACHING ALL LEARNERS

ROLE PLAY Pair fluent English speakers with second-language learners. Have pairs role-play a salesperson and a customer. Encourage children to use *has*, *have*, and *had* in their questions and answers. Have pairs write down some of their sentences as dialogue.

"Do you have animal toys?"

"I have a bear. It has brown fur."

Language Play

How Many Do I Have?
● Play this game with a few other players.
● The first player hides some counters in a fist. Then the player asks the other players, "How many do I have?"
● The player whose guess is closest then takes a turn at hiding the counters.
● After all the players have had one turn, talk about the number of counters they had. Who had the most? Who had the fewest? Make sure you use *have*, *has*, and *had* correctly.

Writing Connection

Time Line A time line shows things that have happened over time. Make a time line of your life. Use this time line as a model.

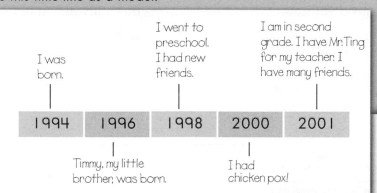

I was born.

I went to preschool. I had new friends.

I am in second grade. I have Mr. Ting for my teacher. I have many friends.

| 1994 | 1996 | 1998 | 2000 | 2001 |

Timmy, my little brother, was born.

I had chicken pox!

215

Language Play

Have children play the game on page 215 in small groups. Give each group a handful of counters. Have children go around the group to make guesses. Make sure every child gets a chance to hide the counters.

Writing Connection

Time Line Check to see that children have successfully written a time line by using the criteria below.

CRITERIA
☑ Begins with the year he or she was born.
☑ Writes the correct form of the verb to tell about the past.
☑ Writes the correct form of the verb *have* that agrees with the naming part.
☑ Ends with the present year.

📁 **PORTFOLIO OPPORTUNITY** You may want to have children share their time lines with the group and then place them in their portfolios.

PRACTICE page 59

Name _____

Extra Practice

A. Read each sentence. Underline the verb.

1. The cat has whiskers.
2. The kittens have closed eyes.
3. They had a nap earlier.

B. Circle the verb that completes each sentence.

4. The kittens (has, **have**) a soft bed.
5. The bed (**has**, have) a pillow.
6. Yesterday, the cat (has, have, **had**) a small ball.
7. Today, the kittens (has, **have**, had) the ball.

C. Decide if *has, have,* or *had* is used correctly in each sentence. Write the incorrect sentences correctly.

8. I has a cat, too.
   I have a cat, too.

9. My cat has short fur.

10. Last summer, I have another cat.
    Last summer, I had another cat.

Practice • *Forms of Have*   Unit 3 • Chapter 17   59

CHALLENGE

TELL ABOUT A TRIP Ask children to write about a real or imaginary trip. Have them describe what they had with them and what they did. Have them tell why they think people should visit the place or places they have written about. Invite children to draw a picture of the place.

Chapter Review

OBJECTIVES

- To review when to use *has, have,* and *had*
- To use available technology such as word processing to revise pieces of writing

DAILY LANGUAGE PRACTICE

TRANSPARENCY 33

1 Did you had a good time at the play last week. (have; week?)

2 Jane and yoshi has a cousin in New York. (Yoshi; have)

BRIDGE TO WRITING Peter (form of *have*) three dogs now.

STANDARDIZED TEST PREP

Read the directions with children to make sure they understand how to complete the page. You may wish to have children complete this page independently before you use it as an assessment.

TEST PREPARATION TIP

Item Type: Multiple Choice

 TIP

Model this strategy to help children determine the correct answer:

First I read the sentence. Then I read the underlined word. I ask myself: Can I use this verb in the sentence? Next I read the naming part of the sentence to see whether it tells about one or about more than one. Then I check the sentence for a time word to find whether it tells about now or about the past. I look at the answer choices. I choose the answer that goes best with the naming part and the time.

Forms of *Have*

Chapter Review STANDARDIZED TEST PREP

Choose the best answer for each underlined word.

1. Yesterday the owl <u>had</u> a hurt wing.
   a. have
   b. has
   <u>c. correct as is</u>

2. At that time, its wing <u>has</u> dirt on it.
   a. have
   <u>b. had</u>
   c. correct as is

3. Now the owl <u>have</u> a clean, mended wing.
   <u>a. has</u>
   b. had
   c. correct as is

4. We <u>have</u> other animals in the shelter today.
   a. had
   b. has
   <u>c. correct as is</u>

5. The animals <u>had</u> a good vet now.
   a. has
   <u>b. have</u>
   c. correct as is

6. Today the vet <u>had</u> a busy day ahead of her.
   <u>a. has</u>
   b. have
   c. correct as is

 Visit our website for more activities with *has, have,* and *had.*

www.harcourtschool.com

216

Language Skills Assessment

• •

PORTFOLIO ASSESSMENT
Have children select their best work from the following activities:

- **Writing Connection,** pages 211, 215; TE activities, pages 211 and 215.

ONGOING ASSESSMENT
Evaluate the performance of 4-6 children using appropriate checklists and record forms from pages R65–R68 and R77–R79.

 INTERNET Activities and exercises to help children prepare for state and standardized assessments appear on *The Learning Site!*

www.harcourtschool.com

■ Technology ■

Editing on a Computer

A word processing program can help you revise and edit your writing and organize notes. You can use it to move words from one place in a document to another. To move words, you need to highlight them, <u>Cut</u> or <u>Copy</u> them, and then <u>Paste</u> them in the new place.

Practice

Type these notes on your computer. Then move the words to put them in a better order. Add numbers and any other words you need. Some parts are done for you.

Notes
gets bigger, taller
body grows, changes
gets stronger, heavier

adult   child
teenager   baby

people grow, change

Document 1

1. The body grows and changes.
   - gets bigger and taller
   - gets stronger and heavier
2. People grow and change.
   - baby
   - child
   - teenager
   - adult

217

■ Technology ■

Editing on a Computer

TEACH/MODEL

Read the explanation to the children. Explain that children must highlight the words they want to copy, cut, or move. If they click *copy*, the words will be repeated wherever they put their cursors and click *paste*. If they click *cut*, the high-lighted words will be cut out. Cut-out words can be pasted somewhere else by moving the cursor and clicking *paste*. You may want to demonstrate these commands on a computer to make sure children understand how to cut and paste text.

PRACTICE When children have finished, have volunteers make up sentences and type the words in mixed-up order. Ask other children to put the words in the correct order using the cut-and-paste commands on the computer.

WRAP-UP/ASSESS

SUMMARIZE Ask children to tell what they have learned about editing on a computer.

REACHING ALL LEARNERS — PRACTICE page 60

Name _____

Editing on a Computer

Follow the directions using a computer.

1. Type the following sentence:
   Birds fly south.

2. Add the words *in the winter* so that the sentence says:
   Birds fly south in the winter.

3. Add the word *Many* so that the sentence says:
   Many birds fly south in the winter.

4. Move *in the winter* so that the sentence says:
   in the winter Many birds fly south.

5. Make the letter *I* capital and the letter *M* lowercase so that the sentence says:
   In the winter many birds fly south.

6. Add a comma so that the sentence says:
   In the winter, many birds fly south.

TRY THIS! Use your computer skills to add, delete, or move text in a piece of your own writing.

60   Unit 3 • Chapter 17   Practice • Forms of *Have*

REACHING ALL LEARNERS — CHALLENGE

COMPUTER REVISION Have children select a piece of writing from their portfolios. Have them use the computer to type their work, edit it, and then check the spelling and grammar. Tell children to keep revising until they are happy with their writing. Have them print their text and share it with the group.

LESSON ORGANIZER	DAY **1**	DAY **2**
DAILY LANGUAGE PRACTICE *TRANSPARENCY 34*	1. i are in the second grade. (I am) 2. we share our favorite books yesterday (We shared; yesterday.)	1. yesterday I were inside. (Yesterday; was) 2. it were cold and wet (It was; wet.)
ORAL WARM-UP *Listening/Speaking*	Recall Animal Stories p. 218	Take a Poll p. 228
TEACH/MODEL *WRITING* 	**Literature Model:** "Two Greedy Bears," pp. 218–224 • To read and respond to a story as a model for writing • To identify the beginning, middle, and ending of a story **Reading-Writing Connection:** Parts of a Story p. 225 **A Student Model** pp. 226–227	**GUIDED WRITING** ✔ **Prewriting** pp. 228–229 • To brainstorm and select a story idea • To use a story map to plan a beginning, middle, and ending **Transparency** 35
Reaching All Learners	**Options for Reading** p. 219 **ESL:** Dramatize p. 222 *ESL Manual* pp. 90–91	**Interactive Writing** p. 228 **Challenge:** Write a Story p. 229 **ESL:** *ESL Manual* p. 90
GRAMMAR	**Unit 3 Review** pp. 236–237	**Unit 3 Review** pp. 236–237
CROSS-CURRICULAR/ ENRICHMENT	**Math Connection:** Dividing Into Equal Parts p. 220 **School-Home Connection:** Story Fest p. 221 **Writer's Craft:** Using Dialogue p. 221 **Social Studies Connection:** Good Appetite p. 222	**Vocabulary Power** Related Words p. 218 *Vocabulary Power* book p. 52 📷 **Vocabulary activity**

KEY
✔ = tested writing form/skill

creatures, beasts, beings, critters, varmints
See *Vocabulary Power* book.

DAY 3

1. has you ever read a fable.
   (Have; fable?)
2. They is stories that teach a lesson
   (are; lesson.)

Summarize Favorite Stories p. 230

GUIDED WRITING
✔ **Drafting** pp. 230–231
• To draft a story that contains
  a beginning, a middle, and an
  ending
• To create characters, a problem, and a solution

Transparency 36

Interactive Writing p. 231
ESL:
  ESL Manual p. 90

Unit 3 Review pp. 236–237

Writer's Craft: Repetiton
  p. 231

Vocabulary Power

Expand Word Meaning p. 218
Vocabulary Power book p. 53

DAY 4

1. the fox helpt the bears share the
   cheese. (The; helped)
2. she divideded it evenly
   (She divided; evenly.)

Review the Elements of a Story p. 232

GUIDED WRITING
✔ **Revising and Proofreading**
  pp. 232–233
• To revise a story
• To proofread a story for capitalization, punctuation, grammar, and spelling
• To use Editor's Marks to make
  revisions and corrections

Transparencies 36, 36a, 36b

ESL:
  ESL Manual p. 90

Unit 3 Review pp. 236–237

Spelling Connection:
  Spelling Strategies p. 233

Vocabulary Power

Regionalisms p. 218
Vocabulary Power book p. 54

Vocabulary activity

DAY 5

1. Carlos like my story about the bone
   (likes; bone.)
2. pam erase the first pictures she made
   (Pam erased; made.)

Talk About Sharing Stories p. 234

GUIDED WRITING
✔ **Publishing** p. 234
• To make final copies of
  revised stories
• To share stories with an
  audience
Scoring Rubric p. 234
Handwriting: Using Margins
  p. 235

ESL: Using Story Props p. 235
  ESL Manual p. 90

Unit 3 Review pp. 236–237

LISTENING AND SPEAKING:
  Telling a Story p. 235

Vocabulary Power

Word Usage p. 218

Assessment Strategies and Resources

FORMAL ASSESSMENT

If you want to know more about a child's mastery of the language and writing skills taught in Unit 3, **then** administer the first *Language Skills and Writing Assessment* for Unit 3. The test consists of two parts:

Language Skills: present- and past-tense verbs, forms of *be*, forms of *have*, and **dialogue**

Writing Task: Write a **story.** Scoring guidelines and model papers are included.

You can also use Cumulative Assessment: Units 1–3.

INFORMAL ASSESSMENT TOOLS

 Using Portfolios

During a conference with children, discuss their stories and review what they chose to include in their **writing portfolios.** Have children present a review of the writing in their portfolios to demonstrate how their writing has improved over time. Then ask the following types of questions about children's stories:

- What did you do to plan your story?
- Where and when does your story take place?
- Who is the main character?
- What is the problem of the story?
- What do your characters do to solve the problem?

You can also check children's understanding of **grammar** by evaluating it in their writing. Look for these points:

- Are *s* and *es* correctly added to present-tense verbs?

- Is *ed* correctly added to past-tense verbs?
- Are *am, is,* and *are* used correctly?
- Are *was* and *were* used to tell about the past?
- Are *have, has,* and *had* used correctly?

Oral Language Assessment

Use these guidelines:

Listening and Speaking

- Listens to enjoy and appreciate
- Asks relevant questions
- Adapts spoken language to the purpose, including rate and volume

Informal Assessment Reminder

If you used the pre-instruction writing prompt suggested in Teaching Grammar from Writing, **then** remember to compare the results with the writing done by children after the grammar and writing instruction.

Unit 4

Grammar
- All About Adjectives

Writing
- Poem
- Paragraph That Describes

Snowflakes

Snowflakes are like feathers
but smaller.
Snowflakes are like soap flakes
but wetter.
Snowflakes are like raindrops
but colder.
Snowflakes are like confetti
but icier.
Snowflakes are like tiny stars
falling quietly at night.

Unit 4

Grammar • All About Adjectives
Writing • Poem
• Paragraph That Describes

Introducing the Unit, pp. 240–241

Chapters	Grammar	Writing	Listening/ Speaking/Viewing
19 **Adjectives** pp. 242–251	**What Is an Adjective?** Usage and Mechanics: Adjectives That Tell What Kind, Writing Longer Sentences Extra Practice Chapter Review Daily Language Practice	**Writing Connections** Writing a Description Revising Riddle Fun	**"Red Riding Hood"** **Activities** Describe Red Riding Hood and Her House Language Play **Use Prior Knowledge** Play I Spy
20 **More Adjectives** pp. 252–261	**Words That Tell About the Senses** Usage and Mechanics: Adjectives for Taste, Smell, Feel, and Sound; Using Synonyms in Writing Extra Practice Chapter Review Daily Language Practice	**Writing Connections** Write a Description Revising Write a Shape Poem	**"August Afternoon"** **Activities** Talk About What You Hear, Feel, Smell, and Taste Language Play **Use Prior Knowledge** Play Pass the Soup, Please
21 **Short Process Writing:** **Poem** pp. 262–269	Daily Language Practice	**Poem** Prewriting and Drafting Editing Writer's Craft: Using Colorful Words Writing and Thinking: Reflect	**"Busy," "The Wind Is Cool and Swift"** **Sharing a Poem** **Activities** Read and Respond to the Model Reflect **Use Prior Knowledge**
22 **Adjectives for Size and Number** pp. 270–279	**Words for Size and Number** Usage and Mechanics: Adjectives That Tell How Many, Using a and an Extra Practice Chapter Review Daily Language Practice	**Writing Connections** Functional Writing: Breakfast Menu Revising Functional Writing: List of Materials	**"The Cow"** **Activities** Describe an Animal Language Play **Use Prior Knowledge** Play I'm Going on a Picnic Create Riddles
23 **Adjectives That Compare** pp. 280–289	**Words That Compare** Usage and Mechanics: Adding er and est, Writing to Compare Extra Practice Chapter Review Daily Language Practice	**Writing Connections** Colorful Adjectives Writing and Revising Functional Writing: Shopper's Report	**"Spring Rain"** **Activities** Talk About the Weather Language Play **Use Prior Knowledge** Building Blocks Making Comparisons
24 **Long Process Writing:** **Paragraph That Describes** pp. 290–307	Daily Language Practice	**Paragraph** Prewriting Drafting Revising Proofreading Publishing **Reading-Writing Connection:** Parts of a Paragraph	Reading Like a Writer Read and Respond to the Model Making Announcements **Use Prior Knowledge**

Unit Wrap-Up   Writing Across the Curriculum: Science and Literature, pp. 310–311

Vocabulary Power

Words of the week: *considerate*, *courteous, mannerly, polite, thoughtful*
Study Skill: Using a Thesaurus
🏆 **Technology:** Writing Connection

Vocabulary Power

Words of the week: *appetizing, delicious, flavorful, **luscious**, savory*
Vocabulary: Antonyms
🏆 **Technology:** Writing Connection

Vocabulary Power

Words of the week: *coil, swirl, twirl, twist, **whirl***
Handwriting: Making Letters the Correct Size
Hands-on Activities, pp. 239I–239J

Vocabulary Power

Words of the week: *countless, endless, **infinite**, unlimited, vast*
🏆 **Technology:** Using Spell-Check
Writing Connection

Vocabulary Power

Words of the week: *hasty, **quicker**, rapid, speedily, swiftest*
Study Skill: Using Pictographs and Bar Graphs
🏆 **Technology:** Writing Connection

Vocabulary Power

Words of the week: ***dignified**, formal, noble, regal, royal*

Language Minutes

- **Describe** an object you see using only **adjectives.** Have your partner look around and find it. SPEAKING/LISTENING/VIEWING

- **Draw** something you like to eat. **Write adjectives** to tell how it looks, feels, tastes, smells, or sounds. VIEWING/WRITING

- **Write** a poem about a place where you like to go. Remember to **use adjectives** and **colorful words** in your poem. Then read it to a partner. WRITING/SPEAKING

- **Make up** a strange animal. **Describe** it to a partner. **Use adjectives** that tell **what kind** and adjectives for **size and number.** Have your partner draw the animal you described. SPEAKING/LISTENING

- **Change** seats with a partner. Use adjectives to **compare** what you see around you now with what you usually see. VIEWING/SPEAKING

- **Write a paragraph that describes** something you like to have with you. WRITING

Technology Resources

Grammar Jingles™ **CD, Primary**
Grammar Practice and Assessment **CD-ROM**
Writing Express **CD-ROM**
Media Literacy and Communication Skills **Package**
🏆 **Visit** *The Learning Site!*
www.harcourtschool.com

Reaching All Learners

Intervention

SUPPORT ACTIVITIES To help you meet the needs of children who require extra support, use the following activity with individual children or small groups.

- Tell children to look for objects that are similar, but have different sizes, such as books, chalk sticks, or pencils. Invite children to sort and compare the groups of objects, using adjectives that tell size and number, and adjectives that compare.

INTERACTIVE WRITING Show children a picture of mountains or a scenic spot in your state. Have children brainstorm words to tell about the picture. Children can help you record them in a web or chart. Then have children help you write a description. Tell them their descriptions can be a poem, a song, or sentences.

Challenge

Use these suggestions with children who would benefit from more challenging activities.

- **DESCRIBE A PAINTING** Have children find a picture of a painting and make a list of adjectives that describe it. Children then write a caption for the painting.

- **WRITE A POEM** Ask children to think of a favorite animal within its habitat. Have them list words to describe how their animal looks, sounds, feels, and smells. Have children write a poem about their animal using vivid adjectives.

- **MAKE A POSTER** Have children make a math poster, using adjectives that describe shape, color, size, and number. For example, a poster might include a round red ball, a square blue block, a large book, and a larger book. Children can label each item.

English as a Second Language

ESL STRATEGIES Use these strategies and activities to help children use adjectives.

- Describe something you want children to draw, such as a small red cap or two big, brown dogs. Pause to give children time to draw after each sentence. Have volunteers tell about their drawings.

- Draw one large and one small tree on the board or on chart paper. Draw two round, red apples under the trees. Then draw three brown worms to illustrate small, smaller, and smallest. Model the language. Then invite volunteers to tell about the pictures. Encourage their efforts to use adjectives that compare.

Inclusion

VISUALLY IMPAIRED To help visually-impaired children, gather items of different sizes and textures, such as cotton, silk, aluminum foil, adhesive notes, pine cones, sandpaper, sponges, scouring pads, and rocks. Place the items in a box. Have children take turns touching the items. Ask them to use adjectives to tell about the items.

HEARING IMPAIRED To help hearing impaired children work with comparative adjectives, show them photographs of objects that can be compared. Have them use adjective word cards with -er and -est to describe the objects.

Teaching Grammar from Writing

PRETEST
Use the following prompt as a pretest to assess children's ability to use adjectives to describe and to compare in writing.

WRITING PROMPT
Think about your favorite meal. Write sentences that describe that meal to your teacher. Tell how the meal looks, tastes, feels, and smells.

EVALUATE AND PLAN
Analyze children's writing to determine how you can best meet their individual needs for instruction. Use the chart below to identify and remedy problems.

COMMON PROBLEMS	CHAPTERS TO USE
Does not use adjectives in writing.	Chapter 19: Adjectives
Does not use sensory details in writing.	Chapter 20: More Adjectivies
Rarely uses colorful, vivid words to describe.	Chapter 21: Using Colorful Words
Writes general descriptions that lack words for size number.	Chapter 22: Adjectives for Size and Number
Does not use *a* and *an* correctly.	Chapter 22: Adjectives for Size and Number
Uses incorrect wording when writing comparisons.	Chapter 23: Adjectives That Compare

Classroom Management

DURING...	SOME CHILDREN CAN...
Grammar Reteaching	Work on the Writing Across the Curriculum project.
Independent Practice	Begin the Writing Connection. Participate in Language Centers.
Portfolio Conferences	Complete Self-Evaluation forms. (See pages R78–R79 in this *Teacher's Edition*.) Participate in peer conferences.

Drama

LANGUAGE ARTS IN THE CLASSROOM

Incorporating drama in the classroom results in the development of enthusiastic readers and writers. When engaged in drama, children gain meaning through an interaction between who they are, what they know and have experienced, and what they read and understand in print.

STORY DRAMATIZATION Drama is an effective way to make stories and poetry come alive for children. In the classroom, drama can be a creative experience with little or no preparation at all or a very elaborate production with costumes, scenery, and props. The following examples show how literature, drama, and movement come together to develop and support literacy.

STORY PARTICIPATION As a familiar story is shared, have children participate by making sounds, gestures, or repeating a line during appropriate moments.

STORY REENACTMENT Children can re-create or "play" a favorite story by acting out. This type of informal drama differs from dramatic play since the action and dialogue children use are from a story they have shared. There can be but need not be an audience.

MINI-PERFORMANCES A mini-performance takes reader's theatre and a story reenactment one step further. After a story is shared with children, a script is developed, but it is a narration written and read by the teacher. The children follow a story line and become the characters, but they decide using their own words what the characters will say. Songs and simple movements can be used as well as simple costumes and props.

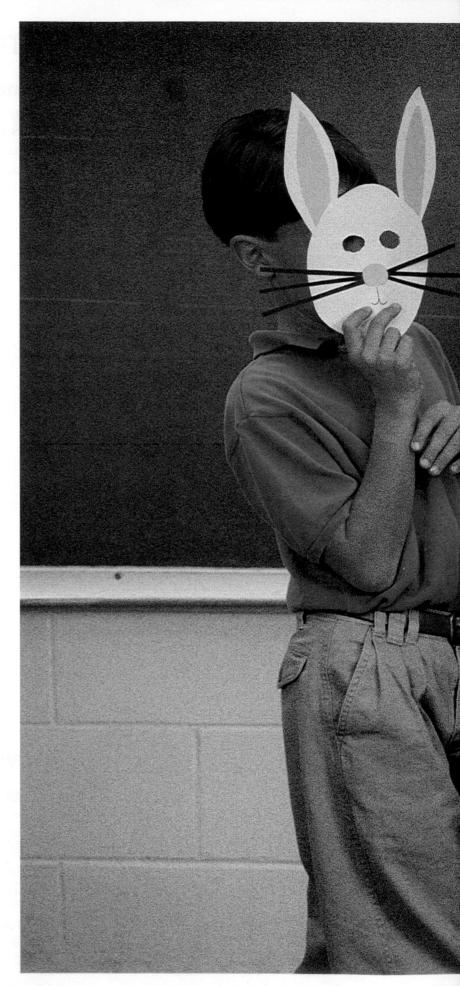

Hands-on Activities

What Am I?

MATERIALS: classroom objects

DIRECTIONS:

1. Have children gather several classroom objects. List the objects on the board.

2. Ask a volunteer to choose and describe one of the objects, using only adjectives that tell what kind. After several adjective clues, the volunteer asks, "What Am I?"

3. Have children guess the object, and then recall some of the adjectives used to describe it. Write one or two of the adjectives next to the object's name on the board.

globe	round, blue, green, and brown
dictionary	blue, yellow, red, green
pencil	orange, pointed
wastebasket	green, round

Adjective Collage

MATERIALS: pictures of things, foods, and animals, poster board, glue

DIRECTIONS:

1. Provide small groups with pictures and poster board to make a collage.

2. Invite children to select pictures and label them using adjectives for taste, smell, touch, or sound.

3. Have children arrange and then glue their pictures and words onto the poster board.

4. Display collages.

School Numbers Search

MATERIALS: note pads, index cards

DIRECTIONS:

1. Have small groups generate and write questions they can ask school personnel to find out different numbers about the school. For example, questions might include *How many books are there in the library?* or *How old is the school building?*

2. Then have children plan and conduct their investigation, asking the appropriate people the questions, or looking through school information books. Tell children to use index cards to take notes.

3. Ask children to compile their results in an illustrated class poster or a booklet. Ask them to use adjectives for size and number to label their findings.

Size-and-Number Matching Game

MATERIALS: index cards, yarn, hole punch

DIRECTIONS:

1. Label five index cards with nouns, such as *feet, giraffe, elephant, sugar, toes.*

2. Label five other index cards with adjectives that tell about size or number that can match the nouns, such as *two, big, tiny, some, ten.*

3. Display the noun cards in a column and the adjective cards in random order on the opposite side.

4. Attach a piece of yarn to each noun.

5. Have children take turns matching the noun to an adjective by attaching the yarn.

Spin and Compare

MATERIALS: 6-inch tagboard circle, tagboard spinner, metal fastener, crayons or markers, index cards

DIRECTIONS:

1. Write six different adjectives in the sections of a 6-inch tagboard circle. Attach a spinner to the center of the circle. Then write *–er* and *–est* on two index cards.

2. Have children choose a card and then spin the spinner. Have them use the adjective and the ending they chose in a sentence that makes a comparison.

Ice is colder than liquid water.

Listening to Literature

Night Sounds, Morning Colors

BY ROSEMARY WELLS

WHEN I WAKE UP

Outside my window
there is a morning mist, hiding everything
but a big droopy spiderweb
loaded with emerald raindrops.
At breakfast the sun appears through the clouds suddenly.
It shines right into the stream of gold honey
that spins from my spoon to my biscuit.
In the morning I garden with my mother.
The violets we plant are so bright
in their deep black earth
that my mother is sure they are laughing and singing.
She washes my hands.
I watch Jim, our goldfish,
weave in and out the windows of his pagoda.
My father cuts fruits of four colors for my lunch.
After lunch my sister dances the tango for me.

NIGHT SOUNDS

After supper Grandpa reads to me.
His quiet voice rolls up and down like ocean waves.
Through the screen door I hear the rain
pattering and popping on the leaves outside.
My mother makes me an egg-cup ice cream sundae.
The spoon clinks against the china.
The chocolate sauce sounds thick and sleepy.
Next I listen to my mother's footsteps
tapping down the hallway. She runs my bath.
The water gushes into the tub.
After my bath my father turns out the light
and hums "Danny Boy" to me.
Through my window drift the night songs
of creatures I can't see.
They whirr and hoot and chuckle and click.
Far away I can hear a train come and go.
Its whistle mixes with the wind.

IN MY KITCHEN

Grandma takes me to the bakery.
The whole store smells of new, warm bread.
She buys poppy seed rolls, my mother's favorite.
The baker gives me a pumpkin cookie.
It tastes of Halloween.
Next door we buy roses for my mother's birthday.

Building Background

As a child, Rosemary Wells was encouraged to draw and remembers doing little else. She says, "It's a writer's job to have ideas." Noisy Nora and Max, both child-like animals, are among the most popular characters in her 60 books. Rosemary Wells has her own web site at *http://www.rosemarywells.com*

INTRODUCE THE LISTENING SELECTION You may wish to read aloud only a part of the reading selection. Introduce the selected part to children, telling them what the topic is. Prompt children to listen for colorful words that describe the topic.

Determine a Purpose for Listening

Tell children that this is a story about familiar times and places. It is filled with colorful words that will get them to use their senses. Ask children to decide whether their purpose for listening is

- to listen for information
- to solve problems
- to enjoy and appreciate. (to enjoy and appreciate)

While Grandma decides, she lets me hold her wallet.
Creaky, strong, and worn shiny,
it has the secret smell of old leather.
When we get home, Grandma makes a birthday cake.
All around the stove is a zone
of vanilla and butter and chocolate.
When the cake is done, Grandma opens a new bag
of Kentucky Kitchen coffee. "It's the kind
my grandmother bought," she tells me.
"Breathe it in and smell the mountains of home."
Everyone kisses my mother at her birthday dinner.
Her flowers have opened in the warm air,
and they fill the room with sweetness.
My mother puts me to bed.
I smell of clean towels and soap.
She smells just of herself.

WINTER WALK

My brother wants to look for a ball he lost
this summer behind the hill.
He tells me to wear my thick woolly sweater
and my heavy socks.
Bingo comes with us.
A gust of freezing wind blows right through my hair.
I pick an icicle. It is almost sharp,
but the point melts in my hand.
We go through a pine grove.

Under our feet there are a million dry needles,
spongy and springy as a mattress.
Suddenly I walk right into a prickly bush.
A thorn rips through my pants and cuts me, and I cry.
My brother hugs me.
He gives me a feather
he says is from a dove's wing.
He runs its velvety softness along my cheek.
We cannot find the ball.
I have a hard, cold stone in my sock.
My cut stings and my sweater itches.
My brother carries me home.
He makes me hot toast
with smooth shivering jelly on top.
I lie on the sunny window seat.
Next to me lies Bingo. Her warm tummy is softer even
than the dove's feather, softer than sleep.

Listening Comprehension

LISTEN FOR COLORFUL WORDS
Explain to children that in this story, the writer uses many colorful words to describe typical events in a day. The story is broken up into four parts; each part focuses on one particular sense.

PERSONAL RESPONSE *What are some of the colorful words that stand out most clearly in your mind?*
(Responses will vary. Possible responses: droopy spiderweb loaded with emerald raindrops; quiet voice rolls up and down like ocean waves; zone of vanilla and butter and chocolate; clean towels and soap; a million dry needles spongy and springy as a mattress; velvety softness.)
INFERENTIAL: INTERPRET FIGURATIVE LANGUAGE

Unit 4

Grammar
- All About Adjectives

Writing
- Poem
- Paragraph That Describes

Introducing the Unit

ORAL LANGUAGE/VIEWING

DISCUSS THE IMAGES Tap children's prior knowledge by inviting them to describe the scene they see on pages 240–241. Ask children to pretend they are part of the scene, playing in the snow.

- **How does the snow feel?** (cold, wet, soft)
- **Imagine you are walking in deep drifts of snow. Show me how you would walk.**
- **A big gust of wind just blew. Show me what happens.**
- **What sounds do you hear?** (Responses will vary.)
- **What does the snow look like? Compare it to something else. What are some of those things?** (white and clean, cotton, clouds)

ENCOURAGE CHILDREN'S QUESTIONS Have children brainstorm words and phrases to describe snow and snowflakes. Encourage them to use sensory details. Then have them write questions they might have about snow in their journals. Encourage them to use resources to research answers to their questions.

Unit 4

Grammar
- All About Adjectives

Writing
- Poem
- Paragraph That Describes

240

Viewing and Representing
• • • • • • • • • • • • • • • • • •

COMPARE/CONTRAST PRINT AND VISUAL MEDIA Have small groups of children choose words or phrases they might use in a poem or description of a winter scene. Children can show the words in a collage or illustrate them. Some children may want to write the words on a poster or as a list. Have children share their words and the images they create in their minds.

For evaluation criteria, see the checklist on page R77.

MEDIA LITERACY AND COMMUNICATION
SKILLS PACKAGE Use the video to extend children's oral and visual literacy. See pages 6–7 of the *Teacher's Guide*.

Snowflakes

Snowflakes are like feathers
but smaller.
Snowflakes are like soap flakes
but wetter.
Snowflakes are like raindrops
but colder.
Snowflakes are like confetti
but icier.
Snowflakes are like tiny stars
falling quietly at night.

Previewing the Unit

Read and discuss the unit contents list with children. Ask them to tell what they already know about *adjectives* and give examples. Tell them that in this unit they will learn about the kinds of adjectives and how to use adjectives to compare things. They will learn how to add adjectives to their writing to make it better. Discuss with them how they might use adjectives to write a poem and a descriptive paragraph.

SCIENCE/MATH CONNECTION Children will be exposed to a variety of science/math topics in this unit:

- Shapes
- Color
- Animals
- The five senses
- Size
- Numbers
- Quantities

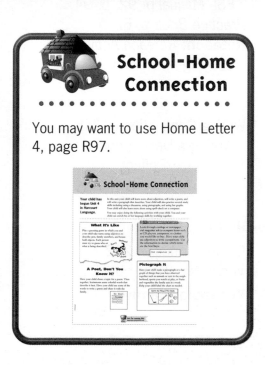

School-Home Connection

You may want to use Home Letter 4, page R97.

LESSON ORGANIZER	DAY 1	DAY 2
DAILY LANGUAGE PRACTICE  TRANSPARENCIES 37-38	1. I has a test tooday. (have; today) 2. my friend have two tests. (My; has) **Bridge to Writing** When do you <u>(form of *have*)</u> a test?	1. lucy lives in a smalle house. (Lucy; small) 2. Who lives in the scari house. (scary; ?) **Bridge to Writing** Red Riding Hood has a <u>(adjective for color)</u> coat.
ORAL WARM-UP *Listening/Speaking*	Describe a Fairy Tale Character p. 242	Name Colors p. 244 *Grammar Jingles*™ CD, Primary, Track 12
TEACH/MODEL **GRAMMAR** **KEY** ✔ = tested skill	✔ **WHAT IS AN ADJECTIVE?** pp. 242-243 • To understand that adjectives describe nouns • To use adjectives in writing	✔ **ADJECTIVES THAT TELL WHAT KIND** pp. 244-245 • To identify adjectives that tell about color and shape • To use adjectives for color and shape in writing
Reaching All Learners	*Practice Book* p. 61 **Challenge:** Activity Card 13 p. R53 **ESL:** *ESL Manual* pp. 92–93 **Reteach:** *Reteach Activities Copying Masters* p. 37	**Modified Instruction** Below-Level: Identify Nouns Above-Level: Rewrite Sentences **Challenge:** Wanted Poster p. 245 **ESL:** Color and Shape p. 244 *ESL Manual* p. 92, p. 94 *Practice Book* p. 62 **Reteach:** *Reteach Activities Copying Masters* p. 38
WRITING	Write Adjectives p. 243 Summarize/Reflect	Writing Connection p. 245 Writing a Description Summarize/Reflect
CROSS-CURRICULAR/ ENRICHMENT	**Vocabulary Power** Word Meaning p. 242 **considerate,** courteous, mannerly, polite, thoughtful See ***Vocabulary Power*** book.	**Vocabulary Power** Context Clues p. 242 *Vocabulary Power* book p. 55 **Vocabulary activity**

Visit *The Learning Site!*
www.harcourtschool.com
WRITING ACTIVITIES
Writing Express CD-ROM

DAY 3	DAY 4	DAY 5
1. Do you have a grean crayon. (green; ?) 2. look in that skuare box. (Look; square) **Bridge to Writing** May I borrow your <u>(adjective for color)</u> pencil?	1. Max sits on a rownd gray rock (round; .) 2. The young boy catches a larj broun fish. (large; brown) **Bridge to Writing** How <u>(adjective for shape)</u> the wolf's teeth are!	1. Did you see that yello bird. (yellow; ?) 2. it flew to that flatt gray rock. (It; flat) **Bridge to Writing** I have a <u>(adjective)</u> dog with <u>(adjective)</u> spots.
Give Color and Shape Clues p. 246 *Grammar Jingles™* CD, Primary, Track 12	Play I Spy p. 248	
✔ **WRITING LONGER SENTENCES** pp. 246-247 • To compose longer sentences by adding adjectives • To use adjectives in writing	**EXTRA PRACTICE** p. 248 • To recognize that an adjective describes a noun • To elaborate on a topic by using adjectives that tell what kind 🏆 **Practice and Assessment**	**TEST PREP** **CHAPTER REVIEW** p. 250 • To review adjectives for color and shape • To locate synonyms and antonyms in a thesaurus 🏆 **Test Preparation**
Modified Instruction Below-Level: Work in Pairs Above-Level: Write Additional Sentences **Challenge:** Story Time p. 247 **ESL:** Adding Adjectives p. 246 *ESL Manual* p. 92, p. 95 *Practice Book* p. 63 **Reteach:** *Reteach Activities Copying Masters* p. 39	**Challenge:** Crosswords p. 249 **ESL:** Riddles p. 248 *ESL Manual* pp. 92, 96 *Practice Book* p. 64	**Challenge:** Use a Thesaurus to Revise p. 251 **ESL:** *ESL Manual* p. 92, p. 97 *Practice Book* p. 65

Writing Connection p. 247
  Revising
  Summarize/Reflect
	Writing Connection p. 249
	  Riddle Fun
		Study Skill p. 251
		  Using a Thesaurus

Vocabulary Power Antonyms p. 242 *Vocabulary Power* book p. 56 🏆 **Vocabulary activity**	**Vocabulary Power** Word Endings p. 242 *Vocabulary Power* book p. 57 Language Play p. 249 🏆 **Vocabulary activity**	**Vocabulary Power** Related Words p. 242

What Is an Adjective?

OBJECTIVES
• To understand that adjectives describe nouns
• To use adjectives in writing

What Is an Adjective?

Read this paragraph from the book
Red Riding Hood.

Red Riding Hood
retold and illustrated by James Marshall

A long time ago in a simple cottage beside the deep, dark woods, there lived a pretty child called Red Riding Hood. She was kind and considerate, and everybody loved her.

242

DAILY LANGUAGE PRACTICE

TRANSPARENCY 37

1 I has a test tooday. (have; today)

2 my friend have two tests. (My; has)

BRIDGE TO WRITING When do you (form of *have*) a test?

ORAL WARM-UP

USE PRIOR KNOWLEDGE Ask volunteers to name favorite fairy tale characters. Then have children suggest words to describe them. Set up an **Adjective Word Wall**. Have children add their words to the list.

TEACH/MODEL

Have children turn to page 242 and predict what the paragraph will be about. Read the paragraph aloud, asking children to listen carefully to see if their predictions are correct. As you reread the paragraph, pause after each adjective and have children call out the noun described.

DEVELOP ORAL LANGUAGE Ask children to recall the words that tell about Red Riding Hood. Ask questions such as these:

• **What do you think it means to be kind and considerate?**
• **In what ways do you think Red Riding Hood is kind and considerate?**

Remind children that the paragraph has words that describe the cottage, woods, and child. Call on volunteers to add these words to the **Word Wall**.

Vocabulary Power

DAY 1 WORD MEANINGS Introduce and define *considerate*. **What are some examples of considerate things that people do for each other?**

DAY 2 CLASSIFY/CATEGORIZE Say: ***The considerate student helped her friend.*** Have partners act out situations that show considerate behavior. (See also *Vocabulary Power*, page 55.)

DAY 3 ANTONYMS Write *considerate* and *thoughtless* on the board. Explain that these two words have opposite meanings. What other antonym pairs can you name? (See also *Vocabulary Power*, page 56.)

DAY 4 WORD FAMILIES Write *consider/considerate* on the board. **What ending was added to *consider*?** Have a volunteer underline it. Explain that *consider* means "to think about." The *-ate* changes the meaning to "acting in a way that thinks [about others]." (See also *Vocabulary Power*, page 57.)

DAY 5 RELATED WORDS Have children make a word map for *considerate*. They should add adjectives that describe a considerate person.

Talk about Red Riding Hood. Tell what she is like. Then write words that describe her.

> An **adjective** describes, or tells about, a noun.
>
> Red Riding Hood lives in a **small** cottage. Her cape is **red**.

Write an adjective that describes each underlined noun. Possible responses are given.

1. Red Riding Hood has a <u>basket</u> of food.
   big
2. The food is for her <u>grandmother</u>.
   lovable
3. Red Riding Hood walks through the <u>woods</u>.
   dark, scary
4. She picks <u>flowers</u> along the way.
   pretty
5. Why is the <u>wolf</u> hiding behind the tree?
   bad, hungry

243

WRITE After talking about Red Riding Hood, have children generate a list of words that could describe her clothes or her house. Invite volunteers to read their word lists aloud. Remind children that the describing words they listed are adjectives. Read the definition in the box and talk about the example sentences. Add any new words to the **Word Wall**.

Then read the first item at the bottom of page 243 together. Have children think of adjectives to describe a basket and then choose one. Have children complete the items and share with a partner.

WRAP-UP/ASSESS

SUMMARIZE Reread the paragraph with children. Then have them reflect on what they have learned about adjectives. You may want them to write their reflections in their journals.
REFLECTION

REACHING ALL LEARNERS
RETEACH

INTERVENTION Lessons in **visual, auditory,** and **kinesthetic** modalities: p. R29 and *Reteach Activities Copying Masters,* p. 37.

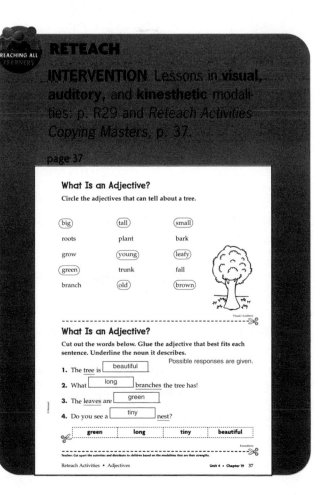

Adjectives That Tell What Kind

OBJECTIVES
- To identify adjectives that tell about color and shape
- To use adjectives for color and shape in writing

DAILY LANGUAGE PRACTICE

TRANSPARENCY 37

1 lucy lives in a smalle house. (Lucy; small)

2 Who lives in the scari house. (scary; ?)

BRIDGE TO WRITING Red Riding Hood has a _____ (adjective for color) coat.

ORAL WARM-UP

USE PRIOR KNOWLEDGE Have a volunteer pick out a crayon from a box. Ask everyone who is wearing something of that color to stand up. Call on volunteers to name the article of clothing and its color. Repeat with other colors.

Grammar Jingles™ **CD Primary** Use Track 12 for review and reinforcement of adjectives.

TEACH/MODEL

Introduce the concept of adjectives for color and shape by using the explanation and the examples. Ask questions such as these:

- **What noun is described in the sentence?** (*cottage/windows*)
- **Which word describes it?** (*white/square*) **What do the adjectives describe?** (*color/shape*)

GUIDED PRACTICE Work with children to complete each sentence. Encourage them to tell if the adjective in each sentence describes color or shape.

Adjectives That Tell What Kind

> Adjectives describe nouns. Some adjectives describe **color** and **shape**. They tell *what kind*.
>
> Who lives in the **white** cottage?
> Look at the **square** windows.

Guided Practice

Choose an adjective from the box to complete each sentence. Write the new sentence. Possible responses are given.

flat	red	green	orange	crooked

1. The girl with the ___red___ cape lives there.
2. Do you see her ___orange___ cat?
3. Does the cat have a ___crooked___ tail?
4. The cat sits on a ___flat___ stump.
5. ___Green___ grass is by the cat.

244

Vocabulary Power page 55

Name _____

Classify/Categorize

The following words have similar meanings. They all describe ways people can be considerate, or nice to each other.

mannerly   courteous   polite   thoughtful

How do you show you are considerate? Are you mannerly, courteous, polite, and thoughtful? Draw pictures. You can add speech balloons, too.

A friend is not feeling well. Show how to be thoughtful. Responses will vary. Accept reasonable responses.	Someone has trouble opening a door. Show how to be courteous.
Someone gives you a gift that you don't like. Show how to be polite.	A family member wants to take a nap. Show how to be considerate.

Vocabulary Power   Unit 4 • Chapter 19   55

ESL

REACHING ALL LEARNERS

COLOR AND SHAPE Pass around something colorful or with a distinctive shape, such as an orange or a diskette. Have children describe the object. Record all the adjectives they suggest on the chalkboard. Then ask children to read the words, and circle each one that describes color or shape.

Independent Practice

Choose an adjective from the box to complete each sentence. Write the new sentence.
Possible responses are given.

yellow	white	gray	black	green
pointed	round	straight	flat	purple

6. Look at these __purple__ flowers.

7. That flower has __round__ petals.

8. Its center is __yellow__.

9. Look how __straight__ the stems are!

10. Each leaf has a __pointed__ tip.

11. The leaves are also __flat__.

12. I see a __gray__ squirrel.

13. It is in the tall __green__ grass.

14. Do you see the __white__ fur on its belly?

15. How __black__ its eyes are!

Writing Connection

Writing a Description Draw a picture of a butterfly. Then write a paragraph about it. Use adjectives to tell about its color and shape.

You can use your computer to help you draw and color your picture.

245

Independent Practice

Have children complete the Independent Practice, or modify it by using the following suggestions:

MODIFIED INSTRUCTION

BELOW-LEVEL STUDENTS Before children choose an adjective, have them identify the noun they need to describe and then look for an appropriate adjective.

ABOVE-LEVEL STUDENTS After children are finished, challenge them to rewrite the sentences using an adjective for shape instead of color or an adjective for color instead of shape.

Writing Connection

Writing a Description Have children use adjectives to compose sentences with interesting, elaborated subjects. After they have completed the activity, display several butterfly pictures. Then ask volunteers to read their descriptions. Challenge the class to guess which butterfly each description most closely matches.

WRAP-UP/ASSESS

SUMMARIZE Ask children to reflect on and summarize what they have learned about adjectives that tell what kind.

REFLECTION

RETEACH

INTERVENTION Lessons in **visual**, **auditory**, and **kinesthetic** modalities: p. R29 and *Reteach Activities Copying Masters*, p. 38.

page 38

PRACTICE page 62

REACHING ALL

Name_____

Adjectives That Tell What Kind

A. Circle the adjective in each sentence. Write it on the line.

1. Look at your (yellow) pencil.   yellow

2. Does it have a (pointy) tip?   pointy

3. Is the other end (flat?)   flat

4. Use your (brown) ruler.   brown

5. Draw a (straight) line.   straight

B. Write an adjective from the box to complete each sentence. Underline the noun the adjective describes.

round	silver	black	square	red

Responses may vary. Samples are given.

6. I need __square__ paper.

7. Do you have my __black__ marker?

8. Your __round__ eraser is under the table.

9. I can't find my __red__ pencil.

10. Did you look in that __silver__ can?

TRY THIS! Write three sentences about items you use in art class. Use adjectives that tell about color and shape.

62 Unit 4 • Chapter 19   Practice • Adjectives

CHALLENGE

REACHING ALL

WANTED POSTER Ask children to design a "Wanted" poster of the wolf in *Red Riding Hood* or of another story character of their choice. Have them draw the character and write sentences such as: *Look out for a big gray wolf. Wolf has _____ teeth and a _____ tail.* Invite children to display their posters and give dramatic readings as if broadcasting a news bulletin.

Adjectives That Tell What Kind

Read each sentence. Follow the directions to make a snowman. Then underline the word in each sentence that describes a color or a shape.

1. Draw a snowman in the box. Make its body round.

2. Make its glasses square.

3. Use a crayon to give the snowman a black hat.

4. Draw a red scarf on the snowman.

Visual / Auditory

Adjectives That Tell What Kind

Cut out the words below. Glue the adjective that best fits each sentence. Circle the noun it describes

1. The __white__ (snow) was falling fast.

2. I put on my __green__ (snowsuit).

3. I finally found my __round__ (sled.)

4. We took the __crooked__ (path) to the top of the hill.

crooked	white	green	round

Kinesthetic

Teacher: Cut apart the activities and distribute to children based on the modalities that are their strengths.

38 Unit 4 • Chapter 19   Reteach Activities • Adjectives

Writing Longer Sentences

OBJECTIVES
- To compose longer sentences by adding adjectives
- To use adjectives in writing

DAILY LANGUAGE PRACTICE
TRANSPARENCY 37

1 Do you have a grean crayon. (green; ?)

2 look in that skuare box. (Look; square)

BRIDGE TO WRITING May I borrow your <u>(adjective that tells about color)</u> pencil?

ORAL WARM-UP

USE PRIOR KNOWLEDGE Display several colorful paper shapes. Tell children, "I am looking at a ____ shape." Add adjectives until children identify the shape. Call on volunteers to describe a shape for the class to identify. Ask them to add adjectives to make their sentences more descriptive.

Grammar Jingles™ **CD Primary** Use Track 12 for review and reinforcement of adjectives.

TEACH/MODEL

Have children read the explanation and the sentences. Have children discuss which sentence they think is more interesting and why. Then point out how adjectives help give a clearer picture of a topic.

GUIDED PRACTICE Work through the first item together. Have children identify the two nouns and think of adjectives that could be added to the sentence. Repeat the procedure with the remaining items.

Writing Longer Sentences

Adjectives can make your writing more interesting. They give more information about nouns. Use adjectives to create better word pictures.

> I see a snake on that rock.
> I see a **black** snake on that **big flat** rock.

Guided Practice

Add adjectives to describe the noun or nouns in each sentence. Write the new sentence.
Possible responses are given.

1. I put on my jacket with the pockets.
   I put on my red jacket with the big square pockets.
2. Dad and I walked down to the pond.
   Dad and I walked down to the big round pond.
3. We saw flowers in the water.
   We saw beautiful white flowers in the warm blue water.
4. I looked at the leaves.
   I looked at the flat brown leaves.
5. Fish swam by us.
   Some little orange fish swam by us.

246

Vocabulary Power page 56

ESL

Name_____ **Antonyms**

Antonyms are words that have opposite meanings.

| happy | connect | careful |
| unhappy | disconnect | careless |

Circle the word that is the opposite of the word in dark print.

1. polite
   politely
   (impolite)
   replace

2. courteous
   courtroom
   courteously
   (discourteous)

3. behave
   (misbehave)
   behaving
   act

4. thoughtful
   thoughts
   (thoughtless)
   rethought

5. friendly
   (unfriendly)
   friendship
   friends

6. kind
   kindly
   (unkind)
   kindness

7. well-mannered
   manners
   mannerly
   (ill-mannered)

8. pleased
   (displeased)
   pleasantly
   pleasingly

9. hopeless
   hoping
   hopping
   (hopeful)

Choose a pair of opposites. Draw and label pictures to show the meanings.

56   Unit 4 • Chapter 19   Vocabulary Power

ADDING ADJECTIVES Write each word in this sentence on a separate card: *I have a coat with buttons.* Place the cards on the board ledge. Have children brainstorm adjectives that can describe a coat with buttons. Write each adjective on a card. Ask children to add adjective cards to the sentence and read each aloud. Repeat the procedure. Children may illustrate one of the sentences.

Remember Add adjectives to describe nouns to make your writing more interesting.

Independent Practice

Add adjectives to describe the noun or nouns in each sentence. Write the new sentence.
Possible responses are given.

6. I stood on a rock.
   I stood on a big flat rock.

7. I fed the ducks.
   I fed the brown ducks.

8. Dad pointed to a turtle.
   Dad pointed to a green turtle.

9. It had marks on its shell.
   It had orange marks on its rough shell.

10. I once saw a snake here.
    I once saw a small green snake here.

11. Do all snakes have fangs?
    Do all snakes have sharp, pointed fangs?

12. Dad saw a spider.
    Dad saw a big black spider.

13. A fly was in its web.
    A little red fly was in its sticky web.

14. Then a butterfly landed on me!
    Then a blue butterfly landed on me!

15. It had spots on its wings.
    It had tiny round spots on its wings.

Writing Connection

Revising Choose a piece of writing from your Writing Portfolio. Find the nouns in your sentences. Add adjectives to make your sentences more interesting.

Use your computer to revise your writing.

247

Independent Practice

Have children complete the Independent Practice, or modify it by using the following suggestions:

MODIFIED INSTRUCTION

BELOW-LEVEL STUDENTS Have pairs identify the nouns and then think of and test adjectives orally before writing the new sentence.

ABOVE-LEVEL STUDENTS After children are finished, invite them to write four sentences without adjectives, trade sentences with a partner, and then add adjectives to make longer, more interesting sentences.

Writing Connection

Revising Suggest children underline the nouns in their sentences and list possible adjectives to add to their sentences. Encourage them to make precise word choices as they select adjectives from their lists.

WRAP-UP/ASSESS

SUMMARIZE Have children reflect on what they have learned about writing longer sentences and then summarize when and how to do it.

REFLECTION

RETEACH

INTERVENTION Lessons in **visual, auditory,** and **kinesthetic** modalities: p. R29 and *Reteach Activities Copying Masters*, p. 39.

PRACTICE page 63

Name _____

Writing Longer Sentences

A. Read each sentence. Circle the adjectives that tell about the underlined noun.

1. Here is a (round blue) button.
2. I found it on the (big red) chair.
3. It was under the (square yellow) pillow.
4. I'll check my (big white) shirt.

B. Add adjectives to describe the nouns in each sentence. Write the new sentence. Sentences may vary. Sample responses are provided.

5. I have a coat.
   I have a new purple coat.

6. My coat has pockets.
   My coat has big square pockets.

7. It has buttons.
   It has round black buttons.

TRY THIS! Write a sentence about something you are wearing. Then rewrite the sentence as many times as you can. Add a new adjective each time.

Practice • Adjectives   Unit 4 • Chapter 19 63

CHALLENGE

STORY TIME Have children select a short passage from a story, such as *Three Little Pigs or Red Riding Hood*. Have them write the sentences without the adjectives. Then ask them to rewrite the passage, this time with new adjectives, and share it.

Who is afraid of the great mean wolf?

---

page 39

Writing Longer Sentences

Add an adjective from the box to describe the noun in each sentence. Read your sentences to a partner. Possible responses are given.

| long | sick | big | warm |

1. I have a __long__ cape.
2. This is my __big__ basket.
3. I visit my __sick__ grandmother.
4. The __warm__ sun feels good.

Visual/Auditory

Writing Longer Sentences

Cut out the adjectives from the bottom of the page. Glue a word to describe the noun in each sentence. Possible responses are given.

1. Do you like my __new__ cape?
2. It has __red__ buttons.
3. Look at the __square__ pocket.
4. I like the __pointed__ hood.

| square | pointed | red | new |

Kinesthetic

Teacher: Cut apart the activities and distribute to children based on the modalities that are their strengths.

Reteach Activities • Adjectives   Unit 4 • Chapter 19 39

Extra Practice

OBJECTIVES

- To recognize that an adjective describes a noun
- To elaborate on a topic by using adjectives that tell what kind

DAILY LANGUAGE PRACTICE

TRANSPARENCY 38

1 Max sits on a rownd gray rock (round; .)

2 The young boy catches a larj broun fish. (large; brown)

BRIDGE TO WRITING How (adjective for shape) the wolf's teeth are!

ORAL WARM-UP

USE PRIOR KNOWLEDGE Play "I spy" with children, using the following as a model: *I spy something round and orange. What do I spy?* The first child to guess what you spy then gives clues for something he or she sees in the classroom. Remind children to adapt their volume and rate of speech as they give their clues.

TEACH/MODEL

Read each set of directions, making sure children understand how to complete each section. Have children share their answers with a partner before you read aloud the answers.

WRAP-UP/ASSESS

SUMMARIZE Have children reflect on and discuss any problems they had in completing the practice exercises. Then have them summarize what they have learned.

ADDITIONAL PRACTICE Extra Practice items are provided on page 472 of the *Pupil Edition (Teacher's Edition R5).*

TECHNOLOGY

Grammar Practice and Assessment CD-ROM

Writing Express CD-ROM

INTERNET Visit *The Learning Site!*
www.harcourtschool.com

Adjectives

Extra Practice

Write the adjective in each sentence.

1. What a <u>beautiful</u> day it is!
2. Ben goes for a <u>long</u> walk.
3. He puts on his <u>old</u> boots.
4. The path is <u>muddy</u>.

Choose an adjective from the box to complete each sentence.
Possible responses are given.

long	yellow	round	black
straight	brown	flat	orange

5. Ben jumps into a pile of __yellow__ leaves.
6. Ben sees a small __flat__ rock.
7. He uses a __long__ stick to lift the rock.
8. Ben finds a __black__ bug.

Add adjectives to describe the noun in each sentence.

Write the new sentence.
Possible responses are given.

9. Ben sees a deer.
   Ben sees a little brown deer.
10. It has spots.
    It has round white spots.

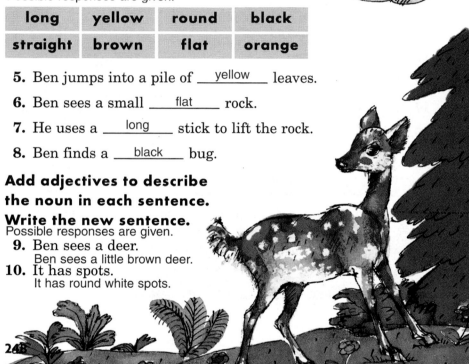

248

Vocabulary Power page 57

Name_____ Word Families

Words that have the same base word belong to the same word family. Underline the word <u>friend</u> in each of these words.

friends   friendly   unfriendly   friendship   friendless

Add prefixes and endings to the words in dark print to make word families. Possible responses are given.

1. consider	2. polite
considerate	impolite
reconsider; consideration	politeness
3. manner	**4. courteous**
mannered	discourteous
mannerly	courteously
5. thought	**6. please**
thoughtful	pleases; pleasure
thoughtfulness	pleasing; displease

Write one sentence. Use any three of the words you wrote.

_____

_____

Vocabulary Power   Unit 4 • Chapter 19   57

ESL

REACHING ALL LEARNERS

RIDDLES Gather a variety of classroom items that can be easily described and arrange them on a table. As you hold up each item, ask volunteers to tell what it is, how it is used, and what its color or shape is. Then have children work with a partner to write a riddle, following the directions on page 249.

Language Play

Adjective Trail
- Sit in a circle with a few classmates.
- Say a sentence about an animal. Put one adjective in your sentence.
- The next person adds one more adjective and says the new sentence.
- Go around the circle until each person has added an adjective. Write the whole sentence.
- Draw a picture to go with the sentence.

> Use these sentences to get started. Don't forget to add an adjective.
> I saw a _____ frog.
> Look at the _____ snake!
> He has a _____ dog.

Writing Connection

Riddle Fun Think of an object, and list adjectives to tell about its color and shape. Then use the adjectives to write a riddle on one side of a card. Write the answer on the back. Read the riddle to a classmate.

> I can be any color.
> I am made of wax.
> I can write.
>
> A crayon.

249

Language Play

Have children form groups of three or four and sit in a circle. You may want to model how to add adjectives with the following sentences: *I have a gray cat. I have a big gray cat. I have a big, gray, fluffy cat.* Instruct children to slow their rate of speech as more adjectives are added. This will give the next group member time to remember the new, longer sentence. After children have completed the activity, invite groups to read their sentences.

Writing Connection

Riddle Fun Check to see that children have successfully written a riddle by using the criteria that follow.

CRITERIA
- ☑ Writes each clue as a sentence.
- ☑ Includes an adjective for color or shape in at least one clue.
- ☑ Begins each sentence with a capital letter.
- ☑ Punctuates the sentences correctly.

📁 **PORTFOLIO OPPORTUNITY** You may want to have children place their writing in their portfolios or create a class riddle book.

PRACTICE page 64

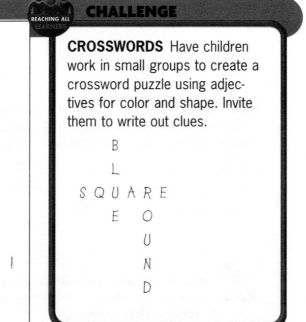

Name _____

Extra Practice

A. Underline the adjective in each sentence. Circle the noun it describes.
1. How <u>dark</u> the (woods) are today!
2. The <u>tall</u> (trees) block the sunlight.
3. The (leaves) are <u>green</u>.

B. Write an adjective from the box to complete each sentence.

> pointy   black   gray

4. Have you ever seen a ___gray___ wolf?
5. Its tail has a ___black___ tip.
6. What sharp ___pointy___ fangs it has!

C. Add adjectives to describe the noun in each sentence. Write the new sentence. Sentences will vary. Sample responses are provided.
7. Do you see the owl?
   Do you see the big white owl?
8. It is on the tree.
   It is on the tall oak tree.

64 Unit 4 • Chapter 19   Practice • Adjectives

CHALLENGE

CROSSWORDS Have children work in small groups to create a crossword puzzle using adjectives for color and shape. Invite them to write out clues.

```
    B
    L
S Q U A R E
    E
    O
    U
    N
    D
```

Chapter Review

OBJECTIVES
- To review adjectives for color and shape
- To locate synonyms and antonyms in a thesaurus

DAILY LANGUAGE PRACTICE

TRANSPARENCY 38

1 Did you see that yello bird. (yellow; ?)

2 it flew to that flatt gray rock. (It; flat)

BRIDGE TO WRITING I have a __(adjective)__ dog with __(adjective)__ spots.

STANDARDIZED TEST PREP

Read each set of directions with children to make sure they understand how to complete each section. You may wish to have children complete this page independently and use it as an assessment.

TEST PREPARATION TIP
Item Type: Multiple Choice

TIP

Model this strategy to help children determine the correct answer:

First I carefully read the sentence. Then I read the answer choices for *a*, *b*, and *c*. I know the correct answer isn't *a* or *b* because *I* is a pronoun and *see* is a verb. I know that *brown* is a word for color and that it describes the spider in this sentence, so I choose *c*.

Chapter Review

Find the adjective in each sentence. Choose the answer that shows that adjective.

1. I see a brown spider.
   - **a.** I
   - **b.** see
   - **c. brown**

2. Its body is round.
   - **a.** body
   - **b. round**
   - **c.** Its

3. The spider has pointed fangs.
   - **a. pointed**
   - **b.** fangs
   - **c.** has

4. The spider's web looks like white thread.
   - **a.** web
   - **b.** thread
   - **c. white**

5. A green bug is in a web.
   - **a. green**
   - **b.** bug
   - **c.** web

6. It wiggles its small body.
   - **a.** body
   - **b. small**
   - **c.** wiggles

Add adjectives to the sentences.
Write the new sentences. Possible responses are given.

7. A spider makes a web.
   A big black spider makes a round sticky web.

8. The spider has legs.
   The brown spider has eight fuzzy legs.

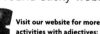 Visit our website for more activities with adjectives:
www.harcourtschool.com
250

Language Assessment

. . . .

PORTFOLIO ASSESSMENT
Have children select their best work from the following activities:

- **Writing Connection,** pages 245, 247, 249; TE activities, pages 243, 245, 247, 249.

ONGOING ASSESSMENT
Evaluate the performance of 4-6 children using appropriate checklists and record forms from pages R65–R68 and R77–R79.

 INTERNET Activities and exercises to help children prepare for state and standardized assessments appear on *The Learning Site:*
www.harcourtschool.com

■ Study Skills ■

Using a Thesaurus

A **thesaurus** is a list of words in alphabetical order. Each word in a thesaurus is called an **entry word**. The thesaurus lists synonyms for each entry word. A **synonym** is a word that means the same or almost the same as another word. Sometimes a thesaurus lists **antonyms**, or opposites, too.

Practice

Use the Thesaurus at the back of your book to answer each question.

1. On what page can you find the entry word *pretty*? page 497

2. Does the word *pretty* come before or after the word *nice*?   after

3. What words mean almost the same as *pretty*? beautiful, lovely

4. What words are opposites for *pretty*? ordinary, plain, ugly

5. What entry word comes after *pretty*? run

251

■ Study Skills ■

Using a Thesaurus

TEACH/MODEL

Write the following sentences on the board and have children read them aloud: *I have a little cat; Your dog is not as little as my cat. My cat is little; Your dog is not little.* Call on a volunteer to underline the word *little* in each sentence. Tell children that to make the sentences more interesting, they can find synonyms for the word *little* in a word book called a thesaurus. Have children turn to page 251. Read the paragraph together and talk about how to use a thesaurus. To review the terms *entry word* and *alphabetical order*, see pages 43 and 189.

PRACTICE Have children work together to answer the questions. Then have them use the thesaurus at the end of their books to find synonyms for the word *little*, and rewrite the last three sentences on the board.

WRAP-UP/ASSESS

SUMMARIZE Ask children to tell what they have learned about the thesaurus and discuss how they can use it to make their writing better and more interesting.

PRACTICE page 65

REACHING ALL LEARNERS

Name_____

Using a Thesaurus

A. Read the entry for *nice* in your Thesaurus on pages 494–498. Write a synonym for *nice* that best completes each sentence. Possible responses are given.
1. A cool breeze is ____lovely____ on a hot day.

2. We saw a ____beautiful____ yellow bird on the feeder.

3. Meg is a ____kind____ person, so she has many friends.

4. Thank you for the ____beautiful____ gift.

5. Grandma had a ____lovely____ visit with the children.

B. Read the entry for *eat* in your Thesaurus on pages 494–498. Write a synonym for *eat* that best completes each sentence. Possible responses are given.
6. My sister will ____taste____ spaghetti for the first time tonight.

7. After school Carrie and Ted ____munch____ on carrots.

8. My dogs always ____gobble____ their food quickly.

TRY THIS! Write three sentences that use *good* to describe someone or something. Then rewrite each sentence using a synonym for *good*. Use your Thesaurus.

Practice • Adjectives   Unit 4 • Chapter 19   65

CHALLENGE

USE A THESAURUS TO REVISE
Suggest that children select a piece of writing from their writing portfolios and replace some of the adjectives they used with more colorful or exact synonyms. Encourage children to use the thesaurus at the back of their books.

LESSON ORGANIZER	DAY 1	DAY 2
DAILY LANGUAGE PRACTICE TRANSPARENCIES 39, 40	1. my sister picked some pruple flowers. (My; purple) 2. How pointd the petals are? (pointed; !) **Bridge to Writing** The leaves are _(adjective that tells what kind)_ and _(adjective that tells what kind)_.	1. The children is noysy. (are; noisy) 2. The grapes are swit, (sweet; .) **Bridge to Writing** The _(adjective for sound)_ sound of the alarm woke us up.
ORAL WARM-UP Listening/Speaking	Describe Pictures p. 252	Act Out Adjectives p. 254 *Grammar Jingles™* CD, Primary, Track 12
TEACH/MODEL GRAMMAR **KEY** ✔ = tested skill	✔ **WORDS THAT TELL ABOUT THE SENSES** pp. 252-253 **Literature:** "August Afternoon" by Marion Edey • To interpret a poem • To write adjectives that tell about the senses	✔ **ADJECTIVES FOR TASTE, SMELL, FEEL, AND SOUND** pp. 254-255 • To identify adjectives for taste, smell, feel, and sound • To use adjectives for taste, smell, feel, and sound in writing
Reaching All Learners	*Practice Book* p. 66 **Challenge:** Activity Card 14, p. R54 **ESL:** *ESL Manual* pp. 98–99 **Reteach:** *Reteach Activities Copying Masters* p. 40	**Modified Instruction** Below-Level: Identify Nouns Above-Level: Rewrite Sentences **Challenge:** Travel Poster p. 255 **ESL:** The Senses p. 254 *ESL Manual* pp. 98, 100 *Practice Book* p. 67 **Reteach:** *Reteach Activities Copying Masters* p. 41
WRITING	Write Adjectives p. 253 Summarize/Reflect	Writing Connection p. 255 Write a Description Summarize/Reflect
CROSS-CURRICULAR/ ENRICHMENT	**Vocabulary Power** Word Meaning p. 252 **luscious,** appetizing, delicious, flavorful, savory See *Vocabulary Power* book.	**Vocabulary Power** Synonyms p. 252 *Vocabulary Power* book p. 58 **Vocabulary activity**

Visit *The Learning Site!*
www.harcourtschool.com
WRITING ACTIVITIES
Writing Express CD-ROM

DAY 3	DAY 4	DAY 5
1. they follow a bumpi trail. (They; bumpy) **2.** What a smokie campfire. (smoky; !) **Bridge to Writing** Feel how (adjective for *feel*) this rock is.	1 A squirrel have sofft fur. (has; soft) 2. It eats ard acorns (hard; .) **Bridge to Writing** This banana is good and (synonym for *good*).	1. Is a snake's skin slimee (slimy; ?) 2. Do not sits on that weit log. (sit; wet) **Bridge to Writing** This glass of water is fresh and (synonym for *cold*) .
Synonym Game p. 256 *Grammar Jingles*™ CD, Primary, Tracks 12 and 13	Play "Pass the Soup, Please" p. 258	
✔ **USING SYNONYMS IN WRITING** pp. 256-257 • To recognize and select exact words • To use available technology to find synonyms	**EXTRA PRACTICE** pp. 258, 259 • To identify adjectives that tell about the senses • To use adjectives for taste, smell, feel, and sound in writing **Practice and Assessment**	**TEST PREP CHAPTER REVIEW** p. 260 • To review adjectives for taste, smell, feel, and sound • To identify and select the more exact adjective • To identify and use antonyms **Test Preparation**

Modified Instruction
  Below-Level: Work in Pairs
  Above-Level: Write Sentences
Challenge: Acrostic p. 257
ESL: Synonyms p. 256
  ESL Manual pp. 98, 101
Practice Book p. 68
Reteach: *Reteach Activities Copying Masters* p. 42
	Challenge: Make a Menu p. 259
	ESL: What Is It? p. 258
	  ESL Manual pp. 98, 102
	Practice Book p. 69
		Practice Book p. 70
		Challenge: Antonym Puzzles p. 261
		ESL: *ESL Manual* pp. 98, 103

Writing Connection p. 257
  Revising
 Summarize/Reflect
	Writing Connection p. 259
	  Write a Shape Poem
		Writing Application p. 261
		  Sentences with Antonyms

Vocabulary Power
  Related Words p. 252
Vocabulary Power book p. 59
Vocabulary activity
	Vocabulary Power
	  Expand Word Meaning p. 252
	Vocabulary Power book p. 60
	Vocabulary activity
	  Language Play p. 259
		Vocabulary: Antonyms p. 261
		Vocabulary Power
		  Content-Area Words p. 252

Words That Tell About the Senses

OBJECTIVES

• To listen critically to interpret and evaluate a poem
• To write adjectives that tell about the senses

DAILY LANGUAGE PRACTICE

TRANSPARENCY 39

1 my sister picked some pruple flowers. (My; purple)

2 How pointd the petals are? (pointed; !)

BRIDGE TO WRITING The leaves are __(adjective that tells what kind)__ and __(adjective that tells what kind)__ .

ORAL WARM-UP

USE PRIOR KNOWLEDGE Display picture cards showing things such as a lemon, a peach, a rose, and a trumpet. Ask children to tell how each thing tastes, feels, sounds, or smells. List the adjectives children use on an **Adjectives Word Wall.**

TEACH/MODEL

Have children turn to page 252, read the title, and predict what the poem is about. Then read the poem aloud, asking children to listen for three questions and the answers. Invite volunteers to dramatically interpret the poem as others join in to reread it with you.

DEVELOP ORAL LANGUAGE Ask children to describe a summer afternoon they have experienced and then compare it with the one in the poem. Encourage them to tell what they heard, felt, smelled, and tasted. Add the adjectives children use to tell about senses to the **Word Wall.**

Words That Tell About the Senses

Read the poem.

August Afternoon

Where shall we go?
What shall we play?
What shall we do
On a hot summer day?

We'll sit in the swing.
Go low. Go high.
And drink lemonade
Till the glass is dry.

One straw for you,
One straw for me,
In the cool green shade
Of the walnut tree.

Marion Edey

252

Vocabulary Power

DAY 1 WORD MEANINGS Introduce and define *luscious* (delicious, tasty). Discuss luscious foods.

DAY 2 RELATED WORDS Write *luscious* on the board. Help children name words with similar meanings. (See also *Vocabulary Power*, page 58.)

DAY 3 RELATED WORDS Discuss what makes food luscious, such as sweetness. (See also *Vocabulary Power*, page 59.)

DAY 4 EXPAND WORD MEANING Remind children that *luscious* describes foods. Discuss what other things *luscious* might describe. (See also *Vocabulary Power*, page 60.)

DAY 5 CONTENT-AREA WORDS Ask children to write a menu that contains their favorite foods. Suggest that they use words such as *luscious* to describe the dishes.

What are the adjectives the poet uses in "August Afternoon"? What do you hear, feel, smell, and taste during your favorite month? Talk with a partner. Write down the adjectives you use.

> Some adjectives tell about the senses.
>
> What shall we do on a **hot** summer day?
> We will listen to the **noisy** birds.
> We will drink **sweet** lemonade.

Write an adjective that describes each underlined noun. Possible responses are given.

Warm <u>Weather</u>

What shall we do today?

We will drink ___icy___ <u>lemonade</u>

and listen to the ___busy___ <u>bees</u>.

We will sit on a ___white___ <u>bench</u>

and eat ___sweet___ <u>fruit</u>

in the ___cool___ <u>shade</u>

of the ___cherry___ <u>tree</u>.

253

WRITE Use children's discussions about the things they hear, feel, smell, and taste during their favorite month to help them generate words that tell about the senses. Invite volunteers to read aloud their word lists. Remind children that they already know about adjectives for color and shape. Read aloud the definition in the box and talk about the example sentences.

Then read the poem at the bottom of page 253 together. Use the title, "Warm Weather," to explain the directions. After children have added an adjective before each underlined noun, have them read the revised poems to partners.

WRAP-UP/ASSESS

SUMMARIZE Reread the poem on page 252 with children. Then ask them to reflect on what they have learned about adjectives. Have children write their reflections in their journals. **REFLECTION**

RETEACH

INTERVENTION Lessons in **visual, auditory,** and **kinesthetic** modalities: p. R30 and *Reteach Activities Copying Masters,* p. 40.

page 40

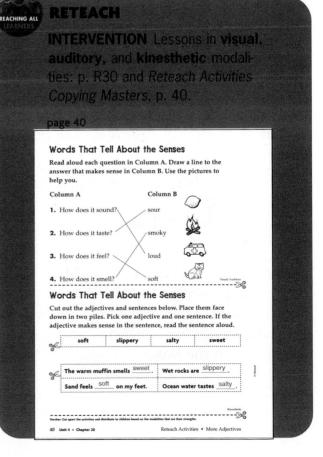

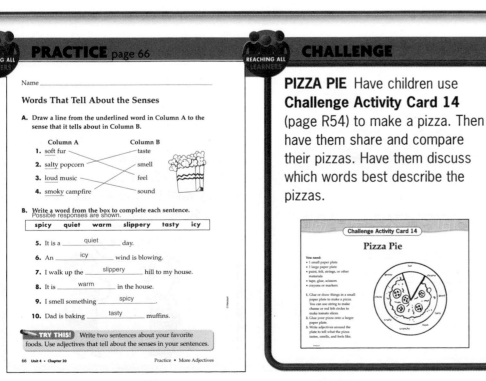

Adjectives for Taste, Smell, Feel, and Sound

OBJECTIVES
- To identify adjectives for taste, smell, feel, and sound
- To use adjectives for taste, smell, feel, and sound in writing

DAILY LANGUAGE PRACTICE

TRANSPARENCY 39

1 The children is noysy. (are; noisy)

2 The grapes are swit, (sweet; .)

BRIDGE TO WRITING The ____(adjective for sound)____ sound of the alarm woke us up.

ORAL WARM-UP

USE PRIOR KNOWLEDGE Have volunteers take turns acting out eating something sweet, sour, hot, or smelly. Ask others to suggest adjectives that tell about the foods. Add any new adjectives to the **Word Wall**.

Grammar Jingles™ **CD, Primary** Use Track 12 for review and reinforcement of adjectives.

TEACH/MODEL

Introduce the concept of adjectives for taste, smell, feel, and sound by using the explanation and the examples. Ask questions such as these:

- **Which words in the sentences are adjectives?** (sweet, fresh, bumpy, noisy)
- **What do they tell about?** (how something tastes, smells, feels, and sounds)

GUIDED PRACTICE Work with children to complete the sentences. Have them decide whether they need an adjective for taste, smell, feel, or sound and then look for it in the box.

Adjectives for Taste, Smell, Feel, and Sound

Some adjectives tell how something tastes, smells, feels, or sounds.

We pick some **sweet** blueberries.
The air smells **fresh**.
We sit on a **bumpy** log.
I listen to the **noisy** birds.

Guided Practice

Write a word from the box to complete each sentence. Possible responses are given.

noisy	warm	quiet	firm	sticky

1. The forest is ___quiet___.
2. It is a ___warm___ day.
3. Three rangers walk on the ___firm___ ground.
4. They hear some ___noisy___ bees.
5. The rangers see a hive filled with ___sticky___ honey.

254

Vocabulary Power page 58

Name _____

The words in the box have similar meanings. Read the words. How do they make you feel? Hungry?

appetizing	delicious
flavorful	luscious
	savory

Draw pictures to show the meaning of the underlined words. Share your pictures with classmates. Compare your ideas.

an appetizing breakfast	a delicious lunch
a flavorful salad	a luscious dessert
a savory dinner	a tasty snack

58 Unit 4 • Chapter 20   Vocabulary Power

REACHING ALL **ESL**

THE SENSES Help children identify which sense an adjective tells about. Have children point to their mouth, nose, hands, and ears as you say various adjectives for taste, smell, feel, and sound. You may want to have volunteers act out some of the adjectives.

SMOKY

Remember Some adjectives tell how things taste, smell, feel, or sound.

Independent Practice

Write a word from the box to complete each sentence. Possible responses are given.

cool	crunchy	fresh	hard	quiet
slippery	soft	bitter	sticky	tasty

6. The rangers now walk on __slippery__ rocks.

7. A rock falls and scares a __quiet__ rabbit.

8. The rangers find a plant with a __bitter__ smell.

9. The plant has __sticky__ leaves and berries.

10. The rangers pick some __fresh__ berries.

11. They put the fruit in a __soft__ bag.

12. Back home the rangers keep the bag in a __cool__ place.

Writing Connection

Write a Description Think about a fruit you like. Draw a picture of it. Then write sentences that tell how it tastes, smells, feels, and sounds when you eat it.

You can use a computer to print out your sentences.

255

Independent Practice

Have children complete the Independent Practice, or modify it by using the following suggestions:

MODIFIED INSTRUCTION

BELOW-LEVEL STUDENTS Before choosing an adjective, suggest that children first identify the noun they are describing. Then have them decide whether they can taste, smell, feel, or hear it.

ABOVE-LEVEL STUDENTS After children are finished, invite them to list other adjectives they can use to complete the sentences and then rewrite each sentence, using a different adjective.

Writing Connection

Write a Description Remind children that when writing a description, they should begin with a topic sentence that tells what the paragraph is about. Ask volunteers to read their descriptions. Instruct the audience to decide whether the adjectives helped create a good word picture.

WRAP-UP/ASSESS

SUMMARIZE Invite children to summarize what they have learned about adjectives for taste, smell, feel, and sound.

REACHING ALL

RETEACH

INTERVENTION Lessons in visual, auditory, and kinesthetic modes, Lessons pp. 45 and Reteach Activities Copying Masters p. 41

PRACTICE page 67

Name _____

Adjectives for Taste, Smell, Feel, and Sound

A. Underline the adjective in each sentence. Write it on the line.

1. It's a <u>hot</u> afternoon at the beach. — hot
2. <u>Noisy</u> gulls look for food. — Noisy
3. A man races across the <u>burning</u> sand. — burning
4. This seaweed has a <u>fishy</u> smell. — fishy
5. How <u>salty</u> the air is today! — salty

B. Write a word from the box to complete each sentence. Possible responses are shown.

| shrill | sticky | fruity | slippery | fresh |

6. Don't climb on the __slippery__ rocks.
7. A lifeguard's __shrill__ whistle warns swimmers.
8. This sunscreen is __sticky__!
9. A __fresh__ breeze blows across the beach.
10. A child enjoys a __fruity__ ice cone.

TRY THIS! Write two sentences about a summer day at the beach, lake, or pool. Use adjectives for taste, feel, sound, and smell.

Practice • More Adjectives — Unit 4 • Chapter 20 67

REACHING ALL CHALLENGE

TRAVEL POSTER Provide children with old travel brochures or magazines to make a travel poster for an imaginary summer vacation spot. Suggest that they cut out trees, animals, beaches, and so on, to make a collage showing what the place looks like. Have children write sentences about the place, using adjectives about the senses.

Hear the soft sound of the sea.

Adjectives for Taste, Smell, Feel, and Sound

Add an adjective to each sentence. Share your answers. Possible responses are given.

1. The grill smells __smoky__
2. The pickle tastes __sour__
3. The tree bark feels __rough__
4. An airplane sounds __loud__

Visual/Auditory

Adjectives for Taste, Smell, Feel, and Sound

Cut out the words at the bottom of the page. Glue the adjective that best fits each sentence. Circle the noun it describes.

1. A __noisy__ (squirrel) chatters at us.
2. We put our blanket on the __hard__ (ground).
3. I need to wash my __sticky__ (hands).
4. How __sweet__ this (lemonade) is!

| sticky | noisy | hard | sweet |

Kinesthetic

Teacher: Cut apart the activities and distribute to children based on the modalities that are their strengths.

Reteach Activities • More Adjectives — Unit 4 • Chapter 20 41

Using Synonyms in Writing

OBJECTIVES
- To recognize and select exact words
- To use available technology to find synonyms

SPIRAL REVIEW

DAILY LANGUAGE PRACTICE

TRANSPARENCY 39

❶ they follow a bumpi trail. (They; bumpy)

❷ What a smokie campfire. (smoky; !)

BRIDGE TO WRITING Feel how (adjective for feel) this rock is.

ORAL WARM-UP

USE PRIOR KNOWLEDGE Tell children they will be playing a word game. For each word you say, children say words with almost the same meaning. Say words such as *cold, tasty, little, wet, nice*.

Grammar Jingles™ **CD, Primary** Use Tracks 12 and 13 for review and reinforcement of adjectives and synonyms.

TEACH/MODEL

Have children read the definition and the examples. Discuss the differences between *loud* and *noisy*, and between *tasty* and *sweet* in the sentences. Ask children to name other synonyms for these adjectives.

GUIDED PRACTICE Work through the first sentence together. Invite a volunteer to read aloud the sentence using the word *rainy* and then repeat it using the word *wet*. Discuss with children which word better describes the weather (*rainy*) and explain why they think so. Repeat the procedure with the remaining sentences.

Using Synonyms in Writing

A **synonym** is a word that means the same or almost the same as another word. Some synonyms are adjectives.

> The birds in the forest are **loud**.
> The birds in the forest are **noisy**.

Choose the synonyms to tell exactly what you mean to say.

> I like to eat **tasty** blueberries.
> I like to eat **sweet** blueberries.

The adjective *sweet* gives a better idea of how the blueberries taste.

Guided Practice

Choose the more exact adjective to finish each sentence.

1. The (rainy, wet) weather ends.
2. Water falls from the (bent, droopy) tree branches.
3. I sit on a (soggy, wet) log.
4. My dad gives me a (hot, spicy) sandwich.
5. It has some (crunchy, hard) carrots in it.

256

Vocabulary Power page 59

Name _____

The following words have similar meanings. They all describe foods we enjoy—foods that look good, smell good, and taste good.

appetizing   delicious   flavorful   luscious   savory

What foods do these words make you think of? Draw and label pictures.

sweet, creamy, cold	salty, crispy, crunchy
hot, spicy, chunky	juicy, tender, rich

Draw two of your favorite foods. Use three or more words from the box to describe each food.

sweet	creamy	crispy	hot
juicy	sour	smooth	crunchy
warm	hearty	spicy	lumpy
tender	cold	thick	salty
chunky	fluffy	icy	rich

Vocabulary Power   Unit 4 • Chapter 20   59

ESL

REACHING ALL LEARNERS

SYNONYMS Children may need help differentiating and choosing between synonyms. Write synonyms such as *cold/icy*, *soft/furry*, and *sweet/tasty* on separate index cards. Invite children to taste something sweet, hold an ice cube, and touch a furry stuffed animal. Have children match the synonym pairs, and then choose the more exact adjective to describe each item. Invite them to discuss their choices.

Remember Some synonyms are adjectives. Choose synonyms that tell exactly what you mean to say.

Independent Practice

Choose the more exact adjective to finish each sentence.

6. My father gives me some (<u>sweet</u>, tasty) berries to eat.

7. I drink some (cool, <u>icy</u>) water.

8. I pick up a (<u>silky</u>, soft) leaf.

9. A (cold, <u>chilly</u>) wind blows.

10. (Big, <u>Huge</u>) raindrops fall again.

11. I slip on a (<u>slimy</u>, wet) rock.

12. My foot touches a (soft, <u>furry</u>) thing.

13. It is a (<u>fuzzy</u>, hairy) chipmunk.

14. The chipmunk has (<u>sparkly</u>, bright) eyes.

15. It hides under a (rough, <u>bumpy</u>) root.

Writing Connection

Revising Choose a piece of writing from your Writing Portfolio. Check to see which adjectives you can replace with more exact synonyms.

Use your computer's thesaurus to help you find more synonyms.

257

Independent Practice

Have children complete the Independent Practice, or modify it by using the following suggestions:

MODIFIED INSTRUCTION

BELOW-LEVEL STUDENTS Tell children to work with a partner. Have them read the sentence aloud with each adjective, and then answer the following question: *Which adjective tells me more about the noun?*

ABOVE-LEVEL STUDENTS When children are finished, invite them to rewrite two of the sentences using another pair of synonyms. Have them trade sentences with a partner and choose the more exact adjective for each sentence.

Writing Connection

Revising Help children select appropriate pieces of writing to revise, as needed. Tell them to underline the adjectives and then decide which ones they can replace with more exact synonyms.

WRAP-UP/ASSESS

SUMMARIZE Have children summarize and reflect about why choosing a more exact synonym is important to their writing.

REFLECTION

RETEACH

INTERVENTION Lessons in **visual**, **auditory**, and **kinesthetic** modalities: p. R30 and *Reteach Activities Copying Masters*, p. 42.

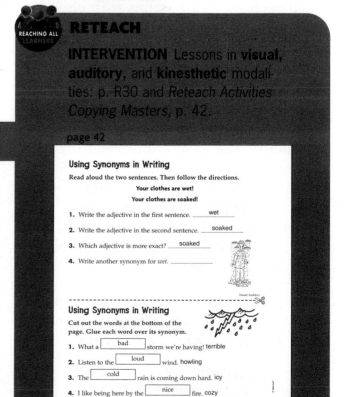

Extra Practice

OBJECTIVES
- To identify adjectives that tell about the senses
- To use adjectives for taste, smell, feel, and sound in writing

DAILY LANGUAGE PRACTICE

TRANSPARENCY 40

① A squirrel have sofft fur. (has; soft)

② It eats ard acorns (hard; .)

BRIDGE TO WRITING This banana is good and __(synonym for *good*)__ .

ORAL WARM-UP

PLAY "PASS THE SOUP, PLEASE" Pretend you are eating a spoonful from a bowl of soup. Say an adjective that tells how the soup tastes, smells, or feels. Then pass the imaginary bowl to children who take turns sipping the soup and telling about it. Repeat with other dishes.

TEACH/MODEL

Read each set of directions with children. Then have children share their answers with a partner or in small groups before you read aloud the answers.

WRAP-UP/ASSESS

SUMMARIZE Have children reflect on and discuss any special problems they had when completing the page. Then have children summarize what they have learned about adjectives that tell about the senses and about choosing more exact adjectives. **REFLECTION**

ADDITIONAL PRACTICE Extra practice items are provided on pages 472–473 of the *Pupil Edition* (*Teacher's Edition* R5).

TECHNOLOGY
Grammar Practice and Assessment CD-ROM
Writing Express CD-ROM

INTERNET Visit *The Learning Site!*
www.harcourtschool.com

More Adjectives

Extra Practice

Write the adjective in each sentence.

1. The squirrel has <u>soft</u> fur.
2. I watch it eat <u>hard</u> nuts.
3. It climbs the <u>bumpy</u> branches.
4. It has a <u>warm</u> nest in a tree.
5. The <u>quiet</u> squirrel sleeps.

Write a word from the box to complete each sentence.

juicy	furry	flat	sharp	fresh

6. I sit on a ___flat___ log and watch a squirrel.
7. It has a ___furry___ tail.
8. It also has ___sharp___ teeth.
9. The squirrel bites into a ___juicy___ berry.
10. It sniffs the ___fresh___ air.

Choose the more exact synonym.

11. I have a (bright, <u>shiny</u>) apple.
12. I see a (little, <u>tiny</u>) animal.
13. The animal wants my (<u>sweet</u>, tasty) apple.
14. It has (<u>black</u>, dark) fur.
15. I gave it a (hard, <u>crisp</u>) piece of apple.

258

Vocabulary Power page 60

REACHING ALL LEARNERS   ESL

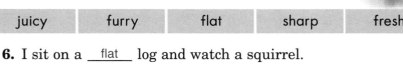

Name _____
Expand Word Meaning

Words that describe foods can be used to describe other things—things that are totally different from food.

Rock candy tastes <u>sweet</u>.
My friend Candy is a <u>sweet</u> person.

Draw and label pictures to answer the questions. Share your pictures with classmates. Compare ideas. Responses will vary.

It's a hot, hot day. What would be a <u>luscious</u> way to get cool?	You're looking for a good book. What topic would be <u>appetizing</u>?
You've worked hard. You're tired. What would look <u>delicious</u> to you?	It's been a rough day. You're cranky. You have a <u>sour</u> look on your face.

60   Unit 4 • Chapter 20   Vocabulary Power

WHAT IS IT? To reinforce vocabulary, display picture cards showing things such as an ice cube, a log, a furry animal, an apple, and a campfire. Say sentences such as "What is smoky?" and have children pick the picture that matches the description (campfire). Use adjectives that tell about the senses in your sentences.

Language Play

Food Clues
- Take turns with a partner. Think of a food you like, but don't tell its name.
- Tell your partner how the food feels, tastes, and smells. You can also tell how it sounds when you eat it. Be sure to use exact adjectives.
- Have your partner guess the food.

Writing Connection

Write a Shape Poem Think about something you like, such as a flower or a fruit. Write a shape poem about it. Use adjectives to tell how it smells, feels, sounds, or tastes. Copy your poem onto a sheet of paper shaped like your topic.

Apples

I eat juicy apples.

I like crisp apples.

I bite crunchy apples.

An apple is a

great food!

259

Language Play

Have children play "Food Clues" in pairs or in small groups. You may wish to make "food flash cards." Cut out magazine pictures of foods and glue them onto large index cards. Then have children place them face down in a pile and take turns choosing a card and describing the food on it. Remind children to speak in a volume that is appropriate for the size of their group.

Writing Connection

Write a Shape Poem Check to see that children have successfully written a shape poem by using the criteria below.

CRITERIA
- ☑ Writes the poem in the shape of the object described.
- ☑ Includes adjectives that tell about the senses.
- ☑ Punctuates sentences correctly.
- ☑ Begins each sentence with a capital letter.

PORTFOLIO OPPORTUNITY You may want to have children place their writing in their portfolios or compile the poems into a class book.

PRACTICE page 69

REACHING ALL LEARNERS

Name _____

Extra Practice

A. Underline the adjective in each sentence. Then write each word in the puzzle.

1. Come sit by the <u>warm</u> campfire.
2. The ground is <u>damp</u> over there.
3. Dad adds a <u>dry</u> log to the fire.

Puzzle:
1. W A R
3. D A M P / R / Y
(entry 2. connected)

B. Write an adjective from the box to finish each sentence.

| feathery | quiet | spicy |

4. The woods are _____quiet_____ tonight.
5. I finish the last of Mom's _____spicy_____ stew.
6. We listen for our _____feathery_____ friend.

C. Circle the more exact adjective to finish each sentence. Write the new sentence.

7. Owls have (soft, (fluffy)) feathers.
   Owls have fluffy feathers.

8. The owl's ((hooked) bent) beak and claws are strong.
   The owl's hooked beak and claws are strong.

Practice • More Adjectives   Unit 4 • Chapter 20   69

CHALLENGE

REACHING ALL LEARNERS

MAKE A MENU Have children work in small groups to create a menu. They can draw or cut out magazine pictures of their favorite dishes and then write sentences to describe them, using adjectives from pages 254–255 and from the Word Wall. Then invite children to share and compare their completed menus.

Menu

You will love this crunchy taco.

Chapter Review

OBJECTIVES

- To review adjectives for taste, smell, feel, and sound
- To identify and select the more exact adjective
- To identify and use antonyms

DAILY LANGUAGE PRACTICE

TRANSPARENCY 40

1 Is a snake's skin slimee (slimy?)

2 Do not sits on that weit log. (sit; wet)

BRIDGE TO WRITING This glass of water is fresh and (synonym for *cold*) .

STANDARDIZED TEST PREP

Read the directions with children to make sure they understand how to complete the items. You may wish to have children complete this page independently and use it as an assessment.

TEST PREPARATION TIP
Item Type: Multiple Choice

TIP

Model this strategy to help children determine the correct answer.

 I know that *tasty* tells how the blueberries taste. I read the answer choices to find a word with almost the same meaning as *tasty*. *Hard* and *loud* do not mean the same as *tasty*. I know that blueberries are not *spicy*. I choose answer *a* because *sweet* means almost the same as *tasty*.

 Read the sentences again with children, having them substitute *sweet* for *tasty* to be sure it makes sense.

Chapter Review STANDARDIZED TEST PREP

Choose the best synonym for each underlined adjective.

1. We ate some tasty blueberries.

   a. sweet

   b. spicy

   c. hard

   d. loud

2. Now we sit outside in the cold night.

   a. sharp

   b. sweet

   c. dull

   d. chilly

3. Our campfire has a burnt smell.

   a. smoky

   b. loud

   c. cool

   d. cold

4. We hear a big clap of thunder.

   a. tasty

   b. huge

   c. crunchy

   d. hot

5. Cold rain begins to fall on our camp.

   a. Sharp

   b. Smooth

   c. Icy

   d. Noisy

6. We all run into our small tents.

   a. tiny

   b. open

   c. big

   d. large

Visit our website for more activities with adjectives:

www.harcourtschool.com

260

Language Skills Assessment

• •

PORTFOLIO ASSESSMENT
Have children select their best work from the following activities:

- **Writing Connection,** pages 255, 257, 259; TE activities, pages 253, 255, 257, 259

ONGOING ASSESSMENT
Evaluate the performance of 4-6 students using appropriate checklists and record forms from pages R65–R68 and R77–R79.

INTERNET Activites and exercises to help children prepare for state and standardized assessments appear on *The Learning Site:*

www.harcourtschool.com

■ Vocabulary ■

Antonyms

> **Antonyms** are words that have opposite meanings.
>
> The campfire is **hot**.
> It is not **cold**.
>
> *Hot* and *cold* are antonyms.

Practice

Write an antonym from the box for each underlined adjective.

Antonyms

dry	wet	heavy	light	soft	hard	warm	cool
good	bad	large	small	sweet	sour	tall	short

1. Many <u>large</u> plants grow in the forest.
   small
2. I learned about one plant that grows in <u>wet</u> places.
   dry
3. This plant likes <u>cool</u> weather.
   warm
4. In spring its flowers smell <u>good</u>.
   bad
5. Then in summer its fruit is <u>sour</u>.
   sweet

261

■ Vocabulary ■

Antonyms

TEACH/MODEL

On the board, list the adjectives *warm*, *bumpy*, *sweet*, and *loud* in one column, and *bitter*, *soft*, *cool*, and *smooth* in another column. Ask volunteers to draw lines to connect the adjectives that have opposite meanings and then read them aloud. Explain that words that have opposite meanings are called *antonyms*.

PRACTICE When children are finished, have volunteers share their sentences with classmates.

WRAP-UP/ASSESS

SUMMARIZE Ask children to tell what they have learned about antonyms and to name a pair of words that are antonyms.

ACHING ALL **PRACTICE** page 70

Name _____

Antonyms

A. Draw a line from each word in Column A to its antonym in Column B.

Column A   Column B

1. cold   quiet
2. wet   large
3. small   high
4. low   hot
5. loud   dry

B. Read each question. Underline the antonyms. Then write a sentence to answer each question.

6. Are blueberries <u>sweet</u> or <u>sour</u>?
   Blueberries are sweet.

7. Is most tree bark <u>rough</u> or <u>smooth</u>?
   Most tree bark is rough.

TRY THIS! Write three sentences that use the words *tall*, *hot*, and *bad*. Then write three sentences using their antonyms.

70 Unit 4 • Chapter 20   Practice • More Adjectives

REACHING ALL **CHALLENGE**

ANTONYM PUZZLES Provide groups of children with index cards. Have children write two antonyms on each card, and then cut each card so that there is one antonym on each half. Put the pairs of cards for each group in two paper bags. Then switch sets of bags among groups and have groups put together the pairs of antonym cards.

Writing a Poem

pages 262–269

LESSON ORGANIZER

	DAY 1	DAY 2
DAILY LANGUAGE PRACTICE TRANSPARENCY 41	1. it are a cute squirrel. (It is) 2. see how busy they is. (See; it)	1. luna are a playful pet. (Luna is) 2. she have a droopy tail. (She has)
ORAL WARM-UP Listening/Speaking	Share Favorite Poems p. 262	Describe Objects p. 264
TEACH/MODEL WRITING	✔ **WRITING A POEM** **Literature Model:** "Busy" p. 262, "The Wind Is Cool and Swift" p. 263 **WRITER'S CRAFT** • To read and respond to a poem as a model for writing • To recognize and use colorful words **Think About It** p. 263	**GUIDED WRITING** **Writing Colorful Words** pp. 264–265 • To use colorful words to describe nouns • To complete a poem with colorful words **Writing and Thinking:** Reflect p. 265
Reaching All Learners	**ESL:** Building Vocabulary p. 263 *ESL Manual* pp. 104–105	**ESL:** Building Vocabulary p. 265 *ESL Manual* p. 104
GRAMMAR	**Unit 4 Review** pp. 308–309	**Unit 4 Review** pp. 308–309
CROSS-CURRICULAR/ ENRICHMENT	**Science Connection:** Nature Notes p. 263 **Vocabulary Power** Word Meaning p. 262 coil, swirl, twirl, twist, **whirl** See *Vocabulary Power* book. **Self-Initiated Writing** p. 263	**School-Home Connection:** My Luna p. 264 **Art Connection:** Portrait of Luna p. 265 **Vocabulary Power** Synonyms p. 262 *Vocabulary Power* book, p. 61 **Vocabulary activity**

KEY
 ✔ = tested writing form/skill

DAY 3	DAY 4	DAY 5
1. My buny is black and white (bunny; white.)	**1.** what is your favorite animal (What; animal?)	**1.** April have three sister. (has; sisters)
2. It have a pink noze. (has; nose)	**2.** I sow a hippo at the zo. (saw; zoo)	**2.** what a busy family they are? (What; !)
Oral Descriptions p. 266	Review the Features of a Poem p. 268	Discuss Letter Size p. 269
GUIDED WRITING ✔ **Applying the Craft** pp. 266–267 • To use a poem as a model for writing • To prewrite and draft an original poem **Read and Respond to the Model** p. 266	**GUIDED WRITING** **Editing Your Poem** p. 268 • To peer conference in editing a poem • To edit a poem and share it aloud	**HANDWRITING** **Making Letters the Correct Size** p. 269 • To practice making letters the correct size
Interactive Writing Model Drafting p. 267 **Challenge:** Write a Poem p. 267 **ESL:** *ESL Manual* p. 104	**Peer Conferencing** p. 268 **ESL:** *ESL Manual* p. 104	**Writing Resource:** Writing Frames p. 269 **ESL:** *ESL Manual* p. 104
Unit 4 Review pp. 308–309	**Unit 4 Review** pp. 308–309	**Unit 4 Review** pp. 308–309
Vocabulary Power Rhyming Words p. 262 *Vocabulary Power* book, p. 62	**LISTENING AND SPEAKING:** Poems p. 268 **Vocabulary Power** Blended Words p. 262 *Vocabulary Power* book, p. 63 🏆 **Vocabulary activity**	**Vocabulary Power** Figurative Language p. 262

Adjectives for Size and Number

LESSON ORGANIZER	DAY 1	DAY 2
DAILY LANGUAGE PRACTICE  TRANSPARENCIES 42, 43	**1.** this oatmeal is too lummpy! (This; lumpy) **2.** Who will eat the brunt toast (burnt; toast?) **Bridge to Writing** I like (adjective) orange juice.	**1.** an octopus has aight arms. (An; eight) **2.** How larg the eyes of a giant squid are (large; are!) **Bridge to Writing** Did you see the (adjective) fish in the tank?
ORAL WARM-UP Listening/Speaking	Tell About Size and Number p. 270	Play "I'm Going on a Picnic" p. 272 *Grammar Jingles™* CD, Primary, Track 12
TEACH/MODEL GRAMMAR **KEY** ✔ = tested skill	✔ **WORDS FOR SIZE AND NUMBER** pp. 270–271 • To listen critically to interpret and evaluate a poem • To recognize that some adjectives tell about size and some adjectives tell about number	✔ **ADJECTIVES THAT TELL HOW MANY** pp. 272–273 • To identify adjectives that tell how many • To use adjectives that tell how many in writing
Reaching All Learners	Practice Book p. 71 **Challenge:** Activity Card 15, p. R55 **ESL:** *ESL Manual* pp. 106–107 **Reteach:** *Reteach Activities Copying Masters* p. 43	**Modified Instruction** Below-Level: Identify Adjectives Above-Level: Write Sentences **Challenge:** Write Directions p. 273 **ESL:** *ESL Manual* pp. 106, 108 *Practice Book* p. 72 **Reteach:** *Reteach Activities Copying Masters* p. 44
WRITING	Write Adjectives That Tell Size and Number p. 271 Summarize/Reflect	Writing Connection p. 273 Functional Writing: Breakfast Menu Summarize/Reflect
CROSS-CURRICULAR/ ENRICHMENT	**Vocabulary Power** Word Meaning p. 270 **infinite,** countless, endless, unlimited, vast See *Vocabulary Power* book.	**Vocabulary Power** Synonyms p. 270 *Vocabulary Power* book p. 64 **Vocabulary activity**

DAY 3

1. We need wone or twoo big boxes. (one; two)

2. Aren't there a fue boxs in the basement? (few; boxes)

Bridge to Writing The children found (how many) boxes in the attic.

Use Correct Articles p. 274

 Grammar Jingles™ CD, Primary, Track 14

✔ **USING A AND AN** pp. 274–275
 • To understand when to use *a* and *an*
 • To use *a* and *an* in writing

Modified Instruction
 Below-Level: Identify Vowels
 Above-Level: Correct Articles
Challenge: Finishing Stories p. 275
ESL: *ESL Manual* pp. 106, 109 *Practice Book* p. 73
Reteach: *Reteach Activities Copying Masters* p. 45

Writing Connection p. 275
 Revising
 Summarize/Reflect

Vocabulary Power

 Word Families p. 270
 Vocabulary Power book p. 65
 Vocabulary activity

DAY 4

1. I put a orange scarf on an doll's head. (an; a)

2. A icicle is not an snowflake. (An; a)

Bridge to Writing I have (a, an) old wooden sled.

Create Riddles p. 276

EXTRA PRACTICE p. 276–277
 • To identify and use adjectives that tell size and number
 • To use adjectives that tell size and number in writing
 Practice and Assessment

Challenge: Silly Sentences p. 277
ESL: Shared Writing p. 276
 ESL Manual pp. 106, 110
 Practice Book p. 74

Writing Connection p. 277
 Functional Writing: List of Materials

Vocabulary Power

 Figurative Language p. 270
 Vocabulary Power book p. 66
Language Play p. 277
 Vocabulary activity

DAY 5

1. it snowed sevin inches last night. (It; seven)

2. I poured sum cocoa in a old mug. (some; an)

Bridge to Writing We had (a or an) excellent time playing in the snow.

TEST PREP **CHAPTER REVIEW** p. 278
 • To review adjectives that tell size and number; review *a* and *an*
 • To use available technology for aspects of writing, such as spell-checking
 Test Preparation

ESL: *ESL Manual* pp. 106, 111 *Practice Book* p. 75
Challenge: Spell-Check vs. the Dictionary p. 279

Writing Application p. 279

Technology: Using Spell-Check

Vocabulary Power

 Suffixes p. 270

Words for Size and Number

OBJECTIVES
- To listen critically to interpret and evaluate a poem
- To recognize that some adjectives tell about size and some adjectives tell about number

SPIRAL REVIEW

DAILY LANGUAGE PRACTICE

TRANSPARENCY 42

1 this oatmeal is too lummpy! (This; lumpy)

2 Who will eat the brunt toast (burnt toast?)

BRIDGE TO WRITING I like ___(adjective) orange juice.

ORAL WARM-UP

USE PRIOR KNOWLEDGE Have children talk about the books in the classroom. Have volunteers tell how many books they have near them and describe their sizes. Write some of the sentences on the board. Have volunteers underline the adjectives that tell about size and number. Add to the **Adjectives Word Wall**.

TEACH/MODEL

Tell children you will read aloud a poem called "The Cow." Ask them to pay attention to the description of the cow. After reading the poem once, have children open to page 270, look at the illustration, and join in as you reread the poem.

DEVELOP ORAL LANGUAGE Have children recall how the cow is described in the poem. Then ask them to think of other things about a cow the poet didn't mention. (possible responses: two eyes, big body) Continue to add adjectives that tell size and number to the **Word Wall**.

Words for Size and Number

Read the poem.

The Cow

There's a cow on the mountain,
The old saying goes;
At the end of her legs
Are four feet and eight toes.
Her tail hangs behind
At the end of her back,
And her head sticks out front
At the end of her neck.

Chinese Mother Goose Rhyme

*illustration by
Ed Young*

270

Vocabulary Power

DAY 1 WORD MEANING Introduce and define: *infinite* (too big to measure or count). **Look at the picture for the poem "The Cow." Is this sentence true:** *The cow has an infinite number of legs.* **Why is it untrue?**

DAY 2 SYNONYMS Write: *There is an endless number of stars.* **What word has the same meaning as** *infinite?* (See also *Vocabulary Power*, page 64.)

DAY 3 WORD FAMILIES Write: *infinite, infinity, infant.* **Which words belong to the same word family? Why?** (See also *Vocabulary Power*, page 65.)

DAY 4 FIGURATIVE LANGUAGE Write: *It will take until infinity to finish this work!* **What does this sentence mean?** (See also *Vocabulary Power*, page 66.)

DAY 5 SUFFIXES Write: *endless.* Have children brainstorm a list of other words that end with -*less*. Encourage children to draw pictures to illustrate some of their words.

With a partner, make a list of words from the poem that tell what the cow looks like. Then talk about an animal you like. Describe it. Tell about its size and things like legs, ears, and wings.

> Some adjectives tell about size.
>
>   I see a **big** cow and a **small** calf.
>
> Some adjectives tell how many.
>
>   The cow has **four** legs and **two** ears.

Think about an animal. It can be real or made up. Write its name on the first line of this new poem. Then write adjectives that tell about its size and body. Responses will vary.

There is a _____ on the mountain.

At the end of _____ legs

are _____ feet and _____ toes.

A _____ head sticks out front

with _____ ears and _____ eyes

at the end of a _____ neck.

271

WRITE Invite volunteers to read their lists aloud. Ask which words on their lists tell about size and number. Then give partners several minutes to talk about animals they like before reading the definition in the box and talking about the example sentences.

Then have children look at the bottom of page 271. Talk about how the pattern is similar to "The Cow." Have children take turns reading their poems to their partners. You may wish to have children illustrate the animals described in their partner's poem.

WRAP-UP/ASSESS

SUMMARIZE Reread the poem with children and have volunteers read their poems. Then ask children to summarize and reflect on what more they have learned about adjectives. Have children write their reflections in their journals, as well as write the adjectives they used while completing the page.

RETEACH

INTERVENTION Lessons in **visual**, **auditory**, and **kinesthetic** modalities: p. R31 and *Reteach Activities Copying Masters*, p. 43.

PRACTICE page 71

Name _____

Words for Size and Number

A. Write a word from the box to finish each sentence. Possible responses are given.

seven	little	twenty	many	big

1. I read a ____big____ book with my mother.
2. The book has ____twenty____ pages.
3. It is about a ____little____ girl named Lucy.
4. She is ____seven____ years old.
5. She has ____many____ friends.

B. Circle the adjectives that tell size or number.

6. Lucy lives on a (huge) farm.
7. She has (some) animals.
8. (Five) horses live in a stable.
9. Her goat just had (three) kids.
10. The kids are (small).

TRY THIS! Write sentences about a book you read. Describe the characters and the story. Use adjectives that tell size and number.

Practice • Adjectives for Size and Number   Unit 4 • Chapter 22 71

CHALLENGE

MAKE A CREATURE Have children use **Challenge Activity Card 15** (page R55) to make an imaginary animal. Then have them write a new rhyme that includes words for size and shape, based on the poem on page 270. Children can share and act out their rhymes.

Challenge Activity Card 15

Make a Creature

---

page 43

Words for Size and Number

Talk about each picture. Use an adjective from the box to complete each sentence. Possible responses are given.

short	tall	nine	five

1. Aubree makes a ____tall____ building.
2. She uses ____nine____ blocks.
3. Greg makes a ____short____ building.
4. He uses ____five____ blocks.

- -

Words for Size and Number

Cut out the words below. Glue an adjective that fits each sentence. Write whether it tells about size or number.

1. Cara brings a ____big____ bag of blocks. ____size____
2. Each friend gets ____ten____ blocks. ____number____
3. Greg builds ____one____ building. ____number____
4. Cara builds many ____small____ buildings. ____size____

big	small	one	ten

Teacher: Cut apart the activities and distribute to children based on the modalities that are their strengths.

Reteach Activities • Adjectives for Size and Number   Unit 4 • Chapter 22 43

Adjectives That Tell How Many

OBJECTIVES
- To identify adjectives that tell how many
- To use adjectives that tell how many in writing

DAILY LANGUAGE PRACTICE

TRANSPARENCY 42

1 an octopus has aight arms. (An; eight)

2 How larg the eyes of a giant squid are (large; !)

BRIDGE TO WRITING Did you see the (adjective) fish in the tank?

ORAL WARM-UP

PLAY "I'M GOING ON A PICNIC" Invite children to an imaginary picnic. Say: *I'm bringing six salami sandwiches. What are you bringing?* Have children answer with a word that tells how many, followed by one or two more words that begin with the same sound/letter, such as *two tomatoes* or *eight excellent eggs*. Add the adjectives that tell how many to the **Word Wall**.

Grammar Jingles™ **CD, Primary** Use Track 12 for review and reinforcement with adjectives that tell how many.

TEACH/MODEL

Introduce the concept of adjectives that tell how many by using the explanation and the examples. Ask questions such as: **Which word tells exactly how many in the first sentence?** (*four*) **Which word tells about how many in the second sentence?** (*some*) **What other words can you use to tell about how many?** (*few, many*)

GUIDED PRACTICE Work with children to complete each item. After they identify the adjective that tells how many, ask children if it tells exactly how many or about how many.

Adjectives for Size and Number

Adjectives That Tell How Many

Some adjectives tell how many. You can tell exactly how many with number words such as **one** and **two**.

The **four** children want breakfast.

You can tell about how many with words such as **few**, **some**, and **many**.

Dad will make **some** pancakes.

Guided Practice

Write the adjective that tells how many.

1. Cindy and Paul get <u>one</u> bag of flour.
2. They put <u>two</u> cups of flour in a bowl.
3. I add a <u>few</u> spoonfuls of water.
4. Jeff puts in <u>three</u> eggs.
5. Dad mixes the batter for <u>ten</u> seconds.

272

Vocabulary Power page 64

Name _____   Synonyms

These words have similar meanings.	!!!!! NEWS FLASH !!!!!
countless endless infinite unlimited vast	To understand these words, it's helpful to understand the meaning of limited. Something that's limited has a beginning and an end. I have 15 minutes to talk. My time is limited. We can't all fit in this elevator. Space is limited.

Show the meaning of the underlined word. Draw a picture, write words, or do both. Share your ideas with classmates.

limited	unlimited
infinite	countless
endless	vast

64 Unit 4 • Chapter 22   Vocabulary Power

REACHING ALL LEARNERS **ESL**

TELL HOW MANY Point to objects and groups of objects, such as books on a table, the door, plants, paper clips, or a pencil sharpener. Ask volunteers to identify the objects and tell exactly how many or about how many.

Independent Practice

Write the adjective that tells how many.

6. My <u>two</u> brothers hand Dad the frying pan.

7. Dad puts <u>four</u> drops of oil in the pan.

8. Then he pours in <u>some</u> of the batter.

9. It will make <u>one</u> pancake.

10. It takes <u>two</u> minutes to cook.

11. He makes <u>many</u> more.

12. Each person gets <u>three</u> pancakes.

13. Mom cuts <u>four</u> oranges into slices.

14. She puts <u>some</u> slices on each plate.

15. The breakfast will be ready in a <u>few</u> minutes.

Writing Connection

Functional Writing: Breakfast Menu
Imagine that you will make breakfast for your family. Think about how many people are in your family. Make a list of what you need. Use adjectives that tell how many.

- four eggs
- four pieces of toast
- some butter
- some jelly

Use your computer to help you write your menu.

273

Independent Practice

Have children complete the Independent Practice, or modify it by using the following suggestions:

MODIFIED INSTRUCTION

BELOW-LEVEL STUDENTS Have children work in pairs to identify and circle the adjectives that tell how many.

ABOVE-LEVEL STUDENTS Ask children to write five sentences that could have adjectives that tell how many but do not, for example *I have books.* Then have them trade sentences and rewrite them, adding adjectives that tell how many.

Writing Connection

Functional Writing: Breakfast Menu Remind children that an adjective can tell exactly how many as well as about how many. Call on volunteers to read their lists.

WRAP-UP/ASSESS

SUMMARIZE Ask children to reflect on and summarize what they have learned about adjectives that tell how many.

REFLECTION

RETEACH

INTERVENTION Lessons in **visual**, **auditory**, and **kinesthetic** modalities, p. R31 and *Reteach Activities Copying Masters*, p. 44.

PRACTICE page 72

Name _____

Adjectives That Tell How Many

A. Write a word from the box to finish each sentence.

| four | few | some | many | five |

1. My neighbor is ___five___ years old.

2. She has ___many___ tea parties.

3. Every day she puts out four plates and ___four___ cups.

4. She has ___some___ play food.

5. I sit on the floor because there are ___few___ chairs.

B. Fill in each blank with an adjective that tells how many.
Possible responses are given.

6. Carrie always invites ___three___ stuffed animals.

7. Her mother lets her have ___some___ cookies.

8. She puts ___one___ cookie on each plate.

9. After the party, she cleans ___many___ of the dishes.

10. She will have another party in ___seven___ days.

TRY THIS! Write two sentences about a snack you enjoy. Use adjectives that tell how many.

72 Unit 4 • Chapter 22   Practice • Adjectives for Size and Number

CHALLENGE

WRITE DIRECTIONS Ask groups of children to write general directions for making something. Encourage them to use adjectives that tell how many. Invite children to illustrate and then share their directions with the class.

Making Cookies
You mix a cup of flour with some butter. You add many chocolate chips. You bake for ten minutes.

---

page 44

Adjectives That Tell How Many

Talk about the picture. Read the sentences. Use an adjective from the box to complete each sentence.

| one | Two | Five | many |

1. Jason has ___many___ rocks.

2. He uses them to make ___one___ face.

3. ___Two___ rocks are used for eyes.

4. ___Five___ rocks are used for a smile.

Adjectives That Tell How Many

Cut out the words below. Glue the adjective that best fits each sentence. Underline the noun it describes.

1. A ___few___ friends come by.

2. They watch Jason make ___some___ faces.

3. ___Four___ people make bodies for the rock faces.

4. They play for a ___long___ time.

| Four | few | long | some |

Teacher: Cut apart the activities and distribute to children based on the modalities that are their strengths.

44 Unit 4 • Chapter 22   Reteach Activities • Adjectives for Size and Number

Using *a* and *an*

OBJECTIVES
- To understand when to use *a* and *an*
- To use *a* and *an* in writing

DAILY LANGUAGE PRACTICE

TRANSPARENCY 42

① We need wone or twoo big boxes. (one; two)

② Aren't there a fue boxs in the basement? (few; boxes)

BRIDGE TO WRITING The children found (adjective that tells about how many) boxes in the attic.

ORAL WARM-UP

USE PRIOR KNOWLEDGE Tell children to imagine that they went on a treasure hunt. Ask: **What did you find?** Have a volunteer start by saying *I found a (an) ____.* Have the next child say something else. Record the things children name. Continue until each child has had a turn. Then read the list, using the correct articles.

Grammar Jingles™ **CD, Primary** Use Track 14 for review and reinforcement of *a* and *an*.

TEACH/MODEL

Introduce the concept by using the explanation and the examples. As you read aloud each example, encourage children to explain why *a* or *an* is used. Invite volunteers to give examples, using *a* and *an*.

GUIDED PRACTICE Work through the first sentence with children, asking whether *rocket* begins with a consonant or a vowel (consonant) and which article belongs before the word *(a)*. Have children write the correct article. Call on a volunteer to read aloud the completed sentence. Repeat the procedure with the remaining items.

Using *a* and *an*

> **A** and **an** are special adjectives that mean "one." Use **a** before a word that begins with a consonant.
>
> > Astronauts ride in **a** space shuttle.
>
> Use **an** before a word that begins with a vowel.
>
> > **An** adventure in space sounds like fun.

Guided Practice

Write *a* or *an* to complete each sentence.

1. I have always wanted to ride in __a__ rocket.
2. First I will get __an__ old box.
3. I will build __a__ special rocket.
4. On one side of the box, I make __a__ window.
5. Now I am __an__ astronaut!

274

Vocabulary Power page 65

Name _____

Word Families

Words that have the same base word belong to the same word family. Underline the base word *agree* in the following words.

agreeing   agreement   disagreement   agreeable

Make new words. Circle words that have the same meaning.

1. end + ed = _____ ended
   end + ing = _____ ending
   end + less = _____ (endless)
   un + end + ing = _____ (unending)
   Circle the words that mean "without end."

2. limit + ed = _____ limited
   un + limit + ed = _____ (unlimited)
   limit + less = _____ (limitless)
   Circle the words that mean "without limit."

3. count + s = _____ counts
   count + ing = _____ counting
   count + less = _____ (countless)
   count + able = _____ countable
   un + count + able = _____ (uncountable)
   Circle the words that mean "can't be counted."

Vocabulary Power   Unit 4 • Chapter 22   65

REACHING ALL LEARNERS ESL

CHOOSE AN ARTICLE Review the meanings of *vowel* and *consonant* and the rules for using *a* and *an*. Then display familiar objects or their pictures, and have volunteers identify each one and tell which article to use. List the names of the objects on the board and have volunteers write *a* or *an* before each one. Have children read aloud the list together.

> **Remember** Use *a* before words that begin with a consonant. Use *an* before words that begin with a vowel.

Independent Practice

Write *a* or *an* to complete each sentence.

6. I use __a__ brush for a microphone.

7. __An__ orange hat becomes my helmet.

8. I find __an__ old shoe box.

9. The shoe box makes __a__ good seat.

10. I use __a__ skateboard for wheels.

11. I hear __an__ engine roar.

12. It takes __a__ minute to get into space.

13. I see __a__ planet.

14. Isn't it __an__ amazing sight?

15. __An__ imaginary trip is fun!

> **Writing Connection**
>
> **Revising** Choose a piece of writing from your Writing Portfolio. Check whether you have used *a* and *an* correctly. Change words in your sentences, if you need to do so.

Use your computer to revise the sentences.

275

Independent Practice

Have children complete the Independent Practice, or modify it by using the following suggestions:

MODIFIED INSTRUCTION

BELOW-LEVEL STUDENTS Have children write the alphabet on a paper strip and circle all the vowels. Suggest that they refer to the alphabet strip to remind them when to use *a* and *an*.

ABOVE-LEVEL STUDENTS Have children write four sentences with *a* or *an*. Have partners add an adjective after the article in each sentence. Tell them to decide whether the article stays the same or changes.

> **Writing Connection**
>
> **Revising** Help children select appropriate pieces of writing to revise. Suggest that they underline *a* and *an* and decide whether they used them correctly.

WRAP-UP/ASSESS

SUMMARIZE Have children summarize what they know about using *a* and *an* and how it helps when they are writing.

RETEACH

INTERVENTION Lessons in **visual**, **auditory**, and **kinesthetic** modalities: p. R31 and *Reteach Activities Copying Masters*, page 45.

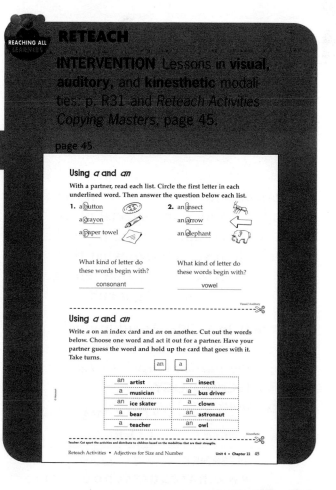

PRACTICE page 73

Name _____

Using *a* and *an*

A. Write *a* or *an* to complete each sentence.

1. There is __a__ library in Don's town.

2. __An__ older woman works there.

3. She shows Don __a__ special shelf.

4. Don sees __an__ unusual book.

5. There is __a__ river on the cover.

B. Decide if *a* or *an* is used correctly in each sentence. Write the incorrect sentences correctly.

6. Inside the book is a animal. __Inside the book is an animal.__

7. The animal has a furry body. _____

8. It is called a otter. __It is called an otter.__

TRY THIS! Write two nouns that begin with a consonant. Then write two nouns that begin with a vowel. Write sentences using these words. Be sure to use *a* and *an* correctly.

Practice • Adjectives for Size and Number   Unit 4 • Chapter 22 73

CHALLENGE

FINISHING STORIES Have children write the beginning of a fairy tale, without giving any nouns. Provide the following as a model to help them get started: *Once there was an ____ who lived in an ____ by a ____. One day, a ____ walked by.* Have children trade story starters with partners and then add the missing nouns. Call on volunteers to read the completed stories.

---

page 45

Using *a* and *an*

With a partner, read each list. Circle the first letter in each underlined word. Then answer the question below each list.

1. a button   2. an insect
   a crayon   an arrow
   a paper towel   an elephant

What kind of letter do these words begin with?
__consonant__

What kind of letter do these words begin with?
__vowel__

Using *a* and *an*

Write *a* on an index card and *an* on another. Cut out the words below. Choose one word and act it out for a partner. Have your partner guess the word and hold up the card that goes with it. Take turns.

| an | a |

an artist		an insect
a musician		a bus driver
an ice skater		a clown
a bear		an astronaut
a teacher		an owl

Teacher: Cut apart the activities and distribute to children based on the modalities that are their strengths.

Reteach Activities • Adjectives for Size and Number   Unit 4 • Chapter 22 45

Extra Practice

OBJECTIVES
- To identify and use adjectives that tell size and number
- To use adjectives that tell size and number in writing

DAILY LANGUAGE PRACTICE

TRANSPARENCY 43

1 I put a orange scarf on an doll's head. (an; a)

2 A icicle is not an snowflake. (An; a)

BRIDGE TO WRITING I have (a, an) old wooden sled.

ORAL WARM-UP

CREATE RIDDLES Have children create riddles with adjectives that tell about size and number. You may wish to use the following as a model: *What has many short legs, no arms, and one head and becomes a butterfly?* (a caterpillar) Try to work a Vocabulary Power word into the game.

TEACH/MODEL

Read each set of directions to help children understand how to complete each section. Have children share their answers with a partner or in small groups before you read aloud the answers to them.

WRAP-UP/ASSESS

SUMMARIZE Encourage children to reflect on and talk about any special problems they had in completing the page. Then have children summarize what they have learned about adjectives that tell size and number and about using *a* and *an*.

ADDITIONAL PRACTICE An additional page of Extra Practice is provided on page 473 of the *Pupil Edition* (*Teacher's Edition* R5).

TECHNOLOGY

Grammar Practice and Assessment CD-ROM

Writing Express CD-ROM

INTERNET Visit *The Learning Site!*
www.harcourtschool.com

Adjectives for Size and Number

Extra Practice

Write an adjective from the box to complete each sentence. Possible responses are given.

| tiny |
| tall |
| three |
| four |
| one |

1. __Tiny__ snowflakes fell on the lawn.

2. _____ inches of snow fell. Three, Four

3. Jenny made _____ snowballs. three, four

4. She aimed for the __tall__ tree on the hill.

5. She threw __one__ snowball that hit the tree.

Write the adjective that tells how many.

6. Jenny found <u>many</u> rocks for her snowman.

7. She used <u>some</u> rocks for buttons.

8. <u>Two</u> rocks made the eyes.

9. A <u>few</u> small rocks made the mouth.

10. <u>One</u> carrot was the nose.

Choose *a* or *an*. Write the new sentence.

11. Jenny found (a, <u>an</u>) old sled.

12. Then she got (a, <u>an</u>) idea.

13. Her mom climbed (<u>a</u>, an) hill with her.

14. Jenny took (<u>a</u>, an) trip down on the sled.

15. Jenny had (<u>a</u>, an) fun time sledding.

276

Vocabulary Power page 66

Name _____

We often use words to express strong feelings.

"I am so happy today! My happiness is <u>unlimited</u>!"

Someone whose happiness is <u>unlimited</u>, is very, very, very happy.

Answer the questions. Draw pictures, write, or do both.

1. "I have so much to do! It's <u>endless</u>!"
   What has seemed <u>endless</u> to you?

2. "Don't slam the door. I have told you <u>countless</u> times!"
   What has someone told you <u>countless</u> times?

3. "This is <u>infinitely</u> beautiful!"
   What seems <u>infinitely</u> beautiful to you?

66 Unit 4 • Chapter 22   Vocabulary Power

REACHING ALL LEARNERS — ESL

SHARED WRITING Have small groups write lines for "The Twelve Days of School." Review the ordinal numbers *first* through *twelfth*, writing them on the board. Have children brainstorm a list of things that classmates might give to one another during the school day. Children can dictate their lines to more proficient English speakers. Have children read aloud their verses together.

Language Play

The Twelve Days of School

● Take turns with a classmate. Make up and add new lines to a song.

● Begin with these lines:
> On the **first** day of school
> my classmate gave to me
> **one** sharpened yellow pencil.

● Complete the ending of the next lines:
> On the **second** day of school
> my classmate gave to me, **two** _____.

● Keep going until you have made up lines for twelve days of school.

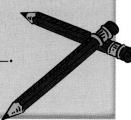

Writing Connection

Functional Writing: List of Materials Think about something you know how to make. Then think about what you need to make it. Write a list of things.

> ## Paper-Plate Mask
> • One paper plate
> • One pair of scissors
> • One pencil
> • Some markers and crayons
> • Two pieces of string

277

Language Play

Have children work with a partner to write "The Twelve Days of School." Remind children that in each line they are to write an adjective that tells how many things and an adjective that tells which day it is. Ask partners to act out their completed verses, displaying the correct number of props as they say their lines.

Writing Connection

Functional Writing: List of Materials Have children identify the most effective features of their list by using the criteria below.

CRITERIA

☑ Writes a title that tells the purpose of the list.

☑ Writes adjectives that tell how many.

☑ Uses *a* and *an* correctly.

☑ Begins each line with a capital letter.

Portfolio Opportunity You may want to have children place their lists in their portfolios or in the Sharing Basket.

PRACTICE page 74

REACHING ALL LEARNERS

Name _____

Extra Practice

A. Circle the words that tell size or number.

1. Angel made her room into a (large) zoo.
2. She used (many) stuffed animals.
3. She had (six) pens.
4. She used her bed for a (small) pen.

B. In each sentence, write an adjective that tells how many. Possible responses are given.

5. _____Four_____ bears were on her bed.

6. _____Two_____ pens had monkeys in them.

7. Angel had only _____one_____ zebra.

C. Decide if *a* or *an* is used correctly in each sentence. Write the incorrect sentences correctly.

8. Two friends took a look at the zoo. _____

9. They thought it was a interesting idea. They thought it was an interesting idea.

10. Kira wanted to borrow an bear. Kira wanted to borrow a bear.

74 Unit 4 • Chapter 22   Practice • Adjectives for Size and Number

---

CHALLENGE

REACHING ALL LEARNERS

SILLY SENTENCES Ask children to write and illustrate a silly sentence about wintertime fun. Invite them to use as often as they can adjectives that tell how many and words that begin with the same sound as the adjective. Have children share their sentences in small groups.

> Six sisters sat on a slippery sled.

Chapter Review

OBJECTIVES
- To review adjectives that tell size and number and the articles *a* and *an*
- To use available technology for aspects of writing, such as spell-checking

DAILY LANGUAGE PRACTICE

TRANSPARENCY 43

1 it snowed sevin inches last night. (It; seven)

2 I poured sum cocoa in a old mug. (some; an)

BRIDGE TO WRITING We had (*a* or *an*) excellent time playing in the snow.

STANDARDIZED TEST PREP

Read the directions with children. Make sure they understand what they have to do. You may wish to use this page as an assessment after children have completed it independently.

TEST PREPARATION TIP
Item Type: Multiple Choice

TIP

Model this strategy to help children determine the correct answer:

First I read the directions to make sure I know what to do. Then I carefully read the first sentence and think, "Which word best completes the sentence?" I know it isn't *some* or *large* because when I say either word in the sentence, it doesn't make sense. Answer *b* is the only choice left, so the word *a* is the correct answer.

Have children read the sentence aloud, inserting their answer choice to be sure it makes sense.

 Adjectives for Size and Number

Chapter Review
STANDARDIZED TEST PREP

Choose the word that best completes the sentence.

1. We make _____ snow fort.
   a. some
   b. a
   c. large

2. _____ of my friends join me.
   a. Some
   b. Big
   c. Small

3. Yuri brings _____ iron shovel.
   a. many
   b. a
   c. an

4. We make a _____ pile of snow.
   a. few
   b. large
   c. five

5. _____ people add more snow.
   a. A
   b. Less
   c. Four

6. The fort is _____.
   a. tall
   b. two
   c. a

 Visit our website for more activities with adjectives:
www.harcourtschool.com

278

Language Skills Assessment

PORTFOLIO ASSESSMENT
Have children select their best work from the following activities:

- **Writing Connection** *pages 271, 273, 277;* TE activities, *pages 273, 275, 277, and 279.*

ONGOING ASSESSMENT
Evaluate the performance of 4-6 students using appropriate checklists and record forms from pages R65–R68 and R77–R79

 INTERNET Activities and exercises to help students prepare for state and standardized assessments appear on *The Learning Site:*

www.harcourtschool.com

■ Technology ■

Using Spell-Check

You can use spell-check on your computer to find words that are misspelled. The spell-check gives you a choice of words that could fix the misspelled word. You click on the correctly spelled word. The computer replaces the misspelled word for you.

Spell-Check

Word to Check: spel

replace
cancel

spell
spill
sped

Practice

Read each sentence. The misspelled word is underlined. Choose the correct spelling in (). You can use your computer's spell-check to check.

1. You can write a <u>storey</u>. (<u>story</u>, starry, store)

2. Write about clouds and <u>rane</u>. (ran, <u>rain</u>, rang)

3. Be <u>shure</u> to use a frog and fish. (share, shore, <u>sure</u>)

4. Give <u>yor</u> characters names. (<u>your</u>, or, you)

5. Draw a <u>pickture</u>, too. (picketer, <u>picture</u>, pick)

279

REACHING ALL LEARNERS

PRACTICE page 75

Name _____

Using Spell-Check

Read the sentences. The misspelled words are underlined. Look at the choices in spell-check. Circle the word you would choose.

1. Jessie is a <u>grat</u> athlete.
   Replace with: (great) grape grated

2. She is good at <u>sockr</u>.
   Replace with: sock (soccer) soaker

3. It is her <u>favorit</u> sport.
   Replace with: favor (favorite) fantastic

4. She goes to camp in the <u>sumer</u>.
   Replace with: sum something (summer)

5. They play <u>gaimes</u> each day.
   Replace with: gems gains (games)

6. This year her <u>taem</u> won the camp award.
   Replace with: (team) tam meat

TRY THIS! Type a story from your portfolio on a computer. Use the spell-check program to check it for misspelled words. Correct each one.

Practice • Adjectives for Size and Number   Unit 4 • Chapter 22 75

REACHING ALL LEARNERS

CHALLENGE

SPELL-CHECK VS. THE DICTIONARY Have pairs compare using a computer and a dictionary to check spelling. Have them write in two columns the advantages and disadvantages of both methods.

Dictionary   Computer
slow   fast
has pictures

■ Technology ■

Using Spell-Check

TEACH/MODEL

Write on the board the following paragraph with misspelled words. Have children follow along as you read it aloud. *What fun my frends and I had today! It snowed aight inches last night. It was our furst big snow of the winter. We didn't have skool, so we played outside all day.* Ask children to identify four misspelled words. *(frends, aight, furst, skool)*

Call on volunteers to circle the words and spell them correctly, using a dictionary if necessary. Explain to children that there is an easier way to find misspelled words if they are writing on a computer. Have children read the information about using spell-check. You may want to demonstrate by typing and spell-checking the above paragraph.

PRACTICE When children are finished, have volunteers share their sentences with classmates.

WRAP-UP/ASSESS

SUMMARIZE Ask children to tell what they have learned about adjectives. Discuss how using adjectives can make their writing more exact and interesting.

LESSON ORGANIZER	DAY 1	DAY 2
DAILY LANGUAGE PRACTICE TRANSPARENCIES 44, 45	1. we got som books. (We; some) 2. Who got to dinosaur books (two; ?) **Bridge to Writing** I have ___(adjective that tells how many)___ books about horses.	1. Snow iz colderer than rain. (is; colder) 2. tim is the smartestest boy. (Tim; smartest) **Bridge to Writing** The weather is ___(adjective that compares)___ in winter.
ORAL WARM-UP Listening/Speaking	Use Adjectives That Compare p. 280	Building Blocks p. 282 *Grammar Jingles™* CD, Primary, Track 15
TEACH/MODEL GRAMMAR **KEY** ✔ = tested skill	✔ **WORDS THAT COMPARE** pp. 280–281 **Literature:** *"Spring Rain"* • To listen critically to interpret and evaluate a poem • To identify adjectives that compare	✔ **ADDING ER AND EST** pp. 282–283 • To understand that an adjective with er compares two and an adjective with est compares more than two • To use adjectives that compare in writing
Reaching All Learners	*Practice Book* p. 76 **Challenge:** Activity Card 16, p. R56 **ESL:** *ESL Manual* pp. 112–113 **Reteach:** *Reteach Activities Copying Masters* p. 46	**Modified Instruction** Below-Level: Use Key Words Above-Level: Rewrite Sentences **Challenge:** Weather Report p. 283 **ESL:** Compare p. 282 *ESL Manual* pp. 112, 114 *Practice Book* p. 77 **Reteach:** *Reteach Activities Copying Masters* p. 47

WRITING	Write Adjectives p. 281
	
	  Summarize/Reflect
		Writing Connection p. 283
		 Colorful Adjectives
		  Summarize/Reflect

CROSS-CURRICULAR/ ENRICHMENT	**Vocabulary Power** Word Meaning p. 280 **quicker,** hasty, rapid, speedily, swiftest See *Vocabulary Power* book.	**Vocabulary Power** Related Words p. 280 *Vocabulary Power* book p. 67 **Vocabulary activity**

Visit *The Learning Site!*
www.harcourtschool.com

WRITING ACTIVITIES
Writing Express CD-ROM

DAY 3

1. Who is the younger child of all in your family. (youngest; ?)

2. my sister is oldest than I am. (My; older)

Bridge to Writing I am the (adjective that compares) one in my family.

Act Out Comparisons p. 284

 Grammar Jingles™ CD Track 15

✔ **WRITING TO COMPARE**
pp. 284–285
• To understand when to add *er* or *est* to an adjective
• To use adjectives that compare in writing

Modified Instruction
Below-Level: Use a Mnemonic
Above-Level: Write Sentences
Challenge: Ads p. 285
ESL: Completing Sentences p. 284
ESL Manual pp. 112, 115
Practice Book p. 78
Reteach: *Reteach Activities Copying Masters* p. 48

Writing Connection p. 285
Writing and Revising
 Summarize/Reflect

Vocabulary Power
Word Families p. 280
Vocabulary Power book p. 68
🏆 **Vocabulary activity**

DAY 4

1. My dog is the smarter dog of all? (smartest; .)

2. My cat is oldest thar your cat. (older; than)

Bridge to Writing Ann's brothers are tall, but Ann is the (adjective that compares) of all.

Making Comparisons p. 286

EXTRA PRACTICE p. 286–287
• To understand when to add *er* and *est* to an adjective
• To use adjectives that compare in writing
🏆 **Practice and Assessment**

Challenge: Buildings p. 287
ESL: Adjective Check p. 286
ESL Manual pp. 112, 116
Practice Book p. 79

Writing Connection p. 287
Functional Writing: Shopper's Report

Vocabulary Power
Synonyms p. 280
Vocabulary Power book p. 69
🏆 **Vocabulary activity**
Language Play p. 287

DAY 5

1. What is the taller building in the world! (tallest; ?)

2. Your book is than oldest mine. (older than)

Bridge to Writing I wrote a (adjective) story, but yours is the (adjective that compares) one of all.

TEST PREP **CHAPTER REVIEW** p. 288
• To review when to add the endings *er* or *est* to adjectives
• To interpret graphic sources: pictographs and bar graphs
🏆 **Test Preparation**

Practice Book p. 80
Challenge: Compare Graphs p. 289
ESL: *ESL Manual* pp. 112, 117

Vocabulary Power
Abbreviations p. 280
Study Skill p. 289
Using Pictographs and Bar Graphs

Words That Compare

OBJECTIVES

- To listen critically to interpret and evaluate a poem
- To identify adjectives that compare

DAILY LANGUAGE PRACTICE

SPIRAL REVIEW

TRANSPARENCY 44

1. we got som books. (We; some)

2. Who got to dinosaur books (two; books?)

BRIDGE TO WRITING I have (adjective that tells how many) books about horses.

ORAL WARM-UP

USE PRIOR KNOWLEDGE Ask children to imagine that a big storm is coming and to then describe how the sky, clouds, air, and wind change as the storm gets closer. List adjectives that compare, such as *darker* or *colder*, in a three-column chart (adjective, + *er*, + *est*) or add these to your **Adjectives Word Wall.**

TEACH/MODEL

Have children turn to page 280, look at the illustration, and read aloud the poem title. Have them use the illustration and title to predict what the poem is about. Then read aloud the poem, asking children to listen to find out what happens in the rain. Next, invite volunteers to read the poem aloud dramatically.

DEVELOP ORAL LANGUAGE Ask

- **What word in the poem rhymes with slicker?** (quicker)
- **What word rhymes with better?** (wetter)

Mention that *quicker*, *better*, and *wetter* are adjectives; they tell what something is like. Invite children to think of more adjectives, such as *smaller*, *taller*, *shorter*, and *colder*, and add these adjectives to the chart or to the **Word Wall**.

Words That Compare

Read the poem.

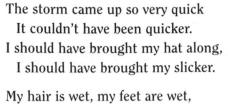

Spring Rain

The storm came up so very quick
  It couldn't have been quicker.
I should have brought my hat along,
  I should have brought my slicker.

My hair is wet, my feet are wet,
  I couldn't be much wetter.
I fell into a river once
  But this is even better.

Marchette Chute

280

Vocabulary Power

DAY 1 WORD MEANING Write: *quicker*. **Find this word in the poem "Spring Rain." Why couldn't the rain have been quicker?**

DAY 2 RELATED WORDS Write: *quicker — size? speed? shape?* **What does the word *quicker* tell about: something's size, speed, or shape?** (See also *Vocabulary Power*, page 67.)

DAY 3 WORD FAMILIES Write: *quicker, quacking, quickest.* **Which two words belong in the same word family? Why?** (See also *Vocabulary Power*, page 68.)

DAY 4 SYNONYMS Write: *hasty, rapid, slow.* **Which two words have a similar meaning?** (See also *Vocabulary Power*, page 69.)

DAY 5 ABBREVIATIONS **Writing the abbreviation is often quicker than writing the complete word. Make a list of all the abbreviations you know. Hint: think about titles of people, days of the week, and months of the year.**

Talk with a group about different kinds of weather. How are they alike? How are they different? Use adjectives, like *warmer,* to tell how weather can be different.

> You can use adjectives to **compare**.
>
> Summer rain can be **warmer** than spring rain.
>
> Winter rain is the **coldest** of all.

Add new lines to the poem. To finish each sentence, write an adjective that compares.

The rain came up so very **fast**.
   It couldn't have been ___faster___.

The wind came up so very **strong**.
   It couldn't have been ___stronger___.

The fog came up so very **thick**.
   It couldn't have been ___thicker___.

My hair is damp, my feet are **damp**.
   I couldn't be much ___damper___.

I walked in the **cold** snow once,
   but this is even ___colder___!

281

WRITE As children talk, continue to list the adjectives they use on the chart or on the **Word Wall**. Then have children read the adjectives aloud, reminding them that an adjective tells about a noun. Read the definition in the box, and discuss the example sentences, pointing out the *er* and *est* endings.

Then read the first item at the bottom of page 281 together. Explain that the word *faster* is an adjective that compares and is formed by adding *er* to the adjective *fast.* Point out the pattern from the poem. Have children complete the items and share with a partner.

WRAP-UP/ASSESS

SUMMARIZE Reread the poem with children. Then have them reflect on and write what they have learned about adjectives that compare. Children may want to record adjectives they generated while completing the page and write them in their journals.

REFLECTION

REACHING ALL LEARNERS
RETEACH

INTERVENTION Lessons in **visual,** **auditory,** and **kinesthetic** modalities: p. R32 and *Reteach Activities Copying Masters,* p. 46.

page 46

REACHING ALL LEARNERS
PRACTICE page 76

Name _____

Words That Compare

A. Underline the adjectives that compare.

   1. We just had the <u>warmest</u> summer ever.
   2. August was <u>warmer</u> than it was last year.
   3. We stayed in the pool <u>longer</u> today than yesterday.
   4. Sue can swim <u>faster</u> than I can.
   5. Melinda is the <u>fastest</u> swimmer of all.

B. Write an adjective from the box to finish each sentence.

coldest	cooler	brighter	longer	highest

   6. The sun seems ___brighter___ in the spring and summer.
   7. The sun is ___highest___ in the sky in the summer.
   8. Fall air is ___cooler___ in the evening than in the afternoon.
   9. Winter is the ___coldest___ season of all.
   10. It seems to last ___longer___ than the other seasons.

TRY THIS! Write two sentences that tell how seasons are different. Use adjectives that compare.

76   Unit 4 • Chapter 23   Practice • Adjectives That Compare

---

REACHING ALL LEARNERS
CHALLENGE

SEASON PENNANT Have children use **Challenge Activity Card 16** (page R56) to make pennants that show their favorite seasons. Make sure they use adjectives that compare in their sentences. Then have children display and compare their pennants.

Challenge Activity Card 16

Season Pennant

You need:
• paper
• felt, cotton balls, or other materials
• tape, glue, scissors
• crayons or markers

1. Cut out a large triangle.
2. On one side, draw a picture that shows your favorite season. You can also glue on pieces of felt, cotton, or other things.
3. On the other side, write sentences about the season. Use adjectives that compare.

Winter is colder than summer.
I made the largest snowman.
Winter is the greatest season!

Words That Compare

Talk about the picture. Use a word from the box to finish each sentence.

lighter	darkest	taller	tallest

1. Harry has the ___darkest___ hair.
2. Mike is the ___tallest___.
3. Lauren is ___taller___ than Harry.
4. Mike has ___lighter___ hair than Harry.

Mike Lauren Harry

Visual / Auditory

Words That Compare

Cut out the words below. Glue each adjective where it fits best. Circle the ending that makes it compare.

1. Lauren is the [oldest]
2. Harry has [darker] hair than Mike.
3. Mike is [older] than Harry.
4. Lauren's hair is the [longest]

Mike Lauren Harry

darker	older	oldest	longest

Kinesthetic

Teacher: Cut apart the activities and distribute to children based on the modalities that are their strengths.

46   Unit 4 • Chapter 23   Reteach Activities • Adjectives That Compare

Adding *er* and *est*

OBJECTIVES
- To understand adjectives that end with *er* compare two things and that adjectives that end with *est* compare more than two things
- To use adjectives that compare in writing

DAILY LANGUAGE PRACTICE

TRANSPARENCY 44

1 Snow iz colderer than rain. (is; colder)

2 tim is the smartestest boy. (Tim; smartest)

BRIDGE TO WRITING The weather is __(adjective that compares)__ in winter.

ORAL WARM-UP

BUILDING BLOCKS Have three volunteers use blocks to build towers of different heights. Then have children compare the three towers. Ask children to identify the adjectives they used and add them to the **Word Wall**.

Grammar Jingles™ **CD, Primary** Use Track 15 for review and reinforcement of adjectives that compare.

TEACH/MODEL

Read the explanation and the examples on page 282 with children. Have children identify the adjective (fast) and what things are compared in the first two sentences. (a car and an airplane) Then have them discuss what is being compared in the third and fourth sentences. (a jet to two other things and a rocket to all other things)

GUIDED PRACTICE Work with children to complete each sentence. Have them decide how many things are being compared before choosing the form of the adjective.

Adding *er* and *est*

> An adjective that ends with **er** compares two things.
>
> A car is **fast**.
> An airplane is **faster**.
>
> An adjective that ends with **est** compares more than two things.
>
> A jet is the **fastest** of the three.
> A rocket is **fastest** of all.

Guided Practice

Write the correct form of the adjective in ( ) to finish each sentence.

1. This science fair is the (greater, <u>greatest</u>) of all.

2. Tina made her model (<u>faster</u>, fastest) than Jim did.

3. Her sea model is (<u>deeper</u>, deepest) than Jim's pond.

4. His model is much (<u>smaller</u>, smallest) than her model.

5. Aldo's steamboat is the (louder, <u>loudest</u>) thing of all.

282

Vocabulary Power page 67

Name _____

The following words are related. They describe how fast someone or something is.

hasty   quicker   rapid   speedily   swiftness

Draw pictures to show the meaning of the words in dark print. Write a sentence to describe each picture.

1. quicker

2. rapid

3. hasty

4. swiftness

5. speedily

Vocabulary Power   Unit 4 • Chapter 23   67

REACHING ALL LEARNERS   ESL

COMPARE Display three cutouts of different sizes. Model comparing them using the words *small*, *smaller*, and *smallest*. Then display different cutouts and have children compare them using other adjectives. Write on the board the adjectives said by children. Have children repeat the correct responses while you point at the written adjectives.

Remember
Add *er* to most adjectives to compare two nouns. Add *est* to most adjectives to compare more than two nouns.

Independent Practice

Write the correct form of the adjective in ( ) to finish each sentence.

6. Dana's ant farm has (<u>fewer</u>, fewest) ants than mine.

7. My ant farm is (<u>newer</u>, newest) than her farm.

8. Mario brought the (older, <u>oldest</u>) fossil of all.

9. It's the (smaller, <u>smallest</u>) of all the shells I have ever seen.

10. Sandy's recycled paper is (<u>stronger</u>, strongest) than cardboard.

11. It is also (<u>darker</u>, darkest) than cardboard.

12. This science fair is (<u>greater</u>, greatest) than the one we had last year.

Writing Connection
Colorful Adjectives Think about three things you find outside. Draw pictures and write sentences to compare them. Be sure to use colorful adjectives and to add *er* or *est* correctly.

Use your computer to write and revise your sentences.

283

Independent Practice
Have children complete the Independent Practice, or modify it by using the following suggestions:

MODIFIED INSTRUCTION

BELOW-LEVEL STUDENTS Suggest that children use clues such as *than* (signals the comparison of two things) and of *all* (signals the comparison of more than two things) to help them decide which response is correct.

ABOVE-LEVEL STUDENTS When children have finished, have them rewrite each sentence so that it compares two things instead of more than two, or more than two things instead of two.

Writing Connection
Colorful Adjectives Have volunteers write their sentences on the board using the same format as the sentences in Independent Practice. Then display the drawings and have children choose the correct forms of the adjectives in the sentences.

WRAP-UP/ASSESS
SUMMARIZE Ask children to summarize what they have learned about adjectives that compare.

RETEACH

REACHING ALL LEARNERS

INTERVENTION Lessons in visual, auditory, and kinesthetic modalities: p. R32 and *Reteach Activities Copying Masters*, p. 47.

page 47

PRACTICE page 77

REACHING ALL LEARNERS

Name_____

Adding *er* and *est*

A. Circle the ending that was added to each adjective that compares. Then write whether it compares two things or more than two things.

1. This is the tall(est) redwood tree! — more than two

2. Is it old(er) than the tree next to it? — two

3. It makes the long(est) shadow of all. — more than two

4. This tree has a thick(er) bark than that one. — two

5. The needles are short(er) than my finger! — two

B. Circle the correct form of the adjective in ( ) to finish each sentence.

6. A redwood has (softer, softest) wood than an elm tree.

7. Are redwood seeds the (smaller, smallest) of all?

8. Which tree has (darker, darkest) bark than this one?

9. This pine tree has the (sharper, sharpest) needles of all.

10. Our pine tree has (greener, greenest) needles than this one.

TRY THIS! Draw pictures of three trees. Write sentences telling how they are different. Use adjectives with *er* and *est*.

Practice • Adjectives That Compare   Unit 4 • Chapter 23 77

CHALLENGE

REACHING ALL LEARNERS

WEATHER REPORT Have children take turns reporting the day's weather and then predict what tomorrow's weather will be, using adjectives that compare. You may wish to tape-record children's weather reports. Replay them later, and have children identify the adjectives they used that compare.

Adding *er* and *est*

Talk about the pictures. Use a word from the box to finish each sentence.

short	shorter	shortest

1. The turtle's line is _____shorter_____ than the dog's line.

2. The rabbit's line is the _____shortest_____ line of all.

3. All three lines are _____short_____.

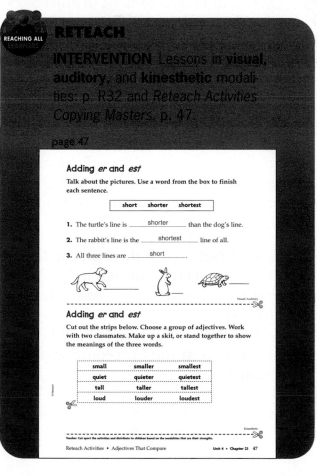

Adding *er* and *est*

Cut out the strips below. Choose a group of adjectives. Work with two classmates. Make up a skit, or stand together to show the meanings of the three words.

small	smaller	smallest
quiet	quieter	quietest
tall	taller	tallest
loud	louder	loudest

Teacher: Cut apart the activities and distribute to children based on the modalities that are their strengths.

Reteach Activities • Adjectives That Compare   Unit 4 • Chapter 23 47

Writing to Compare

OBJECTIVES
- To understand when to add *er* or *est* to an adjective that compares
- To use adjectives that compare in writing

DAILY LANGUAGE PRACTICE

TRANSPARENCY 44

1 Who is the younger child of all in your family. (youngest; family?)

2 my sister is oldest than I am. (My; older)

BRIDGE TO WRITING I am the (adjective that compares) one in my family.

ORAL WARM-UP

USE PRIOR KNOWLEDGE Provide three volunteers with a varying number of books, between two and six. Have children make comparisons using the word *few*. Repeat the activity with the words *light*, *large*, and *small*.

Grammar Jingles™ CD, Primary Use Track 15 for review and reinforcement of adjectives that compare.

TEACH/MODEL

Read with children the explanation and the examples. Draw three stick figures on the board and label them Ben, Jan, and Sara. Call on volunteers to draw each child's rock, using the information in the sentences. Discuss how using adjectives that compare can give readers a clearer picture.

GUIDED PRACTICE Work through the first item together. Have children tell whether to add *er* or *est* to *smooth* and explain why. (Only two things are compared.) Call on a volunteer to read both sentences. Repeat the procedure with the remaining items.

Adjectives That Compare Grammar-Writing Connection

Writing to Compare

You can use adjectives that compare to help tell how things are different from each other. This will give your readers a clear picture of the things you are comparing.

> The children are looking for **large** rocks.
> Ben found a rock that is **larger** than Jan's rock.
> Sara found the **largest** rock of all.

Guided Practice

Read each item. Then add *er* or *est* to the adjective in dark letters to complete the second sentence.

1. Most of the rocks are **smooth.**
   My rock is __smoother__ than Jeff's rock.

2. Some of the rocks are **dark.**
   Sam's rock is the __darkest__ of all.

3. Jack and Lisa found **small** rocks.
   Lisa's rock is __smaller__ than Jack's rock.

4. Maria, Tanya, and Rick found **round** rocks.
   Tanya's rock is the __roundest__ of all.

284

Vocabulary Power page 68

Name _____   Word Families

These words belong to the same word family.

haste: hasty hastily hastiest hastiness

Add endings to the words in dark print to make word families.
Possible responses are given.

1. quick	2. speed
quickly	speedy
quickest	speedily
quicken	speediness

3. rapid	4. swift
rapidly	swiftly
rapidness	swifter
	swiftest

5. slow	6. slack
slowness	slackness
slowly	slacken
slowing	slackly

Which two base words mean the opposite of quick?

slow _____   slack _____

68 Unit 4 • Chapter 23   Vocabulary Power

REACHING ALL LEARNERS **ESL**

COMPLETING SENTENCES

Display pictures of three girls with long hair of varying lengths. Provide children with word cards for *long, longer,* and *longest* and three sentence strips with the following: *All three girls have ____ hair. Lisa has ____ hair than Anna. Tina has the ____ hair of all.* Have children complete the sentences and then tell which girl is which.

Remember Add *er* to most adjectives to compare two things. Add *est* to compare more than two.

Independent Practice

Read each item. Then add *er* or *est* to the adjective in dark letters to complete the second sentence.

5. Miss Lee had a **smart** idea for the rocks. The class had an even ___smarter___ idea.

6. Everyone made **small** rock animals. Who made the ___smallest___ one of all?

7. Dan made a **short** tail for his animal. Ann made a ___shorter___ tail than Dan did.

8. Beth, Lisa, and Al painted **bright** eyes. My rock animal has the ___brightest___ eyes of all.

9. Ed put **long** ears on his rock animal. Maria's had ___longer___ ears than his.

10. Ted and Lisa painted **thick** stripes. Ted painted ___thicker___ stripes than Lisa did.

Writing Connection

Writing and Revising Draw three rock animals you might like to make. Write sentences to compare them.

Use your computer to check and revise your spelling.

285

Independent Practice

Have children complete the Independent Practice, or modify it by using the following suggestions:

MODIFIED INSTRUCTION

BELOW-LEVEL STUDENTS Suggest that children use the following; *Use er with two letters to compare two. Use est with three letters to compare three or more.*

ABOVE-LEVEL STUDENTS After children have finished, invite them to write sentences in the same format. Have children trade sentences with a partner and complete each other's sentences.

Writing Connection

Writing and Revising Remind children that using adjectives to compare helps readers picture the things being compared. As volunteers display their pictures and read aloud their sentences, have children identify which rock animal is which.

WRAP-UP/ASSESS

SUMMARIZE Have children reflect on what they have learned about writing to compare and summarize. **REFLECTION**

RETEACH

INTERVENTION Lessons in **visual, auditory,** and **kinesthetic** modalities: p. R32 and *Reteach Activities Copying Masters,* p. 48.

page 48

Writing to Compare

Read aloud each sentence. Circle the adjectives that compare.

1. My brother Jack is the (oldest) of all.
2. I am (taller) than both of them.
3. My (older) brother Lee is (shorter) than my brother Jack.
4. Isn't that the (oddest) thing of all?
5. Lee is the (fastest) runner.
6. Jack is (faster) than I am.

Visual/Auditory

Writing to Compare

Read each sentence. Fill in the blank with the name of a classmate. Then cut out the letters below. Glue them in place to complete the sentences.

1. _____ is tall [er] than I am.
2. _____ is young [er] than I am.
3. _____ has the neat [est] writing in the class.
4. _____ is the fast [est] runner in the class.

[er : er : est : est]

Kinesthetic

Teacher: Cut apart the activities and distribute to children based on the modalities that are their strengths.

48 Unit 4 • Chapter 23   Reteach Activities • Adjectives That Compare

---

PRACTICE page 78

Name _____

Writing to Compare

A. Add *er* or *est* to a word from the box to finish each sentence.

| long | tall | smooth |

1. Are giraffes the ___tallest___ animals of all?
2. Does a frog have ___smoother___ skin than a toad?
3. Does an alligator have a ___longer___ snout than a crocodile?

B. Read each sentence pair. Then add *er* or *est* to the underlined word to complete the second sentence.

4. Cheetahs, lions, and zebras are fast.
   Cheetahs are the ___fastest___ runners of all.

5. Ostriches have long necks.
   Giraffes have ___longer___ necks than ostriches.

6. Turtles are slow animals.
   Snails are even ___slower___ than turtles.

TRY THIS! Write three questions that compare animals. Use adjectives with *er* and *est*.

78 Unit 4 • Chapter 23   Practice • Adjectives That Compare

CHALLENGE

ADS Provide children with advertisements, coupon fliers from the Sunday papers, or store catalogs. Have them find and cut out sentences and catchphrases with adjectives that compare as well as pictures of the products. Have children glue their examples on paper and then share their findings.

Extra Practice

OBJECTIVES
- To understand when to add *er* and *est* to an adjective that compares
- To use adjectives that compare in writing

DAILY LANGUAGE PRACTICE

TRANSPARENCY 45

1 My dog is the smarter dog of all?
(smartest; all.)

2 My cat is oldest thar your cat. (older; than)

BRIDGE TO WRITING Ann's brothers are tall, but Ann is the (adjective that compares) of all.

ORAL WARM-UP

MAKING COMPARISONS Display pictures from *Goldilocks and the Three Bears*. Have children make up sentences to compare the bears, the bowls, the chairs, and the beds.

TEACH/MODEL

Read each set of directions, and make sure children understand how to complete each section. Have children share their answers with partners before you read aloud the correct answers to them.

WRAP-UP/ASSESS

SUMMARIZE Have children reflect on and discuss any specific problems they had in completing the exercises. Then have them summarize what they have learned about adjectives that compare.

ADDITIONAL PRACTICE Extra practice items are provided on page 473 of the *Pupil Edition (Teacher's Edition R5)*.

TECHNOLOGY

Grammar Practice and Assessment CD-ROM
Writing Express CD-ROM

INTERNET Visit *The Learning Site!*
www.harcourtschool.com

Adjectives That Compare

Extra Practice

Write the adjective that compares in each sentence. Then circle the letters that were added.

1. Who painted the tall**est** tree?
2. Ann's tree is short**er** than my tree.
3. This tree has few**er** branches than that tree.
4. Sam's tree has the small**est** leaves of all.

Write the correct form of the adjective in ( ) to finish each sentence.

5. Sue painted the (taller, <u>tallest</u>) buildings of all!
6. Max made a (<u>higher</u>, highest) mountain than Jill made.
7. Is the ocean (<u>deeper</u>, deepest) than the lake?
8. Jed made the (light, <u>lightest</u>) clouds of all.

Add *er* or *est* to the adjective in ( ). Then write the new sentence.

9. Mark painted the (bright) stars of all!   brightest
10. We made a (long) rainbow than the third graders made.   longer

286

Vocabulary Power page 69

Name _____   Synonyms

Words that have similar meanings are called synonyms.

quick—fast   quicker—faster   quickness—fastness

Read the word in dark print. Circle the letter beside the synonym.

1. speedier	2. swiftness	3. quicker
A slow	A quickly	A haste
B faster	B slowness	B runner
C quickest	C rapid	**C** swifter
D fasten	**D** quickness	D slower
4. rapidly	5. hasty	6. swiftly
A quickly	A slow	A speed
B hurry	B silly	B slackly
C zoom	**C** fast	C faster
D quicker	D jog	**D** rapidly
7. quickness	8. speedily	9. quick
A running	**A** hastily	A fasten
B speediness	B vastly	B slowly
C speeder	C swifter	**C** speedy
D speedier	D unlimited	D swiftness
10. slowness	11. huge	12. swirly
A restful	A tiniest	A squarely
B slackness	B wildly	B roundness
C quickness	**C** vast	C untwist
D sleepiness	D unforgettable	**D** whirly

Vocabulary Power   Unit 4 • Chapter 23   69

REACHING ALL LEARNERS   **ESL**

ADJECTIVE CHECK Before children make their cards, be sure they understand the words listed on page 287. As children write their cards, ask them to give an example of being loud, to find and to touch something smooth, to name something that tastes sweet, and so on. As children play, record their sentences on chart paper. Then ask children to read aloud their sentences and identify the adjectives that compare.

Language Play

Create a Group Story

- Write each word on an index card. Then put the cards in a pile.
- Cut six more index cards in half. Write **+ er** on half of the cards and **+ est** on the other half. Put these cards in another pile.
- Take turns with two or three players. The first player picks a card from each pile and says the adjective in a sentence. He or she uses it to start a story.
- The next player picks cards. He or she says a sentence to add to the story.

loud	small
long	short
tall	high
deep	smooth
sweet	dark
strong	smart

Writing Connection

Functional Writing: Shopper's Report Cut out pictures from ads for two items of clothing or toys you might buy. Compare the items. Which one Is cheaper? Which one is bigger? Tell which one is better and why. Write a Shopper's Report like this one.

> I want a new teddy bear. I saw two bears in a catalog. The brown bear has longer arms, brighter eyes, and softer fur than the blue bear. It is also cheaper. I think the brown bear is better.

287

PRACTICE page 79

REACHING ALL LEARNERS CHALLENGE

Name_____

Extra Practice

A. Underline the adjectives that compare.

1. We are putting on the <u>greatest</u> puppet show ever.
2. Mary made the <u>smallest</u> puppet of all!
3. Steven's puppet has <u>longer</u> hair than mine.
4. Your puppet has <u>fewer</u> buttons than his.

B. Underline the adjectives that compare two nouns. Circle the adjectives that compare more than two nouns.

5. My puppet has the (brightest) smile of all.
6. Ann wants a <u>smaller</u> part than Luis.
7. Luis is <u>bolder</u> than she is.

C. Add er or est to a word from the box to finish each sentence.

loud	soft	quiet

8. She has the ____softest____ voice in our class.
9. Ann is ____quieter____ than everyone else.
10. Ann did such a good job that her puppet got the ____loudest____ laughs of all.

Practice • Adjectives That Compare   Unit 4 • Chapter 23 **79**

BUILDINGS Have children find pictures of three buildings in a magazine and then cut them out. Invite them to paste the pictures on a blank sheet of paper and write sentences to compare them, using adjectives. Children can then display their pictures and read aloud their sentences.

This building is the tallest. The house is older than the tall building.

Organize children into small groups. You may want to use the following sentence as an example of a story starter for the word *smallest: I have the smallest dog in the world.* Suggest that each group choose one person to record the group's sentences. When children have completed the activity, invite groups to read aloud their stories.

Writing Connection

Functional Writing: Shopper's Report Check to see that children have successfully written a Shopper's Report by using the criteria that follow.

CRITERIA

- ☑ Writes complete sentences
- ☑ Writes and correctly uses adjectives that compare
- ☑ Begins each sentence with a capital letter
- ☑ Punctuates the sentences correctly

 PORTFOLIO OPPORTUNITY You may want to have children place their writing in their portfolios or create a bulletin board display.

Chapter Review

OBJECTIVES

• To review when to add the endings *er* or *est* to adjectives
• To interpret graphic sources, such as pictographs and bar graphs

DAILY LANGUAGE PRACTICE

TRANSPARENCY 45

❶ What is the taller building in the world! (tallest; world?)

❷ Your book is than oldest mine. (older than)

BRIDGE TO WRITING I wrote a _(adjective)_ story, but yours is the _(adjective that compares)_ one of all.

STANDARDIZED TEST PREP

Read the directions with children to make sure they understand how to complete the page. You can have them complete the page independently and use it as an assessment.

TEST PREPARATION TIP

Item Type: Multiple Choice

TIP

Model this strategy to help children check their answers.

Before I hand in the page, I need to make sure I chose the correct answers. I carefully read each sentence again. I check to see whether it compares two or more than two things. I know that when you compare two things, you add *er* to an adjective. When you compare more than two things, you add *est*. Next, I reread my answer choices. I reread the whole sentence, adding the word I chose, just to be sure.

Adjectives That Compare

Chapter Review   STANDARDIZED TEST PREP

Choose the word that correctly completes each sentence.

1. Dad planned the _____ tree house I've ever seen.
   a. great
   b. greater
   c. greatest

2. He buys the _____ wood of all at the lumberyard.
   a. strong
   b. stronger
   c. strongest

3. We need _____ nails than the ones we have at home.
   a. long
   b. longer
   c. longest

4. Dad chooses the _____ tree of all in our yard.
   a. old
   b. older
   c. oldest

5. Is this branch _____ than the other one?
   a. thick
   b. thicker
   c. thickest

6. Dad is a _____ worker than I am.
   a. fast
   b. faster
   c. fastest

 Visit our website for more activities with adjectives that compare:
www.harcourtschool.com

288

---

 288 UNIT 4

Language Skills Assessment

• •

PORTFOLIO ASSESSMENT
Have children select their best work from the following activities:

• **Writing Connection,** *pages 283, 285, and 287;* TE activities, *pages 282 and 287.*

ONGOING ASSESSMENT
Evaluate the performance of 4-6 students using appropriate checklists and record forms from pages R65–R68 and R77–R79.

 INTERNET Activities and exercises to help children prepare for state and standardized assessments appear on *The Learning Site:*
www.harcourtschool.com

■Study Skills■

Using Pictographs and Bar Graphs

Graphs make it easy to compare numbers of things. A **pictograph** uses pictures to show how many. A **key** tells you how many each picture stands for in the graph.

A **bar graph** also shows how many.

Pictograph

Books Read in October

Tom	📖 📖 📖 📖
Ann	📖 📖
Sam	📖 📖 📖 📖 📖
Beth	📖 📖 📖

Key: 📖 = 1 book

Bar Graph

Books Read in October

	1	2	3	4	5
Tom					
Ann					
Sam					
Beth					

Practice

Use the graphs to answer the questions.

1. What do both graphs show?
   how many books were read in October
2. How many children are shown on each graph?
   four children
3. How many books did Sam read? five books

4. Who read the fewest books? Ann

5. Which graph do you think is easier to read? Why?
   Possible response: the pictograph, because you can actually count the pictures of books

289

■ Study Skills ■

Using Pictographs and Bar Graphs

TEACH/MODEL

Have four volunteers stand in a row holding varying numbers of pencils (or books). Ask the group to tell who has the most pencils and who has the fewest pencils. Then have children turn to page 289. Read the information together, and talk about how to use pictographs and bar graphs to compare things.

PRACTICE When children have completed the activity, call on volunteers to share their responses with classmates.

WRAP-UP/ASSESS

SUMMARIZE Ask children to tell what they have learned about pictographs and bar graphs and to explain how they can be used to compare things.

REACHING ALL LEARNERS **PRACTICE** page 80

Name _____

Using Pictographs and Bar Graphs

Use the information on the pictograph and the bar graph to answer the questions.

Favorite Ice Cream	
Chocolate	🍦 🍦 🍦 🍦
Strawberry	🍦 🍦 🍦
Vanilla	🍦 🍦 🍦 🍦 🍦
Key: 🍦 = 1 vote	

Favorite Ice Cream						
Chocolate						
Strawberry						
Vanilla						
	1	2	3	4	5	6

1. How many children's votes are shown on each graph?
   12

2. Did more children choose chocolate or vanilla?
   vanilla

3. Which flavor did only three children choose?
   strawberry

4. How many children voted for chocolate?
   4

TRY THIS! Write directions that explain how to use one of the graphs above.

80 Unit 4 • Chapter 23   Practice • Adjectives That Compare

REACHING ALL LEARNERS **CHALLENGE**

COMPARE GRAPHS Invite groups of children to make a pictograph or bar graph to compare numbers of another thing. Display the graphs and compare the results.

Number of Pets

	1	2	3	4	5
Juan					
Sara					
Austin					
Kyra					

LESSON ORGANIZER	DAY 1	DAY 2
DAILY LANGUAGE PRACTICE  TRANSPARENCY 86	1. a penguin is a interesting bird (A; an; bird.) 2. it looks like an waiter with a suit (It; a; suit.)	1. what is a iceberg. (What; an iceberg?) 2. it is an chunk of ice (It; a chunk; ice.)
ORAL WARM-UP Listening/Speaking	Tell About Descriptions p. 290	Talk About Kinds of Descriptions p. 300
TEACH/MODEL WRITING 	**Literature Model:** "Penguins!," pp. 290–296 • To read and respond to a description as a model for writing • To identify important details for writing a description **Reading-Writing Connection:** Parts of a Paragraph That Describes p. 297 **A Student Model** pp. 298–299	**GUIDED WRITING** ✔ **Prewriting** pp. 300–301 • To brainstorm and select a description idea • To use a word web to plan a paragraph that describes **Transparency** 47
Reaching All Learners	**Options for Reading** p. 291 **ESL:** Illustrate Descriptive Details p. 294 *ESL Manual* pp. 118–119	**Interactive Writing** p. 301 **ESL:** *ESL Manual* p. 118
GRAMMAR	**Unit 4 Review** pp. 308–309	**Unit 4 Review** pp. 308–309
CROSS-CURRICULAR/ ENRICHMENT	**Science Connection:** Birds of a Feather p. 292 **Writer's Craft:** Sensory Words p. 293 **Science Connection:** Food Chain Lineup p. 294 **School-Home Connection:** Family Field Trip p. 295 **Vocabulary Power** dignified, formal, noble, regal, royal See *Vocabulary Power* book.	**Writer's Craft:** Audience p. 301 **Vocabulary Power** Context Clues p. 290 *Vocabulary Power* book p. 70 **Vocabulary activity**

KEY
✔ = tested writing form/skill

DAY 3

1. the South Pole is cold than here
   (The; colder; here.)
2. places near the equator are warmer
   of all (Places; warmest; all.)

Tell About Details p. 302

GUIDED WRITING

✔ **Drafting** pp. 302–303
   • To draft a descriptive para-
     graph that includes a topic sen-
     tence and details
   • To use sensory details

 Transparency 48

Interactive Writing p. 303
ESL:
   Shared Writing p. 303
   ESL Manual p. 118

Unit 4 Review pp. 308–309

 Vocabulary Power

   Classify/Categorize p. 290
   Vocabulary Power book p. 71

DAY 4

1. an penguin cannot fly (A; fly.)
2. a ostrich is another bird that does
   not fly (An; fly.)

Review the Elements of a Description
   p. 304

GUIDED WRITING

✔ **Revising and Proofreading**
   pp. 304–305
   • To revise a paragraph that
     describes
   • To proofread a descriptive para-
     graph for capitalization, punctu-
     ation, grammar, and spelling
   • To use Editor's Marks to make
     revisions and corrections

Transparencies 48, 48a, 48b

Proofreading practice

ESL:
   ESL Manual p. 118

Unit 4 Review pp. 308–309

Spelling Connection:
Spelling Strategies p. 305

Vocabulary Power

   Titles for People p. 290
   Vocabulary Power book p. 72

Vocabulary activity

DAY 5

1. penguins are funniest birds
   (Penguins; funny; birds.)
2. some penguins are tall than others
   (Some; taller; others.)

Talk About Descriptions in Media
   p. 306

GUIDED WRITING

✔ **Publishing** p. 306
   • To make final copies of revised
     descriptive paragraphs
   • To share paragraphs with an
     audience
   Scoring Rubric p. 306
   Handwriting: Size and Spacing
   p. 307

Practice and assessment

CHALLENGE:
Reporting the News p. 307
ESL:
   ESL Manual p. 118

Unit 4 Review pp. 308–309

LISTENING AND SPEAKING:
Making Announcements p. 307

Vocabulary Power

   Perform p. 290

Assessment Strategies and Resources

FORMAL ASSESSMENT

If you want to know more about a child's mastery of the language and writing skills taught in Unit 4, **then** administer the first *Language Skills and Writing Assessment* for Unit 4. The test consists of two parts:

Language Skills: adjectives that tell what kind; adjectives for taste, smell, touch, and sound; adjectives for size and number; adjectives that compare; and using colorful words

Writing Task: Write a **paragraph that describes.** Scoring guidelines and model papers are included.

INFORMAL ASSESSMENT TOOLS

 Using Portfolios

During a conference with children, discuss their paragraphs that describe and what they chose to include in their **writing portfolios.** Ask the following types of questions:

- What is the topic of your paragraph? How did you choose that topic?
- Which part of your description do you think shows your best writing?
- What details did you decide to include in your paragraph? Why?
- What are some of the colorful words you used to describe your topic?

You can also check children's understanding of **grammar** by evaluating it in their writing. Look for these points:

- Are *a* and *an* used correctly?
- Is the ending *er* added to adjectives to compare two things?
- Is the ending *est* added to adjectives to compare more than two things?

Oral Language Assessment

Use these guidelines to evaluate oral language:

Listening and Speaking

- Listens attentively to announcements
- Listens to obtain information
- Listens and retells a spoken message by summarizing
- Uses verbal communication in effective ways when making announcements
- Chooses appropriate language
- Adapts rate and volume

Informal Assessment Reminder

If you used the pre-instruction writing prompt suggested in Teaching Grammar from Writing, **then** remember to compare the results with the writing done by children after the grammar and writing instruction.

Unit 5

Grammar
- More About Verbs

Writing
- Directions
- How-to Paragraph

Make a Photo Mobile

1. Get a hanger, paints, crayons, markers, yarn, paper, glue, a paper punch, and some photographs.

2. Glue the photographs onto different shapes of paper. Paint or color the borders.

3. Punch a hole at the top of each picture.

4. Use yarn to tie your pictures to the hanger. Hang up your mobile!

Reaching All Learners

Intervention

SUPPORT ACTIVITIES To help you meet the needs of children who require extra support, use the following activities with individual children or small groups.

- Provide children with newspaper articles. Have them work in pairs to find helping and main verbs. Tell them to circle the main verbs and underline the helping verbs.

- Work with children to make a list of adverbs that can be pantomimed. Then have children take turns acting them out. Ask others to guess the adverb.

INTERACTIVE WRITING Share pictures of people doing activities. Have children brainstorm adverbs to tell about the actions they see. Ask groups of children to write sentences about the pictures. Sentences should include main and helping verbs as well as adverbs.

English as a Second Language

ESL STRATEGIES Use these strategies with children who need help with helping verbs.

- Have children pick a word or picture card showing an action verb. Then invite them to pick a card with *has*, *have*, or *had* and combine them to make sentences.

- To provide practice with forming the past-tense verbs of *come, run, give, go, do,* and *see,* pair children with different proficiencies. Give one verb to each pair. Invite them to make up sentences using the verb to tell about something they did in the past.

Challenge

Use these suggestions to provide challenging activities for children.

- **BE AN ANNOUNCER** Have children work in pairs to role-play radio announcers. Invite them to choose an event to announce, such as a sporting event or a contest. Tell them to use main verbs and helping verbs in their announcement as well as adverbs that tell *how, when,* and *where* the event takes place. Then have volunteers present their broadcast to the class.

- **PLAY A MATCHING GAME** Have children work in groups of six. Provide each child with two cards. Assign each child one of these verbs: *come, run, give, go, do,* or *see.* Have each child write on the cards the present and past tense form of the verb. Then have groups use the cards to play a matching game.

- **TURN ADJECTIVES TO ADVERBS** Have pairs of children list some adjectives that can be rewritten as adverbs by adding *-ly.* Have them record the adverbs on a chart next to the matching adjectives. Then have partners take turns using the adverbs in sentences.

Multi-Age Classroom

Pair younger and older children to create flashcards for the verbs *come, run, give, go, do,* and *see.* Younger partners can draw a picture illustrating each word. Then on the back of each card, older partners can write the past-tense form. Partners can use the cards to quiz each other.

Teaching Grammar from Writing

PRETEST

Use the following prompt as a pretest to assess children's ability to use *come, run,* and *give; go, do,* and *see;* main and helping verbs; and adverbs in writing.

WRITING PROMPT

Write a paragraph to tell about an interesting place you have visited. Tell when you went. Describe what you saw and did. Use the verbs *come, run,* and *go* somewhere in your writing.

EVALUATE AND PLAN

Analyze children's writing to determine how you can best meet their individual needs for instruction. Use the chart below to identify and remedy problems.

COMMON PROBLEMS	CHAPTERS TO USE
Incorrectly uses forms of *come, run,* or *give*	Chapter 25: *Come, Run,* and *Give*
Uses *I does* or *I sees* instead of the correct form of *see* and *do*	Chapter 26: *Go, Do,* and *See*
Does not use commas between the city and state in place names	Chapter 26: *Go, Do,* and *See*
Misplaces commas in dates	Chapter 26: *Go, Do,* and *See*
Uses helping verbs incorrectly	Chapter 28: Helping Verbs
Does not use adverbs in writing	Chapter 29: Adverbs

Classroom Management

DURING...	SOME CHILDREN CAN...
Grammar Reteaching	Work on the Writing Across the Curriculum project.
Independent Practice	Begin the Writing Connection. Participate in Language Centers.
Portfolio Conferences	Complete Self-Evaluation forms. (See pages R77–R79 in this *Teacher's Edition.*) Participate in peer conferences.

Celebrations!

LANGUAGE ARTS IN THE CLASSROOM

Make an ordinary day at school an extraordinary day by focusing on a reason to celebrate! Create a one-hour or one-day mini-unit. Use the celebration as the focal point for activities that provide opportunities for oral language and develop children's reading, writing, speaking, listening, thinking, and motor skills.

Discuss and plan special programs and projects to celebrate the events. Each celebration can include some or all of the following parts, depending on the amount of time you wish to spend.

WARM UP WITH LITERATURE Begin each celebration with a piece of literature that serves as a springboard for the rest of the activities. Find ways to have children interact as you read or reread the selection and follow up with a response activity.

GROUP-TIME ACTIVITIES Plan creative projects for children to engage in that reinforce the theme of the celebration. You can make these activities range from quick and simple to more elaborate.

ON THE MOVE Creative movement and structured games are a way to promote the theme of the celebration through physical development and social play.

WAYS TO INCORPORATE A CELEBRATION THEME

- **Choose books that reflect the theme of your celebration to display.**
- **Use the theme of the celebration to decorate your classroom door, a bulletin board, your room, or to make special tags for children to wear.**
- **Adapt classroom routines, songs, rhymes, games, or interactive charts to reflect the theme.**
- **Carry over the celebration theme into each area of the curriculum.**
- **Alert families beforehand by sending home a message telling about the celebration, asking for certain items, or encouraging children to bring something special for Sharing Time.**

Book Fair

Hands-on Activities

Now and the Past

MATERIALS: colored chalk

DIRECTIONS:

1. Write pairs of sentences on the chalkboard, such as these:

   My brother runs two miles.
   My brother ran two miles.

   The children come home after school.
   The children came home after school.

   Tina gives me a present.
   Tina gave me a present.

2. Call on a volunteer to read the first pair of sentences and circle the verbs.

3. Have children decide if each sentence tells about the present or the past. Ask volunteers to underline the present and past-tense verbs with different colored chalk. Repeat with the remaining sentences.

How Animals Move

MATERIALS: tagboard strips, modeling clay

DIRECTIONS:

1. On tagboard strips, write adverbs that tell how, such as *slowly, heavily, quickly, softly, quietly, loudly*. Place the strips in a basket.

2. Have children pick an adverb from the basket. Tell them to make clay animals that move in a way described by the adverb.

3. Invite children to use their clay models to act out a sentence they make up about their animal. Make sure they include the adverb they chose in the sentence.

Where To Go, What To Do, Who To See

MATERIALS: drawing paper, crayons, markers

DIRECTIONS:

1. Ask children to make a list of places they can go, things they can do, and people or animals they can see. Record their lists on the board.

2. Have children choose a place to go, something to do, and someone to see. Ask them to draw a picture of each thing they chose.

3. Ask children to write and then say a sentence about each picture, using the verbs *go, do,* and *see*.

4. Call on volunteers to repeat some of the sentences, changing the verbs so that they tell about the past.

I go to the store.

Helping-Verb Chain

MATERIALS: poster board

DIRECTIONS:

1. On a large piece of poster board, draw a chain with two links. Write the helping verbs *has* and *have* in the links.

2. Attach the helping-verb chain poster to the board. Then write a naming part to the left of the chain. Write a main verb and a telling part to the right.

3. Have a volunteer go to the board, choose, and write in the helping verb that makes the sentence correct.

4. Repeat with other sentences.

has have

The girls _____ cooked dinner.

Pockets of Adverbs

MATERIALS: large tagboard sheet divided into three sections, index cards, envelopes, stapler

DIRECTIONS:

1. Have children write adverbs that tell how, where, and when on separate index cards.

2. Label each section of the tagboard sheet with one of the following words: how, where, when. Then attach the envelopes to make a pocket for each section.

3. Have children sort the adverbs on the cards into the pocket chart.

4. Call on volunteers to pick an adverb and use it in a sentence.

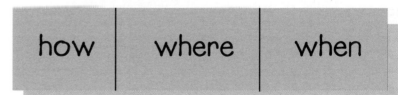

| how | where | when |

Writing It Down

BY VICKI COBB

DO YOU WANT TO DRAW a picture? Do you want to write your name? The tools you need are all handy. Get some paper and a pencil or a pen or crayons. You are now ready to write.

Imagine what would happen if we suddenly didn't have writing tools. Writing tools didn't always exist. Someone had to invent them.

PAPER

Paper is very flat and smooth, yet all paper is made of fuzz. Prove it to yourself. Tear a sheet of paper and hold a torn edge up to the light. Look closely at the torn edge. Try different kinds of paper. Sure enough, there's always fuzz! Scientists call the fuzz in paper *fibers*. Paper is made with fibers and a secret ingredient: namely, water.

A Chinese man named Ts'ai Lun (*say lun*) thought up this great idea. Ts'ai Lun worked for a Chinese emperor about 1,800 years ago. Ts'ai Lun put bamboo and rags and fishnets in water. He beat them with clubs until they were fibers. Then he lifted out the fibers on a flat screen.

The water drained away, leaving behind a flat, thin sheet.

Ts'ai Lun brought his new writing material to his emperor. No one had ever seen anything like it before. Ts'ai Lun's invention changed the world.

Before Ts'ai Lun invented paper, most people wrote on mats made of dried plant stems. These mats were called *papyrus* (*puh-PIE-rus*). Papyrus is very thick. Long pieces of papyrus were rolled up into scrolls. Papyrus was too thick to be piled in sheets, so there were no books.

Thin sheets of Ts'ai Lun's paper could be piled one on top of another. The sheets could be stuck together along one edge. That's how books came to be.

It's easy to open a book in the middle. Books replaced papyrus scrolls. Today the word *paper* comes from the word *papyrus*.

Paper was made by hand for more than 1,500 years. Then, about two hundred years ago, a papermaking machine was invented. Instead of making paper sheet by sheet, the machine made huge rolls of paper.

When the machine was first invented, most paper fibers

Building Background

Author Vicki Cobb was a science teacher before she became a writer. Her curiosity about science and technology led her to write several award-winning books for children and create *The Science Game,* an educational television series. Her many books include *Dirt and Grime Like You've Never Seen, This Place Is Wild,* and *Don't Try This at Home: Science Fun for Kids on the Go.*

INTRODUCE THE LISTENING SELECTION Tell children that they will listen to a nonfiction selection about two main topics: paper and pencils. Suggest that they think about how the writer's exact words help provide information.

Determine a Purpose for Listening

Tell children that this nonfiction selection tells about some writing tools they use every day. Ask children to decide whether their purpose for listening is

• to gain information (to gain information)
• to solve problems
• to enjoy and appreciate.

came from cloth rags. But now paper companies needed more fibers than they could get just from rags.

An inventor once got a great idea from a wasp nest. Wasps make paper nests from wood fibers. Their saliva dissolves the gluelike material holding wood fibers together. Today, paper pulp factories first chop up wood and then add chemicals to get out the fibers. Tons of fibers from the forests of the world become paper.

PENCILS

In the days when pen and ink were the main writing tools, people still needed a dry writing tool. Workers who measured land to make a road couldn't very well dip a feather pen into ink while the wind was blowing. It was too messy. Some people used lead, a soft metal, as a dry writing tool. It made a very light mark.

People also knew about a very soft black stone that looked like a piece of coal, only it was much softer. When the stone was rubbed against another surface, it left behind a black mark that was much darker than the lead marks. The stone could be used for writing or drawing. We call this stone *graphite*.

Pure graphite is very dirty to use. Also, pure graphite is too soft to keep a point. When you write, you need a point to make a fine line. How could graphite be turned into a useful writing tool?

About two hundred years ago, people mixed powdered graphite with fine clay and shaped it into thin sticks. After baking the sticks, they glued them between flat sticks of wood. The wood and graphite sandwich could be sharpened with a knife. It was a pencil! The graphite-and-clay stick is its lead. It is called *lead* because of the lead metal that at one time was used to write with.

Writing tools are used by people who create art and tell stories. You can be an artist or storyteller too.

Listening Comprehension

LISTEN FOR EXACT WORDS
Explain to children that in this passage, the writer uses exact words to tell about the history of making paper and pencils. Suggest that they listen for exact words that tell about how writing tools were first made, how they changed, and how they are made now.

	PAPER	PENCILS
FIRST		
NEXT		
NOW		

PERSONAL RESPONSE *Tell something new you learned about paper and pencils. Use exact words in your response.*
(Possible responses: I was surprised that fiber in paper used to come from rags. I thought pencils have real lead in them, but they have graphite.) INFERENTIAL: IMPORTANT DETAILS

Unit 5

Grammar
● More About Verbs

Writing
● Directions
● How-to Paragraph

Introducing the Unit

ORAL LANGUAGE/VIEWING

DISCUSS THE IMAGES Tap children's prior knowledge by inviting them to describe the items they see on pages 316–317. (colored paper, paint, paint jars, crayons, ruler) Have children share what they have made from these materials. Ask questions such as these:

- **How did you decide what to make? What materials did you use?** (Responses will vary.)
- **Did you have directions? How did you know how to make your object?** (Responses will vary.)
- **How did you feel about making your object? Did you share it with others? How did they feel?** (Responses will vary.)

ENCOURAGE CHILDREN'S QUESTIONS Have children think of questions they would have about something they would like to make. Have them write their questions in journals to research.

Unit 5

Grammar
● More About Verbs

Writing
● Directions
● How-to Paragraph

316

Viewing and Representing

• • • • • • • • • • • • • • • • • • •

COMPARE/CONTRAST PRINT AND VISUAL MEDIA Have small groups of children decide on an art project to make. Then have them make a list of the steps to follow. Children can share their steps with the class in a variety of ways, such as a chart, a poster, or a comic strip. Children can explain the steps.

For evaluation criteria, see the checklist on page R77.

MEDIA LITERACY AND COMMUNICATION
SKILLS PACKAGE Use the video to extend children's oral and visual literacy. See pages 6–7 of the *Teacher's Guide.*

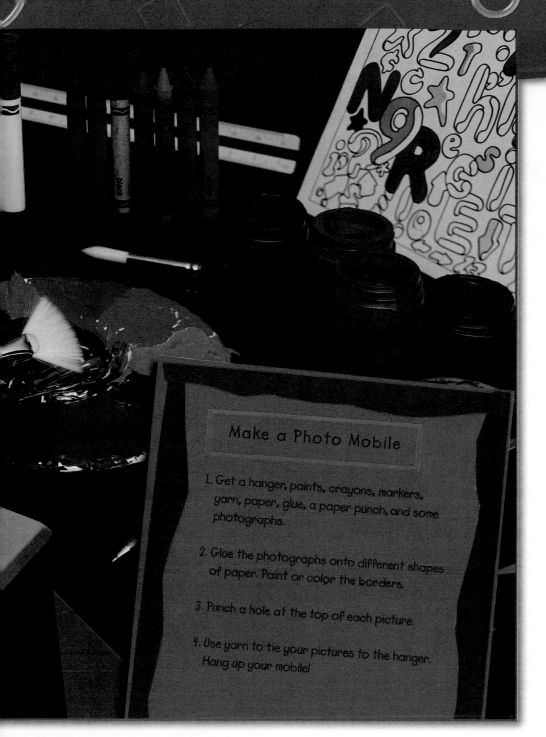

Make a Photo Mobile

1. Get a hanger, paints, crayons, markers, yarn, paper, glue, a paper punch, and some photographs.

2. Glue the photographs onto different shapes of paper. Paint or color the borders.

3. Punch a hole at the top of each picture.

4. Use yarn to tie your pictures to the hanger. Hang up your mobile!

Previewing the Unit

Read and discuss the unit contents list with children. Tell them that in this unit they will learn more about verbs, particularly how to change some verbs to tell about the past. They will also learn about words that tell *how*, *when*, and *where*. Then have children tell how learning to write directions will help in writing a how-to paragraph.

FINE ARTS CONNECTION Children will be exposed to a variety of fine arts topics in this unit:

- Museum
- Art show
- Theater
- Concert

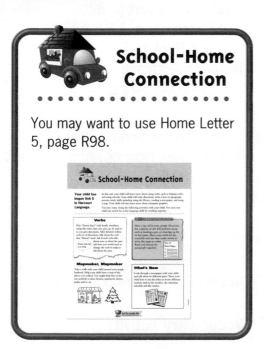

School-Home Connection

You may want to use Home Letter 5, page R98.

LESSON ORGANIZER	DAY **1**	DAY **2**
DAILY LANGUAGE PRACTICE *TRANSPARENCIES 49, 50*	1. The bestest place to swim is the pacific ocean. (best; Pacific) 2. The other oceans is smallest than the Pacific. (are; smaller) **Bridge to Writing** The ocean is (form of *cold*) than the lake.	1. Me comes home. (I come) 2. I runs the hole way. (run; whole) **Bridge to Writing** The champion (form of *run*) very fast.
ORAL WARM-UP **Listening/Speaking**	Play Charades p. 318	Identify Incorrect Uses of *Come, Run,* and *Give* p. 320 *Grammar Jingles*™ CD, Primary, Track 16
TEACH/MODEL **GRAMMAR** **KEY** ✔ = tested skill	✔ **THE VERBS *COME, RUN,* AND *GIVE*** pp. 318-319 **Literature:** "This Is My Rock" by David McCord • To listen critically to interpret and evaluate a poem • To understand that *come, run,* and *give* tell about now	✔ **USING *COME, RUN,* AND *GIVE*** pp. 320-321 • To use the correct forms of the verbs *come, run,* and *give* in the present and past tenses • To use the correct forms of *come, run,* and *give* in writing

Reaching All Learners	*Practice Book* p. 81
	Challenge: Activity Card 17, p. R57
	ESL: *ESL Manual* pp. 120, 121
	Reteach: *Reteach Activities Copying Masters* p. 49
		Modified Instruction
		  Below-Level: Identify Time Words
		  Above-Level: Write Sentences
		Challenge: Interview p.321
		ESL: Use a Chart p. 320
		  ESL Manual pp. 120, 122
		  Practice Book p. 82
		Reteach: *Reteach Activities Copying Masters* p. 50

WRITING	Complete a Poem p. 319 Summarize/Reflect	Writing Connection p. 321 Telling About Now or About the Past Summarize/Reflect

CROSS-CURRICULAR/ ENRICHMENT	**Vocabulary Power**
	  Word Meaning, p. 318
	
	action, connection, **contribution**, prediction, transportation
	See *Vocabulary Power* book.
		Vocabulary Power
		  Word Families, p. 318
		  Vocabulary Power book, p. 73
		
		🏆 **Vocabulary activity**

DAY 3

1. Juanita cames with us Yesterday. (came; yesterday)
2. Yesterday I give Mark a bok. (gave; book)

Bridge to Writing My dad (form of *run*) five miles last Sunday.

Using *And* p. 322

Grammar Jingles™ CD, Primary, Track 17

✔ **JOINING SENTENCES**
   pp. 322-323
• To use *and* to join whole sentences that tell about the same thing
• To join sentences to make a piece of writing more interesting

Modified Instruction
   Below-Level: Work in Pairs
   Above-Level: Join Sentences
Challenge: Parents and Teachers p. 323
ESL: Joining Sentences p. 322
ESL Manual, pp. 120, 123
Practice Book p. 83
Reteach: *Reteach Activities Copying Masters* p. 51

Writing Connection p. 323
Revising
Summarize/Reflect

Vocabulary Power
   Suffixes, p. 318
   Vocabulary Power book, p. 74
 Vocabulary activity

DAY 4

1. Our class is putting on a play and, You want to be in it. (play, and you)
2. The play is fun, And we, all love it. (and we)

Bridge to Writing I love to read. (join sentences) My teacher gives me books.

Theme Sentences p. 324

EXTRA PRACTICE p. 324-325
• To recognize and use the verbs *come, run,* and *give* in the present and past tenses and to join whole sentences
• To write lists to record
 Practice and Assessment

Challenge: Taking Polls p. 325
ESL: Shared Writing p. 324
   ESL Manual, pp. 120, 124
Practice Book p. 84

Writing Connection p. 325
   Making Lists

Vocabulary Power
   Analogies, p. 318
   Vocabulary Power book, p. 75
 Vocabulary activity
Language Play, p. 325

DAY 5

1. gina gaves a report now. (Gina; gives)
2. Diego give's me a kard. (gives; card)

Bridge to Writing Jeff (form of the verb *come*) to the desk now.

TEST PREP **CHAPTER REVIEW** p. 326
• To review *come, run,* and *give* and how to join sentences
• To understand how to use a newspaper and the different parts of an article
 Test Preparation

Practice Book p. 85
Challenge: School News p. 327
ESL: *ESL Manual,* pp. 120, 125

Writing Application p. 327
Newspaper Articles

STUDY SKILLS
   Using a Newspaper p. 327
Vocabulary Power

   Graphics/Art, p. 318

CHAPTER **25** 317B

The Verbs *Come, Run,* and *Give*

OBJECTIVES

- To listen critically to interpret and evaluate a poem
- To understand that the verbs *come, run,* and *give* tell about now

DAILY LANGUAGE PRACTICE

TRANSPARENCY 49

1. The bestest place to swim is the pacific ocean. (best; Pacific)

2. The other oceans is smallest than the Pacific. (are; smaller)

BRIDGE TO WRITING The ocean is ____ (form of *cold*) than the lake.

ORAL WARM-UP

PLAY CHARADES Have three volunteers each act out one of the three verbs *come, run,* and *give.* Have the other children decide what they are doing. Write the three words on chart paper or set up a **Word Wall.**

TEACH/MODEL

Tell children to open their books to page 318. Have them describe the illustration. Then have them read the title and use the illustration to predict what the poem will be about. Read the poem aloud. Then reread the poem again with children.

DEVELOP ORAL LANGUAGE Ask children to recall how the poet got to the rock. Ask if there are other ways he could have gotten to the rock. Write children's sentences with the verbs *run* or *come* on the board.

The Verbs *Come, Run,* and *Give*

Read the poem.

This Is My Rock

This is my rock,
And here I run
To steal the secret of the sun;

This is my rock,
And here come I
Before the night has swept the sky;

This is my rock,
This is the place
I meet the evening face to face.

David McCord

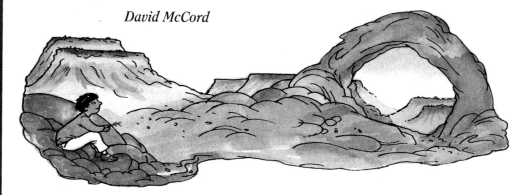

318

Vocabulary Power

DAY 1 WORD MEANINGS Introduce and define *contribution* (something given). **How can you make a contribution when we talk about a book?**

DAY 2 WORD FAMILIES Write: *contribute, contribution.* **Are these two words in the same word family? How do you know?** (See also *Vocabulary Power,* page 73.)

DAY 3 SUFFIXES Write: *act, acted, action.* **What is the base word? What endings have been added to the base word?** (See also *Vocabulary Power,* page 74.)

DAY 4 ANALOGIES Write: *A contribution is something you give. An action is something you _____.* (do) **What word completes this sentence?** (See also *Vocabulary Power,* page 75.)

DAY 5 GRAPHICS/ART Invite children to make a book about different kinds of transportation. Have each child label his or her contribution.

Tell why you think the rock is special to the poet. Then talk with a classmate about a place that is special to you.

> The verbs **come**, **run**, and **give** tell about now. Add **s** to tell what one person, animal, or thing does. Do not add **s** when using **I**.
>
> I **come** home.
> The sun **comes** out now.
> Ramon **runs** to Maria's house.
> He **gives** her a drawing of the sun.

Write a poem like the one you just read. Write the name of your special place in the first line. Use the verbs come, run, and give in some of the other lines if you can. Responses will vary.

319

WRITE Help children realize that a special place can be small or large. A person needs to feel secure and safe there. Invite volunteers to share places they like to go. Then read the explanation and talk about the example sentences in the box.

Help children get started writing their poem by suggesting that they begin the first two lines using the following sentence frame: *This is my ____, and here I ____.* Invite children to share their completed poems with a partner.

WRAP-UP/ASSESS

SUMMARIZE Reread the poem with children. Then have them reflect on what they have learned about the verbs *come*, *run*, and *give*. Be sure children talk about when to add an *s* to each verb and when not to do so. You may want children to write their reflections and sentences in their journals. **REFLECTION**

RETEACH

INTERVENTION Lessons in **visual**, **auditory**, and **kinesthetic** modalities: p. R33 and *Reteach Activities Copying Masters*, p. 49.

REACHING ALL LEARNERS

PRACTICE page 81

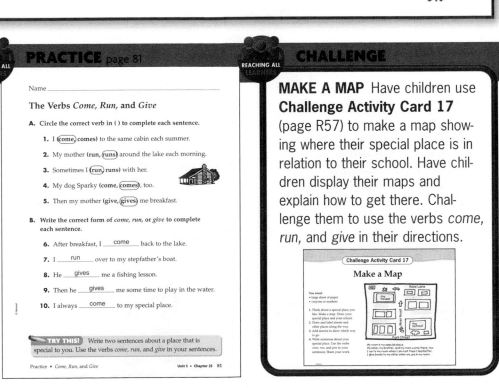

Name _____

The Verbs *Come, Run,* **and** *Give*

A. Circle the correct verb in ( ) to complete each sentence.

1. I (**come**, comes) to the same cabin each summer.
2. My mother (run, **runs**) around the lake each morning.
3. Sometimes I (**run**, runs) with her.
4. My dog Sparky (come, **comes**), too.
5. Then my mother (give, **gives**) me breakfast.

B. Write the correct form of *come, run,* or *give* to complete each sentence.

6. After breakfast, I ___come___ back to the lake.
7. I ___run___ over to my stepfather's boat.
8. He ___gives___ me a fishing lesson.
9. Then he ___gives___ me some time to play in the water.
10. I always ___come___ to my special place.

> **TRY THIS!** Write two sentences about a place that is special to you. Use the verbs *come, run,* and *give* in your sentences.

Practice • *Come, Run, and Give*   Unit 5 • Chapter 25 81

CHALLENGE

MAKE A MAP Have children use **Challenge Activity Card 17** (page R57) to make a map showing where their special place is in relation to their school. Have children display their maps and explain how to get there. Challenge them to use the verbs *come, run,* and *give* in their directions.

Challenge Activity Card 17

Make a Map

page 49

The Verbs *Come, Run,* **and** *Give*
Read aloud each sentence. Circle the verb.

1. A horse (comes) into the stable.
   I (come) out of the stall.
2. I (run) to see the horse.
   It (runs) away from me.
3. I (give) the horse a carrot.
   My friend (gives) it some water.
4. The horse (runs) out of the stable.
   I (run) out, too.

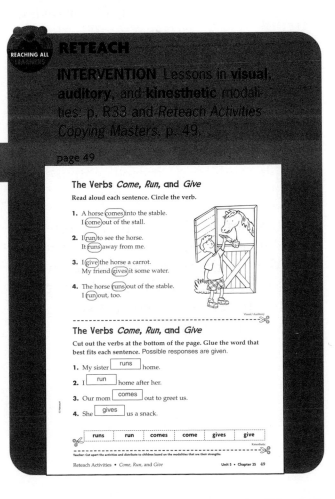

The Verbs *Come, Run,* **and** *Give*

Cut out the verbs at the bottom of the page. Glue the word that best fits each sentence. Possible responses are given.

1. My sister ___runs___ home.
2. I ___run___ home after her.
3. Our mom ___comes___ out to greet us.
4. She ___gives___ us a snack.

| runs | run | comes | come | gives | give |

Teacher: Cut apart the activities and distribute to children based on the modalities that are their strengths.
Reteach Activities • *Come, Run, and Give*   Unit 5 • Chapter 25 49

Using *Come, Run,* and *Give*

OBJECTIVES
- To use the correct forms of the verbs *come*, *run*, and *give* in the present and past tenses
- To use the correct forms of the verbs *come*, *run*, and *give* in writing

SPIRAL REVIEW

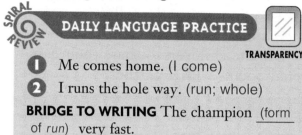

DAILY LANGUAGE PRACTICE

TRANSPARENCY 49

1 Me comes home. (I come)

2 I runs the hole way. (run; whole)

BRIDGE TO WRITING The champion ___(form of *run*)___ very fast.

ORAL WARM-UP

USE PRIOR KNOWLEDGE Ask children to identify what is wrong with sentences you say. Use incorrect tenses of *come*, *run*, and *give*. Have children repeat the sentences using the correct verbs.

Grammar Jingles™ **CD, Primary** Use Track 16 for review and reinforcement of verbs.

TEACH/MODEL

Introduce the lesson by reading the instruction box. Point out that sentences may give time words as clues. Have volunteers identify the time words in the examples and decide if each sentence tells about now or about the past.

GUIDED PRACTICE Work with children to complete each sentence. Tell them to first identify the time word and then choose the correct verb. Use the instruction box to review the correct verb forms, as necessary.

Using *Come, Run,* and *Give*

The verbs **come**, **run**, and **give** tell about now.

> Today we **come** to the theater by bus.
> We **run** to the bus stop.
> We **give** our tickets to the bus driver.

The verbs **came**, **ran**, and **gave** tell about the past.

> Yesterday we **came** into the city by train.
> We **ran** to catch the train.
> We **gave** our tokens to the conductor.

Guided Practice

Write the correct verb in ( ) to complete each sentence.

1. I (<u>come</u>, came) to the museum today.
2. Last month my mom (give, <u>gave</u>) me some tickets.
3. She now (<u>comes</u>, came) to the museum to work.
4. Now she (<u>gives</u>, gave) me a tour of Dinosaur Hall.
5. I (<u>run</u>, ran) to see the dinosaurs right now!

320

Vocabulary Power page 73

Name _____

Word Families

Words in the same word family have related meanings. Draw a line from each word in dark print to other words in the same word family.

action — contribute, contributed
connection — predict, predicting
contribution — act, acted, acting
prediction — transport, transports
transportation — connect, connected

Draw pictures to show the meaning of the underlined words.

1. a silly action	2. a weather prediction
3. an important connection	4. a large contribution
5. forms of transportation	

Vocabulary Power   Unit 5 • Chapter 35   73

REACHING ALL LEARNERS

ESL

USE A CHART Create a two-column chart with the headings *Today* and *Yesterday*. Have children as a group talk about and list the present-tense and past-tense forms of the verbs *come*, *run*, and *give* in the chart. Challenge volunteers to use the verbs in sentences to tell about themselves.

> I ran to the bus stop yesterday.

Use *come*, *run*, and *give* to tell about now. Use *came*, *ran*, and *gave* to tell about the past.

Independent Practice

Write the correct verb in ( ) to complete each sentence.

6. Last week I (<u>ran</u>, run) to the museum.

7. My uncle (<u>gave</u>, give) me a free ticket.

8. Now I (<u>come</u>, came) to the museum again.

9. I walk in and (run, <u>ran</u>) to meet my uncle.

10. I greet him and (give, <u>gave</u>) him a hug.

11. Now we (<u>run</u>, ran) to the Dinosaur Hall.

12. My uncle (come, <u>came</u>) here to draw last weekend.

13. He (give, <u>gave</u>) me his drawings last Sunday.

14. Now he (<u>gives</u>, gave) me a pencil and some paper.

15. He (<u>comes</u>, came) with me now to draw a dinosaur.

Writing Connection

Telling About Now or About the Past
Think about an interesting place you visited. Write a few sentences about it. Use the verbs *come*, *run*, *give*, or *came*, *ran*, *gave*.

To print your sentences, you may be able to choose Print from the File menu.

321

Independent Practice

Have children complete the Independent Practice, or modify it by using the following suggestions:

MODIFIED INSTRUCTION

BELOW-LEVEL STUDENTS Have children circle the time word(s). Then have them choose the correct verb, referring to page 320 if needed.

ABOVE-LEVEL STUDENTS After children are finished, have them write sentences using time words and leaving out the verbs. Have them trade sentences with a partner and fill in the verbs.

Writing Connection

Telling About Now or About the Past Remind children to use time words to make their writing clearer. Have volunteers place their sentences in the Sharing Basket to share with others.

WRAP-UP/ASSESS

SUMMARIZE Ask children to summarize and reflect on what they have learned about *come*, *run*, and *give*. **REFLECTION**

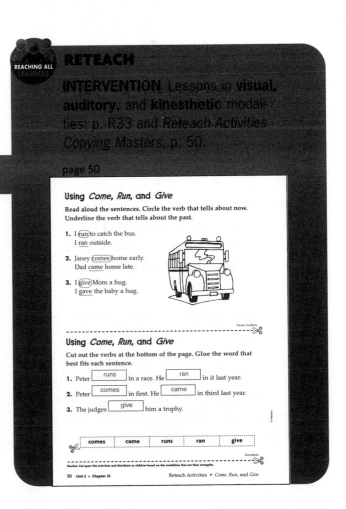

RETEACH

INTERVENTION Lessons in **visual**, **auditory**, and **kinesthetic** modalities: p. R33 and *Reteach Activities Copying Masters*, p. 50.

page 50

Using *Come, Run*, and *Give*

Read aloud the sentences. Circle the verb that tells about now. Underline the verb that tells about the past.

1. I (run) to catch the bus.
   I <u>ran</u> outside.

2. Janey (comes) home early.
   Dad <u>came</u> home late.

3. I (give) Mom a hug.
   I <u>gave</u> the baby a hug.

Using *Come, Run*, and *Give*

Cut out the verbs at the bottom of the page. Glue the word that best fits each sentence.

1. Peter [runs] in a race. He [ran] in it last year.

2. Peter [comes] in first. He [came] in third last year.

3. The judges [give] him a trophy.

| comes | came | runs | ran | give |

PRACTICE page 82

Name _____

Using *Come, Run*, and *Give*

A. Change the verb in ( ) to tell about the past.

1. I (come) _came_ to school early.

2. I (run) _ran_ from the bus stop.

3. I (give) _gave_ my friend help before class.

4. Jake (gives) _gave_ a report.

5. He (comes) _came_ early to help me, too.

B. Underline the correct verb in ( ) to complete each sentence.

6. Last year Jake (gives, <u>gave</u>) me a special birthday card.

7. Now I (<u>come</u>, came) to his house each day.

8. I (<u>run</u>, ran) there after school.

9. I (give, <u>gave</u>) him his favorite book last month.

10. Now he (come, <u>comes</u>) to my house on the weekends.

TRY THIS! Write two sentences about a person who is special to you. What things do you do together? Use the past-tense and present-tense of the verbs *come*, *run*, and *give* in your sentences.

82 Unit 5 • Chapter 25   Practice • *Come, Run, and Give*

CHALLENGE

INTERVIEW Have children interview someone they know. Ask them to find out which interesting places the person has visited. Children can ask questions, take notes, and write a paragraph about one of the places. Remind them to use time words and the verbs *came*, *ran*, or *gave*. Encourage them to draw pictures of the place before they share their paragraphs.

Joining Sentences

OBJECTIVES
- To use *and* to join two whole sentences that tell about the same thing
- To join sentences in a piece of writing to make it more interesting

DAILY LANGUAGE PRACTICE

TRANSPARENCY 49

1 Juanita cames with us Yesterday. (came; yesterday)

2 Yesterday I give Mark a bok. (gave; book)

BRIDGE TO WRITING My dad ___ (form of *run*) five miles last Sunday.

ORAL WARM-UP

USE PRIOR KNOWLEDGE Write the word *and* on the chalkboard. Ask volunteers to tell two things about themselves, using *and* in their sentences.

Grammar Jingles™ **CD, Primary** Use Track 17 for review and reinforcement of how to join sentences.

TEACH/MODEL

Read the instruction box with children. Ask them to discuss how the two example sentences tell about the same thing. (They tell about preparing for an art show.) Explain that when joining two sentences in writing, they must add a comma before the joining word *and*. Point out that the first letter of the second sentence no longer begins with a capital letter.

GUIDED PRACTICE Work through the first item together. Ask children to show how to combine the two sentences using a comma followed by *and*. Remind children to change the first capital letter at the beginning of the second sentence. Do the same with the remaining sentences.

Joining Sentences

You can use **and** to join two sentences that tell about the same thing. Add a **comma (,)** before **and** to separate the ideas.

The teacher set up the table for the art show. The children sorted their drawings.

The teacher set up the table for the art show, **and** the children sorted their drawings.

Guided Practice

Use *and* to join the sentences. Remember to use a *comma (,)* before *and*.

1. The clock said 9:00.
   People came to our show.
   The clock said 9:00, and people came to our show.
2. We were in the museum.
   People came to look at our art. We were in the museum, and people came to look at our art.
3. My parents walked in.
   I showed them my drawings.
   My parents walked in, and I showed them my drawings.
4. The art teacher came by.
   My parents talked to her.
   The art teacher came by, and my parents talked to her.

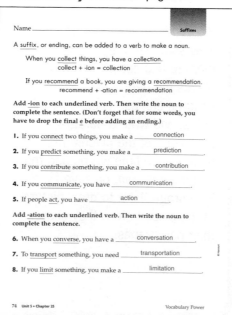

322

Vocabulary Power page 74

Name _____

Suffixes

A suffix, or ending, can be added to a verb to make a noun.

When you collect things, you have a collection.
collect + -ion = collection

If you recommend a book, you are giving a recommendation.
recommend + -ation = recommendation

Add -ion to each underlined verb. Then write the noun to complete the sentence. (Don't forget that for some words, you have to drop the final e before adding an ending.)

1. If you connect two things, you make a ___ connection
2. If you predict something, you make a ___ prediction
3. If you contribute something, you make a ___ contribution
4. If you communicate, you have ___ communication
5. If people act, you have ___ action

Add -ation to each underlined verb. Then write the noun to complete the sentence.

6. When you converse, you have a ___ conversation
7. To transport something, you need ___ transportation
8. If you limit something, you make a ___ limitation

74   Unit 5 • Chapter 25   Vocabulary Power

REACHING ALL LEARNERS   ESL

JOINING SENTENCES Provide children with pairs of pictures from magazines. A pair should show the same thing or event. Ask children to say a sentence about each picture. Then hand out two cards, one with a comma and one with *and*. Have children orally join their sentences as they put their pictures and word cards in order.

Remember Use *and* to join two sentences that tell about the same thing. Put a *comma (,)* before *and*.

Independent Practice

Use *and* to join the sentences. Remember to use a *comma (,)* before *and*.

5. My teacher talked about my work.

   Dad thanked her. My teacher talked about my work, and Dad thanked her.

6. Dad looked at more drawings.

   Mom took pictures of the show. Dad looked at more drawings, and Mom took pictures of the show.

7. Diego showed his dinosaur poster to a girl.

   She liked it very much. Diego showed his dinosaur poster to a girl, and she liked it very much.

8. The director of the museum came by.

   I ran to say hello. The director of the museum came by, and I ran to say hello.

9. The director is also a teacher.

   I study art with him. The director is also a teacher, and I study art with him.

10. Many people came to the show.

    We were very proud. Many people came to the show, and we were very proud.

Writing Connection

Revising Choose a story you like from your Writing Portfolio. Where can you join sentences? Revise your writing to make it more interesting.

To type a comma (,) using the computer, press ⟨ , ⟩.

323

Independent Practice

Have children complete the Independent Practice, or modify it by using the following suggestions:

MODIFIED INSTRUCTION

BELOW-LEVEL STUDENTS In pairs, have one child orally read the new sentence using *and*. The other writes it including the comma.

ABOVE-LEVEL STUDENTS After children are finished, have them write two sentences that tell about the same thing. Have them swap with a friend to join the sentences.

Writing Connection

Revising As children revise their selected stories, have them think about how they can achieve and maintain a sense of audience by joining only sentences that their audience would associate with each other.

WRAP-UP/ASSESS

SUMMARIZE Have children summarize and reflect on what they have learned about joining sentences. After children write about their experiences, have them meet in small groups to share information. **REFLECTION**

REACHING ALL LEARNERS

RETEACH

INTERVENTION Lessons in **visual, auditory,** and **kinesthetic** modalities: p. R33 and *Reteach Activities Copying Masters,* p. 51.

page 51

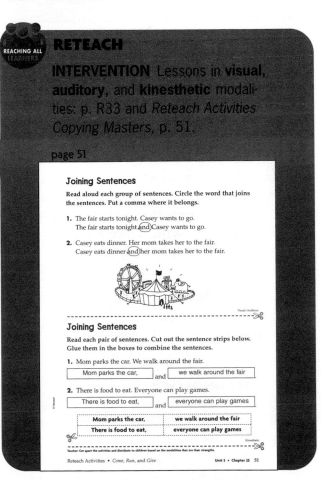

REACHING ALL LEARNERS

PRACTICE page 83

REACHING ALL LEARNERS

CHALLENGE

PARENTS AND TEACHERS Ask children to think of a time when parents, teachers, and children are together in your school. Have them write a story describing the event. When they are finished, have them revise their story by joining sentences. If possible, have them use the computer to write and illustrate their final drafts.

Extra Practice

OBJECTIVES

- To recognize and use the verbs *come*, *run*, and *give* in the present and past tenses and to join whole sentences
- To write lists to record

DAILY LANGUAGE PRACTICE

TRANSPARENCY 50

1 Our class is putting on a play and, You want to be in it. (play, and you)

2 The play is fun, And we, all love it. (and we)

BRIDGE TO WRITING I love to read. (join sentences) My teacher gives me books.

ORAL WARM-UP

USE PRIOR KNOWLEDGE Display word cards with time words and the verbs *come*, *run*, and *give*. Give a theme to children, such as school or movies. Display a time word and a verb and have children make up sentences about the theme.

TEACH/MODEL

Read each set of directions to help children understand how to complete each section. Have children share their answers in small groups before you read aloud the answers.

WRAP-UP/ASSESS

SUMMARIZE Ask children to reflect on and discuss any special problems they had in completing the practice before you have them summarize what they have learned about the verbs *come*, *run*, and *give*.

ADDITIONAL PRACTICE Additional items of Extra Practice are provided on page 474 of the *Pupil Edition* (*Teacher's Edition* R6).

TECHNOLOGY

Grammar Practice and Assessment CD-ROM

Writing Express CD-ROM

INTERNET Visit *The Learning Site!* www.harcourtschool.com

Come, Run, and Give

Extra Practice

Write the correct verb in ( ) to finish each sentence.

1. Last week my uncle (give, <u>gave</u>) me a note about a play.

2. Now I (<u>come</u>, came) to the play with my parents.

3. We (<u>run</u>, ran) now because we are late.

Change the verb in each sentence to tell what happened yesterday.

4. We come into the city.   came

5. We run to the theater.   ran

6. My parents give money for the tickets.   gave

Use *and* to join the sentences. Remember to use a comma (,) before *and*.

7. My uncle was in a play.
I wanted to see him.
My uncle was in a play, and I wanted to see him.

8. The play was about animals.
My uncle played a lion.
The play was about animals, and my uncle played a lion.

9. I asked my parents if we could go.
They got tickets.
I asked my parents if we could go, and they got tickets.

10. My uncle was a great lion.
It was fun to watch him.
My uncle was a great lion, and it was fun to watch him.

324

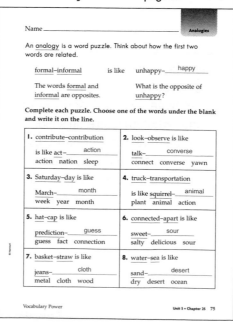

Vocabulary Power page 75

Name_____

Analogies

An *analogy* is a word puzzle. Think about how the first two words are related.

formal–informal   is like   unhappy–__happy__

The words *formal* and *informal* are opposites.   What is the opposite of *unhappy*?

Complete each puzzle. Choose one of the words under the blank and write it on the line.

1. contribute–contribution is like act–__action__ action nation sleep	2. look–observe is like talk–__converse__ connect converse yawn
3. Saturday–day is like March–__month__ week year month	4. truck–transportation is like squirrel–__animal__ plant animal action
5. hat–cap is like prediction–__guess__ guess fact connection	6. connected–apart is like sweet–__sour__ salty delicious sour
7. basket–straw is like jeans–__cloth__ metal cloth wood	8. water–sea is like sand–__desert__ dry desert ocean

Vocabulary Power   Unit 5 • Chapter 35   75

REACHING ALL LEARNERS — **ESL**

SHARED WRITING Some children may need help thinking of things to list for the Writing Connection. You may wish to pair up children to discuss and list what they give and receive. Children may write a wish list of things they would like to give to other people. Remind them to use the lists on page 325 as a model for their own writing.

Sentence Time
- Use the game board below.
- Take turns with a partner. Roll a number cube.
- Find the matching number in the chart. Make up a sentence using the verb. Use the clue *today* or *yesterday* to know whether to change the verb.
- Keep playing until each player has used each word in a sentence.

	come	run	give
today	1	2	3
yesterday	4	5	6

Writing Connection

Making Lists Making lists can help you remember. Write sentences to list the things you often give to your friends and family. Then list what people have given you in the past. This list can help you remember to whom to write a thank-you note.

I give cards.
I give hugs.

Sue gave me a Valentine's Day card.
Tom gave me a book.

325

Language Play

Have children play "Sentence Time" in pairs. Model how to roll the cube and use the chart to make up sentences.

Writing Connection

Making Lists Check to see that children have successfully written a list by using the criteria below.

CRITERIA
- ☑ Writes two lists.
- ☑ Writes the correct forms of the verb *give* to tell about now and about the past.
- ☑ Begins each proper noun with a capital letter.
- ☑ Begins the sentence with a capital letter and ends with the correct punctuation.

📁 **Portfolio Opportunity** You may want to have children place their writing in their portfolios or take it home to share with family members.

PRACTICE page 84
REACHING ALL LEARNERS

Name _____

Extra Practice

A. Circle the correct verb in ( ) to complete each sentence.

1. We (come, comes) to this museum each year.
2. I (run, runs) to catch up to Mike and Tony.
3. Our teacher (give, gives) us a paper.

B. Change the verb in ( ) to tell about the past.

4. The paper (gives) _____gave_____ dinosaur facts.
5. We (come) _____came_____ to the dinosaur room.
6. A tiny model dinosaur (runs) _____ran_____ through a maze.
7. A tour guide (gives) _____gave_____ us a tour.

C. Use *and* to join the sentences. Remember to use a comma before *and*.

8. The museum was big. I couldn't see everything.
   The museum was big, and I couldn't see everything.
9. I loved everything I saw. I want to go back.
   I loved everything I saw, and I want to go back.

84 Unit 5 • Chapter 25   Practice • *Come, Run, and Give*

CHALLENGE
REACHING ALL LEARNERS

TAKING POLLS Have children divide a page into three columns labeled *come*, *run*, and *give*. Then invite them to ask their classmates where they come and run, and what they give. Have children record the answers. Then ask the class to work together to tally the results in three class lists.

COME	RUN	GIVE
Sally comes to school.	Jose runs home.	

Chapter Review

OBJECTIVES

- To review the verbs *come*, *run*, and *give* and how to join whole sentences
- To understand how to use a newspaper and the different parts of an article

DAILY LANGUAGE PRACTICE

TRANSPARENCY 50

① gina gaves a report now. (Gina; gives)

② Diego give's me a kard. (gives; card)

BRIDGE TO WRITING Jeff _____ (form of the verb *come*) to the desk now.

STANDARDIZED TEST PREP

Read the directions with children to make sure they understand how to complete page 326. You may wish to use this page as an assessment after children have completed it independently.

TEST PREPARATION TIP

Item Type: Multiple Choice

TIP

Model this strategy to help children determine the correct answer:

First I read the sentence. I look at the underlined part. Then I read the answer choices. I look at the same part of the sentence to see if it makes better sense. It is not correct to put a comma after *and*, so *a* is wrong. There is no capital letter in *and*, so *b* is also wrong. I look at the first sentence again and I choose *c*, because the sentence is correct.

Come, Run, and Give

Chapter Review

Choose the best answer for each underlined word.

1. It was Thanksgiving, and all my family was there.

   a. It was Thanksgiving and, all my family was there.

   b. It was Thanksgiving And all my family was there.

   c. correct as is

2. My cousin Amy gave me a book And I smiled.

   a. My cousin Amy gave me a book, and I smiled.

   b. My cousin Amy gave me a book and, I smiled

   c. correct as is

3. She come to Thanksgiving dinner with her brother.

   a. Come

   b. came

   c. correct as is

4. Now she come for New Year's Eve.

   a. comes

   b. came

   c. correct as is

5. I gave her a card now.

   a. give

   b. gaves

   c. correct as is

6. Now she ran outside to show her brother.

   a. Ran

   b. runs

   c. correct as is

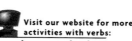 Visit our website for more activities with verbs:
www.harcourtschool.com

326

Language Skills Assessment

• •

PORTFOLIO ASSESSMENT
Have children select their best work from the following activities:

- **Writing Connection** pages 321 and 325; TE activities, pages 321, 323, and 325.

ONGOING ASSESSMENT
Evaluate the performance of 4-6 children using appropriate checklists and record forms from pages R65–R68 and R77–R79.

 INTERNET Activities and exercises to help students prepare for state and standardized assessments appear on *The Learning Site:*

www.harcourtschool.com

■ Study Skills ■

Using a Newspaper

A newspaper gives the news. It can tell what is happening around the world and in your town.

A newspaper tells about many subjects. It can tell what is happening in neighborhoods, sports, art, and the weather.

---

author →

The story tells *who, what, where, when, and why.*

Class Trip to the Museum
by Bob Parker

Yesterday, Mrs. Soto took a bus to Mapletown with her class. They all came to the museum to see the new Dinosaur Hall. The guide talked about the fossils and about how the dinosaurs lived. After the visit, the guide gave out pictures of dinosaurs.

The title of a news story is called a *headline.*

Practice

Use the news story to answer the questions.
Possible responses are given.
1. Who is the story about?
   It is about Mrs. Soto and her class.
2. What did they do?
   They went to the museum.
3. Where is the museum?
   It is in Mapletown.
4. When did the class go there?
   They went there yesterday.
5. Why did they go to the museum?
   They wanted to see the new Dinosaur Hall.

327

■ Study Skills ■

Using a Newspaper

TEACH/MODEL

Read about using a newspaper. Allow children to discuss where they have seen newspapers and who may have been reading them. You may also want to bring in a newspaper. Be sure to talk about the fact that all newspaper articles tell *who, what, where, when,* and *why.* Then read the sample article together.

PRACTICE You may want to have children use different-colored pencils to underline the *who, what, where, when,* and *why* of the article. When children are finished, have volunteers share their answers with the class.

WRAP-UP/ASSESS

SUMMARIZE Ask children to tell what they have learned about using a newspaper. Be sure they discuss how the newspaper gives news and tells about many things that happen around the world and in your town. They should also say that newspaper stories should always tell *who, what, where, when,* and *why.*

PRACTICE page 85

Name _____

Using a Newspaper

Read the newspaper story. Use it to answer each question below.

Student Starts Club
by Shennell Barnes
In September James Terry started a club at Prescott Elementary School. It's called the Clean School Club. He started it because he wanted to have a clean playground at school. At first he was the only member. Then he invited classmates to help him. Now the club has fifty members.

1. Who is this article about? James Terry

2. What did he do? He started a club called the Clean School Club.

3. Where did James Terry start his club? at Prescott Elementary School

4. When did he start the club? in September

5. Why did James start the club? He wanted to have a clean playground at school.

TRY THIS! Write a newspaper story about something exciting that happened to you. Remember to answer the questions *who, what, when, where,* and *why* in your story.

Practice • *Come, Run, and Give*   Unit 5 • Chapter 25 85

CHALLENGE

SCHOOL NEWS Provide children with several short articles from your local newspaper as models. Ask children to write a news article about a school event or happening. Have them choose a topic and then find out and write the answers to *Who? What? When? Where?* and *Why?* Remind children to include a headline and a byline.

LESSON ORGANIZER	DAY 1	DAY 2
DAILY LANGUAGE PRACTICE TRANSPARENCIES 51, 52	1. yesterday I runned all the way to the playground. (Yesterday; ran) 2. My brother always come whit me. (comes; with) **Bridge to Writing** Sam <u>(form of the verb give)</u> me an apple last week.	1. Our class go to the art sho yesterday. (went; show) 2. we see John's painting at the art show yesterday. (We saw) **Bridge to Writing** We <u>(form of the verb do)</u> this last month, too.
ORAL WARM-UP Listening/Speaking	Recall a Vacation p. 328	Using *Went* and *Saw* p. 330 *Grammar Jingles*™ CD, Primary, Track 18
TEACH/MODEL GRAMMAR **KEY** ✔ = tested skill	✔ **THE VERBS *GO*, *DO*, AND *SEE*** **Literature:** "Where I Went" pp. 328-329 • To listen critically to a poem • To understand that the spellings of *go*, *do*, and *see* change to tell about the past	✔ **USING *GO*, *DO*, AND *SEE*** pp. 330-331 • To use the correct forms of the verbs *go*, *do*, and *see* for present and past tense • To use the different forms of the verbs *go*, *do*, and *see* correctly in writing
Reaching All Learners	*Practice Book* p. 86 **Challenge:** Activity Card 18, p. R58 **ESL:** *ESL Manual* pp. 126, 127 **Reteach:** *Reteach Activities Copying Masters* p. 52	**Modified Instruction** Below-Level: Identify Time Words Above-Level: Rewrite Sentences **Challenge:** Write a Checklist p. 331 **ESL:** Use Time Words p. 330 *ESL Manual* pp. 126, 128 *Practice Book* p. 87 **Reteach:** *Reteach Activities Copying Masters* p. 53
WRITING	Changing Verbs to the Past Tense p. 329 Summarize/Reflect	Writing Connection p. 331 Sentences About an Experience Summarize/Reflect
CROSS-CURRICULAR/ ENRICHMENT	**Vocabulary Power** Word Meaning, p. 328 frayed, **ragged,** shaggy, tattered, uneven See *Vocabulary Power* book.	**Vocabulary Power** Synonyms, p. 328 *Vocabulary Power* book, p. 76  **Vocabulary activity**

DAY 3

1. last week I go to New York. (Last; went)

2. Now you saw pictures form our trip. (see; from)

Bridge to Writing I (form of the verb *do*) a report about our trip.

Using Commas in Place Names p. 332
Grammar Jingles™ CD, Primary, Track 18

✔ **COMMAS IN PLACE NAMES AND DATES** pp. 332-333
- To understand where commas are placed when writing names of places and dates
- To use commas correctly

Modified Instruction
 Below-Level: Identify Comma
  Placement
 Above-Level: Add Commas
Challenge: Story Problems p. 333
ESL: Putting Dates in Order p. 332
 ESL Manual pp.126, 129
Practice Book p. 88
Reteach: *Reteach Activities Copying Masters* p. 54

Writing Connection p. 333
 Neighborhood Sentences
 Summarize/Reflect

 Vocabulary Power
 Figurative Language, p. 328
 Vocabulary Power book, p. 77
 Vocabulary activity

DAY 4

1. Was yesterday's date January 16 2001 (16, 2001;?)

2. my grandma flew from El Paso Texas. (My; El Paso, Texas)

Bridge to Writing On (tomorrow's date), we are going to (city and state) .

Follow Directions p. 334

EXTRA PRACTICE p. 334-335
- To recognize the correct forms of *go*, *do*, and *see*
- To use commas in place names and dates
- To use the correct forms of *go*, *do*, and *see* in writing
 Practice and Assessment

Challenge: Write a Journal Entry p. 335
ESL: Postcards p. 334
 ESL Manual pp. 126, 130
Practice Book p. 89

Writing Connection p. 335
 Write a Postcard

Vocabulary Power
 Rhyming Words, p. 328
 Vocabulary Power book, p. 78
 Language Play p. 335
 Vocabulary activity

DAY 5

1. We do many funn things yesterday. (did; fun)

2. We goes to Orlando Florida this week. (go; Orlando,)

Bridge to Writing On (yesterday's date) we saw a rocket launch.

TEST PREP **CHAPTER REVIEW** p. 336
- To review the use of *go*, *do*, and *see* and the use of commas
- To recognize that a map shows a place on paper and to understand a map key

 Test Preparation

Practice Book p. 90
Challenge: Make a Map p. 337
ESL: *ESL Manual* pp. 126, 131

Writing Application p. 337
 Maps

STUDY SKILLS
 Using a Map p. 337
 Vocabulary Power

 Alliteration, p. 328

The Verbs *Go*, *Do*, and *See*

OBJECTIVES
- To listen critically to interpret and evaluate a poem
- To understand that the spellings of *go*, *do*, and *see* change to *went*, *did*, and *saw* to tell about the past

DAILY LANGUAGE PRACTICE

TRANSPARENCY 51

1 yesterday I runned all the way to the playground. (Yesterday; ran)

2 My brother always come whit me. (comes; with)

BRIDGE TO WRITING Sam ___(form of the verb *give*)___ me an apple last week.

ORAL WARM-UP

USE PRIOR KNOWLEDGE Have children recall what they do when they are on vacation. Ask them to discuss where they go and what they see and do.

TEACH/MODEL

Have children turn to page 328 in their books. Ask them to identify and describe the animals in the illustration. Discuss where each animal can be found in nature. Then read the poem aloud, telling children to listen carefully to where the speaker in the poem sees each animal. Reread the poem, having children join in.

DEVELOP ORAL LANGUAGE Ask children what two verbs the poet used throughout the poem. Have children tell what else they could have seen if they went up the hill, down by the running rill, out to the roaring sea, or under the green tree. Add *went* and *saw* to the **Word Wall**.

The Verbs *Go*, *Do*, and *See*

Read the poem.

Where I Went

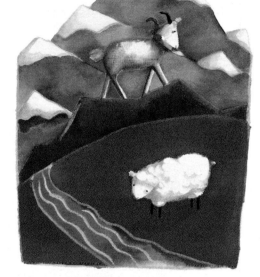

I went up the high hill,
There I saw a climbing goat;
I went down by the running rill,
There I saw a ragged sheep;
I went out to the roaring sea,
There I saw a tossing boat;
I went under the green tree,
There I saw two doves asleep.

from The Mother Goose Treasury
by Raymond Briggs

328

Vocabulary Power

DAY 1 WORD MEANING Write: *ragged*. **Find this word in the poem "Where I Went." How do you think a "ragged sheep" looks?**

DAY 2 SYNONYMS Write: *ragged, neat, shaggy*. **Which two words have similar meanings?** (See also *Vocabulary Power*, page 76.)

DAY 3 FIGURATIVE LANGUAGE Write: *I look like a Raggedy-Andy*. **What does this sentence mean? When might someone say such a sentence?** (See also *Vocabulary Power*, page 77.)

DAY 4 RHYMING WORDS Write: *ragged, jagged*. **How are these words alike? Name other words that rhyme.** (See also *Vocabulary Power*, page 78.)

DAY 5 ALLITERATION Write: *I ran down a ragged-rugged-rough-rocky road*. **Make a list of words that begin like frayed. Write a sentence using your words to describe a *friend*, *fruit*, or *french fry*.**

Read the poem again with a partner. Then talk about where the poet went and what he saw.

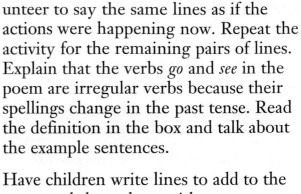

The verbs **go**, **do**, and **see** tell about the present, or now.

> I **go** to the beach.
> I **do** a cartwheel in the sand.
> I **see** a boat on the water.

The verbs **went**, **did**, and **saw** tell about the past.

> I **went** to the lake.
> I **did** some swimming.
> I **saw** two frogs jumping.

Think about places you have gone and what you saw there. Then write an ending to each sentence to add new lines to the poem.

I went to the park.

There I saw a leaping squirrel.

Responses will vary.

I _____.
There I _____.
I _____.
There I _____.

329

WRITE Call on a volunteer to say the first two lines of the poem. Ask another volunteer to say the same lines as if the actions were happening now. Repeat the activity for the remaining pairs of lines. Explain that the verbs *go* and *see* in the poem are irregular verbs because their spellings change in the past tense. Read the definition in the box and talk about the example sentences.

Have children write lines to add to the poem and share them with a partner.

WRAP-UP/ASSESS

SUMMARIZE Reread the poem on page 328 with children and have volunteers read aloud their new lines. Then tell children to summarize and reflect on what they have learned about the verbs *go*, *do*, and *see*. Have them write their reflections in their journals.

RETEACH

INTERVENTION Lessons in **visual, auditory,** and **kinesthetic** modalities. p. R34 and *Reteach Activities Copying Masters*, p. 52.

page 52

PRACTICE page 86

Name_____

The Verbs *Go, Do,* and *See*

A. Use a word from the box to complete each sentence.

| did | see | go | do | saw |

1. I ___go___ to the library on Saturdays with my father.
2. We ___see___ interesting things.
3. We ___saw___ a funny puppet show last month.
4. Sometimes I ___do___ my homework there.
5. Last Saturday, I ___did___ my whole science project.

B. Circle the correct verb in ( ) to complete each sentence.

6. One time I (sees, **saw**) an exciting video.
7. It was about a man who (go, **goes**) to different countries.
8. He (**did**, do) a dangerous thing to save a tiger cub.
9. Someone (**saw**, see) the cub trapped on a cliff.
10. The man (go, **went**) to the cliff and set the cub free.

TRY THIS! Write three sentences about characters in your favorite book or video. Use the verbs *go, do* and *see* in your sentences.

86 Unit 5 • Chapter 26   Practice • *Go, Do, and See*

CHALLENGE

MAKE PUPPETS Have children use **Challenge Activity Card 18** (page R58) to make puppets of the animals and things mentioned in the poem. Have small groups use the puppets to act out the poem on page 328. Encourage children to add new lines to the poem.

Challenge Activity Card 18
Make Puppets

You need:
• old magazines
• construction paper
• scissors
• glue
• craft sticks

1. Find and cut out pictures of the animals and things from the poem on page 328.
2. Glue each picture onto paper.
3. Glue each picture to a craft stick to make a puppet.
4. Use your puppets to act out the poem.

The Verbs *Go, Do,* and *See*

Read aloud each sentence. Underline each verb. Draw a line from each sentence that tells about now to the *Now* circle. Draw a line from each sentence that tells about the past to the *Past* circle.

1. I go to the mall.
   I went to the movies.

2. I do my shopping.
   I did not finish the popcorn.

   (Now)
   (Past)

3. I see many things.
   I saw a good film.

Visual/Auditory

----------------------✂

The Verbs *Go, Do,* and *See*

Cut out the verbs at the bottom of the page. Glue the word that best fits each sentence.

1. Yesterday I [went] to the store. I often [go] on Fridays.
2. I [saw] a book. I always [see] good books.
3. I [did] not have enough money this time. Sometimes I [do] buy a book.

| go | went | do | did | see | saw |

Kinesthetic

Teacher: Cut apart the activities and distribute to children based on the modalities that are their strengths.

52 Unit 5 • Chapter 26   Reteach Activities • *Go, Do, and See*

Using *Go*, *Do*, and *See*

OBJECTIVES
- To use the correct forms of the verbs *go*, *do*, and *see* for present and past tense
- To use the different forms of the verbs *go*, *do*, and *see* correctly in writing

DAILY LANGUAGE PRACTICE

TRANSPARENCY 51

1 Our class go to the art sho yesterday. (went; show)

2 we see John's painting at the art show yesterday. (We saw)

BRIDGE TO WRITING We _____ (form of the verb *do*) this last month, too.

ORAL WARM-UP

USE PRIOR KNOWLEDGE Tell children to list the places to which they and people they know have gone. Encourage them to tell when they went and what they saw.

***Grammar Jingles*™ CD, Primary** Use Track 18 for review and reinforcement for the verbs *go*, *do*, and *see*.

TEACH/MODEL

Introduce the present and past-tense forms of the verbs *go*, *do*, and *see* by using the explanation and the examples. Have children identify the verb and the time of the action in each sentence. Discuss when the spelling of a verb changes and how.

GUIDED PRACTICE Work with children to complete each item. Have them look for words in the sentences that tell whether the actions are happening now or in the past. Ask how children know which form of the verb is correct.

Using *Go*, *Do*, and *See*

> The verbs **go**, **do**, and **see** tell about now.
>
> I **go** to art class today.   She **goes** with me.
> I **do** a good job.   He **does** well, too.
> I **see** other children.
>
> The verbs are spelled **went**, **did**, and **saw** to tell about the past.
>
> My sister **went** to a drawing class last week.
> She **did** three drawings.
> We **saw** her pictures.

Guided Practice

Choose the correct verb to finish each sentence.

1. Last week I (go, <u>went</u>) to a concert.
2. I (see, <u>saw</u>) a school band at the concert.
3. Now I (<u>go</u>, went) to music class.
4. I (<u>see</u>, saw) my teacher every day.
5. She says I always (<u>do</u>, did) a good job.

330

Vocabulary Power page 76

Name _____

These words are synonyms. They have similar meanings.

rayed   ragged   shaggy   tattered   uneven

Draw a picture to show the meaning of the word in dark print. Label your picture. For example: a shaggy dog.

1. frayed	2. ragged
3. shaggy	4. tattered
5. uneven	6. even

76   Unit 5 • Chapter 26   Vocabulary Power

REACHING ALL LEARNERS   **ESL**

USE TIME WORDS Explain that some words can help you know which form of a verb to use. Write time words such as *yesterday*, *last week*, *now*, and *today* on index cards. Write *now* and *past* on the board. Have volunteers pick a card, decide whether it tells about now or the past, and use the time word in a sentence. Children can write the sentences on the board.

Remember Use *go*, *do*, and *see* to tell about now. Use *went*, *did*, and *saw* to tell about the past.

Independent Practice

Choose the correct verb to finish each sentence.

6. Right now my parents and I (<u>go</u>, went) into a concert hall.

7. Today we (<u>see</u>, saw) people play music.

8. We (do, <u>did</u>) this last month, too.

9. I (see, <u>saw</u>) a great guitar player last time.

10. He (do, <u>did</u>) some funny things.

11. Later I (see, <u>saw</u>) him play a toy guitar.

12. Now the guitar player (<u>does</u>, did) a song I love.

13. He (<u>sees</u>, saw) me and smiles at me.

14. The show is over, and we (go, <u>went</u>) backstage.

15. Now I (<u>see</u>, saw) the guitar player and thank him for the song.

Writing Connection

Sentences About an Experience Think about a time you went to a show. Write sentences about what you saw and did. Check your verbs.

Use a computer to type your sentences. Save your work.

331

Independent Practice

Have children complete the Independent Practice, or modify it by using the following suggestions:

MODIFIED INSTRUCTION

BELOW-LEVEL STUDENTS Suggest that children circle time-word clues as they read each sentence to help them decide which form of the verb to choose.

ABOVE-LEVEL STUDENTS Have children rewrite each sentence so that it tells about now instead of the past or the past instead of now. Remind them to change time words, too.

Writing Connection

Sentences About an Experience Remind children that to tell about the past, they must change the spellings of the verbs *go*, *do*, and *see*. Have them edit their sentences to be sure the verbs are in the appropriate tense.

WRAP-UP/ASSESS

SUMMARIZE Ask children to summarize what they have learned about the verbs *go*, *do*, and *see*. Have them write in their journals sentences using different forms of these verbs.

RETEACH

INTERVENTION Lessons in **visual**, **auditory**, and **kinesthetic** modalities: p. R34 and *Reteach Activities Copying Masters*, p. 53.

page 53

REACHING ALL LEARNERS

PRACTICE page 87

Name_____

Using *Go*, *Do*, and *See*

A. Change the verb in ( ) to tell about the past.

1. I (go) ___went___ to a dance recital.

2. I (see) ___saw___ beautiful ballerinas.

3. They (do) ___did___ graceful turns.

4. One dancer (do) ___did___ a hard jump.

5. I (see) ___saw___ him smile when he landed.

B. Circle the correct verb to finish each sentence.

6. I (go, went) to dance class tomorrow.

7. Last week I (go, went) for the first time.

8. Dancers must (do, did) a lot of practicing.

9. I practice often since I (see, saw) the dancers.

10. I hope I (do, did) beautiful dances like them one day.

TRY THIS! Write three sentences that use *go*, *do*, and *see*. Trade papers with a classmate. Write your classmate's sentences using verbs that tell about the past.

Practice • *Go, Do, and See*   Unit 5 • Chapter 26   87

REACHING ALL LEARNERS

CHALLENGE

WRITE A CHECKLIST Have children write a list of things they have to do, places they have to go, and people they have to see this week. As they complete a task, have them check it off. Then have children write sentences to tell what they did, where they went, and whom or what they saw.

Do a book report.   ☑

Go to the library.   ☐

I did a book report last night.

Using *Go*, *Do*, and *See*

Read aloud each pair of sentences. Circle the verb that tells about now. Underline the verb that tells about the past.

1. I go to school.
   I <u>went</u> to class.

2. I do my math test.
   I <u>did</u> my homework.

3. I see the teacher.
   I <u>saw</u> the movie.

4. I go to lunch.
   I <u>went</u> home.

Visual/Auditory

Using *Go*, *Do*, and *See*

Cut out the verbs at the bottom of the page. Glue the word that best fits each sentence.

1. Last week I ___went___ to a museum.

2. I ___saw___ a painting.

3. I ___did___ not know who painted it.

4. Today my teacher ___sees___ the name.

| went | did | sees | saw |

Kinesthetic

Teacher: Cut apart the activities and distribute to children based on the modalities that are their strengths.

Reteach Activities • *Go, Do, and See*   Unit 5 • Chapter 26   53

Commas in Place Names and Dates

OBJECTIVES

- To understand that a comma is placed between the names of a city and a state, and between the day and the year in a date
- To use commas correctly when writing names of places and dates

SPIRAL REVIEW

DAILY LANGUAGE PRACTICE

TRANSPARENCY 51

1 last week I go to New York. (Last; went)

2 Now you saw pictures form our trip. (see; from)

BRIDGE TO WRITING I ___ (form of the verb *do*) a report about our trip.

ORAL WARM-UP

USE PRIOR KNOWLEDGE Display a United States map and ask children what places they have visited. Point out the places on the map. Then have volunteers record the names of the cities and states on the board. Note whether they use commas, and save the list.

Grammar Jingles™ **CD, Primary** Use Track 18 for review and reinforcement of the verbs *go*, *do*, and *see*.

TEACH/MODEL

Read the explanations in the box. Then read aloud each example, pausing slightly for the commas. Ask a few volunteers to write the place and date of their birth on the board.

GUIDED PRACTICE Identify the first item as the heading on the postcard. Have children tell the rule for placing a comma and then write the date correctly. Call on a volunteer to write the date correctly on the board and read it aloud. Have children complete the practice and check the dates and places they recorded earlier on the board.

Go, Do, and See **Usage and Mechanics**

Commas in Place Names and Dates

> Always use a **comma (,)** between the names of a city and a state.
>
> We went to **Dallas, Texas**.
>
> Always use a **comma (,)** between the day and the year in a date.
>
> My brother was born on **April 11, 1999**.

Guided Practice

Write the dates and the names of places correctly.

(1) March 16, 2001

Dear Betty,
We love the big city of (2) Denver, Colorado. Yesterday we went to see a play. It was very funny. We will go to a concert in (3) Sedona, Arizona on (4) March 20, 2001.

Your friend,
Jen

Betty Baker
10 James Street
(5) Ocean City, Maryland 21842

332

Vocabulary Power page 77

Name _____

Figurative Language

Which sayings have you heard? What do they mean?

look like a Raggedy-Ann   even–Steven

Draw pictures to show what these sayings mean.

1. shaggy dog look	2. uneven numbers
3. ragged corners	4. frayed cuffs

Make up your own saying.

Vocabulary Power   Unit 5 • Chapter 16   77

REACHING ALL LEARNERS   **ESL**

PUTTING DATES IN ORDER
When writing the date in certain cultures, the day is sometimes written before the month instead of after it. Write the names of a month, a day, and a year on separate cards. Make another card with a comma on it. Mix them up, and then have children discuss and arrange the parts in the correct order and read the date aloud. Repeat with different dates.

Remember

Put a *comma (,)* between the names of a city and a state. Put a *comma (,)* between the day and the year in a date.

Independent Practice

Write the dates and the names of places correctly.

(6) July 10, 2001

Dear Terry,

I am having fun on my trip. First we went to (7) Dallas, Texas. Next we went to (8) Austin, Texas. After that, my dad drove to (9) Santa Fe, New Mexico. We saw an art museum and went to a concert there. I will be back soon!

Your friend,
Steve

Terry Jordan
326 North Verde Street
(10) Tempe, Arizona 85280

Writing Connection

Neighborhood Sentences Draw a picture of a place that you have visited in your neighborhood. Write sentences about where you went, when you went, and what you did and saw. Remember to use commas (,) correctly.

Some programs add the date for you. Click on **Date and Time** under the **Insert** menu.

333

Independent Practice

Have children complete the Independent Practice, or modify it by using the following suggestions:

MODIFIED INSTRUCTION

BELOW-LEVEL STUDENTS Suggest that children first state the rule and point to the space where the comma belongs. After they write each date and place name, have children circle the comma.

ABOVE-LEVEL STUDENTS After children are finished, invite them to write one sentence with a place name and another with a date, both without commas. Have a partner add the commas.

Writing Connection

Neighborhood Sentences Remind children to use the correct form of the verbs *go, do,* and *see.* Display volunteers' drawings. Have these children read aloud their sentences and ask others to decide about which drawing the sentences tell.

WRAP-UP/ASSESS

SUMMARIZE Have children summarize what they know about using commas in place names and dates. Have them list the birthdays of family and friends in their journals.

RETEACH

INTERVENTION Lessons in **visual, auditory,** and **kinesthetic** modalities: p. R34 and *Reteach Activities Copying Masters,* p. 54.

page 54

Commas in Place Names and Dates

Read each item to a partner. Put a comma in the correct place.

1. January 22, 2002
2. Boise, Idaho
3. San Antonio, Texas
4. March 5, 2001
5. Portland, Oregon
6. July 9, 1995

January					
	1	2	3	4	5
6	7	8	9	10	11	12
13	14	15	16	17	18	19
20	21	22	23	24	25	26
27	28	29	30	31		

- -

Commas in Place Names and Dates

Work with a partner. Cut out the parts of the first sentence. Put the parts in the correct order, and read the sentence aloud. Glue the sentence onto a sheet of paper. Repeat with the other sentences.

I was born	1993.	on June 9	,
in Norfolk	,	I live	Virginia.
visit Chicago	Illinois soon.	,	I will

Teacher: Cut apart the activities and distribute to children based on the modalities that are their strengths.

54   Unit 5 • Chapter 26   Reteach Activities • *Go, Do, and See*

PRACTICE page 88

Name_____

Commas in Place Names and Dates

A. Add commas to write the dates and the names of places correctly.

(1) May 4, 2001

Dear Beth,
I like being in (2) Seattle, Washington. It rains more than in (3) Austin, Texas. We will be home soon.
Amy

Beth Pardie
935 West End Avenue
(4) Baltimore, Maryland 21228

B. Fill in the chart with the dates and the names of places.
Responses will vary.

	When (date)	Where (place name)
The day you were born	5.	6.
A trip you went on	7.	8.
A person you visited	9.	10.

TRY THIS! Use the chart to write sentences about the day you were born, a special trip, and a special visit. Remember to use commas.

88   Unit 5 • Chapter 26   Practice • *Go, Do, and See*

CHALLENGE

STORY PROBLEMS Have children write a story problem that includes dates and the names of places. You may wish to use the following as a model: *Today is May 10, 2001. Sam used to live in Dallas, Texas. Two days ago, he moved to Milo, Maine. On what date did he move?* Have children trade problems with a partner and solve them.

Extra Practice

OBJECTIVES

- To recognize the correct forms of the verbs *go*, *do*, and *see* for present and past tense
- To use commas in place names and dates
- To use the correct forms of the verbs *go*, *do*, and *see* in writing

DAILY LANGUAGE PRACTICE

TRANSPARENCY 52

1 Was yesterday's date January 16 2001 (January 16, 2001?)

2 my grandma flew from El Paso Texas. (My; El Paso, Texas)

BRIDGE TO WRITING On <u>(tomorrow's date)</u> , we are going to <u>(city and state)</u> .

ORAL WARM-UP

FOLLOW DIRECTIONS Write directions on index cards, such as: *Do jumping jacks. Go to the board and write the date.* Have volunteers choose and then act out a task. Other children tell what each person did, using the correct form of the verbs go, do, and see. Try to work a Vocabulary Power word into the game.

TEACH/MODEL

Read aloud each set of directions. When they have finished, have children share their answers with a partner or in small groups. Then read aloud the correct answers.

WRAP-UP/ASSESS

SUMMARIZE Ask children to reflect on and discuss any special problems they had in completing the practice. Then have them summarize what they know about using the verbs *go*, *do*, and *see*, and about writing place names and dates. **REFLECTION**

ADDITIONAL PRACTICE Extra practice items are on page 474 of the *Pupil Edition* (*Teacher's Edition* R6).

TECHNOLOGY

Grammar Practice and Assessment CD-ROM

Writing Express CD-ROM

INTERNET Visit *The Learning Site!* www.harcourtschool.com

Extra Practice

Choose the correct verb to finish each sentence.

1. My parents let me (<u>do</u>, did) fun things.
2. We often (<u>see</u>, saw) plays.
3. Last month I (go, <u>went</u>) out with my parents.
4. We (see, <u>saw</u>) a great play then.
5. The actors we saw (do, <u>did</u>) a great job.

Rewrite the sentences. Put commas in the names of places and in the dates.

6. You can see many shows in New York, New York.
7. I will see a show on November 22, 2002.
8. Two actors in the show come from Los Angeles, California.
9. Then I will go to Tampa, Florida with my parents.
10. We will see a dance show on December 22, 2002.

334

Vocabulary Power page 78

Name _____

Rhyming Words

Some rhyming words have similar spellings. Others have different spellings.

road   load   sewed   code   showed

Some words that have similar spellings don't rhyme.

hugged–rugged   some–home   have–save

Write rhyming words for the word in dark print. Some of the words may have a different spelling. Remember: Words with similar spellings may or may not rhyme.
Possible responses include:

1. tatter	2. frayed
spatter, matter, flatter	made, maid, stayed
scatter, batter, patter	paid, played, weighed
3. lagged	4. shaggy
wagged, bagged, sagged	baggy, saggy, raggy
dragged, tagged, nagged	Maggie, Aggie, craggy
5. ragged	6. even
jagged	Steven

78   Unit 5 • Chapter 26   Vocabulary Power

ESL

REACHING ALL LEARNERS

POSTCARDS You may wish to help children complete the writing activity on page 335. Bring in travel brochures for places in the United States. Have children look through the brochures to choose a place, and then write sentences about it. Peer readers can help make sure the writers correctly use the verbs *go, do, see* and write commas correctly in the dates and place names.

Language Play

Guess Where I Went!
- Think of two places you have visited and two places you want to visit. Make a chart like the one below.
- Take turns with a partner.
- Use the verbs *go*, *do*, and *see* to give hints about a place on your chart.
- Keep playing until both partners have guessed all the places.

Where I Went	Where I Want to Go
I went to the zoo. I went to Chicago, Illinois.	I want to go to New York, New York. I want to go to Mars.

Writing Connection

Write a Postcard Write a postcard about a town you like. Tell about what you do and see there and the places you go. Make sure you use verbs and commas (,) correctly.

July 22, 2001

Dear Anita,
    I went to Santa Cruz, California. I left on July 10, 2001. I saw my grandpa and my grandma. We had fun!

        Your friend,
        Sara

Anita Ortega
245 West Street
New York, New York 10019

335

Language Play

Have children play "Guess Where I Went!" in pairs. Model how to give clues about a place you have visited and how to keep score. Suggest that children include clues that tell about the special things they did and saw in the place they chose.

Writing Connection

Write a Postcard Check to see that children have successfully written a postcard by using the criteria below.

CRITERIA
- ☑ Includes a heading, greeting, body, closing, and signature.
- ☑ Writes commas correctly in dates and names of places.
- ☑ Writes the correct forms of the verbs *go*, *do*, and *see*.
- ☑ Begins each proper noun with a capital letter.

📁 **PORTFOLIO OPPORTUNITY** You may want to have children share their postcards with classmates before placing them in their portfolios.

REACHING ALL LEARNERS

Name _____

Extra Practice

A. Write a word from the box to complete each sentence.

sees	goes	do

1. My sister ___goes___ to the ballet often.

2. She ___sees___ dancers leaping and spinning.

3. The dancers ___do___ hard moves.

B. Circle the correct verb in each sentence.

4. Sometimes she (**does**) did) the same steps as the dancers.

5. I (go, (**went**)) to a ballet class with my sister last month.

6. She still ((**goes**) went) to class to get better.

C. Rewrite the sentences. Put commas in the dates and names of places.

7. We live in Kansas City Missouri.
   We live in Kansas City, Missouri.

8. We saw a ballet on October 31 2003.
   We saw a ballet on October 31, 2003.

Practice • *Go, Do, and See*   Unit 5 • Chapter 26   89

REACHING ALL LEARNERS

WRITE A JOURNAL ENTRY
Have children pick a favorite story character. Have them use what they know of the character and story to write a journal entry telling what the character did and saw, and where he/she went. Invite children to illustrate their entries before sharing them with the class.

Yesterday I went to Grandma's house. I saw a big wolf.

Chapter Review

OBJECTIVES
- To review the use of the verbs *go*, *do*, and *see* in the present and past tenses and the use of commas in place names and dates
- To recognize that a map shows a place on paper and to understand a map key

DAILY LANGUAGE PRACTICE

TRANSPARENCY 52

1 We do many funn things yesterday. (did; fun)

2 We goes to Orlando Florida this week. (go; Orlando,)

BRIDGE TO WRITING On (yesterday's date) we saw a rocket launch.

STANDARDIZED TEST PREP

Read the directions with children to make sure they understand how to complete the page. You may wish to use this page as an assessment after children have completed it independently.

TEST PREPARATION TIP
Item Type: Multiple Choice

TIP

Model this strategy to help children determine the correct answer:

First I read the directions to make sure I understand what to do. Then I carefully read number 1. I know that the underlined verb *sees* can't be right because it tells about now and the sentence begins with *Last week*. The verb should tell about the past. I know that *saw* tells about the past, so I choose *a* as my answer. Remind children to reread the sentence with their answer choice to be sure the answer makes sense and sounds right.

Chapter Review STANDARDIZED TEST PREP

Choose the best answer for each underlined word or words.

1. Last week we <u>sees</u> singers at our school.
   - **a.** saw
   - **b.** saws
   - **c.** see
   - **d.** correct as is

2. The singers came from <u>Danville Virginia</u>.
   - **a.** Danville virginia
   - **b.** Danville, Virginia
   - **c.** danville, Virginia
   - **d.** correct as is

3. They <u>did</u> a great show.
   - **a.** dids
   - **b.** does
   - **c.** done
   - **d.** <u>correct as is</u>

4. It was on <u>May 11 2000</u>.
   - **a.** May, 11 2000
   - **b.** <u>May 11, 2000</u>
   - **c.** May, 11, 2000
   - **d.** correct as is

5. We <u>sees</u> them every year.
   - **a.** saw
   - **b.** sees
   - **c.** <u>see</u>
   - **d.** correct as is

6. The next show will be <u>May 9, 2001</u>.
   - **a.** May, 9, 2001
   - **b.** May, 9 2001
   - **c.** May 9 2001
   - **d.** <u>correct as is</u>

 Visit our website for more activities with verbs:
www.harcourtschool.com

336

Language Skills Assessment

PORTFOLIO ASSESSMENT
Have children select their best work from the following activities:

- **Writing Connection,** *pages 329, 331, 333, 335;* TE activities, *pages 331, 333, and 335.*

ONGOING ASSESSMENT
Evaluate the performance of 4-6 students using appropriate checklists and record forms from pages R65–R68 and R77–R79.

INTERNET Activities and exercises to help students prepare for state and standardized assessments appear on *The Learning Site:*
www.harcourtschool.com

■ Study Skills ■

Using a Map

A **map** shows a place on paper. It can show a city, a state, or a country. A map is too small to show how things look. It uses little drawings instead. The **map key** tells what the drawings mean.

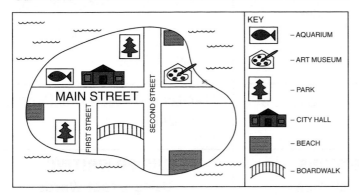

Practice
Use the map to answer the questions.
Possible responses are given.

1. How many beaches are there? three

2. How many parks are there? two

3. Where can you find a boardwalk?
   between First Street and Second Street

4. Where is the city hall? on Main Street

5. How would you walk from the aquarium
   to the art museum?
   I would walk down Main Street.

337

■ Study Skills ■

Using a Map

■ Study Skills ■

Using a Map

TEACH/MODEL

Display several maps, such as maps of the United States, your state, community, and a nearby mall, and, if possible, an atlas. Invite children to examine the maps for several minutes. Write *map* on the board and ask children how they would define the term. Record their ideas. Then read about maps at the top of page 337 with children. Have them locate the map key on each map you displayed and note the symbols.

PRACTICE When children have finished, have volunteers share their answers. Then ask children to use the map to explain how to get from one point to another.

WRAP-UP/ASSESS

SUMMARIZE Ask children to tell what they have learned about maps and about using a map key.

PRACTICE page 90

REACHING ALL LEARNERS

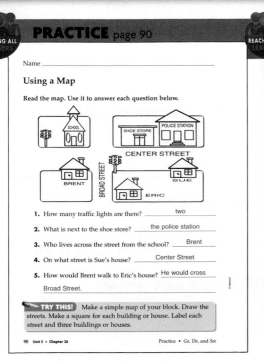

Name _____

Using a Map

Read the map. Use it to answer each question below.

1. How many traffic lights are there? two
2. What is next to the shoe store? the police station
3. Who lives across the street from the school? Brent
4. On what street is Sue's house? Center Street
5. How would Brent walk to Eric's house? He would cross Broad Street.

TRY THIS! Make a simple map of your block. Draw the streets. Make a square for each building or house. Label each street and three buildings or houses.

90 Unit 5 • Chapter 26   Practice • Go, Do, and See

CHALLENGE

REACHING ALL LEARNERS

MAKE A MAP Have pairs of children make a map of the school to help new students find the gym, office, library, cafeteria, and other places. Encourage children to use symbols, such as a book for the library, and to include a map key that shows what each symbol means. Have children share and talk about their school maps.

Writing Directions

LESSON ORGANIZER

	DAY 1	DAY 2
DAILY LANGUAGE PRACTICE TRANSPARENCY 53	1. A firetruck goed by my hoose. (went; house) 2. i seen it through the window. (I; saw)	1. kenny gived me a card. (Kenny; gave) 2. It camme in the, mail. (came; the)
ORAL WARM-UP Listening/Speaking	Talk About Directions for Crossing a Street p. 338	Discuss and Follow Oral Directions p. 340
TEACH/MODEL WRITING 	✔ **WRITING DIRECTIONS** **Literature Model:** "Fire Fighters" pp. 338–339 **WRITER'S CRAFT** • To read and respond to directions as a model for writing • To recognize exact words in sentences **Think About It** p. 339	**GUIDED WRITING** **Using Exact Words** pp. 340–341 • To rewrite directions using exact words • To use exact words to complete directions **Writing and Thinking:** Reflect p. 341
Reaching All Learners 	**ESL** *ESL Manual* pp. 132–133 **Think About It** p. 339	**Challenge:** More Exact Words p. 340 **ESL** Word Bank p. 341 *ESL Manual* p. 132
GRAMMAR	**Unit 5 Review** pp. 384–385	**Unit 5 Review** pp. 384–385
CROSS-CURRICULAR/ ENRICHMENT	**Social Studies Connection:** Career Day p. 339 **School-Home Connection:** Fire Escape Plan p. 339 **Vocabulary Power** Word Meaning p. 338	**Vocabulary Power** Related Words p. 338 *Vocabulary Power* book, p. 79 Vocabulary activity

KEY
✔ = tested writing form/skill

demonstrate, display, illustrate, model, present
See also *Vocabulary Power* book.

DAY 3	DAY 4	DAY 5
1. My skhool is in Chicago Illinois. (school; Chicago,) **2.** Please comes visit Us. (come; us)	**1.** Didd you follow the directions already (Did; ?) **2.** What go after the first step! (goes; ?)	**1.** She see me yesterday? (saw; .) **2.** mickey do his homework. (Mickey does)
Talk About Written Directions p. 342	Discuss Order of Steps p. 344	Discuss Careful Retracing p. 345
GUIDED WRITING ✔ **Applying the Craft** pp. 342–343 • To use a model for writing directions • To prewrite and draft a set of directions **Read and Discuss the Model** p. 342	**GUIDED WRITING** **Using Exact Words** p. 344 • To peer conference in editing directions • To edit directions and share them aloud	**HANDWRITING** **Retracing Letters** p. 345 • To retrace letters correctly
Interactive Writing: Model Drafting p. 343 **ESL** *ESL Manual* p. 132	**Peer Conferencing** p. 344 **ESL** *ESL Manual* p. 132	**Writing Resource:** Retracing Letters p. 345 **ESL** *ESL Manual* p. 132
Unit 5 Review pp. 384–385	**Unit 5 Review** pp. 384–385	**Unit 5 Review** pp. 384–385
Vocabulary Power Multi-Meaning Words p. 338 *Vocabulary Power* book, p. 80 🏆 **Vocabulary activity**	**LISTENING AND SPEAKING:** Directions p. 344 **Vocabulary Power** Homographs p. 338 *Vocabulary Power* book, p. 81 🏆 **Vocabulary activity**	**Vocabulary Power** Perform p. 338

Writer's Craft
Using Exact Words

OBJECTIVES
- To read and respond to directions as a model for writing
- To recognize exact words in sentences

DAILY LANGUAGE PRACTICE

TRANSPARENCY 53

① A firetruck goed by my hoose. (went; house)

② i seen it through the window. (I; saw)

ORAL WARM-UP

USE PRIOR KNOWLEDGE Discuss with children how they know what to do when they want to cross a street that has a traffic light. Talk about the exact words that are part of the directions they follow for crossing at a light.

TEACH/MODEL

Read and discuss the introductory text on page 338, and have children read the model literature excerpt.

ANALYZE THE LITERATURE Use these questions for discussing the directions.

1. **What do the directions tell you how to do?** (They tell how to act if your clothing catches on fire.) **LITERAL: MAIN IDEA**

2. **Why should you protect your face?** (Possible response: This will help keep your face from getting burned.) **INFERENTIAL: DRAW CONCLUSIONS**

Writer's Craft

Using Exact Words

Directions give steps to tell how to make or do something. The steps are written as commands.

Read these directions. Look at how the writer uses exact words to tell what to do.

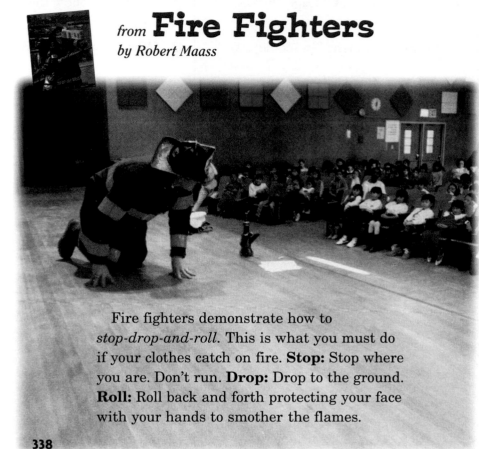

from **Fire Fighters**
by Robert Maass

Fire fighters demonstrate how to *stop-drop-and-roll*. This is what you must do if your clothes catch on fire. **Stop:** Stop where you are. Don't run. **Drop:** Drop to the ground. **Roll:** Roll back and forth protecting your face with your hands to smother the flames.

338

Vocabulary Power

DAY ① WORD MEANINGS Write: *demonstrate.* **Find this word in the first sentence about fire fighters. What does *demonstrate* mean?** (show how to do something)

DAY ② RELATED WORDS Write *demonstrate, explain, teachers.* **These words go together. Which words have similar meanings? Why does the word *teachers* belong in this group?** (See also *Vocabulary Power*, page 79.)

DAY ③ Multi-Meaning Words Write *I can ̲i̲l̲l̲u̲s̲t̲r̲a̲t̲e̲ how to swim. I can ̲i̲l̲l̲u̲s̲t̲r̲a̲t̲e̲ a story.* Discuss the two meanings of *illustrate.* (See also *Vocabulary Power*, page 80.)

DAY ④ HOMOGRAPHS Write: *I'd like to ̲p̲r̲e̲s̲e̲n̲t̲ you a ̲p̲r̲e̲s̲e̲n̲t̲ .* (See also *Vocabulary Power*, page 81.) **How are the underlined words alike? How are they different?**

DAY ⑤ PERFORM Invite volunteers to demonstrate how to do or make something.

Directions should be clear and easy to understand. **Exact words** tell readers what to do for each step. The steps should be easy for readers to picture in their minds.

Read these numbered directions.

In Case of Fire

1. Line up quietly.

2. Walk quickly to the nearest exit.

3. Go outside. Listen for instructions.

Think About It

1. How are both sets of directions alike? How are they different?

2. Could you picture the steps in your mind? Act out the first set of directions. Draw pictures for the second set of directions.

339

USING EXACT WORDS Explain that writers use exact words when they write directions to help readers understand clearly what to do. Have children discuss some of the exact words that are included in the directions.

Think About It

1. Have children describe similarities and differences between the two sets of directions. They should mention that both tell what to do step by step, but only the second set numbers the steps. **INFERENTIAL:** COMPARE AND CONTRAST

2. Have children demonstrate their understanding by acting out and drawing the directions. **LITERAL:** IMPORTANT DETAILS

SELF-INITIATED WRITING Have children respond to the directions they just read through self-initiated writing, which might include writing a summary or generating ideas for writing by using prewriting techniques such as listing key thoughts, among others. You might also want to allow children to respond through other methods, such as drama.

WRAP-UP/ASSESS

SUMMARIZE Have children talk about why writers use exact words when they write directions. They can record their reflections in their journals. **REFLECTION**

Social Studies Connection

· · · · · · · · · · · · · · ·

CAREER DAY Invite parents and others who are employed as community workers to visit the class and tell about their jobs. Encourage visitors to make their presentations interactive, and have children prepare questions they would like to ask the guests.

School-Home Connection

· · · · · · · · · · · · · · · · ·

FIRE ESCAPE PLAN You might want to suggest that families prepare and practice emergency escape plans in case of fire, including a meeting place outside the home.

Writer's Craft
Using Exact Words

OBJECTIVES
- To rewrite directions using exact words
- To use exact words to complete directions

SPIRAL REVIEW

DAILY LANGUAGE PRACTICE

TRANSPARENCY 53

1. kenny gived me a card. (Kenny; gave)
2. It camme in the, mail. (came; the)

ORAL WARM-UP

USE PRIOR KNOWLEDGE Give a simple set of oral directions, such as *Walk around the room.* Then give a more detailed set of directions, such as *Walk in single file around the outside of the desks.* Have children discuss which directions were clearer and why. Have children take turns giving simple directions with exact words.

GUIDED WRITING

ADDING EXACT WORDS Read and discuss the introductory material. Tell children that they will add exact words to complete written directions in exercises A and B.

USE THE WORD BANK Have children complete exercise A by adding exact words such as those in the Word Bank.

Using Exact Words

Exact words help readers follow directions correctly. When writers use exact words, readers can picture what to do at each step.

Roll: Roll back and forth protecting your face with your hands to smother the flames.

If the writer said only to roll, the reader would not know exactly what to do and why. This sentence tells the reader exactly how to roll.

A. Rewrite the directions below. Use exact words in place of the underlined word or words. Use the Word Bank for help.
Responses will vary.

1. This is how to make <u>something</u>.
2. Find <u>things</u>.
3. <u>Make</u> the paper in half.
4. Write <u>something on it</u>.
5. <u>Finish</u> the card.

Word Bank
- bright-colored paper
- stickers
- a greeting on the front
- fold
- markers
- decorate
- a message inside
- a card

340

Vocabulary Power page 79

Name _____

These words are related because they all have to do with teaching or explaining something.

demonstrate   display   illustrate   model   present

Draw pictures to show the meaning of the underlined words.

1. I can <u>demonstrate</u> how to dance.	2. I can <u>display</u> my favorite books.
3. I can <u>illustrate</u> ways to tie knots.	4. I can <u>model</u> how to add numbers.
5. I can <u>present</u> a book report.	6. This is my favorite <u>teacher</u>.

Vocabulary Power   Unit 5 • Chapter 37   79

REACHING ALL LEARNERS   **CHALLENGE**

MORE EXACT WORDS Have children brainstorm alternative exact words for the underlined words in exercise A and then follow their directions to make the item.

B. Use exact words to complete these directions about how to mail a letter.
Responses will vary.

How to Mail a Letter

1. Put your letter in an envelope.

2. <u>1.   </u> the envelope.

3. Write the first and <u>2.   </u> name of the person to whom you are sending it.

4. Write the address <u>3.   </u>.

5. Put a stamp on the <u>4.   </u> corner of the envelope.

6. Drop the letter in a <u>5.   </u>.

Writing and Thinking

Reflect Tell what helped you think of exact words. Did you picture the steps in your mind before you wrote? Write your ideas. Share your ideas in a small group.

341

WRITE EXACT WORDS Read the directions for exercise B together. You may wish to do the first example together. Children can complete the exercise independently or with a partner. Provide time for children to share and compare their exact words with classmates.

Writing and Thinking

Reflect Children can record in their journals their reflections on thinking of exact words. Then they can discuss ideas with group members. **REFLECTION**

WRAP-UP/ASSESS

SUMMARIZE Ask volunteers to summarize what they know about using exact words to write directions.

ESL
REACHING ALL LEARNERS

WORD BANK Children who are acquiring English may have difficulty adding exact words to their directions. You may want to provide them with aids similar to the Word Bank as they write their own directions with a partner.

Writer's Craft
Applying the Craft

OBJECTIVES
- To use a model for writing directions
- To prewrite and draft a set of directions

DAILY LANGUAGE PRACTICE

TRANSPARENCY 53

❶ My skhool is in Chicago Illinois. (school; Chicago,)

❷ Please comes visit Us. (come; us)

ORAL WARM-UP

USE PRIOR KNOWLEDGE Ask children how they know what to do at the beginning of school each day. Talk about how written directions can be helpful in situations like this.

TEACH/MODEL

THINK ABOUT THE MODEL Read and discuss the model. Ask if children would know what to do if these directions were for their school.

Looking at the Model

1. Children may note that exact words such as those that tell where or how are a helpful part of directions.
   CRITICAL: MAKE JUDGMENTS
2. Children may suggest that without exact words, readers might be confused about what they should do.
   INFERENTIAL: DRAW CONCLUSIONS

Applying the Craft

Read these directions. Think about how the exact words that are underlined help the reader know just what to do.

> **What to Do When the Morning Bell Rings**
>
> I. Line up by the <u>front door</u>. Stand in <u>ABC order by last name</u>.
>
> 2. March <u>single file</u> into the classroom.
>
> 3. Sit in your <u>assigned seat</u>.

Looking at the Model

1. Which parts of these directions give the reader the best idea of what to do? Why?
2. What could happen if the writer had not used exact words? Why?

342

Vocabulary Power page 80

Name _____

Some words have many different meanings.

> The buttons are <u>attached</u> to the coat.
> My friend and I are very <u>attached</u>.

Write the word in dark print to complete each phrase. Circle one of the phrases and draw a picture to show its meaning.

1. illustrate
   _____ a picture
   _____ a dance

2. model
   _____ a coat
   make a _____

3. display
   present a _____
   _____ happiness

4. present
   _____ a report
   _____ a prize

80   Unit 5 • Chapter 27   Vocabulary Power

EVALUATION CRITERIA

WRITING PROMPT Work with children to establish criteria for what makes good directions. Encourage children to add additional criteria. Children should apply criteria to their writing.

- Directions use exact words to help the reader know what to do.
- Directions follow a logical order.
- Directions include all the steps necessary to do the task.

Your Turn

Write directions for a new student about how to do something in your school.

Prewriting and Drafting

STEP 1 Develop your ideas.

Ask yourself these questions.

- What must be done first, next, and last?
- What are the best words to tell how to do each step?

STEP 2 Brainstorm exact words.

Make a flowchart. Add exact words to show your reader what to do.

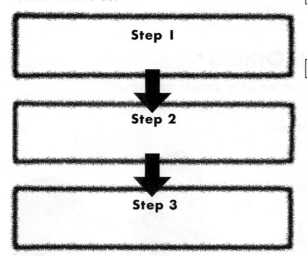

```
┌─────────────────────────────┐
│          Step 1             │
└─────────────────────────────┘
              ↓
┌─────────────────────────────┐
│          Step 2             │
└─────────────────────────────┘
              ↓
┌─────────────────────────────┐
│          Step 3             │
└─────────────────────────────┘
```

STEP 3 Write your draft.

Use your chart and What Good Writers Do to write a draft of your directions.

What Good Writers Do

 Remember to tell your readers exactly what to do.

 Put your ideas in the correct order.

Student Handbook

Use the thesaurus on page 494 to help you think of exact words.

343

Your Turn Explain to children they will use the prewriting and drafting steps and What Good Writers Do to write directions for a new student at school.

Prewriting and Drafting Read the directions and the steps with children. Suggest that once they select a topic, they try to picture themselves going through the activity step by step. They can make notes about the steps on a chart and then add exact words to the chart. Then read What Good Writers Do and suggest that children think about these tips during the prewriting and drafting steps.

You may wish to have children use word-processing software to compose their drafts.

PORTFOLIO Have children store their first drafts in their Writing Portfolios.

WRAP-UP/ASSESS

SUMMARIZE Ask volunteers to summarize the process they used to prewrite and draft their directions. You may want to have children record in their journal their reflections on writing directions.

REFLECTION

INTERACTIVE WRITING

MODEL DRAFTING Invite children to suggest a topic for writing directions. Have them brainstorm steps. Prompt them with words such as first, next, then, last. List their steps and model beginning to write a draft. "Share the pen" by having volunteers write the steps.

Writer's Craft
Using Exact Words

OBJECTIVES
- To peer conference in editing directions
- To edit directions and share them aloud

DAILY LANGUAGE PRACTICE

TRANSPARENCY 53

1 Didd you follow the directions already (Did; ?)

2 What go after the first step! (goes; ?)

ORAL WARM-UP

Give a set of simple directions with the steps out of order, such as turn off the water. Fill a glass. Turn on the water. Discuss why the order of steps is important in giving directions.

GUIDED WRITING

EDITING YOUR DIRECTIONS Have volunteers read aloud the directions and the checklist. Review the Editor's Marks.

PEER CONFERENCING Have children use the checklist and the Editor's Marks in their peer editing conference.

SHARING WITH OTHERS Have volunteers share their edited directions in small groups. Provide time and materials for children to follow the steps in selected directions.

WRAP-UP/ASSESS

SUMMARIZE Volunteers can summarize the process they used to draft and edit the directions they wrote. Have children evaluate their final copy using a scale of 1-4 on a self-stick note. Children can attach their ratings to their writing and place it in their Writing Portfolio.

Writer's Craft

Editing Your Directions

Share your draft with a few classmates. Together, talk about how you can make your directions better. Use the checklist and the Editor's Marks to help you revise your directions.

✔ My directions are in the correct order.

✔ My directions use exact words so that my reader knows what to do.

Editor's Marks

∧ Add.

⋏ Change.

℘ Take out.

= Use a capital letter.

⊙ Add a period.

◯ Check the spelling.

Sharing with Others

Meet with a partner or in a small group. Read your directions aloud. Have others follow the directions.

344

Vocabulary Power page 81

Name _____

Homographs are words that have the same spelling, but they are pronounced differently and they have different meanings.

I'm keeping a <u>record</u> of different birds I see.
Let's use this tape to <u>record</u> some music.

Draw pictures to show the meaning of the underlined words.

1. This <u>present</u> is for you.	**2.** We will <u>present</u> a play.
3. <u>Wind</u> the clock.	**4.** The <u>wind</u> is blowing.
5. <u>Lead</u> the parade.	**6.** A <u>lead</u> pipe.

Vocabulary Power   Unit 5 • Chapter 27   81

LISTENING AND SPEAKING

DIRECTIONS If group members are to follow directions that are read aloud, tell speakers to allow time for the audience to respond before reading each next step. Have children use props, when possible, to clarify directions.

•Handwriting•

Retracing Letters Correctly

> Follow these tips to make sure your letters with retraced strokes are formed correctly.
>
> | correct | incorrect |
> |---------|-----------|
> | 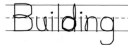 | Building |
>
> ✓ Try not to lift your pencil from the paper.
>
> ✓ Retrace along the same line.
>
> ✓ Do not put any loops in these letters or leave any spaces.
>
> ✓ Make the strokes smooth and even.

Write these letters and words. Use your best handwriting. Follow the tips to make the strokes correctly.

B h m n r u

Build a tree house.

Bake the muffins.

345

Writing Resource
. . . .

RETRACING LETTERS Suggest that children who need additional practice retracing letters could try to write more slowly until they are able to produce neater letters.

EVALUATION CRITERIA

Have children revisit the evaluation criteria they established earlier and informally rate their writing of directions by writing their score (on a 1–4 scale) on the corner of their papers or by raising their fingers.

•Handwriting•

Retracing Letters Correctly

OBJECTIVES
- To retrace letters correctly

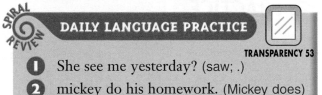

SPIRAL REVIEW

DAILY LANGUAGE PRACTICE

TRANSPARENCY 53

1 She see me yesterday? (saw; .)

2 mickey do his homework. (Mickey does)

TEACH/MODEL

Explain that as we write certain letters, we retrace over lines that we have already written. Retracing carefully makes it easier for others to read what we write.

Have volunteers read the tips aloud. Have children copy the practice letters and words on page 345, keeping in mind the retracing tips.

You may wish to have children refer to the handwriting models on pages 490-493 in their handbooks (see also R92-R93).

CURSIVE WRITING Have children who write in cursive apply the concepts in this lesson to their writing.

WRAP-UP/ASSESS

SUMMARIZE Ask volunteers to summarize the handwriting tips. You may wish to have children make name tags for their desks, paying special attention to the way they retrace letters.

LESSON ORGANIZER	DAY 1	DAY 2
DAILY LANGUAGE PRACTICE 	1. she go to the art show yesterday. (She went) 2. Pete and mark does a lot of work now. (Mark; do) **Bridge to Writing** The painter (past-tense form of see) the pretty sky at sunset yesterday.	1. He have worked hard (has; .) 2. we has learned a play. (We have) **Bridge to Writing** Laura (form of have) cleaned her room yesterday.
ORAL WARM-UP Listening/Speaking	Discuss Past Experiences p. 346	Use Past-Tense Verbs p. 348 *Grammar Jingles*™ CD Track 19
TEACH/MODEL GRAMMAR **KEY** ✔ = tested skill	✔ **WHAT IS A HELPING VERB?** pp. 346–347 • To understand that a helping verb works with the main verb to tell about an action • To present a dramatic interpretation of a play	✔ **USING *HAS*, *HAVE*, AND *HAD*** pp. 348–349 • To understand that *has*, *have*, and *had* work with verbs to show past actions • To use the helping verbs *has*, *have*, and *had* in writing
Reaching All Learners	**Challenge:** Activity Card 19, p. R59 *Practice Book* p. 91 **ESL:** *ESL Manual* pp. 134–135 **Reteach:** *Reteach Activities Copying Masters* p. 55	**Modified Instruction** Below-Level: Identify Subject Above-Level: Rewrite Sentences **Challenge:** Where Have You Been? p. 349 **ESL:** Helping-Verb Action p. 348 *ESL Manual* pp. 134, 136 *Practice Book* p. 92 **Reteach:** *Reteach Activities Copying Masters* p. 56

WRITING	Identify Helping Verbs p. 347
	
	  Summarize/Reflect
		Writing Connection p. 349
		 Writing a Summary
		  Summarize/Reflect

CROSS-CURRICULAR/ ENRICHMENT	**Vocabulary Power** Word Meaning p. 346 **guided,** advise, direct, led, taught See *Vocabulary Power* book.	**Vocabulary Power** Related Words p. 346 *Vocabulary Power* book p. 82 **Vocabulary activity**

DAY 3

1. he hadd learned how to paint. (He had)

2. They has paintd many pictures. (have painted)

Bridge to Writing Maria (form of have + form of play) the piano for me.

Brainstorm Details p. 350

 Grammar Jingles™ CD Track 19

✔ **KEEPING TO ONE MAIN IDEA** pp. 350-351
• To identify the main idea in a paragraph
• To revise a paragraph to make sure that all the sentences tell about the main idea

Modified Instruction
Below-Level: Fill In a Web
Above-Level: Write the Main Idea
Challenge: Detail Add-Ons p. 351
ESL: Main-Idea Items p. 350
ESL Manual pp. 134, 137
Practice Book p. 93
Reteach: *Reteach Activities Copying Masters* p. 57

Writing Connection p. 351
Revising
 Summarize/Reflect

Vocabulary Power
Expand Word Meaning p. 346
Vocabulary Power book p.83
Vocabulary activity

DAY 4

1. Mara have create a poster. (has created)

2. pete hads used watercolors for his painting. (Pete had/has)

Bridge to Writing We (helping verb have) visited the museum.

Play Charades p. 352

EXTRA PRACTICE p. 352-353
• To identify and write the correct forms of the helping verb *have*
• To revise a paragraph so that all the sentences tell about the main idea
Practice and Assessment

Challenge: Match Up p. 353
ESL: Shared Writing p. 352
ESL Manual pp. 134, 138
Practice Book p. 94

Writing Connection p. 353
Functional Writing: Job Chart

Vocabulary Power
Homophones p. 346
Vocabulary Power book p. 84
Vocabulary activity
Language Play p. 353

DAY 5

1. We had movd in april. (moved; April)

2. Mike have visite a big city. (has; visited)

Bridge to Writing That boy (form of have + form of finish) his work.

TEST PREP **CHAPTER REVIEW** p. 354
• To review helping verbs
• To use appropriate fonts and graphics to publish writing
Test Preparation

Challenge: Computer Poster p. 355
Practice Book p. 95
ESL: *ESL Manual* pp. 134, 139

Writing Application p. 355
Using Computer Graphics

Vocabulary Power
Comparison p. 346
Technology: Using Computer Graphics p. 355

What Is a Helping Verb?

OBJECTIVES

- To understand that a helping verb works with the main verb to tell about an action
- To present a dramatic interpretation of a play

DAILY LANGUAGE PRACTICE

TRANSPARENCY 54

1 she go to the art show yesterday. (She went)

2 Pete and mark does a lot of work now. (Mark; do)

BRIDGE TO WRITING The painter (past-tense form of *see*) the pretty sky at sunset yesterday.

ORAL WARM-UP

USE PRIOR KNOWLEDGE Have children discuss their past experiences with paints, brushes, and pencils. Write their responses in sentences that include the helping verbs *have*, *had*, and *has*. Then add the verbs to the **Verb Word Wall**.

TEACH/MODEL

Have children open their books to page 346. Ask them to use the characters, time, and setting to predict what the play will be about. Have volunteers read the parts aloud. Remind them to read expressively in a loud and clear voice.

DEVELOP ORAL LANGUAGE Discuss each character's contribution to the painting. Point out that the play showed how each character helped the artist make the painting. Ask children to discuss ways they have helped someone complete an activity. Write verb phrases with *has*, *had*, and *have* and a main verb on the board.

What Is a Helping Verb?

Read this short play.

Who Has Made the Painting?

Characters:	brush, paint, pencil
Time:	evening
Setting:	in the artist's toolbox

Brush: I have painted the mural on the wall.

Paint: Not true! I have painted it. I have covered the wall with beautiful colors.

Pencil: I had started it. I had traced the lines of the drawings.

Paint: I have filled those lines with color. The brush has helped me, but it did not paint.

Brush: How would you get on the wall without me? You need me.

Pencil: Let's not argue! I think we forgot a few things.

Brush and Paint: What?

Pencil: The artist has guided me on the wall. She has picked the paint, and she has brushed it on. The *artist* has created the painting!

346

Vocabulary Power

DAY 1 WORD MEANINGS Write: *guided*. **Find this word at the end of the play on Page 346. Who guided the pencil? What does *guided* mean?**

DAY 2 RELATED WORDS List: *guided, taught, school*. **These words go together. Which two words have similar meanings? Why does the word *school* belong in this group?** (See also *Vocabulary Power*, page 82.)

DAY 3 EXPAND WORD MEANING Write: *My mom is a museum guide*. **What does *guide* mean in this sentence?** (See also *Vocabulary Power*, page 83.)

DAY 4 HOMOPHONES Write: *Led, lead*. **Led means "guided." Lead is a metal. How are the two words the same? How are the words different?** (See also *Vocabulary Power*, page 84.)

DAY 5 COMPARISON **If you were learning to ride a two-wheel bike, would you want someone to guide you or direct you? Why?**

Read the play aloud with two partners. Act out each action.

> A **helping verb** works with the main verb to tell about an action.
>
> The artist **has** <u>painted</u> the flower red.
>
> *Has* is the helping verb.

Write a helping verb and a main verb to complete each new line of the play.

Possible responses are given.

Brush: First the artist __has__ __mixed__ the paint.

Paint: Next she __has__ __traced__ the lines with the pencil.

Pencil: Then she __has__ __dipped__ the brush into the paint.

Think about what might happen next. Work with your partners to add new lines to the play. Include helping verbs.

347

WRITE Continue to have children discuss a time when they helped someone do something and how they helped. Invite them to list the action verbs they used. Explain that sometimes we use the verb *has* in front of a main verb. A verb that helps tell what was done is called a **helping verb**. Tell children to read the definition in the box and then identify the helping and main verb in the example.

Read the first item at the bottom of page 347 with children. Ask them to point out what is missing in the sentence (a helping verb and a main verb). Brainstorm with children action verbs they could use. Have them pick the one that best completes the sentence.

WRAP-UP/ASSESS

SUMMARIZE Have children summarize and reflect on what they have learned about helping verbs. Tell children to write their reflections in their journals. **REFLECTION**

RETEACH

INTERVENTION Lessons in **visual**, **auditory**, and **kinesthetic** modalities: p. R35 and *Reteach Activities Copying Masters*, p. 55.

page 55

REACHING ALL LEARNERS

PRACTICE page 91

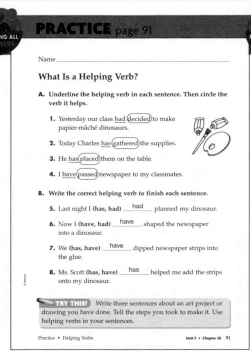

Name _____

What Is a Helping Verb?

A. Underline the helping verb in each sentence. Then circle the verb it helps.

1. Yesterday our class had (decided) to make papier-mâché dinosaurs.
2. Today Charles has (gathered) the supplies.
3. He has (placed) them on the table.
4. I have (passed) newspaper to my classmates.

B. Write the correct helping verb to finish each sentence.

5. Last night I **(has, had)** __had__ planned my dinosaur.
6. Now I **(have, had)** __have__ shaped the newspaper into a dinosaur.
7. We **(has, have)** __have__ dipped newspaper strips into the glue.
8. Ms. Scott **(has, have)** __has__ helped me add the strips onto my dinosaur.

TRY THIS! Write three sentences about an art project or drawing you have done. Tell the steps you took to make it. Use helping verbs in your sentences.

Practice • Helping Verbs   Unit 5 • Chapter 28 91

CHALLENGE

MAKE A PUPPET Have children use **Challenge Activity Card 19** (page R59) to make a puppet representing their favorite character in the play. Then have children reread the play and use their puppets to act it out. Encourage them to add lines to the play that use helping verbs.

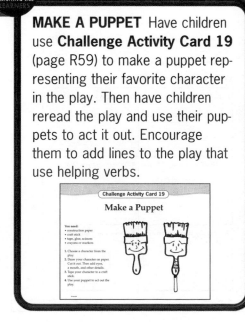

Challenge Activity Card 19

Make a Puppet

You need:
• construction paper
• craft stick
• tape, glue, scissors
• crayons or markers

1. Choose a character from the play.
2. Draw your character on paper. Cut it out. Then add eyes, a mouth, and other details.
3. Tape your character to a craft stick.
4. Use your puppet to act out the play.

What Is a Helping Verb?

Read each sentence aloud. Circle the helping verbs.

EXAMPLE: Ben and Joey (have) played all day.

1. They (have) tossed a ball.
2. Ben (has) looked for shells.
3. They (had) played here last week, too.
4. Ben (had) gathered many shells.
5. Joey (had) watched the waves.

- -

What Is a Helping Verb?

Cut out the words below. Glue the helping verb that best fits each sentence. Underline the main verb.

1. Yesterday Joey __had__ collected sea glass.
2. They __have__ created a huge sand castle today.
3. Ben __has__ stacked shells all around the castle.
4. Ben's mom __has__ snapped a picture of the sand castle.

| has | has | had | have |

Teacher: Cut apart the activities and distribute to children based on the modalities that are their strengths.

Reteach Activities • Helping Verbs   Unit 5 • Chapter 28 55

Using *Has, Have,* and *Had*

OBJECTIVES

- To understand that the helping verbs *has, have,* and *had* work with other verbs to show actions that happened in the past
- To use the helping verbs *has, have,* and *had* in writing

DAILY LANGUAGE PRACTICE

TRANSPARENCY 54

1 He have worked hard (has; .)

2 we has learned a play. (We have)

BRIDGE TO WRITING Laura ___(form of have)___ cleaned her room yesterday.

ORAL WARM-UP

USE PRIOR KNOWLEDGE Display a picture of children playing. On the board, write: *The child has* <u>played</u>. *The children have* <u>played</u>. *The child had* <u>played</u>. Show pictures of children doing other things, such as cooking, cleaning, walking, or dancing. Ask children to say different *-ed* words to replace the verb *played.*

***Grammar Jingles*™ CD, Primary** Use Track 19 for review and reinforcement of helping verbs.

TEACH/MODEL

Read the first example sentence and have children identify the helping verb (*has*) and the main verb (*helped*). Use the explanation and sentences to help children understand when to use *has, have,* and *had.*

GUIDED PRACTICE Help children as needed to complete the sentences. Have them decide whether to use a verb that tells about one or about more than one.

Using *Has, Have,* and *Had*

Use the helping verbs **has**, **have**, and **had** with other verbs to show action that happened in the past.

- **Has** tells about one.
  Tim **has helped** our teacher.

- **Have** tells about more than one and is used with *I*.
  All the children **have worked** hard.
  I **have worked** hard, too.

- **Had** tells about one or more than one.
  Tanya **had cleaned** her desk before.
  Don and Felipe **had helped** yesterday.

Guided Practice

Choose the correct helping verb to finish each sentence.

1. The children (<u>have</u>, has) cleaned the classroom.

2. The teacher (<u>had</u>, have) asked them to do so.

3. David (<u>has</u>, have) picked up the trash.

4. Victor and Yoko (<u>had</u>, has) wiped the board.

5. The children (<u>have</u>, has) washed everything.

348

Vocabulary Power page 82

Name _____

These words are related because they all have something to do with teaching or leading.

advise   direct   guided   led   taught

Write or draw to demonstrate the meaning of the underlined word.

1. I <u>led</u> the way.	**2.** The signs <u>guided</u> me home.
3. The officer will <u>direct</u> traffic.	**4.** Who <u>taught</u> you how to read?
5. I will <u>advise</u> you when to stop.	**6.** Please <u>direct</u> me to the gym.

82 Unit 5 • Chapter 28   Vocabulary Power

REACHING ALL LEARNERS   ESL

HELPING-VERB ACTION To familiarize children with the use of helping verbs, write on the board verbs such as *cleaned, danced, listened, walked, painted.* Have one or two volunteers act out one of these action verbs. Then ask, *What (has, have) he/she/they done?* Encourage children to answer in complete sentences, using *has* or *have.*

She has danced.

Remember Use *has, have,* and *had* with other verbs to show action that happened in the past.

Independent Practice

Choose the correct helping verb to finish each sentence.

6. The parents (<u>have</u>, has) walked into our classroom.

7. Our teacher (<u>has</u>, have) talked to the parents.

8. Pablo (<u>had</u>, have) asked to sing a song.

9. My dad (<u>had</u>, have) wished to see my work.

10. He (<u>has</u>, have) stopped by my desk with my mom.

11. First my parents (has, <u>have</u>) listened to Pablo's song.

12. Then they (has, <u>have</u>) looked at my papers.

Writing Connection

Writing a Summary Think about a story you like. Write a few sentences to tell the main events that happened. Use the helping verbs *has, have,* and *had.*

The Lost Island

Write your summary on your computer. Save it and label the disk to help you find the document later.

349

Independent Practice

Have children complete the Independent Practice, or modify it by using the following suggestions:

MODIFIED INSTRUCTION

BELOW-LEVEL STUDENTS Have children circle the word that tells who did the action to decide whether the verb tells about one or more than one.

ABOVE-LEVEL STUDENTS Have children rewrite several of the sentences. Tell them to change the word that tells who did the action so that the helping verb in each sentence changes.

Writing Connection

Writing a Summary Remind children that when writing a summary they are retelling only the most important parts of a story. Have volunteers place their summaries in the Sharing Basket.

WRAP-UP/ASSESS

SUMMARIZE Have children reflect about helping verbs and summarize what they have learned in their journals.
REFLECTION

RETEACH

INTERVENTION Lessons in **visual, auditory,** and **kinesthetic** modalities; p. R35 and *Reteach Activities Copying Masters,* p. 56.

page 56

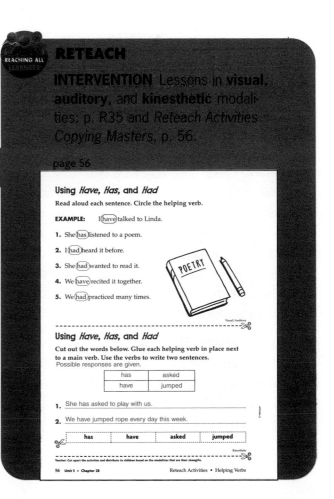

Using *Have, Has,* and *Had*

Read aloud each sentence. Circle the helping verb.

EXAMPLE: I(have)talked to Linda.

1. She(has)listened to a poem.
2. I(had)heard it before.
3. She(had)wanted to read it.
4. We(have)recited it together.
5. We(had)practiced many times.

Using *Have, Has,* and *Had*

Cut out the words below. Glue each helping verb in place next to a main verb. Use the verbs to write two sentences.
Possible responses are given.

has	asked
have	jumped

1. She has asked to play with us.

2. We have jumped rope every day this week.

has	have	asked	jumped

56 Unit 5 • Chapter 28   Reteach Activities • Helping Verbs

PRACTICE page 92

Name

Using *Has, Have,* and *Had*

A. Read each sentence. Fill in each blank with *have* or *has.*

1. Richie __has__ picked up the camera today.
2. Mom __has__ told him not to touch it.
3. Now she __has__ put it on a high shelf.
4. Sandy and I __have__ used it.
5. We __have__ followed directions.

B. Underline the correct helping verb to finish each sentence.

6. I (**have**, has) used a camera before.
7. Last week Dad (have, **had**) shown me how.
8. Yesterday we (**had**, has) developed the film.
9. Now I (**have**, has) seen all the pictures.
10. Dad (have, **has**) taken them to show Mom.

TRY THIS! Write three sentences about using a camera or having your picture taken. Use helping verbs in your sentences.

92 Unit 5 • Chapter 28   Practice • Helping Verbs

CHALLENGE

WHERE HAVE YOU BEEN?

Have pairs of children each think about a place they have visited, such as a museum, or something they have watched or listened to, such as a movie or a concert. Ask children to use helping verbs as they take turns telling their partners about the experience.

Keeping to One Main Idea

OBJECTIVES
- To identify the main idea in a paragraph
- To revise a paragraph to make sure that all the sentences tell about the main idea

DAILY LANGUAGE PRACTICE

TRANSPARENCY 54

1. he hadd learned how to paint. (He had)
2. They has paintd many pictures. (have painted)

BRIDGE TO WRITING Maria (form of have + form of play) the piano for me.

ORAL WARM-UP

USE PRIOR KNOWLEDGE Write this web on the board.

Singing a Song

Explain that singing a song is the main idea. Have children brainstorm details that tell about it. Write them in the web.

Grammar Jingles™ CD, Primary Use Track 19 for review and reinforcement of helping verbs.

TEACH/MODEL

Use the example to explain to children what a paragraph is. Discuss why a paragraph should have only one main idea. Help children understand that including details that do not tell about the main idea might confuse the reader.

GUIDED PRACTICE Read the paragraph aloud. Have children identify the main idea and the sentences that tell about the main idea. Call on a volunteer to point out the sentence that does not belong.

Keeping to One Main Idea

A paragraph is a group of sentences that tell about one *main idea*. The first sentence of a paragraph often gives the main idea. The other sentences give *details*. They tell more about the main idea.

Painting a picture takes time. First think about what you want to paint. Next make a few drawings in pencil. Pick the best drawing, and draw it again on good paper. Then mix your colors and paint your picture.

My Cat

Guided Practice

Write the paragraph. Underline the main idea. Leave out the sentence that does not tell about the main idea.

1. Paintings can be found in many different places. You can see them at a museum or an art gallery. You can also go to an art show in a park or at school. ~~Red roses are beautiful flowers.~~ Paintings are in books, too.

350

Vocabulary Power page 83

Name _____

Some words can be used in many different ways.

You can run. You can hit a home run.
You can be a model. You can model how to skip.

Read the sentence pairs. Think about the meanings of the underlined words. Then follow the directions.

1. Dad has to park the car. We are visiting a wildlife park. Show or describe what a wildlife park is.

2. The signs direct us to the park. This path is the most direct. Show or describe a direct path.

3. The man can guide us. He is a park guide. Show or describe what a park guide does.

4. The guide taught us birdsongs. The lesson was well-taught. Show or describe what well-taught means.

Vocabulary Power   Unit 5 • Chapter 28   83

ESL

REACHING ALL LEARNERS

MAIN-IDEA ITEMS To help children understand the concept of a main idea, show a paintbrush, paints, water, paper, paper clips, and a plastic bag. Then write on the board and say: *I have all the materials I need to paint a picture.* Ask children to discuss and then choose only materials that tell about your main-idea sentence.

💡 **Remember** In a paragraph, all sentences should tell more about the main idea.

Independent Practice

Write each paragraph. Underline the main idea. Leave out the sentence that does not tell about the main idea.

2. I have made a penguin puppet. First I picked some black and white felt. ~~I like ducks, too.~~ I used the felt to make the body. Then I added a piece of orange paper for the beak and two little paper eyes. Last I glued some black felt on each side to make the wings.

3. I worked hard to get ready for my part in the play. Before the show, I had learned my lines. I also had practiced many times with my partners. I had learned how to move on stage. ~~My friend made a penguin puppet.~~ By the day of the play, I was ready to go.

Writing Connection

Revising Choose a paragraph from your Writing Portfolio. Make sure all the sentences tell about one main idea. Cross out any sentences that do not tell about the main idea.

Press **tab** once to indent a paragraph on your computer.

351

Independent Practice

Have children complete the Independent Practice, or modify it by using the following suggestions:

MODIFIED INSTRUCTION

BELOW-LEVEL STUDENTS Suggest that children fill in a web or chart to show which details go with the main idea.

ABOVE-LEVEL STUDENTS Have children write a paragraph with one sentence that doesn't tell about the main idea. Have them trade paragraphs, underline the main-idea sentence, and cross out the sentence that does not tell about the main idea.

Writing Connection

Revising Help children to select appropriate pieces of writing to revise as needed. Have them use different colored pencils to underline the main idea and the details that tell about it.

WRAP-UP/ASSESS

SUMMARIZE Have children record their reflections about writing paragraphs and an example paragraph in their journals.

REFLECTION

RETEACH

INTERVENTION Lessons in **visual, auditory,** and **kinesthetic** modalities: p. R35 and *Reteach Activities Copying Masters,* p. 57.

page 57

Keeping to One Main Idea

Read each paragraph aloud. Draw a line through the sentence that does not tell about the main idea.

1. There was music in the park this month. A different band played every day. ~~Children played on the swings.~~ Many people listened to the music.

2. The park is a wonderful place for a picnic. People sell tasty snacks. There are picnic tables and grills. ~~There are slides in the park.~~

Visual/Auditory

Keeping to One Main Idea

Read each group of sentences. Cut out the sentences at the bottom of the page. Glue each sentence where it belongs.

1. Artists show their paintings. People come to see the paintings.

   | People buy the artists' work. |

2. There are plays in the summer. People bring chairs and watch.

   | The plays are at night. |

   People buy the artists' work.
   The plays are at night.

Kinesthetic

Teacher: Cut apart the activities and distribute to children based on the modalities that are their strengths.

Reteach Activities • Helping Verbs   Unit 5 • Chapter 28   **57**

Name

Keeping to One Main Idea

A. Read the paragraph. Cross out two sentences that do not keep to the main idea.

1. I have drawn a picture. It is red, blue, yellow, and green. My picture shows flowers and fruit. ~~Pears are my favorite fruit to eat. In the summer, I like to eat grapes.~~ It took me only one day to draw the picture.

B. Underline the main idea in each paragraph. Cross out the sentence that does not tell about the main idea.

2. I found a fun room at the Baker Art Museum last week. A woman told me about the new children's room. ~~She wore a red dress and black shoes.~~ The room had pretty pictures that I could touch. An artist was there, too. He answered my questions about painting.

3. Making papier-mâché animals is easy. First, bend newspaper into the shape of an animal. ~~My father loves to read the newspaper.~~ Next, soak newspaper strips in glue and water. Then, wrap the strips around your animal shape. Last, paint your animal when it is all dry.

TRY THIS! Write four sentences about a painting or a picture you like. Use a main idea sentence and detail sentences. Keep to one main idea.

Practice • Helping Verbs   Unit 5 • Chapter 28   93

CHALLENGE

DETAIL ADD-ONS Have children work in groups of three or four. One child writes a main-idea sentence on a sheet of paper. A second child writes a detail sentence about the main idea. The other children do the same until everyone in the group has added a sentence. Have children take turns writing the main-idea sentence.

I have painted a card. First I used a pencil.

Extra Practice

OBJECTIVES

- To identify and write the correct forms of the helping verb *have*
- To revise a paragraph so that all the sentences tell about the main idea

DAILY LANGUAGE PRACTICE

TRANSPARENCY 55

1 Mara have create a poster. (has created)

2 pete hads used watercolors for his painting. (Pete had/has)

BRIDGE TO WRITING We (helping verb have) visited the museum.

ORAL WARM-UP

PLAY CHARADES Have volunteers pantomime simple actions for the class. Other children guess the action and describe it, using a sentence that includes a helping verb. Try to work a Vocabulary Power word into the game.

TEACH/MODEL

Read each set of directions to ensure that children understand how to complete each section. Have children share their answers in small groups before you read aloud the correct answers.

WRAP-UP/ASSESS

SUMMARIZE Ask children to reflect on and discuss any problems they had in completing a section of the page. Then have them summarize what they have learned about helping verbs and the main idea of a paragraph. **REFLECTION**

ADDITIONAL PRACTICE Extra Practice items are on page 475 of the *Pupil Edition* (*Teacher's Edition* R6).

TECHNOLOGY

Grammar Practice and Assessment CD-ROM

Writing Express CD-ROM

INTERNET Visit *The Learning Site!*
www.harcourtschool.com

Extra Practice

Copy each sentence. Underline the helping verb. Then circle the verb it helps.

1. We <u>have</u> (decided) to recycle.
2. Our teacher <u>had</u> (talked) to us about it.
3. We <u>have</u> (placed) three trash cans in the classroom.

Choose the correct helping verb to finish each sentence.

4. The children (<u>have</u>, has) reused old things.
5. Tim and Laura (<u>have</u>, has) cleaned old cans.
6. They (has, <u>have</u>) used them to hold pencils.
7. Kim (<u>had</u>, have) wanted a box for stickers.
8. She (had, <u>has</u>) made a box from egg cartons.
9. The children (has, <u>have</u>) helped their school.

Write the paragraph. Underline the main idea. Leave out the sentence that does not tell about the main idea.

10. <u>My brother and I had worked in the park last Saturday.</u> We put out seeds for the birds. ~~My mom reads often.~~ We weeded the flower garden.

352

Vocabulary Power page 84

REACHING ALL LEARNERS **ESL**

Name _____

Homophones are words that sound the same, but they have different spellings and different meanings.

read–reed   loan–lone   seam–seem   taught–taut

Draw and label pictures to illustrate the meanings of these homophones.

1. led–lead

2. road–rode

3. write–right

4. grown–groan

84   Unit 5 • Chapter 28   Vocabulary Power

SHARED WRITING Children may write the job chart on page 353 as a shared writing activity. You may refer children to the Word Wall or to page 348 to help them think of jobs. Have children write jobs on separate cards. Place the cards in a paper bag and have each child pick a card. Children work together to record the jobs they picked on chart paper. Then they write their names next to the jobs to make a group list.

Helping Verbs Calendar
- Write *have*, *has*, and *had* on three strips of paper. Place them in a bag.
- Find or draw a calendar showing the past week.
- Take turns with a partner. Pick a helping verb. Use it in a sentence. Tell about one helpful thing you did last week.
- Keep playing until you have each said a sentence for each day of the week.

Sunday	Monday	Tuesday	Wednesday	Thursday	Friday	Saturday

Writing Connection

Functional Writing: Job Chart Make a list of jobs for you and your classmates. Share it with the group. Decide who does each job. Then hang up the job chart.

Job Chart	
wipe board	Joe
water the plants	Tara
pick up trash	Susana
clean hamster cage	Chris

353

Have partners make "Helping Verbs Calendars." Tell them to use their first names instead of the pronoun I. For variety, have them say sentences using both their names or the names of other classmates in some sentences.

Writing Connection

Functional Writing: Job Chart Encourage children to brainstorm ways they may have helped others as well as ways to form the verb phrases. Check to see that children have successfully written a job list by using the criteria below.

CRITERIA
- ☑ Includes an action verb in each item.
- ☑ Capitalizes names correctly.
- ☑ Spells words correctly.

📁 **Portfolio Opportunity** You may want to have children place their writing in the Sharing Basket to share with classmates before they put it in their portfolios.

PRACTICE page 94

REACHING ALL LEARNERS

Name_____

Extra Practice

A. Underline the helping verb in each sentence. Then circle the verb it helps.

1. Jill has worked hard on her painting.
2. She has entered it in the art show.
3. She had won second place in the show last year.
4. Her brother Mark has helped her carry the painting.

B. Write *has* or *have* to make each sentence correct.

5. Mark ___has___ bought two tickets to the show.
6. He ___has___ invited a friend.
7. Today they ___have___ used the tickets.

C. Underline the main idea. Cross out the sentence that does not tell about the main idea.

8. Mark liked the art show. He arrived early. Then he walked around and looked closely at each painting. It was raining outside. Mark liked the colorful paintings best. He also liked the drawings of animals.

94 Unit 5 • Chapter 28   Practice • Helping Verbs

CHALLENGE

REACHING ALL LEARNERS

MATCH UP Have children work in pairs. One child writes six different subjects on separate index cards. The other child writes six verb phrases on separate cards using *has*, *have*, or *had*. Partners try to match subjects and verb phrases and write down sentences. Suggest that they add more words to complete the sentences.

Chapter Review

STANDARDIZED
TEST PREP

OBJECTIVES
• To review helping verbs
• To use appropriate fonts and graphics to publish writing

DAILY LANGUAGE PRACTICE

TRANSPARENCY 55

1 We had movd in april. (moved; April)

2 Mike have visite a big city. (has; visited)

BRIDGE TO WRITING That boy *(form of have + form of finish)* his work.

STANDARDIZED TEST PREP

Read the directions aloud to children. Make sure they understand what they need to do to complete the page. You may wish to have children complete this page independently and use it as an assessment.

TEST PREPARATION TIP
Item Type: Multiple Choice

TIP

Model this strategy to help children determine the correct answer.

I read the first sentence. Then I look to find who is doing the action. I understand that one person, the mayor, is doing the action. So I know that the helping verb in the sentence needs to be *has* or *had* because *has* and *had* tell about one. The answer is *d, correct as is,* because the sentence is the only choice that includes *had* or *has*.

Have children reread the sentence to be sure the answer is correct.

Helping Verbs

Chapter Review

STANDARDIZED
TEST PREP

Choose the best answer for the underlined words.

1. Last month, the mayor <u>had walked</u> in the park.
   a. have walked
   b. hads walked
   c. haves walked
   d. correct as is

2. She saw that children <u>has used</u> a dirty park.
   a. had used
   b. haves used
   c. have used
   d. correct as is

3. She <u>have planned</u> a "Park Clean-Up Day."
   a. haves planned
   b. has planned
   c. hads planned
   d. correct as is

4. My friends <u>has cleaned</u> the playground last year.
   a. had cleaned
   b. haves cleaned
   c. have has cleaned
   d. correct as is

5. This year we <u>have started</u> to work in the park.
   a. haves started
   b. hads started
   c. has started
   d. correct as is

6. The mayor <u>have agreed</u> to help.
   a. has agreed
   b. haves agreed
   c. hads agreed
   d. correct as is

 Visit our website for more activities with helping verbs:
www.harcourtschool.com

354

Language Skills Assessment

PORTFOLIO ASSESSMENT
Have children select their best work from the following activities:

• **Writing Connection**, *pages 347, 349, 353; TE activities, pages 351, 353, and 355.*

ONGOING ASSESSMENT
Evaluate the performance of 4-6 students using appropriate checklists and record forms from pages R65–R68 and R77–R79.

 INTERNET Activities and exercises to help students prepare for state and standardized assessments appear on *The Learning Site:*
www.harcourtschool.com

354 UNIT 5

■ Technology ■

Using Computer Graphics

You can use your computer to add graphics, or pieces of art, to your writing.

- **Use different kinds of type.** Using different kinds of type and different colors makes writing fun to read.

- **Add pictures to a story.** Use pictures from your word processing program, or use a separate drawing program. Add art to your story to make a book.

- **Add frames and borders.**

- **Add charts or graphs to a report.** Use your computer to make charts and graphs. Show them as you share your report with your classmates.

Practice

1. Pick a piece of writing from your Writing Portfolio.

2. Add graphics and publish your writing.

355

■ Technology ■

Using Computer Graphics

Before class, prepare a sample computer-generated page. Use three or four different kinds of type, and highlight important words in color. If possible, also include a frame or border, at least one graphic, and a chart. During class, show your sample page, explaining how each element helps add interest to the writing. For example, color can be used to emphasize information. Large typefaces can set off the most important information or titles.

PRACTICE Compile children's work into a class booklet so that they have a chance to observe the work of others.

WRAP-UP/ASSESS

SUMMARIZE Ask children to tell what they have learned about using the computer to create graphics to add to their writing. Have them create a list of suggestions for improving the look of a written page. Post the list on a classroom bulletin board or wall.

PRACTICE page 95

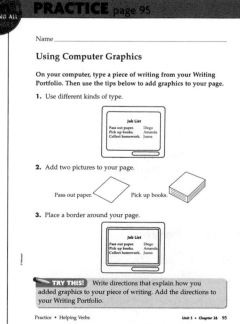

Name _____

Using Computer Graphics

On your computer, type a piece of writing from your Writing Portfolio. Then use the tips below to add graphics to your page.

1. Use different kinds of type.

Job List
Pass out paper.   Diego
Pick up books.   Amanda
Collect homework.   Juana

2. Add two pictures to your page.

Pass out paper.   Pick up books.

3. Place a border around your page.

Job List
Pass out paper.   Diego
Pick up books.   Amanda
Collect homework.   Juana

TRY THIS! Write directions that explain how you added graphics to your piece of writing. Add the directions to your Writing Portfolio.

Practice • Helping Verbs   Unit 5 • Chapter 28   95

CHALLENGE

COMPUTER POSTER Have groups of children make computer-generated posters to advertise a school event or a class assignment. Encourage groups to use various kinds of type, graphics, and frames.

■ Class Trip! ■

When? On January 23

Where? To the zoo!

Come see the animals!

LESSON ORGANIZER	DAY 1	DAY 2
DAILY LANGUAGE PRACTICE TRANSPARENCIES 56, 57	**1.** they has asked a question. (They; have) **2.** The ticher have answered. (teacher has) **Bridge to Writing** Jane (form of *have*) listened to the answer.	**1.** jack laughs happily (Jack; happily.) **2.** Cathy cries saddely (sadly; .) **Bridge to Writing** The class cheers (adverb).
ORAL WARM-UP **Listening/Speaking**	Guess the Adverb p. 356	List and Act Out Adverbs p. 358 *Grammar Jingles*™ CD, Primary, Track 20
TEACH/MODEL **GRAMMAR** **KEY** ✔ = tested skill	✔ **WHAT IS AN ADVERB?** pp. 356-357 • To recognize that an adverb can tell how, when, or where • To use vocabulary to clearly describe feelings	✔ **USING ADVERBS** pp. 358-359 • To recognize and write adverbs that tell how, where, or when • To use adverbs in writing
Reaching All Learners	*Practice Book* p. 96 **Challenge:** Activity Card 20 p. R60 **ESL:** *ESL Manual* pp. 140–141 **Reteach:** *Reteach Activities Copying Masters* p. 58	**Modified Instruction** Below-Level: Identify Adverbs Above-Level: Add Adverbs **Challenge:** New Tales p. 359 **ESL:** How to Identify an Adverb p.358 *ESL Manual* p. 140, p. 142 *Practice Book* p. 97 **Reteach:** *Reteach Activities Copying Masters* p. 59

WRITING	Write Adverbs p. 357
	
	  Summarize/Reflect
		Writing Connection p. 359
		 Lively Adverbs
		  Summarize/Reflect

CROSS-CURRICULAR/ ENRICHMENT	**Vocabulary Power** Word Meaning p. 356 **angrily**, gracefully, hungrily, noisily, playfully See **Vocabulary Power** book.	**Vocabulary Power** Context Clues p. 356 *Vocabulary Power* book p. 85 🏆 **Vocabulary activity**

Visit *The Learning Site!*
www.harcourtschool.com

WRITING ACTIVITIES
Writing Express **CD-ROM**

DAY **3**	DAY **4**	DAY **5**
1. The gently wind blew, (blew gently.) **2.** I raked the leaves kwickly? (quickly.) **Bridge to Writing** There is no rain (adverb).	**1.** Does Rosa sing welle (well?) **2.** she yesterday sang. (She sang yesterday.) **Bridge to Writing** My friend sings (adverb).	**1.** jason reads always books. (Jason always reads) **2.** He go to the library ofen. (goes; often) **Bridge to Writing** The library closes (adverb).
Tell About Holidays Using Adverbs p. 360 *Grammar Jingles*™ CD Track 20	Play a Game p. 362	
✔ **WRITING WITH ADVERBS** pp. 360-361 • To write and refine ideas in sentences using adverbs • To revise a selected piece of writing to include adverbs	**EXTRA PRACTICE** p. 362-363 • To identify adverbs that tell how, when, or where • To express experiences adequately in writing **Practice and Assessment**	**TEST PREP** **CHAPTER REVIEW** p. 364 • To identify and review adverbs • To use the library to find fiction and nonfiction books **Test Preparation**
Modified Instruction Below-Level: Work in Pairs Above-Level: Write Additional Sentences **Challenge:** Magazine Strips p. 361 **ESL:** Play Opposites p. 360 *ESL Manual* p. 140, p. 143 *Practice Book* p. 98 **Reteach:** *Reteach Activities Copying Masters* p. 60	**Challenge:** News Story p. 363 **ESL:** Write Poems p. 362 *ESL Manual* p. 140, p. 144 *Practice Book* p. 99	**Challenge:** Library Trip p. 365 **ESL:** *ESL Manual* p. 140, p. 145 *Practice Book* p. 100
Writing Connection p. 361 Revising	Writing Connection p. 363 News Story	
Vocabulary Power Suffixes p. 356 *Vocabulary Power* book p. 86 **Vocabulary activity**	**Vocabulary Power** Antonyms p. 356 *Vocabulary Power* book p. 87 Language Play p. 363 **Vocabulary activity**	**Study Skills:** p. 365 Using the Library **Vocabulary Power** Onomatopoeia p. 356

What Is an Adverb?

OBJECTIVES

- To recognize that an adverb can tell how, when, or where
- To use vocabulary to clearly describe feelings

DAILY LANGUAGE PRACTICE

TRANSPARENCY 56

1 they has asked a question. (They have)

2 The ticher have answered. (teacher has)

BRIDGE TO WRITING Jane (form of *have*) listened to the answer.

ORAL WARM-UP

USE PRIOR KNOWLEDGE Secretly give volunteers adverbs that describe ways to speak, such as *loudly, softly, angrily, joyfully, quickly.* Tell the volunteers to say their names using the appropriate tone of voice. Other children listen and tell how the volunteer is speaking. Begin a list of adverbs on chart paper, or begin an **Adverb Word Wall**.

TEACH/MODEL

Have children use the illustration and title to predict what the poem will be about. Read the poem aloud to the group, asking children to listen for the words that tell how the characters ask each question. Have volunteers read the poem again, using tones suggested by the adverbs.

DEVELOP ORAL LANGUAGE Ask children to recall the ways the three bears asked their questions (crossly, weepily, angrily). Have children suggest other ways to ask the mama bear's question. List the adverbs on the board. Add new adverbs to the chart paper or the **Word Wall**.

What Is an Adverb?

Read the dialogue.

Who's Been Sleeping in My Porridge?

"Who's been sitting in my bed?"
    said the mama bear crossly.
"Who's been eating my chair?"
    said the baby bear weepily.
"Who's been sleeping in my porridge?"
    said the papa bear angrily.
"Wait a minute," said Goldilocks.

"Why can't you guys just stick
    to the script? Now let's try it
    again and this time, no messing around."

Colin McNaughton

356

Vocabulary Power

DAY 1 WORD MEANING Write: *angrily.* **Find this word in the poem on page 356. What does the word *angrily* mean?** Have volunteers ask the question angrily.

DAY 2 CONTEXT CLUES Write: *The boy shouted and angrily slammed the door.* **What clues help you understand the meaning of *angrily*?** (See also *Vocabulary Power,* page 85.)

DAY 3 SUFFIXES List: *angry, angrily.* **How does adding the ending -ly change the meaning of *angry*?** (See also *Vocabulary Power,* page 86.)

DAY 4 Antonyms Write: *angrily, sweetly.* **Do these two words have the same or opposite meanings?** Ask volunteers to say "I know" angrily and then sweetly. (See also *Vocabulary Power,* page 87.)

DAY 5 ONOMATOPOEIA Have children make a growling sound such as *g-r-r-r.* Ask volunteers to growl angrily . . . hungrily . . . noisily . . . playfully.

Words like *angrily* and *happily* can help describe how someone does something. Think about times you have felt sad, happy, or excited. Show or tell about the different ways you can say something. Then list words that tell the ways you felt.

> An **adverb** describes a verb. It can tell *how*, *when*, or *where* an action takes place.
>
> I sang **joyfully**.
> I **quietly** whispered.

Add a new part to the dialogue. Write what the character says. Write an adverb to tell how the character says it. Then act out your new lines with a partner.
Possible responses are given.

"Who's been ___running in my bed___?"

said the mama bear ___loudly___.

"Who's been ___dancing in my milk___?"

said the baby bear ___softly___.

"Who's been ___reading my cereal___?"

said the papa bear ___angrily___.

357

WRITE As necessary, help children think of ways they have felt by prompting them with hypothetical situations. Invite volunteers to add adverbs to the list on the board or to the **Word Wall**. Then read the definition in the box. Point out the verb in each example. Ask questions such as *How can you sing?* Then have volunteers point out each adverb. Have children read the sentences first without, and then with the adverbs. Ask how the adverbs help make the sentences more specific.

Then read the directions to children. Have children complete the items and then share their work with a partner.

WRAP-UP/ASSESS

SUMMARIZE Reread the poem with children. Have children reflect on the use of adverbs in the poem. Discuss how the adverbs add to the poem. **REFLECTION**

REACHING ALL LEARNERS
RETEACH

INTERVENTION Lessons in **visual**, **auditory**, and **kinesthetic** modalities: p. R36 and *Reteach Activities Copying Masters*, p. 58.

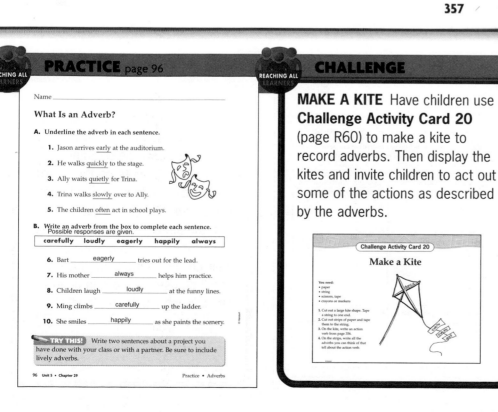

REACHING ALL LEARNERS
PRACTICE page 96

Name _____

What Is an Adverb?

A. Underline the adverb in each sentence.

1. Jason arrives early at the auditorium.
2. He walks quickly to the stage.
3. Ally waits quietly for Trina.
4. Trina walks slowly over to Ally.
5. The children often act in school plays.

B. Write an adverb from the box to complete each sentence.
Possible responses are given.

carefully	loudly	eagerly	happily	always

6. Bart ___eagerly___ tries out for the lead.
7. His mother ___always___ helps him practice.
8. Children laugh ___loudly___ at the funny lines.
9. Ming climbs ___carefully___ up the ladder.
10. She smiles ___happily___ as she paints the scenery.

TRY THIS! Write two sentences about a project you have done with your class or with a partner. Be sure to include lively adverbs.

96 Unit 5 • Chapter 29   Practice • Adverbs

REACHING ALL LEARNERS
CHALLENGE

MAKE A KITE Have children use **Challenge Activity Card 20** (page R60) to make a kite to record adverbs. Then display the kites and invite children to act out some of the actions as described by the adverbs.

Challenge Activity Card 20
Make a Kite

You need:
• paper
• string
• scissors, tape
• crayons or markers

1. Cut out a large kite shape. Tape a string to one end.
2. Cut out strips of paper and tape them to the string.
3. On the kite, write an action verb from page 39a.
4. On the strips, write all the adverbs you can think of that tell about the action verb.

---

page 58

What Is an Adverb?

Read aloud each sentence. Circle each adverb. Underline the verb it describes.

EXAMPLE: Rabbits <u>hop</u> (quickly).

1. Monkeys <u>climb</u> (quietly).
2. Elephants <u>stomp</u> (loudly).
3. Birds <u>chirp</u> (happily).
4. Owls <u>hoot</u> (softly).
5. Lions <u>run</u> (swiftly).

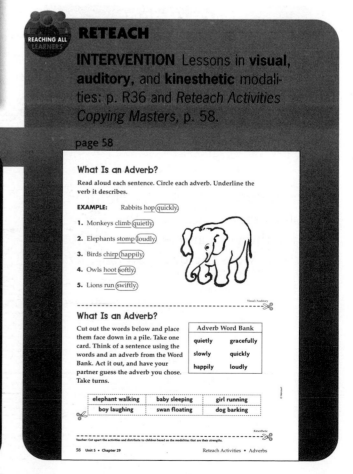

Visual/Auditory

What Is an Adverb?

Cut out the words below and place them face down in a pile. Take one card. Think of a sentence using the words and an adverb from the Word Bank. Act it out, and have your partner guess the adverb you chose. Take turns.

Adverb Word Bank	
quietly	gracefully
slowly	quickly
happily	loudly

elephant walking	baby sleeping	girl running
boy laughing	swan floating	dog barking

Kinesthetic

Teacher: Cut apart the activities and distribute to children based on the modalities that are their strength.

58 Unit 5 • Chapter 29   Reteach Activities • Adverbs

Using Adverbs

OBJECTIVES
• To recognize and write adverbs that tell how, where, or when
• To use adverbs in writing

DAILY LANGUAGE PRACTICE

TRANSPARENCY 56

1 jack laughs happily (Jack; happily.)

2 Cathy cries saddely (sadly.)

BRIDGE TO WRITING The class cheers (adverb) .

ORAL WARM-UP

USE PRIOR KNOWLEDGE Ask *How can you walk?* List responses on the board. Have a volunteer secretly choose one way from the list to act out. The child who correctly guesses chooses and acts out another way.

Grammar Jingles™ **CD, Primary** Use Track 20 for review and reinforcement of adverbs.

TEACH/MODEL

Introduce the concept of adverbs using the explanation and sample sentences in the box on page 358. Then read the headings and examples in the chart. Invite children to replace the adverbs in the sample sentences with examples from the chart and discuss new sentences.

GUIDED PRACTICE Work with children to complete each sentence. Model how to identify the verb and decide whether the adverb answers the question *how, where,* or *when.*

Using Adverbs

Use an adverb to tell *how, when,* or *where* an action takes place.

The child played **quietly**. *how*
She played **inside**. *where*
Her aunt visited **today**. *when*

Here are some more adverbs.

How?	When?	Where?
loudly	always	far
carefully	sometimes	near
proudly	often	inside
softly	soon	outside

Guided Practice

Look at the adverb in each sentence. Write *how, when,* or *where* for each adverb.

1. We want to put on a play <u>soon</u>. when
2. We have to practice <u>often</u>. when
3. We all say our lines <u>loudly</u>. how
4. Our teacher <u>carefully</u> chooses the actors. how
5. We will try on our costumes <u>inside</u>. where

358

Vocabulary Power page 85

Name _____ Context Clues

These words describe ways you can do something.

angrily   gracefully   hungrily   noisily   playfully

Use the context clues to help you understand the meaning of the underlined words. Answer the questions by drawing or writing.

1. The dancers move gracefully. What can you do gracefully?	2. The cat watches the bird hungrily. What do you look at hungrily?
3. The dogs bark noisily. What can you do noisily?	4. The baby gurgles playfully. What can you do playfully?
5. Bees buzz angrily. What else buzzes angrily?	6. The fish swam gracefully. What else moves gracefully?

Vocabulary Power   Unit 5 • Chapter 29   85

REACHING ALL LEARNERS ESL

HOW TO IDENTIFY AN ADVERB Explain to children that many adverbs that tell *how* end in *-ly*. To help children recognize such adverbs, write on the board the words *quick, slow, loud, soft, quiet, sad*. Then hand out cards with the suffix *-ly*. Ask a volunteer to add the suffix to a word of their choice to make an adverb and then use the word in a sentence, such as: "I sing loudly."

Remember An adverb describes a verb and answers the questions *how, when,* or *where.*

Independent Practice

Look at the adverb in each sentence. Write *how, when,* or *where* for each adverb.

6. Carmen waited <u>near</u> the stage. where
7. She <u>slowly</u> walked up to the stage. how
8. Carmen said her lines <u>proudly</u>. how
9. Jenny draws <u>beautifully</u>. how
10. Ms. Brown chose her <u>yesterday</u> to draw scenery. when
11. <u>Today</u> we start practicing. when
12. We practiced <u>inside</u> our classroom. where
13. The first practice went <u>badly</u>. how
14. <u>Sometimes</u> we forgot our lines. when
15. We learned our lines <u>quickly</u>. how

Writing Connection

Lively Adverbs Draw a picture or choose one from an old magazine. Write sentences to tell what is happening. Use a lively adverb in each sentence to describe the action.

Use your computer to help you add adverbs to your sentences.

359

Independent Practice

Have children complete the Independent Practice, or modify it by using the following suggestions:

MODIFIED INSTRUCTION

BELOW-LEVEL STUDENTS Have children identify each adverb and ask themselves the question *Does [adverb] tell when, how, or where?* to complete each item.

ABOVE-LEVEL STUDENTS After children have finished, challenge them to include another adverb that would work in each sentence.

Writing Connection

Lively Adverbs Remind children that adverbs make sentences more interesting. Have volunteers place their sentences and pictures in the Sharing Basket to share with others.

WRAP-UP/ASSESS

SUMMARIZE Encourage children to reflect on how adverbs answer the questions *how, where,* or *when* in a sentence. Have them summarize what they have learned in their journals. **REFLECTION**

RETEACH

INTERVENTION Lessons in **visual, auditory,** and **kinesthetic** modalities: p. R36 and *Reteach Activities Copying Masters,* p. 59.

page 59

Using Adverbs

Read the sentence aloud. Answer each question with an adverb from the sentence.

Today the boy ran outside quickly.

1. How did the boy run? _quickly_
2. When did the boy run? _today_
3. Where did the boy run? _outside_

Using Adverbs

Cut out the adverbs at the bottom of the page. Glue the word that best answers each question. Possible responses are given.

1. How did the girl hold the umbrella? _tightly_
2. When did the woman sing? _often_
3. Where did the boy study? _inside_
4. How did the firefighter work? _bravely_

| tightly | often | bravely | inside |

Reteach Activities • Adverbs   Unit 5 • Chapter 29   59

PRACTICE page 97

Name_____

Using Adverbs

A. Decide whether each adverb from the box tells *how, when,* or *where.* Write it on the chart.

| inside | sometimes | slowly |
| never | above | sadly |

Tells *How*	Tells *When*	Tells *Where*
1. slowly	3. never	5. inside
2. sadly	4. sometimes	6. above

B. Circle the adverb in each sentence. Write whether it tells *how, when,* or *where.*

7. The workbench (downstairs) has many tools. _where_
8. (Yesterday,) my dad and I worked on the set for the play. _when_
9. He used the hammer (carefully.) _how_
10. We (often) build things together. _when_

TRY THIS! Write four sentences to describe something you do when school is out. Be sure to use adverbs that tell *how, when,* and *where.* Draw a picture to go with the sentences.

Practice • Adverbs   Unit 5 • Chapter 29   97

CHALLENGE

NEW TALES Have pairs of children choose two characters from a favorite fairy tale. Tell them to use the format of the poem on page 356 to write lines for each character, including an adverb that tells how the character feels or speaks. Then pairs act out their dialogue for a group.

Writing with Adverbs

OBJECTIVES

- To write and refine ideas in sentences using adverbs
- To revise a selected piece of writing to include adverbs

 DAILY LANGUAGE PRACTICE

TRANSPARENCY 56

❶ The gently wind blew. (blew gently.)

❷ I raked the leaves kwickly? (quickly.)

BRIDGE TO WRITING There is no rain (adverb) .

ORAL WARM-UP

USE PRIOR KNOWLEDGE Talk with children about what they do on their favorite holiday. Have them use both verbal and nonverbal communication to show how, when, and where they do different things.

 Grammar Jingles™ **CD, Primary** Use Track 20 for review and reinforcement of adverbs.

TEACH/MODEL

Introduce the concept by reading aloud the information in the box on page 360. Model the principle for children by saying a simple sentence such as *Casey sings.* Invite children to give more details describing the singing by adding an adverb. Write the new sentences on the board, and have children discuss how the adverbs add to the sentences.

GUIDED PRACTICE Aid children as needed to think of appropriate words to answer the questions for each sentence. Encourage volunteers to share their revised sentences with the group.

Adverbs   **Grammar-Writing Connection**

Writing with Adverbs

> Adverbs always give more details. When you tell *how, when,* or *where,* you give more information to the reader.

Guided Practice

Add an adverb that answers the question in ( ). Write the new sentence.
Possible responses are given.

1. Debbie reads her lines. (How?)
   Debbie reads her lines quickly.
2. Mr. Reed checks the lights. (When?)
   Mr. Reed checks the lights today.
3. Tammy puts on make-up. (How?)
   Tammy puts on make-up carefully.
4. Joey ties the sash on his costume. (How?)
   Joey ties the sash on his costume neatly.
5. Ms. Brown plays her piano. (Where?)
   Ms. Brown plays her piano here.

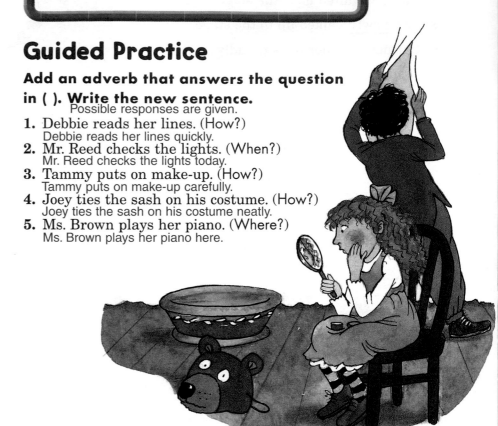

360

Vocabulary Power page 86

Name _____   Suffixes

A suffix is an ending that is added to a base word. Some words have one suffix. Other words have two suffixes.

anger + y = angry   anger + y + ly = angrily
play + ful = playful   play + ful + ly = playfully

1. Add the following suffixes: y y + ly	**2.** Add the following suffixes: ful ful + ly
speed	**grace**
speedy	graceful
speedily	gracefully
noise	**hope**
noisy	hopeful
noisily	hopefully
anger	**rest**
angry	restful
angrily	restfully
hunger	**help**
hungry	helpful
hungrily	helpfully

86 Unit 5 • Chapter 29   Vocabulary Power

REACHING ALL LEARNERS   **ESL**

PLAY OPPOSITES Create word cards with opposite adverbs, such as: *quickly=slowly, sadly=happily, badly=well, loudly=softly, inside=outside, far=near, often=never.* Provide each child with one card. Have children find a partner with a card that has an opposite adverb. Invite pairs to use their adverbs in sentences.

Independent Practice

Add an adverb that answers the question in ( ). Write the new sentence. Possible responses are given.

6. Josh wrote the program. (When?)
Josh wrote the program yesterday.
7. Ms. Brown made copies of the program. (How?)
Ms. Brown made copies of the program happily.
8. Sam passed out the programs. (When?)
Sam passed out the programs today.
9. The teacher moved the scenery. (Where?)
The teacher moved the scenery inside.
10. The actors were waiting. (Where?)
The actors were waiting outside.
11. People came to the theater. (When?)
People came to the theater early.
12. They gave their tickets to Sam. (How?)
They gave their tickets to Sam quickly.
13. The people sat. (How?)
The people sat quietly.
14. The lights went out. (How?)
The lights went out suddenly.
15. The curtain went up. (When?)
The curtain went up soon.

Writing Connection

Revising Look through your Writing Portfolio to find a piece of writing you like. Where can you add more details that tell *how, where,* and *when?* Revise your writing. Use adverbs.

Use your computer to write. Then it's easy to make changes until you are happy with your writing.

361

Independent Practice

Have children complete the Independent Practice, or modify it by using the following suggestions:

MODIFIED INSTRUCTION

BELOW-LEVEL STUDENTS Have children work in pairs to read each sentence and question and think of possible answers. Children may refer to the chart on top of page 358 or to the **Word Wall** to help them think of appropriate adverbs.

ABOVE-LEVEL STUDENTS After children have finished, have them write other sentences that use an adverb to answer a question not originally asked.

Writing Connection

Revising Help children select appropriate pieces of writing to revise. Have them look for images that they can make more vivid by adding adverbs.

WRAP-UP/ASSESS

SUMMARIZE Have children summarize what they know about adverbs. Be sure they discuss the idea that adverbs give more information to the reader and add details to their sentences. **REFLECTION**

RETEACH

INTERVENTION Lessons in **visual, auditory,** and **kinesthetic** modalities: p. R36 and *Reteach Activities Copying Masters,* p. 60.

page 60

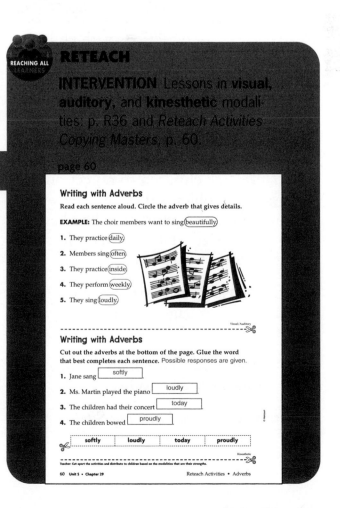

Writing with Adverbs

Read each sentence aloud. Circle the adverb that gives details.

EXAMPLE: The choir members want to sing (beautifully)

1. They practice (daily)
2. Members sing (often)
3. They practice (inside)
4. They perform (weekly)
5. They sing (loudly)

Writing with Adverbs

Cut out the adverbs at the bottom of the page. Glue the word that best completes each sentence. Possible responses are given.

1. Jane sang [softly]
2. Ms. Martin played the piano [loudly]
3. The children had their concert [today]
4. The children bowed [proudly]

| softly | loudly | today | proudly |

60 Unit 5 • Chapter 29   Reteach Activities • Adverbs

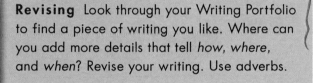

PRACTICE page 98

Name _____

Writing with Adverbs

A. Circle the adverb that answers the question.

1. How? The lights shone (brightly) here).
2. Where? Lisa stood (near) proudly) the stage.
3. How? She cleared her throat (softly) today).
4. When? Lisa (often) quickly) gets shy in front of people.
5. When? The feeling (slowly, (soon) goes away.

B. Add an adverb that answers the question in ( ). Write the new sentence. Possible responses are given.

6. Then Lisa walked onstage. (How?)
Then Lisa walked onstage calmly.
7. Everyone was quiet. (Where?)
Everyone was quiet there.
8. She said her lines. (How?)
She said her lines clearly.

TRY THIS! Change your sentences from Part B. Write new sentences using different adverbs. Think of adverbs that mean the opposite of the adverb you choose.

98 Unit 5 • Chapter 29   Practice • Adverbs

CHALLENGE

MAGAZINE STRIPS Point out that writers for magazines often use adverbs in their sentences. Have children look through old magazines and cut out sentences that include adverbs. Then have the class sort the sentences into three groups: *how, where, when,* based on the question each adverb answers. Children can add the adverbs they found to the **Word Wall**.

Extra Practice

OBJECTIVES

- To identify adverbs that tell how, when, or where
- To express experiences adequately in writing

SPIRAL REVIEW

DAILY LANGUAGE PRACTICE

TRANSPARENCY 57

❶ Does Rosa sing welle (well?)

❷ she yesterday sang. (She sang yesterday.)

BRIDGE TO WRITING My friend sings <u>(adverb)</u>.

ORAL WARM-UP

PLAY A GAME Invite children to play a game in which they act out the action in a sentence you say only if the sentence includes an adverb. Use sentences such as "Walk slowly" or "Dance around the room." Try to work a Vocabulary Power word into your sentences.

TEACH/MODEL

Read each set of directions with children. Be sure they understand how to complete each section. When they finish, invite children to share and discuss their answers in groups.

WRAP-UP/ASSESS

SUMMARIZE Ask children to reflect on and discuss any problems they may have had in completing the practice. Then have them summarize what they have learned about adverbs. **REFLECTION**

ADDITIONAL PRACTICE Extra practice items are provided on page 475 of the *Pupil Edition (Teacher's Edition* R6).

 TECHNOLOGY *Grammar Practice and Assessment* CD-ROM

INTERNET Visit *The Learning Site!* www.harcourtschool.com

Extra Practice

Underline the adverb in each sentence.

1. The principal <u>warmly</u> welcomed the people.
2. The music started <u>softly</u>.
3. Each actor spoke <u>loudly</u>.
4. Children moved the scenery <u>quietly</u>.

Look at the adverb in each sentence. Write *how*, *when*, or *where* for each adverb.

5. The people laughed <u>happily</u> at the funny parts. how
6. They listened <u>quietly</u> at the sad parts. how
7. Sam helped with costumes <u>behind</u> the curtain. where
8. <u>Soon</u> Ms. Brown played the music. when

Add an adverb to each sentence to give more details. Possible responses are given.

9. The children were smiling.
   The children were smiling happily.
10. Everyone was clapping.
    Everyone was clapping loudly.

362

Vocabulary Power   page 87

Name _____   Antonyms

Antonyms are words that have opposite meanings.

   give–take   sink–float   empty–full

Write an antonym for each word. Use the words in the box.

noisy	slow	playful	polite
graceful	unsteady	noisily	slowly
playfully	politely	gracefully	unsteadily

1. clumsy – graceful   clumsily – gracefully
2. quiet – noisy   quietly – noisily
3. serious – playful   seriously – playfully
4. swift – slow   swiftly – slowly
5. steady – unsteady   steadily – unsteadily
6. rude – polite   rudely – politely

Choose two pairs of antonyms. Draw and label pictures to show the opposite meanings.

Vocabulary Power   Unit 5 • Chapter 29   87

REACHING ALL LEARNERS   **ESL**

WRITE POEMS Have small groups of children use adverbs that end in *-ly* to make up short poems about what they do. Invite children to illustrate and share their poems.

> I walk slowly,
> but I run quickly.
> I dance badly,
> but I sing beautifully.

Language Play

Adverb Challenge

- Take turns with a partner. Roll a number cube.
- Choose an adverb from the correct column. Use it in a sentence. You get one point if you use the adverb correctly.
- The first player with 5 points wins.

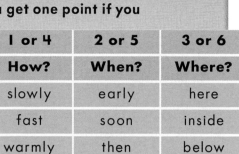

I or 4	2 or 5	3 or 6
How?	**When?**	**Where?**
slowly	early	here
fast	soon	inside
warmly	then	below
loudly	now	far
clearly	next	down

Writing Connection

News Story A news story tells about something that really happened. It answers the questions *who, what, when, where, why,* and *how.* Write a short news story about something you saw. Use adverbs. Use this news story as a model.

Heavy Rain Falls in River City

Yesterday the rain began suddenly. People ran quickly to find shelter. The storm moved through fast. Soon the sun shone brightly in the sky again.

363

Language Play

Have children play "Adverb Challenge" in pairs. Model how to roll and read a number cube, choose a correct adverb, and use it in a sentence. Have partners evaluate their sentences based on what they have learned about adverbs.

Writing Connection

News Story Have children identify the most effective features of their news story by using the criteria below.

CRITERIA

- ☑ Answers the questions *who, what, where, when, why,* and *how.*
- ☑ Tells about something that happened.
- ☑ Uses at least two adverbs in the story.
- ☑ Begins each sentence with a capital letter.

📁 **PORTFOLIO OPPORTUNITY** You may want to have children place their writing in their portfolios or take it home to share with family members.

PRACTICE page 99

REACHING ALL LEARNERS

Name _____

Extra Practice

A. Circle the adverb in each sentence.
1. The rest of the play went (smoothly.)
2. The students perform (well.)
3. They feel proud of themselves (today.)

B. Write the adverb in each sentence. Then write *how, when,* or *where* for each adverb.
4. Soon the show was over.   Soon; when
5. The actors changed out of the costumes quickly.   quickly; how
6. Then they went outside to see their families.   outside; where

C. Add an adverb to each sentence to give more details. Write the new sentence.
Possible responses are given.
7. Lisa's grandmother was waiting.

   Lisa's grandmother was waiting inside.

8. Her grandmother hugged her.

   Her grandmother hugged her proudly.

Practice • Adverbs   Unit 5 • Chapter 29   99

CHALLENGE

REACHING ALL LEARNERS

NEWS STORY Provide children with a short, simple article from a newspaper. Tell children that good news articles answer the questions *who, what, where, when, why,* and *how.* Ask children to locate the answers to these questions in the article and to record them in a chart, using adverbs.

Who?	Diego Manuel
What?	ran well
Where?	in the park
When?	yesterday
Why?	to win a race
How?	He ran quickly.

Chapter Review

OBJECTIVES

- To identify and review adverbs
- To use the library to find fiction and nonfiction books

DAILY LANGUAGE PRACTICE

TRANSPARENCY 57

1 jason reads always books. (Jason always reads)

2 He go to the library ofen. (goes; often)

BRIDGE TO WRITING The library closes (adverb).

STANDARDIZED TEST PREP

Read the directions on page 364 with children to make sure they understand how to complete the exercises. You may wish to have children complete this page independently and use it as an assessment.

TEST PREPARATION TIP

Item Type: Multiple Choice

TIP

Model this strategy to help children use their time wisely:

I look at all the questions and their answer choices. I answer the questions I think are easy first. I skip the questions that seem difficult. I will have time to go back and look at them again. When I do, I read the sentence three times, putting each choice in the blank space. I choose the answer that makes the most sense to complete the sentence.

Adverbs

Chapter Review

Choose the best answer to finish each sentence.

1. Ms. Brown praised the class _____.
   a. warm
   b. warmly
   c. under

2. The children had worked _____.
   a. hard
   b. difficult
   c. ever

3. They want to start another play _____.
   a. coldly
   b. above
   c. soon

4. They finish their schoolwork _____.
   a. far
   b. quickly
   c. around

5. The children are _____ reading plays.
   a. eagerly
   b. near
   c. last

6. They hope to choose a new play _____.
   a. tomorrow
   b. near
   c. last

Visit our website for more activities with adverbs:

www.harcourtschool.com

364

Language Skills Assessment

• •

PORTFOLIO ASSESSMENT
Have children select their best work from the following activities:

- **Writing Connection,** *pages 359, 361, and 363*; TE activities, *pages 357, 359, 361, and 363.*

ONGOING ASSESSMENT
Evaluate the performance of 4-6 students using appropriate checklists and record forms from pages R65–R68 and R77–R79.

INTERNET Activities and exercises to help students prepare for state and standardized assessments appear on *The Learning Site:*

www.harcourtschool.com

■ Study Skills ■

Using the Library

The library puts books in a special order. It also puts fiction books and nonfiction books in separate places.

- **Fiction books** are made-up stories. They are in ABC order by the author's last name.
- **Nonfiction books** are about things that are real. They are put in order by topic and then by their special numbers.

 You can use a computer to help you find books in a library.

Practice

In which part of the library would you find each book? Write *fiction* or *nonfiction*.

fiction

nonfiction

1. 582 *Endangered Plants* by Jeff Sanders
   nonfiction
2. *Digger Dog* by Tom McNeal
   fiction
3. 419 *The Handtalk School* by Mary Beth Miller
   nonfiction
4. *Swimmy* by Leo Lionni
   fiction

Look at the books in items 1- 4.

5. Write the fiction book titles in ABC order.
   Swimmy by Leo Lionni, Digger Dog by Tom McNeal
6. Write the nonfiction book titles in order.
   419 The Handtalk School, 582 Endangered Plants

365

■ Study Skills ■

Using the Library

TEACH/MODEL

Read aloud the information about library books. Point out where the information is located on the spine of each book. Tell children that authors' last names are used to order fiction books and that nonfiction books are ordered by numbers assigned to them according to their topics. If possible, share with children actual books from your school library as well.

PRACTICE When children have finished, have them share their answers with classmates.

WRAP-UP/ASSESS

SUMMARIZE Ask children to tell what they know about organizing books in a library. Be sure they understand that fiction titles are arranged alphabetically by author's last name, and that nonfiction titles are arranged by number.

PRACTICE page 100

Name _____

Using the Library

A. Write *fiction* or *nonfiction* to tell where you would find each book in the library.

1. *The Stories Huey Tells*
   by Ann Cameron — fiction

2. *510 Math Puzzles for Your Brain*
   by Tom Harris — nonfiction

3. *Cloudy with a Chance of Meatballs*
   by Judi Barrett — fiction

4. *590 Spooky Spiders*
   by Jackie Thiel — nonfiction

5. *570 Evergreen Trees*
   by Robert Sherman — nonfiction

6. *Frog and Toad Are Friends*
   by Arnold Lobel — fiction

B. Look at the books in items 1–6.

7. Write the fiction book titles in ABC order by the author's last name. *Cloudy with a Chance of Meatballs, The Stories Huey Tells, and Frog and Toad Are Friends*

100 Unit 5 • Chapter 29   Practice • Adverbs

CHALLENGE

LIBRARY TRIP Set up a time when children can go to the school library or to a library branch. Have children write two nonfiction titles and their numbers as well as the names of the authors of two fiction titles. Then have children swap lists with a partner and locate the books on the library shelves.

Writing a How-to Paragraph
pages 366–383

LESSON ORGANIZER	DAY **1**	DAY **2**
DAILY LANGUAGE PRACTICE *TRANSPARENCY 58*	1. I seen Andy this morning? (saw; morning.) 2. He just comed back from Orlando Florida. (came; Orlando, Florida)	1. Have he done his homework. (Has; homework?) 2. Please comes to a party on April 12 2001. (come; April 12, 2001)
ORAL WARM-UP Listening/Speaking	Talk About Following Steps p. 366	Talk About Following Steps p. 376
TEACH/MODEL WRITING	**Literature Model:** "Jalapeño Bagels," pp. 366–372 • To read and respond to a how-to paragraph as a model for writing • To identify the steps in how-to writing **Reading-Writing Connection:** Parts of a How-to Paragraph p. 373 **A Student Model** pp. 374–375	**GUIDED WRITING** ✔ **Prewriting** pp. 376–377 • To brainstorm and select a writing topic • To use a flowchart to plan a how-to paragraph **Transparency** 59
Reaching All Learners	**Options for Reading** p. 367 **ESL:** *ESL Manual* pp. 146–147 Pantomime Action Verbs p. 370	**ESL:** *ESL Manual* p. 146 **Interactive Writing** p. 377
GRAMMAR	**Unit 5 Review** pp. 384–385	**Unit 5 Review** pp. 384–385
CROSS-CURRICULAR/ ENRICHMENT	**Health Connection:** Food Pyramid p. 368 **Math Connection:** Measuring Up p. 370 **School-Home Connection:** Family Recipes p. 371 **Vocabulary Power** international, interact, intercom, interleaf, internet. See *Vocabulary Power* book.	**Writer's Craft:** Time-Order Words p. 377 **Vocabulary Power** Context Clues p. 366 *Vocabulary Power* book, p. 88 🏆 **Vocabulary activity**

KEY
✔ = tested writing form/skill

DAY 3

1. Walk quick to the door? (quickly; door.)
2. please speak loud. (Please; loudly *or* louder)

Describe a Process p. 378

GUIDED WRITING
✔ **Drafting** pp. 378–379
  • To draft a how-to paragraph that lists the topic and materials needed
  • To write steps for completing a task

 Transparency 60

ESL: *ESL Manual* p. 146
Interactive Writing p. 379

Unit 5 Review pp. 384–385

Vocabulary Power

Prefixes p. 366
Vocabulary Power book, p. 89

DAY 4

1. Where did that dog goed (go?)
2. he always run away. (He; runs)

Review Elements of a How-to Paragraph p. 380

GUIDED WRITING
✔ **Revising and Proofreading** pp. 380–381
  • To revise a how-to paragraph
  • To proofread writing for capitalization, punctuation, grammar, and spelling
  • To use Editor's Marks to make revisions and corrections

 Transparencies 60, 60a, 60b

ESL: *ESL Manual* p. 146

Unit 5 Review pp. 384–385

Spelling Connection: Spelling Strategies p. 381

Vocabulary Power

Clipped Words p. 366
Vocabulary Power book, p. 90

🎙 **Vocabulary activity**

DAY 5

1. Your skate runned over my toe? (ran; toe!)
2. Who gived you those skates. (gave; skates?)

Review Formats for How-to Writing p. 382

GUIDED WRITING
✔ **Publishing** p. 382
  • To make final copies of revised how-to paragraphs
  • To share how-to writing with others
  Handwriting p. 383
  Scoring Rubric p. 382

ESL: *ESL Manual* p. 146

Unit 5 Review pp. 384–385

LISTENING AND SPEAKING:
  Giving and Following Directions p. 383

Vocabulary Power

Jargon p. 366

Writing a How-to Paragraph

Read the Literature

OBJECTIVES
- To read and respond to a how-to paragraph as a model for writing
- To identify the steps in how-to writing

DAILY LANGUAGE PRACTICE

TRANSPARENCY 58

1 I seen Andy this morning? (saw, morning.)

2 He just comed back from Orlando Florida. (came; Orlando, Florida)

ORAL WARM-UP

USE PRIOR KNOWLEDGE Tell children that they will read a how-to selection to prepare for their own writing.

Read the introductory statement on page 366 with children. Invite them to tell about times they have heard or read steps to follow in order to do or make something.

PREREADING STRATEGIES

VOCABULARY Have children read the title of the story. Ask if they have ever tasted jalapeño peppers or bagels. Ask volunteers to describe each food. Lead children to understand that jalapeño peppers are hot and spicy, and that a bagel is a kind of bread.

PREVIEW/SET PURPOSE Have children preview the pictures in the selection. Discuss their predictions based on the pictures, title, and the discussion you have had.

How can you tell someone how to do something? One way is to explain the steps. Pablo helps to make different kinds of bread in this story. Find out the steps he follows.

from # Jalapeño Bagels

by Natasha Wing   illustrated by Robert Casilla

"What should I bring to school on Monday for International Day?" I ask my mother. "My teacher told us to bring something from our culture."

366

Vocabulary Power

DAY 1 WORD MEANING Point out the words *International Day* on page 366. Use the story context to define *international*. (relating to different nations, countries, cultures) Ask children to name countries they know about.

DAY 2 CONTEXT CLUES Write: *Everyone in the world likes to dance. Dancing is* _international_. **What clues help you understand the meaning of** _international_**?** (See also *Vocabulary Power*, page 88.)

DAY 3 PREFIXES Write: *Each country has one* _national_ *anthem, but singing is* _international_. Help children understand that *national* refers to one country, and *international* refers to many different countries. (See also *Vocabulary Power*, page 89.)

DAY 4 CLIPPED WORDS Write: _intercommunication_. **How is the word** _inter-com_ **like an** _abbreviation_**?** (See also *Vocabulary Power*, page 90.)

DAY 5 JARGON Write: The _Internet_ _is_ _international_. With children, brainstorm a list of words that relate to communicating by computer.

"You can bring a treat from the *panaderia*," she suggests. Panaderia is what Mama calls our bakery. "Help us bake on Sunday—then you can pick out whatever you want."

"It's a deal," I tell her. I like helping at the bakery. It's warm there, and everything smells so good.

Early Sunday morning, when it is still dark, my mother wakes me up.

"Pablo, it's time to go to work," she says.

We walk down the street to the bakery. My father turns on the lights. My mother turns on the ovens. She gets out the pans and ingredients for *pan dulce*. Pan dulce is Mexican sweet bread.

I help my mother mix and knead the dough. She shapes rolls and loaves of bread and slides them into the oven. People tell her she makes the best pan dulce in town.

"Maybe I'll bring pan dulce to school," I tell her.

367

OPTIONS FOR READING

DIRECTED READING Use the questions to guide reading and discussion.

PARTNER READING Partners can whisper-read the story together.

INDEPENDENT READING Have children read the story silently. After reading, small groups can share reactions to the story.

READING LIKE A WRITER

Pages 366–367 Tell children that they may often learn how to do or make something by reading a story. Have them examine the pictures and make predictions about what they might learn as they read the story.

1. **What kind of work do Pablo's parents do?** (They work in their own panaderia, or bakery.) **INFERENTIAL: IMPORTANT DETAILS**

2. **What are the first steps in making *pan dulce*?** (First you mix and knead the dough.) **INFERENTIAL: SEQUENCE**

3. **Would *pan dulce* be a good choice for Pablo to take to school?** (Possible response: Yes, because it is an international food.) **CRITICAL: MAKE JUDGMENTS**

SELECTION SUMMARY

FICTION: STORY Pablo must choose something to bring to school for International Day— something that represents his culture. He helps his parents in the family bakery as they make jalapeño bagels, which represent a mix of his Jewish and Mexican heritage.

ABOUT THE AUTHOR

Natasha Wing says that her writing is influenced by her surroundings, and in fact, this story is based on a real bakery in her community in California. Wing is writing another book about holidays celebrated by the multi-cultural family introduced in *Jalapeño Bagels*. Some of her other books include *The Night Before Halloween* and *Hippity Hop, Frog on Top*.

READING LIKE A WRITER

Pages 368–369 Have children examine the pictures and discuss what Pablo and his father are making. Then have them read the text to confirm their predictions.

1. **Where did Pablo probably learn the Yiddish words he knows?** (Possible response: from his father or other family members) **CRITICAL: SPECULATE**

2. **How is cooking bagels different from making most other baked items?** (Most baked items are only baked, but bagels are boiled first and then baked.) **INFERENTIAL: COMPARE AND CONTRAST**

3. **Why is Pablo probably thinking of bringing bagels to school for International Day?** (Bagels represent his father's culture.) **INFERENTIAL: DRAW CONCLUSIONS**

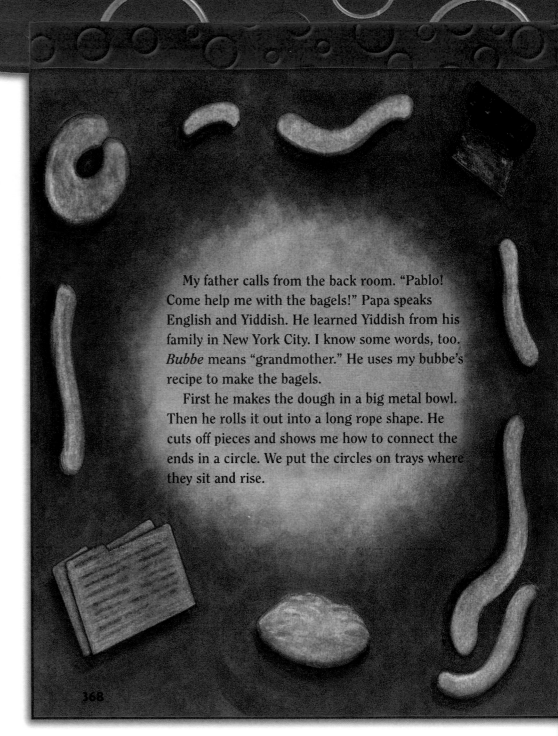

My father calls from the back room. "Pablo! Come help me with the bagels!" Papa speaks English and Yiddish. He learned Yiddish from his family in New York City. I know some words, too. *Bubbe* means "grandmother." He uses my bubbe's recipe to make the bagels.

First he makes the dough in a big metal bowl. Then he rolls it out into a long rope shape. He cuts off pieces and shows me how to connect the ends in a circle. We put the circles on trays where they sit and rise.

368

Health Connection

FOOD PYRAMID Explain to children that most bakery items are in the bread, grains, and cereal food group. Display a food pyramid and point out the number of grain servings that should be consumed each day. Have children keep a log for one day, noting the number of servings they eat in each food group.

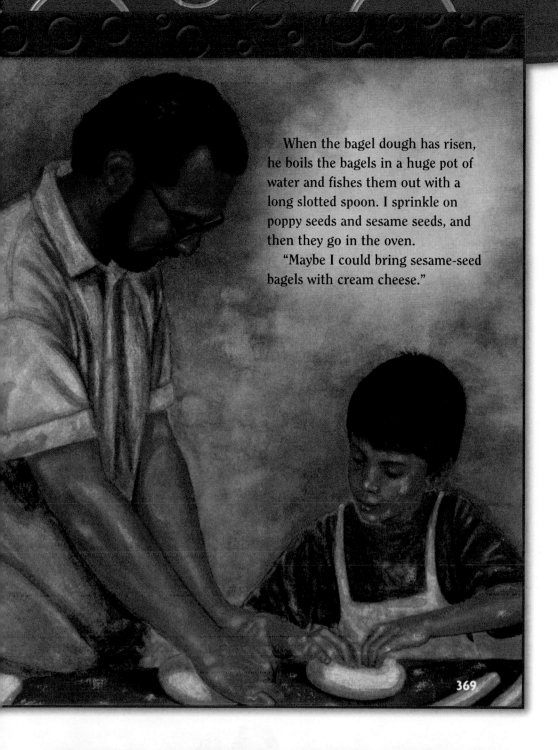

When the bagel dough has risen, he boils the bagels in a huge pot of water and fishes them out with a long slotted spoon. I sprinkle on poppy seeds and sesame seeds, and then they go in the oven.

"Maybe I could bring sesame-seed bagels with cream cheese."

369

Strategies Good Readers Use

SEQUENCE EVENTS Discuss why the sequence, or order, of events is especially important in "Jalapeño Bagels." Elicit the following: Much of the story tells about how bagels are made. Understanding the order of the steps is an important part of understanding the order of the entire story. Ask volunteers to review the steps described on pages 368 and 369.

Pages 370–371 Have children look over the pictures and discuss what they think Pablo will choose to bring for International Day.

1. **How does Pablo's family work as a team to make the jalapeño bagels?**
(Pablo and his father make, shape, and cook the dough for the first batch. Then Mama chops the chiles while Papa makes the dough for the next batch. Together they cut and shape the dough.) **INFERENTIAL: SUMMARIZE**

2. **What would you choose to take to school from the bakery? Explain.**
(Answers will vary.) **CRITICAL: EXPRESS PERSONAL OPINIONS**

My mother joins us and helps my father make another batch of bagels—*jalapeño* bagels. My parents use their own special recipe. While Papa kneads the dough, Mama chops the jalapeño *chiles*. She tosses them into the dough and adds dried red peppers. We roll, cut, make circles, and let them rise. I can't wait until they are done because I am getting hungry.

370

Math Connection

• • • • • • • • • • • • • • •

MEASURING UP Select a simple recipe for children to follow that requires measurement. Review common cooking measurements such as *cup, teaspoon,* and *table-spoon*. Have children talk about how they would measure the ingredients if they were to double the recipe.

ESL

REACHING ALL LEARNERS

PANTOMIME ACTION VERBS
On the board, list each of the verbs in the steps given for making bagels. Have a volunteer act out each verb in order and give the group an opportunity to follow the leader. Then repeat the action words in random order and have children quickly mime the action.

"Have you decided what you're going to bring to
school?" asks Mama.

"It's hard to choose. Everything is so good," I tell her.

"You should decide before we open," warns Mama, "or
else our customers will buy everything up."

I walk past all the sweet breads and bagels.

I think about my mother and my father and all the
different things they make in the bakery.

371

School-Home Connection

· ·

FAMILY RECIPES Have children
discuss with family members
something that represents their
culture. They can bring in an
object, draw a picture of it, or
write about it, including an explanation of why it is their
choice.

Page 372 Ask children to predict how the story will end. Then have them read to check their predictions.

1. In what way is Pablo like the jalapeño bagels? (Both Pablo and the bagels are a mix of his mother and father.)
INFERENTIAL: COMPARE AND CONTRAST

Think About It

Ask volunteers to retell the steps in making bagels.

1. Children tell their opinions of Pablo's choice. Possible response: It was a good one because jalapeño bagels show different parts of his culture. **CRITICAL:** EXPRESS PERSONAL OPINIONS
2. Possible response: I didn't know you had to boil bagels. **CRITICAL:** MAKE JUDGMENTS

Suddenly I know exactly what I'm going to bring.
"Jalapeño bagels," I tell my parents. "I'll spread them with cream cheese and jam."
"Why jalapeño bagels?" asks Papa.
"Because they are a mixture of both of you. Just like me!"

Think About It

1. What do you think of Pablo's choice for what to bring for International Day?

2. What was the most surprising thing you learned about making bagels?

372

Response to Literature

WRITING PROMPT You may want to have children write in response to "Jalapeño Bagels." Use the following writing prompt, or another you choose. Before you begin, review that a news story answers the questions *who, what, where, when, why, and how.*

Imagine that you go to Pablo's school. It's the day after International Day. You are a writer for the school newspaper. Write a news story about Pablo and his jalapeño bagels.

Informal Assessment You can use children's writing to assess informally their understanding of the story and their ability to write a cohesive piece. Note areas where children might benefit from instruction in writing and grammar.

Parts of a How-to Paragraph

In a **how-to paragraph**, a writer gives steps to tell how to make or do something.

- The first sentence tells what the paragraph will explain how to do.
- The second sentence tells all the things you need.
- The **steps** are written in the order they should be done. Time-order words make their order clear.

Reread this how-to paragraph from the story. Then, on a sheet of paper, complete the flowchart.

First he makes the dough in a big metal bowl. Then he rolls it out into a long rope shape. He cuts off pieces and shows me how to connect the ends in a circle. We put the circles on trays where they sit and rise.

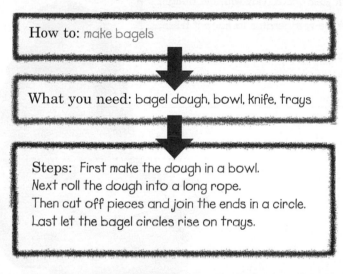

How to: make bagels

What you need: bagel dough, bowl, knife, trays

Steps: First make the dough in a bowl.
Next roll the dough into a long rope.
Then cut off pieces and join the ends in a circle.
Last let the bagel circles rise on trays.

373

Parts of a How-to Paragraph

ANALYZE THE LITERATURE Discuss the elements of a how-to paragraph. Explain that a good how-to paragraph tells what the topic is, what materials are needed, and what the steps are in order.

Model how to complete the flowchart by working through the first few steps with children. Then discuss the steps described in the text on page 369, eliciting children's ideas on where the steps should be listed on the flowchart. Have children complete the remaining boxes of the flowchart for making bagels.

WRAP-UP/ASSESS

Invite children to share their flowcharts. Have them tell the steps for making bagels, using words such as *first*, *next*, and *last*.

Informal Assessment

You can informally assess children's **comprehension** of the story and their knowledge of the **structure of a how-to paragraph** by encouraging them to retell the events of "Jalapeño Bagels" or, more specifically, how to make bagels.

A Student Model

READ AND RESPOND TO THE MODEL Tell children that you will read Maria's how-to paragraph aloud, and have them identify their purpose for listening. (to be informed) Then read the how-to aloud, and discuss whether Maria does a good job of writing a paragraph that teaches how to do something. Ask children to point out parts of the story that they found surprising. Tell children that they can use this published student piece as a model for their own writing.

FOCUS ON ORGANIZATION Have children reread the paragraph to themselves, using the sidenotes to identify the main parts of the how-to. Then ask volunteers to identify and tell something about each part in their own words. Point out that how-to paragraphs that tell how to make something nearly always include materials and steps to follow.

FOCUS ON WRITER'S CRAFT Have children find and read aloud the exact words that Maria uses to make her directions clear. (The directions tell to use two cups of flour and two cups of salt. The word *next* tells when to add the salt and flour. When everything is in the bowl, you mix it together with your hands.)

A Student Model

Maria enjoyed learning how to make bagels. She thought of something she could teach her classmates to make. Read her how-to paragraph, and see how she put the important parts in order.

How to Make Fun Dough

You can make your own fun dough. You need two cups of salt, two cups of warm water, two cups of flour, a bowl, and food coloring. First put the water in the bowl and add a little food coloring. Next put the salt and flour slowly into the bowl. Then mix the dough with your hands. Play with the dough, or put it in the refrigerator to keep it fresh.

The **title** tells what the paragraph will help the reader make.

The **materials** are what you need to do the activity.

The **steps** tell what to do in the correct order.

374

LISTENING AND SPEAKING

GENERATE QUESTIONS Have small groups compare "Jalapeño Bagels" and Maria's how-to. Write a list of questions for discussion, such as these:
- What are some steps that you follow in both how-tos?
- What ingredients are used to make both bagels and play dough?

Instruct children to ask other questions they have and to make contributions within their groups.

EVALUATION CRITERIA

ESTABLISH CRITERIA FOR WRITING Have children locate the rubric for a how-to paragraph in their handbooks on page 486. Explain that if their how-tos reflect all of the items on the list, this shows that they have done their best work. Have children talk about each item and identify and generate others. Remind children to refer to this rubric as they write. (See also pages 382 and R75 in this Teacher's Edition.)

Looking at the Model

1. What is Maria's paragraph about?
2. What do you need to make fun dough?
3. What is the first step?
4. What is the second step?
5. What do you do after everything is in the bowl?

Writer's Craft

Using Exact Words

Maria made sure her how-to paragraph was easy to understand. She used exact words to show how and when to do all the steps. Find the parts of Maria's paragraph that have exact words.

- How much salt and flour do you need? How do you know?
- How do you know when to add flour and salt?
- When do you mix everything together? What do you use to mix the dough?

375

Looking at the Model

1. **What is Maria's paragraph about?** (how to make fun dough)
2. **What do you need to make fun dough?** (salt, water, flour, a bowl, and food coloring)
3. **What is the first step?** (Put the water and a little food coloring in the bowl.)
4. **What is the second step?** (Put the salt and flour into the bowl.)
5. **What do you do after everything is in the bowl?** (Mix it by hand.)

SELF-INITIATED WRITING Have children choose a way to respond to the models they just read, which may include self-initiated writing or another method such as art. Children may choose to generate their own ideas for writing by using techniques such as listing key thoughts.

WRAP-UP/ASSESS

Invite children to share their flowchart from page 373. Have them tell one of the most interesting or surprising things they read in "Jalapeño Bagels" and in Maria's paragraph, explaining their choice.

TAKE-HOME BOOK 5 provides additional models of how-to paragraphs and home activities. See *Practice Book* pages 129–130.

Prewriting

OBJECTIVES
- To brainstorm and select a writing topic
- To use a flowchart to plan a how-to paragraph

DAILY LANGUAGE PRACTICE

TRANSPARENCY 58

1. Have he done his homework. (Has; homework?)
2. Please comes to a party on April 12 2001. (come; April 12, 2001.)

ORAL WARM-UP

USE PRIOR KNOWLEDGE Have children discuss some of the things they have learned to do by watching, listening, or reading about the steps to follow. List their ideas on the board.

GUIDED WRITING

TALK ABOUT A FLOWCHART Explain to children that a flowchart is a helpful way to organize information for writing a how-to paragraph. Have children talk about what Maria did in the prewriting stage. Discuss the following questions.

1. **What did Maria probably do before she wrote anything on her paper?** (She thought about who would read her writing and what topic might interest them.)

2. **How did making a flowchart probably help Maria before she began to write her paragraph?** (It helped her think about all the steps and the order in which she would write about them.)

Use Transparency 59 for an additional way to model the prewriting stage.

Prewriting

Before Maria wrote her how-to paragraph, she planned it. She knew it was important to list all the materials and steps. She used a flowchart to plan her paragraph and put her ideas in order.

> **How to:** make fun dough
>
> ⬇
>
> **What you need:** two cups of salt, two cups of warm water, two cups of flour, a bowl, food coloring
>
> ⬇
>
> **Steps:** First put the water in the bowl. Add food coloring.
> Next put the salt and flour into the bowl.
> Then mix the dough with your hands.
> Last play with the dough, or put it in the refrigerator to keep it fresh.

376

TRANSPARENCY 59

PREWRITING:
HOW-TO PARAGRAPH

How to:

What you need:

Steps:

Harcourt Language
Grade 1   59   PREWRITING: How-to Paragraph   Chapter 30

Vocabulary Power page 88

Name _____

Read the following words. Circle the words you know.

interact   intercom   interleaf   international   Internet

For boxes 1–5, use context clues to figure out the meaning of the underlined word. Draw or write to answer the question. For box 6, answer the question.

1. When people interact, they communicate. What are some ways in which people interact?	2. I use my computer to find things on the Internet. What do you know about the Internet?
3. Everyone in the world sings. Singing is international. What other things are international?	4. This book has an interleaf at the end. It is blank on the front and back. What is an interleaf?
5. The principal talked to us over the intercom. What is an intercom? Does your classroom have one?	6. Look at the words you circled at the top of the page. Did you learn anything new about the words? What?

88   Unit 5 • Chapter 30   Vocabulary Power

Your Turn

STEP 1 **Think of things you can make or do.** Make a list of snacks or crafts you like to make. Write or draw your ideas.

STEP 2 **Choose one thing about which to write.** Choose something your classmates would like to learn to do.

STEP 3 **Complete a flowchart.**

What Good Writers Do

☑ Remember for whom you are writing and why.

☑ Make a plan that shows the steps in the order in which you will write them.

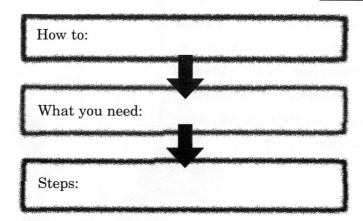

How to:

⬇

What you need:

⬇

Steps:

Your Turn Share the information at the top of the page with children to review the steps needed to construct a flowchart. Explain that children will follow the same process as Maria in planning their own how-to paragraph. Tell them to begin by brainstorming possible topics and selecting one. Then have them complete the flowchart.

WRAP-UP/ASSESS

SUMMARIZE Encourage volunteers to summarize the process they followed in preparing their flowcharts. Invite them to reflect on how this kind of prewriting helps them plan their writing. Have them consider what changes they might make the next time they prepare a flowchart.

 Have children write their reflections about prewriting in their journals. **REFLECTION**

377

INTERACTIVE WRITING

SHARE THE PEN You may want to work through the writing process together to write a group how-to paragraph. To plan the paragraph, use **Transparency 59** or a group flowchart recorded on chart paper. Model how to brainstorm and organize ideas. Encourage children to participate, and have them write their ideas.

Writer's Craft

• • • • • • • • • • • • •

TIME-ORDER WORDS Hand out a number of cards with sequence words such as *first, next, then,* and *last.* Have children holding the cards arrange themselves in order in a line across the front of the room.

Then ask the group to explain the steps involved in a simple task such as making a peanut-butter sandwich. Instruct each child in turn to state one step, beginning with the sequence word on the card he or she is holding.

Continue with a new group of volunteers and a new how-to topic.

Drafting

OBJECTIVES
- To draft a how-to paragraph that lists the topic and materials needed
- To write steps for completing a task

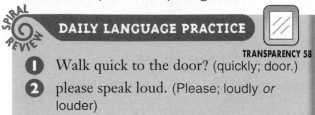

SPIRAL REVIEW

DAILY LANGUAGE PRACTICE

TRANSPARENCY 58

1 Walk quick to the door? (quickly; door.)

2 please speak loud. (Please; loudly *or* louder)

ORAL WARM-UP

USE PRIOR KNOWLEDGE Invite volunteers to describe a process they use for preparing a simple snack or craft. Tell them to describe the steps in order.

GUIDED WRITING

DISCUSS FIRST DRAFTS Remind children that a first draft does not need to be perfect. Use the writing model to talk about how to write a first draft. Ask questions such as the following about Maria's how-to paragraph.

- **In which part of the paragraph does Maria tell what the topic is? Does this match the flowchart?** (in the beginning, yes)
- **What are some ways to make this paragraph better?** (Accept reasonable responses.)

If children point out spelling and punctuation errors, remind them that these types of errors will be corrected later in the Proofreading step.

 Use **Transparency 60** for an additional teaching model.

Writing a How-to Paragraph

Drafting

Maria used her flowchart to help her write a first draft. She wrote her ideas quickly. Later she could go back over her work and correct any mistakes.

DRAFT

How to Make Fun Dough

You can make your own fun dough. You need two cups of salt, two cups of warm water, two cups of flour, a bowl, and food coloring. First put the water in the bowl and add a little food coloring. And then put the salt and flour slowly into the bowl. Play with the dough. Mix the dough with your hands.

378

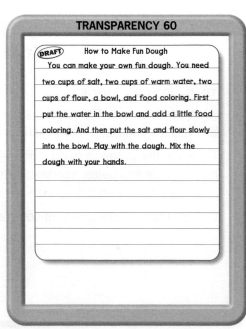

TRANSPARENCY 60

DRAFT   How to Make Fun Dough

You can make your own fun dough. You need two cups of salt, two cups of warm water, two cups of flour, a bowl, and food coloring. First put the water in the bowl and add a little food coloring. And then put the salt and flour slowly into the bowl. Play with the dough. Mix the dough with your hands.

Vocabulary Power page 89

Name _____

Prefixes

These words begin with the same prefix. Underline inter- in each word.

interact   intercom   interleaf   international   Internet

Complete each sentence. Use a word from above.

1. Something known among many nations is
   ___international___

2. When people talk among themselves, they
   ___interact___

3. A blank page at the beginning or end of a book is called an
   ___interleaf___

Add inter- to the words. Draw pictures for labels.

1. connected	2. twined
interconnected telephones	intertwined ropes

Vocabulary Power   Unit 5 • Chapter 30   89

Look at the way Maria's how-to paragraph follows her flowchart so far. What else can she add to make it complete?

What Good Writers Do

☑ Think about who will read your paragraph and why.

☑ Follow your plan and write your important ideas. You can fix any mistakes later.

How to: *make fun dough*

↓

What you need: *two cups of salt, two cups of warm water, two cups of flour, a bowl, food coloring*

↓

Steps: *First put the water in the bowl. Add food coloring.*

Next put the salt and flour into the bowl.

Then mix the dough with your hands.

Last play with the dough, or put it in the refrigerator to keep it fresh.

Your Turn

Use your flowchart and What Good Writers Do to write a draft of a how-to paragraph.

Remember to put the date on your draft. It will help you tell which draft is newer.

379

Your Turn Tell children that they will use their flowcharts and What Good Writers Do to work on their first drafts. Read over What Good Writers Do with children. Remind children to work from their flowcharts as they write their drafts. Suggest that they work quickly to get their ideas down. Later they will have a chance to fix any mistakes or make other changes.

 Demonstrate for children how to use the automatic date function on the computer to input the date in a heading on their draft.

 PORTFOLIO Remind children to put their drafts in their Working Portfolios.

WRAP-UP/ASSESS

SUMMARIZE Invite volunteers to tell what elements should be included in a first draft.

You may wish to have children record their thoughts on writing a draft in their journals.
REFLECTION

INTERACTIVE WRITING

SHARE THE PEN Guide children to develop a draft. Model how to expand the steps into sentences in a paragraph. Start a draft and have volunteers add to it.

Assessment Strategies and Resources

FORMAL ASSESSMENT

If you want to know more about a child's mastery of the language and writing skills taught in Unit 5, **then** administer the first *Language Skills and Writing Assessment* for Unit 5. The test consists of two parts:

Language Skills: the verbs *come, run, give, go, do,* and *see;* the helping verbs *has, have, had;* adverbs; and **using exact words**

Writing Task: Write a **how-to paragraph.** Scoring guidelines and model papers are included.

INFORMAL ASSESSMENT TOOLS

 Using Portfolios

During a conference with children, discuss their self-assessments (see pages R78–R79) as well as their how-to paragraphs and other writing included in their **writing portfolios.** Ask the following types of questions about their how-to paragraphs:

- What is the topic of your how-to paragraph?
- For whom are you writing this how-to paragraph?
- What materials do you need?
- How did you decide the order of the steps?
- What are some of the time-order words you used?

You can also check children's understanding of **grammar** by evaluating it in their writing. Look for these points:

- Are the verbs *come, run,* and *give* used correctly?
- Are the verbs *go, do,* and *see* used correctly?

- Are the helping verbs *has, have,* and *had* used correctly?
- Are adverbs used appropriately?
- Are commas included in place names and dates?

Oral Language Assessment
Use these guidelines to evaluate oral language:

Listening and Speaking
- Listens for information
- Responds appropriately and courteously to directions
- Uses verbal communication in effective ways when giving directions
- Clarifies directions using appropriate props, such as objects or pictures

Informal Assessment Reminder
If you used the pre-instruction writing prompt suggested in Teaching Grammar from Writing, **then** remember to compare the results with the writing done by children after the grammar and writing instruction.

Unit 6

Grammar
- Usage Wrap-Up

Writing
- Book Report
- Research Report

All About Dinosaurs

The word *dinosaur* means "terrible lizard." The first dinosaurs lived more than 200 million years ago. The dinosaurs died out about 65 million years ago, though. Scientists learn about dinosaurs from fossils they find in the ground.

See

- Dinosaur Family Tree

- The Biggest and Smallest Dinosaurs

- What Happened to the Dinosaurs?

Cross-Curricular Writing

LANGUAGE ARTS IN THE CLASSROOM

Searching for ways to integrate language arts into content areas will provide children with many opportunities to experience reading and writing for information. Writing experiences across the curriculum provide endless opportunities for children to think on paper, to reinforce concepts about print and the conventions of language, and to develop how writers think, plan, and write to learn.

MAKING LISTS Be it science, social studies, or math, children like to make lists and the longer the better. List making reinforces classification and vocabulary expansion. Lists can generate questions for inquiry. Have children make their own lists, in picture or written form.

USING IDEA CHARTS Using interactive writing, model how writers use different ways to write down what they know, what they learn from reading, and how to plan what they will write. As a chart is added to or revised, children understand that writers return to their writing to change or add ideas.

USING CLASS LEARNING LOGS Create a class learning log using rings and large sheets of newsprint or oaktag. Place the learning log onto an easel to explain its purpose and have children suggest a title for the log. Show how each entry will begin with the day of the project or experiment and the date. (A date stamp works well.) Children will discuss what they did each day and how that experience can be recorded in the log. Have children read entries aloud from the log periodically.

Unit 6

Grammar
● Usage Wrap-Up

Writing
● Book Report
● Research Report

Introducing the Unit

ORAL LANGUAGE/VIEWING

DISCUSS THE IMAGES Have children describe the most important things on pages 388–389. (fossil of a dinosaur in a museum and computer screen with information about dinosaurs) Have children pretend that they live back in the time when there were still dinosaurs.

- **How did the dinosaurs move? Show me.**
- **What could you hear when the dinosaurs moved? How does it feel outside, hot or cold?** (Accept reasonable responses.)
- **What kind of dinosaurs do you see?** (Accept reasonable responses.)
- **If you wanted to find out more about dinosaurs, where could you find the information?** (look in books, magazines, and on a computer)

ENCOURAGE CHILDREN'S QUESTIONS. Have children list questions about dinosaurs and discuss ways to find answers to them.

Unit 6

Grammar
● Usage Wrap-Up

Writing
● Book Report
● Research Report

388

Viewing and Representing

COMPARE/CONTRAST PRINT AND VISUAL MEDIA Have groups of children decide on a topic to explore. Then have them use classroom or school resources to locate information on their topic from two different sources. Children can share their findings in a variety of ways, such as with notes, a printout of information on a computer screen, or a display of pages in a book or magazine. Have children tell which sources they like using most, and why.

For evaluation criteria, see the checklist on page R77.

MEDIA LITERACY AND COMMUNICATION SKILLS PACKAGE Use the video to extend children's oral and visual literacy. See pages 6-7 of the *Teacher's Guide.*

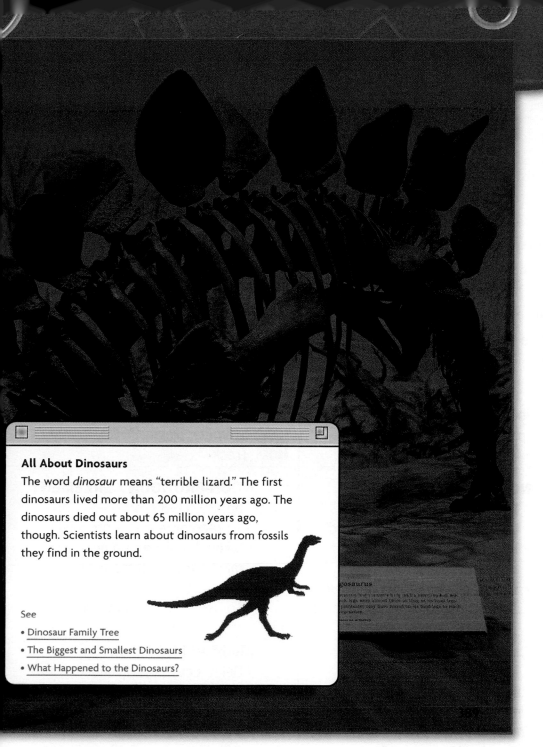

All About Dinosaurs

The word *dinosaur* means "terrible lizard." The first dinosaurs lived more than 200 million years ago. The dinosaurs died out about 65 million years ago, though. Scientists learn about dinosaurs from fossils they find in the ground.

See

• Dinosaur Family Tree

• The Biggest and Smallest Dinosaurs

• What Happened to the Dinosaurs?

Previewing the Unit

Read and discuss the unit contents list with children. Ask them to tell in their own words the terms they already recognize, such as *noun*, *verb*, and *pronoun*. Tell them that in this unit they will learn more about how to find and fix sentence problems to make their writing and speaking better. Discuss with them how they might use these skills to polish their writing and speaking as they do a report.

SCIENCE CONNECTION Children will be exposed to a variety of science topics in this unit:

• Plants and animals
• Weather
• Health and fitness
• Earth's resources
• The sun, moon, and stars
• Changes in matter
• Forces and motion

School-Home Connection

You may want to use Home Letter 6, page R99.

LESSON ORGANIZER	DAY 1	DAY 2
DAILY LANGUAGE PRACTICE TRANSPARENCIES 61, 62	1. Grandma all-ways walks slowy. (always; slowly) 2. She offen sings soft. (often; softly) **Bridge to Writing** I (adverb) read books.	1. The boy has a bike. It likes he. (He; it) 2. Itt is red, and He rides it a lot. (It; he) **Bridge to Writing** Tiffany makes soup. (pronoun) is a good cook.
ORAL WARM-UP Listening/Speaking	Describe a Picture Using Pronouns p. 390	Replace Nouns with Pronouns p. 392 *Grammar Jingles*™ CD, Primary, Track 7
TEACH/MODEL GRAMMAR **KEY** ✔ = tested skill	✔ **NOUNS AND PRONOUNS TOGETHER** pp. 390-391 **Literature:** "The Mockingbird" • To listen critically to interpret and evaluate a poem • To understand what a pronoun is; to use pronouns in sentences	✔ **NOUN-PRONOUN AGREEMENT** pp. 392-393 • To recognize that a pronoun takes the place of a noun and must agree with the noun it replaces • To use pronouns in writing
Reaching All Learners	**Challenge:** Activity Card 21, p. R61 **ESL:** *ESL Manual* pp. 148–149 *Practice Book* p. 101 **Reteach:** *Reteach Activities Copying Masters* p. 61	**Modified Instruction** Below-Level: List Pronouns Above-Level: Write Sentences **Challenge:** Story Time p. 393 **ESL:** Use Pronouns p. 392 *ESL Manual* pp. 148, 150 *Practice Book* p. 102 **Reteach:** *Reteach Activities Copying Masters* p. 62
WRITING	Write Pronouns 391 Summarize	Writing Connection p. 393 Revising Summarize
CROSS-CURRICULAR/ ENRICHMENT	**Vocabulary Power** Word Meaning p. 390 anteater, groundhog, **mockingbird**, starfish, stingray See *Vocabulary Power* book.	**Vocabulary Power** Compound Words p. 390 *Vocabulary Power* book p. 91 **Vocabulary activity**

Visit *The Learning Site!*
www.harcourtschool.com
WRITING ACTIVITIES
Writing Express CD-ROM

DAY 3

1. Dora went to florida. He visited her grandma. (Florida; She)
2. Dora and Grandma went to the beach. We both got wet? (They; .)

Bridge to Writing The water was salty. (pronoun) was warm, too.

Identify Pronouns p. 394
Grammar Jingles™ CD, Primary, Track 7

✔ **WORD ORDER FOR PRO-NOUNS** 394-395
• To understand that when a pronoun is used with a noun, the two must be in order
• To use pronouns and nouns in order in sentences

Modified Instruction
  Below-Level: Identify Nouns and Pronouns
  Above-Level: Write Sentences
Challenge: Write a Poem p. 395
ESL: Talk About Yourself p. 394
  ESL Manual pp. 148, 151
Practice Book p. 103
Reteach: *Reteach Activities Copying Masters* p. 63

Writing Connection p. 395
  Using Clear Pronouns
Summarize/Reflect

Vocabulary Power
  Classify/Categorize p. 390
  Vocabulary Power book p. 92
  Vocabulary activity

DAY 4

1. I and Von swam inn the lake. (Von and I; in)
2. Von splashd at me and Maria. (splashed; Maria and me)

Bridge to Writing (noun and I) have fun when we go to the lake, too.

Shout It p. 396

EXTRA PRACTICE 396-397
• To identify pronouns and to recognize the order of pronouns in sentences
• To use pronouns when writing dialogue
Practice and Assessment

Challenge: Play Dialogue p. 397
ESL: Listen Up p. 396
  ESL Manual pp. 148, 152
Practice Book p. 104

Writing Connection p. 397
  Play Dialogue

Vocabulary Power
  Regionalisms p. 390
  Vocabulary Power book p. 93
Language Play p. 397
  Vocabulary activity

DAY 5

1. Laura likes hats, And it has many. (and she)
2. Laura lent me and Bev two hat. (Bev and me; hats)

Bridge to Writing Bev and I wore the hats to school. (pronoun) looked great.

TEST PREP **CHAPTER REVIEW** 398
• To review how to use nouns and pronouns correctly
• To understand how to use a telephone book
Test Preparation

Challenge: Make a Telephone Book p. 399
ESL Manual pp. 148, 153
Practice Book p. 105

Writing Application p. 399
  Write Answers to Questions

STUDY SKILL
Using a Telephone Book p. 399

Vocabulary Power

Compound Words p. 390

Nouns and Pronouns Together

OBJECTIVES
- To listen critically to interpret and evaluate a poem
- To understand that a pronoun is a word that takes the place of a noun and to use pronouns in sentences

SPIRAL REVIEW

DAILY LANGUAGE PRACTICE

TRANSPARENCY 61

1 Grandma all-ways walks slowy. (always; slowly)

2 She offen sings soft. (often; softly)

BRIDGE TO WRITING I ___(adverb)___ read books.

ORAL WARM-UP

USE PRIOR KNOWLEDGE Show children a picture of a mockingbird. Ask volunteers to describe what they see and to imagine what the bird might be like. Encourage children to use pronouns in their sentences. You may want to start a **Pronouns Word Wall.**

TEACH/MODEL

Have children look at page 390 and describe the illustration. Have them use the title and illustration to predict what the poem is about. Read the poem aloud once. Then reread it with children.

DEVELOP ORAL LANGUAGE Ask children to recall some of the sentences from the poem. Prompt them with questions such as: *What does the mockingbird do in the morning?* Encourage children to use pronouns in their answers. Invite volunteers to demonstrate or say other sentences that might describe the mockingbird in the poem. Add the pronouns they use to the **Word Wall.**

Nouns and Pronouns Together

Read the poem.

The Mockingbird

The mockingbird, the mockingbird,
In the morning he speaks, in the morning
  he sings.
For the sake of the people in the morning
  he speaks,
In the morning he sings.

from the Acoma nation

390

Vocabulary Power

DAY 1 WORD MEANING Write: *mock, mocking, mockingbird.* Reread "The Mockingbird." **One meaning of *mock* is "to copy." How do you think the mockingbird got its name?** (Mockingbirds can mimic, or copy, the calls of other birds.

DAY 2 COMPOUND WORDS Write: *mocking + bird = mockingbird.* **Mockingbirds mock the sounds of other birds. Do you think *mockingbird* is a good name for this bird?** (See also *Vocabulary Power,* page 91.)

DAY 3 CLASSIFY/CATEGORIZE List: *crow, mockingbird, robin.* **What kind of animal do these words name? What other animals fly?** (See also *Vocabulary Power,* page 92.)

DAY 4 REGIONALISMS Write: _Groundhogs_ are also called _woodchucks_. **Why do you think the same animal has a different name in a different place?** (See also *Vocabulary Power,* page 93.)

DAY 5 COMPOUND WORDS Have children dictate a list of animal names. Use these words to make your own list of compound words.

Read the poem with a partner. Talk about what the bird in the poem does. Then tell about other things birds do at different times of the day.

A **pronoun** is a word that takes the place of a noun. *I*, *he*, *she*, *they*, and *it* are pronouns. Each pronoun in a sentence should go with the noun it replaces.

> **Teresa** watches a **mockingbird**.
> **She** draws a picture of **it**.

Think about a person you like. Write this person's name twice on the first line. Then add new lines to the poem. Use some pronouns to tell what the person does. Responses will vary.

_____, _____,

In the morning _____, in the morning

_____.

For the sake of the people in the morning

_____,

In the morning _____.

391

WRITE Write children's sentences on the board. Have children practice reading them. Underline the pronouns. Explain that a **pronoun** is a word that takes the place of a noun. Read the definitions in the box and talk about the example sentences. You might want to point out that although the poet has used the pronoun *he* to take the place of *mockingbird*, it is generally correct to use the pronoun *it* to talk about animals.

Then read the first item at the bottom of page 391 together. Have children complete the sentences and then share them with a partner. Have volunteers read their sentences aloud.

WRAP-UP/ASSESS

SUMMARIZE Have children summarize what they have learned about pronouns. They can write their reflections in their journals, as well as record sentences they brainstormed. **REFLECTION**

RETEACH

INTERVENTION Lessons in **visual, auditory,** and **kinesthetic** modalities: p. R37 and *Reteach Activities Copying Masters*, p. 61.

page 61

Nouns and Pronouns Together

Read each group of sentences aloud. Circle the noun in the first sentence. Circle the pronoun in the second sentence.

EXAMPLE: (Jim) climbs.
(He) gets to the top.

1. (Beth) jumps.
   (She) doesn't miss.
2. The (children) play.
   (They) form two teams.
3. The (bell) rings.
   (It) is loud.

Nouns and Pronouns Together

Cut out the pronouns at the bottom of the page. Glue them in place to complete the second sentence in each pair.

1. The children stop playing. | They | line up.
2. Beth gets in line. | She | holds her jump rope.
3. The jump rope is long. | It | drags on the ground.
4. Jim taps Beth on the shoulder. | He | tells her the rope is dragging.

| He | She | They | It |

Teacher: Cut apart the activities and distribute to children based on the modalities that are their strengths.

Reteach Activities • Using Nouns and Pronouns Correctly   Unit 6 • Chapter 31   61

PRACTICE page 101

Name_____

Nouns and Pronouns Together

A. Underline the pronoun in each sentence.

1. They have a good breakfast each morning.
2. Today she eats oatmeal.
3. It is delicious.
4. He has cereal and fruit.
5. She tastes his breakfast.
6. They like to share.

B. Write a pronoun from the box to complete each sentence.
Possible responses are given.

| she | They | He | It |

7. __He__ finishes his cereal first.
8. __It__ is his favorite breakfast.
9. Then __she__ finishes her oatmeal.
10. __They__ clean the dishes together.

TRY THIS! Write three sentences about your favorite meal of the day. What do you eat? Who eats with you? Use pronouns in your sentences.

Practice • Using Nouns and Pronouns Correctly   Unit 6 • Chapter 31   101

CHALLENGE

MAKE AN ANIMAL MOBILE Have children use **Challenge Activity Card 21** (page R61) to make mobiles. Encourage children to draw wild animals or pets they like. Remind them to use pronouns in all the sentences. Display the mobiles. Have volunteers read and act out sentences and ask the classmates to guess the animal.

Challenge Activity Card 21
Make an Animal Mobile

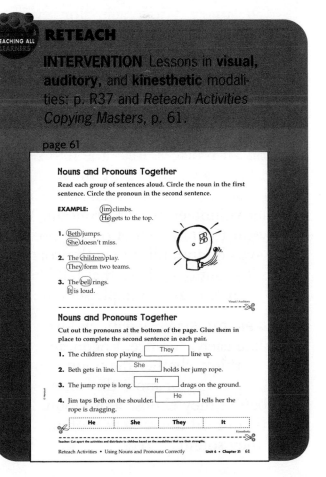

Noun-Pronoun Agreement

OBJECTIVES
- To recognize that a pronoun takes the place of a noun and must agree with the noun it replaces
- To use pronouns in writing

DAILY LANGUAGE PRACTICE

TRANSPARENCY 61

❶ The boy has a bike. It likes he. (He; it)

❷ Itt is red, and He rides it a lot. (It; he)

BRIDGE TO WRITING Tiffany makes soup.
<u>(pronoun)</u> is a good cook.

ORAL WARM-UP

SAY IT BACK Say sentences such as *Bill and Kara have red shirts.* Have a volunteer say the sentence back to you replacing the names with a pronoun. Continue until everyone has had a turn. Add the pronouns to the **Word Wall**.

***Grammar Jingles*™ CD, Primary** Use Track 7 for review and reinforcement of pronouns.

TEACH/MODEL

Use the explanation and examples to explain that a pronoun must agree with the noun it replaces. Read the first sentence. Have a volunteer say the noun. Then read the second sentence. Have another volunteer say the pronoun. You may want to draw a chart on the board and have children fill it in with pronouns that tell about one, those that tell about more than one, and example sentences.

GUIDED PRACTICE Work with children to complete each sentence. Encourage them to think whether the noun names one (I, he, she, it) or more than one (we, they) before they choose a pronoun. Also have them read the sentences aloud to see if they sound correct.

Using Nouns and Pronouns Correctly

Noun-Pronoun Agreement

A pronoun is a word that takes the place of a noun. A pronoun should agree with, or go with, the noun it replaces.

> **Ms. Gomez** is a scientist.
> **She** studies rocks.
>
> **The rocks** are rough.
> **They** are hard to climb.

Guided Practice

Write the pronoun that agrees with the underlined noun in each set of sentences.

1. The <u>families</u> went camping.
   <u>　They　</u> had a good time.

2. <u>Maria</u> took her sleeping bag.
   <u>　She　</u> knew it would keep her warm.

3. <u>José</u> brought a telescope.
   <u>　He　</u> wanted to see stars.

4. The <u>telescope</u> was small and black.
   <u>　It　</u> helped José see stars and planets.

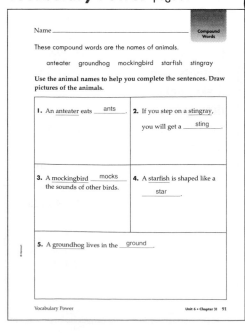

392

Vocabulary Power page 91

Name _____   Compound Words

These compound words are the names of animals.

anteater   groundhog   mockingbird   starfish   stingray

Use the animal names to help you complete the sentences. Draw pictures of the animals.

1. An anteater eats <u>ants</u>.	2. If you step on a stingray, you will get a <u>sting</u>
3. A mockingbird <u>mocks</u> the sounds of other birds.	4. A starfish is shaped like a <u>star</u>
5. A groundhog lives in the <u>ground</u>	

Vocabulary Power   Unit 6 • Chapter 31   91

USE PRONOUNS Prepare a set of picture cards that show people and objects. On the back of each card write the pronoun that would replace the noun. Give children the cards. Have them say sentences about the pictures, first using a noun, and then replacing the noun with a pronoun. Have them check their answers by looking at the back of the card.

Remember A pronoun should agree with the noun it replaces.

Independent Practice

Write the pronoun that agrees with the underlined noun in each set of sentences.

5. The <u>grown-ups</u> set up the tents.
   ___They___ worked hard.

6. The <u>tents</u> were large.
   ___They___ were big enough for four people.

7. <u>Barbara</u> went to collect wood.
   ___She___ came back with many dry sticks.

8. <u>Mr. Johnson</u> built a fire in the fire pit.
   Then ___he___ lit the fire with a match.

9. The <u>wood</u> crackled as it burned.
   ___It___ made a warm fire.

10. <u>Mrs. Johnson</u> unpacked the food.
    Then ___she___ helped make dinner.

Writing Connection

Revising Choose a piece of writing from your Writing Portfolio. Find nouns that you can replace with pronouns. Make sure your pronouns agree.

You can use your computer to edit. Erase a letter or word by pressing the **delete** key.

393

Independent Practice

Have children complete the Independent Practice, or modify it by using the following suggestions:

MODIFIED INSTRUCTION

BELOW-LEVEL STUDENTS List pronouns on chart paper so that children can refer to it. Ask them to say each sentence aloud to see if the pronoun they selected sounds correct.

ABOVE-LEVEL STUDENTS After children finish, have them write at least two sentences using pronouns.

Writing Connection

Revising Have children underline the nouns. Then have them rewrite on another sheet of paper using pronouns. Suggest that volunteers place their writing in the Sharing Basket to share with others.

WRAP-UP/ASSESS

SUMMARIZE Ask children to summarize what they have learned about pronouns.

RETEACH

INTERVENTION Lessons in **visual, auditory,** and **kinesthetic** modalities: p. R37 and *Reteach Activities Copying Masters,* p. 62.

page 62

Noun-Pronoun Agreement

Read each sentence aloud. Underline the naming part. Draw a line to the pronoun it matches.

1. <u>Bobby</u> likes to go to the beach.
2. <u>Allison</u> likes to swim in the ocean.
3. <u>Bobby and Allison</u> run quickly into the water.
4. The <u>water</u> is very cold.

They
It
He
She

Noun-Pronoun Agreement

Cut out the words below. Place them face down on a table. Have a partner point to one of the pronouns. Then turn over a word. If your partner's pronoun can take the place of the noun, place the word aside. If not, turn the word face down again. Take turns.

he	she	it	they

grandparents	Mrs. James	a butterfly	my dog Skip
Angie	Tom and Amy	Jim	a kitten
my uncle	games	my sister	Mr. Smith

62 Unit 6 • Chapter 31   Reteach Activities • Using Nouns and Pronouns Correctly

PRACTICE page 102

Name _____

Noun-Pronoun Agreement

A. Circle the pronoun that could replace the underlined noun in each sentence.

1. <u>Charles</u> likes to go camping. (She, **He**)
2. <u>Denise</u> enjoys camping, too. (It, **She**)
3. The <u>children</u> like camping because it teaches them about nature. (**it**, they)

B. Write the pronoun that agrees with the underlined noun or nouns in each set of sentences.

4. The <u>campground</u> is large.
   ___It___ is twenty miles wide.
5. <u>Charles</u> knows this campground well.
   ___He___ first came here when he was five.
6. <u>Charles and Denise</u> set up their tent.
   ___They___ finish quickly.

TRY THIS! Write three sentences about something your friends like to do. Use a pronoun in each sentence.

102 Unit 6 • Chapter 31   Practice • Using Nouns and Pronouns Correctly

CHALLENGE

STORY TIME Show children a picture of a group of people engaged in an activity. Have children write a short story about the picture. Remind them to use pronouns in their writing.

Mr. and Mrs. Selandia took their children to the beach. They all swam in the sea. Then Victor built a castle in the sand. It was very big.

Word Order for Pronouns

TRANSPARENCY 61

OBJECTIVES
- To understand that when a pronoun is used with a noun, the two must be in order
- To use pronouns and nouns in order in sentences

DAILY LANGUAGE PRACTICE

1 Dora went to florida. He visited her grandma. (Florida; She)

2 Dora and Grandma went to the beach. We both got wet? (They; .)

BRIDGE TO WRITING The water was salty. (pronoun) was warm, too.

ORAL WARM-UP

USE PRIOR KNOWLEDGE Write two sentences on the board such as *Marco and I have brown hair* and *Mr. Marks gave the book to Jill and me.* Read them aloud with children. Underline the pronouns. Ask volunteers to say sentences about themselves and a classmate modeled after the sample sentences.

Grammar Jingles™ **CD, Primary** Use Track 7 for review and reinforcement of pronouns.

TEACH/MODEL

Read the explanation and example sentences in the instruction box together. Then invite children to recall sentences they said during the warm-up activity.

GUIDED PRACTICE Work through the sentences together. Have children identify the nouns and pronouns in the phrases in parentheses. Ask them to tell which phrase is correct and why.

Word Order for Pronouns

When you talk or write about another person and yourself using ***I*** or ***me***, always name yourself last. Use ***I*** in the naming part of the sentence.

> **Bob and I** went to the store.

Use ***me*** in the telling part.

> Mr. Flores gave apples to **Bob and me**.

Guided Practice

Write the correct words in ( ) to complete each sentence.

1. (My family and I, I and my family) flew to the Grand Canyon.

2. My sister Lisa sat next to (my mother and me, me and my mother) on the jet.

3. (I and Lisa, Lisa and I) had never been to the Grand Canyon.

4. My mother read a book about it to (me and Lisa, Lisa and me).

394

Vocabulary Power page 92

These animals can be grouped into many different categories.

anteater   groundhog   mockingbird   starfish   stingray

Write the animal names above in at least one category. Add other animal names to complete each category. *Additional responses will vary.*

BIRDS	FISH
mockingbird	starfish
	stingray

MAMMALS	ANIMALS THAT FLY
anteater	mockingbird
groundhog	

ANIMALS THAT EAT INSECTS	ANIMALS THAT STING
anteater	stingray

92   Unit 6 • Chapter 31   Vocabulary Power

ESL

TALK ABOUT YOURSELF Have children work in pairs. One child says a sentence to tell what he/she likes to do or what other people do with him/her. (*I like to write stories. The teacher helps me.*) The second child repeats the sentence, adding his or her partner's name. (*Linda and I like to write stories. The teacher helps Linda and me.*) The second child then begins the next round.

Remember
When you talk or write about another person and yourself, always name yourself last.

Independent Practice

Write the correct words in ( ) to complete each sentence.

5. (<u>My family and I</u>, I and my family) hiked to the bottom of the canyon.

6. My mother let (<u>Lisa and me</u>, me and Lisa) carry our own water.

7. (I and my father, <u>My father and I</u>) saw a mule.

8. My mother asked (<u>my sister and me</u>, me and my sister) if we wanted to ride it.

9. (<u>Lisa and I</u>, I and Lisa) took turns riding.

10. (<u>My family and I</u>, I and my family) had a great trip.

Writing Connection

Using Clear Pronouns Write sentences about a trip you took. Tell about things you did and with whom you did them. Make sure the pronouns and nouns you use together are in the correct order.

Use your computer to help you write. Save your writing, and add more details later.

395

Independent Practice

Have children complete the Independent Practice, or modify it by using the following suggestions:

MODIFIED INSTRUCTION

BELOW-LEVEL STUDENTS Have children circle the noun and underline the pronoun in the phrases in parentheses. Then have them choose the answer in which the pronoun (underline) comes after the noun (circle).

ABOVE-LEVEL STUDENTS After children finish, have them write additional sentences that use the pronouns *I* and *me* with nouns.

Writing Connection

Using Clear Pronouns Have children trade sentences so they can edit each other's work. Instruct them to check for standard usage, including pronoun agreement and order.

WRAP-UP/ASSESS

SUMMARIZE Ask children to summarize and reflect on what they have learned about using the pronouns *I* and *me*. **REFLECTION**

RETEACH

INTERVENTION Lessons in **visual, auditory,** and **kinesthetic** modalities: p. R37 and *Reteach Activities Copying Masters,* p. 63.

page 63

PRACTICE page 103

Name_____

Word Order for Pronouns

A. Write the correct words in ( ) to complete each sentence.

1. **(I and Brad, Brad and I)** like to read.   Brad and I

2. Mom reads to **(Brad and me, me and Brad)** each night.   Brad and me

3. **(Dad and I, I and Dad)** tell great stories.   Dad and I

B. Put the underlined words in the correct order. Write the new sentence.

4. <u>I and my brother</u> went to the library.
   My brother and I went to the library.

5. Brad looked at books with <u>me and the librarian</u>.
   Brad looked at books with the librarian and me.

6. <u>I and Brad</u> found a book about the Grand Canyon.
   Brad and I found a book about the Grand Canyon.

TRY THIS! Write two sentences about something you and your friends do after school. Use at least one pronoun in each sentence.

Practice • Using Nouns and Pronouns Correctly   Unit 6 • Chapter 31 103

CHALLENGE

WRITE A POEM Have children write poems about themselves and a classmate. Remind them to use the pronoun *I* or *me* in each sentence. Then have them illustrate their poems before sharing them with the class.

Luis and I are friends.
Luis plays ball with me.
Luis and I have fun.
I like Luis, you see!

Word Order for Pronouns

With a partner, read each sentence. Circle the words in ( ) that are in the correct order.

1. (Felix and I,) Felix and me) went to a fair.

2. My mom took (Felix and I, (Felix and me)) to a fair.

3. (My mom and I,) My mom and me) went on the roller coaster.

4. Felix heard (my mom and I, (my mom and me)) scream.

Word Order for Pronouns

Cut out the words at the bottom of the page. Glue the words that best complete each sentence.

1. [Felix and I] went on the water slide.

2. [My mom and I] watched Felix on the Ferris wheel.

3. My mom told [Felix and me] it was time to go.

4. Felix thanked [my mom and me]

| Felix and I | My mom and I |
| my mom and me | Felix and me |

Reteach Activities • Using Nouns and Pronouns Correctly   Unit 6 • Chapter 31 63

Extra Practice

OBJECTIVES
- To identify pronouns and to recognize the order of pronouns in sentences
- To use pronouns when writing dialogue

TRANSPARENCY 62

DAILY LANGUAGE PRACTICE

1 I and Von swam inn the lake. (Von and I; in)

2 Von splashd at me and Maria. (splashed; Maria and me)

BRIDGE TO WRITING (noun and I) have fun when we go to the lake, too.

ORAL WARM-UP

SHOUT IT Say a noun and have children as a group or as individual volunteers shout out the pronoun that agrees with it. Use a variety of nouns, such as: the girl, a bird, children, cars, the bench, the teacher, a mail carrier.

TEACH/MODEL

Read each set of directions to help children understand how to complete each section. Have children share their answers in small groups before you read aloud the correct answers.

WRAP-UP/ASSESS

SUMMARIZE Ask children to reflect on and discuss any special problems they had in completing the practice before you have them summarize what they have learned about using nouns and pronouns. You may want children to write their reflections in their journals.

ADDITIONAL PRACTICE Extra practice items are provided on page 476 of the *Pupil Edition* (*Teacher's Edition* R7).

TECHNOLOGY
Grammar Practice and Assessment CD-ROM

Writing Express CD-ROM

INTERNET Visit *The Learning Site!*
www.harcourtschool.com

Using Nouns and Pronouns Correctly

Extra Practice

Write the pronoun that agrees with the underlined noun in each set of sentences.

1. The <u>children</u> went hiking with their parents.

   ___They___ carried backpacks.

2. <u>Cindy</u> had the map.

   ___She___ led the way.

3. First the <u>path</u> went by two lakes.

   Next ___it___ passed through the woods.

4. An <u>eagle</u> flew in the sky.

   Then ___it___ landed in a tall tree.

5. <u>Tom and Kim</u> were last.

   ___They___ had to run to catch up.

Write the correct words in ( ) to complete each sentence.

6. (<u>Luis and I</u>, I and Luis) saw a deer.

7. The deer walked close to (<u>Luis and me</u>, me and Luis).

8. (<u>Wu and I</u>, I and Wu) listened to the birds.

9. The birds sang to (me and Wu, <u>Wu and me</u>).

10. (<u>Pat and I</u>, I and Pat) watched the chipmunks.

396

Vocabulary Power page 93

Name_____

Regionalisms

The same animal can have different names in different places.

Which name do you use? groundhog or woodchuck?

Read the words. Circle the word or words you use. Draw a picture.

1. peanuts   goobers
    ground nuts
	2. sub hoagie
	    grinder

3. soda tonic pop	4. spuds potatoes taters

Vocabulary Power   Unit 6 • Chapter 31   93

ESL

REACHING ALL LEARNERS

LISTEN UP Have groups of children do the "Play Dialogue" on page 397 as a shared writing activity. Ask children to tape-record their conversation. They can listen to see if their sentences make sense and to check their use of pronouns before they write the conversation in play form.

Language Play

Pronoun Partners

- **Write sentences on cards.**
- **Pick a card. Read the sentence to a partner.**
- **Your partner changes one noun in the sentence to a pronoun and says the new sentence.**
- **Then switch places with your partner.**
- **You get one point for each correct sentence.**

> Many ducks swim in the lake.

> Diane and Paul are going to the lake.

> Liz likes to watch birds.

> The boy and his family went to the park.

Writing Connection

Play Dialogue Work with a classmate. Talk to each other about something that you and other classmates did together. Use pronouns when you talk. Write what you say in play form.

	Teresa: Han and I went to the park yesterday.
	Stella: Beth and I did, too. She and I fed the ducks.
	Teresa: Han and I saw the ducks, too! He told me
	about the different kinds of ducks.

Language Play

Have children play "Pronoun Partners" in pairs. As an example, write a sentence on the board. Read the sentence aloud. Model how to change one noun in the sentence to a pronoun. Then read the sentence again.

Have children play "Pronoun Partners" in pairs. As an example, write a sentence on the board. Read the sentence aloud. Model how to change one noun in the sentence to a pronoun. Then read the sentence again.

Writing Connection

Play Dialogue You may want to have children turn to page 481 in their handbooks, where they can refer to additional models of play dialogue. After children write their dialogues, have them identify the most effective features of their writing by using the criteria below.

CRITERIA
- ☑ Writes the name of the speaker before each sentence.
- ☑ Writes pronouns correctly.
- ☑ Uses pronouns with nouns in the correct order.
- ☑ Begins each proper noun with a capital letter.

PORTFOLIO OPPORTUNITY Have volunteers perform their dialogues before they place them in their portfolios.

PRACTICE page 104

Name _____

Extra Practice

A. Underline the pronoun in each sentence. Then find and circle it in the puzzle. Words can go up, down, across, or backwards.

1. He went to camp for the first time.
2. It was a lonely place.
3. Then she became his first friend.
4. They had lots of fun.

```
O   B   S   C
N   E   H   N
T   H E   Y
P   T I   L
```

B. Write the pronoun that agrees with the underlined noun in each set of sentences.

5. Todd joined the art class at camp.
   He made a wooden parrot.

6. The parrot was colorful.
   It had yellow and blue wings.

7. Tammy sat next to Todd.
   She worked on a drawing of a kitten.

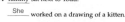

CHALLENGE

PLAY DIALOGUE Invite volunteers to practice and present their play dialogues. As they rehearse, encourage children to write more sentences or to elaborate on their writing.

Chapter Review

OBJECTIVES
- To review how to use nouns and pronouns correctly
- To understand how to use a telephone book

DAILY LANGUAGE PRACTICE

TRANSPARENCY 62

1 Laura likes hats, And it has many. (and; she)

2 Laura lent me and Bev two hat. (Bev and me; hats)

BRIDGE TO WRITING Bev and I wore the hats to school. (pronoun) looked great.

STANDARDIZED TEST PREP

Read the directions with children. Make sure they understand what they have to do. You may wish to use this page as an assessment after children have completed it independently.

TEST PREPARATION TIP
Item Type: Multiple Choice

TIP

Model this strategy to help children determine the correct answer:

First I read the sentence. I read the underlined pronoun *He.* I look to see which noun it replaces. It takes the place of *Matt.* I know that *Matt* is a boy's name and that it names only one. I look at the answer choices. *She* takes the place of a girl's name, and *It* takes the place of the name of a thing or an animal. So I choose *c.* because I know that *He* is correct.

Chapter Review

Choose the best answer for the underlined word or words.

1. Matt went to camp. <u>He</u> had never been there before.
   a. She
   b. It
   c. correct as is

2. Matt and Donny wanted to go to the lake. <u>It</u> hoped to catch fish.
   a. She
   b. They
   c. correct as is

3. The children sat around a campfire. <u>She</u> listened to stories.
   a. It
   b. They
   c. correct as is

4. The campers did a skit. <u>They</u> played the parts of a rabbit and a bear.
   a. It
   b. He
   c. correct as is

5. <u>I and Matt</u> took a hike with Ms. Jones.
   a. Matt and I
   b. Matt
   c. correct as is

6. She showed <u>me and Matt</u> new trails.
   a. Me
   b. Matt and me
   c. correct as is

Visit our website for more activities with using nouns and pronouns:
www.harcourtschool.com

398

Language Skills Assessment

PORTFOLIO ASSESSMENT
Have children select their best work from the following activities:

- **Writing Connection** *pages 391, 395, and 397;* TE activities, *pages 393 and 395.*

ONGOING ASSESSMENT
Evaluate the performance of 4-6 children using appropriate checklists and record forms from pages R65–R68 and R77–R79.

INTERNET Activities and exercises to help children prepare for state and standardized assessments appear on *The Learning Site:*

www.harcourtschool.com

■ Study Skills ■

Using a Telephone Book

A **telephone book** has the phone numbers and addresses of people and businesses. Use the guide words at the top of the page to find the page you need. The people's last names are in alphabetical order.

Hale—Hapford	
HALE Nathan 1 Elm St 555-0198	**HALFORD Sally** 22 West St 555-0164
HALE Robert 24 Main St 555-0110	**HALGAN Chris** 774 Oak St 555-0151
HALEY Bill 36 South St . . . 555-0156	**HALLER G.** 7 South St 555-0192
HALFON Tom 4 North St 555-0103	**HAO David** 43 Main St 555-0122

Practice

Use the telephone book page above to answer each question.

1. What is Nathan Hale's telephone number? 555-0198

2. Who lives at 774 Oak Street? Chris Halgan

3. Who else could be on this page — Stephen Glenn, Carol Hall, or Howard Jackson? Carol Hall

4. Where would Kim Hammond go on this page? between G. Haller and David Hao

399

■ Study Skills ■

Using a Telephone Book

TEACH/MODEL

Before you begin the page, ask children to share what they already know about the telephone book. You may want to bring in a telephone book and have children look through it and discuss what they see and read. Then read the explanation on page 399 together.

PRACTICE Have children use the sample page on page 399 to complete the questions. After children finish, have them share and discuss their answers.

WRAP-UP/ASSESS

SUMMARIZE Ask children to tell what they have learned about using a telephone book. Invite them to discuss how they think a telephone book might help them.

PRACTICE page 105

REACHING ALL LEARNERS

Name_____

Using a Telephone Book

Use the page from a telephone book to answer each question.

Samuels - Suarez	
SAMUELS, Cindy 34 West St. 555-0112	SMITH, K. 5 Thomas Circle 555-0120
SANBORN, George 62 Fifth Ave. 555-0122	SMITH, Shawna 267 Arcadia Place 555-0115
SANTOS, Lauren 19 Withers Ave. 555-0173	STANTON, Len 315 Rose Lane 555-0123
SEARLE, Lee 82 Park St. 555-0164	SUAREZ, N. 78 Branch St. 555-0103

1. What is Lee Searle's phone number? 555-0164

2. Who else could be on this page—Monica Stevens, Stanley Thomas, or John Swift? Monica Stevens

3. Who lives at 19 Withers Ave? Lauren Santos

4. Where would Tanisha Scard go on this page? between Lauren Santos and Lee Searle

5. Why are the guide words for this page Samuels - Suarez? They are the first and last names on the page.

> **TRY THIS!** Make your own telephone book. Write the names and phone numbers of ten people you know. Then put the names in ABC order.

Practice • Using Nouns and Pronouns Correctly   Unit 6 • Chapter 31   105

CHALLENGE

REACHING ALL LEARNERS

MAKE A TELEPHONE BOOK
Have children make a class telephone directory. Invite them to write the names, phone numbers, and addresses of places that interest them, such as the library, a museum, a sports store, or a bookstore. Remind them to put the names in alphabetical order. Have them include guide words at the top of each page.

LESSON ORGANIZER	DAY 1	DAY 2
DAILY LANGUAGE PRACTICE TRANSPARENCIES 63 64	1. I and my sister sees a frog. (My sister and I; see) 2. The frog is cute. We is grean. (It; green) **Bridge to Writing** My sister and I like pets, but (pronoun) don't have one.	1. our dog always bark at the squirrels. (Our; barks) 2. The squirrels runs away qwickly. (run; quickly) **Bridge to Writing** This squirrel (verb) an acorn.
ORAL WARM-UP Listening/Speaking	Imitate Animal Sounds p. 400	Act Out and Identify Verbs p. 402 *Grammar Jingles™* CD, Primary, Track 5
TEACH/MODEL GRAMMAR **KEY** ✔ = tested skill	✔ **SUBJECT-VERB AGREEMENT** pp. 400–401 **Literature:** "Sun Song" by Pat Mora • To evaluate a poem • To match a verb with the naming part and to write verbs	✔ **CHANGING Y TO I** pp. 402–403 • To understand that if a verb ends in a consonant plus *y*, *y* changes to *i* before *es* is added • To correctly write verbs to match naming parts
Reaching All Learners	**Challenge:** Activity Card 22, p. R62 **ESL:** *ESL Manual* pp. 154, 155 **Reteach:** *Reteach Activities Copying Masters* p. 64 *Practice Book* p. 106	**Modified Instruction** Below-Level: Identify Naming Parts Above-Level: Write Sentences **Challenge:** Write a Riddle p. 403 **ESL:** Act Out Sentences p. 402 *ESL Manual* pp. 154, 156 *Practice Book* p. 107 **Reteach:** *Reteach Activities Copying Masters* p. 65
WRITING	Identify Naming Parts and Verbs p. 401 Summarize/Reflect	Writing Connection p. 403 Writing a Paragraph Summarize/Reflect
CROSS-CURRICULAR/ ENRICHMENT	**Vocabulary Power** Word Meaning p. 400 bellow, **croak,** hoot, warble, yowl See *Vocabulary Power* book.	**Vocabulary Power** Related Words p. 400 *Vocabulary Power* book p. 94 **Vocabulary activity**

Visit *The Learning Site!*
www.harcourtschool.com

WRITING ACTIVITIES
Writing Express **CD-ROM**

DAY 3 | DAY 4 | DAY 5

DAY 3

1. my sister hurrys home after the storm. (My; hurries)

2. Ed and Al tries to jump over an puddle. (try; a)

Bridge to Writing Ann (form of the verb *try*) to open her old umbrella.

Use *Can Not* and *Can't* p. 404

Grammar Jingles™ CD, Primary, Track 21

✔ **WRITING CONTRACTIONS**
pp. 404–405
- To understand that a contraction is a way to write two words
- To use an apostrophe to replace a letter in a contraction and to use contractions in writing

- - - - - - - - - - - - - - - - - -

Modified Instruction
Below-Level: Write Contractions
Above-Level: Write Additional
 Sentences
Challenge: Write a Comic Strip
p. 405
ESL: Look for Contractions p. 404
ESL Manual pp. 154, 157
Reteach: *Reteach Activities Copying Masters* p. 66
Practice Book p. 108

- - - - - - - - - - - - - - - - - -

Writing Connection p. 405
 Giving Reasons
 Summarize/Reflect

Vocabulary Power

Onomatopoeia p. 400
Vocabulary Power book p. 95
Vocabulary activity

DAY 4

1. Why does'nt Eva like snakes! (doesn't; ?)

2. snakes really arn't so scary. (Snakes; aren't)

Bridge to Writing I (contraction for *do not*) like snakes either.

Talk About Animals p. 406

EXTRA PRACTICE p. 406–407
- To match a verb with the naming part and to write verbs that end with a consonant plus *y*
- To use contractions in writing

Practice and Assessment

- - - - - - - - - - - - - - - - - -

Challenge: Contraction Chart
p. 407
ESL: Play Match-Up p. 406
ESL Manual pp. 154, 158
Practice Book p. 109

- - - - - - - - - - - - - - - - - -

Writing Connection p. 407
 Do and Don't Chart

Vocabulary Power

Descriptive Words p. 400
Vocabulary Power book p. 96
Vocabulary activity
Language Play p. 407

DAY 5

1. My brother hurry too the window. (hurries; to)

2. He cant w'ait to go out in the snow. (can't; wait)

Bridge to Writing Why (contraction for *does not*) your little sister like snow?

TEST PREP **CHAPTER REVIEW** p. 408
- To review how to use verbs and contractions correctly
- To learn how to use an atlas

Test Preparation

- - - - - - - - - - - - - - - - - -

Challenge: Writing Facts p. 409
ESL: *ESL Manual* pp.154, 159
Practice Book p. 110

- - - - - - - - - - - - - - - - - -

Writing Application p. 409
 Maps

Study Skills p. 409
 Using an Atlas

Vocabulary Power

Synonyms p. 400

Subject-Verb
Agreement

OBJECTIVES

- To listen critically to interpret and evaluate a poem
- To understand that a verb must agree with the naming part of a sentence and to write verbs correctly

SPIRAL REVIEW

DAILY LANGUAGE PRACTICE

TRANSPARENCY 63

1 I and my sister sees a frog. (My sister and I; see)

2 The frog is cute. We is grean. (It; green)

BRIDGE TO WRITING My sister and I like pets, but ___(pronoun)___ don't have one.

ORAL WARM-UP

USE PRIOR KNOWLEDGE Ask volunteers to think of some animals and imitate the sounds they make. Have others guess the animals and say sentences, such as *A coyote howls.* Begin a list of animal-sound action words on chart paper or add them to your **Verb Word Wall**.

TEACH/MODEL

Tell children you will read a poem called "Sun Song." Ask them to listen carefully to discover who hears the sun's song and what they do when they hear it. Then have children turn to page 400, look at the illustration, and tell which of the animals are *ranitas* (little frogs). Reread the poem, having children join in with you.

DEVELOP ORAL LANGUAGE Ask children to recall who hears the sun's first song and what they do when they hear it. Call on volunteers to imitate the birds, the frogs, the bees, and the wind. Then add the verbs to the list on chart paper or to the **Word Wall**.

Subject-Verb Agreement

Read the poem.

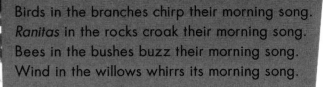

Birds in the branches hear the sun's first song.
Ranitas in the rocks hear the sun's first song.
Bees in the bushes hear the sun's first song.
Wind in the willows hears the sun's first song.

Birds in the branches chirp their morning song.
Ranitas in the rocks croak their morning song.
Bees in the bushes buzz their morning song.
Wind in the willows whirrs its morning song.

Sun song. Sun song. Sun song.

Pat Mora

400

Vocabulary Power

DAY 1 WORD MEANING Write: *croak.* **Find the word *croak* in the poem "Sun Song." What animal makes a croaking sound?**

DAY 2 RELATED WORDS Write: *croak, quack, caw.* **How are these words alike? What animals make these sounds?** (See also *Vocabulary Power*, page 94.)

DAY 3 ONOMATOPOEIA Write: *"Ribbet, ribbet," croak the frogs.* Ask volunteers to imitate the croaking sound of frogs. (See also *Vocabulary Power*, page 95.)

DAY 4 DESCRIPTIVE WORDS Read: *"My throat is sore,"* Jenny said. *"My throat is sore,"* Jenny croaked. **Which sentence is more descriptive? Why?** (See also *Vocabulary Power*, page 96.)

DAY 5 SYNONYMS **Make a list of words you might use in your writing in place of the word *said.***

Work with a group. Make up a tune and sing "Sun Song" or act out your favorite part. Then say more sentences to go with the poem.

> A verb should always **agree** with, or go with, the naming part of a sentence. When the naming part of a sentence tells about one, add **s** to the verb.
>
> The cat **meows** its morning song.
>
> When a naming part tells about more than one, do not add **s** to the verb.
>
> Dogs **bark** their morning song.

Write a verb in each sentence. Make sure that the verb agrees with the naming part. Responses will vary.

A duck quacks its morning song.

A frog _____ its morning song.

Frogs _____ their morning song.

A hen _____ its morning song.

Bears _____ their morning song.

401

WRITE After groups sing "Sun Song" and act out their favorite parts, record the sentences they say on chart paper. Call on volunteers to circle the naming part and underline the verb. Read the rules in the box and talk about how the examples and sentences on chart paper follow the rules.

Then have children look at the sample sentence at the bottom of page 401 and tell why *s* was added to the verb. Have children complete the remaining items and then share with a small group.

WRAP-UP/ASSESS

SUMMARIZE Reread the poem on page 400 with children. Then ask them to summarize and reflect on what they know about verbs. Have children write their reflections in their journals along with a pair of sentences they completed on page 401. **REFLECTION**

RETEACH

INTERVENTION Lessons in visual, auditory, and kinesthetic modalities: p. R38 and Reteach Activities Copying Masters, p. 64.

REACHING ALL LEARNERS

PRACTICE page 106

Name _____

Subject-Verb Agreement

A. Write the correct verb to complete each sentence.

1. The baby kangaroo (**ride, rides**) in the pouch. — rides

2. He (**peeks, peek**) out. — peeks

3. The mother kangaroo (**hops, hop**) down the trail. — hops

4. Then she (**stop, stops**) to get food. — stops

5. She (**eat, eats**) quickly. — eats

B. Use a word from the box to complete each sentence.

| swims | look | swing | watch | naps |

6. Jack and Mona ___watch___ the kangaroos.

7. Then the children ___look___ at other animals.

8. A polar bear ___swims___ in the cool water.

9. A goat ___naps___ under a tree.

10. The monkeys ___swing___ from branch to branch.

TRY THIS! Write three sentences about things that zoo animals do. Underline the verbs.

106 Unit 6 • Chapter 32   Practice • Using Verbs Correctly

CHALLENGE

MAKE PAPER BAG ANIMALS Have children use **Challenge Activity Card 22** (page R62) to make puppets of the animals in the poem as well as any other animals they would like to add. Then have children reread and act out the poem, adding new lines for new animals.

Challenge Activity Card 22

Make Paper Bag Animals

---

page 64

Subject-Verb Agreement

Read each sentence aloud. Circle the verb in each sentence. Underline the naming part.

EXAMPLE: The pilot (waves) to the children.

1. Mom and Dad (lift) the suitcases.

2. Gina (helps) the baby.

3. The family (walks) into the airport.

4. A plane (flies) above the airport.

5. The engine (roars) loudly.

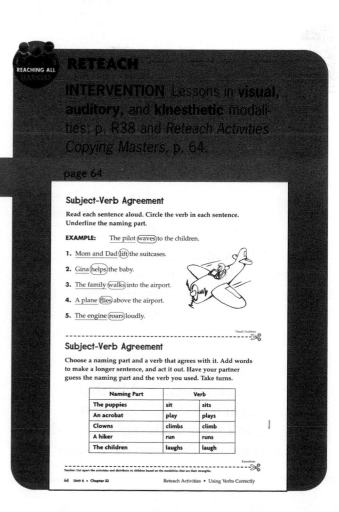

Subject-Verb Agreement

Choose a naming part and a verb that agrees with it. Add words to make a longer sentence, and act it out. Have your partner guess the naming part and the verb you used. Take turns.

Naming Part	Verb	
The puppies	sit	sits
An acrobat	play	plays
Clowns	climbs	climb
A hiker	run	runs
The children	laughs	laugh

Teacher: Cut apart the activities and distribute to children based on the modalities that are their strengths.

64 Unit 6 • Chapter 32   Reteach Activities • Using Verbs Correctly

Changing *y* to *i*

OBJECTIVES

- To understand that if a verb ends in a consonant plus *y*, *y* changes to *i* before *es* is added when telling about one
- To correctly write verbs when the naming parts of sentences tell about one

DAILY LANGUAGE PRACTICE

TRANSPARENCY 63

1 our dog always bark at the squirrels. (Our; barks)

2 The squirrels runs away qwickly. (run; quickly)

BRIDGE TO WRITING This squirrel ___(verb)___ an acorn.

ORAL WARM-UP

USE PRIOR KNOWLEDGE Ask volunteers to pantomime the following for others to guess: a person carrying too many bags, a bird about to fly, a person drying off with a towel, a crying child, a dog burying a bone. Have children describe each action and identify the verb. Add *carry*, *fly*, *dry*, *cry*, and *bury* to the **Verb Word Wall**.

Grammar Jingles™ **CD, Primary** Use Track 5 for review and reinforcement of changing *y* to *i*.

TEACH/MODEL

Introduce the concept by using the explanation and examples. Ask children to identify the verb in each sentence. Have them discuss when the action takes place (now) and if the naming part tells about one or more than one (about one).

GUIDED PRACTICE Work with children to complete each sentence. Ask them to explain in their own words when to change *y* to *i* before adding *es* and when not to. Have children say each sentence aloud.

Changing *y* to *i*

When the naming part of a sentence tells about one, add **s** to the verb. If the verb ends with a consonant plus **y**, change **y** to **i**. Then add **es**.

Tom and Tina **carry** the fishing rods.
Dad **carries** a basket, too.

Guided Practice

Write each verb in ( ) correctly.

1. Mom (study) the map before going to the lake.
   studies
2. Mom (copy) the map onto a sheet of paper.
   copies
3. Tom (hurry) to get ready on time.
   hurries
4. Tina (carry) the sandwiches to the car.
   carries
5. Tom (try) to put the fishing rods in the trunk.
   tries

402

Vocabulary Power page 94

ESL

Name _____

These words are related because they all name sounds.

bellow   croak   hoot   warble   yowl

For boxes 1–5, read the sentence and draw a picture of an animal that makes the sound. For 6, draw a picture showing when you might make one of the sounds.

1. A bellow is deep and roaring.	**2.** A croak is low and hoarse.
3. A hoot is a kind of cry.	**4.** A warble is trilling and song-like.
5. A yowl is a kind of whine.	**6.** I can _____

94   Unit 6 • Chapter 32   Vocabulary Power

REACHING ALL LEARNERS

ACT OUT SENTENCES Have volunteers act out the verbs *carry*, *study*, *cry* while classmates say each volunteer's name and movement, such as *John carries a box*, or *Meg and Don carry a box*. Repeat each sentence, emphasizing the verb. Write the sentence on the board and review the rule for changing *y* to *i* before adding *es*. Have a volunteer circle the naming part and underline the verb.

Remember
When the naming part of a sentence tells about one, add *s* to the verb. If the verb ends with a consonant plus *y*, change *y* to *i*. Then add *es*.

Independent Practice

Write each verb in ( ) correctly.

6. Dad (carry) the fishing rods to the lake.
   carries
7. Mom (try) to catch some fish.
   tries
8. Tina (study) the animals by the lake.
   studies
9. Tom (copy) his sister, and they both watch.
   copies
10. A frog (hurry) out of the water.
    hurries
11. The frog (spy) some bugs.
    spies
12. The bugs (fly) away.
    fly
13. Two birds (dry) their feathers in the sun.
    dry
14. One bird (cry) when it sees a worm.
    cries
15. The worm (bury) itself in the ground.
    buries

Writing Connection

Writing a Paragraph Draw a picture of an animal and write a paragraph about it. Use some of these verbs.

carry   hurry   dry   try   cry   fly

Use the spell-check on your computer to help you check that you spelled the verbs correctly.

403

Independent Practice
Have children complete the Independent Practice, or modify it by using the following suggestions:

MODIFIED INSTRUCTION

BELOW-LEVEL STUDENTS Have children circle the naming part and decide whether it tells about one or about more than one.

ABOVE-LEVEL STUDENTS After children finish, have them write two sentences for two of these verbs: *bury, fry, worry, carry.* The naming part of one sentence should tell about one.

Writing Connection

Writing a Paragraph Have volunteers display their drawings and read aloud their paragraphs. Then ask children to create a final draft of their paragraphs. Remind them to check for subject-verb agreement as they edit.

WRAP-UP/ASSESS

SUMMARIZE Ask children to summarize what they have learned about verbs that end with a consonant plus *y*.

RETEACH

INTERVENTION Lessons in **visual, auditory,** and **kinesthetic** modalities: p. R38 and *Reteach Activities Copying Masters,* p. 65.

PRACTICE page 107

Name _____

Changing *y* to *i*

A. Circle the correct form of the verb.

1. Theresa (**hurries**, hurrys) to the lake.
2. She (carrys, **carries**) a sack.
3. She (**tries**, trys) to climb into the boat.
4. Fred (scurrys, **scurries**) behind her.
5. A bird (flys, **flies**) onto the boat.

B. Write the correct form of the verb in ( ).

6. Another bird (copy) ____copies____ the first bird and lands on the boat.
7. The boat (carry) ____carries____ Theresa and Fred.
8. Fred (study) ____studies____ the sky.
9. Theresa (spy) ____spies____ a fish in the water.
10. She (try) ____tries____ to guess what kind it is.

TRY THIS! Use the following words in sentences that tell about one: *try, fry,* and *carry.* Draw a picture for each sentence.

Practice • Using Verbs Correctly   Unit 6 • Chapter 12   107

CHALLENGE

WRITE A RIDDLE Have children choose some of the verbs from pages 400–403 and use them in riddles. Then ask children to read their riddles for small groups to solve. You may wish to use these as models: What gets wetter as it dries? (a towel) What carries its trunk wherever it goes? (an elephant)

page 65

Changing *y* to *i*

Read aloud each sentence. Underline the verb.

1. I <u>hurry</u> outside.
   Grandma <u>hurries</u> outside, too.
2. A baseball <u>flies</u> by.
   Two more <u>fly</u> by.
3. I <u>try</u> to catch a ball.
   Grandma <u>tries</u> to catch a ball, too.
4. I <u>carry</u> one inside.
   She <u>carries</u> another one inside.

Changing *y* to *i*

Read each sentence. Cut out the verbs at the bottom of the page. Glue the verb that best completes each sentence.

1. Spot [scurries] outside.
2. He [buries] the ball.
3. Grandma [tries] to find the ball.
4. Grandma [spies] it under the tree.

| bury | buries | spy | spies |
| scurry | scurries | try | tries |

Reteach Activities • Using Verbs Correctly   Unit 6 • Chapter 12   65

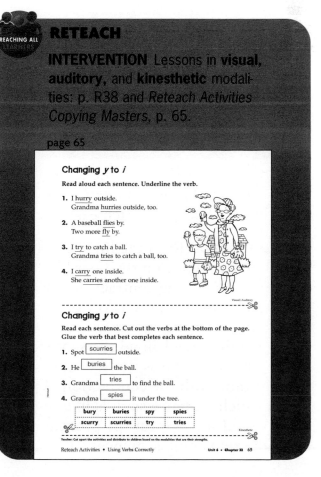

Writing Contractions

OBJECTIVES

- To understand that a contraction is a short way to write two words
- To use an apostrophe to replace a letter or letters in a contraction and to use contractions in writing

DAILY LANGUAGE PRACTICE

TRANSPARENCY 63

1 my sister hurrys home after the storm. (My; hurries)

2 Ed and Al tries to jump over an puddle. (try; a)

BRIDGE TO WRITING Ann (form of the verb _try_) to open her old umbrella.

ORAL WARM-UP

USE PRIOR KNOWLEDGE Ask children to brainstorm things they can and can't do when they play outside. Write two sentences with contractions; then rewrite them using _can not_ instead of _can't_. Have children discuss the differences and think of other contractions they know.

Grammar Jingles™ **CD, Primary** Use Track 21 for review and reinforcement of contractions.

TEACH/MODEL

Read the explanation and the examples with children. Have them name the letters that are left out in each example.

GUIDED PRACTICE Read the first sentence aloud; write _has not_ on the board. Ask a volunteer to say the contraction for _has not_, write it beneath the two words, and circle the letter the apostrophe replaces. Have children read aloud the sentence twice, the first time as written and the second time with the contraction. Ask them which sentence sounds like the one they would say. Repeat the procedure with the remaining sentences.

Writing Contractions

A **contraction** is a short way to write two words. In a contraction, one or more letters are left out. An **apostrophe** (') is a mark that takes the place of the missing letters.

are + not **= aren't**   can + not **= can't**

The seeds **aren't** sprouting.
The seeds **can't** grow in the snow.

Guided Practice

Write the contraction for the underlined words.

1. The snow <u>has</u> <u>not</u> stopped.
   hasn't
2. Eva <u>can</u> <u>not</u> go outside.
   can't
3. The weather <u>is</u> <u>not</u> good.
   isn't
4. Eva <u>did</u> <u>not</u> want to get wet.
   didn't
5. She <u>could</u> <u>not</u> check the seeds she planted.
   couldn't

404

Vocabulary Power page 95

Name _____   Onomatopoeia

There are many words that describe sounds.

bellow   croak   hoot   warble   yowl

Write the above sounds in the following categories. Add other words to complete each category. Accept reasonable additions.

LOUD SOUNDS	QUIET SOUNDS	GRUFF SOUNDS
bang	hush	grunt
bellow		croak
yowl		

ANIMAL SOUNDS	WEATHER SOUNDS	MUSIC SOUNDS
yowl	whoosh	toot-toot
bellow		warble
croak		
hoot		
warble		

Vocabulary Power   Unit 6 • Chapter 32   95

REACHING ALL LEARNERS   **ESL**

LOOK FOR CONTRACTIONS
Display sentences with contractions, such as the following: _I didn't see Ann today. Ann wasn't in school. We haven't seen Ann since Monday. She hasn't been in school all week. My friend isn't feeling well._ Have volunteers read each sentence, identify the contraction, and then say the two words that form the contraction.

Remember A contraction is a short way to write two words. An apostrophe (') takes the place of the letters that are left out.

Independent Practice

Write the contraction for the underlined words.

6. The seeds <u>have</u> <u>not</u> grown in the garden.
   haven't
7. They <u>did not</u> get enough sun.
   didn't
8. Eva <u>had</u> <u>not</u> planted them correctly.
   hadn't
9. The seeds <u>were</u> <u>not</u> in a good spot.
   weren't
10. The soil <u>was</u> <u>not</u> warm enough.
    wasn't
11. Eva <u>is</u> <u>not</u> happy.
    isn't
12. She <u>did</u> <u>not</u> think this would happen.
    didn't
13. Eva <u>should</u> <u>not</u> feel sad.
    shouldn't
14. Eva <u>does</u> <u>not</u> want this to happen again.
    doesn't
15. She <u>can</u> <u>not</u> wait to plant other seeds.
    can't

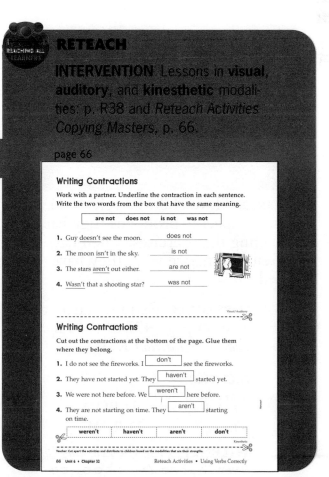

Writing Connection

Giving Reasons Write a few sentences to explain why you think you shouldn't plant seeds in cold, dark places. Use some contractions in your sentences.

To type an apostrophe, push the **"** key.

405

Independent Practice

Have children complete the Independent Practice, or modify it by using the following suggestions:

MODIFIED INSTRUCTION

BELOW-LEVEL STUDENTS Suggest that children circle the letters the apostrophe will replace and write the contraction.

ABOVE-LEVEL STUDENTS Have children write three sentences, leaving a space where the contraction belongs. Children can trade papers with partners and write the contraction.

Writing Connection

Giving Reasons Have children work in small groups to brainstorm reasons why seeds do not grow well in cold, dark places.

WRAP-UP/ASSESS

SUMMARIZE Have children summarize and reflect on what they have learned about contractions. **REFLECTION**

RETEACH

INTERVENTION Lessons in **visual**, **auditory**, and **kinesthetic** modalities: p. R38 and *Reteach Activities Copying Masters*, p. 66.

page 66

Writing Contractions

Work with a partner. Underline the contraction in each sentence. Write the two words from the box that have the same meaning.

are not	does not	is not	was not

1. Guy <u>doesn't</u> see the moon. ___does not___
2. The moon <u>isn't</u> in the sky. ___is not___
3. The stars <u>aren't</u> out either. ___are not___
4. <u>Wasn't</u> that a shooting star? ___was not___

- -

Writing Contractions

Cut out the contractions at the bottom of the page. Glue them where they belong.

1. I do not see the fireworks. I [don't] see the fireworks.
2. They have not started yet. They [haven't] started yet.
3. We were not here before. We [weren't] here before.
4. They are not starting on time. They [aren't] starting on time.

weren't	haven't	aren't	don't

Teacher: Cut apart the activities and distribute to children based on the modalities that are their strengths.

66 Unit 6 • Chapter 32   Reteach Activities • Using Verbs Correctly

---

PRACTICE page 108

Name _____

Writing Contractions

can't	shouldn't	aren't	doesn't	didn't

A. Write a contraction from the box for the underlined words.

1. Steve <u>does not</u> have an umbrella. doesn't
2. He <u>should not</u> play in the rain. shouldn't
3. The others <u>are not</u> outside. aren't
4. They <u>did not</u> bring umbrellas. didn't
5. Steve <u>cannot</u> wait to go out. can't

B. Write a contraction for the underlined words.

6. The rain <u>is not</u> stopping. isn't
7. They <u>were not</u> ready for this. weren't
8. The wind <u>has not</u> stopped blowing. hasn't
9. Lisa <u>cannot</u> walk home in the storm. can't
10. They <u>have not</u> been outside all day. haven't

TRY THIS! Write three sentences about things you do not do when there is bad weather. Use contractions in your sentences.

108 Unit 6 • Chapter 32   Practice • Using Verbs Correctly

CHALLENGE

WRITE A COMIC STRIP Have children work in groups to draw comic strips showing what you should and shouldn't do when eating at the table. Invite children to use contractions in the captions or speech bubbles.

You shouldn't stand on your chair.

Extra Practice

OBJECTIVES
- To recognize that a verb agrees with the naming part of a sentence and to correctly write verbs that end with a consonant plus y
- To use contractions in writing

DAILY LANGUAGE PRACTICE

TRANSPARENCY 64

1 Why does'nt Eva like snakes! (doesn't;?)

2 snakes really arn't so scary. (Snakes; aren't)

BRIDGE TO WRITING I (contraction for *do not*) like snakes either.

ORAL WARM-UP

USE PRIOR KNOWLEDGE Ask children to talk about what some animals do and don't do. Prompt them with questions, such as: *Could a monkey sing?* (No, a monkey couldn't sing. A monkey *could* swing.) or *Could a snake hug and kiss?* (No, it couldn't. It *could* hiss.) Have children form their own questions and answers.

TEACH/MODEL

Read both sets of directions, making sure children understand how to complete each section. Have children share their answers with a partner or in small groups before you read aloud the answers.

WRAP-UP/ASSESS

SUMMARIZE Have children reflect on and share any specific problems they had in completing the exercises. Then have children summarize what they have learned.

ADDITIONAL PRACTICE Extra practice items are provided on page 477 of the *Pupil Edition* (*Teacher's Edition* R7).

TECHNOLOGY
Grammar Practice and Assessment CD-ROM
Writing Express CD-ROM

INTERNET Visit *The Learning Site!*
www.harcourtschool.com

Using Verbs Correctly

Extra Practice

Write each present-tense verb in ( ) correctly.

1. Mario and Luz (copy) their science homework.
   copy
2. Luz (study) the weather.
   studies
3. Mario (want) to learn about sunflowers.
   wants
4. He (bury) some seeds in the soil.
   buries
5. Luz (help) him.
   helps
6. They (try) to grow sunflowers in winter!
   try

Write a contraction for the underlined words.

7. It has not snowed today.
   hasn't
8. Luz thinks the weather was not cold enough.
   wasn't
9. It did not rain either.
   didn't
10. The temperature is not high.
    isn't

406

Vocabulary Power page 96

Name _____
Descriptive Words

Which words are more descriptive? Why?

"Hurray," Mitchell said.   "Ouch," Joan said.
"Hurray," Mitchell bellowed.   "Ouch," Joan yowled.

Substitute another word for said. Write the word on the blank. Draw a picture to illustrate the sentence. Share your ideas with classmates. Possible responses are given. Accept reasonable responses.

1. "Let's play ball," said Juan.	2. "I'm late," said Doris.
shouted	sighed
3. "What time is it?" said Raj.	4. "Help, help!" said Barnie.
asked	screamed
5. "Oink, oink," said the pig.	6. "Grrr, grrr," said the bear.
squealed	growled

96   Unit 6 • Chapter 32   Vocabulary Power

REACHING ALL LEARNERS   ESL

PLAY MATCH-UP Write contractions on one set of index cards. Write the two words that form each contraction on another set of index cards. Display each set of cards randomly. Have volunteers match the cards and then use the contractions in sentences.

Language Play

Act It Out

- Work with a small group. Sit in a circle.
- Think of ways animals move and sound.
- The first person says a sentence that tells how one animal moves or sounds.
- The next person says a sentence that tells how two of one kind of animal move or sound.
- Keep going around the circle until everyone has had at least two chances to say a sentence.

Writing Connection

Do and Don't Chart Make a chart that shows classroom rules. Think about what you should do. Then think about what you should not do. Write these rules in your Do and Don't Chart.

Classroom Rules	
Do	**Don't**
1. Raise your hand if you want to speak. 2. Keep your desk clean.	1. Don't talk out of turn.

407

Language Play

Have children play "Act It Out" in small groups. Remind them to adapt the volume of their voices according to their group's size. Suggest that they reread "Sun Song" for ideas about how birds, frogs, and bees sound. Have the members of each group choose a person to record all the sentences they say. Then ask each group to act out some of its sentences for the other groups.

Writing Connection

Do and Don't Chart Check to see that children have successfully written a chart by using the criteria below.

CRITERIA

- ☑ Begins appropriate sentences with *Don't*, followed by an action verb.
- ☑ Writes the apostrophe in contractions correctly.
- ☑ Writes the sentences in a chart.

 PORTFOLIO OPPORTUNITY You may want to have children place their writing in their portfolios after sharing it with classmates or take it home to share and discuss with family members.

PRACTICE page 109

REACHING ALL LEARNERS

Name _____

Extra Practice

A. Circle the correct verb to complete each sentence.

1. Tiana and her friends (waits, **wait**) with her mom.

2. Mom (point, **points**) to the sky diver.

3. The diver (**glides**, glide) through the sky.

4. Soon the parachute (open, **opens**) wide.

B. Write the correct form of the verb in ( ) on the line.

5. The diver (fly) ____flies____ through the sky.

6. She (carry) ____carries____ a small banner.

7. Tiana (try) ____tries____ to read the banner.

C. Write a contraction for the underlined words.

8. She cannot read the banner yet. ____can't____

9. She does not know it is for her. ____doesn't____

10. Her party was not supposed to start until tomorrow. ____wasn't____

Practice • Using Verbs Correctly   Unit 6 • Chapter 32   109

CHALLENGE

REACHING ALL LEARNERS

CONTRACTION CHART Point out that in this chapter, children have learned about contractions with *not*. Have children work in pairs or small groups to think of other kinds of contractions they know and use. Have them organize the contractions on a chart. To help children get started, write the following on the board: *I'm, I've, I'll, I'd*. Have children share and compare their charts.

Chapter Review

STANDARDIZED TEST PREP

OBJECTIVES

- To review how to use verbs and contractions correctly
- To learn how to use an atlas

DAILY LANGUAGE PRACTICE

TRANSPARENCY 64

1 My brother hurry too the window. (hurries; to)

2 He cant w'ait to go out in the snow. (can't; wait)

BRIDGE TO WRITING Why (contraction for *does not*) your little sister like snow?

STANDARDIZED TEST PREP

Read the directions with children. Make sure they understand what they have to do. You may wish to use this page as an assessment after children have completed it independently.

TEST PREPARATION TIP
Item Type: Multiple Choice

TIP

Model this strategy to help children determine the correct answer:

I read the first sentence and the underlined word. I ask myself if the verb agrees with the naming part. The naming part (the children) **tells about more than one. I know that you do not add *s* to a verb if the naming part tells about more than one. The verb *travel* does not end in *s*. I read the four answer choices and find *d, correct as is*. I see that it makes the most sense of all the choices.**

Using Verbs Correctly

Chapter Review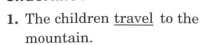

Choose the best answer for each underlined word.

1. The children <u>travel</u> to the mountain.
   - a. travels
   - b. traveling
   - c. traveles
   - **d. correct as is**

2. Alec <u>study</u> the tracks in the snow.
   - **a. studies**
   - b. studys
   - c. study's
   - d. correct as is

3. His friends <u>plays</u> in the snow.
   - a. plaies
   - b. playes
   - **c. play**
   - d. correct as is

4. Maria <u>trys</u> to pick up some snow.
   - a. try
   - **b. tries**
   - c. tryes
   - d. correct as is

5. She <u>doesn't</u> wear gloves.
   - a. do'nt
   - b. doesnt
   - c. don't
   - **d. correct as is**

6. Snow <u>melt</u> in her hands.
   - **a. melts**
   - b. melt's
   - c. melties
   - d. correct as is

 Visit our website
for more activities on
using verbs correctly:
www.harcourtschool.com

408

Language Skills Assessment

PORTFOLIO ASSESSMENT
Have children select their best work from the following activities:

- **Writing Connection,** pages 403, 405, 407; TE activities, pages 403, 405, 409.

ONGOING ASSESSMENT
Evaluate the performance of 4-6 students using appropriate checklists and record forms from pages R65–R68 and R77–R79.

 INTERNET Activities and exercises to help children prepare for state and standardized assessments appear on *The Learning Site:*
www.harcourtschool.com

■ Study Skills ■

Using an Atlas

An **atlas** is a book of maps. An atlas of the United States shows maps of all the states in the country. It may show where cities and bodies of water are. Look in the Table of Contents or the Index to help you find the map you need.

This map is like one you can find in an atlas.

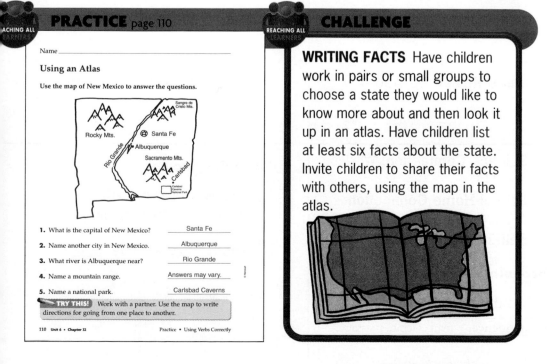

Practice

Use the map of Texas to answer the questions.

1. Why do you think Austin has a star by it?
   Possible response: It is the capital.
2. Which city is closest to Dallas?
   Fort Worth
3. What body of water is Corpus Christi near?
   Gulf of Mexico
4. Which city is farthest west?
   El Paso
5. Imagine that you have an atlas of maps of the United States that are listed in alphabetical order. Would you look near the beginning, middle, or end to find a map of Texas?
   near the end

409

■ Study Skills ■

Using an Atlas

TEACH/MODEL

Remind children that in Chapter 26, they learned about using a map. Have children tell what they can learn about where they live by looking at a map. Then write the word *atlas* on the board, and ask if anyone knows what an *atlas* is. After sharing ideas, have children read about the atlas at the top of page 409. If possible, invite children to look through an actual atlas.

PRACTICE If you have an atlas, call on a volunteer to use the table of contents or the index to find a map of Texas. When children have answered the questions, have volunteers share their answers.

WRAP-UP/ASSESS

SUMMARIZE Ask children to tell what an atlas is and how to use it.

PRACTICE page 110

REACHING ALL LEARNERS

Name _____

Using an Atlas

Use the map of New Mexico to answer the questions.

1. What is the capital of New Mexico? _Santa Fe_
2. Name another city in New Mexico. _Albuquerque_
3. What river is Albuquerque near? _Rio Grande_
4. Name a mountain range. _Answers may vary._
5. Name a national park. _Carlsbad Caverns_

TRY THIS! Work with a partner. Use the map to write directions for going from one place to another.

110 Unit 6 • Chapter 32   Practice • Using Verbs Correctly

CHALLENGE

REACHING ALL LEARNERS

WRITING FACTS Have children work in pairs or small groups to choose a state they would like to know more about and then look it up in an atlas. Have children list at least six facts about the state. Invite children to share their facts with others, using the map in the atlas.

Writing a Book Report

LESSON ORGANIZER	DAY 1	DAY 2
DAILY LANGUAGE PRACTICE TRANSPARENCY 65	1. ask Mr. Blueberry her first name. (Ask; his) 2. He hurryed to write for I. (hurried; me)	1. My dog bury bones in the hyard. (buries; yard) 2. That dog carrys a sticks in its mouth. (carries; stick)
ORAL WARM-UP Listening/Speaking	Talk About Choosing Books p. 410	Talk About Favorite Games p. 412
TEACH/MODEL WRITING	✔ **WRITING A BOOK REPORT** **Literature Model:** Book Report pp. 410–411 **WRITER'S CRAFT** • To read and respond to a book report as a model for writing • To recognize and use examples to support statements made in a book report **Think About It** p. 411	**GUIDED WRITING** **Giving Examples** pp. 412–413 • To give examples to support ideas • To write examples to complete a book report **Writing and Thinking:** Reflect p. 413
Reaching All Learners	**ESL:** *ESL Manual,* pp. 160–161	**Challenge:** Videotape Reviews p. 413 **ESL:** Read With a Partner p. 413 *ESL Manual,* p. 160
GRAMMAR	**Unit 6 Review** pp. 456–457	**Unit 6 Review** pp. 456–457
CROSS-CURRICULAR/ ENRICHMENT	**Science Connection:** Whales p. 411 **School-Home Connection:** Find Out About Books p. 411 **Self-Initiated Writing** p. 411	**Vocabulary Power** Related Words p. 410 *Vocabulary Power* book, p. 97 📷 **Vocabulary activity**

KEY
✔ = tested writing form/skill

Vocabulary Power

Word Meaning p. 410

> **correspondence,** e-mail, memo, message, post
>
> See *Vocabulary Power* book.

DAY 3

1. *Abuela* is one of me favorite storys. (my; stories)

2. Abuela flys around New york City. (flies; York)

Talk About Making Recommendations p. 414

GUIDED WRITING
✔ **Applying the Craft**
pp. 414–415
  • To use a model for writing a book report
  • To prewrite and draft a book report

 Read and Respond to the Model p. 414

- - - - - - - - - - - -

Interactive Writing: Model Drafting p. 415
ESL:
  ESL Manual, p. 160

- - - - - - - - - - - -

Unit 6 Review pp. 456–457

Social Studies Connection: Using Information Books p. 415

Vocabulary Power

  Clipped Words p. 410
  Vocabulary Power book, p. 98

  Vocabulary activity

DAY 4

1. How did your like that book, (you; ?)

2. I cant' read it nwo. (can't; now)

Review What to Include in a Book Report p. 416

GUIDED WRITING
Editing Your Book Report
p. 416
  • To peer conference in editing a book report
  • To edit a book report and share it aloud

- - - - - - - - - - - -

Peer Conferencing p. 416
ESL:
  ESL Manual, p. 160

- - - - - - - - - - - -

Unit 6 Review pp. 456–457

LISTENING AND SPEAKING:
Book Reports p. 416

Vocabulary Power

  Jargon p. 410
  Vocabulary Power book, p. 99

  Vocabulary activity

DAY 5

1. Lets goes to the park. (Let's go)

2. Has you been there before. (Have; before?)

Discuss Correct Letter Formation p. 417

HANDWRITING
Forming Letters Correctly
  p. 417
  • To form letters correctly

- - - - - - - - - - - -

Writing Resource: Tracing Letters p. 417
ESL:
  ESL Manual, p. 160

- - - - - - - - - - - -

Unit 6 Review pp. 456–457

Vocabulary Power

  Technology p. 410

Writer's Craft
Giving Examples

OBJECTIVES
- To read and respond to a book report as a model for writing
- To recognize and use examples to support statements made in a book report

DAILY LANGUAGE PRACTICE

TRANSPARENCY 65

1 ask Mr. Blueberry her first name.
(Ask; his)

2 He hurryed to write it for I.
(hurried; me)

ORAL WARM-UP

USE PRIOR KNOWLEDGE Discuss with children how they choose a book to read for fun. If needed, suggest that we sometimes read books that others recommend.

TEACH/MODEL

Read and discuss the introductory text on page 410 and have children read the model book report.

ANALYZE THE LITERATURE Use these questions for discussing the book report.

1. **Who are the main characters in *Dear Mr. Blueberry*?** (It is about a girl named Emily and her teacher, Mr. Blueberry.) **LITERAL: NOTE DETAILS**

2. **How does the writer of the book report feel about the book? Why?** (The writer likes it because he or she learned a lot about whales from it.) **INFERENTIAL: SUMMARIZE**

Giving Examples

A **book report** tells what a book is about. It names the title and the author of the book. Then it tells who the characters are and what they do.

In a book report a writer tells what he or she thinks about a book. The writer may also include **examples**, or descriptions of parts of the book. Examples can show what a writer means or why a writer thinks a certain way.

Read this book report. What is the book about? What does the writer think about the book? Why?

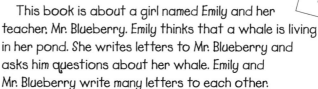
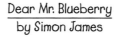

> Dear Mr. Blueberry
> by Simon James
>
> This book is about a girl named Emily and her teacher, Mr. Blueberry. Emily thinks that a whale is living in her pond. She writes letters to Mr. Blueberry and asks him questions about her whale. Emily and Mr. Blueberry write many letters to each other.
>
> I like this book because it is unusual. The whole book is letters that the characters write. I also learned a lot about whales. I learned that whales live in salt water and eat tiny animals. You will like this book if you like whales.

410

Vocabulary Power

DAY 1 WORD MEANING Write: *Emily and Mr. Blueberry had a **correspondence.*** Discuss the meaning of *correspondence*. (communicating by letters)

DAY 2 RELATED WORDS List: *correspondence, letters, memo, message, post, notes.* **How are these words related?** (See also *Vocabulary Power*, page 97.)

DAY 3 CLIPPED WORDS List: *electronic mail, e-mail.* **How is the word e-mail like an abbreviation?** (See also *Vocabulary Power*, page 98.)

DAY 4 JARGON Write: What is your e-mail address? **Is your e-mail address the same as your street address? How is it different?** (See also *Vocabulary Power*, page 99.)

DAY 5 TECHNOLOGY If possible, suggest that children correspond by writing each other e-mail messages about favorite books. Make a collection of their correspondence.

If a book has an illustrator as well as an author, write the illustrator's name under the author's name. You may even want to tell about the book's art in your report. Remember to include examples in your writing about the art.

Think About It

1. What does the writer tell about in the first paragraph of the book report? What does the writer tell about in the second paragraph?

2. Do you think you would like this book? Use examples from the book report to tell why or why not.

411

GIVING EXAMPLES Read the introductory text on page 411. Explain that writers often give examples to help readers better understand what they mean.

Have children find and discuss some of the examples the writer uses in the book report.

Think About It

1. Children should note that the first paragraph of the book report tells what the book is mainly about. The second paragraph tells why the writer of the book report likes the book. **INFERENTIAL:** TEXT STRUCTURE

2. Have children explain whether they think they would like the book and support their answers with examples from the book report. **CRITICAL:** EXPRESS PERSONAL OPINIONS

SELF-INITIATED WRITING Have children respond to the book report they just read through self-initated writing. Give children a writing prompt like the following:

You look out the window and see a whale in *your* yard. It is looking back at you in a curious way. Choose one of the forms listed below to write what happens with the whale.

• news report • story • friendly letter

Children could also respond by other methods, such as through drama or art.

WRAP-UP/ASSESS

SUMMARIZE Have children talk about why writers include examples when they write book reports. They can use their journals to record their reflections. **REFLECTION**

TECHNOLOGY
Additional writing activities are provided on the *Writing Express* CD-ROM

Science Connection

WHALES Have children write questions about whales that can be answered through investigation. Children can find many interesting pictures and facts online about whales and dolphins at websites like the following:

http://whales.ot.com/whales/cetacean/home.html

School-Home Connection

FIND OUT MORE ABOUT BOOKS Suggest that children watch a show about books, such as *Reading Rainbow* on the public broadcasting TV station, together with family members and then look for some of the recommended books at the local library.

Writer's Craft
Giving Examples

OBJECTIVES
- To give examples to support ideas
- To write examples to complete a book report

DAILY LANGUAGE PRACTICE

TRANSPARENCY 65

❶ My dog bury bones in the hyard.
(buries; yard)

❷ That dog carrys a sticks in its
mouth. (carries; stick)

ORAL WARM-UP

USE PRIOR KNOWLEDGE Ask volunteers to tell why they like a particular game, TV show, or computer software program. Ask them to give specific reasons to help classmates understand their choice.

GUIDED WRITING

USE EXAMPLES TO SUPPORT IDEAS Read and discuss the introductory material with children. Explain to them that they will give examples to support ideas. You may wish to do the first item in activity A together. Tell them that they can use the Idea Bank and their own ideas to think of examples. When children are finished, discuss their responses and the reason for the example they used.

Writer's Craft

Giving Examples

Examples show what the writer means.

I like this book because it is unusual. *The whole book is letters.*

The writer could have said only that the book is unusual. The second sentence tells **why** it is unusual.

I also learned a lot about whales. *I learned that whales live in salt water and eat tiny animals.*

The writer could have said only that he or she learned a lot about whales. The second sentence gives an example of **what** the writer learned.

A. Give an example to support each idea below. Use the Idea Bank to help you.

Answers may vary.
1. This book is good.
2. The movie is funny.
3. That board game is fun.
4. The show was boring.

Idea Bank

- **There was no action in the first half.**
- **The main character has an exciting adventure in space.**
- **My whole family can play it together.**
- **The main character tells a funny joke about an apple.**

412

Vocabulary Power page 97

Name _____

These words in dark print are related because they all have something to do with communication.

correspondence e-mail memo message post

Draw pictures or write descriptions to illustrate the meaning of each word.

1. message	2. e-mail
3. post	4. memo
5. correspondence	

Vocabulary Power   Unit 6 • Chapter 33 97

B. Reread "Jalapeño Bagels," on pages 366–372. Then give examples from the story to complete this book report.

Answers may vary somewhat.

Jalapeño Bagels
by Natasha Wing

"Jalapeño Bagels" is about a boy named Pablo. He is trying to choose a food for his class's International Day. Pablo goes to his parents' bakery. At the bakery, Pablo helps his parents make many treats, such as 1. <u>Mexican sweetbread</u>. The 2. <u>rolls and bread</u> look especially good.

I like this book because the foods are interesting. For example, I think it is interesting how Pablo makes 3. <u>bagels</u>. I also think the part about 4. <u>adding</u> <u>jalapeño chiles to bagels</u> is interesting because 5. <u>foods from two cultures are used</u>. You will like this book if you like food.

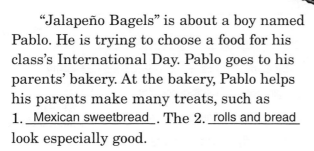

Writing and Thinking

Reflect Tell what helped you think of examples. Write your ideas. Share your ideas in a small group.

413

ADD EXAMPLES Read the directions for activity B together. As needed, have children reread "Jalapeño Bagels" for examples to include in the book report.

Writing and Thinking

Reflect Read the text and discuss children's ideas before they write them. Have children share in small groups what helped them think of good examples to support their ideas. Children can record their thoughts in their journals. Then they can discuss their reflections with group members.

WRAP-UP/ASSESS

SUMMARIZE Ask volunteers to summarize what they know about giving examples in a book report.

CHALLENGE

REACHING ALL LEARNERS

VIDEOTAPE REVIEWS You may want to have some children work on videotaping reviews of favorite books after writing and correcting their own book report drafts.

ESL

REACHING ALL LEARNERS

READ WITH A PARTNER Suggest that children who are acquiring English work with a partner to read and discuss the examples in the Idea Bank and other ideas they may have. Partners can also read and discuss "Jalapeño Bagels."

Writer's Craft
Applying the Craft

OBJECTIVES
- To use a model for writing a book report
- To prewrite and draft a book report

SPIRAL REVIEW

DAILY LANGUAGE PRACTICE

TRANSPARENCY 65

1 *Abuela* is one of me favorite storys.
(my; stories)

2 Abuela flys around New york City.
(flies; York)

ORAL WARM-UP

USE PRIOR KNOWLEDGE Ask children if they have ever watched a TV program or a movie based on a friend's recommendation. Ask: *How might examples from a program or film help you decide whether or not you want to see it?*

GUIDED WRITING

READ AND RESPOND TO THE MODEL Have children read the student model silently. Then have a volunteer read it aloud. Talk about whether the writer did a good job giving examples to support his or her ideas. Then use the questions on page 414 to discuss the book report.

Looking at the Model
1. Children should support their ideas by explaining the examples they select. **CRITICAL:** INTERPRET TEXT STRUCTURE
2. **Possible response:** Without the examples, there isn't much information to explain the writer's ideas. **INFERENTIAL:** DRAW CONCLUSIONS

Writing a Book Report

Writer's Craft
Applying the Craft

Read this student book report. Think about how the examples show what the writer means.

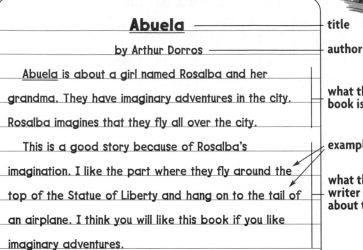

> **Abuela** ——— title
>
> by Arthur Dorros ——— author
>
> Abuela is about a girl named Rosalba and her grandma. They have imaginary adventures in the city. Rosalba imagines that they fly all over the city. ——— what the book is about
>
> This is a good story because of Rosalba's imagination. I like the part where they fly around the top of the Statue of Liberty and hang on to the tail of an airplane. I think you will like this book if you like imaginary adventures. ——— examples / what the writer thinks about the book

Looking at the Model
1. Which example best shows what the writer means? Explain.
2. How do these examples make this book report better?

414

Vocabulary Power page 98

Name _____ Clipped Words

A clipped word is a shortened form of a longer word.

telephone—phone   eyeglasses—glasses

Write the clipped words for these longer words. Write or draw pictures to explain the meanings.

1. memorandum memo
2. electronic mail e-mail
3. stereophonic stereo
4. gymnasium gym
5. rhinoceros rhino
6. hippopotamus hippo

98 Unit 6 • Chapter 11   Vocabulary Power

EVALUATION CRITERIA

BOOK REPORT Review the criteria that make up a good book report that children should apply to their writing:

- tells about the characters and what the book is mainly about
- tells feelings about the book.
- includes examples.

Ask children to establish additional criteria. Possible ideas might include examples of dialogue or a picture of a favorite scene from the book.

Your Turn

Write a book report about a book you have read. Be sure to give examples that show what you mean.

Prewriting and Drafting

STEP 1 **Develop your ideas.**

Ask yourself these questions.

- Why do I like or not like this book?
- What examples can I give to support my ideas?
- What can I tell my readers to make them want to read this book or not want to read it?

STEP 2 **Brainstorm examples.**

Make a chart. Write examples that tell why you did or did not like the book.

About My Book

Title _____

Author _____

Please check correct box.

☐ I liked this book.

☐ I did not like this book.

Give two examples why you did or did not like the book. _____

_____

_____

STEP 3 **Write your draft.**

Use your chart and What Good Writers Do to write a draft of your book report.

What Good Writers Do

✓ Remember to use examples to show your readers why you think a certain way.

✓ Plan your ideas.

415

INTERACTIVE WRITING

MODEL DRAFTING Using a book that all children have read, model how to develop a chart to record examples, and then use the notes to create a draft of a book report. Invite children's ideas and let them write them on the chart and in the draft.

Social Studies Connection

• • • • • • • • • • •

USING INFORMATION BOOKS
Children can use reference books and nonfiction books in the library to find out more about the Statue of Liberty and other places that Rosalba visits. Have them take notes and report their findings to the class.

Your Turn Explain to children that they will use the prewriting and drafting steps and What Good Writers Do to write a book report about a book they have read.

Prewriting and Drafting Have children read the directions and steps silently. Then have volunteers read them aloud. Discuss the steps with the group.

Tell children that they may choose to write about a book that they did or did not enjoy reading. They can make notes about their reasons on a chart and then use these prewriting notes in their draft.

Read What Good Writers Do aloud and suggest that children think about these tips during the prewriting and drafting steps.

 Have children use word processing software to compose their drafts.

 PORTFOLIO Have children save their work in their Writing Portfolios.

WRAP-UP/ASSESS

 SUMMARIZE Ask volunteers to summarize the process they used to prewrite and draft their book reports. Children can record in their journal their reflections on writing book reports that give examples. **REFLECTION**

Writer's Craft
Editing Your Book Report

OBJECTIVES
- To peer conference in editing a book report
- To edit a book report and share it aloud

DAILY LANGUAGE PRACTICE

TRANSPARENCY 65

1 How did your like that book, (you; ?)

2 I cant' read it nwo. (can't; now)

ORAL WARM-UP

Review with children the kind of information that should be included in a good book report.

GUIDED WRITING

EDITING YOUR BOOK REPORT Have a volunteer read the directions and the checklist aloud. Remind children to use the Editor's Marks as they polish their drafts.

PEER CONFERENCING Have children work with partners on improving their drafts.

SHARING WITH OTHERS Volunteers may share their edited book reports with a partner or in small groups. Have children show the actual books, if possible. Children discuss the books and respond to one another's reports.

WRAP-UP/ASSESS

SUMMARIZE Volunteers can summarize the steps they followed in creating their book reports. Children can reflect on their effort on a scale of 1–4 on a self-stick note. Children can attach their ratings to their writing. Ask volunteers to share their scores and the reasons for the scores. Then have children place their book reports in their Writing Portfolio.

Writing a Book Report — Writer's Craft

Editing Your Book Report

Share your draft with a few classmates. Together, think about how you can make your book report better. Use the checklist and the Editor's Marks to help you revise your book report.

Editor's Marks	
∧	Add.
∕\	Change.
℘	Take out.
≡	Use a capital letter.
⊙	Add a period.
⬭	Check the spelling.

✓ My book report tells the title of the book and the author's name.

✓ My book report tells what I think about the book. I give examples that show why I think this way.

Sharing with Others

Meet with a partner or a small group. Share your book report. Read it aloud.

416

Vocabulary Power page 99

Name _____

Jargon

Jargon is language that is used by a group of people who do the same work or have the same interests. People who work with computers or who are interested in computers use jargon.

Brainstorm things that are related to computers. Add to the items in the box.

e-mail	post a message

Other computer words or phrases: Responses will vary. Accept reasonable responses.

mouse	program	graphics
keyboard	CD-ROM	log on
crash	icon	password

Now draw and label pictures.

Vocabulary Power   Unit 6 • Chapter 11   99

LISTENING AND SPEAKING

BOOK REPORTS As children read their book reports aloud, remind them to read clearly and at the correct speed to make their words sound smooth and easy to understand. If children have a book to show as a prop, remind them to hold it so that everyone in the group can see it.

Listeners should listen carefully for examples that explain why the writer feels as he or she does about the book.

•Handwriting•

Forming Letters Correctly

Follow these tips to make sure your letters are formed correctly.

- Make smooth curves. Close up circle letters.
- Make straight lines correctly.
- Form letters made up of curves and straight lines correctly.
- Make slanted lines correctly.

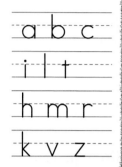

Practice

Write these letters. Use your best handwriting. Follow the tips. Use the Handwriting Models on page 490 to help you.

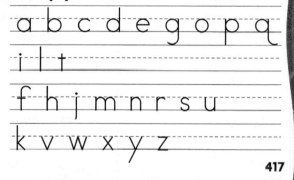

curves

straight lines

combination

slanted lines

417

Writing Resource

TRACING LETTERS Suggest that children who need additional practice trace over photocopied practice letters with a different-colored pencil. Have children trace each letter several times and then write words using the letters they practiced.

EVALUATION CRITERIA

Have children revisit the evaluation criteria you helped them establish earlier and informally rate their writing of sentences about a picture by writing their score (on a 1–4 scale) on the corner of their papers or by raising their fingers.

•Handwriting•

Forming Letters Correctly

OBJECTIVE
- To form letters correctly

 **DAILY LANGUAGE PRACTICE**

TRANSPARENCY 65

❶ Lets goes to the park. (Let's; go)

❷ Has you been there before. (Have; before?)

TEACH/MODEL

Write the word *boy* on the board, but form the letters so that the circle parts are not closed and the strokes in the letter *y* are not connected. Ask children what is wrong with what you have written.

Explain that we try to form letters properly so that others can read our writing.

Have volunteers read the tips aloud. Then have children copy the practice letters on page 417, working to form them properly.

You may wish to have children refer to the handwriting models on pages 490-493 in their handbooks. (See also R92–R93)

CURSIVE WRITING Have children who write in cursive apply the concepts in this lesson to their writing.

WRAP-UP/ASSESS

SUMMARIZE Ask volunteers to restate the handwriting tips in their own words. You may wish to have children recopy a practice exercise and compare their handwriting on the first sample with the copy.

LESSON ORGANIZER	DAY 1	DAY 2
DAILY LANGUAGE PRACTICE  TRANSPARENCIES 66, 67	1. Who has'nt been to the museum yet. (hasn't; ?) 2. you really shoudnt miss it. (You; shouldn't) **Bridge to Writing** I <u>(contraction for could not)</u> go today.	1. I went to the library And thun I did my homework. (and; then) 2. Next we cleared the table and first we did the dishes. (First; next) **Bridge to Writing** First put the ingredients in a bowl. <u>(time-order word)</u> mix them.
ORAL WARM-UP *Listening/Speaking*	Describe Actions in Order p. 418	Combine Sentences p. 420 *Grammar Jingles*™ CD, Primary, Track 23
TEACH/MODEL GRAMMAR **KEY** ✔ = tested skill	✔ **FIXING "AND THEN" SENTENCES** pp. 418-419 • To listen critically to interpret and evaluate cartoon dialogue • To understand that time-order words help tell the order in which things happen	✔ **WRITING LONGER SENTENCES** pp. 420-421 • To combine short sentences into one longer sentence • To look for short sentences that can be combined in a piece of writing and revise accordingly
Reaching All Learners	**Challenge:** Activity Card 23, p. R63 *Practice Book* p. 111 **ESL:** *ESL Manual* pp. 168, 169 **Reteach:** *Reteach Activities Copying Masters* p. 67	**Modified Instruction** Below-Level: Identify Parts Above-Level: Combine Sentences **Challenge:** Chain of Sentences p. 421 **ESL:** Combine Sentences p. 420 *ESL Manual* pp. 168, 170 *Practice Book* p. 112 **Reteach:** *Reteach Activities Copying Masters* p. 68

WRITING	Use Time-Order Words p. 419
	
	  Summarize/Reflect
		Writing Connection p. 421
		 Revising
		  Summarize/Reflect

CROSS-CURRICULAR/ ENRICHMENT	**Vocabulary Power** Word Meaning, p. 418 fabulous, fantastic, **marvelous**, splendid, superb See ***Vocabulary Power*** book.	**Vocabulary Power** Synonyms, p. 418 *Vocabulary Power* book, p. 100 **Vocabulary activity**

Visit *The Learning Site!*
www.harcourtschool.com

WRITING ACTIVITIES
Writing Express CD-ROM

DAY 3

1. The driver stops looks, And listens. (stops, ; and)

2. The children sees a big, shiny, black engine. (see; shiny,)

Bridge to Writing I met the engineer. I met the driver. (combine into one sentence)

Brainstorm Uses for Commas p. 422
Grammar Jingles™ CD, Primary, Track 23

✔ **USING A SERIES COMMA** pp. 422–423
  • To recognize that a comma is used between each item in a list
  • To use commas correctly between items in a series

- - -

Modified Instruction
  Below-Level: Identify Series
  Above-Level: Add Commas
Challenge: Adding Commas p. 423
ESL: Adding Commas p. 422
ESL Manual, pp. 168, 171
Practice Book p. 113
Reteach: *Reteach Activities Copying Masters* p. 69

- - -

Writing Connection p. 423
  Description

Summarize/Reflect

Vocabulary Power
  Word Origins, p. 418
  Vocabulary Power book p.101
  Vocabulary activity

DAY 4

1. Ben Sara, and Tom, Toby followed a butterfly. (Ben, ; Tom, and)

2. Did you see the yellow blue and orange markings on its wings? (yellow, ; blue,)

Bridge to Writing Later (four names) drew pictures of the butterfly.

Discuss Daily Activities p. 424

EXTRA PRACTICE pp. 424–425
  • To use time-order words and to combine short sentences into one longer sentence
  • To use commas correctly when writing a list
  Practice and Assessment

- - -

Challenge: Insect Time p. 425
ESL: Time-Order Practice p. 424
  ESL Manual pp. 168, 172
  Practice Book p. 114

- - -

Writing Connection p. 425
  Sales Poster

Vocabulary Power
  Analogies p. 418
  Vocabulary Power book, p.102
  Vocabulary activity
Language Play p. 425

DAY 5

1. Firsth I did my homework and, then I played for a while. (First; homework. Then)

2. we had chicken mashed potatoes, and green beans for dinner. (We; chicken,)

Bridge to Writing I (three verbs) the dishes.

TEST PREP **CHAPTER REVIEW** p. 426
  • To review time-order words, combining sentences, and using commas in series
  • To understand how suffixes change word meanings
  Test Preparation

- - -

Practice Book p. 115
Challenge: Look for Suffixes p. 427
ESL: *ESL Manual,* pp. 168, 173

- - -

Writing Application p. 427
  Using Suffixes

Vocabulary: Suffixes p. 427
Vocabulary Power
  Classify/Categorize, p. 418

Fixing "And Then" Sentences

OBJECTIVES

- To listen critically to interpret and evaluate cartoon dialogue
- To understand that time-order words help tell the order in which things happen

DAILY LANGUAGE PRACTICE

TRANSPARENCY 66

1 Who has'nt been to the museum yet. (hasn't; ?)

2 you really shoudnt miss it. (You; shouldn't)

BRIDGE TO WRITING I (contraction for *could not*) go today.

ORAL WARM-UP

USE PRIOR KNOWLEDGE Have volunteers tell about things they did yesterday in the order in which they did them. Then ask children to recall any words they used to help tell about that order, such as *first*, *next*, or *then*. Begin a list of such words on chart paper, or add them to your **Word Wall.**

TEACH/MODEL

Read aloud the comic strip with children. Discuss with them what they think is wrong with Bobby's sentences and what could be done to make them "sound" better. Tell children that Bobby should not be using *and then* to begin his sentences and that he can instead use time-order words to make the sentences flow better.

DEVELOP ORAL LANGUAGE Have children reread what Bobby says. Ask volunteers to demonstrate how to say what Bobby did without using "and then." Add any new time-order words to the **Word Wall.**

Fixing "And Then" Sentences

Read the cartoon.

Bobby's Long Weekend...

418

Vocabulary Power

DAY 1 WORD MEANING Write: *Bobby had a marvelous time* _____. Discuss the meaning of *marvelous*. (great, wonderful) Have children dictate phrases to complete the sentence.

DAY 2 SYNONYMS Write: *marvelous, awful, super.* **Which two words have similar meanings? Which word has a meaning opposite to the other two?** (See also *Vocabulary Power*, page 100.)

DAY 3 WORD ORIGINS List *marvelous*, *wonder, terror.* **The word *marvelous* comes from a very old word. What do you think that old word means: *wonder* or *terror*? Why?** (See also *Vocabulary Power*, page 101.)

DAY 4 ANALOGIES Write: Marvelous is the opposite of *terrible. Happy* is the opposite of _____. **What word completes the sentence?** (sad) (See also *Vocabulary Power*, page 102.)

DAY 5 CLASSIFY/CATEGORIZE Have children draw and write about the books they have read. Have them categorize the books as "marvelous," "so-so."

Tell about things that Bobby did at the museum in the order in which they happened. This time use the time-order words *first*, *next*, *then*, and *last* instead of the words *and then*.

Vocabulary Power
marvelous

> Time-order words help tell about the order in which things happen. Use time-order words instead of the words *and then* to tell what happened.
>
> **First** I went to the new science museum.
> **Next** I took a tour and saw a real lizard.

Write the paragraph using time-order words.
Possible responses are given.

Last weekend I helped my grandmother in her garden. I dug a hole in the ground. And then I put in some seeds. And then we covered them up with dirt. And then we watered them.

Last weekend I helped my grandmother in her garden. First I dug a hole in the ground. Next I put in some seeds. Then we covered them. Last we watered them.

419

WRITE Ask children to follow along as you read the paragraph at the bottom of the page. Point out that the paragraph has too many "and then" words. After children rewrite the paragraph using time-order words, have them share ideas with a partner or a small group.

WRAP-UP/ASSESS

SUMMARIZE Ask children to summarize and reflect on what they have learned about fixing "and then" sentences. Have children write their reflections in their journals along with the time-order words they used to rewrite the paragraph. **REFLECTION**

RETEACH

INTERVENTION Lessons in **visual**, **auditory**, and **kinesthetic** modalities: p. R39 and *Reteach Activities Copying Masters*, p. 67.

page 67

Fixing "And Then" Sentences

Read the long sentence aloud. Use the time-order words in the box to write shorter sentences.

First	Next	Last

I took out the pans and then I got the cake mix and then I took out the eggs.

___First___ I took out the pans.

___Next___ I got the cake mix.

___Last___ I took out the eggs.

Fixing "And Then" Sentences

Read the long sentence aloud. Cut out the time-order words. Glue them in place to make shorter sentences.

The timer went off and then my dad took the cakes out and then we let them cool.

First	the timer went off.
Next	my dad took the cakes out.
Last	we let them cool.

First	Next	Last

Reteach Activities • Fixing Sentence Problems   Unit 6 • Chapter 34   67

PRACTICE page 111

Name _____

Fixing "And Then" Sentences

Write each paragraph using time-order words.
Possible responses are given.

1. On Saturday my mother and I made tacos. She heated up beans and then we got lettuce, tomatoes, and cheese and then we put all the food in the taco shells.

   On Saturday my mother and I made tacos. First she

   heated up beans. Next we got lettuce, tomatoes, and

   cheese. Last we put all the food in the taco shells.

2. Jay got a cold last weekend. His throat was sore and then he started to cough and then he took medicine and then he took a nap.

   Jay got a cold last weekend. First his throat was sore.

   Next he started to cough. Then he took medicine. Last he

   took a nap.

TRY THIS! Write a paragraph about something you did one weekend. Use time-order words in your paragraph.

Practice • Fixing Sentence Problems   Unit 6 • Chapter 34   111

CHALLENGE

MAKE A COMIC STRIP Have children use **Challenge Activity Card 23** (page R63) to make a comic strip. Encourage them to draw or cut out fun characters for each frame, such as people, animals, or objects. Have children write several things each character did, using time-order words. Then have them share their comic strips.

Challenge Activity Card 23
Make a Comic Strip

Writing Longer Sentences

OBJECTIVES

- To combine short sentences into one longer sentence
- To look for short sentences that can be combined in a piece of writing and to revise accordingly

DAILY LANGUAGE PRACTICE

TRANSPARENCY 66

1 I went to the library And thun I did my homework. (and; then)

2 Next we cleared the table and first we washed the dishes. (First; next)

BRIDGE TO WRITING First put the ingredients in a bowl. (time-order word) mix them.

ORAL WARM-UP

USE PRIOR KNOWLEDGE Say pairs of sentences with the same naming or telling parts. Have children identify the parts that are the same and then think of a way to make one sentence using the two parts.

Grammar Jingles™ **CD Primary** Use Track 23 for review and reinforcement of sentences.

TEACH/MODEL

Read the explanation in the box. Then have volunteers read aloud the sentences. Discuss how the sentences are alike and different, and what parts were combined to make a longer sentence. Ask how the parts in the longer sentence are separated. (the word *and*)

GUIDED PRACTICE Work with children to complete each sentence. Have them identify the parts that can be combined and the parts that are the same. Then read aloud the original sentences and the new sentence; ask children which sounds better and why.

Fixing Sentence Problems

Writing Longer Sentences

You can combine two short sentences to make one longer sentence.

Combine naming parts.

> **Children** go home. **Parents** go home.
> **Children** and **parents** go home.

Combine telling parts.

> The children **talk**. The children **laugh**.
> The children **talk** and **laugh**.

Combine other words.

> The museum is **big**. The museum is **bright**.
> The museum is **big** and **bright**.

Guided Practice

Combine each set of sentences.

1. A smart guide meets Ms. Li.
   A smart guide meets the class.
   A smart guide meets Ms. Li and the class.
2. Susan asks to see a snake.
   Jeff asks to see a snake.
   Susan and Jeff ask to see a snake.
3. The guide points to a cage.
   The guide reads the sign.
   The guide points to a cage and reads the sign.

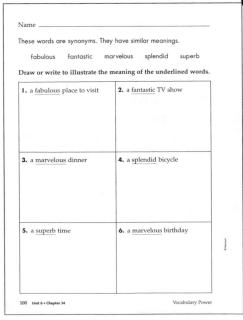

420

Vocabulary Power page 100

Name _____

These words are synonyms. They have similar meanings.

fabulous   fantastic   marvelous   splendid   superb

Draw or write to illustrate the meaning of the underlined words.

1. a <u>fabulous</u> place to visit	2. a <u>fantastic</u> TV show
3. a <u>marvelous</u> dinner	4. a <u>splendid</u> bicycle
5. a <u>superb</u> time	6. a <u>marvelous</u> birthday

100   Unit 6 • Chapter 34   Vocabulary Power

REACHING ALL LEARNERS   ESL

COMBINE SENTENCES Make sentence strips for combinable sentences such as the following: *Max saw a snake. Ann saw a snake.* Give partners a set of sentence strips. Have them cut the sentences apart and then combine the parts to make one longer sentence. Tell them to use a marker to add *and* if necessary. Have the partners read aloud the new sentence.

Independent Practice

Combine each set of sentences.

4. The snake is small.

   The snake is green.
   The snake is small and green.

5. The snake crawls in the cage.

   The snake drinks in the cage.
   The snake crawls and drinks in the cage.

6. The teachers look at a poster.

   The parents look at a poster.
   The teachers and parents look at a poster.

7. They see photos of Jupiter.

   They see photos of Mars.
   They see photos of Jupiter and Mars.

8. Jupiter is a large planet.

   Jupiter is a colorful planet.
   Jupiter is a large and colorful planet.

9. The children ask questions.

   The children take pictures.
   The children ask questions and take pictures.

10. The children line up quietly to go home.

    The children line up quickly to go home.
    The children line up quietly and quickly to go home.

Writing Connection

Revising Find a piece of writing in your Writing Portfolio. Revise sentences that you can combine.

Use cut and paste on your computer to help combine your sentences.

421

Independent Practice

Have children complete the Independent Practice, or modify it by using the following suggestions:

MODIFIED INSTRUCTION

BELOW-LEVEL STUDENTS Have partners identify the sentence parts that are the same and different. Suggest that they circle the word *and*.

ABOVE-LEVEL STUDENTS After children finish, have them write two short sentences, trade them with a partner, and then combine the sentences into one longer sentence.

Writing Connection

Revising Help children choose appropriate pieces of writing to revise as needed. Suggest that they underline any short sentences they can combine into longer sentences.

WRAP-UP/ASSESS

SUMMARIZE Ask children to summarize and reflect on what they have learned about combining sentences. Have small groups meet and discuss what they learned. **REFLECTION**

RETEACH

INTERVENTION Lessons in **visual**, **auditory**, and **kinesthetic** modalities: p. R39 and *Reteach Activities Copying Masters*, p. 68.

page 68

Writing Longer Sentences
Work with a partner. Circle the parts that are the same in each pair of the sentences. Then combine the sentences.

1. The boy (watched a movie.) The girl (watched a movie.)

   The boy and the girl watched a movie.

2. (They) laughed. (They) cried.

   They laughed and cried.

3. (They) ate popcorn. (They) drank juice.

   They ate popcorn and drank juice.

Visual/Auditory

Writing Longer Sentences
Cut out the words at the bottom of the page. Glue them in place to combine the sentences.

1. The sun is bright. The sun is hot.

   The sun is [bright] and [hot]

2. The wind blew the balloons. The wind blew the leaves.

   The wind blew the [balloons] and [leaves]

   | leaves | bright | hot | balloons |

Kinesthetic

Teacher: Cut apart the activities and distribute to children based on the modalities that are their strengths.

68 Unit 6 • Chapter 34   Reteach Activities • Fixing Sentence Problems

---

PRACTICE page 112

Name _____

Writing Longer Sentences

Combine each set of sentences to make one longer sentence. Write the new sentence.

1. The students are ready for the tour.
   The teachers are ready for the tour.

   The students and teachers are ready for the tour.

2. They point at the radio station.
   They stare at the radio station.

   They point and stare at the radio station.

3. The building is tall.
   The building is shiny.

   The building is tall and shiny.

4. They visit the studio.
   They take pictures of the studio.

   They visit and take pictures of the studio.

TRY THIS! Write three short sentences about an adventure you have had. Then combine the sentences into one.

112 Unit 6 • Chapter 34   Practice • Fixing Sentence Problems

CHALLENGE

CHAIN OF SENTENCES Have children form groups of three. The first child writes two short sentences that can be combined. The second child combines the sentences and writes the longer sentence on another sheet of paper. Then the third child rewrites the longer sentence as two short ones and compares them with the first writer's sentences. Have children trade places and repeat.

Using a Series Comma

OBJECTIVES
- To recognize that a comma is used between each item in a list
- To use commas correctly between items in a series

DAILY LANGUAGE PRACTICE

TRANSPARENCY 66

① The driver stops looks, And listens. (stops,; and)

② The children sees a big, shiny black engine. (see; shiny,)

BRIDGE TO WRITING I met the engineer. I met the driver. (combine into one sentence)

ORAL WARM-UP

USE PRIOR KNOWLEDGE Have children brainstorm a list of uses for commas in writing, such as in dates, place names, greetings and closings of letters, and combined sentences. Ask volunteers to give examples in sentences and write them on the board.

Grammar Jingles™ **CD Primary** Use Track 23 for review and reinforcement of commas in a series.

TEACH/MODEL

Introduce the concept by using the explanation and the examples in the box. Ask volunteers to read aloud the sentences, pausing at each comma. Have children identify the words in each series as nouns, verbs, or adjectives.

GUIDED PRACTICE Write the first sentence on the board. Have children listen as you read it aloud without pauses, as written. Ask children to identify the list in the sentence. Then call on a volunteer to write the commas where they belong. Repeat the procedure with the remaining items.

Fixing Sentence Problems — **Usage and Mechanics**

Using a Series Comma

Sometimes a series of three or more nouns, verbs, or adjectives is used in a sentence. Put a comma (,) between the items in a series.

Peter, Judy, Joe, and Carol share a table.
The children draw, paint, and write about the museum.
They use red, yellow, and blue paint.

Guided Practice

Write each sentence correctly using the series comma.

1. Carol shares crayons with Peter Judy and Joe.
   Carol shares crayons with Peter, Judy, and Joe.
2. Joe traces draws and colors with pencils.
   Joe traces, draws, and colors with pencils.
3. Judy writes a story about a small lonely sad planet.
   Judy writes a story about a small, lonely, sad planet.
4. The planet is happy when he meets Earth Mars and Jupiter.
   The planet is happy when he meets Earth, Mars, and Jupiter.
5. He smiles laughs and plays with his new friends.
   He smiles, laughs, and plays with his new friends.

422

Vocabulary Power page 101

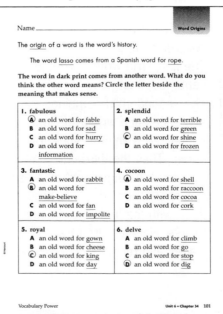

Name _____

Word Origins

The *origin* of a word is the word's history.

The word *lasso* comes from a Spanish word for *rope*.

The word in dark print comes from another word. What do you think the other word means? Circle the letter beside the meaning that makes sense.

1. fabulous	2. splendid
A an old word for *fable*	**A** an old word for *terrible*
B an old word for *sad*	**B** an old word for *green*
C an old word for *hurry*	**C** an old word for *shine*
D an old word for *information*	**D** an old word for *frozen*
3. fantastic	4. cocoon
A an old word for *rabbit*	**A** an old word for *shell*
B an old word for *make-believe*	**B** an old word for *raccoon*
C an old word for *fan*	**C** an old word for *cocoa*
D an old word for *impolite*	**D** an old word for *cork*
5. royal	6. delve
A an old word for *gown*	**A** an old word for *climb*
B an old word for *cheese*	**B** an old word for *go*
C an old word for *king*	**C** an old word for *stop*
D an old word for *day*	**D** an old word for *dig*

Vocabulary Power   Unit 6 • Chapter 34   101

REACHING ALL LEARNERS — **ESL**

ADDING COMMAS Have children write a large comma on an index card. Display sentences such as the ones on page 422. Read each sentence aloud, pausing where commas belong. Have children hold up their comma cards and say *comma*. Call on volunteers to add the commas in the displayed sentences.

Remember Put a comma (,) between the items in a series.

Independent Practice

Write each sentence correctly using the series comma.

6. Next they read study and color a map of the planets.
   Next they read, study, and color a map of the planets.

7. Mercury Venus Earth and Mars are closest to the sun.
   Mercury, Venus, Earth, and Mars are closest to the sun.

8. The largest planets are Jupiter Saturn Neptune and Uranus.
   The largest planets are Jupiter, Saturn, Neptune, and Uranus.

9. The children learn that stars are bright hot and large.
   The children learn that stars are bright, hot, and large.

10. Then they plan draw and color their own maps.
    Then they plan, draw, and color their own maps.

11. They put stars planets and a comet on their maps.
    They put stars, planets, and a comet on their maps.

12. Dan's map shows the Little Dipper the Big Dipper and the sun.
    Dan's map shows the Little Dipper, the Big Dipper, and the sun.

Writing Connection

Description Brainstorm words that describe you. Then write three sentences about yourself. Be sure to use commas correctly.

Use your computer to add any missing commas to your writing.

423

Independent Practice

Have children complete the Independent Practice, or modify it by using the following suggestions:

MODIFIED INSTRUCTION

BELOW-LEVEL STUDENTS Suggest that first children look for three or more adjectives, nouns, or verbs and the word *and*.

ABOVE-LEVEL STUDENTS Have children write a sentence with a list of adjectives, nouns, or verbs. Tell them to leave out the commas. Have them trade

Writing Connection

Description Remind children that commas help make lists easier to understand. Ask volunteers to share their descriptions.

WRAP-UP/ASSESS

SUMMARIZE Have children summarize what they have learned about using commas in sentences with a list. Ask them to reflect on how they can use this information to improve their writing.

REFLECTION

RETEACH

INTERVENTION Lessons in **visual, auditory,** and **kinesthetic** modalities: p. R39 and *Reteach Activities Copying Masters,* p. 69.

page 69

Using a Series Comma

Read the sentences. Circle the commas. Talk about why the commas are there.

1. Gina packs her brush, comb, and hair clips.
2. Zack packs socks, sneakers, a belt, and a tie.
3. Mom packs a dress, a necklace, earrings, and shoes.
4. They forgot sunglasses, hats, and toothpaste.

Using a Series Comma

Cut out the commas at the bottom of the page. Glue them where they belong.

1. Mom bought a book , magazines , and a snack.
2. On the train Zack read , slept , and ate.
3. They rode past cities , towns , and farms.
4. Bob , Joey , and Grandma were at the station.

Teacher Cut apart the activities and distribute to children based on the modalities that are their strength.
Reteach Activities • Fixing Sentence Problems   Unit 6 • Chapter 34   69

PRACTICE page 113

Name_____

Using a Series Comma

A. Underline the sentence in each pair that is written correctly.

1. Our class will create write, and perform skits.
   Our class will create, write, and perform skits.

2. Groups will have two, three, or four people.
   Groups will have two, three or four people.

3. The skits can be funny sad real, or made-up.
   The skits can be funny, sad, real, or made-up.

4. Groups can borrow, make or bring costumes.
   Groups can borrow, make, or bring costumes.

B. Write each sentence correctly.

5. Jamal Reese and Tammy worked in a group.
   Jamal, Reese, and Tammy worked in a group.

6. Their skit was about an owl a chicken and a parrot.
   Their skit was about an owl, a chicken, and a parrot.

TRY THIS! Write three sentences about a project you have worked on with classmates. Use a list in each sentence.

Practice • Fixing Sentence Problems   Unit 6 • Chapter 34   113

CHALLENGE

ADDING COMMAS Write the following sentences on the board: *John Henry Adam James and I sketched colored and outlined our pictures. We used blue green orange red yellow purple and brown markers crayons and pencils.* Have children rewrite the sentences, adding commas where they belong. Then invite groups to make up similar sentences and trade them to add commas.

CHAPTER 34 423

Extra Practice

OBJECTIVES
- To use time-order words and to combine short sentences into one longer sentence
- To use commas correctly when writing a list

DAILY LANGUAGE PRACTICE

TRANSPARENCY 67

1 Ben Sara, and Tom, Toby followed a butterfly. (Ben, ; Tom, and)

2 Did you see the yellow blue and orange markings on its wings? (yellow, ; blue,)

BRIDGE TO WRITING Later (four names) drew pictures of the butterfly.

ORAL WARM-UP

USE PRIOR KNOWLEDGE Have volunteers use time-order words to discuss what they do before coming to school, playing their favorite sports, or going to bed. You may wish to record children's sentences in paragraph form on chart paper and have them identify the time-order words.

TEACH/MODEL

Read each set of directions to make sure children understand how to complete each section. Have children share their answers in small groups before you read aloud the correct answers.

WRAP-UP/ASSESS

SUMMARIZE Have children share any problems they had in completing the exercises. Then have children summarize and reflect on what they have learned about fixing "and then" sentences, combining sentences, and writing lists in sentences.

ADDITIONAL PRACTICE Extra practice items are on page 477 of the *Pupil Edition* (*Teacher's Edition* R7).

TECHNOLOGY
Grammar Practice and Assessment CD-ROM
Writing Express CD-ROM

INTERNET Visit *The Learning Site!*
www.harcourtschool.com

Fixing Sentence Problems

Extra Practice

Write each paragraph using time-order words.
Possible responses are given.

1. We all get teeth the same way. Small teeth grow in when we are babies. And then the baby teeth fall out. And then adult teeth grow in. And then those teeth replace the baby teeth.

   We all get teeth the same way. First small teeth grow in when we are babies. Next the baby teeth fall out. Then adult teeth grow in. Those teeth replace the baby teeth.

2. How does a caterpillar become a butterfly? The caterpillar hatches out of an egg. And then it eats so it can grow. And then its body turns into a shell. And then it breaks out of the shell and is a beautiful butterfly.

   How does a caterpillar become a butterfly? First the caterpillar hatches out of an egg. Next it eats so it can grow. Then its body turns into a shell. Last it breaks out of the shell and is a beautiful butterfly.

Combine the short sentences to make one longer sentence.

3. Butterfly eggs can be green.
   Butterfly eggs can be orange.
   Butterfly eggs can be green and orange.

4. Caterpillars hatch on leaves.
   Caterpillars crawl on leaves.
   Caterpillars hatch and crawl on leaves.

Write the list in each sentence correctly.

5. Caterpillars eat beans fruit leaves and other plants.
   Caterpillars eat beans, fruit, leaves, and other plants.

6. Caterpillars live in cold hot or warm places.
   Caterpillars live in cold, hot, or warm places.

424

Vocabulary Power page 102

Name _____   Analogies

An analogy is a word puzzle. Think about how the first two words are related. Think of a word related to the third word in the same way.

bicycle–two is like tricycle–
A bicycle has two wheels. How many wheels does a tricycle have?

Complete these word puzzles. Share your answers.

1. fabulous–wonderful is like mad–   angry
2. horse–trot is like frog–   hop, leap, jump
3. lumpy–smooth is like awful–   great, marvelous
4. fifteen–number is like purple–   color
5. bellow–loud is like whisper–   soft, quiet
6. tremble–shiver is like splendid–   great, wonderful
7. memorandum–memo is like internetwork–   internet
8. corn–vegetable is like tulip–   flower
9. calf–cow is like cub–   bear
10. France–country is like Texas–   state
11. quickly–quick is like superbly–   superb
12. honey–sweet is like lemon–   sour

102   Unit 6 • Chapter 34   Vocabulary Power

ESL

TIME-ORDER PRACTICE Write time-order words such as *First, Next, Then,* and *Finally* on index cards. Then write the following sentences on strips: *I leave the classroom. I wash my hands. I eat lunch. I go home.* Have pairs of children arrange the sentences in an order that makes sense. Then ask them to add an appropriate time-order word card at the beginning of each sentence. Ask volunteers to read their sentences.

Language Play

Make It Longer

- Play this game with four people. Form two teams.
- Make cards with sets of three verbs, adjectives, and nouns.
- Pick a card. Work with your partner to make up a sentence that uses all three words on the card.
- The next team does the same thing with a different card.
- Play until all the cards are gone. You get one point for each correct sentence.

dogs cats

mice

act speak

write

excited

happy

proud

Writing Connection

Sales Poster Think about a store you have visited. Make a poster that will help sell items in the store. Name and describe the items so that they sound interesting. Use lists of items in your sentences.

> Pat's Art Store on Smith Street has markers, pencils, and crayons.
>
> Walk, run, or drive down to catch the great sales now!

425

Language Play

Have children play "Make It Longer" in groups of four. Suggest that they look back at pages 422-423 for other possible verbs, adjectives, and nouns to use. You may wish to have each team record the sentences they make up during the game. Then invite groups to share their sentences with one another.

Writing Connection

Sales Poster Check to see that children have successfully written a Sales Poster by using the criteria below.

CRITERIA

- ☑ Names and describes items in a store.
- ☑ Includes lists of items in sentences.
- ☑ Adds a comma between items in a list.

📁 **PORTFOLIO OPPORTUNITY** You may wish to have children place their posters in their portfolios after sharing them with classmates.

REACHING ALL LEARNERS

Name _____

Extra Practice

A. Write the sentences using time-order words.

1. The mother bird lays eggs and then she sits on them. And then the eggs hatch.

   First the mother bird lays eggs. Next she sits on them.

   Last the eggs hatch.

B. Combine each set of sentences to make one longer sentence.

2. Robins have red feathers. Robins have orange feathers.

   Robins have red and orange feathers.

3. Robins eat insects. Robins eat fruit.

   Robins eat insects and fruit.

C. Write the sentence correctly.

4. Birds build nests with twigs grass and mud.

   Birds build nests with twigs, grass, and mud.

114 Unit 6 • Chapter 34   Practice • Fixing Sentence Problems

---

CHALLENGE

REACHING ALL LEARNERS

INSECT TIME Have children write about a time they observed insects, such as bees, ants, or ladybugs. Direct children to use time-order words to write at least one sentence that includes a list. Remind children that they can also combine short sentences. Have children illustrate their writing and then share their work in small groups.

Chapter Review

OBJECTIVES

- To review time-order words, how to combine short sentences, and how to use commas in series
- To identify suffixes and understand how they change the meanings of words

DAILY LANGUAGE PRACTICE

TRANSPARENCY 67

1 Firsth I did my homework and, then I played for a while. (First; homework. Then)

2 we had chicken mashed potatoes, and green beans for dinner. (We; chicken,)

BRIDGE TO WRITING I (3 verbs) the dishes.

STANDARDIZED TEST PREP

Read the directions with children. Make sure they understand what they have to do. You may wish to use this page as an assessment after children have completed it independently.

TEST PREPARATION TIP
Item Type: Multiple Choice

 TIP

Model this strategy to help children determine the correct answer:

I carefully read sentence number 1. Next I read all three answer choices. I know *a* isn't the best answer because it doesn't sound right. Answer *b* starts with *And then*, so I know the order is mixed up. I read sentence number 1 again. It tells the order in which things happened in a way that makes sense without using *and then*. I choose *c. correct as is.*

Chapter Review

Read each numbered item. Choose the best answer.

1. Ms. Kim told the class about a trip. Then they cheered.
   a. Ms. Kim told the class about a trip they cheered.
   b. And then Ms. Kim told the class about a trip. Then they cheered.
   c. correct as is

2. First they will take a tour of the museum. Then they will eat.
   a. First they will take a tour of the museum. And then they will eat.
   b. Last they will take a tour of the museum. And then they will eat.
   c. correct as is

3. Donna, Sam and Trish like dinosaurs.
   a. Donna, Sam, and Trish like dinosaurs.
   b. Donna Sam and Trish like dinosaurs.
   c. correct as is

4. One dinosaur is black green, red.
   a. One dinosaur is black green and red.
   b. One dinosaur is black, green, and red.
   c. correct as is

 Visit our website for more activities about fixing sentence problems:
www.harcourtschool.com

Language Skills Assessment

PORTFOLIO ASSESSMENT
Have children select their best work from the following activities:

- **Writing Connection,** *pages 423 and 425;* TE activities, *pages 419, 425, and 427.*

ONGOING ASSESSMENT
Evaluate the performance of 4-6 children using appropriate checklists and record forms from pages R65–R68 and R77–R79.

 INTERNET Activities and exercises to help children prepare for state and standardized assessments appear on *The Learning Site:*
www.harcourtschool.com

■ Vocabulary ■

Suffixes

A **suffix** is a group of letters added to the end of a word. A suffix changes the meaning of a word.

Suffix	Meaning	Words
– less	without	useless, careless
– ful	full of	useful, careful

Practice

Add -ful or -less to the word in ( ). Write the new sentence.

1. Reggie cleaned the chalkboard to be (help).
   helpful
2. He dropped the chalk because he was (care).
   careless
3. A small piece of broken chalk is (use).
   useless
4. His teacher asked him to be more (care).
   careful
5. Reggie was (thank) she was not angry.
   thankful

427

■ Vocabulary ■

Suffixes

TEACH/MODEL

Have children answer the following questions: *If something without color is colorless, what do you call something without taste?* (tasteless) *If someone who is full of joy is joyful, what is someone who is full of hope?* (hopeful)

Write the words *tasteless* and *joyful* on the board, and circle *less* and *ful*. Ask children to say the circled endings and then discuss how they change the words. After sharing their ideas, have children read about suffixes at the top of page 427.

PRACTICE When children are finished, have volunteers share their words with classmates, and then read aloud the sentences.

WRAP-UP/ASSESS

SUMMARIZE Ask children to tell what they have learned about suffixes and to explain how knowing about suffixes might help make their writing more exact and interesting.

REACHING ALL LEARNERS

PRACTICE page 115

Name_____

Suffixes

A. Read each sentence. Add -ful or -less to complete the underlined word.

1. I am not afraid of that harm___less___ bug.

2. A bee can be harm___ful___.

3. Be care___ful___ not to get a bee sting.

4. If you are care___less___, the bee might sting you.

B. Use words from the box to complete the sentences.

careful	useless	colorful	thoughtful

5. Mom was ___thoughtful___ to buy me the book.

6. I will be very ___careful___ with it.

7. If it rips, it will be ___useless___.

8. The book is filled with ___colorful___ pictures.

TRY THIS! Write sentences using each of the following words: *fearless, fearful, restful, restless.* Draw a picture to go with each sentence.

Practice • Fixing Sentence Problems   Unit 6 • Chapter 34 115

REACHING ALL LEARNERS

CHALLENGE

LOOK FOR SUFFIXES Have small groups look through old newspapers and magazines for words that end with the suffixes *less* and *ful*. Invite children to write them down and use some of them to write a paragraph.

The weather was wonderful. The children were cheerful. They played endless games on the beach.

LESSON ORGANIZER	DAY 1	DAY 2
DAILY LANGUAGE PRACTICE TRANSPARENCIES 68, 69	1. I eat pizza And thon I eat pie. (pizza. Then) 2. Fyrst I ate some pizza. Nex I ate some pie. (First; Next) **Bridge to Writing** Maria likes pizza. Peter likes pizza. I like pizza. (combine into one sentence)	1. They have they're own kar. (their; car) 2. There going to Dallas, texas. (They're; Texas) **Bridge to Writing** They like (they're, their, there) school.
ORAL WARM-UP Listening/Speaking	Discuss Giraffes p. 428	Choose the Correct Word p. 430 _Grammar Jingles_™ CD, Primary, Track
TEACH/MODEL GRAMMAR **KEY** ✔ = tested skill	✔ **SPELLING WORDS THAT SOUND ALIKE** pp. 428–429 • To interpret and evaluate a poem • To recognize words that sound the same but have different meanings and spellings.	✔ **USING _THERE_, _THEIR_, AND _THEY'RE_** pp. 430–431 • To understand that _there_, _their_, and _they're_ sound alike but have different meanings and spellings • To use _there_, _their_, and _they're_ in writing

Reaching All Learners	_Practice Book_ p. 116
	Challenge: Activity Card 24, p. R64
	ESL: _ESL Manual_ pp. 168, 169
	Reteach: _Reteach Activities Copying Masters_ p. 70
		Modified Instruction
		  Below-Level: Identify Meaning
		  Above-Level: Complete Sentences
		ESL: Tell the Difference p. 430
		  ESL Manual pp. 168, 170
		Practice Book p. 117
		Challenge: Travel Journal p. 431
		Reteach: _Reteach Activities Copying Masters_ p. 71

WRITING	Favorite Animals p. 429 Summarize/Reflect	Writing Connection p. 431 Write About Classmates Summarize/Reflect
CROSS-CURRICULAR/ ENRICHMENT	**Vocabulary Power** Word Meaning, p. 428 bolt, dawdle, linger, plunge, **scamper** See _Vocabulary Power_ book.	**Vocabulary Power** Synonyms/Antonyms, p. 428 _Vocabulary Power_ book, p. 103 🏆 **Vocabulary activity**

DAY 3

1. There team won the gaim. (Their; game)
2. Theyre the best socker team. (They're; soccer)

Bridge to Writing I like soccer and hockey because (they're, there, their) fun sports.

Use *two, to,* or *too* p. 432

Grammar Jingles™ CD, Primary, Track 24

✔ **USING *TO, TOO,* AND *TWO***
  pp. 432–433
  • To identify the differences between *too, to,* and *two*
  • To identify meaning while listening to troublesome words

Modified Instruction
  Below-Level: Work in Pairs
  Above-Level: Find Sentences
Challenge: Other Words That Sound Alike p. 433
ESL: *ESL Manual,* pp. 168, 171
  Say It, Too p. 432
Practice Book p. 118
Reteach: *Reteach Activities Copying Masters* p. 72

Writing Connection p. 433
  Listen for Troublesome Words

  Summarize

Vocabulary Power

  Compare/Contrast, p. 428
  Vocabulary Power book, p. 104
  Vocabulary activity

DAY 4

1. Derrick goes too the store, two. (to; too)
2. Chuck has too oranges two eat. (two; to)

Bridge to Writing I have (to, too, two) cats and you have one, (to, too, two) .

Make Up Riddles p. 434

EXTRA PRACTICE p. 434–435
  • To identify and use troublesome words
  • To use troublesome words to write tongue twisters
  Practice and Assessment

Challenge: Troublesome Tongue Twister p. 435
ESL: Interactive Writing p. 434
  ESL Manual, pp. 168, 172
Practice Book p. 119

Writing Connection p. 435
  Tongue Twister

Vocabulary Power

  Context Clues, p. 428
  Vocabulary Power book, p. 105
  Vocabulary activity
Language Play p. 435

DAY 5

1. Where are they're hats (their; ?)
2. They're next two our too coats. (to; two)

Bridge to Writing It's (to, too, two) hot to go out without a hat.

TEST PREP CHAPTER REVIEW p. 436
  • To review troublesome words
  • To use the computer to find information
  Test Preparation

Practice Book p. 120
Challenge: Search a Topic p. 437
ESL: *ESL Manual,* pp. 168, 173

Vocabulary Power

  Technology, p. 428
Technology p. 437
  Using a Computer to Get Information

Spelling Words That Sound Alike

OBJECTIVES

- To listen critically to interpret and evaluate a poem
- To recognize words that sound the same but have different meanings and spellings

DAILY LANGUAGE PRACTICE

TRANSPARENCY 68

❶ I eat pizza And thon I eat pie. (pizza. Then)

❷ Fyrst I ate some pizza. Nex I ate some pie. (First; Next)

BRIDGE TO WRITING Maria likes pizza. Peter likes pizza. I like pizza. (combine into one sentence)

ORAL WARM-UP

USE PRIOR KNOWLEDGE Ask children what they know about giraffes. Record responses on the board, using *they're* and *their*: *They're tall. Their necks are long.* You may want to set up a **Troublesome Words Wall.**

TEACH/MODEL

Tell children to turn to page 428. Have them read the title and predict what the poem will be about. Read the poem aloud. Direct attention to the differences in spelling and meaning for the words *they're* and *their*. Point out that the contraction *they're* means *they are* and that *their* describes something the giraffes have such as a trait or object.

DEVELOP ORAL LANGUAGE Ask children to recall different reasons why the poet likes giraffes. Challenge children to come up with other reasons why someone may like giraffes. Be sure children use *their* and *they're* in the responses. Add *their*, *they're*, and *there* to the **Word Wall.**

Spelling Words That Sound Alike

Read the poem.

Giraffes

I like them.
Ask me why.

Because they hold their heads so high.
Because their necks stretch to the sky.
Because they're quiet, calm, and shy.
Because they run so fast they fly.
Because their eyes are velvet brown.
Because their coats are spotted tan.
Because they eat the tops of trees.
Because their legs have knobby knees.
Because
Because
Because. That's why
I like giraffes.

Mary Ann Hoberman

428

Vocabulary Power

DAY ❶ WORD MEANING Write: *Playful monkeys scamper about.* Discuss the meaning of *scamper*. (run quickly and lightly) **Do you think giraffes scamper?**

DAY ❷ SYNONYMS/ANTONYMS Write: *scamper, dash, stroll.* **Which words are synonyms? Which are antonyms?** (See also *Vocabulary Power*, page 103.)

DAY ❸ COMPARE/CONTRAST Write: *scampering squirrel, dawdling snail.* **Which is faster?** (See also *Vocabulary Power*, page 104.)

DAY ❹ CONTEXT CLUES Write: *We'll have to scamper to get this work done in time!* **What does scamper mean?** (See also *Vocabulary Power*, page 105.)

DAY ❺ Technology **Make a list of animals and words that describe the way they move.** Suggest that children use the computer to find information about the way various animals move.

Talk about your favorite animals. Use *they're* and *their* to tell why you like them.

Some words sound the same but have different meanings and spellings.

The giraffes are over **there** by the trees.
Their legs are long and thin.
They're nibbling on the leaves.

Write about another animal to add more lines to the poem. Responses will vary.

I like _____.

because they're _____.

because they're _____.

because their _____.

because their _____.

Because

Because

Because. That's why

I like _____.

429

WRITE Use children's previous responses to help them generate phrases about animals they like. Invite volunteers to share their reasons with the class. Write the sentences with *they're* or *their* on the board. Read the explanation and the example sentences in the box. Have children identify the words that sound the same and then discuss their meanings and spellings.

Read the poem at the bottom of page 429 together. Point out the language pattern. Have children complete the items and share their ideas.

WRAP-UP/ASSESS

SUMMARIZE Reread the poem with children. Have them summarize and reflect on what they have learned about words that sound alike but have different spellings and meanings. Children can write their reflections in their journals.
REFLECTION

RETEACH

INTERVENTION Lessons in **visual**, **auditory**, and **kinesthetic** modalities: p. R40 and *Reteach Activities Copying Masters*, p. 70

PRACTICE page 116

Name _____

Spelling Words That Sound Alike

A. Use the words from the box to complete the sentences.

their	they're	there

1. My friends left a note for me _____there_____.

2. It said _____they're_____ having a party.

3. I want to go to _____their_____ house.

4. But _____there_____ was no address in the note.

5. _____Their_____ friends will not know where to go!

B. Circle the word in ( ) that correctly completes the sentence.

6. (They're) There) getting ready for the party.

7. No one comes to (there, (their)) party, though.

8. Then ((their) they're) phone rings.

9. (They're, Their) going to make new notes.

10. (Their, (There)) will be a new party.

TRY THIS! Write two sentences about a party or a fun place you have been. Use *there, their,* or *they're* in your sentences.

116 Unit 6 • Chapter 35   Practice • Troublesome Words

CHALLENGE

MAKE A STORY LADDER Have children use **Challenge Activity Card 24** (page R64) to write a three-sentence story using words that sound alike. Call on volunteers to display and share their ladders.

Challenge Activity Card 24

Make a Story Ladder

You need:
• 3 index cards
• 2 long cardboard strips
• glue
• markers or crayons

1. Glue three index cards to two cardboard strips to make a ladder.
2. Write one troublesome word on each card.
3. Write a story on the back of the cards. Use the troublesome words. Start your story at the bottom of the ladder. You can add pictures if you want.

too

two

to

She buys one, too.

I buy two toys.

I go to the store with my sister.

---

page 70

Spelling Words That Sound Alike
Write a word from the box to finish each sentence. Share your answers with a partner.

Their	They're	there

1. The party for Veronica and Victor will be ____there____ in the yard.

2. ____Their____ mom is planning it.

3. ____They're____ twins.

4. ____Their____ friends are invited.

You're invited...

- -

Spelling Words That Sound Alike
Make this chart on a separate sheet of paper. Cut out the sentences below. Glue each sentence under the word that best completes it.

Their	They're	there

Two cakes are over there	____Their____ brother put candles on the cakes.
They're eight years old today.	They have gifts over there on the table.
____Their____ friends sing to them.	They're very happy.

Teacher: Cut apart the activities and distribute to children based on the modalities that are their strengths.

70 Unit 6 • Chapter 35   Reteach Activities • Troublesome Words

Using *there, their,* and *they're*

OBJECTIVES

• To understand that *there, their,* and *they're* sound alike but have different meanings and spellings

• To use *there, their,* and *they're* in writing

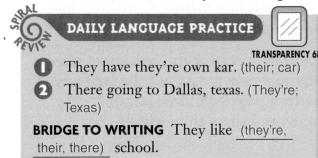

DAILY LANGUAGE PRACTICE

TRANSPARENCY 68

1 They have they're own kar. (their; car)

2 There going to Dallas, texas. (They're; Texas)

BRIDGE TO WRITING They like (they're, their, there) school.

ORAL WARM-UP

USE PRIOR KNOWLEDGE List these words on the board: *there, they're, their.* Have volunteers use one of the words in a sentence about a class trip or event. Ask other volunteers to point to the correct word being used.

Grammar Jingles™ **CD, Primary** Use Track 24 for review and reinforcement of troublesome words.

TEACH/MODEL

Introduce the troublesome words using the explanation and the examples. Show children how to read the chart to find the different meanings. Ask questions such as: *When do you use* **their**? (when something belongs to them) *How is the spelling different?* (The words all start the same but end differently.) *What word means "that place"?* (there)

GUIDED PRACTICE Work with children to complete each sentence. Suggest that they first decide the meaning of the missing word and then use the chart to find the word's correct spelling. Model if necessary.

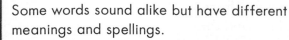

Troublesome Words

Using *there, their,* and *they're*

Some words sound alike but have different meanings and spellings.

Word	Meaning
their	belonging to them
there	that place
they're	contraction for *they are*

The Smiths planned **their** trip to New York. Then a big snowstorm hit **there**. Now **they're** planning another trip.

Guided Practice

Write *their, there,* or *they're* to complete each sentence.

1. On ____their____ trip they will go to Texas.

2. The family will see many things ____there____.

3. The children are excited about ____their____ plane ride.

4. ____Their____ bags are on board.

5. ____They're____ all ready to go.

430

Vocabulary Power page 103

Name _____

Synonyms have similar meanings. Antonyms have opposite meanings. Which word pairs are synonyms? Which are antonyms?

happy — glad   first — beginning   stop — halt
happy — sad   first — last   stop — go

Use the synonyms to help you understand the meaning of the word in dark print. Draw a picture to illustrate the meaning.

1. bolt — hurry — dash	**2. plunge** — dive — jump
3. scamper — run — rush	**4. linger** — stay — dilly-dally

Use the antonyms to help you understand the meaning of the word in dark print. Draw a picture to illustrate the meaning.

5. dawdle — scamper — rush

Vocabulary Power   Unit 6 • Chapter 35   103

ESL

REACHING ALL LEARNERS

TELL THE DIFFERENCE Provide children with 6 index cards. On three cards, write the words *there, their,* and *they're.* On the other three, write the meanings of the words. Children can lay out the three words and discuss how to spell them. Then have children match the words with their meanings and use them in sentences to tell about themselves.

Remember *There, their,* and *they're* sound the same but have different meanings and spellings.

Independent Practice

Write *their, there,* or *they're* to complete each sentence.

6. ___They're___ leaving the airport.

7. They get to ___their___ hotel.

8. The maps are over ___there___.

9. ___Their___ tour bus takes them to the river walk.

10. The children like the sights ___there___.

11. Now ___they're___ hungry.

12. A restaurant is over ___there___ by the river.

13. They get ___their___ meals quickly.

14. At the end of the day, ___they're___ tired.

15. ___Their___ trip was fun.

Writing Connection

Write About Classmates Think about yourself and a group of classmates. Write three sentences about how they are like you. Use *they're, there,* or *their* in the sentences. Draw a picture.

Use your computer to help you write your sentences.

431

Independent Practice

Have children complete the Independent Practice, or modify it by using the following suggestions:

MODIFIED INSTRUCTION

BELOW-LEVEL STUDENTS Work with children to first identify the meaning and then the spelling for the missing word in each sentence. They can refer to the chart on page 430.

ABOVE-LEVEL STUDENTS After children finish, have them write sentences leaving out the troublesome words. They can then trade sentences with a partner and add the words.

Writing Connection

Write About Classmates Ask children to think of what their friends own, do, or are like. Have volunteers place their sentences in the Sharing Basket to share with others.

WRAP-UP/ASSESS

SUMMARIZE Ask children to reflect on what they have learned about words that sound alike. Have them summarize what they have learned. **REFLECTION**

RETEACH

INTERVENTION Lessons in **visual, auditory,** and **kinesthetic** modalities: p. R40 and *Reteach Activities Copying Masters,* p. 71.

PRACTICE page 117

Name _____

Using *there, their,* and *they're*

A. Write each word from the box next to its meaning. Then add the words to the puzzle.

their	they're	there

1. that place ___there___

2. belonging to them ___their___

3. contraction for they are ___they're___

B. Write *there, their,* or *they're* to complete each sentence.

4. ___They're___ planning a picnic.

5. Many people will be ___there___.

6. That's why ___their___ picnics are fun.

7. They set the food over ___there___.

8. ___They're___ ready to eat!

TRY THIS! Write sentences using *there, their,* and *they're.* Leave out these words in each sentence. Ask a friend to fill in the blanks.

Practice • Troublesome Words   Unit 6 • Chapter 35 117

CHALLENGE

TRAVEL JOURNAL Have children recall a time when they went on a trip with others. Have them write several sentences describing the trip. Be sure they use *there, they're* and *their* in the sentences. They can draw a picture to go with the sentences.

---

page 71

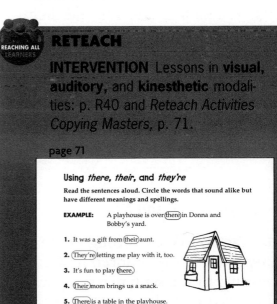

Using *there, their,* and *they're*

Read the sentences aloud. Circle the words that sound alike but have different meanings and spellings.

EXAMPLE: A playhouse is over (there) in Donna and Bobby's yard.

1. It was a gift from (their) aunt.

2. (They're) letting me play with it, too.

3. It's fun to play (there).

4. (Their) mom brings us a snack.

5. (There) is a table in the playhouse.

Using *there, their,* and *they're*

Cut out the words at the bottom of the page. Glue the words that best fit each sentence.

1. Two chairs are ___there___ in the corner.

2. A shelf holds ___their___ games and books.

3. ___They're___ trying to make it special.

4. ___Their___ dad brought us snacks.

there	their	Their	They're

Reteach Activities • Troublesome Words   Unit 6 • Chapter 35 71

Using *to, too,* and *two*

OBJECTIVES

- To identify the differences between *too, to,* and *two*
- To identify meaning while listening to troublesome words

DAILY LANGUAGE PRACTICE

TRANSPARENCY 68

1 There team won the gaim. (Their; game)

2 Theyre the best socker team. (They're; soccer)

BRIDGE TO WRITING I like soccer and hockey because (they're, there, their) fun sports.

ORAL WARM-UP

USE PRIOR KNOWLEDGE Ask children to use the words *two, to,* or *too* in sentences about what is going on in the classroom, such as: *I have two books. You go to the closet to get paper. There is too much talking.* Discuss with children how the words sound the same but mean different things. You may want to add them to your **Word Wall.**

Grammar Jingles™ **CD, Primary** Use Track 24 for review and reinforcement of troublesome words.

TEACH/MODEL

Read the instruction box. Discuss the meanings of *to, too,* and *two.*

GUIDED PRACTICE Work through the first item together. Show children how to use the meaning of the sentence to figure out which word to choose. Do the same with the remaining sentences.

Using *to, too,* and *two*

The words **to**, **too**, and **two** sound the same but have different spellings and meanings.

Word	Meaning
to	in the direction of
too	also
two	one more than one

Ken walks **to** Pat's house.
Maya walks there, **too**.
The **two** of them walk together.

Guided Practice

Choose *to, too,* or *two* to complete each sentence.

1. Sometimes Kevin and Pat walk (<u>to</u>, too, two) the park.

2. Once they heard (to, too, <u>two</u>) kittens.

3. A police officer heard them, (to, <u>too</u>, two).

4. They all ran (<u>to</u>, too, two) see what was the problem.

5. The kittens were stuck on (to, too, <u>two</u>) high tree branches.

432

Vocabulary Power page 104

Name _____

Compare/Contrast

These words name ways to move.

bolt   dawdle   linger   plunge   scamper

Read these descriptions. Do you picture something moving fast or slowly?

a scampering kitten   a plunging kite
a dawdling snail   lingering smoke
a bolting horse   a bolt of lightning
dawdling ducks   scampering children

Write the descriptions above in the correct box. Add other descriptions.

FAST	SLOW
a scampering kitten	a dawdling snail
a bolting horse	dawdling ducks
a plunging kite	lingering smoke
a bolt of lightning	
scampering children	

104   Unit 6 • Chapter 35   Vocabulary Power

ESL

REACHING ALL LEARNERS

SAY IT, TOO Hand out cards with the words *to, too,* and *two.* Have children hold up their cards and say the word as you say sentences such as: *I have <u>two</u> feet. You have two feet, <u>too</u>. Let's walk <u>to</u> the window.* Then invite volunteers to make up and say sentences using those words, and have children hold up the cards.

Remember *To, too,* and *two* sound the same, but have different spellings and meanings.

Independent Practice

Choose *to, too,* or *two* to complete each sentence.

6. Other officers came (<u>to</u>, too, two) the park.

7. Many people were watching, (to, <u>too</u>, two).

8. A fire truck showed up, (to, <u>too</u>, two).

9. Firefighters brought a tall ladder (<u>to</u>, too, two) the tree.

10. The ladder had (to, too, <u>two</u>) cracks in it.

11. Luckily, the truck had (to, too, <u>two</u>) ladders.

12. The other ladder was tall, (to, <u>too</u>, two).

13. (To, Too, <u>Two</u>) officers carried it to the tree.

14. The (to, too, <u>two</u>) kittens were saved!

15. The boys went (<u>to</u>, too, two) see them.

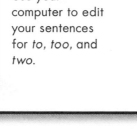

Writing Connection

Listen for Troublesome Words Write three sentences. Use *to, too,* or *two* in them. Read the sentences to a classmate. Ask the classmate to write the correct troublesome words.

Use your computer to edit your sentences for *to, too,* and *two.*

Independent...

Have children complet... modify it by using the fo...

MODIFIED INSTRUCTION...

BELOW-LEVEL STUDENTS Hav... pairs. One child reads the sentenc... answers with *to, two,* or *too.*

ABOVE-LEVEL STUDENTS After childre... invite them to find three sentences in a tex... uses *to, too,* and *two.* Have them write the se... and tell where they found them.

Writing Connection

Listen for Troublesome Words Have children underline or circle the troublesome word in each sentence. This will make it easier when they identify the words.

WRAP-UP/ASSESS

SUMMARIZE Have children summarize what they know about troublesome words.

RETEACH

INTERVENTION Lessons in **visual**, **auditory**, and **kinesthetic** modalities: p. R40 and *Reteach Activities Copying Masters*, p. 72.

page 72

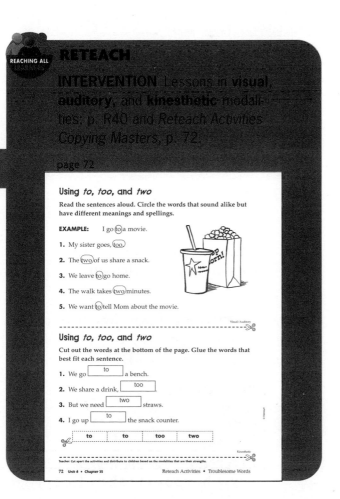

PRACTICE page 118

Name _____

Using *to, too,* and *two*

A. Underline the word in ( ) that correctly completes the sentence.

1. (**To**, **Two**) days ago I went on a day trip.

2. I went (**too**, **to**) my uncle's cabin.

3. My grandpa was there, (**too**, **two**).

4. We went (**to**, **too**) the lake.

5. I caught (**two**, **to**) fish.

B. Write *to, too,* or *two* to complete each sentence.

6. My mom caught some fish, ___too___.

7. ___Two___ friends helped us carry the fish.

8. Then we headed ___to___ my house.

9. It took ___two___ hours to drive home.

10. I would go ___to___ the cabin again.

TRY THIS! Write rules to show how you will use *to, too,* and *two.* Then write a sentence using each word correctly.

118 Unit 6 • Chapter 35   Practice • Troublesome Words

CHALLENGE

OTHER WORDS THAT SOUND ALIKE Have small groups list words that sound alike but have different spellings and meanings. Prepare a list of words such as *blue, sew, knew, one,* and *hi.* Challenge children to write a word next to each item that sounds the same but has a different spelling and meaning. Invite children to make up sentences using the words that sound alike.

DAILY LANGUAGE PRACTICE

TRANSPARENCY 69

1 Derrick goes too the store, two. (to; too)

2 Chuck has too oranges two eat. (two; to)

BRIDGE TO WRITING I have (to, too, two)
cats and you have one, (to, too, two).

ORAL WARM-UP

USE PRIOR KNOWLEDGE Ask volunteers to
make up riddles about troublesome
words. They should say two clues—first
the sound of the word and then the
meaning. Have the group try to guess
and then spell the word. Ask children to
tell what other words sound alike. Try to
work a Vocabulary Power word into the
riddles.

TEACH/MODEL

Read each set of directions to make sure
children understand how to complete
both sections. Have children share their
answers in small groups before you read
aloud the correct answers.

WRAP-UP/ASSESS

SUMMARIZE Ask children to reflect on and
discuss any special problems they had in
completing the practice activities before
you have them summarize what they
have learned about troublesome
words.

ADDITIONAL PRACTICE Extra practice items
are provided on page 477 of the *Pupil
Edition* (*Teacher's Edition* R7).

TECHNOLOGY

*Grammar Practice
and Assessment* CD-ROM

Writing Express CD-ROM

INTERNET Visit *The Learning Site!*
www.harcourtschool.com

Troublesome Words

Extra Practice

**Write *their*, *there*, or *they're* to complete
each sentence.**

1. It is raining out ___there___ at the lake.

2. Most children bring ___their___ raincoats.

3. ___They're___ going to sail anyway.

4. The sails are raised on the boats over
___there___ .

5. Now ___they're___ ready to go.

**Choose *to*, *too*, or *two* to complete
each sentence.**

6. The class went (<u>to</u>, too, two) the dock.

7. (To, Too, <u>Two</u>) boats sailed away.

8. A motorboat went out, (to, <u>too</u>, two).

9. The (to, too, <u>two</u>) sails on each boat
filled with air.

10. The boats sailed (<u>to</u>, too, two) the
other side of the lake.

434

Vocabulary Power page 105

Name _____

Context clues can help you understand different meanings of the
same word.

Hurry! We have to *dash*.
Write a *dash* between the words.

Draw pictures or write to show the meaning of the underlined
words.

1. The mice <u>scamper</u> into their nest.	2. Hurry, Jan. We have to <u>scamper</u>!
3. The penguins <u>plunge</u> into the icy water.	4. Let's try something new. Let's take a <u>plunge</u>.
5. Snails creep and <u>linger</u>.	6. I like to <u>linger</u> at the lake.
7. The dogs <u>bolt</u> out of the yard.	8. Don't forget to <u>bolt</u> the door.

Vocabulary Power   Unit 6 • Chapter 35   105

ESL

INTERACTIVE WRITING You
may wish to have children write
the tongue twisters as an interactive writing activity. Have small
groups decide which troublesome
words they will use. Then have
them dictate names of things and
action words that begin with the
same letter-sound as the troublesome word. List the words. Then
have them dictate and help you
write a tongue twister on the
board or chart paper, using
the examples on page 435 as
models.

Language Play

Which Word?
- Take turns with a partner.
- Pick a word from the list. Do not tell your partner what the word is.
- Say a sentence using the word.
- Have your partner write the word.
- Score one point for each word written correctly. The first player with 5 points wins.

to	there
too	their
two	they're

Writing Connection

Tongue Twister Tongue twisters are fun to say because many of their words begin with the same sound. Write some tongue twisters using troublesome words. Then try reading them aloud. How fast can you read them and still say each word correctly?

Tongue Twisters
Their three friends think they're thrifty.

Tori wore two shoes to town, too.

They're thirsty and their throats throb.

435

Language Play

Have children play "Which Word?" in pairs. Model how to play the game and keep score. Tell children to keep playing until they have used all the words on the list.

Writing Connection

Tongue Twister Check to see that children have successfully written tongue twisters by using the criteria below.

CRITERIA
- ☑ Writes at least one troublesome word in each tongue twister.
- ☑ Writes as many words as possible that begin with the same sound.
- ☑ Begins each tongue twister with a capital letter and ends it with an end mark.

- 📁 **PORTFOLIO OPPORTUNITY** You may want to have children take their writing home to share with family members or place it in their portfolios. Have children review the work in their portfolios to monitor their growth as writers over time.

REACHING ALL LEARNERS

PRACTICE page 119

Name _____

Extra Practice

A. Circle the word in ( ) that correctly completes the sentence.

1. They got a surprise from (there, (their,) they're) mother.

2. (There, Their, (They're)) going on a trip to Texas.

3. It will be hot ((there,) their, they're).

4. (There, (Their,) They're) plane leaves tomorrow.

B. Write there, their, or they're to complete each sentence.

5. ___Their___ plane flew to Dallas.

6. ___They're___ sitting in the front of the plane.

7. They have more space ___there___

C. Write to, too, or two to complete each sentence.

8. They went ___to___ a football game.

9. The ___two___ teams were from Texas.

10. The fans were from Texas, ___too___.

Practice • Troublesome Words   Unit 6 • Chapter 35 119

REACHING ALL LEARNERS

CHALLENGE

TROUBLESOME TONGUE TWISTER Challenge children to write one tongue twister with as many troublesome words in it as they can use. Remind them that the tongue twister must make sense even if it's in a silly way. For example, *Two of their tall trees over there are too tall to climb.* Encourage children to illustrate their writing and share it with the class.

Chapter Review

OBJECTIVES
- To review troublesome words
- To use the computer to find information

DAILY LANGUAGE PRACTICE

TRANSPARENCY 69

1 Where are they're hats (their; ?)

2 They're next two our too coats. (to; two)

BRIDGE TO WRITING It's (to, too, two) hot to go out without a hat.

STANDARDIZED TEST PREP

Read the directions with children to make sure they understand how to complete page 436. You may wish to use this page as an assessment after children have completed it independently.

TEST PREPARATION TIP
Item Type: Multiple Choice

TIP

Model this strategy to help children determine the correct answer:

I read the sentence and the underlined words. I know *they're* means *they are*. When I read *they are* in the first sentence, it doesn't make sense, so I know the answer has to be one of the other choices. *Their* describes someone's things, so I know *b* doesn't work. That leaves *a*. I know *a* is the correct answer. I read the sentence again with *There* to make sure it makes sense.

Chapter Review

STANDARDIZED **TEST PREP**

Choose the best answer for each underlined word.

1. <u>They're</u> is the cave.
   a. There
   b. Their
   c. correct as is

2. Go in with <u>to</u> people.
   a. two
   b. too
   c. correct as is

3. You can't go <u>two</u> the cave alone.
   a. too
   b. to
   c. correct as is

4. The rangers follow <u>their</u> own rule.
   a. they're
   b. there
   c. correct as is

5. <u>They're</u> never alone in the cave.
   a. There
   b. Their
   c. correct as is

6. You have to follow the rule, <u>to</u>.
   a. too
   b. two
   c. correct as is

 Visit our website for more activities with troublesome words
www.harcourtschool.com

436

Language Skills Assessment

• •

PORTFOLIO ASSESSMENT
Have children select their best work from the following activities:

- **Writing Connection,** pages 431, 433, and 435; TE activities, pages 429, 431, 433, 434, and 435.

ONGOING ASSESSMENT
Evaluate the performance of 4-6 students using appropriate checklists and record forms from pages R65–R68 and R77–R79.

 INTERNET Activities and exercises to help children prepare for state and standardized assessments appear on *The Learning Site:*

www.harcourtschool.com

■ Technology ■

Using a Computer to Get Information

You can use a computer's search engine to help you find information. A search engine is a computer's tool for finding different information. Picture **1** shows how to search using a key word. A **key word** tells what your topic is. Type a key word and click on *Go.* Picture **2** shows a guided search. You click on key word choices on the computer screen.

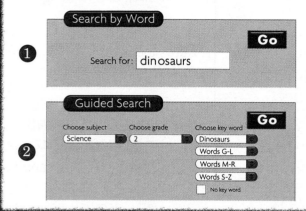

❶
Search by Word

Search for: dinosaurs   **Go**

❷
Guided Search

Choose subject Choose grade Choose key word   **Go**
Science   2   Dinosaurs
                Words G-L
                Words M-R
                Words S-Z
                ☐ No key word

Practice

Write the key word you would use to find answers to each question. Possibe responses are given.

1. What is the biggest city in Texas? Texas

2. How do clouds form? clouds

3. What does a veterinarian do? veterinarian

437

REACHING ALL LEARNERS

PRACTICE page 120

Name _____

Using a Computer to Get Information

Write the key word or words you would use with a search engine to find the answer to each question.

1. What is the capital of England? ___ England
2. What are three types of butterflies? ___ butterflies
3. Where do kangaroos live? ___ kangaroos
4. Who is Alma Flor Ada? ___ Alma Flor Ada
5. What does a biologist do? ___ biologist
6. Where is the Golden Gate Bridge? ___ Golden Gate Bridge
7. What do bats eat? ___ bats
8. When did the Civil War begin? ___ Civil War

TRY THIS! Write three questions about a topic that interests you. Use a search engine to find out more information.

120 Unit 6 • Chapter 35   Practice • Troublesome Words

CHALLENGE

SEARCH A TOPIC Have children use an actual search engine to locate information about a topic of their choice. Have them research different sites and print out a page that gives new information about the topic. Have children locate the e-mail address and then see if they can go back online and locate the site. If going online is not possible, have children use a CD-ROM, such as *Encarta,* to locate information.

■ Technology ■

Using a Computer to Get Information

TEACH/MODEL

Read about how to find information using a computer. Use the illustrations to show children how they have to think about the main topic when they want to use a search engine. Explain that children need to first type in the word or words and then click on *Go.* The computer then will search for all the sites that have to do with dinosaurs. Allow children with experience to discuss searches they have done.

PRACTICE When children finish, have volunteers share the word from each sentence they chose. If possible, have them use a computer to find the answers to the questions.

WRAP-UP/ASSESS

SUMMARIZE Ask children to summarize what they know about using a computer to find information. Be sure they discuss both CD-ROMs and using online search engines.

Writing a Research Report

pages 438-455

LESSON ORGANIZER	DAY 1	DAY 2
DAILY LANGUAGE PRACTICE TRANSPARENCY 70	1. Ann wishes her could sea a dinosaur. (she; see) 2. a diplodocus's neck was longer than he legs. (A; its)	1. Fish dogs and birds all needs water. (Fish, dogs,; need) 2. People uses water for drinking washing and cooking. (use; drinking, washing,)
ORAL WARM-UP Listening/Speaking	Tell Main Ideas of Research Reports or Information Articles p. 438	Retell the Main Idea of a Book or Movie p. 448
TEACH/MODEL WRITING 	**Literature Model:** "Water on Earth" from *You're Aboard Spaceship Earth*, pp. 438-444 • To read and respond to a non-fiction selection as a model for writing • To identify main ideas and details **Reading-Writing Connection:** Parts of a Research Report p. 445 **A Student Model** pp. 446-447	**GUIDED WRITING** ✔ **Prewriting** pp. 448-449 • To brainstorm and select a writing topic • To use an outline to plan main ideas and details **Transparency** 71
Reaching All Learners	**ESL:** *ESL Manual* pp. 174-175 Water-Cycle Terminology p. 440 **Challenge:** Water-Cycle Skit p. 441	**ESL:** *ESL Manual* p. 174
GRAMMAR	**Unit 6 Review** pp. 456-457	**Unit 6 Review** pp. 456-457
CROSS-CURRICULAR/ ENRICHMENT	**Science Connection:** Salt from Sea Water p. 440 **Technology Connection:** Using Water p. 442 **School-Home Connection:** Conservation List p. 442	**Vocabulary Power** Context Clues p. 438 *Vocabulary Power* book, p. 106 **Vocabulary activity**

KEY
✔ = tested writing form/skill

Vocabulary Power

recycled, recount, rethink, retrace, review
See *Vocabulary Power* book.

DAY 3

1. Shannon and Marie left they're books there (their; there.)

2. She hurrys too see to movies. (hurries to; two)

Talk About a News Article p. 450

GUIDED WRITING

✔ **Drafting** pp. 450–451
- To draft a research report
- To write paragraphs with clear main ideas and supporting details

 Transparency 71

ESL: *ESL Manual* p. 174
Interactive Writing p. 451

Unit 6 Review pp. 456–457

Writers Craft: Sentence Variety p. 451

Vocabulary Power

Prefixes p. 438
Vocabulary Power book p. 107

DAY 4

1. We'l return the cans bottles, and newspapers. (We'll; cans,)

2. Its rainy foggy and snowy all at one time. (It's rainy, foggy,)

Review the Elements of a Research Report p. 452

GUIDED WRITING

✔ **Revising and Proofreading** pp. 452–453
- To revise a research report
- To proofread writing for capitalization, punctuation, grammar, and spelling
- To use Editor's Marks to make revisions and corrections

 Transparencies 71, 71a, and 71b

ESL: *ESL Manual* p. 174

Unit 6 Review pp. 456–457

SPELLING CONNECTION: Spelling Strategies p. 453

Vocabulary Power

Content-Area Words p. 438
Vocabulary Power book p. 108

🖥 **Vocabulary activity**

DAY 5

1. Jack said he report are on cars. (his; is)

2. Myself prefer to rite about traveling. (I; write)

Brainstorm Forms of Presenting Research Report Information p. 454

GUIDED WRITING

✔ **Publishing** p. 454
- To make final copies of revised research reports
- To share reports with an audience
Scoring Rubric p. 454
Handwriting p. 455

ESL: *ESL Manual* p. 174

Unit 6 Review pp. 456–457

LISTENING AND SPEAKING: Giving an Oral Report p. 455

Vocabulary Power

Figurative Language p. 438

Read the Literature

OBJECTIVES

- To read and respond to a nonfiction selection as a model for writing
- To identify main ideas and details

DAILY LANGUAGE PRACTICE

TRANSPARENCY 70

1 Ann wishes her could sea a dinosaur. (she; see)

2 a diplodocus's neck was longer than he legs. (A; its)

ORAL WARM-UP

USE PRIOR KNOWLEDGE Explain that children will write their own research reports after they read and discuss one as a group.

Read the introductory paragraph on page 438. Have volunteers tell the main ideas of other research reports or informational articles they have read before.

PREREADING STRATEGIES

VOCABULARY Have children read the title of the selection and brainstorm some ideas about where water comes from and how it is used. Record their ideas on a chart.

Water	
Where It Comes From	How We Use It
rivers, clouds	washing cars, taking baths

PREVIEW/SET PURPOSE Based on the illustrations, selection title, and discussion, ask children to predict what they might learn from the selection.

A research report gives information about a topic. Each paragraph has a main idea and detail sentences that tell more about the topic. As you read this report, think about its main ideas.

You're Aboard Spaceship Earth

by Patricia Lauber
ILLUSTRATED BY HOLLY KELLER

438

Vocabulary Power

DAY 1 WORD MEANING Write: *recycled.* **Find this word on page 439. What does *recycled* mean?** (used over again) **What things do you recycle?**

DAY 2 CONTEXT CLUES Write: *This newspaper will be* <u>recycled</u> *into grocery bags.* **What clues help you understand the meaning of *recycled*?** (See also *Vocabulary Power*, page 106.)

DAY 3 PREFIXES List: *cycle, recycle, use, reuse.* **Which are the base words? What has been added to *cycle* and *use* to make new words? What do the new words mean?** (See also *Vocabulary Power*, page 107.)

DAY 4 CONTENT-AREA WORDS Write: *Music, Art, Math.* **In which class would you recycle scrap paper to make a collage?** (See also *Vocabulary Power*, page 108.)

DAY 5 FIGURATIVE LANGUAGE Discuss the meaning of the following: to *recycle* an idea, to "*reinvent* the wheel," to *rehash* a topic. Ask children to illustrate or give examples.

Water on Earth

Earth has had the same water for billions of years. Plants, animals, and people all use it. Yet Earth doesn't run out of water, because the same water is used over and over again. It is recycled.

439

OPTIONS FOR READING

DIRECTED READING Use the questions.

PARTNER READING Have partners read alternate pages aloud.

INDEPENDENT READING Children can read the selection silently. After reading, they can join a small group to share one or two new things they learned.

READING LIKE A WRITER

Pages 438–439 Tell children that nonfiction writing like this is often organized by main ideas and supporting details. Have them use the picture on these pages to predict the main idea of this selection. Point out to children that to make the topic interesting to readers, the author often tries to start the writing with an interesting fact or question in the first paragraph.

1. **Why doesn't the earth run out of water?** (The same water is used over and over again.) **LITERAL: CAUSE AND EFFECT**

2. **How did the author try to make the beginning of "Water on Earth" interesting to readers right at the beginning?** (She started the writing with an interesting fact.) **METACOGNITIVE: AUTHOR'S CRAFT**

SELECTION SUMMARY

NONFICTION: RESEARCH REPORT This excerpt from a nonfiction trade book describes the water cycle and different ways in which people and other living things use water.

ABOUT THE AUTHOR

Patricia Lauber has written more than 90 children's books. A nonfiction writer, she enjoys nature by hiking and sailing near her Connecticut home. Some of her related titles that might interest children are *Living with Dinosaurs*, *The News About Dinosaurs*, and *Be a Friend to Trees*.

Pages 440–441 Have children look at the pictures and try to trace the path of a drop of water through the water cycle.

1. **How does water get into the air?** (Heat makes it turn into a gas.) **INFEREN-TIAL: IMPORTANT DETAILS**

2. **Where do the oceans get their water?** (from rivers and rainwater) **INFER-ENTIAL: SUMMARIZE**

3. **How does the diagram on pages 440 and 441 help you understand the writing?** (makes the information easier to understand) **METACOGNITIVE: AUTHOR'S CRAFT**

Most of our water comes from the oceans. Water is drawn into the air by the sun's heat. It becomes a gas called water vapor. Salt from the ocean water is left behind.

WATER VAPOR

440

Science Connection

SALT FROM SEA WATER
Obtain several cups of saltwater from a natural source or make saltwater by dissolving a couple of teaspoons of salt in a couple of cups of water. Pour the salt water into a shallow pan, and let it evaporate over several days. Have children examine the salt crystals or salty residue that remains in the pan.

REACHING ALL LEARNERS **ESL**

WATER-CYCLE TERMINOLOGY
Display labeled photographs of several of the terms related to the water cycle to guide children who are acquiring English in understanding important parts of the water cycle. Have children draw and label their own pictures of the cycle and then talk about their drawings in small groups.

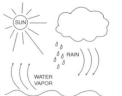

RAIN

Water vapor forms clouds. Rain clouds drop their water on the earth. Some of it falls in the oceans. Some falls on land. There much of the rainwater runs off into streams. The streams flow into rivers. The rivers flow back into the oceans.

Again the sun's heat draws water out of the oceans. Water vapor forms clouds. It falls again as rain.

441

REACHING ALL LEARNERS

CHALLENGE

WATER-CYCLE SKIT Invite children to create an original skit to explain the water cycle. Suggest that they make signs or costumes to help their audience understand each part of the cycle. After they practice the skit, have them present it to the entire class.

SUN

RAIN

WATER VAPOR

Pages 442–443 Have children use the illustrations on these pages to predict where water comes from and how it is used.

1. **Based on this passage, which group—plants, people, or animals—uses water in the greatest number of ways? Explain.** (People; most of the examples of water use are things that people do.) **INFERENTIAL: GENERALIZE**

2. **How can you tell that life would be very different without water?** (The author gives many examples of ways that we use water, so without water many things would be different.) **METACOGNITIVE: AUTHOR'S CRAFT**

Water is used in many ways. The roots of plants draw water from the soil. Animals drink water and bathe in it. So do people.

442

Technology Connection

USING WATER Have children learn about an appliance or a process that relies heavily on the use of water. They can make a labeled diagram to explain how the appliance or the process works and can then present their findings to the class.

School-Home Connection

CONSERVATION LIST Suggest children talk with family members about ways to conserve water at home. Ask them to record for one week ways they saved water at home.

∘ Monday—turned water off while I brushed my teeth

Rushing water can be put to work. It can turn machines that make electricity. Paper mills use water. Other factories do too.

Tugs and barges travel on rivers. So do canoes and rowboats.

Water fills swimming pools. Heated, it warms buildings in cold weather. It washes clothes, dishes, and cars.

How many other uses can you think of?

443

Strategies Good Readers Use

LOOK AT WORD BITS AND PARTS Write the word *electricity* on the board. Help children understand that one strategy they might use to read long words is to look at parts of the word that they already know. Ask children if any parts of the word on the board are familiar. Frame the word part *city*, and ask a volunteer to read this part of the word. Guide children as they decode the word one part at a time.

Page 444 Have children examine the picture and predict what dinosaurs have to do with water on Earth. Then have them read to find the answer.

1. **What does the author mean in the last sentence in this passage?**
(Since the earth doesn't get new water, the water is recycled. The same water has been here for millions of years, even since the time of the dinosaurs.) **INFERENTIAL: DRAW CONCLUSIONS**

Think About It

Ask volunteers to retell the main idea and important details from the selection in their own words.

1. Children share their choice of the most interesting details with a partner. **CRITICAL:** EXPRESS PERSONAL OPINIONS
2. Children list any uses of water described in the selection or from their own experience. Their answer should suggest that they realize that water is essential for life as we know it. **CRITICAL:** SPECULATE

After being used, water goes back into the oceans, is drawn into the air, and falls again as rain. Some of the rain that falls on you probably fell on the dinosaurs.

Think About It

1. What is the most interesting thing you found out about water? Read the sentences that tell about it to a partner.

2. What are some of the uses of water? Why is water important to you?

444

Response to Literature

WRITING PROMPT You may want to have children write to respond to "Water on Earth." Use the writing prompt below, or another you choose. Before children begin, you might want to review important parts of a poster that persuades on page R8.

Now that you've learned about the water cycle, you know that it's important to conserve water and to keep water clean. Use what you have learned to make a poster to persuade others about the importance of water.

Informal Assessment You can use children's posters to informally assess their understanding of the selections and their ability to create a cohesive piece. Note areas where they might benefit from instruction in writing and grammar.

Parts of a Research Report

A research report gives information on a **topic**. The report's **title** tells what the topic is.

Within the report there may be one or more paragraphs. Each paragraph has one **main idea** and sentences that give **details** about the main idea.

Write the main idea shown. It is from the paragraph on page 442. Reread the paragraph. Write details from that paragraph in a list. Then do the same thing with another paragraph in the report.

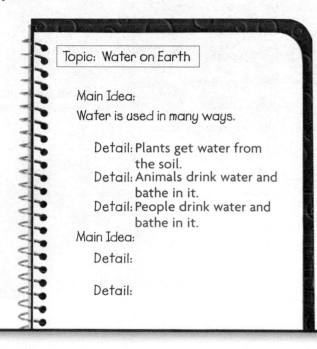

Parts of a Research Report

ANALYZE THE LITERATURE Discuss the elements of a research report. Explain that a good research report has clearly stated main ideas and details, or examples that support each main idea about the topic. Model how to complete the list by filling in a detail for the main idea with children. Demonstrate how to find other details in the text and fill them in on an appropriate spot in the list. Ask volunteers to find additional details in the text to support the main idea. Guide children in writing sentences for these details.

Informal Assessment

• • • • • • • • • • • • • • •

You can informally assess children's **comprehension** of the selection and their knowledge of the **structure of a research report** by having them retell the main ideas and a few details from "Water on Earth."

A Student Model

READ AND RESPOND TO THE MODEL Tell children that you are going to read Jermaine's report aloud. Ask them what their purpose for listening should be. (to be informed) Then read the report aloud. Discuss how effectively Jermaine has written a report that is informative on the topic of dinosaurs. Ask children to identify details that tell about something new they learned from the report. Tell children that they can use this published piece as a model for their own writing.

FOCUS ON ORGANIZATION Have children reread the report silently, using the side notes to identify the main parts of it. Then ask volunteers to identify and explain the main idea of each paragraph in their own words. Point out that main ideas in reports are supported by details.

FOCUS ON WRITER'S CRAFT Have children find and read aloud the examples that Jermaine uses. (He names Tyrannosaurus rex, Stegosaurus, and Troodon: Tyrannosaurus, 1,400 pounds; Stegosaurus, bony plated; Troodon, small dinosaur.)

A Student Model

Jermaine enjoyed reading about how water is used on Earth. He wrote a report about another topic in which he is interested. Read his report, and think about its parts.

Dinosaurs

Dinosaurs lived millions of years ago. The first dinosaurs lived about 245 million years ago. The last dinosaurs died about 65 million years ago. No one is sure why this happened.

Many different kinds of dinosaurs roamed the Earth. Tyrannosaurus rex was big and fierce and weighed more than 1,400 pounds. Stegosaurus had bony plates on its back. Troodon weighed less than 100 pounds, but some scientists think it was one of the smartest dinosaurs.

The **title** tells the topic, or what the report is about.

The **main idea** answers an important question about the topic.

The **details** are examples that tell about the main idea.

LISTENING AND SPEAKING

GENERATE QUESTIONS Have children work in small groups to compare and contrast "Water on Earth" and Jermaine's report. Write a list of questions for discussion, such as these:

- What is similar about the two reports? What is different?
- How does each author give main ideas and details?

Ask children to raise other questions they have for discussion within their groups.

EVALUATION CRITERIA

ESTABLISH CRITERIA FOR WRITING Have children locate the rubric for a research report in their handbooks on page 487. Explain that a "best effort" should address all of the items on the list. Talk about each item and add others determined by children's needs and interests. Remind children to refer to this rubric as they write. (See also pages 454 and R76 in this *Teacher's Edition*.)

Looking at the Model

1. What is the title of Jermaine's report?

2. What is the topic of the report? Why do you think Jermaine chose that topic?

3. When did dinosaurs live? Why did they die out?

4. What is the main idea of the second paragraph? What kinds of dinosaurs does Jermaine write about?

Writer's Craft

Giving Examples

Jermaine used examples to help you understand his main ideas. Find the examples in Jermaine's report.

- What kinds of dinosaurs does Jermaine name?

- How much did Tyrannosaurus weigh?

- What did Stegosaurus look like?

- What kind of dinosaur was Troodon?

447

Looking at the Model

1. **What is the title of Jermaine's report?** (Dinosaurs)

2. **What is the topic of the report?** (dinosaurs) **Why do you think Jermaine chose that topic?** (He probably likes learning about dinosaurs and feels that his audience will, too.)

3. **When did dinosaurs live?** (between 65 and 245 million years ago) **Why did they die out?** (No one is sure why.)

4. **What is the main idea of the second paragraph?** (There were many kinds of dinosaurs.) **About what kinds of dinosaurs does Jermaine write?** (Tyrannosaurus rex, Stegosaurus, and Troodon)

SELF-INITIATED WRITING Have children choose a way to respond to the models they just read, which may include self-initiated writing or another method such as generating ideas for their own writing by drawing or listing key thoughts or writing or dictating questions for investigating further.

WRAP-UP/ASSESS

Invite children to share their lists from page 445. Have them tell which details they read in "Water on Earth" and in "Dinosaurs" were the most interesting. Ask them to explain their choices.

TAKE-HOME BOOK 6 provides an additional model of a research report and home activities. See *Practice Book* pages 131-132.

Prewriting

OBJECTIVES
- To brainstorm and select a writing topic
- To use an outline to plan main ideas and details

SPIRAL REVIEW

DAILY LANGUAGE PRACTICE

TRANSPARENCY 70

1 Fish dogs and birds all needs water. (Fish, dogs,; need)

2 People uses water for drinking washing and cooking. (use; drinking, washing,)

ORAL WARM-UP

USE PRIOR KNOWLEDGE Ask children to state the main idea of a movie they have seen or a book they have read recently. Remind them that a main idea is a thought that links all the information in a story or selection.

GUIDED WRITING

TALK ABOUT AN OUTLINE Explain that an outline is helpful for organizing details about a main idea. Have children examine the outline that Jermaine prepared on dinosaurs. Talk about what Jermaine did in the Prewriting stage. Then discuss these questions.

1. **What things did Jermaine do before he chose a topic?** (He made a list of interesting topics and thought about his audience.)

2. **What is the topic of Jermaine's outline?** (dinosaurs)

3. **How did Jermaine find information about his topic?** (He used the library, went online, and took notes.)

71 Use **Transparency 71** for an additional way to model the prewriting stage.

448 UNIT **6**

Prewriting

Before Jermaine wrote his report, he made a list of topics that interested him. He also thought about his classmates who would read the report. Jermaine knows they like dinosaurs. He decided to write about dinosaurs.

Next Jermaine thought about what he wanted to know about dinosaurs. He wrote each idea as a question on a note card.

Then Jermaine went to the library to find answers to his questions. He read books and used a computer to find information. He wrote the answers on the note cards.

> **When did dinosaurs live?**
> - The last dinosaur died about 65 million years ago.
> - The first dinosaur lived about 245 million years ago.
> - No one knows for sure why they died.

Jermaine put his note cards in an order that made sense. He used the cards to write an outline. An **outline** shows the order of main ideas and details in a piece of writing.

448

TRANSPARENCY 71

**PREWRITING:
RESEARCH REPORT**

Topic:
1.
  a.
  b.
  c.
2.
  a.
  b.
  c.
3.
  a.
  b.
  c.

Harcourt Language
Grade 2   71   Chapter 36
PREWRITING: Research Report

Vocabulary Power page 106

Name _____

These words all mean to do something again.

recount   recycle   rethink   retrace   review

Read the sentences. Use the context clues to figure out the meanings of the underlined words. Write or draw pictures to explain the meanings.

1. We are lost. We have to retrace our steps.	**2.** I'm saving these old newspapers. They can be recycled.
3. I can tell you what happened. I will recount the events.	**4.** This plan will not work. We have to rethink our ideas.
5. We're having a spelling test. Let's review our spelling words.	**6.** You counted 20, and I counted 22. We have to do a recount.

106   Unit 6 • Chapter 36   Vocabulary Power

Dinosaurs Outline

1. When did dinosaurs live?
   a. last dinosaur, 65 million years ago
   b. first dinosaur, 245 million years ago
   c. No one knows why they died.
2. What kinds of dinosaurs were there?
   a. Tyrannosaurus rex
   b. Stegosaurus
   c. Troodon

What Good Writers Do

 Remember for whom you are writing and why.

 Make a plan.

When did dinosaurs live?
- The last dinosaur died about 65 million years ago.
- The first dinosaur lived about 245 million years ago.
- No one knows for sure why they died.

Your Turn

STEP 1 **Think of interesting topics.**
Make a list of topics you think are interesting and would like to know more about.

STEP 2 **Choose one topic.** Think about who will read your report. Pick a topic.

STEP 3 **Use note cards.** Write each question you want to answer on a note card.

STEP 4 **Use your note cards to write an outline.** Put the cards in an order that makes sense. Then write an outline. The questions are the main ideas. The answers are the details about the main ideas.

Use your computer to help organize your notes.

449

Your Turn Read the steps at the top of the page with children to review prewriting strategies for a research paper. Explain that children will follow the same steps that Jermaine did to plan their research report. Have them list topics of interest and narrow the list. Then have them use reference sources such as books and the Internet (with your supervision) to find information and make notes about their topic. They will use an outline to organize their ideas. If possible, have children compile their notes into outlines using available technology to help them.

PORTFOLIO Remind children to put their outlines in their Working Portfolios.

WRAP-UP/ASSESS

SUMMARIZE Ask volunteers to describe the steps they took to prepare an outline for their research report. Then have children think about how these steps helped them organize their work. What might they do differently the next time they use an outline for prewriting?

You may want to have children write their reflections about prewriting a research report.
REFLECTION

Drafting

OBJECTIVES
- To draft a research report
- To write paragraphs with clear main ideas and supporting details

SPIRAL REVIEW

DAILY LANGUAGE PRACTICE

TRANSPARENCY 70

1 Shannon and Marie left they're books there (their; there.)

2 She hurrys too see to movies. (hurries; to; two)

ORAL WARM-UP

USE PRIOR KNOWLEDGE Ask volunteers to identify the topic of a news article they have heard or read recently. Ask them to state a main idea and one or two details about the topic.

GUIDED WRITING

DISCUSS FIRST DRAFTS Remind children that a first draft does not need to be perfect. Use the writing model to talk about how to write a first draft. Ask questions such as the following about Jermaine's research report.

- **What is the main idea of Jermaine's first paragraph?** (Dinosaurs lived long ago.) **Was this idea on the outline?** (no)

- **What are some ways Jermaine could improve this report?** (Accept reasonable responses.)

71 Use **Transparency 71** for an additional teaching model.

Drafting

Jermaine used his outline and notes to help him write a first draft. He used the first question and its answers for the first paragraph. He used the second question and its answers for the second paragraph.

Jermaine wrote in the first draft the most important things he found out. He knew he could add more details later. Read Jermaine's first draft.

> **DRAFT**
>
> ## Dinosaurs
>
> Dinosaurs lived millions of years ago. The last dinosaurs died about 65 million years ago. The first dinosaurs lived about 245 million years ago.
>
> Many different kinds of dinosaurs roamed the Earth. Tyrannosaurus rex was big and fierce. Stegosaurus had plates on its back. Troodon

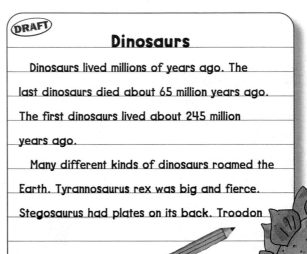

450

TRANSPARENCY 71

> **DRAFT**
>
> ## Dinosaurs
>
> Dinosaurs lived millions of years ago. The last dinosaurs died about 65 million years ago. The first dinosaurs lived about 245 million years ago.
>
> Many different kinds of dinosaurs roamed the Earth. Tyrannosaurus rex was big and fierce. Stegosaurus had plates on its back. Troodon

---

Vocabulary Power page 107

Name _____ Prefixes

These words start with the same prefix. Underline re- in each word.

rethink means "to think again"   recount means "to count again"
retrace means "to trace again"   review means "to view again"

Add re- to each word. Write or draw a picture to explain the meaning of the new word.

1. use ____ reuse	2. turn ____ return
3. write ____ rewrite	4. unite ____ reunite
5. paint ____ repaint	6. read ____ reread
7. heat ____ reheat	8. play ____ replay

Vocabulary Power   Unit 6 • Chapter 36   107

Look at Jermaine's outline and notes. What other details could he add to the report?

Dinosaurs Outline

1. When did dinosaurs live?

    a. last dinosaur, 65 million years ago

    b. first dinosaur, 245 million years ago

    c. No one knows why they died.

2. What kinds of dinosaurs were there?

    a. Tyrannosaurus rex

    b. Stegosaurus

    c. Troodon

When did dinosaurs live?
- The last dinosaur died about 65 million years ago.
- The first dinosaur lived about 245 million years ago.
- No one knows for sure why they died.

 Your Turn

Use your notes, outline, and What Good Writers Do to write a draft of your research report.

What Good Writers Do

✓ Follow your outline to write the first draft.

✓ Don't worry about mistakes. You can fix them later.

 Double-space your draft so you have room to mark changes on your printout.

451

 Your Turn Tell children that they will work with their outlines and What Good Writers Do to develop a first draft of their research report. Read over What Good Writers Do with children. Remind them to work quickly to get their ideas down on paper. Let them know that they will have an opportunity later to fix any mistakes.

 Demonstrate for children how to adjust the computer to double-space automatically rather than using the Return key.

 PORTFOLIO Remind children to put their drafts in their Working Portfolios.

WRAP-UP/ASSESS

SUMMARIZE Have a volunteer summarize what should be included in a first draft of a research report.

 You may wish to have children use their journals to record their thoughts on writing a draft. **REFLECTION**

INTERACTIVE WRITING

SHARE THE PEN Guide children to develop a draft. Model how to develop main ideas and details from an outline into paragraphs. Begin by asking children to make up a main idea sentence from the information in the outline. Invite volunteers to make suggestions and participate in the writing. You might also use **Transparency 71** to demonstrate how to create a draft.

Writer's Craft

SENTENCE VARIETY Explain that good writers keep their readers' attention by using different kinds of sentences. For example, they might use a question to involve readers, even in a research report.

Write several sentences from "Water on Earth" on sentence strips. Give a different sentence to each group of three or four children. Ask the groups to think of new ways to use the same information in a different type of sentence. Then have the group members present the original sentences and their alternates to the class.

Remind children to try to use varied sentence types in their own writing.

Revising

OBJECTIVES

- To revise a research report
- To proofread writing for capitalization, punctuation, grammar, and spelling
- To use Editor's Marks to make revisions and corrections

SPIRAL REVIEW

DAILY LANGUAGE PRACTICE

TRANSPARENCY 70

1 We'l return the cans bottles, and newspapers. (We'll; cans,)

2 Its rainy foggy and snowy all at one time. (It's rainy, foggy,)

ORAL WARM-UP

Review the elements of a well-written research report, such as ideas that flow clearly and smoothly and enough details to help readers thoroughly understand the subject.

TEACH/MODEL

DISCUSS REVISING Discuss the revisions Jermaine made to his report, and encourage children to share ideas on how it might be improved.

Use **Transparencies 71** and **71a** to model how to revise.

Y☺ur Turn Provide time for children to work in small groups to read their drafts aloud. Have group members offer constructive criticism.

REVISIT EVALUATION CRITERIA Have children use the rubric for writing a research report, as well as the evaluation criteria they established earlier in responding constructively to their own and each other's writing.

Revising

Jermaine and a partner talked about how to make the draft better. Then Jermaine added details. He also changed the order of some sentences to make the information clearer.

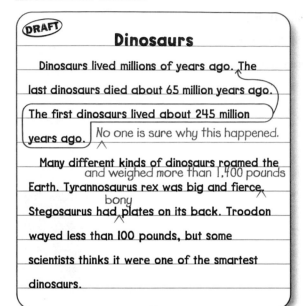

Dinosaurs

Dinosaurs lived millions of years ago. The last dinosaurs died about 65 million years ago.

The first dinosaurs lived about 245 million years ago. No one is sure why this happened.

Many different kinds of dinosaurs roamed the and weighed more than 1,400 pounds Earth. Tyrannosaurus rex was big and fierce, bony Stegosaurus had plates on its back. Troodon wayed less than 100 pounds, but some scientists thinks it were one of the smartest dinosaurs.

Y☺ur Turn

Talk with a partner about how your draft could be better. Use What Good Writers Do and the Editor's Marks to make changes.

452

What Good Writers Do

 Decide if your writing is clear. Do you need to change any sentences?

 Can you add details to tell more about your topic?

Editor's Marks

∧ Add.

⋀ Change.

ℐ Take out.

◡ Move.

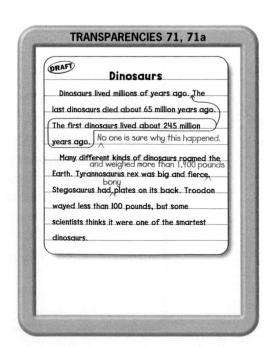

TRANSPARENCIES 71, 71a

Dinosaurs

Dinosaurs lived millions of years ago. The last dinosaurs died about 65 million years ago. The first dinosaurs lived about 245 million years ago. No one is sure why this happened.

Many different kinds of dinosaurs roamed the and weighed more than 1,400 pounds Earth. Tyrannosaurus rex was big and fierce, bony Stegosaurus had plates on its back. Troodon wayed less than 100 pounds, but some scientists thinks it were one of the smartest dinosaurs.

Vocabulary Power page 108

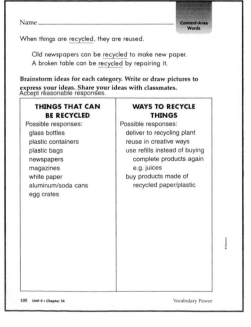

Name_____

Content-Area Words

When things are recycled, they are reused.

Old newspapers can be recycled to make new paper.
A broken table can be recycled by repairing it.

Brainstorm ideas for each category. Write or draw pictures to express your ideas. Share your ideas with classmates.
Accept reasonable responses.

THINGS THAT CAN BE RECYCLED	WAYS TO RECYCLE THINGS
Possible responses:	Possible responses:
glass bottles	deliver to recycling plant
plastic containers	reuse in creative ways
plastic bags	use refills instead of buying
newspapers	complete products again
magazines	e.g. juices
white paper	buy products made of
aluminum/soda cans	recycled paper/plastic
egg crates	

108 Unit 6 • Chapter 36   Vocabulary Power

Proofreading

Jermaine read his report once more to look for mistakes. Why did Jermaine make each change in red?

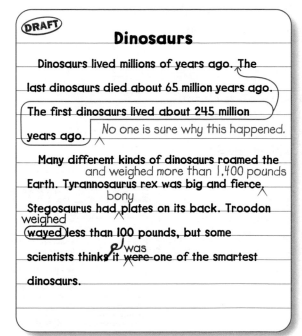

DRAFT

Dinosaurs

Dinosaurs lived millions of years ago. The last dinosaurs died about 65 million years ago. The first dinosaurs lived about 245 million years ago. _No one is sure why this happened._ Many different kinds of dinosaurs roamed the Earth. _and weighed more than 1,400 pounds_ Tyrannosaurus rex was big and fierce. Stegosaurus had _bony_ plates on its back. Troodon ~~wayed~~ _weighed_ less than 100 pounds, but some scientists thinks it ~~were~~ _was_ one of the smartest dinosaurs.

 Your Turn

Now read your story once more. Use What Good Writers Do and the Editor's Marks to fix any mistakes.

What Good Writers Do

✓ Make sure each verb agrees with the subject.

✓ Be sure each sentence begins with a capital letter and ends with an end mark.

✓ Check your spelling. Look up words that sound alike.

Editor's Marks

⬭ Check the spelling.

⋀ Change.

𝒆 Take out.

Use your computer's spell-check to help you find any spelling mistakes.

453

Proofreading

MODEL PROOFREADING Write a sentence on the board that contains errors in spelling, such as: _Dinasers lived milyons of years ago._ Have children work in groups to identify the errors. Others may challenge any responses they think are incorrect.

REVIEW THE EDITOR'S MARKS Have children examine the revision to discuss any new corrections Jermaine made. Discuss the reasons for the corrections.

 Display **Transparencies 71, 71a, and 71b** to model how to proofread a story. Discuss why each change was made.

 Your Turn Explain that even good writers sometimes overlook errors in their own work. As children bring their reports to final form, suggest that they read carefully to look for errors in spelling, capitalization, and punctuation.

 Tell children to think about the correct meanings of words that sound alike to be sure they have used the correct ones. Point out that the computer spell-checker will not detect these errors.

WRAP-UP/ASSESS

SUMMARIZE Have children reflect on what they have learned about how to revise a research report and why they need to proofread first drafts. **REFLECTION**

 Visit _The Learning Site!_ www.harcourtschool.com

TRANSPARENCIES 71, 71a, 71b

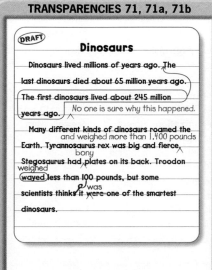

DRAFT

Dinosaurs

Dinosaurs lived millions of years ago. The last dinosaurs died about 65 million years ago. The first dinosaurs lived about 245 million years ago. _No one is sure why this happened._ Many different kinds of dinosaurs roamed the Earth. _and weighed more than 1,400 pounds_ Tyrannosaurus rex was big and fierce. Stegosaurus had _bony_ plates on its back. Troodon ~~wayed~~ _weighed_ less than 100 pounds, but some scientists thinks it ~~were~~ _was_ one of the smartest dinosaurs.

Spelling Connection

SPELLING STRATEGIES Provide sidewalk chalk for children to practice writing difficult spelling words on a paved area. Send home pieces of chalk in plastic baggies and a list of spelling words. Children can practice writing on pavement near their homes for homework.

Publishing

OBJECTIVES
- To make final copies of revised research reports
- To share reports with an audience

DAILY LANGUAGE PRACTICE

TRANSPARENCY 70

1 Jack said he report are on cars. (his; is)

2 Myself prefer to rite about traveling. (I; write)

ORAL WARM-UP

Ask children to brainstorm some ways they have seen research report information presented. (magazine articles, newspaper articles, television documentaries)

GUIDED WRITING

Discuss how Jermaine shared his report with others.

Your Turn Have children make a final copy of their reports. Have them choose a publishing format.

- **Make a poster report.** Suggest that children arrange all parts of the poster before gluing them.
- **Make a magazine-style article.** See patterns on pages R90–R91 for additional ideas.

WRAP-UP/ASSESS

SHARE Invite volunteers to share their reports with the class. Have children place their final reports in their Writing Portfolios. Have children also review the contents of their Portfolios to monitor their growth as writers.

☑ **Writing Conference Checklist,** page R67.

TECHNOLOGY
Grammar Practice and Assessment CD-ROM
Writing Express CD-ROM

INTERNET Visit *The Learning Site!*
www.harcourtschool.com

Writing a Research Report

Publishing

Jermaine made a clean copy of his report. He also drew pictures of dinosaurs and labeled them to show some of the information.

Your Turn

Write your report neatly on a clean sheet of paper. Make the changes. Use a computer if you like. Here are some more publishing ideas.

- **Make a magazine-style article.**
  Type your report on your computer. Then make drawings or find photos for the report. Add them to your report by using Cut and Paste or by scanning them. Write a caption for each one.

- **Make a poster report.**
  Draw pictures that show information from your report. Arrange and glue them on a poster. Then write a caption for each picture. Attach a copy of the report to the poster.

Dinosaurs
— of Long Ago —

Dinosaurs lived millions of years ago. The first dinosaurs lived about 245 million years ago. The last dinosaurs died about 65 million years ago. No one is sure why this happened.

Many different kinds of dinosaurs roamed the Earth. Tyrannosaurus rex was big and fierce and weighed more than 1,400 pounds. Stegosaurus had bony plates on its back. Troodon weighed less than 100 pounds, but some scientists think it was one of the smartest dinosaurs.

Add your finished research report to your Writing Portfolio.

454

SCORING RUBRIC

4 ADVANCED	**3** PROFICIENT	**2** BASIC	**1** LIMITED
Planning: Discusses, uses outline to plan.	**Planning:** Listens and uses outline to plan.	**Planning:** Makes limited use of outline or reference sources.	**Planning:** Fails to make use of planning resources.
Content: Responds to task, uses reference sources to locate information.	**Content:** Responds to task.	**Content:** Does not completely respond to task.	**Content:** Does not respond to task.
Organization: Report is organized by main ideas and details.	**Organization:** Information is organized in a logical manner.	**Organization:** Some important details are missing or out of logical order.	**Organization:** Little attempt to organize ideas into coherent paragraphs.
Mechanics: Few or no errors in punctuation, capitalization, and grammar.	**Mechanics:** Some errors in punctuation, capitalization, and grammar.	**Mechanics:** Several errors in punctuation, capitalization, and grammar.	**Mechanics:** Lacks meaningful use of punctuation, capitalization, and grammar.

For information on adapting this rubric to 5- or 6-point scales, see pages R69–70.

Listening and Speaking

Giving an Oral Report

> **You can give an oral report on research you have done. Practice these tips.**
>
> ### Tips for Oral Reports
>
> - Make drawings, charts, or models. Point to the pictures and models to help explain.
> - Use notes to give your report. When you speak, look at your notes and then at your classmates.
> - Speak slowly and clearly.
> - Speak loudly enough so everyone can hear you.

> **Practice these tips when listening to a report.**
>
> ### Listening Tips
>
> - Listen for the topic.
> - Take notes to help you sum up and remember main ideas.
> - Listen for details.
> - Write down questions you have. Ask the questions after the report is given.

455

Handwriting
. . . .

For children who need extra practice, provide extra help in reviewing proper letter formation. Encourage them to use fine-tip markers or harder or softer pencils, as their grip dictates for improved penmanship. Rubber pencil grips may aid children who grasp the pencil awkwardly or too firmly. Remind children also that they should use good spacing and leave margins in their final drafts.

Listening and Speaking

Giving an Oral Report

OBJECTIVES
- To present an oral report
- To listen carefully to oral presentations

ORAL WARM-UP

Invite volunteers to share their experiences listening to others present oral reports, such as speakers at clubs, at school, or at a museum.

TEACH/MODEL

REVIEW THE TIPS Explain that using natural speech is more likely to interest an audience than reading a report or reciting it from memory. Also, using drawings or props such as models or charts will help the audience understand the report topic more clearly. Have volunteers read the listening and speaking tips.

Children can work with partners to rehearse their oral presentations before presenting them to the entire group.

WRAP-UP/ASSESS

SUMMARIZE Have children summarize what they learned about presenting and listening to oral reports.

☑ **Listening and Speaking Evaluation Forms,** pages R65 and R77.

OBJECTIVES

- To write pronouns to take the place of nouns in sentences
- To identify the correct word order for pronouns in sentences
- To change *y* to *i* when writing verbs that tell about now
- To use contractions in writing

Unit Review

Have children complete the exercises, or modify them using these suggestions:

MODIFIED INSTRUCTION

BELOW-LEVEL STUDENTS Ask children to review and discuss pronouns before they complete items 1-3.

Have children recall the correct word order for pronouns before they complete items 4-5.

Suggest children tell in their own words how to change *y* to *i* when writing verbs to help them complete items 6-7.

Invite children to write the underlined words in items 8-10 on strips. Then have them cut out and paste the words to form contractions, adding apostrophes where needed.

ABOVE-LEVEL STUDENTS Encourage children to create a chart with pronouns on the left side and examples of nouns that can be replaced by each pronoun on the right.

After children have finished items 6-7, challenge them to write sentences with naming parts that tell about more than one and with verbs that end in *y*. Then have them trade sentences with a partner and change the naming parts and verbs to tell about one.

After they have completed items 8-10, have children look through a newspaper and write down all the contractions they read. Have them write out the two words that make up each contraction.

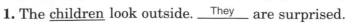

Noun-Pronoun Agreement pages 392–393

Write the pronoun that agrees with the underlined noun in each set of sentences.

1. The <u>children</u> look outside. <u>They</u> are surprised.

2. <u>Snow</u> fell last night. <u>It</u> is a foot deep.

3. <u>Ann</u> can't wait. <u>She</u> gets her snowsuit.

Word Order for Pronouns pages 394–395

Write the correct words in ( ) to complete each sentence.

4. Ed calls (<u>Ted and me</u>, me and Ted) early.

5. (<u>Ted and I</u>, I and Ted) will help Ed study snow.

Changing *y* to *i* pages 402–403

Write each verb in ( ) correctly.

6. Ed and Ann (hurry) over to meet us. hurry

7. Ted (try) to take a picture of a snowflake. tries

Writing Contractions pages 404–405

Write the contraction for the underlined words.

8. Rosa and Tom <u>can not</u> go outside. can't

9. They <u>are not</u> ready. aren't

10. Rosa <u>has not</u> finished her breakfast. hasn't

456

 TEST PREP

TIP

Children should use a pencil when completing a test. This makes it easier to go back and change an answer if needed.

 **Activity**

Divide a large paper plate in six sections. Write the following labels, one per section: *Anita, Yoko and Jack, my house, my friend and I, the boy, the nieces.* Then have children place a paper clip on the tip of a pencil at the center of the plate. Tell them to spin the paper clip. They should make a sentence, replacing the noun pointed at by the clip with a pronoun.

Writing Longer Sentences pages 420–421

Combine each set of sentences.

11. The children saw tracks.
    The parents saw tracks.
    The children and parents saw tracks.

12. We saw deer.
    We saw rabbits.
    We saw deer and rabbits.

Using a Series Comma pages 422–423

Write each sentence correctly using the series comma.

13. Bears,beavers,and turtles sleep all winter.

14. Deer eat roots,berries,and any other food they can find.

Using *there*, *their*, and *they're* pages 430–431

Write *there*, *their*, or *they're* to complete each sentence.

15. The children are over ___there___.

16. ___They're___ having fun in the snow.

17. Are they all wearing ___their___ hats?

Using *to*, *too*, and *two* pages 432–433

Write *to*, *too*, or *two* to complete each sentence.

18. Ted and I go ___to___ the ice-skating rink.

19. Ann and Ed want to go, ___too___.

20. We are all going to skate at ___two___ o'clock.

457

TEST PREP

Activities and exercises to help children prepare for state and standardized assessments appear on our website.

Visit *The Learning Site!*
www.harcourtschool.com

OBJECTIVES
- To use *and* to join sentences
- To use commas in a series
- To use troublesome words in writing

Unit Review

Have children complete the exercises, or modify them using these suggestions:

MODIFIED INSTRUCTION

BELOW-LEVEL STUDENTS Have children write the pairs of sentences in items 11-12 on strips, and then add a comma and the word *and* to combine them.

Before completing items 13-14, have children review comma usage.

Have children discuss the meaning of each word needed to complete items 15-20.

ABOVE-LEVEL STUDENTS Have children write two original sentences that have the same telling part. Then ask them to trade sentences with a partner and combine them using the word *and*.

After children complete items 13-14, have them work in pairs to brainstorm items that they would take on a picnic. Ask pairs to write sentences listing the items.

For items 15-20, challenge children to write one sentence with at least two troublesome words that sound alike. Ask children to read their sentences aloud. Call on volunteers to spell the troublesome words as they hear them.

Assessment

SKILLS ASSESSMENT

Use the **Language and Writing Skills Tests** to assess the grammar and writing skills taught in this unit. Model papers are included.

PORTFOLIO ASSESSMENT

Schedule portfolio conferences with individual students while others are completing the Unit Review exercises. Have each child complete the Self-Evaluation Checklists on pages R78-R79 and place them with the unit's writing in the Portfolio.

Safe Summer Fun

OBJECTIVES

- To take notes from relevant sources including information books and media sources

- To write and publish a summer safety tips book

INTRODUCE THE PROJECT

USE PRIOR KNOWLEDGE Read the introduction aloud with children. Have them discuss what they do during the summer. Invite them to discuss what activities are different from the ones they do at other times of the year and why.

GENERATE QUESTIONS Invite children to think about how to be safe while doing some of the summertime activities, and generate questions about this topic. Encourage them to answer each other's questions.

Plan Your Book

Invite children to list places they usually go to in the summer and things they do. Ask them to compile their lists in a class chart. Have children use the chart to decide on the categories for their book. Then have them form groups to work on each category for a chapter in the book. Ask them to discuss the safety tips they already know and record on note cards questions about what else they need to learn. Have them use the information to write an outline.

Safe Summer Fun

Social Studies Summer is almost here, and you will do many things outdoors. While you are having fun, you need to stay safe. Make a class book of summer safety tips to get ready for summer fun.

Plan Your Book

- Brainstorm a list of things you might do and places you might go this summer. Then sort the items into shorter lists for chapters in your book. For example, *pool* and *beach* may go into the "safe swimming" chapter.

- Write questions about safety for each item in every chapter. Then find answers to your safety questions. Look in books, use your computer, and talk to people such as lifeguards.

- Write the answers on note cards. Use the note cards to help you write an outline.

Write and Publish Your Book

- Use your outline and notes to write your chapters. Then revise and proofread them.

- If a chapter will have pictures, make sketches to show what will be in each one.

458

Technology

. . . .

RECORD INFORMATION Invite children to use tape recorders to record their interviews. Demonstrate how to use the equipment and how to replay and stop a tape in order to write down the information.

School-Home Connection

. . . .

SAFETY BOOK Family members can help children make a Home Safety Tips book. Have them list safety tips that apply to activities done at home. Together, they can find out more about home safety from library books or internet sites, and then record them in a book. Drawings and photographs can be used to illustrate their tips.

- Write a clean copy of your book. Use a computer if you want. Make a title page, a table of contents, and a cover for your book.

- Use your sketches to make final drawings. Add them to your chapters.

- Make copies of your book for classmates and your family members.

Books to Read

Willie Takes a Hike
by Gloria Rand
Fiction
Willie, a mouse, learns how important it is to be prepared when he takes a hike.
Award-Winning Author

Officer Buckle and Gloria
by Peggy Rathmann
Fantasy
A police dog named Gloria helps a police officer give safety tips to children.
Caldecott Medal

459

REACHING ALL

VISUAL SAFETY TIPS Children acquiring English may enjoy making a pictorial safety booklet, using symbols and drawings to show several tips. Have them think of safety signs they have seen, such as "children crossing" or "no swimming", and then think of ways to represent various tips relating to summer activities.

Write and Publish Your Book

Point out to children that they can use their notes to add details to each of their topics or chapter pages. When the chapter is written, suggest that each group member reads it and offers ideas for revisions. Suggest that children make sketches of their pictures first so they can figure out how large the pictures should be and how they will be arranged on the page. Then have children finish the book, including a title page, a table of contents, and a cover.

Children may wish to make a display in the media center to show how they made their book. The display may include resource material, notes, outlines, sketches, layouts, and drafts to show the steps involved in creating the book. If available, have children reformat the book to post it on the school's web site.

WRITING You may want to have children write about their experiences making the book, reflecting on what they liked best and what they found difficult. Ask them what was hard about writing safety tips and why. Children can add their writing to their display in the media center.

STUDENT SELF-ASSESSMENT

Ask children to determine whether their book includes the most important safety tips for each activity. Have them decide whether the information presented is clear. Ask children to discuss other ways they could have presented the information.

Books to Read Children can use these books to expand their knowledge of safety as well as ways to share safety tips. Discuss additional questions children have about safety and how using these books may help them find the answers.

Unit I: All About Sentences

Unit 2: All About Nouns

Use the Cumulative Review to assess children's continued mastery of language concepts and skills presented in Units 1–6. Refer to the pages listed after each section title to review any concepts and skills children have not mastered.

OBJECTIVES

- To order the words in a sentence so that they make sense and to identify the naming parts and telling parts of sentences
- To use *and* to combine parts of sentences
- To identify nouns

UNITS 1 AND 2 REVIEW

Have children complete the exercises, or modify them using these suggestions:

MODIFIED INSTRUCTION

BELOW-LEVEL STUDENTS Remind children that a sentence tells a complete thought, begins with a capital letter, and ends with an end mark. Children may find it easier to read aloud the words in items 1–4 before putting them in order.

For items 5–7, ask children to say the parts that are the same in both sentences. Have children join the naming parts using *and*. Then they should write the telling part that was common to both sentences.

For items 8–11, have children read aloud the nouns before they write them.

ABOVE-LEVEL STUDENTS After children have finished items 5–7, suggest they brainstorm how some animals move, where they live, and what they eat. Have them write sentences about the animals, such as *Rabbits eat grass. Cows eat grass.* Then ask children to combine some of the sentences.

Unit I: All About Sentences

Sentences pages 24–29, 36–37

Write each group of words to make a sentence. Then circle the naming part. Underline the telling part.

1. to store the goes (Lian) Lian goes to the store.
2. a book buys (she) She buys a book.
3. about an owl (the book) is The book is about an owl.
4. in tree a lives (the owl) The owl lives in a tree.

Combining Parts of Sentences pages 38–39

Use *and* to join each pair of sentences. Write the new sentence.

5. Kate went to the park. Sam went to the park.
   Kate and Sam went to the park.
6. Eric played with them. I played with them.
   Eric and I played with them.
7. The trees were pretty. The flowers were pretty.
   The trees and flowers were pretty.

Unit 2: All About Nouns

Nouns pages 96–97, 124–125

Write each sentence. Underline each noun. Write if it is a person, place, animal, or thing.

8. My family is at the zoo. thing, place
9. Seals are playing in the water. animal, thing
10. A girl feeds the seals some food. person, animal, thing
11. My sister pets an elephant. person, animal

460

COMBINING SENTENCES

Display a picture or a poster showing people doing various activities. Have one child say a simple sentence about the poster. Ask another child to make up a sentence with a different naming part, but the same telling part. A third child then combines the two sentences using *and*.

Using Possessive Nouns pages 100–101
Use 's to rewrite the underlined words.

12. <u>The ball of the dog</u> is under the chair. The dog's ball

13. My game is in <u>the room of my brother</u>. my brother's room

14. <u>The computer of Emily</u> is easy to use. Emily's computer

Using *He, She, It,* and *They* pages 136–137
Write each sentence. Use a pronoun for the underlined words.

15. <u>My sister Julie</u> gave me a puzzle. She gave me a puzzle.

16. <u>The puzzle</u> has many pieces. It has many pieces.

17. <u>John</u> puts some pieces together. He puts some pieces together.

18. <u>My friends</u> help me, too. They help me, too.

Unit 3: Verbs

Using the Correct Verb pages 172–173, 202–203
Write the correct verb to finish each sentence.

19. Three deer (was, <u>were</u>) feeding in the field.

20. Some rabbits (<u>hop</u>, hops) nearby.

21. A fox (chase, <u>chases</u>) one of the rabbits.

22. The rabbit (<u>was</u>, were) faster than the fox.

Adding *ed* to Verbs pages 182–185
Rewrite each sentence. Write the verb in ( ) to tell about the past.

23. We (look) for shells along the beach. looked

24. Rico (collect) four colorful shells. collected

25. Suddenly, one of the shells (move)! moved

461

Unit 2 (continued): All About Nouns

Unit 3: Verbs

OBJECTIVES
- To write possessive nouns correctly
- To use the pronouns *he, she, it,* and *they* to take the place of nouns
- To write the correct verbs in sentences
- To add *ed* to verbs to tell about the past

UNITS 2 AND 3 REVIEW

Have children complete the exercises, or modify them using these suggestions:

MODIFIED INSTRUCTION

BELOW-LEVEL STUDENTS For items 12–14, suggest children point to the word that tells the owner in each sentence. Remind children that an apostrophe and an *s* are added to a word to show ownership.

Ask children to tell if the underlined nouns in items 15–18 tell about one or more than one before they decide which pronoun to use.

For items 19–22, have children read aloud the naming part and decide if it tells about one or more than one. Suggest they read each sentence aloud and listen for which verb fits in the sentence.

ABOVE-LEVEL STUDENTS After children have finished items 12–18, challenge partners to write a conversation that includes possessive nouns and pronouns. Ask partners to read their conversations aloud. Have other children identify the pronouns and possessive nouns they hear.

TIP

POSSESSIVES OR CONTRACTIONS? Some children may confuse a possessive with a contraction because they both have an apostrophe. On the board, write four words and phrases such as *can't; don't; cat's food; girl's dress.* Have volunteers read them and identify which are contractions and which are possessives. Discuss how the apostrophe in a contraction takes the place of letters instead of showing ownership.

Unit 4: All About Adjectives

Unit 5: More About Verbs

OBJECTIVES
- To write adjectives in sentences
- To add *er* or *est* to adjectives that compare
- To recognize the correct verb forms in sentences

UNITS 4 AND 5 REVIEW

Have children complete the exercises, or modify them using these suggestions:

MODIFIED INSTRUCTION

BELOW-LEVEL STUDENTS Tell children to point to and read the nouns in items 26–31 before they choose adjectives to describe them.

To help children complete items 32–35, have them decide how many things are being compared in each sentence.

Have children work in pairs to complete items 36–37. One partner underlines the time-order word in the sentence, if any. Then both partners decide if the sentence tells about now or about the past.

ABOVE-LEVEL STUDENTS After children have finished items 26–35, challenge them to write slogans for favorite products using adjectives. Children may want to illustrate their slogans.

Unit 4: All About Adjectives

Adjectives pages 244–245, 254–255, 272–273

Choose an adjective from the box to complete each sentence. Write each sentence.

sour leafy sweet three small yellow

Possible responses are given.

26. Joey has __three__ lemons.

27. The lemons are __yellow__.

28. Lemon juice has a __sour__ taste.

29. Lemons grow on __leafy__ trees.

30. They come from __small__ flowers.

31. Lemon flowers have a __sweet__ smell.

Adding *er* and *est* pages 282–283

Write the correct adjective in ( ) to complete each sentence.

32. A robin is (shorter, shortest) than an owl.

33. A hummingbird is the (smaller, smallest) of all.

34. A hawk's beak is (sharper, sharpest) than a duck's.

35. An ostrich has the (longer, longest) legs of any bird.

Unit 5: More About Verbs

Using the Correct Verb pages 320–321, 330–331

Write the correct verb in ( ) to complete each sentence.

36. Last week, Dad (give, gave) me running shoes.

37. I (do, done) exercises before I run.

462

HANDS ON Activity

ADJECTIVE HUNT Have pairs of children look through old newspapers or magazines for headlines that contain adjectives. Have them underline the adjectives and decide whether they compare, tell what kind, tell about the senses, or tell how many.

Joining Sentences pages 322–323

Use *and* to join the sentences. Remember to use a comma (,) before *and*.

38. Leon plays the piano. Sara plays the violin.
Leon plays the piano, and Sara plays the violin.
39. I liked the concert. Mary liked it, too.
I liked the concert, and Mary liked it, too.
40. They took a bow. The audience applauded.
They took a bow, and the audience applauded.

Using Adverbs pages 358–359

Write the adverb in each sentence. Then write *how*, *when*, or *where* for each adverb.

41. The play begins <u>soon</u>. when

42. It is exciting <u>here</u>. where

43. The audience sits <u>quietly</u>. how

Unit 6: Usage Wrap-Up

Noun–Pronoun Agreement pages 392–393

Write the pronoun that agrees with the underlined noun in each pair of sentences.

44. <u>Dad</u> looks out the window. __He__ calls to us.

45. Look at those <u>bears</u>! __They__ are brown bears.

46. One <u>bear</u> is larger. __It__ is the mother bear.

Writing Contractions pages 404–405

Write the contraction for the underlined words.

47. Snakes <u>can not</u> walk or run. can't

48. Ostriches <u>do not</u> fly. don't

49. Whales <u>are not</u> fish. aren't

463

Unit 5 (continued): More About Verbs

Unit 6: Usage Wrap-Up

OBJECTIVES
- To use *and* to join two sentences
- To identify adverbs
- To use pronouns that agree with nouns
- To write contractions with *not*

UNITS 5 AND 6 REVIEW

Have children complete the exercises, or modify them using these suggestions:

MODIFIED INSTRUCTION

BELOW-LEVEL STUDENTS Ask children to read the sentences in items 38–40 aloud and decide where they should add *and*. Remind them to write a comma before *and*.

Have children ask the questions *how? when? where?* for each sentence in items 41–43 to help them identify the adverbs.

For items 44–46, ask children to first decide if the underlined nouns tell about one or more than one.

Have pairs complete items 47–49. Children can write the verbs and *not* on strips of paper, and then cut and glue them to form contractions.

ABOVE-LEVEL STUDENTS After children have finished all the items on the page, suggest that they write sentences with blanks in place of the nouns and verbs. The missing nouns might be a pronoun, and the missing verb can be a form of *be* or *have*. Have children trade papers and complete the sentences.

TIP

JOINING SENTENCES Remind children that not just any two sentences can be joined. The different sentences must have related ideas to be joined, or the new sentence will be a run-on sentence.

Standardized Test Prep

OBJECTIVES
- To recognize different types of sentences
- To identify the correct forms of *be* and of *have* in sentences
- To practice using standardized test format

STANDARDIZED TEST PREP The format used on this page helps prepare children for standardized tests. Read the first set of directions aloud with children. You may want to model answering the first question: *I read the sentence and look at the end mark. I know that this end mark is used to end a statement or a command. I read the sentence again. It doesn't tell someone to do something. That means it is a statement. So I choose* c. statement *as my answer.*

Have children complete the remaining items independently.

Then have them read the directions for the next sections and complete the items. When they are finished, ask questions such as:

1. **What was hard to understand in the directions? Why?**

2. **Which items did you answer first? Why?**

3. **How did you check your answers to be sure you chose the best ones?**

Standardized Test Prep

Kinds of Sentences pages 54–55, 64–65

Read each sentence. Choose the answer that tells the kind of sentence it is.

50. We went shopping.
    a. question
    b. command
    c. <u>statement</u>

51. Do you like this store?
    a. <u>question</u>
    b. exclamation
    c. statement

52. What a great toy!
    a. question
    b. command
    c. <u>exclamation</u>

53. Pay the clerk.
    a. statement
    b. <u>command</u>
    c. exclamation

Using *Am*, *Is*, and *Are* pages 200–201

Choose the correct verb for each sentence.

54. The children _____ outside.
    a. am   b. is   c. <u>are</u>

55. I _____ collecting rocks.
    a. <u>am</u>   b. is   c. are

56. Tina _____ looking at plants.
    a. am   b. <u>is</u>   c. are

57. We _____ at nature camp.
    a. am   b. is   c. <u>are</u>

Using *Has*, *Have*, and *Had* pages 210–213

Choose the correct verb for each sentence.

58. Once I _____ a hamster.
    a. has   b. have   c. <u>had</u>

59. Now I _____ a dog.
    a. has   b. <u>have</u>   c. had

464

TEST PREP

TIP

TEST-TAKING STRATEGIES
Before giving standardized tests to children, you may want to share the following:

- Read the directions carefully.
- Read each item carefully. Read all answer choices before choosing the best one.
- Answer the easiest items first.

Commas in Place Names and Dates pages 332–333

Choose the best answer for the underlined words.

60. Today is <u>July 21 2001</u>.

    a. <u>July 21, 2001</u>

    b. July, 21 2001

    c. correct as is

62. He will be back on <u>August 2, 2001</u>.

    a. August 2 2001

    b. August, 2, 2001

    c. <u>correct as is</u>

61. Dad is in <u>Tucson Arizona</u>.

    a. <u>Tucson, Arizona</u>

    b. Tucson, Arizona,

    c. correct as is

63. We live in <u>Bangor Maine</u>.

    a. <u>Bangor, Maine</u>

    b. Bangor, Maine,

    c. correct as is

Using *there, their,* and *they're* pages 430–431

Choose the correct word for each sentence.

64. Look at the birds over _____.

    a. <u>there</u>   **b.** their   **c.** they're

65. See _____ colorful feathers.

    a. there   **b.** <u>their</u>   **c.** they're

Using *to, too,* and *two* pages 432–433

Choose the correct word to complete each sentence.

66. Joe wants to go _____ the science fair.

    a. <u>to</u>   **b.** too   **c.** two

67. He has _____ free tickets for us.

    a. to   **b.** too   **c.** <u>two</u>

68. Loni wants to go, _____.

    a. to   **b.** <u>too</u>   **c.** two

465

HANDS ON Activity

TEST TRY-OUTS Provide multiple-choice test items on cards. Have pairs take turns answering the items and checking their answers. Then discuss the items with children, and work together to create a list of test-taking strategies.

Standardized Test Prep

OBJECTIVES

- To use commas in place names and dates correctly
- To identify and use troublesome words in sentences
- To practice using standardized test format

STANDARDIZED TEST PREP The format used on this page helps prepare children for standardized tests. Read each set of directions aloud with children. Point out that in the first section, they must choose the best answer for the words that are underlined in the sentence. For the remaining two sections they need to choose the words that make the most sense to complete the sentences.

Complete one item in each section with children. Then have children work independently to complete the rest of the test items. After they have finished, ask questions such as:

1. How did you decide which answer to choose in the first section?

2. How did you decide which words to choose to complete the sentences in the two other sections?

3. Which part of the test was easiest? Why?

4. What would you do differently next time?

Assessment Strategies and Resources

FORMAL ASSESSMENT

If you want to know more about a child's mastery of the language and writing skills taught in Unit 6, **then** administer the first *Language Skills and Writing Assessment* for Unit 6. The test consists of two parts:

Language Skills: noun-pronoun agreement; subject-verb agreement; using commas in a series; using troublesome words such as *there, they're, their,* or *to, too, two;* and giving examples

Writing Task: Write a **research report.** Scoring guidelines and model papers are included.

You can also use the Cumulative Assessment: Units 4–6.

INFORMAL ASSESSMENT TOOLS

 Using Portfolios

During a portfolio conference with children, discuss their research reports and other writing they chose to include in their **writing portfolios.** Ask the following types of questions about their research reports:

- What is the title of your research report? Why did you use that title?
- Where did you find information for your report?
- How did you plan and organize your report?
- How did you decide what details to add to your report?

You can also check children's understanding of **grammar** by evaluating it in their writing. Look for these points:

- Do pronouns agree with the nouns they replace?
- Are pronouns written in the correct order?

- Do verbs agree with their subjects?
- Are commas used correctly in series?
- Are *there, they're,* and *their* used correctly? Are *to, too,* and *two*?

Oral Language Assessment

Use these guidelines to evaluate oral language:

Listening and Speaking

- Listens attentively and courteously
- Listens critically to evaluate
- Chooses spoken language appropriate to the occasion and the audience
- Supports spoken message using appropriate props

Informal Assessment Reminder

If you used the pre-instruction writing prompt suggested in Teaching Grammar from Writing, **then** remember to compare the results with the writing done by children after the grammar and writing instruction.

Resources

All About Sentences
pages 24–89

Extra Practice

What Is a Sentence? pages 24–25
Write each group of words that is a sentence.

1. wants a puppy
2. Kim goes to the pet store.   Kim goes to the pet store.
3. The puppies play and bark.   The puppies play and bark.

Word Order in a Sentence pages 26–27
Beginning and Ending a Sentence pages 28–29
Write each group of words in an order that makes sense. Begin and end each sentence correctly.

4. one puppy Kim to runs   One puppy runs to Kim.
5. its little tail wags it   It wags its little tail.
6. on the hand it licks Kim   It licks Kim on the hand.

Naming Parts and Telling Parts pages 36–37
Write each sentence. Circle the naming part. Underline the telling part.

7. (Kim) takes the puppy home.
8. (The puppy) plays with a ball.

Combining Parts of Sentences pages 38–39
Use *and* to join the pair of sentences. Write the sentence.

9. The puppy went to sleep. Kim went to sleep.   The puppy and Kim went to sleep.

466

Using Statements and Questions pages 54–55
Write each sentence correctly.

10. have you named your puppy   Have you named your puppy?
11. i call her Sadie   I call her Sadie.
12. where did you get her   Where did you get her?

Sentences That Go Together pages 56–57
Write the sentences that belong. Leave out the sentence that does not belong.

13. I like my puppy, Sadie. We have a lot of fun. I give her food and water every day. ~~My birthday is tomorrow.~~ I take her for walks.

Exclamations and Commands pages 64–65
Write each sentence correctly.

14. how funny puppies are   How funny puppies are!
15. watch her chase the ball   Watch her chase the ball.
16. give her a pat on the head   Give her a pat on the head.

Using Different Kinds of Sentences pages 66–67
Change each sentence into the kind of sentence shown in ( ). Write the new sentence.

17. I may play with your puppy. (question)   May I play with your puppy?
18. Would you throw the ball for her? (command)   Throw the ball for her.

467

Extra Practice

Nouns for People, Places, Animals, and Things pages 98–99

Write each sentence. Underline each noun that names a person, place, or thing.

1. The <u>family</u> lives next to the <u>school</u>.
2. They have a <u>yard</u> with a <u>fence</u> around it.

Using Possessive Nouns pages 100–101

Use 's to rewrite the underlined words.

3. <u>The house of my friend</u> is across the street.   My friend's house
4. I ride my bike to <u>the store of Grandpa</u>.   Grandpa's store

Making Nouns Plural pages 108–109

Write the noun in ( ) so it names more than one.

5. I saw several of my (friend).   friends
6. I bought six (peach) at the market.   peaches
7. Two (bus) passed me on the street.   buses

Plural Nouns That Change Spelling pages 110–111

Write the noun in ( ) to mean more than one.

8. Three (child) were playing in the park.   children
9. They had sneakers on their (foot).   feet
10. Two (woman) said hello to me.   women

468

People, Places, and Animals pages 126–127

Write the proper noun in ( ) correctly. Then write if it is a person, a place, or an animal.

11. My neighbor (mario perez) has a dog.   Mario Perez; person
12. His dog's name is (boxer).   Boxer; animal
13. Boxer came from (stony brook).   Stony Brook; place

Days, Months, and Holidays pages 128–129

Write each proper noun correctly.

14. Our family went on vacation in may.   May
15. We came back on the first saturday of june.   Saturday, June
16. Next monday is flag day.   Monday, Flag Day
17. My birthday is on july 10.   July

He, She, It, and They pages 136–137

Write a pronoun for the words in ( ).

18. (Summer vacation) is my favorite time.   It
19. (My brother and sister) are going to camp.   They
20. (My sister) went to camp last year.   She
21. (My brother) is going for the first time.   He

I and Me pages 138–139

Write the correct pronoun in ( ) to complete each sentence.

22. (<u>I</u>, me) stay home during the summer.
23. My mother finds things for (I, <u>me</u>) to do.
24. My friends and (<u>I</u>, me) play together.

469

Extra Practice

Adding *s* or *es* to Verbs pages 172–173

Write the correct verb to finish each sentence.

1. I (<u>walk</u>, walks) in the woods with my class.

2. Our guide (teach, <u>teaches</u>) us about nature.

3. My friends and I (<u>learn</u>, learns) many things.

Combining Sentences with Verbs pages 174–175

Use *and* to combine each pair of sentences. Write the new sentence.

4. We stop at the stream. We look for animals.
   We stop at the stream and look for animals.

5. Adam spots a frog. Adam points to it.
   Adam spots a frog and points to it.

Adding *ed* to Verbs pages 182–183

Rewrite each sentence. Change the verb to tell about the past.

6. We <u>walk</u> along the stream.   walked

7. I <u>point</u> at a turtle in the stream.   pointed

8. Everyone <u>looks</u> at the turtle.   looked

Changing Verbs That End with *e* pages 184–185

Write the verb in ( ) to tell about the past.

9. Adam (poke) at a rock in the water.   poked

10. He (surprise) a crayfish.   surprised

470

Using *Am*, *Is*, and *Are* pages 200–201

Write *am*, *is*, or *are* to finish each sentence.

11. A crayfish _____ hard to find.   is

12. Turtles and frogs _____ easy to spot.   are

13. I _____ a good hiker.   am

Using *Was* and *Were* pages 202–203

Write *was* or *were* to finish each sentence.

14. We _____ hiking all day.   were

15. The animals _____ exciting to watch.   were

16. I _____ looking for a hawk.   was

17. Sam _____ watching for a raccoon.   was

Using *Has*, *Have*, and *Had* pages 210–211

Write *has*, *have*, or *had* to finish each sentence.

18. I _____ my backpack last time.   had

19. Adam _____ his backpack now.   has

20. Do you and your friends _____ places to hike?   have

21. We _____ to look for deer now.   have

Agreement with *Has*, *Have*, and *Had* pages 212–213

Write each sentence correctly.

22. Many parks <u>has</u> hiking trails.   have

23. Last year our park <u>have</u> one trail.   had

24. Now it <u>had</u> three hiking trails.   has

471

Extra Practice

Adjectives That Tell What Kind   pages 244–245

Choose an adjective from the box to complete each sentence. Write the sentence. Possible responses are given.

| small   tall   round |

1. The _____ pond is filled with water. round
2. Two _____ goldfish swim in the pond. small
3. A _____ plant pokes through the water. tall

Writing Longer Sentences   pages 246–247

Add adjectives to describe the underlined nouns in the sentences. Write each new sentence. Possible responses are given.

4. I see a <u>frog</u> on a <u>rock</u>. I see a large frog on a green rock.
5. A <u>turtle</u> is swimming in the <u>water</u>.
   A green turtle is swimming in the still water.

Adjectives for Taste, Smell, Feel, and Sound

pages 254–255

Choose an adjective from the box to complete each sentence. Write the sentence. Possible responses are given.

| smooth   cool   gentle   wet |

6. The water feels _____ and _____. wet, cool
7. The frog has a _____ skin. smooth
8. I hear the _____ sound of a waterfall. gentle

Using Synonyms in Writing   pages 256–257

Choose the more exact adjective to finish each sentence.

9. A (<u>soggy</u>, wet) log rests by the pond.
10. A (large, <u>huge</u>) rock is in the water.

Adjectives That Tell How Many   pages 272–273

Write the adjective that tells how many.

11. I see three hawks in the sky. three
12. Many birds are at the bird feeder. Many
13. There are two woodpeckers on the tree. two
14. Several robins look for worms. Several

Using *a* and *an*   pages 274–275

Write *a* or *an* to complete each sentence.

15. I saw _____ owl in the forest. an
16. It was sitting on the branch of _____ tree. a
17. It did not move _____ feather. a
18. Then it made _____ eerie hooting sound. an

Adding *er* and *est*   pages 282–283

Write the correct form of the adjective in ( ) to finish each sentence.

19. A sparrow is (<u>smaller</u>, smallest) than an owl.
20. An ostrich is the (taller, <u>tallest</u>) bird of all.
21. A toucan's beak is (<u>longer</u>, longest) than my hand.
22. Parrots are the (smarter, <u>smartest</u>) birds of all.

Extra Practice

Using *Come*, *Run*, and *Give* pages 320–321
Write the correct verb in ( ) to complete each sentence.

1. Now Mom and Tina (<u>come</u>, came) home from shopping.
2. Let's (<u>run</u>, ran) outside to greet them.
3. Last month Dad (give, <u>gave</u>) us tickets for a play.

Joining Sentences pages 322–323
Use *and* to join the sentences. Remember to use a comma (,) before *and*.

4. I get ready to go. We all leave together.
   I get ready to go, and we all leave together.
5. We get into the car. Dad drives to the play.
   We get into the car, and Dad drives to the play.
6. Mom shows our tickets. We go into the theater.
   Mom shows our tickets, and we go into the theater.

Using *Go*, *Do*, and *See* pages 330–331
Write the correct verb in ( ) to complete each sentence.

7. We never (go, <u>went</u>) to the theater before last year.
8. Now we (<u>see</u>, saw) three plays each year.
9. We even (does, <u>did</u>) a children's play in school.
10. I hope we (<u>do</u>, did) another play soon!

474

Commas in Place Names and Dates pages 332–333
Write the date and the name of the place correctly.

11. Mom saw a play in Chicago Illinois. Chicago, Illinois
12. She will see another one on July 12 2002. July 12, 2002

Using *Has*, *Have*, and *Had* pages 348–349
Write the correct verb in ( ) to complete each sentence.

13. Dad (<u>has</u>, have) tickets to a movie museum.
14. Mom (<u>had</u>, has) a ticket last week.
15. Now we (has, <u>have</u>) one extra ticket.

Keeping to One Main Idea pages 350–351
Write the paragraph. Underline the main idea. Leave out the sentence that does not tell about the main idea.

16.   <u>Today we go to the movie museum.</u> We will learn how movies are made. We will see some movies from the past. There is no school tomorrow. I want to learn about children in the movies.

Using Adverbs pages 358–359
Write the adverb in each sentence. Then write *how*, *when*, or *where* for each adverb.

17. We arrived early in the morning.   early, when
18. We walked slowly into the museum.   slowly, how
19. People listened quietly to the person speaking.   quietly, how
20. I learned many things there. there, where

475

Extra Practice

Noun-Pronoun Agreement pages 392–393

Write the pronoun that agrees with the underlined noun in each set of sentences.

1. The <u>children</u> get on the bus. _____ are excited. They
2. The <u>bus</u> starts to move. _____ heads for the beach. It
3. <u>Joe</u> can't wait. _____ wants to find a starfish. He
4. <u>Liz</u> is excited, too. _____ wants to look for shells. She

Word Order for Pronouns pages 394–395

Write the correct words in ( ) to complete each sentence.

5. Tim goes on a trip with (me and Liz, <u>Liz and me</u>).
6. (<u>Liz and I</u>, I and Liz) see the beach.
7. (<u>The teacher and I</u>, I and the teacher) get off the bus first.

Changing y to i pages 402–403

Write each verb in ( ) correctly.

8. Liz (hurry) to the shore. hurries
9. Tim (carry) his camera to take pictures. carries
10. A seagull (fly) over our heads. flies

Writing Contractions pages 404–405

Write the contraction for the underlined words.

11. Joe <u>has not</u> found a starfish. hasn't
12. Tim <u>is not</u> ready to take pictures yet. isn't

Writing Longer Sentences pages 420–421

Combine each set of sentences to make one longer sentence. Write the new sentence.

13. Boys swim. Girls swim.   Boys and girls swim.
14. Joe found a feather. Joe found a pretty shell.
    Joe found a feather and a pretty shell.

Using a Series Comma pages 422–423

Write each sentence correctly using the series commas.

15. Liz found an orange black and red shell.
    Liz found an orange, black, and red shell.
16. Tim took a picture of Liz Joe Sam and me.
    Tim took a picture of Liz, Joe, Sam, and me.

Using *there*, *their*, and *they're* pages 430–431

Write *there*, *their*, or *they're* to complete each sentence.

17. Look at all the crabs over _____! there
18. _____ running across the sand. They're

Using *to*, *too*, and *two* pages 432–433

Write *to*, *too*, or *two* to complete each sentence.

19. We were at the beach for _____ hours. two
20. Liz and Joe wanted _____ stay longer. to

Handbook

Contents

Additional Writing Models

Invitation

In an **invitation**, a writer invites someone to come somewhere or to do something. An invitation has five parts.

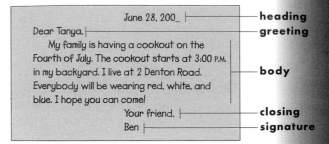

June 28, 200_ — **heading**

Dear Tanya, — **greeting**

My family is having a cookout on the Fourth of July. The cookout starts at 3:00 P.M. in my backyard. I live at 2 Denton Road. Everybody will be wearing red, white, and blue. I hope you can come! — **body**

Your friend, — **closing**

Ben — **signature**

An **envelope** is used to send a letter.

Ben Bradshaw
2 Denton Road
Spring Lake, NJ 07762 — **return address**

Tanya Jackson
111 Hicks Street
Brooklyn, NY 11201 — **mailing address**

Poster That Persuades

A **poster that persuades** shows how a problem can be solved. The writer draws a picture and writes words to show how the problem could be solved.

1. Decide on a topic. What is the problem? How could it be solved?

2. Draw a picture.

3. Write your ideas about the picture. Use some catchy words.

Keep this park beautiful.

put your litter in the trash can.

Play

In a **play,** a writer gives the setting, the characters' names, and what each character says.

1. Think of a title for your play. Write it at the top of the page.

2. Think about where the play takes place. This is the setting. Write the setting under the title.

3. Write each character's name at the beginning of a line.

4. Write what each character says. Think about how you talk with your friends and family members to help you.

The Ladybug Picnic

Setting: in a park

Characters: Linda Ladybug, Larry Ladybug, and Lee Ladybug

Linda: I hear that some people are having a picnic.

Larry: We should see what they brought.

Lee: I hope they have sandwiches.

Linda: Me, too. I love to eat the bread crumbs.

Larry: Let's go check out the picnic.

All Ladybugs: Yes! Let's go!

Writing Rubrics

How to Use Rubrics

The next six pages have checklists you can use to make your writing better. Each kind of writing has its own checklist. Here is how you can use them.

Before writing Look at the checklist to find out what your piece of writing should have.

During writing Check your draft against the list. Use the list to see how to make your writing better.

After writing Check your finished work against the list. Does your work show all the points?

Personal Story

Score of 4

★ My personal story tells about something that happened in my life. It uses words such as *I*, *me*, and *my*.

★ My personal story is complete and has a title.

★ My personal story uses time-order words to show the order in which things happened.

★ My personal story has few or no mistakes in punctuation, capitalization, or grammar.

Friendly Letter

Before writing Look at the checklist to find out what your letter should have.

During writing Check your draft against the list. Use the list to see how to make your writing better.

After writing Check your finished work against the list. Does your work show all the points?

Score of 4

★ My letter is written to someone I know. It tells the person about something I did.

★ My letter has all five parts. It has a heading, greeting, body, closing, and signature.

★ The body of my letter is clear. It has details that make it interesting to the reader.

★ My letter has few or no mistakes in punctuation, capitalization, or grammar.

Story

Before writing Look at the checklist to find out what your story should have.

During writing Check your draft against the list. Use the list to see how to make your writing better.

After writing Check your finished work against the list. Does your work show all the points?

Score of 4

★ My story is complete. It has a title and a beginning, middle, and ending.

★ My story has a problem that the story characters solve.

★ My story has exact words and details that help the reader understand the story events.

★ My story has few or no mistakes in punctuation, capitalization, or grammar.

Paragraph That Describes

Before writing Look at the checklist to find out what your paragraph that describes should have.

During writing Check your draft against the list. Use the list to see how to make your writing better.

After writing Check your finished work against the list. Does your work show all the points?

Score of 4

★ My paragraph that describes tells how something looks, sounds, smells, feels, or tastes.

★ My description has a topic sentence that tells what the paragraph is about. It has detail sentences that tell more about the topic.

★ My description uses details and colorful words that help the reader see what I am describing.

★ My description has few or no mistakes in punctuation, capitalization, or grammar.

How-to Paragraph

Before writing Look at the checklist to find out what your how-to paragraph should have.

During writing Check your draft against the list. Use the list to see how to make your writing better.

After writing Check your finished work against the list. Does your work show all the points?

Score of 4 ★★★★

★ My how-to paragraph is complete. It tells what the topic is, lists the materials first, and tells the steps to follow.

★ My how-to gives the steps in order. It uses time-order words to make the order clear.

★ My how-to has exact words and details that help the reader understand the steps.

★ My how-to has few or no mistakes in punctuation, capitalization, or grammar.

Research Report

Before writing Look at the checklist to find out what your research report should have.

During writing Check your draft against the list. Use the list to see how to make your writing better.

After writing Check your finished work against the list. Does your work show all the points?

Score of 4 ★★★★

★ My research report is about only one topic. Each main idea is stated in a sentence in a paragraph.

★ My report has details that help the reader understand the information.

★ My report is about something that is true. All the information is written in my own words.

★ My report has few or no mistakes in punctuation, capitalization, or grammar.

Spelling

Spelling Strategies

Here are five strategies that will help you spell many words.

1 If a word ends in a short vowel and a consonant, double the final consonant when you add an ending that begins with a vowel.

run + ing = running   hop + ed = hopped

2 If a word ends in *e*, drop the *e* when you add an ending that begins with a vowel.

make + ing = making   race + ed = raced

Keep the *e* when you add an ending that begins with a consonant.

nice + ly = nicely

3 If a word ends in a vowel and *y*, keep the *y* when you add an ending.

say + ing = saying   gray + est = grayest

4 If a word ends in a consonant and *y*, keep the *y* when adding *ing*.

cry + ing = crying

Change the *y* to *i* when you add other endings.

lady + es = ladies   try + ed = tried
funny + er = funnier

5 If a word ends in *s*, *x*, *ch*, or *sh*, add *es*.

bus + es = buses   wash + es = washes

Commonly Misspelled Words

again	it's	running
another	know	second
because	maybe	someone
better	might	their
broke(n)	missed	there
catch	off	third
caught	other	threw
children	people	too
didn't	please	trying
friend(s)	ready	were
happen(ed)	right	where

Manuscript Alphabet

A B C D E F G H
I J K L M N O P
Q R S T U V W
X Y Z

a b c d e f g h
i j k l m n o p
q r s t u v w
x y z

490

Cursive Alphabet

A B C D E F G H
I J K L M N O P
Q R S T U V W
X Y Z

a b c d e f g h
i j k l m n o p
q r s t u v w
x y z

491

D'Nealian Manuscript Alphabet

A B C D E F G H
I J K L M N O P
Q R S T U V W
X Y Z

a b c d e f g h
i j k l m n o p
q r s t u v w
x y z

492

D'Nealian Cursive Alphabet

A B C D E F G H
I J K L M N O P
Q R S T U V W
X Y Z

a b c d e f g h
i j k l m n o p
q r s t u v w
x y z

493

Thesaurus

Using a Thesaurus

Get to Know It! This **thesaurus** lists words and their **synonyms**. It also gives definitions and shows how a word is used in a sentence. The words in a thesaurus are in ABC order, or alphabetical order. Synonyms, which are words that have the same meaning, come after the example sentence. The opposites of most words are also listed.

Learn How to Use It! A good time to use the **thesaurus** is when you write and you are looking for a more interesting or more exact word. For example, find a better word for *big*. First find the *B* words and locate *big*. Then look at the list of **synonyms**, and pick the word that comes the closest to what you want to say. *Big* is on page 495.

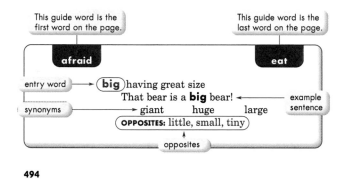

This guide word is the first word on the page.

This guide word is the last word on the page.

afraid   eat

entry word → **big** having great size
That bear is a **big** bear! ← example sentence
synonyms → giant   huge   large
OPPOSITES: little, small, tiny
↑ opposites

494

---

afraid filled with fear
 The mouse is **afraid** of the cat.
  frightened scared
 OPPOSITES: brave, fearless, unafraid

bad not good
 The skunk has a **bad** smell.
  awful dreadful horrible terrible
 OPPOSITES: good, nice, pleasant, wonderful

big having great size
 That bear is a **big** bear!
  giant huge large
 OPPOSITES: little, small, tiny

cold having a low temperature
 The weather is **cold** in the winter.
  chilly cool freezing icy
 OPPOSITES: hot, warm

cry to shed tears
 Most babies **cry** when they are hungry.
  sob wail weep
 OPPOSITES: chuckle, giggle, laugh

eat to take food into the body
 I like to **eat** a snack after school.
  gobble munch nibble taste

495

---

fat heavy; not skinny
 We always have a **fat** turkey for Thanksgiving.
  chubby husky plump stout
 OPPOSITES: skinny, slender, thin, trim

fun enjoyable
 There were many **fun** rides at the park.
  amusing exciting
 OPPOSITES: boring, dull

get to earn something
 I hope I **get** an A on my test.
  earn obtain receive
 OPPOSITES: give, lose, send

go to move away from or toward a place
 I **go** to the park on Saturdays.
  hop jump race ride
 OPPOSITES: halt, remain, stay, stop

good pleasing or correct
 That was a **good** movie.
  fine nice pleasant

happy pleased
 Sunny days make me feel **happy**.
  cheerful delighted glad merry
 OPPOSITES: displeased, sad, unhappy

hard not easy
 It is **hard** to learn a new sport.
  difficult tough
 OPPOSITES: easy, simple

496

---

little not big in size
 Kathy's doll was **little**.
  short small tiny
 OPPOSITES: big, huge, large, tall

make to cause something to happen
 The workers **make** a house.
  build create shape

nice pleasant or good
 We go to the park when it is **nice** outside.
  beautiful kind lovely
 OPPOSITES: awful, bad, mean, unpleasant

pretty nice-looking
 Janet wore a **pretty** dress.
  beautiful lovely
 OPPOSITES: ordinary, plain, ugly

run to move quickly
 I **run** after my brother.
  dash hurry race

497

---

sad unhappy
Michael was **sad** when he lost his hat.
  blue gloomy miserable sorry
OPPOSITES: cheerful, glad, happy

see to use your eyes to look at something
We **see** animals at the zoo.
  notice stare watch

take to move or carry something
Take your toys upstairs.
  carry get move

walk to move by using the feet
Ana and Carlos **walk** to the store.
  step stroll

well in a good or correct way
My sister plays sports **well**.
  easily skillfully
OPPOSITES: badly, poorly

Glossary

Using the Glossary

Get to Know It! The **glossary** gives the meanings of grammar and writing terms that are highlighted in *Harcourt Language*. It also gives sentences that have examples of the terms. The words in the **glossary** are in ABC order, or **alphabetical order**.

Learn How to Use It! If you want to find the word *exclamation* in the **glossary**, you should first find the *E* words. *E* is near the beginning of the alphabet, so the *E* words are near the beginning of the **glossary**. Then you can use the guide words at the top of the page to help you find the entry word *exclamation*.

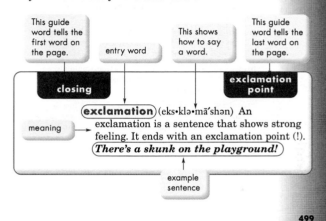

This guide word tells the first word on the page.

entry word

This shows how to say a word.

This guide word tells the last word on the page.

closing   exclamation point

meaning

exclamation (eks·klə·mā′shən) An exclamation is a sentence that shows strong feeling. It ends with an exclamation point (!). *There's a skunk on the playground!*

example sentence

 A

abbreviation (ə·brē·vē·ā′shən) An abbreviation is a short way of writing a word. *Mr. Johnson went to work.*

adjective (aj′ik·tiv) A word that tells about a noun. An adjective can compare or tell how many or what kind. *I have three sisters.*

adverb (ad′vûrb) An adverb tells about a verb. An adverb can tell when, where, or how. *My team played baseball yesterday.*

antonym (an′tə·nim) A word that has an opposite meaning of another word is an antonym. *Plain and fancy are antonyms.*

apostrophe (ə·pos′trə·fē) An apostrophe (') takes the place of missing letters in a contraction or shows possession in a possessive noun. *Molly's sister can't come today.*

atlas (at′ləs) An atlas is a book of maps. *Use the atlas to see where India is.*

B

body (bod′ē) The body of a letter is the friendly message. *Write about your trip in the body of your letter.*

C

characters (kar′ək·tərz) The people or animals in a story are the characters. *Who are the main characters in this story?*

---

closing (klō′zing) The closing of a letter is the part that says good-bye. *Maria ended her letter by writing the closing Your friend.*

command (kə·mand′) A command is a sentence that tells someone to do something. *Please close the door.*

contraction (kən·trak′shən) A contraction is a short way to write two words. *I can't wait for you to come!*

 D

details (dē·tālz′) Details are examples that help explain a main idea. *Tony added details to make his report interesting.*

draft (draft) A first try at writing something is a draft. *Pam made changes to the first draft of her story.*

 E

exclamation (eks·klə·mā′shən) An exclamation is a sentence that shows strong feeling. It ends with an exclamation point (!). *There's a skunk on the playground!*

exclamation point (eks·klə·mā′shən point) An exclamation point (!) at the end of a sentence shows strong feeling. *Look out for that ball!*

fiction books (fik'shən bŏŏks) Fiction books are made-up stories. **I read a fiction book about going to Jupiter.**

greeting (grēt'ing) The greeting of a letter is the part that says hello. **The greeting of Beth's letter was** *Dear Grandpa.*

heading (hed'ing) The heading of a letter tells the date and the writer's address. **Put the date in the heading of your letter.**

helping verb (help'ing vûrb) A helping verb works with the main verb to tell about an action. **I** *have* **learned about plants.**

homophones (hom'ə·fōnz) Words that sound alike but have different meanings are homophones. *Pear* **and** *pair* **are homophones.**

how-to paragraph (hou tŏŏ' par'ə·graf) A how-to paragraph is one in which a writer tells how to make or do something. **Ying told how to bake cookies in her how-to paragraph.**

main idea (mān i·dē'ə) The main idea is the most important idea in a paragraph. **What is the main idea of Adolfo's paragraph?**

naming part (nām'ing pärt) The naming part of a sentence tells who or what the sentence is about. *Frances* **went to the movies.**

noun (noun) A noun is a word that names a person, place, animal, or thing. **The** *boy* **brought his** *ball* **to the** *park.*

nonfiction books (non·fik'shən bŏŏks) Nonfiction books tell about things that are real. **Janie read a nonfiction book about snakes.**

outline (out'līn) An outline shows the order of main ideas and details in a piece of writing. **Check your outline for all the parts of your report.**

paragraph (par'ə·graf) A group of sentences that all tell about a main idea is a paragraph. **Mikey's paragraph is about dogs.**

period (pir'ē·əd) Use a period (.) at the end of a statement or a command. **I saw the monkeys.**

possessive noun (pə·zes'iv noun) A noun that shows ownership. *Pablo's* **book is on the** *teacher's* **desk.**

pronoun (prō'noun) A word that takes the place of a noun is a pronoun. **I played soccer, and** *he* **watched.**

proper noun (prop'ər noun) A noun that tells the special name of a person, a place, or an animal is a proper noun. It begins with a capital letter. *Hector* **lives in** *New York.*

question (kwes'chən) A question is a sentence that asks something. It ends with a question mark (?). *Where is my other shoe?*

question mark (kwes'chən märk) Use a question mark (?) at the end of a question. **Do you like to play soccer?**

sentence (sen'təns) A sentence is a group of words that tells a complete thought. Every sentence begins with a capital letter and ends with an end mark. *The children ride the bus to school.*

setting (set'ing) The setting is where and when a story takes place. **The setting of the story is long ago in the woods.**

signature (sig'nə·chər) The signature of a letter is the writer's handwritten name at the end. **I wrote my signature at the end of my letter.**

statement (stāt'mənt) A statement is a sentence that tells something. It ends with a period (.). *I like grape juice.*

synonym (sin'ə·nim) A word that means the same or almost the same as another word. *Beautiful* **is a synonym for** *pretty.*

telling part (tel'ing pärt) The telling part of a sentence tells what someone or something is or does. **Jasmine** *walks her dog.*

thesaurus (thə·sôr'əs) A thesaurus lists words in alphabetical order and gives synonyms for each word. **Look up the word in the thesaurus to find words with the same or almost the same meaning.**

verb (vûrb) A verb is a word that tells what someone or something is or does. **The frog** *jumps* **from spot to spot.**

Vocabulary Power

angrily My brother slammed the door **angrily**.

ambassador Mrs. Ruiz is an **ambassador** of Mexico.

burrow The rabbits **burrow** underground.

cocoons Caterpillars turn into moths in their **cocoons**.

considerate It was **considerate** of you to clean my room.

consulting He was **consulting** the teacher about what to do.

contribution Her **contribution** made the class better.

correspondence They had a written **correspondence**.

countryside The **countryside** has many trees.

creatures Different **creatures** live in the rain forest.

croak The frogs in the pond **croak** loudly.

demonstrate Marcy will **demonstrate** how to bake a cake.

dignified The mayor looked important and **dignified**.

explored My cousin and I **explored** my attic.

fastened She **fastened** the baby's jacket.

flutter They saw the baby bird **flutter** its wings.

glossiest My book has the **glossiest** cover.

guided The leader **guided** his tour group.

harmony The singers sang in perfect **harmony**.

infinite The universe seems **infinite**.

international The singer is an **international** success.

lullaby Grandma sang me a **lullaby** every night.

luscious I ate a tasty, **luscious** peach yesterday.

marvelous We had a **marvelous** time at the party!

mockingbird I saw a **mockingbird** in the tree.

quicker The cheetah is **quicker** than a lion.

ragged The worn-out old doll wore a **ragged** coat.

rattlesnake A **rattlesnake** is very poisonous.

recycled We **recycled** all of our old newspapers.

revolving My sister got stuck in a **revolving** door!

rodeo My uncle rides bulls at the **rodeo**.

scamper The mice **scamper** into their hole.

seize Will the player **seize** the ball?

species Are whales an endangered **species**?

whirl Watch the dancers **whirl** and twirl!

wholly It is **wholly** likely that the team will lose.

506

507

Index

508

509

Acknowledgments

For permission to reprint copyrighted material, grateful acknowledgment is made to the following sources:

Atheneum Books for Young Readers, an imprint of Simon & Schuster Children's Publishing Division: "August Afternoon" from *Open the Door* by Marion Edey and Dorothy Grider. Published by Charles Scribner's Sons, NY, 1949. From *Jalapeño Bagels* by Natasha Wing, illustrated by Robert Casilla. Text copyright © 1996 by Natasha Wing; illustrations copyright © 1996 by Robert Casilla.

Candlewick Press, Cambridge, MA: "Who's Been Sleeping in My Porridge?" and illustration from *Who's Been Sleeping in My Porridge?* by Colin McNaughton. Copyright © 1990 by Colin McNaughton.

Creative Type, Arcata, CA, www.losbagels.com: Recipe for "Jalapeño Bagels" from *Los Bagels Recipes & Lore.* Copyright © 1991 by Los Bagels.

Dial Books for Young Readers, a division of Penguin Putnam Inc.: Cover illustration by Leo and Diane Dillon from *Why Mosquitoes Buzz in People's Ears* by Verna Aardema. Illustration copyright © 1975 by Leo and Diane Dillon. From *Red Riding Hood* by James Marshall. Copyright © 1987 by James Marshall.

Phyllis Halloran: "Busy" by Phyllis Halloran. Text copyright © 1989 by Phyllis Halloran.

Harcourt, Inc.: "Little Silk Worms" from *Dragon Kites and Dragonflies* by Demi Hitz. Copyright © 1986 by Demi. Cover illustration from *Check It Out! The Book About Libraries* by Gail Gibbons. Copyright © 1985 by Gail Gibbons. "Giraffes" from *The Llama Who Had No Pajama: 100 Favorite Poems* by Mary Ann Hoberman. Text copyright © 1973 by Mary Ann Hoberman. Cover illustration by Ted Rand from *Willie Takes a Hike* by Gloria Rand. Illustration copyright © 1996 by Ted Rand.

HarperCollins Publishers: Cover illustration from *How a Book Is Made* by Aliki. Copyright © 1986 by Aliki Brandenberg. "Tommy" from *Bronzeville Boys and Girls* by Gwendolyn Brooks. Text copyright © 1956 by Gwendolyn Brooks Blakely. Cover illustration from *Feel the Wind* by Arthur Dorros. Copyright © 1989 by Arthur Dorros. From *You're Aboard Spaceship Earth* by Patricia Lauber, illustrated by Holly Keller. Text copyright © 1996 by Patricia G. Lauber; illustrations copyright © 1996 by Holly Keller. From *Red Dancing Shoes* by Denise Lewis Patrick, illustrated by James E. Ransome. Text copyright © 1993 by Denise Lewis Patrick; illustrations copyright © 1993 by James E. Ransome. "I Am Running in a Circle" from *New Kid on the Block* by Jack Prelutsky. Text copyright © 1984 by Jack Prelutsky. "Something Big Has Been Here" from *Something Big Has Been Here* by Jack Prelutsky. Text copyright © 1990 by Jack Prelutsky. Cover illustration from *The Acorn Tree and Other Folktales,* retold and illustrated by Anne Rockwell. Copyright © 1995 by Anne Rockwell. Cover illustration by Steven Kellogg from *If You Made a Million* by David M. Schwartz. Illustration copyright © 1989 by Steven Kellogg.

Elizabeth Hauser: "Spring Rain" from *Around and About* by Marchette Chute. Text copyright 1957 by E. P. Dutton; text copyright renewed 1985 by Marchette Chute.

Holiday House, Inc.: From *Penguins!* by Gail Gibbons. Copyright © 1998 by Gail Gibbons. Cover illustration from *Weather Words and What They Mean* by Gail Gibbons. Copyright © 1990 by Gail Gibbons. Cover illustration from *Who's Who in My Family?* by Loreen Leedy. Copyright © 1995 by Loreen Leedy.

Houghton Mifflin Company: Cover illustration by Blair Lent from *Why the Sun and the Moon Live in the Sky* by Elphinstone Dayrell. Copyright © 1968 by Blair Lent, Jr. "The Flying Machine" from *George and Martha* by James Marshall. Copyright © 1972 by James Marshall.

Ideals Children's Books, Nashville, Tennessee: From *Don't Forget to Write* by Martina Selway. Copyright © 1992 by Martina Selway.

Hettie Jones: Untitled poem (retitled: "The Mockingbird") by Acoma from *The Trees Stand Shining: Poetry of the North American Indians* by Hettie Jones. Text copyright © 1971 by Hettie Jones.

Alfred A. Knopf, a Division of Random House Inc.: "April Rain Song" by Langston Hughes from *Collected Poems* by Langston Hughes. Text copyright © 1994 by the Estate of Langston Hughes.

Lee & Low Books, Inc., 95 Madison Avenue, New York, NY 10016: "Sun Song" from *Confetti: Poems for Children* by Pat Mora, illustrated by Enrique O. Sanchez. Text copyright © 1996 by Pat Mora; illustration copyright © 1996 by Enrique O. Sanchez.

Little, Brown and Company (Inc.): "This Is My Rock" from *Far and Few* by David McCord. Text copyright 1929 by David McCord. Originally published in *The Saturday Review.*

Margaret K. McElderry Books, an imprint of Simon & Schuster Children's Publishing Division: From *Dear Mr. Blueberry* by Simon James. Copyright © 1991 by Simon James.

Pearson Education: Cover illustration by Randy Verougstraete from *A Money Adventure: Earning, Saving, Spending, Sharing* by Neale S. Godfrey. Copyright © 1996 by Children's Financial Network, Inc. Published by Modern Curriculum Press.

Philomel Books, a division of Penguin Putnam Inc.: Illustration by Eric Carle from *Animals Animals,* edited by Laura Whipple. Illustration copyright © 1989 by Eric Carle. "There's a Cow on the Mountain" (retitled: "The Cow") and illustration by Ed Young from *Chinese Mother Goose Rhymes,* selected and edited by Robert Wyndham. Text copyright © 1968 by Robert Wyndham; illustration copyright © 1968 by Ed Young.

G. P. Putnam's Sons, a division of Penguin Putnam Inc.: Cover illustration from *Officer Buckle and Gloria* by Peggy Rathmann. Copyright © 1995 by Peggy Rathmann.

Marian Reiner: "Hurry" from *Out Loud* by Eve Merriam. Text copyright © 1973 by Eve Merriam. "On Our Way" from *Catch a Little Rhyme* by Eve Merriam. Text copyright © 1966 by Eve Merriam; text © renewed 1994 by Dee Michel and Guy Michel.

Scholastic Inc.: From *Fire Fighters* by Robert Maass. Copyright © 1989 by Robert Maass.

Simon & Schuster Books for Young Readers, an imprint of Simon & Schuster Children's Publishing Division: From *Kate Heads West* by Pat Brisson, illustrated by Rick Brown. Text copyright © 1990 by Pat Brisson; illustrations copyright © 1990 by Rick Brown. From *Two Greedy Bears* by Mirra Ginsburg, illustrated by Jose Aruego and Ariane Dewey. Text copyright © 1976 by Mirra Ginsburg; illustrations copyright © 1976 by Jose Aruego and Ariane Dewey. From *I Have a Pet!* by Shari Halpern. Copyright © 1994 by Shari Halpern. Cover illustration by Diane Greenseid from *Wilson Sat Alone* by Debra Hess. Illustration copyright © 1994 by Diane Greenseid.

United Indians of All Tribes Foundation: "The Wind is Cool and Swift" by Tanu Frank from *Daybreak Star Indian Reader.*

Photo Credits

Unit One:
Pages 22-23: Ken Kenzie/Harcourt.

Unit Two:
Pages 94-95: Index Stock Photography.

Unit Three:
Pages 168-169: Harcourt.

Unit Four:
Pages 240-341: Steve Terrill/The Stock Market NY.

Unit Five:
Pages 316-317: Harcourt;
FireFighters photos, pages 338-339: Robert Maass.

Unit 6:
Pages 388-389: Michael Yamashita/Woodfin Camp & Associates.

Other photos: Harcourt.

Illustration Credits
Andrea Tachiera pp. 24, 25; Marsha Winborn pp. 36, 38, 39, 40, 41, 42, 43, 96, 96, 134, 135, 318, 356, 357, 358, 359, 360, 361, 362, 365; Margeaux Lucas pp. 46, 47, 48, 53, 81, 193, 194, 195, 196, 261, 280, 281, 282, 284, 285, 288, 302, 305, 306, 319, 330, 331, 334, 336, 375, 377, 378, 379, 380, 383, 420, 422, 423, 424, 427, 443; Deirdre Newman pp. 52, 58, 105, 131, 141, 337, 409; Alexi Natchev pp. 54, 55, 56, 57, 58, 60, 244, 245, 246, 247, 248, 249, 250; Benton Mahan pp. 63, 64, 65, 66, 67, 68, 70, 208, 209, 346, 347, 348, 349, 350, 351, 352, 353, 354; Dave Winter pp. 71, 198, 199, 271, 272, 273, 274, 275, 276, 278, 418; Myron Grossman pp. 106, 107, 110, 112, 137, 140, 142; Randy Chewning pp. 124, 125, 126, 127, 128, 129, 130, 132, 200, 202, 203, 204, 205, 206, 228, 229, 230, 231, 232, 234, 235, 265, 266, 267, 435, 436, 438, 448, 450; Janet Broxon pp. 208, 209, 270; Laura Huliska-Beith pp. 210, 211, 254, 255, 256, 257, 258, 260, 328, 329, 401, 402, 403, 404, 405, 406, 408; Dawn Appelby pp. 320, 321, 322, 323, 324, 326; Ande Cook pp. 390, 391; George Thompson pp. 392, 393, 394, 395, 396, 398; Bart Rivers pp. 428, 429, 430, 432, 434, 436; Ethan Long p. 481

Reteach

	What Is a Sentence? **Objective:** to recognize that a sentence tells a complete thought	Word Order in a Sentence **Objective:** to identify and use correct word order in a sentence	Beginning and Ending a Sentence **Objective:** to begin a sentence with a capital letter and end it with an end mark
Visual	Display a magazine picture and two groups of words that tell about the picture. One group should be a complete sentence. The other should be lacking a subject or a verb. Ask children to choose the complete sentence and to explain their choice. Repeat with other pictures and sentences.	Write a sentence with the words in jumbled order on the board. Ask volunteers to write number one above the first word, two above the next, and so on. Follow the numbers to rewrite the sentence under the jumbled sentence. Have the group decide if the words are now in the correct order.	On the board, write several sentences. Use lowercase letters to begin the sentences and leave off the end marks. Give children a different color chalk to make corrections to the beginning of the first words and to add the end marks.
Auditory	Read aloud a list of complete sentences mixed with groups of words that are not complete sentences. Ask children to show thumbs up when they hear a complete sentence and thumbs down when they hear a group of words that does not form a complete sentence.	Have children make two cards, one with a happy face, one with a sad face. Read several sentences, some that are in correct order and some that are mixed up. Ask children to listen as you read one sentence at a time and display the happy face for correct sentences or the sad face for the jumbled groups of words.	Read a sentence to children. Have children tell which word starts with a capital letter and which word is followed by an end mark. Write the sentence on the board as they repeat their answers.
Kinesthetic	Write complete and incomplete sentences on sentence strips. Place the sentence strips on the floor around the room. Call out *complete sentence* or *incomplete sentence* and have children stand by a corresponding sentence. Then challenge them to explain how they made their choice.	Provide small groups of children with word cards that can be used to form simple sentences. Have children use the cards to form a sentence and share their completed sentences with other groups.	Give each child four cards. Have them write a period on one and the letters *W*, *L*, and *I* on the others. Write some sentences that begin with *we*, *let's*, and *it*. Begin the sentences with lowercase letters and leave off the periods. Ask children to hold up the two cards that would make the sentence correct.

Reteach

	What Are the Parts of a Sentence? **Objective:** to understand that a sentence has two parts	Naming Parts and Telling Parts **Objective:** to identify the naming and telling parts of a sentence	Combining Parts of Sentences **Objective:** to use and to join sentences with the same telling parts
Visual	Show a magazine picture of a person or animal. Ask children to identify the subject of the picture. Then ask children to make up a phrase that tells what the person or thing is doing.	Write several naming and telling parts of sentences on chart paper in random order. Have children circle all of the naming parts in one color and the telling parts in a different color. Then ask them to draw arrows to link the parts to make complete sentences.	Write two sentences next to each other on the board with the same telling parts. Ask children to cross out the repeated part, write the word *and* to join the naming parts, and read the new sentence.
Auditory	Read a simple sentence. Ask children to tell who or what the sentence is about. Then ask a volunteer to tell what that person or thing does or is.	Write several sentences on a sheet of paper. Call on children to read one sentence at a time as others listen. The reader then calls on volunteers to restate the naming and telling parts.	Read aloud two closely related sentences. Ask children to use the word *and* to join the ideas. Call on volunteers to tell the new sentence.
Kinesthetic	Divide the classroom into groups, labeled naming part and telling part. Read a simple sentence aloud. As they hear the parts of the sentence, have the matching groups stand up and move to the center of the classroom. Switch the group labels and repeat.	Write naming parts and telling parts of sentences on sentence strips. Place the strips face down on a table. Have children turn the strips over and sort them into two groups, naming parts and telling parts.	Hand out pairs of sentences written on sentence strips, some with the same telling parts, some with different telling parts. Have partners link arms when a pair of sentences can be combined and say the new sentence aloud together.

Reteach

	Different Kinds of Sentences **Objective:** to recognize statements and questions	Using Statements and Questions **Objective:** to use correct end marks for statements and questions	Sentences That Go Together **Objective:** to identify sentences that do not belong to a paragraph
Visual	Display a group of statements and questions one by one in random order. Ask children to read each one and tell if it is a question or a statement.	Show a magazine picture. Have children write one statement and one question about the picture. Remind them to use the correct end marks.	Show children a brief paragraph in which one sentence does not belong with the others. Children can use a highlighter to mark the sentences that belong together.
Auditory	Give children two different noisemakers. Read a statement or question. Have children sound only the noisemaker you have designated for that sentence type. Discuss differing opinions. Repeat with a new sentence.	Place several statements and questions on slips of paper in a bag. One child chooses and reads a sentence aloud, as others write it on the board or on paper, using correct end marks.	Read short groups of three or four sentences, one of which does not belong with the others. Have children tell which sentence does not have a topic that relates to the others.
Kinesthetic	Read statements and questions aloud one by one as children listen in teams. The team that first identifies the sentence type gets to toss a ball into a basket.	Give each child a marker and large sheets of chart paper. Have children place the sheets on the floor in front of them. Read a statement or a question aloud. Each child draws a large end mark for the sentence type you read.	Prepare small paragraphs in which one sentence does not tell about the topic. Tell children to cut the sentences apart, remove the one that does not belong, and reassemble the remaining sentences.

Reteach

	More Kinds of Sentences **Objective:** to recognize and use exclamations and commands	Exclamations and Commands **Objective:** to correctly punctuate exclamations and commands	Using Different Kinds of Sentences **Objective:** to identify and use statements, questions, exclamations, and commands
Visual	Write a list of topics related to preparing a meal, such as cutting food, cooking it, being careful with tools, and eating. Have children use the list to brainstorm exclamations and commands that are related to the topic. Record their ideas on a chart.	Have children write the letter *C* on a card to stand for *command* and write *E* on a card to stand for *exclamation.* Write sentences on the board and have children read them and display the corresponding card.	Write some statements on the board. Have children take turns spinning a spinner divided into three sections—questions, exclamations, and commands. Invite them to read a statement and restate it to match the sentence type on the spinner.
Auditory	Have children pretend that they are playing a game. Ask them to make up commands and exclamations they might use in teaching others to play the game. Have others listen and identify each sentence type.	Read several sentences, one at a time, mixing commands and exclamations. Use intonation to suggest the sentence type. Have children write the sentences, including end marks to reflect the sentence type.	Read a sentence aloud. Ask children to identify the sentence type. Then name a different sentence type. Have children recast the original sentence to fit the new type. Guide children in using an appropriate tone of voice as they dramatically retell the changed sentence.
Kinesthetic	Have children play "Simon Says." Tell the child who plays Simon to give commands and say some exclamatory sentences. Tell the group that when they hear Simon give a command, they should obey the command, but when they hear an exclamation, they should draw an exclamation mark in the air.	Write some commands and exclamatory sentences on the board. Write periods and exclamation marks on separate self-stick notes. Invite children to read the sentences and place the punctuation marks where they belong.	Label papers with the words *command, question,* and *exclamation* and hang them in the room. Invite children to stand by the sign of their choice. Then say a statement and call on children to restate it to match the form written on the sign nearest to them.

Reteach

	What Is a Noun? **Objective:** to understand that nouns are words that name people, places, and things	Nouns for People, Places, Animals, Things **Objective:** to identify nouns for people, places, animals, and things	Using Possessive Nouns **Objective:** to use the possessive to show ownership
Visual	Cut out several pictures of people, places, and things. Have children identify and label what they see in the pictures. Invite them to color code their labels, using red to write nouns for people, green for places, and blue for things.	Make a 5-column chart on the board with the headings *People, Places, Nouns, Animals,* and *Things.* In the nouns column list several nouns of each type. Call on volunteers to read a noun and write it in the column in which it belongs.	Write a list of possesive phrases such as: *the ears of my dog.* Have children circle the owner and underline what is owned. Then have children rewrite the phrase in its possessive form.
Auditory	Sing a familiar song or nursery rhyme with children. Then have children repeat the song. Ask them to sing each noun in the song louder than the other words.	Have children make word cards labeled *person, place, animal,* and *thing.* Read a list of nouns. For each word, have children hold up the corresponding card that identifies the type of noun.	Read to children a possesive phrase such as *the purse of my Mom.* Call on a volunteer to restate the phrase as a possesive. (My Mom's purse) Next, have the volunteer say a possesive phrase and call on a classmate to restate it as the game continues.
Kinesthetic	Write a word on each of ten sheets of paper and include five nouns. Tape the papers in a row on the floor. Tell children to walk or hop down the row, stepping only on the words that are nouns.	Prepare a deck of 16 cards. Write 4 nouns for people, 4 for places, 4 for animals, and 4 for things. Have children use the cards to play "concentration". Children make matched pairs by selecting two nouns of the same type.	Give children small sticky notes and strips of masking tape on which to write their names in permanent marker. Then have them add s and an apostrophe in a different color and attach the labels to their possessions, such as chairs, desks, backpacks, and cubbies.

Reteach

	Nouns That Name More Than One **Objective:** to use nouns that name more than one	Making Nouns Plural **Objective:** to add s and es correctly to nouns that name more than one	Plural Nouns That Change Spelling **Objective:** to understand that some nouns change spelling to name more than one
Visual	Give children a copy of a one-page story. Have them use a transparent marker to highlight all the nouns that name more than one.	Create a chart or bulletin board display with the headings *s endings* and *es endings*. Under the *es* heading write the letters *s, ch, sh, x*. Then have children look for and paste pictures to show words that end in *s, ch, sh, x*, such as *bus* and *box*. Have children label the pictures, writing each noun so it names more than one. Repeat with the *s endings* column.	Write a column of singular nouns that change spelling in the plural. In the right hand column, write two plural forms for each noun, one spelled correctly, one with the letter s added to the noun. Have children take turns drawing lines to match the singular form with the correct plural form.

Auditory	Read a story aloud. Have children raise two hands when they hear a noun that names more than one and one hand when they hear a noun that names only one.	Teach children this rhyme to the tune of "Mary Had a Little Lamb:"
		  S, ch, sh, or x.
		  S, ch, sh, or x.
		  S, ch, sh, or x.
		All take es endings.
			Have a spelling bee. Give children the singular form of a noun. Children will spell the plural form. Include some words with spelling changes in the plural form.

Kinesthetic	One child in a pair names a singular noun and tosses a foam ball to a partner, who quickly says the plural form. Invite children to take turns naming singular and plural nouns.	On the sides of a cube, write the letters *s, ch, sh, x, e, and t.* Ask children to toss the cube and name a noun with the ending that falls face up. Then have them tell whether to add s or es to the noun they said to name more than one.	On a tic-tac-toe grid, write singular words that have spelling changes in the plural form. Invite pairs of children to play tic-tac-toe. Each player claims a box by writing the plural form of the noun correctly. Provide answers on the back of the page for self-checking.

Reteach

	What Is a Proper Noun? **Objective:** to distinguish and use proper nouns	People, Places, and Animals **Objective:** to understand that proper nouns are special names that begin with capital letters	Days, Months, and Holidays **Objective:** to recognize that the names of days, months, and holidays are proper nouns
Visual	Give each child a travel catalog page to paste on paper. Have them think of then write proper nouns to label the people, places, and animals they see. Suggest that they make up the proper nouns. Invite children to display and share their labeled pages.	Write several proper nouns on the board using only lowercase letters. Give children colored chalk or markers. Have them erase the incorrect letters and replace them with capital letters in the second color.	Have children work in groups to look at the pages of a calendar. Invite them to take turns writing all the proper nouns they find in a chart.
Auditory	Name pairs of nouns, such as *TV show* and *Sesame Street,* in which one noun is common and one is proper. Children raise one finger or two to show whether the first or second noun named is the proper noun.	Name a common noun, such as *boy, pet, street,* or *city.* Encourage children to name proper nouns to identify special people, places, and animals for each common noun.	Have children work with partners or in small groups to make up a chant to remember the names of days, months, and holidays. Have them tell which letters are capitalized in each. They can share their chants with others. You may want to model the following: *Monday, today is Monday.* *We begin Monday with* *a capital M.*
Kinesthetic	Have groups of children sit in a circle. One child says either a common noun or a proper noun. If the noun is a proper noun, group members stand up. If it is a common noun, they stay seated. Continue around the circle.	Say *person, place,* or *animal.* Toss a yarn ball around a circle. Each child who catches the ball says a proper noun that fits the category you name.	Write the names of days of the week and months of the year in random order on a grid, omitting the first letter of each word. Make copies and have children add the missing capital letters, cut the words apart, and sequence them by category and chronological order.

Reteach

	What Is a Pronoun? **Objective:** to recognize that pronouns take the place of nouns	***He, She, It,* and *They*** **Objective:** to use the pronouns *he, she, it,* and *they* correctly	***I* and *Me*** **Objective:** to use pronouns *I* and *me* correctly
Visual	Write several sentences on the board using the pronouns *he, she, they,* and *it.* Call on volunteers to draw small stick figures of one or more persons, animals, or things above each pronoun. The stick figures should show the number indicated by the pronoun.	Write a paragraph on the board using nouns where you would commonly use pronouns. Have children find each noun, cross it out, and replace it with an appropriate pronoun.	Write a paragraph on the board, replacing the pronouns *I* and *me* with blanks. Call on volunteers to read the sentences and write in the missing pronouns.
Auditory	Read a paragraph or two with several subject pronouns. Tell children to listen for pronouns and clap their hands each time they hear one. Then have children make up their own sentences as others listen for pronouns.	Give each child a name tag with the pronoun *he, she, it,* or *they.* Slowly read sentences or a story using nouns. Each time children hear a noun that can be replaced with their pronoun, they stand up. Call on volunteers to repeat the sentence, replacing the noun with the pronoun.	Read sentences with singular subject and object pronouns, but sound a bell in place of naming the pronoun. Ask children to tell whether *I* or *me* belongs where the bell was sounded.
Kinesthetic	Write sentences on sentence strips. Leave blanks in place of subject nouns. Write corresponding subject nouns on cards, with a matching pronoun on the other side. Display the sentences on a bulletin board with the cards pinned to the blanks. Have children flip the cards and read the sentences, first with the noun, and then with the pronoun.	Make a spinner with the pronouns *he, she, it,* and *they.* Have children take turns spinning the spinner. Children should use the pronoun the spinner points to in an oral sentence.	Have small groups of children sit in a circle. The first one hands an object to the next, saying, "I give it to you." The one who receives the item says, "You gave it to me." Have children continue repeating these sentences as the item is passed around the circle.

Reteach

	What Is a Verb? **Objective**: to recognize action verbs	Adding *s* or *es* to Verbs **Objective**: to add s or es to verbs that tell about one person or thing	Combining Sentences with Verbs **Objective**: to join sentences with the same naming parts
Visual	Hand out copies of the sports pages from a newspaper. Have children work in groups to high-light the action verbs they read. Have groups use some of the verbs to write about sports they play.	List action verbs in a chart, including several that end with *s* or *es*. Cover each verb with a sticky note. Write a singular or a plural subject on each sticky note. Have children select a box, uncover the verb, and tell what form of the verb goes with the subject on the note.	Write two sentences on the board with the same naming parts. Ask a volunteer to put a large X though the repeated part and write the word *and* in the correct place to join the telling parts. Have the child read the new sentence. Repeat with other sentence pairs.
Auditory	Call on volunteers to make up sentences to tell how some ani-mals move. Invite other children to listen for the action word and to repeat it when they hear it.	Have group members brain-storm a list of verbs that tell what they do to get ready for school. Then have children use the verbs to tell a story about a child getting ready for school. Encourage each child to add a sentence. Ask others to identify each action verb and tell whether it ends with *s* or *es*.	Say two sentences with the same subject, such as, *Bees live in hives. Bees make honey.* Ask children to raise their hands when they can tell the new sentence that is formed by joining their telling parts.
Kinesthetic	Have volunteers act out some action verbs such as: *dance, walk, run, hop, turn, skid, skate, fly, swim.* The first child who guess-es what the verb is, uses it in a sentence then takes the next turn.	Write the following verbs on cards: *brush, kiss, wash, stretch, catch, touch, dress, sing, eat, read, waddle, swim, march.* Invite chil-dren to take turns picking a card and pantomiming the word. Group members guess the action and use the verb in a sen-tence. Others in the group tell if the verb ends in *s* or *es*.	Give children sentence strips having sentences with the same naming parts and a card with the word *and*. Have children fold the sentence strips and join them with the *and* card to form one sentence.

Verbs That Tell About the Past	Adding *ed* to Verbs	Changing Verbs That End with *e*
Objective: to recognize verbs that tell about the past	**Objective:** to understand that most verbs that tell about the past end with *ed*	**Objective:** to understand how to write verbs that end with e to tell about the past

Visual

Display a picture from a history book showing people in the past. Have children describe what they see in the picture. Encourage them to use verbs that tell about the past. Write their sentences on the board. Then call on volunteers to circle the verbs that tell about the past.

Write on the board the verbs *plant, water, watch, pack, walk,* and *look.* Challenge small groups to use the group of verbs to write a short story about something that happened in the past. Invite them to illustrate and share their stories.

Demonstrate how to form the past tense of verbs that end with *e* by writing a word such as *save.* Use a second color to cross out the *e* and add *ed.* Write additional present-tense verbs and have volunteers make the same kinds of changes.

Auditory

Have each child make two signs: *Now* and *In the Past.* As you tell a story, have children hold up the *Now* sign when they hear a verb that tells about now. Have them hold up the *In the Past* sign when they hear a verb that tells about the past.

Say a sentence in the present tense, such as, *Today I walk.* Invite a child to restate it, starting the sentence with the word *yesterday.* Repeat with other sentences.

Teach children this couplet:
*You drop the **e***
*Before you add **ed**.*
Remind children to say this to themselves as they change verbs ending in *e* to the past tense.

Kinesthetic

Hand out cards with present- and past-tense verbs. Make sure each verb has two forms (present and past). Have children sort themselves into groups based on the tense of the verbs they are holding. Then ask them to form two facing lines so that matching verb pairs face each other. Have partners read off their present and past pairs and make up two sentences.

Create a game board with a pathway of boxes filled with present-tense verbs. Have partners take turns tossing a number cube and moving that many spaces. They must tell the correct past-tense form of the verb in the box. Keep playing until all players reach the finish line.

Have children work with partners. One child uses letter tiles to form a verb that ends with e. Then the partner removes the final *e* and adds the letter tiles *ed* to form the past tense. Children switch roles and repeat. You may want to write a list of verbs that end in e on the board to help children.

Reteach

	The Verbs *Am*, *Is*, and *Are* **Objective:** to understand that the verbs *am*, *is*, and *are* tell what someone or something is like	Using *Am*, *Is*, and *Are* **Objective:** to recognize that the verbs *am*, *is*, and *are* tell about now	Using *Was* and *Were* **Objective:** to use *was* and *were* correctly
Visual	Display one or more toys. Have children make up sentences using forms of be to tell what the toy is like. Continue with volunteers who wish to describe themselves.	Write the words *am, is,* and *are* on three large paper plates, one verb per plate. Turn over and mix the plates. Then have a volunteer pick a plate and write on the plate a simple sentence using the verb. Mix the plates again and repeat until each child has a turn.	Write a sentence on the board using the verb *was* or *were*. Write two naming parts, one above the other. One naming part should name one and the other more than one. Call on a volunteer to circle the verb and the correct naming part. If children agree, have the child erase the wrong naming part and read the correct sentence. Repeat with other sentences.

Auditory	Invite children to make up poems orally about themselves and someone they know. Have them use the following pattern:
	    I am (Mary).
	    You are (my friend).
	    It is (funny).
	    We are (happy).
		Have children work in groups of three. Give each group a list of questions that can be answered with *is, am,* or *are.* Children take turns asking the questions. The others try to answer using *is, am,* and *are.* Ask questions such as these: *Who is the oldest? Who is 7? Who is hungry? Who is nice? Where are your shoes? What are the red things on your desk?*	Invite pairs of children to make up questions using *was* or *were,* such as *Were the boys outside? Were you here yesterday? Was it Monday yesterday? Who was with you at the bus stop?* Encourage partners to use *was* or *were* in their answers.

Kinesthetic	Make a simple hopscotch board with the words *is, am,* and *are,* each on two squares. Tell children to take turns tossing markers and jumping around the board. They must use the word the marker lands on in a sentence as they jump around the board.	Prepare a cube with the words *is, am,* and *are,* each written on two sides. Children take turns tossing the cube and using the word that lands facing up in a sentence.	Send a child to stand by your desk. Ask, *Where is (child's name)?* Prompt children to answer: *He/she is by the desk.* Call the child back and ask: *Where was he/she? He/She was by the desk.* Repeat by asking individuals or pairs to go to different places, such as by the board, on the chair, under the desk, by the window, at the door.

Reteach

	The Verbs *Has, Have,* and *Had* **objective:** to understand that the verb *have* does not tell about action	Using *Has, Have,* and *Had* **objective:** to use the forms of *have* correctly	Agreement With *Has, Have,* and *Had* **objective:** to use the correct forms of *have*
Visual	Show a picture from a magazine or storybook. Have each child make up a sentence about the picture using the verb *has, have,* or *had.*	Write the letters *h* and *a* next to each other on the board. Call on volunteers to add the letters *s, ve,* or *d* to correctly complete a sentence you start, such as: *Yesterday, I (had) a good time. Today I (have) work to do. Now my friend (has) a new science book.*	On sentence strips, write sentences using the words *has, have,* and *had.* Erase the words *has, have,* and *had.* Read the first sentence. Ask a child to fill in the missing word. Remind him or her to pay attention to the naming part. Repeat with other sentences.
Auditory	Have children close their eyes and listen as you read a paragraph or two with the verbs *has, have,* and *had.* Have children keep their eyes closed and raise their hands each time they hear a form of *have.* Invite them to say it aloud.	Tape record several children as they read sentences with *has, have,* and *had.* Play the recording. Ask if each verb they hear tells about now or the past, and if it tells about one or more than one. Discuss how they know the answer.	Make up a story about something you did earlier. When you get to a place to use *has, have,* or *had,* point to a child in the group to fill in the correct word.
Kinesthetic	Fill foam trays with a small amount of sand. Tell children to write the letter *h* in the sand with their fingers when they hear the word *have, has,* or *had* in a sentence you read.	Make a four-square grid with the words *now/past /one/more than one.* Ask children to toss a beanbag at the grid, and then decide which form of *have* matches the clue in the box they hit. Have them use that form of *have* in a sentence.	Have children take part in a relay race in which they carry a cotton ball in a soup spoon from one place to another. Say Stop periodically and call on children to use *have, has,* or *had* to tell about the race. For example: *Jamie and Kelly have the spoon. Kenny had a spoon before Jamie.*

Reteach

	What Is an Adjective? **Objective:** to understand that adjectives describe nouns	Adjectives That Tell What Kind **Objective:** to use adjectives that describe color and shape	Writing Longer Sentences **Objective:** to use adjectives to make longer sentences
Visual	Invite children to write sentences on chart paper that describe things they see around them. Then ask volunteers to underline the adjectives and draw arrows to link them with the nouns they describe.	Have children take turns holding an object of their choice. Invite volunteers to give adjectives for color and shape that describe each object displayed. Write their adjectives on the board. After children are finished, read the adjectives aloud and ask the class to remember which object it describes.	Write a simple sentence on a large piece of chart paper, such as *I see a bird.* Call on a volunteer to draw the item described. Then have children add adjectives to the sentence and draw the item again. Repeat with other sentences, such as: *He has a hat. We like flowers. This is a tree.*
Auditory	Read simple sentences to children, such as *I like apples, or This is a lion.* Have children take turns adding adjectives to the sentence. Invite the class to repeat the sentence with the adjectives.	Have children list orally all the colors and shapes they see in the classroom. Write the adjectives they say on the board. Then ask children to use the adjectives in sentences. Encourage them to tell about different things that can be described with the adjectives.	Read aloud a simple sentence without adjectives and write it on the board. Then read a list of adjectives and have children choose the ones that best describe the nouns in the sentence. Call on a volunteer to dictate the longer sentence as you write it on the board.
Kinesthetic	Write the following sentence on a sentence strip: *The red balloon popped.* Ask a volunteer to find the adjective and circle it. Repeat with other similar sentences.	Organize the class into small groups. Hand out three cards with adjectives for color and three cards with adjectives for shape to each group. Then have children go on a treasure hunt around the classroom to find things that can be described by the adjectives on the cards.	Make strips with short sentences. Have children rewrite their sentence on another strip using an appropriate adjective. Ask children to share their sentence strips and show what adjective they used.

Reteach

	Words That Tell About the Senses	Adjectives for Taste, Smell, Feel and Sound	Using Synonyms in Writing
	Objective: to note that some adjectives describe taste, smell, feel, and sound	**Objective:** to use adjectives for taste, smell, feel, and sound	**Objective:** to identify and use adjectives that are synonyms
Visual	Gather together several objects with different texture, sound, smell, and taste. Display them for children to see. Have a volunteer describe one of the objects using an adjective that tells about the senses. Challenge the other children to name the object that the first child describes. Repeat until all objects are described.	Write adjectives for taste, smell, feel, and sound on the board. Have children choose one adjective and draw an example of something that word describes. Have children trade papers with partners. Ask partners to look at the picture and lable the correct adjective.	Show a picture. Have a volunteer describe an object in the picture. Write the sentence on the board. Challenge the other children to describe the same object using a synonym for the first adjective. Write the synonyms they say on the board. Discuss with children which adjective is more exact and why.
Auditory	Ask children to answer the following questions that describe objects: How does a cookie taste? How does an orange smell? How does a blanket feel? How does a train sound? Write the adjectives on the board. Challenge children to use those adjectives in other sentences.	Tell a "What am I?" riddle. Give two different clues, each using an adjective for taste, smell, feel or sound. The child who solves the riddle correctly can make up another riddle for the class, such as *I am creamy and cold. What am I? (ice-cream)*	Tell an adjective to children. Challenge them to call out synonyms for the adjective they heard. Repeat the procedure with several adjectives.
Kinesthetic	Have each child choose an object and bring it up for all to see. Ask the child to point to his/her mouth, ear, nose, or hand. Have a volunteer use an adjective that tells about the sense suggested to describe the object.	Provide each child with a card that has an adjective for the senses on it. Write sentences on chart paper that are missing adjectives. Read the sentences and have children come up and tape their cards in the correct place. Repeat until all sentences are completed.	Prepare a set of cards with at least 10 pairs of synonyms. Have children play "Synonym Concentration." The player with the most pairs at the end of the game wins.

Reteach

	Words for Size and Number **Objective:** to understand that adjectives can tell about size and number	Adjectives That Tell How Many **Objective:** to use adjectives that tell how many	Using a and an **Objective:** to understand when to use a and an
Visual	Display a catalog picture that has several objects of varying size and number in it. Ask children to choose one thing they see in the picture and describe it, using an adjective for size or number. Repeat with other things in the picture.	Lay six pencils out in a row. Ask children to describe the pencils using an adjective that tells how many. Challenge them to say a simple sentence such as, There are six pencils. Repeat, adding or removing pencils. Repeat with other classroom objects.	Write several nouns on the chalkboard including words that begin with vowels, such as igloo, eraser, apple. Ask volunteers to come up to the board, underline the first letter of the noun, and then write a or an in front of the noun listed.
Auditory	Tell children you will give two clues to describe an object – one for size and one for how many. For example, What looks like a small bicycle and has three wheels? (tricycle) Make up other riddles for children to answer. Challenge children to think of their own riddles.	Tell children to listen as you ask questions. Tell them that the answers all have adjectives that tell how many. Children can volunteer to answer by raising their hands. Ask questions such as these: * How many days in a week? * How many months in a year? * How many boys in class? Girls? Adults? * How old are you?	Say a noun twice, first with *a* in front of it and then with *an*, such as a elephant and an elephant. Challenge children to identify which form is correct and tell why. Repeat with several nouns.
Kinesthetic	Create several groups of classroom objects around the room such as books or pencils. Describe one of the groups. Have a volunteer name it. If the volunteer is correct, have her choose another group describing it using a clue about size or number.	Provide children with a variety of classroom objects they can use as manipulatives, such as pencils or books. Tell children to sort the objects into groups. Have children move around the room to tell how many items are in each group.	Give each child a pair of cards, one with a and one with an. List three nouns that begin with a vowel and three nouns that begin with a consonant on the chalkboard. Point to the first noun. Ask children to hold up the correct card. Repeat with other nouns.

Reteach

	Words That Compare	Adding er and est	Writing to Compare
	Objective: to understand that adjectives can be used to compare	**Objective:** to add er and est to adjectives to compare two or more things	**Objective:** to recognize that using adjectives that compare helps make writing better
Visual	Display a newspaper and a magazine. Have children discuss how they are alike and different. Encourage children to use words that compare. List all words that compare on the chalkboard. Repeat with other objects.	Have three children of various heights stand next to each other in front of the class. Write the words tall, taller, and tallest on the chalkboard behind them. Challenge the other children to write sentences to describe the height of each child.	Show children pictures of two different cars. Write a simple sentence on the board to describe one car. Then have a volunteer add a sentence, comparing one car to the other. Repeat with more comparisons.
Auditory	Tell children you are thinking of a basketball and a football. Invite children to make comparisons, using adjectives you give them, such as round (The basketball is rounder.)	Tell children to hold up either two or three fingers to identify if you are comparing two or more than two things. You may want to say sentences such as: My chair is larger than Danny's chair. My desk is the biggest. Repeat with other items to compare.	Give each child two cards – one with er on it and another with est written on it. Say a sentence that uses an adjective that ends in er. Tell children to hold up the card that shows the ending of the comparing word you used in the sentence. Repeat this with several sentences using either words that end in er or est.
Kinesthetic	Gather together and display several different objects. Have each child choose two of the objects to take to his or her desk. Allow them time to compare the two objects. Call on each child to share how the objects are different.	In a large paper sack place the following items: ruler, chalkboard eraser, tissue, ball, and a paper clip. Have volunteers reach into the bag. Ask: • Which object is the smallest? • Which object is the longest? • Pick out two objects. Which is heavier? Repeat after adding more objects to the bag.	Give pairs or small groups a set of cards with three comparison words, such as small, smaller, and smallest. Give each group a different set of adjectives. Ask children to choose three things to compare. Then tape the correct cards onto the three objects. Allow time for children to share.

Reteach

	The Verbs *Come, Run,* and *Give* **Objective:** to understand that the verbs *come, run,* and *give* tell about now	Using *Come, Run,* and *Give* **Objective:** to use the correct forms of *come, run,* and *give*	Joining Sentences **Objective:** to use *and* to join whole sentences
Visual	Display pictures showing the verbs *come, run,* and *give.* Have small groups make charts with three columns labeled *come, run,* and *give.* Invite children to write sentences about the pictures they see in the chart under appropriate headings.	Call on volunteers to change past-tense sentences into sentences that tell about now. Children can erase the letter *a* in the verbs and replace it with *u* (run), *i* (give), or *o* (come). Remind them to add s if the verb tells about one.	Write two simple sentences on chart paper. Below it, join the sentences but leave out the capital letter, the word *and,* the lowercase letter of the second sentence, and the comma before *and.* Ask children to finish the sentence by filling in the missing items. Repeat with other sentences.
Auditory	Have children give a thumbs up or down when they hear sentences using *come, give,* and *run.* For instance, first say "I give a test." Then say, "I gives a test." Discuss with children why the verb is incorrect. Repeat the procedure with the verbs *come* and *run.*	Tell children you will use a clue word such as yesterday or today in a sentence with one of the verbs *come, run,* or *give.* If the sentence tells about now, have children point their finger on their desk. If the sentence tells about the past, have children point their finger over their shoulders. Repeat with several sentences.	Say two simple sentences about a favorite story. Make sure the sentences tell about the same thing. Ask children to join the two sentences using a comma and the word *and.* Repeat with several sentences. Then switch roles and challenge children to come up with the sentences. You join the sentences with a comma and the word *and.*
Kinesthetic	Have one child run in place. Ask the children to tell what is happening. (*Joe runs.*) Write the verb *runs* on the board. Then instruct two children to run in place. Write what the children see. (*The girls run.*) Repeat the activity using the verbs *comes, come, gives,* and *give.*	Write sentences on chart paper using *come, came, run, ran, give,* and *gave.* Leave out the vowels such as c_me, r_n, g_ve. Give each child a card with *o, a, u,* or *i* on it. Have children tape the letter in the correct space. Read the sentences to make sure they are correct.	Write pairs of sentences on strips, one sentence per strip. Shuffle the strips, and hand them out to children. Tell children to find a partner that has a similar sentence. After they have paired up, have children link arms and say aloud their combined sentences.

Reteach

	The Verbs *Go*, *Do*, and *See* **Objective:** to recognize the correct forms of the verbs *go*, *do*, and *see*	Using *Go*, *Do*, and *See* **Objective:** to use the correct forms of *go*, *do*, and *see* to tell about now and about the past	Commas in Place Names and Dates **Objective:** to add commas in place names and dates correctly
Visual	Show a picture of a school bus. Invite children to use all the forms of *go*, *do*, and *see* to make sentences about the picture. Write the sentences on the board. Then have volunteers circle the verbs that tell about now, and underline the verbs that tell about the past.	Use a large sheet of chart paper. Draw a chart with four columns: now/one, now/more than one, past/one, past/more than one. Add 3 rows labeled: *go*, *do*, *see*. Have children fill in a chart with all the forms of the verbs *go*, *do*, and *see*.	Show children actual addresses from mailings, letters, and envelopes. Have children circle the commas in the place names and dates. Ask them to add commas in red if some are missing.
Auditory	Make up or say a rhyme with children such as the following: *I go to my bunk.* *I see a skunk.* *I do a jump!* After children have memorized it, have them say it again, this time changing it so that each verb tells about the past. You may want to repeat with other rhymes.	Use all nine verbs (*go, goes, went, do, does, did, see, sees, saw*) in sentences. If you use the verb correctly, have children show thumbs up. If you use the verb incorrectly, have children show thumbs down. If a sentence is thumbs down, have a volunteer repeat the sentence using the correct verb.	Tell children you are going to say a place name (city and state) and a date. Remind them that when you take a pause in speaking, it means a comma is there. Challenge children to repeat the phrase, saying "comma" where one would be used. Repeat with several place names and dates.
Kinesthetic	Have pairs of children play "*go, do, see*" tic-tac-toe on large sheets of chart paper. Tell pairs of children to use different forms of the same verb to play. For example, go and went, or do and did instead of "x" and "o."	Write the words "now" and "past" next to each other in the center of chart paper. All around the two words in no particular order, write the verbs *go, goes, went, do, does, did, see, sees,* and *saw*. Challenge children to draw a line or tape a piece of string from each verb to the word in the center.	Say place names and dates to children. Each time you reach a comma, pause and have children skywrite a comma. Repeat, this time calling on volunteers to say their dates of birth, and where they live.

Reteach

	What Is a Helping Verb? **Objective:** to identify helping verbs	Using *Has, Have,* and *Had* **Objective:** to use *has, have,* and *had* to help show past actions	Keeping to One Main Idea **Objective:** to identify sentences that do not belong to one paragraph
Visual	Write the sentence below on the board. Have children read it, circle the helping verb, and draw an arrow between the helping verb and the main verb. *Kyle has asked for a sandwich and milk.*	Write a sentence on chart paper leaving out the helping verb. Ask a volunteer to decide which helping verb (*has, have,* or *had*) belongs in the sentence. Repeat by writing other sentences.	Write a paragraph on the chalkboard. Include a sentence that does not belong. Ask a volunteer to come up and circle the sentence that tells the main idea. Ask another child to draw a line through the sentence that does not belong.
Auditory	Give children a main verb form, such as *painted* or *helped.* Challenge them to make up sentences using the verb and a form of *have.* Repeat with other main verb forms.	Read sentences with *have,* as a helping verb and as a simple verb. Have children repeat a sentence only if *have* is used as a helping verb. You may want to use sentences such as these: *Mark has helped Tanya.* *This jacket has big buttons.* *You had talked to her before.* *We have danced together.* *You have a pet dog.*	Read a paragraph to the children that includes a main idea statement and one sentence that does not belong. Pause after each sentence. Ask children to say "main idea," after the main idea statement, "yes" if the sentence belongs to the paragraph, and "no" if the sentence doesn't belong.
Kinesthetic	Provide each child with word cards that can form sentences using forms of the helping verb *have.* Mix the cards. First have children sort the cards into groups: main verb, helping verb, telling part, naming part. Then have them arrange the cards to form correct sentences.	Tell children to go on a helping verb treasure hunt. Provide children with old newspapers and magazines. Invite them to cut out all helping verbs and main verbs they find. Then have them tape the verbs on tag board and add cut-out words to make up sentences.	Write each sentence from a paragraph on a sentence strip. Include a sentence that does not belong. Have children put the sentences in order and leave out the sentence strip that should not be in the paragraph.

Reteach

	What Is an Adverb? **Objective:** to recognize adverbs	Using Adverbs **Objective:** to understand that adverbs tell more about verbs	Writing with Adverbs **Objective:** to use adverbs in writing
Visual	Write the sentences below on the board. Call on volunteers to circle an appropriate adverb. Then have children write the complete sentence. *I sing (loudly/softly).* *We dance (well/badly).* *The bear runs (fast/slowly).*	Write a sentence on chart paper that has an adverb in it. Ask a volunteer to circle the adverb and then tell whether the adverb answers *how, when,* or *where.* Invite children to list other adverbs that answer the question and write them on the board.	Create a chart with the headers *how, when,* and *where.* Have children look through story books to find adverbs and write them in the chart under the correct headings.
Auditory	Say a simple sentence that uses an adverb, such as *Jennie sings softly.* Challenge children to call out the adverb in the sentence. Repeat with other sentences.	Ask questions using the words *how, when,* and *where.* Call on volunteers to answer the questions with adverbs. Then review with children that adverbs tell *how, when,* and *where* about an action. You may want to ask the following questions: *How does the bell ring? (Loudly) Where is the ocean? (far from here)*	Read a sentence aloud that does not have an adverb in it. Challenge children to tell more by adding an adverb to the sentence. Accept all reasonable answers. Repeat with other sentences.
Kinesthetic	Provide each child with a card that has a verb and an adverb on it. Be sure the children can act out each action. Have a volunteer act out what is on the card. The other children guess the adverb. Repeat until all children have had a turn.	Organize the class in three groups: *how, when,* and *where.* Say sentences that include adverbs. Each time they hear an adverb, children from the appropriate group raise their hands. Ask one child from that group to use the adverb in a sentence. Keep playing until all children have gone.	Write several sentences alternating adverbs that tell *how, where,* or *when* on sentence strips. Place them around the room. Ask a volunteer to stand next to a sentence that has an adverb that answers *how.* Repeat with *when* and *where.*

Reteach

	Nouns and Pronouns Together **Objective:** to understand that pronouns can take the place of nouns	Noun-Pronoun Agreement **Objective:** to use pronouns correctly	Word Order for Pronouns **Objective:** to use the correct word order with nouns and pronouns
Visual	Write several sentences on the board, leaving out the naming part. Have children list pronouns that could be used as naming parts for each sentence. Write them on the board.	Display a picture or poster with well-known people or characters. First have children name the people and any objects they see. List their responses on the chalkboard. Then ask children to erase each noun and write the pronoun that can replace it.	Have each child write two sentences on a piece of paper, one using *I,* and one using *me.* Tell children to erase the pronouns. Then have children trade sentences with a partner and fill in the blanks. Children should trade sentences again and check for the correct pronouns.
Auditory	Talk about someone the class knows. Say one sentence at a time. After each sentence, ask a volunteer to repeat the sentence, replacing the noun of the person with the correct pronoun. For example, *Mrs. Jones is our school nurse. She is our school nurse.*	Say two sentences—the first using a noun and the second using a pronoun. If the noun and pronoun agree, have children say, "agree." If the noun and pronoun do not agree, have children say, "do not agree." Call on a volunteer to correct the noun/pronoun agreement.	Chant the following rhyme with children several times: *I like Rudy,* *Rudy likes me.* *Rudy and I like Lucy.* *Lucy likes Rudy and me.* Then remind children how to write pronouns and nouns together. Challenge children to make up new rhymes orally, based on the one above.
Kinesthetic	Write several sentences on chart paper with nouns as naming parts. Give each child a card with a pronoun on it. Read the first sentence. Have the child with the corresponding pronoun tape it over the noun in the sentence. Repeat until all children have had a turn.	Write four pairs of sentences on sentence strips. The sentences should be related to each other. The first sentence uses a noun. The second sentence uses a pronoun. Give the children the sentence strips. Challenge them to pair up the sentences.	Provide children with magnetic letters *I, m,* and *e.* Write a sentence, omitting the pronouns *I* or *me.* Have children volunteer to fill in the missing pronoun by placing the appropriate letters. The child then erases and writes another sentence to be completed by a volunteer.

Reteach

	Subject-Verb Agreement **Objective:** to understand that a verb agrees with the naming part	Changing *y* to *i* **Objective:** to use and write correctly verbs that end in *y*	Writing Contractions **Objective:** to understand how and when to use contractions
Visual	Show children a picture with several groups of people. Ask children to tell what they see. Write down their sentences. Call on volunteers to circle and explain the endings of the verbs.	Write a sentence on the board, such as *The girls try.* Erase the s at the end of the word *girls.* Discuss how to change the verb to agree with the naming part. Ask a volunteer to erase the *y* and write *i* before adding *es.* Repeat with other verbs that end in *y.*	On the board, write a list of pairs of words that can become contractions. Then have small groups write out all the contractions. The first group to finish wins. Review all the contractions with children, and have them write out a rule on chart paper to display in the classroom.
Auditory	Give children several naming parts and verbs orally. Have them combine the two in simple sentences. Tell children to stress the final s of verbs when the naming part tells about one. You may want to use the following words: *the cat - meow, two dogs - bark, one dinosaur - run, the lions - roar.*	Have children list orally verbs that end with a consonant plus *y.* Invite them to make up a chant about how to change these verbs. Have them tell the chant before using the verbs they listed in simple sentences with naming parts that name one.	Say two words that can become a contraction, such as *do not.* Have children say the contraction. Review with them that an apostrophe takes the place of missing letters. Challenge children to tell which letters are not in a contraction that are in the original two words.
Kinesthetic	Organize the class into small groups. In front of each group, place a large paper *1* and a large paper *2.* Then read aloud short sentences. Have children move next to the appropriate paper number to tell if the naming part tells about one or more than one.	Write the following verbs on individual index cards: *study, stay, carry, copy, buy, try, spy, cry, play, fly, dry, enjoy.* Have a child choose a card. Ask the child to use the verb with a naming part that tells about one and spell it. Repeat until each child has a turn.	Write two words that can form a contraction, using magnetic letters such as: *are not.* Call on a volunteer to shuffle and remove letters to write a contraction, adding an apostrophe. Repeat with other words, such as *should not, has not, did not, could not, is not.*

Reteach

	Fixing "And Then" Sentences **Objective:** to use time-order words to avoid "and then" sentences	Writing Longer Sentences **Objective:** to combine sentences with the same naming or telling parts	Using a Series Comma **Objective:** to correctly punctuate lists of three or more nouns, verbs, or adjectives in sentences
Visual	Write a run-on sentence on the board. Have children read the sentence. Ask them to erase and replace the "and then" phrases with time-order words. Remind children to use proper punctuation and capital letters for new sentences. Repeat with other "and then" sentences.	Display a picture showing several people doing the same thing. Have children share what they see. Write several small sentences on chart paper. Have a volunteer write a long sentence, combining two shorter ones. Repeat with other items from the picture.	Show children a plant and ask them to describe it. List children's adjectives on the board without punctuation or the word and. Then invite children to write a sentence about the plant, adding commas in the list of adjectives.
Auditory	Tell children a long sentence that uses the phrase "and then" three times. Have children list time-order words they can use to shorten the sentence. Have them use the time-order words to shorten the long sentence.	Say two short sentences with the same verbs, but with different naming parts. Challenge children to make a longer sentence by combining the naming parts. Repeat with other short sentences, some with the same telling parts and some with the same naming parts.	Tell children a riddle, such as *What honks, steers, and drives? (a car)* Repeat the riddle, pausing where a comma would be. Have children say "comma" at the appropriate place. Then invite children to solve the riddle. Repeat with other riddles.
Kinesthetic	Write several "and then" sentences on sentence strips. Give each child a set of cards with time-order words on them. Have children tape the cards in the correct place to make smaller sentences. Remind children to be sure they have a capital letter and correct punctuation.	Give small groups of children sets of cards that can make two short sentences. Then give children a second set of cards that can make a longer sentence. Have children arrange the cards so the longer sentence is below the shorter sentences.	Write a sentence that lists several nouns without commas on chart paper. Provide children with cards that have commas on them. Ask children to tape the commas where they belong in the sentence. Repeat with other sentences.

Reteach

	Spelling Words That Sound Alike **Objective:** to note words that sound alike but have different spellings	Using *There*, *Their*, and *They're* **Objective:** to note that some words sound alike and have different meanings	Using *To*, *Too*, and *Two* **Objective:** to distinguish between the words *to*, *too*, and *two*
Visual	Write *they're*, *there*, and *their* on the board. Invite children to discuss what is different about the spellings. Point out that the spelling of the word is directly related to the meaning of the word. Challenge groups of children to write sentences using all three words.	Make a two-column chart with the headers *word* and *meaning*. Have children fill it in with the words *there*, *their*, and *they're* and include example sentences.	Have small groups of children write three sentences, with *to*, *too*, and *two*. Have children display their sentences, then fill in a chart on the board showing the words *to*, *too*, and *two*, their meanings, and example sentences.
Auditory	Tell children to listen carefully as you read aloud three sentences with *there*, *they're*, and *their*. Have children tell which words sound the same. Then repeat each sentence, asking them to spell the troublesome word. How do they know its correct spelling?	Have children identify the words *their*, *there*, and *they're* they hear in sentences by calling out the word's meaning of "belonging," "place," or "contraction." Say sentences such as: *I would like to go there. Their drawings are colorful. They're very tired. Who was there?*	Tell the children the rhyme: *Two boys go to the igloo.* *Two girls go to the igloo, too.* Repeat each line, asking children to spell out the troublesome words they hear and discuss their meanings. Invite children to make up other rhymes using *to*, *too*, and *two*.
Kinesthetic	Write three sentences on chart paper. Leave out the words *there*, *their*, and *they're*. Give children cards with the spelling words on them. Have them tape the cards in the correct spaces.	Write several sentences using *their*, *there*, and *they're* on pieces of paper. Place the papers around the room. Call out the meaning of one of the words. Children stand next to one of the sentences that uses the word correctly.	Write *to*, *too*, and *two* on pieces of paper. Place the papers around the room. Call out the meaning of one of the words. Have children go stand next to the matching word. Invite them to use it in a sentence about themselves.

Make a Turtle Box

You need:
- clay
- shoebox with lid
- paints
- crayons or markers

1. Use a shoebox to make the box where the turtle in the poem lives. Paint and draw pictures on the outside and the inside of the box.

2. Use clay to make the things and animals from the poem.

3. Write the poem on the shoebox. Use your clay models to act it out.

The Little Turtle
There was a Little turtle.
He lived in a box.

©Harcourt

Make a Sentence Umbrella

You need:

- colored paper
- old magazines
- scissors, glue
- crayons or markers
- cardboard strip
- tape

1. Cut out a large shape of an umbrella.

2. Find pictures of things you use or see when it rains. Glue them on your umbrella.

3. Write a sentence by each picture.

4. Tape your umbrella to a cardboard handle and display it.

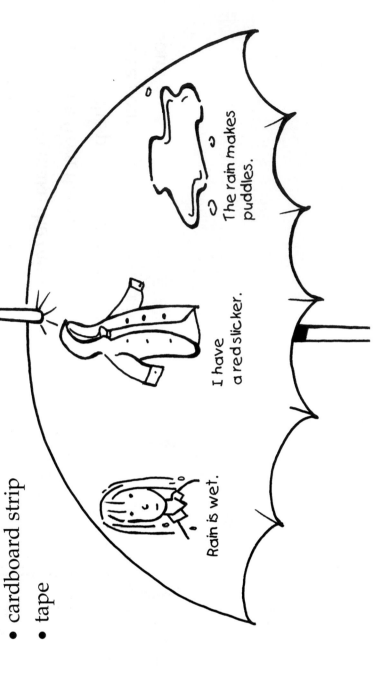

The rain makes puddles.

I have a red slicker.

Rain is wet.

©Harcourt

Make a City Quilt

You need:
- large index cards
- large piece of felt or material
- glue

1. Choose a place you like in your city.

2. Write the name of the place on an index card. Write a question about it. Write the answer.

3. You can also draw a picture of the place.

4. Glue your card onto the class quilt.

The Park
Who takes care of the park?
The rangers take care of the park.

My Street
How is my street? It is sunny and it has many trees.

The Toy Store
Where is the toy store?
It is on Elm Street.

©Harcourt

Make a Robot

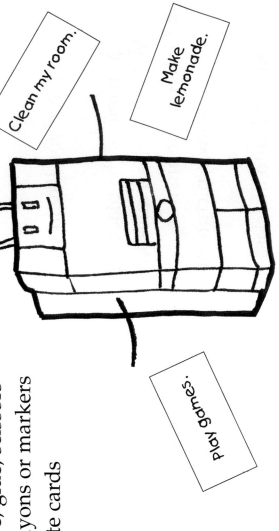

Clean my room.

Make lemonade.

Play games.

You need:

- box
- foil, pipe cleaners, or other materials
- tape, glue, scissors
- crayons or markers
- note cards

1. Draw a robot on a box.
2. Use foil, pipe cleaners, and other things to finish your robot. You can add arms, eyes, and feet.
3. Write commands on note cards to tell what you would like your robot to do.
4. Put the cards inside your robot.
5. Take turns with classmates. Pretend to be a robot and act out a command.

©Harcourt

Make a House of Nouns

You need:
- paper
- crayons or markers
- scissors

1. Draw your house. Show the different rooms.
2. Label the rooms. Write nouns to name the people and things in each room. You can also add pictures.
3. Cut out your house. Write your name on it. Share your house with classmates.

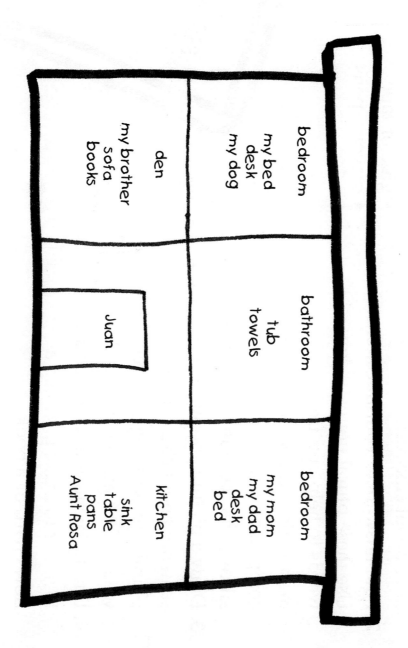

bedroom
my bed
desk
my dog

bathroom
tub
towels

bedroom
my mom
my dad
desk
bed

den
my brother
sofa
books

Juan

kitchen
sink
table
pans
Aunt Rosa

©Harcourt

Find Out About Silkworms

You need:
- paper
- glue or tape
- crayons, pens

1. Write a list of questions you have about silkworms.

2. Find answers to your questions. Use these plural nouns as key words to help you find information in books or using a computer.
   silkworms   cocoons   threads

3. Draw a picture and write a sentence about each of the plural nouns in Step 2 to tell what information you found.

4. Put the pictures and sentences together to make a poster, a flow chart, or a book.

©Harcourt

Make a Holiday Chart

1. Set up your chart like the one here. Write the name of the month at the top.
2. Use a reference book to find out which holidays happen during this month.
3. Write the name and the date of each holiday. Draw a picture if you want.

You need:
- paper
- markers

OCTOBER	DATE
Columbus Day	12

©Harcourt

Make a Pronoun Wheel

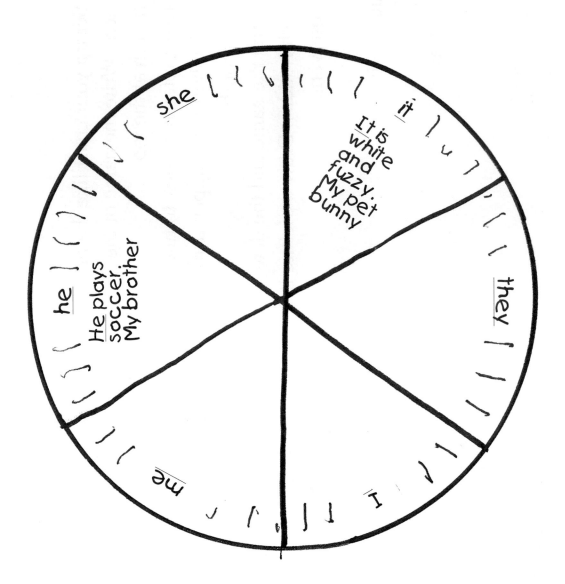

You need:
- paper plate
- crayons or markers

1. Fold a paper plate in half. Fold two more times to make six parts.

2. Write a pronoun in each part.

3. Use the pronoun to write a sentence about a person, an animal, or a thing you like. Write the name the pronoun replaces, too. You can draw a picture if you want.

©Harcourt

Make an Animal Mask

Materials:
- paper plate
- crayons or markers
- paper scraps
- glue

1. Choose an animal from the poem.
2. Draw the animal's face.
3. Add eyes, ears, and other details.
4. Use your mask to act out the poem.

©Harcourt

Yesterday

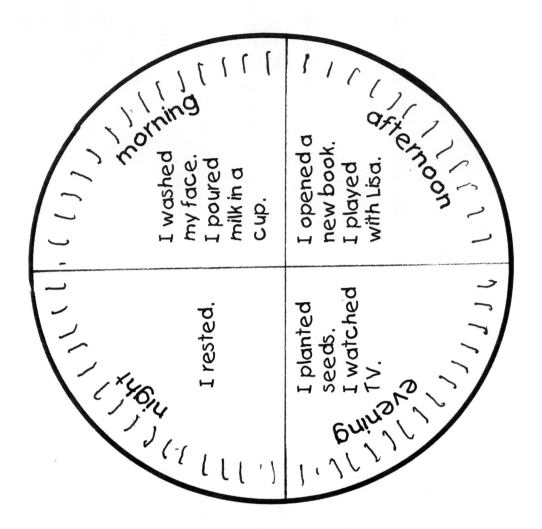

You need:
- paper plate
- crayons or markers

1. Draw lines to make four parts on a paper plate.
2. Write a word in each part: *morning, afternoon, evening,* and *night.*
3. In each part, write things you did yesterday at that time.

©Harcourt

Then and Now

You need:
- large piece of paper
- crayons or markers
- glue

1. Fold a large sheet of paper in half.

2. Draw or glue a picture of yourself as a younger child on one side.

3. Draw or glue a picture of yourself as you are today on the other side.

4. Write sentences about each picture.

I was very young.
I was two years old.
My best friends were Sally and Luis.

I am in second grade.
I am a good reader.
My friends are in the same class.

©Harcourt

Make Your Classroom

My Classroom Last Year

Aa Bb Cc

We had blocks. My teacher had big books. I had a blue chair.

You need:

- large piece of paper
- scissors
- crayons or markers

1. Use a large sheet of paper.
2. Label one side "My Classroom Now." Label the other side "My Classroom Last Year." Draw each classroom.
3. Write sentences to tell what you have or what you had in each classroom.

©Harcourt

Make a Book of Leaves

You need:
- leaves
- paper
- glue
- crayons or markers
- yarn and hole punch

1. Find different kinds of leaves.
2. Glue each leaf on a sheet of paper. Write adjectives that tell about its shape and color.
3. Punch holes in the pages.
4. Make a cover. Use yarn to put together your book.

©Harcourt

Pizza Pie

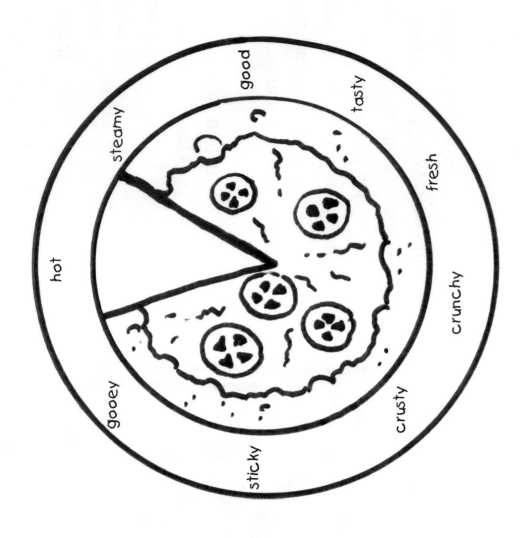

You need:
- 1 small paper plate
- 1 large paper plate
- paint, felt, strings, or other materials
- tape, glue, scissors
- crayons or markers

1. Glue or draw things in a small paper plate to make a pizza. You can use string to make cheese or red felt circles to make tomato slices.

2. Glue your pizza onto a larger paper plate.

3. Write adjectives around the plate to tell what the pizza tastes, smells, and feels like.

©Harcourt

Make a Creature

You need:
- clay
- buttons, pipe cleaners, toothpicks, feathers, fake fur, felt

1. Think of a make-believe creature. Use clay to make its body.
2. Use different things to make the creature's legs, arms, wings, or tail.
3. Add or paint details, such as eyes, teeth, feathers, or fur.
4. Write and act out a new rhyme like "The Cow." Use words to tell about your creature's size, number of legs, and so on.

©Harcourt

Season Pennant

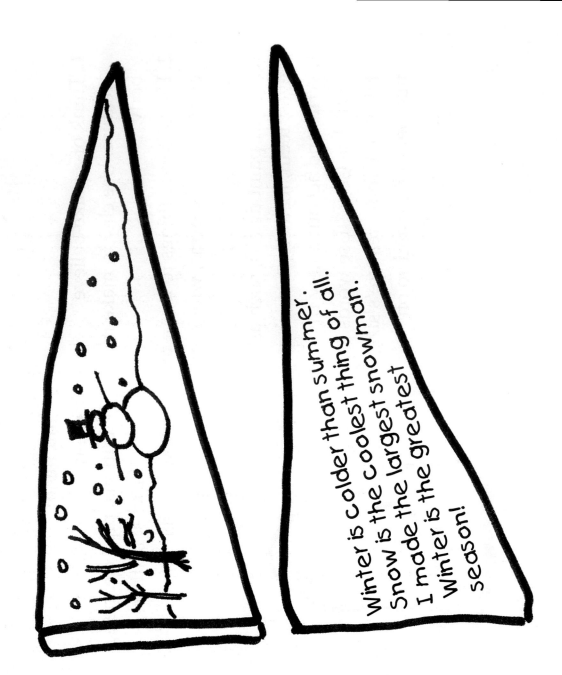

Winter is colder than summer.
Winter is the coolest thing of all.
Snow is the largest snowman.
I made the largest
Winter is the greatest
season!

You need:
- paper
- felt, cotton balls, or other materials
- tape, glue, scissors
- crayons or markers

1. Cut out a large triangle.
2. On one side, draw a picture that shows your favorite season. You can also glue on pieces of felt, cotton, or other things.
3. On the other side, write sentences about the season. Use adjectives that compare.

©Harcourt

Make a Map

You need:
- large sheet of paper
- crayons or markers

1. Think about a special place you like. Make a map. Draw your special place and your school.
2. Draw and label streets and other places along the way.
3. Add arrows to show which way to go.
4. Write sentences about your special place. Use the verbs *come, run,* and *give* in your sentences. Share your work.

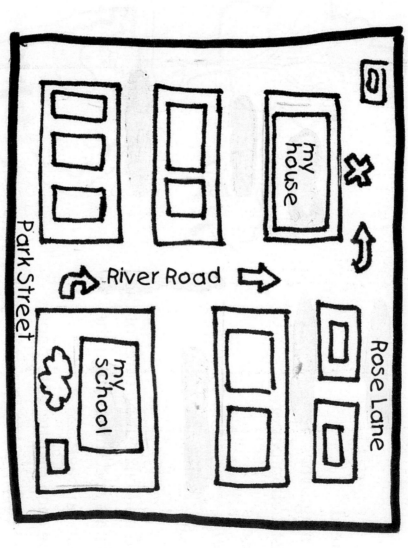

My room is my special place.
My sister, my brother, and my mom come there, too.
I run to my room when I am sad. Then I feel better.
I give books to my sister when we are in my room.

©Harcourt

Make Puppets

You need:
- old magazines
- construction paper
- scissors
- glue
- craft sticks

1. Find and cut out pictures of the animals and things from the poem on page 328.
2. Glue each picture onto paper.
3. Glue each picture to a craft stick to make a puppet.
4. Use your puppets to act out the poem.

©Harcourt

Make a Puppet

You need:
- constrution paper
- craft stick
- tape, glue, scissors
- crayons or markers

1. Choose a character from the play.
2. Draw your character on paper. Cut it out. Then add eyes, a mouth, and other details.
3. Tape your character to a craft stick.
4. Use your puppet to act out the play.

©Harcourt

Make a Kite

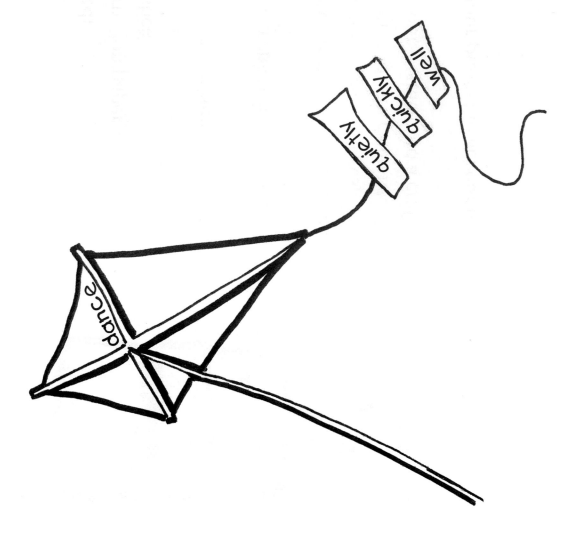

You need:
- paper
- string
- scissors, tape
- crayons or markers

1. Cut out a large kite shape. Tape a string to one end.

2. Cut out strips of paper and tape them to the string.

3. On the kite, write an action verb from page 356.

4. On the strips, write all the adverbs you can think of that tell about the action verb.

©Harcourt

Make an Animal Mobile

You need:
- paper
- crayons or markers
- scissors
- yarn
- coat hanger

1. Draw and label three animals you like. Cut them out.
2. On the back of each picture, write one or two sentences about the animal. Use pronouns.
3. Use yarn to attach each picture to a hanger to make a mobile.

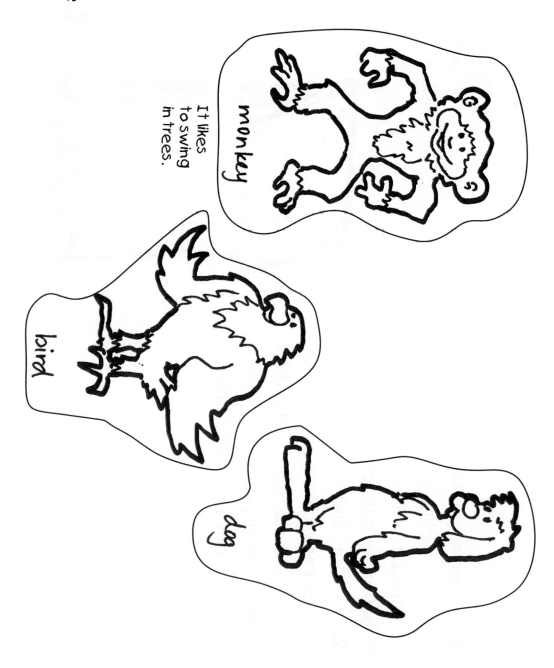

monkey

It likes to swing in trees.

bird

dog

©Harcourt

Make Paper Bag Animals

You need:
- paper lunch bag
- scissors
- glue
- construction paper
- yarn, feathers, trims
- markers or crayons

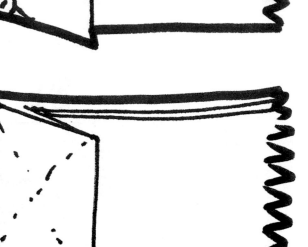

1. Choose an animal from the poem on page 400 or a new animal. Draw its head on the bottom of a lunch bag.

2. Cut, glue, and draw to make eyes, ears, a nose, and a mouth.

3. Use your puppet to act out the poem. To make your puppet "sing," put your hand inside the bag.

©Harcourt

Make a Comic Strip

You need:

- large sheet of paper
- markers or crayons
- glue
- old magazines or comic books

1. Fold a large sheet of drawing paper in half. Then fold it in half again the other way to make four frames.

2. Draw or glue two characters in each frame. Add speech balloons.

3. Write what each character says. Use time-order words to write about the things they did.

©Harcourt

Make a Story Ladder

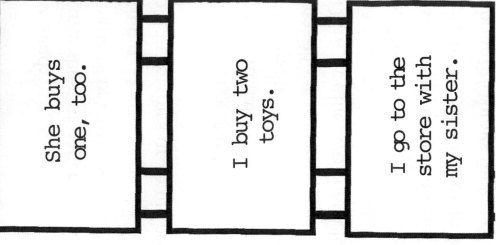

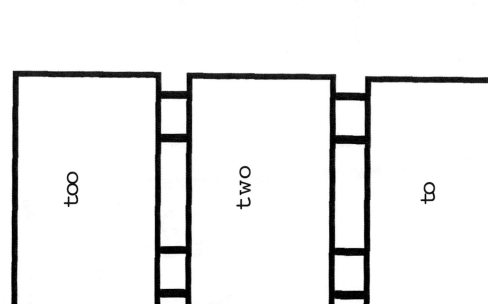

You need:
- 3 index cards
- 2 long cardboard strips
- glue
- markers or crayons

1. Glue three index cards to two cardboard strips to make a ladder.

2. Write one troublesome word on each card.

3. Write a story on the back of the cards. Use the troublesome words. Start your story at the bottom of the ladder. You can add pictures if you want.

©Harcourt

Listening, Speaking, and Viewing Checklist

Child _____ Teacher _____ Grade _____

	Date ____	Date ____	Date ____	Date ____	Date ____	Date ____
LISTENING						
Listens for a purpose						
Listens and responds to a variety of texts						
Listens and responds to peers in small groups; participates in cooperative groups						
Asks questions to clarify a message or explore a topic						
Takes notes, when appropriate, from sources such as classroom guests						
Follows directions						
SPEAKING						
Chooses spoken language appropriate to purpose						
Chooses spoken language appropriate to audience						
Speaks clearly						
Speaks directly to the audience						
Uses appropriate volume and rate						
Uses nonverbal communication effectively						
Asks and answers relevant questions and makes contributions to group discussions						
Demonstrates control of grammar when speaking						
Uses vocabulary to describe clearly ideas, feelings, and experiences						
Participates in retellings, summaries, rhymes, dramatizations						
Gives directions						
Supports spoken messages using props						
Clarifies spoken messages						
VIEWING						
Interprets information from maps, charts, diagrams, photos, and graphs						
Discusses information obtained from illustrations, photos, visuals, media						

Comments:

Key:

N = Not Observed

O = Observed Occasionally

R = Observed Regularly

© Harcourt

Handwriting and Technology Checklist

Child _____ Teacher _____ Grade _____

	Date	Date	Date	Date	Date	Date
HANDWRITING						
Uses correct letter and word spacing						
Uses correct letter formation						
Leaves margins						
Indents paragraphs						
Uses capital and lowercase letters appropriately						
Uses correct posture						
Positions paper and pencil effectively						
TECHNOLOGY						
Uses available technology to support aspects of writing, including word processing						
Uses available technology for spell-checking						
Uses available technology for printing						
Uses technology to compile notes into outlines, reports, summaries, or other written efforts						

Comments:

Key:

N = Not Observed

O = Observed Occasionally

R = Observed Regularly

© Harcourt

Writing Conference Checklist

Child _____ Teacher _____ Grade _____

	Date	Date	Date	Date	Date	Date
CONTENT AND ORGANIZATION						
Selects and uses writing processes for self-initiated and assigned writing						
Uses personal experiences as well as drawing and making lists as a source of writing ideas						
Writes each time for a purpose and an audience						
Constructs several sentences on one topic in a logical order						
Composes sentences with interesting, elaborated subjects						
Joins related sentences into paragraphs						
Stays on topic and sequences ideas						
Shows a beginning, middle, and end in narrative writing						
Uses details in narrative and informational writing						
Uses appropriate word choice						
Revises, edits, and proofreads own work						
Publishes compositions in a variety of ways						
CONVENTIONS AND MECHANICS						
Writes with appropriate word and sentence spacing						
Composes complete sentences						
Uses capitalization and punctuation correctly						
Makes few errors in usage						
Uses penmanship to make messages readable						
SPELLING						
Uses resources to find correct spellings, synonyms, and replacement words						
Uses conventional spelling most of the time						

Comments:

Key:

N = Not Observed

O = Observed Occasionally

R = Observed Regularly

Grammar-in-Writing Checklist

Child _____ Teacher _____ Grade _____

	Date	Date	Date	Date	Date	Date
GRAMMAR AND USAGE						
Uses singular and plural forms of regular nouns correctly						
Edits for pronoun agreement, including pronouns that agree in number						
Edits for subject-verb agreement						
Uses appropriate verb tense						
Uses correct forms and tenses of *to be*						
Composes complete sentences						
Composes sentences with the appropriate end punctuation						
Composes sentences with interesting, elaborated subjects						
Edits writing toward standard grammar and usage in final drafts						
MECHANICS						
Uses appropriate spelling						
Uses basic punctuation correctly						
Uses basic capitalization correctly						
Uses more complex capitalization with increasing accuracy, such as for proper nouns, abbreviations, commas, apostrophes, and quotation marks						

Comments:

Key:

N = Not Observed

O = Observed Occasionally

R = Observed Regularly

© Harcourt

How to Score Writing

Teachers may use a variety of strategies to monitor children's growth as writers. You can adapt the strategies on these pages to your own teaching methods and the requirements of your school or district. Other assessment ideas are provided at point of use in the chapters, on the Assessment Strategies and Resources page at the end of each unit of this *Teacher's Edition,* and in the *Language Skills and Writing Assessment Teacher's Edition.*

USING RUBRICS

Rubrics for the teacher are provided at point of use in the Writing Workshop. Simplified rubrics for the children are provided in the Handbook in the *Pupil Edition.* You can also make photocopies of rubrics for children's use on pages R71–R76.

Work with children to add additional criteria to the rubrics. Children should refer to the rubrics before, during, and after writing. If your school or district uses a 5- or 6-point rating scale, you can use strategies like these to adapt the rubrics.

USING A 5-POINT SCALE

1	2	3	4	5
limited	basic	basic+	proficient	advanced

Use the rubric criteria for a score of 4 to evaluate the papers. Follow these steps to rank them on a 5-point scale.

1. Read through all the papers and sort them into two piles: a score of 2 (basic) and 4 (proficient).

2. Reread the 2 papers, and reconsider them. You may move some into a 3 (basic+) pile. Some papers may be below basic. Move these to a 1 pile.

3. Reread the 4 papers, and reconsider them. You may move some to the 3 pile or make a new pile with a score of 5.

After completing the steps, you should have five piles of papers to be rated 1-5.

USING A 6-POINT SCALE

1	2	3	4	5	6
limited	basic	basic+	proficient	proficient+	advanced

Use the criteria for a score of "4" to evaluate each paper. Then follow these steps to rank them on a 6-point scale: Divide the papers into three piles: below-level, on-level, and above-level. Then reread the papers in each pile and divide those into two piles. You now have six piles of papers to be rated 1-6.

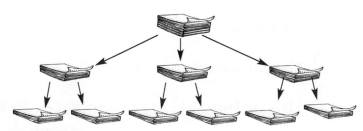

SELF-INITIATED WRITING/ONGOING ASSESSMENT

In addition to assigned writing tasks, establish expectations for self-initiated writing. Tell children that you expect them to write independently on a regular basis, choosing the topic and the form of writing themselves to develop drafts. Meet with individual children and small groups periodically to review their progress. Make one copy of the Writing Conference Checklist (page R67) for each child at each evaluation point, and use it to record your observations and plans for instruction.

The rubrics in *Harcourt Language* can be used to analyze children's work for the traits of good writing.

The Traits of Good Writing

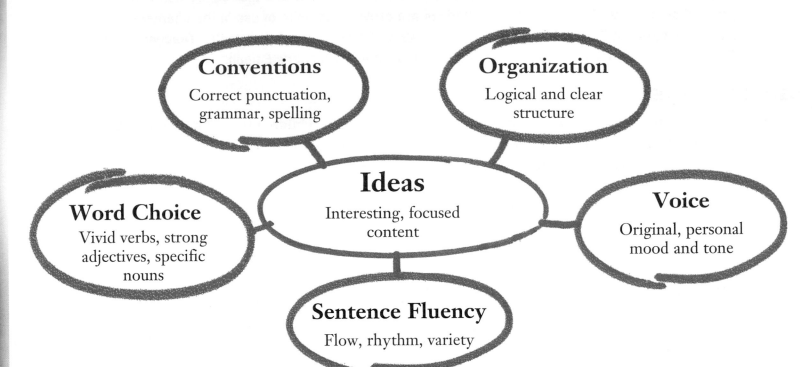

Conventions
Correct punctuation, grammar, spelling

Organization
Logical and clear structure

Word Choice
Vivid verbs, strong adjectives, specific nouns

Ideas
Interesting, focused content

Voice
Original, personal mood and tone

Sentence Fluency
Flow, rhythm, variety

Based on your assessment, target your instruction to emphasize **What Good Writers Do.**

What Good Writers Do

☑ List or draw your ideas before you write.

☑ Remember for whom you are writing and why.

☑ Use your own words.

☑ Use an order that makes sense.

☑ Use different kinds of sentences to make your writing interesting.

☑ Use exact words.

☑ Give examples.

☑ Revise your writing to make it better.

☑ Proofread for grammar, spelling, capitalization, and punctuation.

Look for:

• Writer's Craft chapters for direct instruction in strategies.

• Writing Workshop chapters for application.

Score of 4

My personal story

- tells about something that happened in my life. The events are in the correct order.
- uses the words *I, me,* and *my.*
- has many details and a title.
- has time-order words to show the order in which things happened.
- has complete sentences with capital letters and end marks.

Score of 3

My personal story

- tells about something that happened in my life.
- uses the words *I* and *me* a few times.
- has some details and a title.
- is in the order in which things happened but only has one or two time-order words.
- has a few sentences that need a capital letter in the beginning or an end mark.

Score of 2

My personal story

- tells about something that happened in my life.
- has the word *I,* a few details, and a title.
- needs time-order words to show the order in which events happened.
- needs words added to complete some sentences. Some sentences need a capital letter and an end mark.

Score of 1

My personal story

- tells about something that happened in my life. The events need to be put in the order in which they happened.
- needs details to explain things. It needs a title.
- needs words added to complete some sentences.

Try again!

© Harcourt

Score of 4

My friendly letter

- is written to someone I know. It tells about something I did.
- has a heading, a greeting, a body, a closing, and a signature.
- is clear and has many details that make it interesting.
- has complete sentences. Capital letters and commas are used correctly in all parts of the letter.

Score of 3

My friendly letter

- is written to someone I know. It tells a little about something I did.
- has at least four parts, including a greeting, a body, and a closing.
- is clear and has some details to make it interesting.
- has complete sentences. Capital letters and commas are used correctly in most parts of the letter.

Score of 2

My friendly letter

- is written to someone I know.
- has a body and at least one other part.
- needs sentences added to tell more about something I did.
- needs the parts of the letter that are missing. I need to use capital letters and commas correctly.

Score of 1

My friendly letter

- is written to someone I know.
- has a body, but no other parts.
- needs the parts of the letter that are missing. I need to use capital letters and commas correctly.

Try again!

©Harcourt

Score of 4

My story
- has a title and a beginning, a middle, and an ending.
- has a problem that the story characters solve.
- has exact words and details that help the reader understand the story events.
- has dialogue to show how the characters feel.
- nouns and verbs are used correctly together. They agree.

Score of 3

My story
- has a beginning, a middle, and an ending, but no title.
- has a problem, but it is not clear whether the characters solve it.
- has some exact words and details.
- a few sentences need the noun or verb fixed so that they agree.

Score of 2

My story
- is missing one of these parts: beginning, middle, ending. It does not have a title.
- is unclear. It is not clear whether the characters solve the problem.
- has only a few details.
- some sentences need the noun or verb fixed so that they agree.

Score of 1

My story
- is missing a beginning or an ending. It does not have a title.
- needs a problem for the characters to solve.
- needs sentences, exact words, and details added so that the reader can understand the story.

Try again!

©Harcourt

Score of 4

My paragraph that describes

- tells how something looks, sounds, smells, feels, or tastes.
- has a sentence that tells the main idea. It has enough detail sentences to explain the main idea.
- has colorful words that help the reader see what I am describing.
- has complete sentences and is indented.

Score of 3

My paragraph that describes

- tells how something looks. It needs to tell more about how it sounds, smells, feels, or tastes.
- has a sentence that tells the main idea. It has some detail sentences that tell about the main idea.
- has complete sentences and is indented.

Score of 2

My paragraph that describes

- needs to tell more about how something looks, sounds, smells, feels, or tastes.
- has a sentence that tells the main idea and one or two detail sentences.
- needs more detail sentences and more adjectives.
- needs to be indented. Some sentences need a capital letter or an end mark.

Score of 1

Try again!

My paragraph that describes

- does not describe something.
- has a sentence that tells the main idea. It needs more detail sentences that tell about the main idea.
- needs adjectives added to tell how something looks, sounds, smells, feels, or tastes.

©Harcourt

Score of 4

My how-to paragraph

- tells what the main idea is, lists the materials first, and tells the steps to follow.
- gives the steps in order. It uses time-order words to make the order clear.
- has exact words and enough details.
- has complete sentences and is indented.

Score of 3

My how-to paragraph

- has a sentence that tells what the main idea is and the steps to follow. It is missing the list of materials.
- gives the steps in order. It has some time-order words.
- has some exact words and some details.
- has complete sentences and is indented.

Score of 2

My how-to paragraph

- tells the steps to follow. It is missing the sentence that tells the main idea and the list of materials.
- gives the steps in order. It needs time-order words to make the order clearer.
- needs words added to complete some sentences.

Score of 1

My how-to paragraph

- is missing the sentence that tells the main idea and the list of materials.
- needs the steps put in order. It needs time-order words.
- needs words added to complete sentences.

Try again!

© Harcourt

Score of 4

My research report

- is about only one topic. Each paragraph has a sentence that tells a main idea about the topic.
- has many details. It has a title.
- is about something that is true.
- has each paragraph indented. The sentences are complete and clear.

Score of 3

My research report

- is about only one topic. Most paragraphs have a sentence that tells a main idea about the topic.
- has some details. It has a title.
- is about something that is true.
- has each paragraph indented. The sentences are complete.

Score of 2

My research report

- is about only one topic. Each paragraph needs a sentence to tell a main idea about the topic.
- needs more details to explain the main ideas.
- is about something true. It needs a title.
- needs each paragraph indented.

Score of 1

Try again!

My research report

- is about only one topic. It needs more than one paragraph.
- needs to have a sentence to tell the main idea in each paragraph.
- needs detail sentences to explain each main idea.

© Harcourt

Thinking About My Listening, Speaking, and Viewing

Child:_____ Date:_____ Grade:_____

What I spoke about, listened to, or viewed _____

When I speak,

I use words that my audience will understand.

I speak clearly and look at my audience.

I speak loudly and slowly before a group.

I use objects and movements to help show what I mean.

I answer questions that my audience asks.

I use good grammar.

I use words that describe my ideas and feelings.

When I listen,

I pay attention.

I picture in my mind what the speaker is saying.

I ask questions if I don't understand or want to know more.

I take notes and follow directions.

When I view,

I think about the art or photograph's message.

I describe what I see.

© Harcourt

Thinking About My Writing

Child:_____ Date:_____ Grade:_____

What I wrote _____

When I write,

I think about for whom I am writing and why.

I list or draw my ideas.

I use an order that makes sense.

I write complete sentences.

I indent my paragraphs.

I use different kinds of sentences.

I use exact words.

I give examples.

I use colorful words.

I revise to make my writing better.

I proofread for spelling, capitalization,

   and punctuation.

I use good handwriting.

I do this well. _____

I need to work on this. _____

© Harcourt

Thinking About My Grammar

Child:_____ Date:_____ Grade:_____

What I talked about or wrote _____

When I write or speak,

I use nouns correctly. ☺ 😐 ☹

I use pronouns correctly. ☺ 😐 ☹

I use adjectives correctly. ☺ 😐 ☹

I use adverbs correctly. ☺ 😐 ☹

I use complete sentences. ☺ 😐 ☹

I combine short sentences into longer ones. ☺ 😐 ☹

I use correct capitalization and punctuation when I write. ☺ 😐 ☹

I use correct spelling when I write. ☺ 😐 ☹

I correct what I say or write. ☺ 😐 ☹

I do this well.

_____

_____

_____

I need to work on this.

_____

_____

_____

© Harcourt

Have children make a frame shape book to publish **sentences about a picture**. Children can duplicate the pattern on colorful paper to make a book cover. Children can decorate the frame and attach a drawing inside. Duplicate the frame pattern on paper for the book pages. Punch holes in the top of the frame and use yarn or wire twists to secure the pages.

© Harcourt

Have children make a self-portrait to publish a **personal story**. Duplicate the pattern on paper for children to color or add features to make the person look like himself or herself. Paste the portrait on paper to create a book cover. Add a scene to show the main idea of the story. Staple the story pages to the cover. The portrait can also be mounted on tagboard to make a stick puppet for storytelling, or enlarge the pattern for children to make self-shape books.

© Harcourt

Have children make a fold-out card to publish a **thank-you note**. Duplicate the pattern on paper. Have children cut out the pattern and fold on the solid lines as marked. Then they pull the pie shape down into the folded card. Children can write the thank-you note inside and decorate, glue the card inside a construction-paper cover, and decorate the outside of the card. The thank-you message will pop up when the card is opened.

Have children make fold-and-post stationery to publish a **friendly letter**. Duplicate the pattern on colorful paper. Children can cut out the stationery, write a letter, and color the pencil, if desired. Then they fold the letter in half using the dots as a guide, fold down the pencil flap, and seal with a sticker. Children address the front of the letter, add a stamp, and mail.

© Harcourt

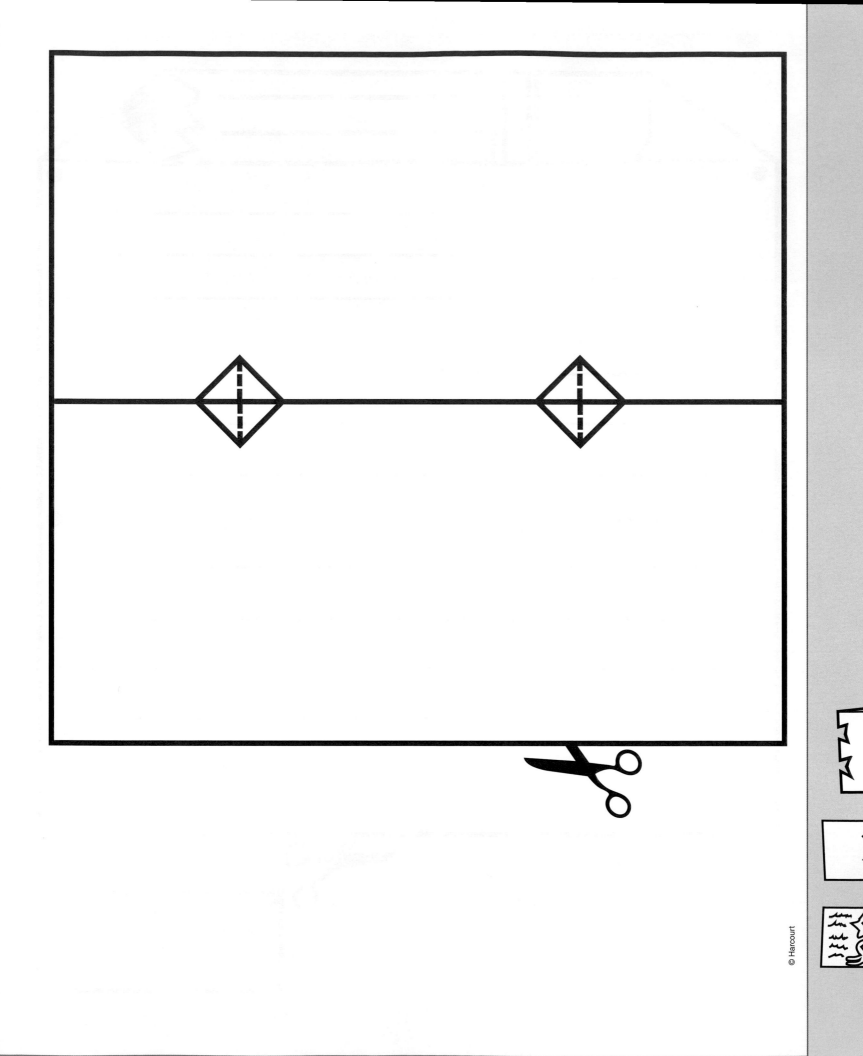

Have children make a talking book to record **dialogue** between two characters or write a **story**. Duplicate the pattern on paper. Have children cut out the pattern and fold on the center line. They can cut along the two short dotted lines, fold back the two flaps by each cut and then fold the flaps inside to make two mouths. Then they can draw a character head for each mouth and glue the characters inside another sheet. The front (and back) of this sheet is for the dialogue.

© Harcourt

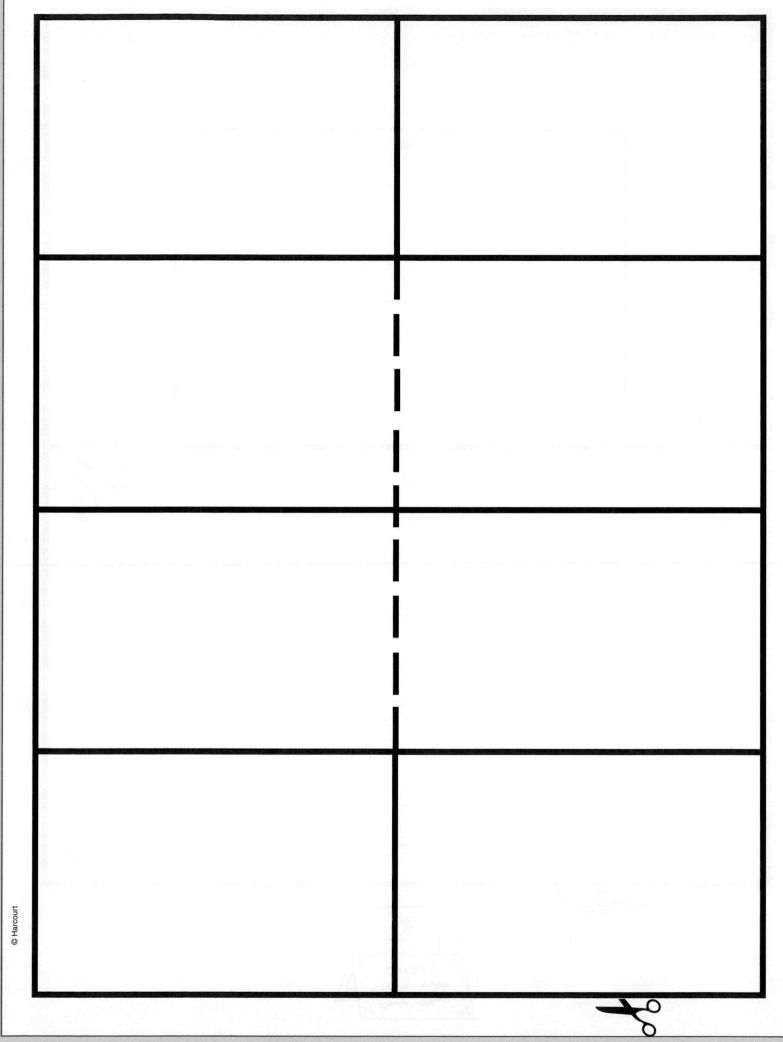

Have children make a fold-it book to publish a **story**. For a mini-book, duplicate and have them cut out the pattern. Model how to fold the pattern in half as shown and cut along the dotted line. Open the pattern and refold lengthwise. Push in the sides, fold over, and crease to make an eight-page booklet. Use the pattern as a model to make any size larger book.

© Harcourt

Have children make a stand-up book to publish a **poem**. Duplicate the pattern and have children cut it out. Children can write their poem on the bottom half. Then they draw a picture to accompany the poem within the dotted lines on the top half. Push the point of a pencil into the dotted lines to make a hole. Carefully push a scissor blade through the hole to cut along the dotted lines. Fold back to make the picture/poem stand.

© Harcourt

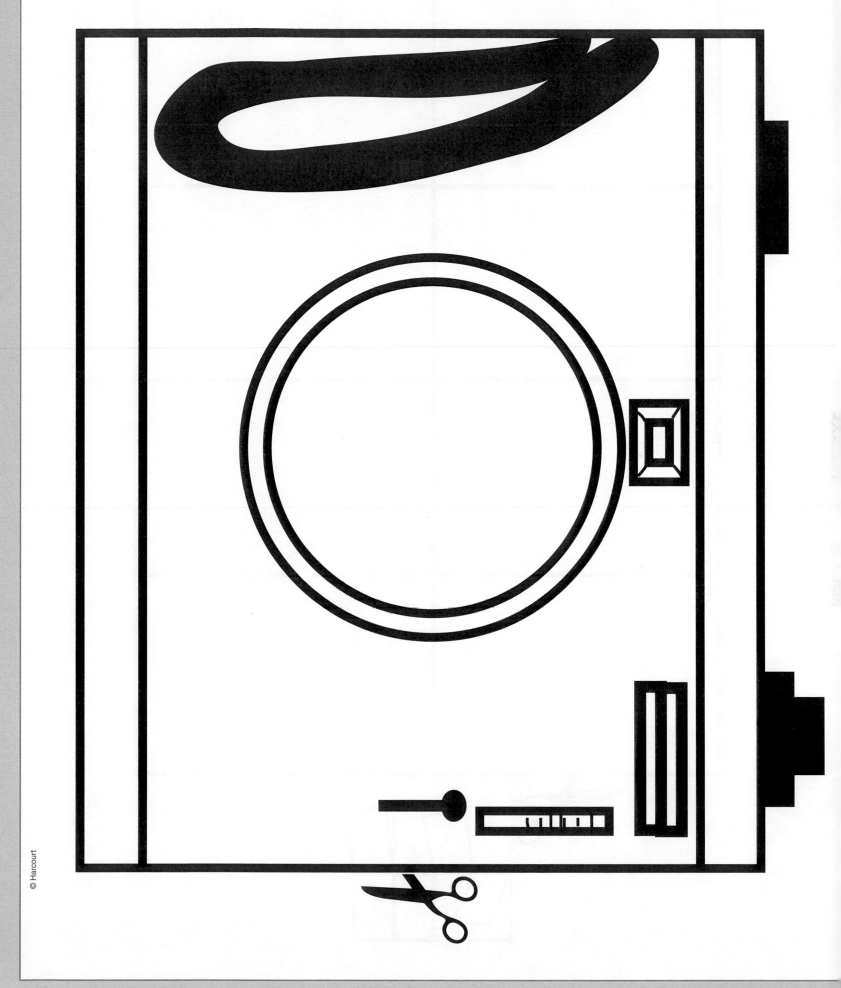

Children can make a camera-shaped book to publish a **paragraph that describes**. Duplicate the pattern on colorful paper for the cover. Children attach a drawing or photograph of the subject inside the lens. Trace and cut out camera-shaped paper for the book pages. Compile the pages and staple at the top.

© Harcourt

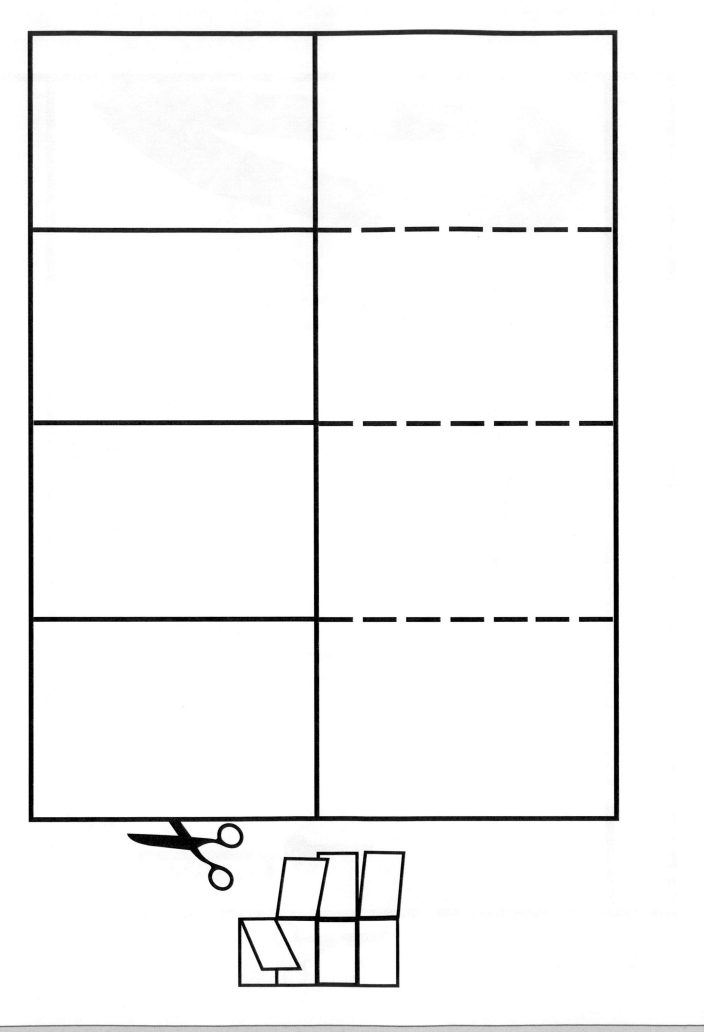

Children can make a flap book to publish **directions**. Duplicate the pattern on paper, or use a full sheet of blank paper. Cut out the pattern and along the three dotted interior lines. Fold each flap down. Write the title at the top of the first flap. Write one step on each flap. Lift the flap and draw a picture to show the step. For more than four steps, tape two patterns together.

© Harcourt

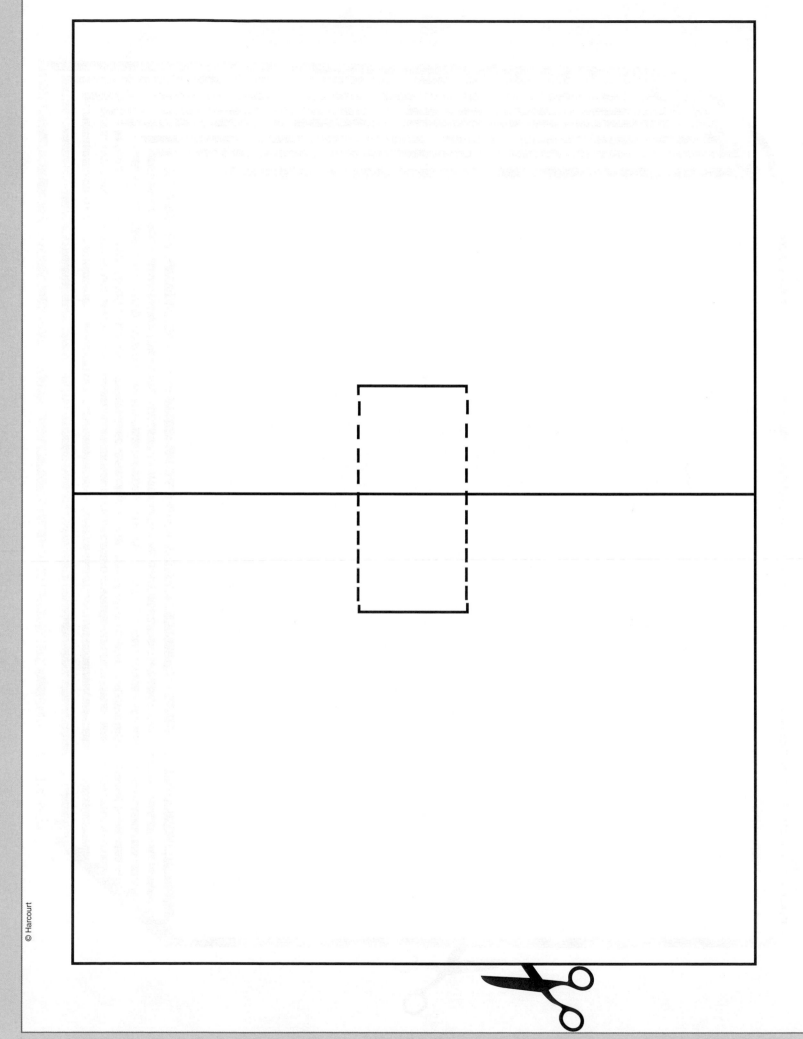

Have children make a pop-up book to publish a **how-to paragraph**. Copy the pattern onto paper. Fold the paper in half and cut long the dotted lines. Help children push the cut area through the fold. Then crease along the solid lines to form the pop-up box. Glue the pop-up page inside blank, folded paper. Have children record the how-to on the blank pages and attach to the front of the pop-up. Children draw a picture and glue to the pop-up box inside.

© Harcourt

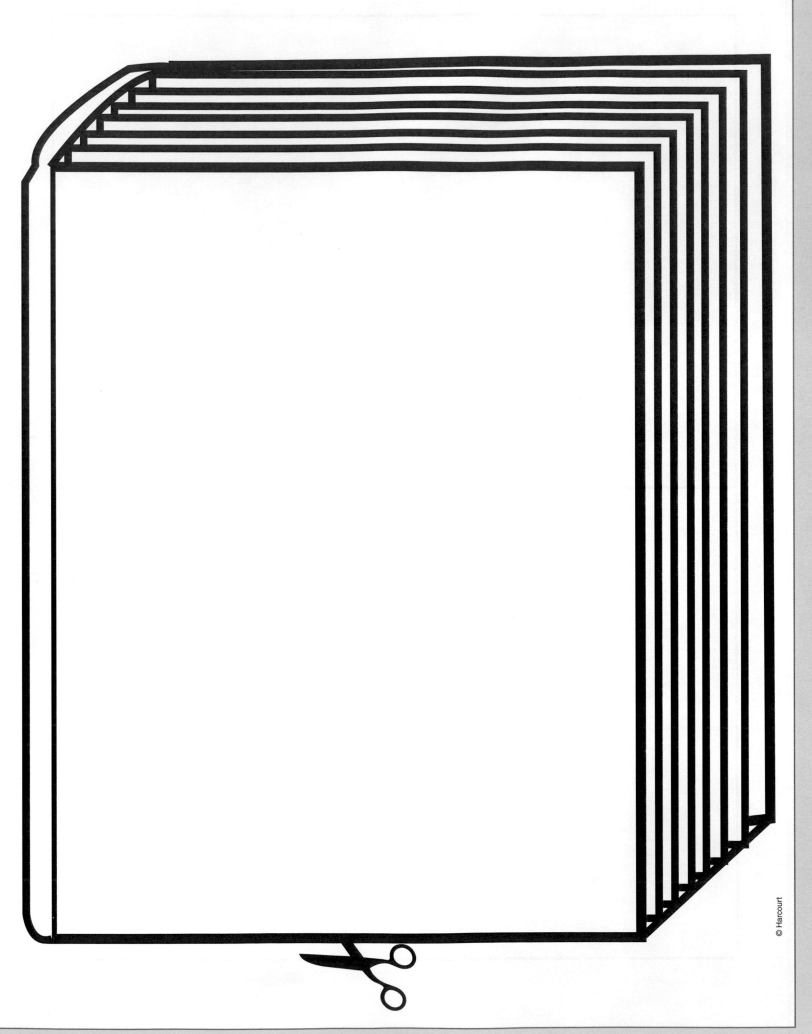

Have children make a shape book to publish a **book report** or **research report**. Duplicate the pattern on colorful paper to make a cover. Cut out. Compile with other pages and staple together. Children decorate the book cover and write final drafts of reports inside.

© Harcourt

Have children make an interlocking stand-up book to publish a **research report**. Duplicate the pattern on tagboard or follow the pattern to make a larger book. Cut out the pattern and fold on the center line. Cut slits for tabs to lock additional panels together as shown. Have children glue paper to each panel to record the report and to draw illustrations. To display, stand up the book as shown.

© Harcourt

Handwriting

Individual children come to second grade with various levels of handwriting skills, but they all have the desire to communicate effectively. To use correct letter formation, they must be familiar with concepts of

- **straight and curved lines.**
- **size (tall, short).**
- **open and closed.**
- **capital and lowercase letters.**
- **letter and word spacing.**
- **punctuation.**

The lessons in *Harcourt Language* build on these concepts in both formal and informal handwriting lessons so that children develop the skills they need to become independent writers.

To assess children's handwriting skills, review samples of their written work. Note whether children use correct letter formation and appropriate size. Note also whether children follow the conventions of print such as correct capitalization and punctuation. Encourage children to proofread and edit their work and to use editing marks. When writing messages, notes, and letters, or when publishing their writing, children should leave adequate margins and indent new paragraphs to help make their work more readable for their audience.

STROKE AND LETTER FORMATION

The shape and formation of letters taught in *Harcourt Language* are based on the way experienced writers write their letters. Most manuscript letters are formed with a contin-uous stroke, so children do not often pick up their pencils when writing a single letter. Models for manuscript, cursive, and D'Nealian Handwriting are used in this program to support different writing systems.

POSITION FOR WRITING

Establishing the correct posture, pencil grip, and paper position for writing will help prevent handwriting problems.

POSTURE Children should sit with both feet on the floor and with hips to the back of the chair. They can lean forward slightly but should not slouch. The writing surface should be smooth and flat and at a height that allows the upper arms to be perpendicular to the surface and the elbows to be under the shoulders.

WRITING INSTRUMENT An adult-sized number-two lead pencil is a satisfactory writing tool for most children. However, use your judgment in determining what type of instrument is most suitable for a child, given his or her level of development.

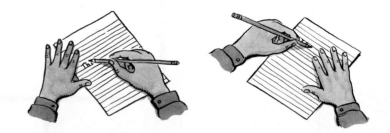

PAPER POSITION AND PENCIL GRIP The paper is slanted along the line of the child's writing arm, and the child uses his or her nonwriting hand to hold the paper in place. The child holds the pencil slightly above the paint line—about one inch from the lead tip.

REACHING ALL LEARNERS

The best instruction in handwriting builds on what children already know and can do. Given the tremendous range in children's writing abilities, a variety of approaches may be needed.

EXTRA SUPPORT For children who need more practice keeping their handwriting legible, one of the first and most important understandings is that print carries meaning and that writing has real purpose. Provide many opportunities for writing in natural settings. For example, children can

- make a class directory listing names and phone numbers of their classmates.
- record observations in science.
- draw and label maps, pictures, graphs, and picture dictionaries.
- write and post messages about class assignments or group activities.

ESL Children learning English as a second language can participate in meaningful print experiences. They can

- write signs, labels for centers, and messages.
- label drawings.
- contribute in group writing activities.
- write independently in journals.

CHALLENGE To ensure continued rapid advancement of children who come to second grade writing fluently, provide

- exposure to a wide range of reading materials.
- opportunities for independent writing on self-selected and assigned topics.

The handwriting strand in *Harcourt Language* teaches correct letter formation, letter and word spacing, and provides a variety of opportunities to help children become fluent, confident writers. Materials and activities include handwriting lessons in the *Pupil's Edition* and handwriting models in the *Pupil's Edition Handbook*.

School-Home Connection

Your child has begun Unit 1 in *Harcourt Language*.

In this unit your child will learn more about sentences, write sentences about a picture, and write a personal story. Your child will also practice several study skills, including using the parts of a book and alphabetical order. In addition, your child will learn more about using a computer.

You may enjoy doing the following activities with your child. You and your child can enrich his or her language skills by working together.

Photo Captions

Look through a collection of family photos or pictures cut out from magazine ads and articles with your child. Talk about the subjects and events pictured. Then have your child write a sentence about the pictures. Read the sentences together. Ask questions like these: What comes at the end of the sentence? What are the different parts of this sentence?

EVERYDAY WRITING ACTIVITY

Look through the weekly supermarket ads with your child, and discuss what you need to purchase. Have your child cut out the names of several items, arrange them in alphabetical order, and copy them to make an alphabetized grocery list.

It Happened to Me!

Think about your last family outing. Brainstorm what happened with your child. Then help your child write a personal story to tell about it. After you have finished, read it aloud. Have your child decide whether all the sentences relate to the topic and whether some could be combined with *and*.

Interview

Look through a magazine or newspaper to find an interview. Read it aloud with your child. Then take turns to role-play interviewer and interviewee based on what you read. Discuss the different kinds of sentences you used such as questions, statements, and exclamations.

© Harcourt

Visit *The Learning Site!* www.harcourtschool.com

School-Home Connection

Your child has begun Unit 2 in *Harcourt Language.*

In this unit your child will learn more about nouns and pronouns, write a thank-you note, and write a friendly letter. Your child will also practice several study skills such as finding words in a dictionary. Your child will also learn more about sending e-mail.

You may enjoy doing the following activities with your child. You and your child can enrich his or her language skills by working together.

Noun of the Day

Each day look with your child for interesting nouns that name people, places, animals, or things. You might find some in the newspaper, in ads, on TV, at school, or at work. Add each noun to a list on the refrigerator. Have your child color-code the nouns by underlining them with different colors such as red for nouns that name people, or green for nouns that name animals. Try to use the nouns in your conversation.

Words at Your Fingertips

Keep a pocket dictionary in the kitchen. You and your child can use it to check on unfamiliar words that come up in conversation, on the radio, or on TV. Discuss the meaning of each word, then have your child write the word and an example to make a personal dictionary.

EVERYDAY WRITING ACTIVITY

Help your child write a thank-you note to a family member for a special outing or gift. Have your child make a drawing or a collage on one side of the note. Then write the note together, address the envelope, apply postage, and mail the note.

Thank You for the Things You Do

If you have a home computer with Internet access, help your child send an e-mail message to a friend or relative. You can also send e-mail on computers at your local library. Ask the reference librarian for assistance as needed.

Visit *The Learning Site!* www.harcourtschool.com

© Harcourt

School-Home Connection

Your child has begun Unit 3 in *Harcourt Language*.

In this unit your child will learn about verbs, will write dialogue, and will write a story. Your child will also practice several study skills including using a dictionary entry and learning how to take a test. Your child will also learn how to use a computer to edit.

You may enjoy doing the following activities with your child. You and your child can enrich his or her language skills by working together.

Character Quotes

Talk with your child about a favorite story or television show. Work together to make up a dialogue between two of the characters. Help your child write the dialogue. Then act it out together.

Tell Me a Story

Take turns telling family stories at the dinner table or on car trips. Children are very interested in hearing what life was like when you were young. Have children tell their own stories or retell yours from a different point of view. Then discuss the verbs you and your child used. Ask questions like these: Does this verb tell about something that happened in the past? Does it tell about now? How would you spell it?

> When I was seven...

Look through a family photo album with your child. Work together to pick a photograph you like. Brainstorm with your child about what happened, who was there, what people were doing, and what the occasion was. Then write a story about it. Be sure your child writes verbs that tell about the past correctly. You may want to put the picture in the story or illustrate it before sharing with other family members.

Dictionary Game

Play a game with your child and family members to guess the meaning of unusual words. Write the words with the possible definitions on paper slips. Read each one aloud. Have each person guess if the meaning is correct. Then look up the word in a dictionary to check the meaning.

lasso: a rope

© Harcourt

Visit **The Learning Site!**
www.harcourtschool.com

School-Home Connection

Your child has begun Unit 4 in *Harcourt Language*.

In this unit your child will learn more about adjectives, will write a poem, and will write a paragraph that describes. Your child will also practice several study skills including using a thesaurus, using pictographs, and using bar graphs. Your child will also learn more about using spell-check on a computer.

You may enjoy doing the following activities with your child. You and your child can enrich his or her language skills by working together.

What It's Like

Play a guessing game in which you and your child take turns using adjectives to describe pets, family members, and household objects. Each person must try to guess who or what is being described.

spotted
furry
noisy
short

© Harcourt

A Poet, Don't You Know It?

Have your child choose a topic for a poem. Then together, brainstorm some colorful words that describe it best. Have your child use some of the words to write a poem and share it with the family.

My Best Friend

EVERYDAY WRITING ACTIVITY

Look through catalogs or newspaper and magazine ads to compare items such as CD players, computers, or clothes you would like to buy. Have your child use adjectives to write comparisons. Use the information to decide which items are the best buys.

One computer is cheaper.
The other is faster.

Pictograph It

Have your child make a pictograph or a bar graph of things that you have observed together such as animals or cars in the neighborhood, sports you watch or play, or fruits and vegetables the family eats in a week. Help your child label the graph as needed.

Sports We Played This Week:				
Hockey				
Skiing				
Basketball				

Visit *The Learning Site!*
www.harcourtschool.com

School-Home Connection

Your child has begun Unit 5 in *Harcourt Language*.

In this unit your child will learn more about using verbs, such as helping verbs, and using adverbs. Your child will write directions, write a how-to paragraph, practice study skills including using the library, reading a newspaper, and using a map. Your child will also learn more about computer graphics.

You may enjoy doing the following activities with your child. You and your child can enrich his or her language skills by working together.

Verbs

Play "Simon Says" with family members, using the verbs *come, run, give, go, do,* and *see* as you give directions. After listeners follow each set of directions, talk about the verb that "Simon" used. Ask if each verb tells about now or about the past. Ask how you would need to change the verb to make it tell about the past.

Simon says run in a circle.

EVERYDAY WRITING ACTIVITY

Have your child write simple directions for a task he or she will perform alone such as feeding a pet, or cleaning up his or her room. Have your child list the materials and use time-order words to write the steps in order. Read and discuss the paragraph together.

How to feed Peppy.
1. ~~~~~
2. ~~~~~
3. ~~~~~

Mapmaker, Mapmaker

Take a walk with your child around your neighborhood. Help your child draw a map of the places you walked. You might help him or her use symbols to show houses, apartments, stores, parks, and so on.

What's New

Look through a newspaper with your child and talk about its different parts. Show your child how to use the index to locate different sections such as the weather, the television schedule and the comics.

© Harcourt

Visit *The Learning Site!*
www.harcourtschool.com

School-Home Connection

Your child has begun Unit 6 in *Harcourt Language*.

In this unit your child will learn more about usage problems, will write a book and will write a research report. Your child will also practice study skills including using a telephone book and using an atlas. Your child will learn more about using a computer to get information.

You may enjoy doing the following activities with your child. You and your child can enrich his or her language skills by working together.

Two Thumbs Up

Have your child pretend to be a reporter reviewing a TV show or a movie you watched together. Encourage your child to use pronouns to give plot highlights and to explain positive and negative things about the movie or show.

Travel Agent Atlas

Plan a real or an imaginary vacation by flipping through an atlas. Talk with your child about some of the features you would like to find in a vacation spot such as a beach, a city, or mountains. Then find out how the atlas represents those features.

EVERYDAY WRITING ACTIVITY

Help your child create a family phone book. It may be written by hand or on the computer. Be sure to list local emergency numbers, and the phone numbers of relatives, neighbors, and family friends. Show your child how to use information in a published phone directory to create your own family version.

Police	911
Fire/Ambulance	911
Uncle Allen	~~
Pat keegan	~~
Dr. knight	~~
Vet's office	~~

Bowl of Words

On small slips of paper, write the names of family members and the pronouns *I, you, he, she, it, we, they*. Place the papers in a bowl. Then write verbs on slips of paper and place them in another bowl. Have your child pick one slip from each bowl and use the words to write sentences. Check to make sure the subjects and verbs agree in number. Keep adding new verbs during the week.

Tanya swims in the lake.

© Harcourt

Visit *The Learning Site!*
www.harcourtschool.com

PREWRITING
Sequence Chart

First

What is this personal story about? What happened?

↓

Next

What happened next?

↓

Last

What happened at the end?

© Harcourt

PREWRITING
Web

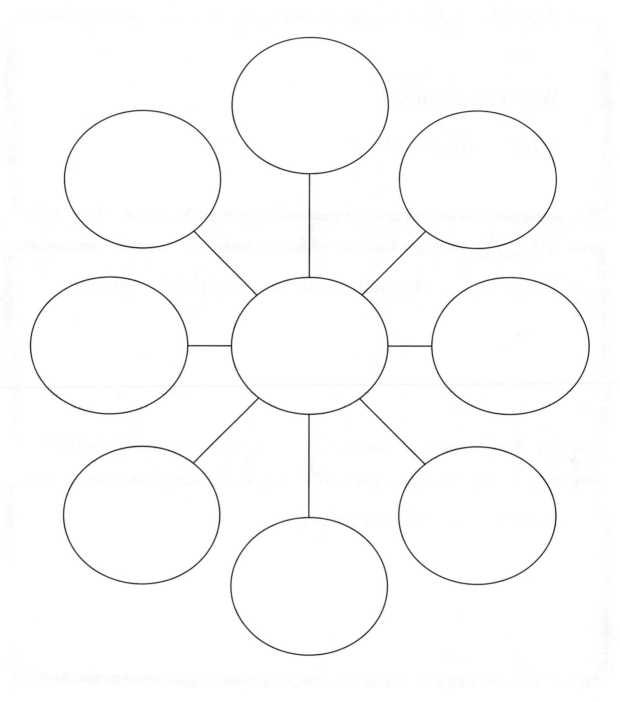

© Harcourt

PREWRITING
Story Map

Beginning

Who?

When and where?

What is the problem?

Middle

What do the characters do to solve the problem?

Ending

How is the problem solved?

© Harcourt

Sentence Strips

Photocopy the page, cut apart the strips, and distribute them to children. One or more sentences can be distributed at a time. You may also need to distribute blanks and punctuation marks. Children can cut the strips apart into cards and can write replacement words on the backs of cards for some activities. Have them use the cards to practice and reinforce word order and other grammatical concepts with activities such as the following:

SENTENCES

- rearrange words in an order that makes sense
- rearrange words to change a statement to a question
- change the sentence type by adding, replacing, or rearranging words
- identify the correct end mark
- combine sentences with the same subjects using *and*
- combine two related sentences using *and*

NOUNS

- replace nouns with different nouns
- replace singular nouns with plural nouns and change the verb to agree
- replace common nouns with proper nouns, and vice versa
- replace general nouns with more exact nouns

PRONOUNS

- replace nouns with pronouns, and vice versa
- use *I* and *me* in the correct positions
- change the pronoun and then change the verb to agree

VERBS

- replace a present-tense verb with a past-tense verb
- combine sentences with the same predicates using *and*
- replace common verbs with more interesting verbs
- change the subject and then change the verb to agree
- replace verbs with a contraction with *not*

ADJECTIVES AND ADVERBS

- add or remove adjectives or adverbs
- replace common adjectives or adverbs with more vivid ones
- experiment with changing the order of two adjectives

The dog played with the ball .

Will Matt give Jimmy the book ?

What a huge dinosaur bone that is !

Please put on your seat belt .

A frog jumps onto the rock .

Two cats climb up the tree .

Boys and girls read their books .

I brush my teeth and go to bed .

They will visit Grandma in July .

She waves to my friend and me .

© Harcourt

He mixes yellow and blue paint .

Last week she painted the fence .

Yesterday we raced to school .

That bug has round , green wings .

We saw an elephant and some bears .

I saw shells , fish , and crabs .

Boys , girls , and parents are at the park .

Carlos is older than his brother .

The owl flies to the tallest tree .

They're going to New York , too .

.	?	!	,	"	"	,	.

© Harcourt

Vocabulary Power Cumulative List

action
adult
advise
agreement
ambassador
anchored
angrily
anteater
anthem
appetizing
attached

beasts
beings
bellow
bolt
brightest
bronco
burrow

capture
category
cattail
cave
chairperson
circular
clutch
cocoons
coil
communicate
confer
connected
connection
considerate

consulting
contribution
converse
correspondence
countless
countryside
courteous
cowhand
creatures
critters
croak
cycle

dawdle
delicious
delve
demonstrate
dignified
direct
disagreement
disharmony
display

e-mail
endless
entirely
explored

fabulous
family
fantastic
farmland
fastened
field

flavorful
flicker
flutter
folk song
formal
frayed

glossiest
grab
gracefully
grasp
groundhog
guided

harmony
hasty
hoot
hungrily

illustrate
infinite
inquire
interact
intercom
interleaf
international
internet

jingle

lair
larvae
lasso

led
linger
lodge
lullaby
luscious

mannerly
marvelous
mayor
meadow
memo
message
mockingbird
model
mostly

noble
noisily

observe
officer
orbit

partly
pasture
pigtail
playfully
plunge
polite
post
prediction
present
president
pupa

quest
quicker
quiver

ragged
rapid
rattlesnake
recommend
recount
recycled
regal
rethink
retrace
review
revolving
rodeo
roost
royal

saddle
savory
scamper
seize
serenade
shaggy
shiver
similar
sleekest
smoothest
species
specimen
speedily
spinning

spiral
splendid
sputter
starfish
steer
stingray
superb
swiftest
swirl

tattered
taught
thoughtful
togetherness
totally
transportation
turtleneck
twirl
twist

uneven
united
unlimited

varmints
vast

warble
whirl
wholly

yowl

Cross-Curricular Connections

Chapter	The Arts						Health						Social Studies						Science				
	Art About People	Art Nearby	Art You Use	Children and Art	Express Yourself	How Artists See	Community and Environmental Health	Disease/Drug/Injury Prevention	Emotional, Intellectual, and Social Health	Family Life, Growth, and Development	Nutrition	Personal Health and Physical Fitness	Being a Good Citizen	Our Neighbors Near and Far	People Make History	We All Work Together	We Belong to Many Groups	Where We Live	Exploring Earth's Surface	Exploring Matter/Energy in Motion	Homes for Living Things	Living Things Grow and Change	Space and Weather
1				•	•																		
2												•											
3																					•	•	
4										•		•				•					•		
5										•	•	•											
6					•				•														
7										•						•							
8																					•		
9														•									
10							•			•			•	•									
11				•	•																	•	
12									•					•									
13																					•	•	
14												•										•	
15																							
16	•				•																•		•
17															•						•	•	
18									•														
19		•				•				•													
20			•																		•		
21																							
22																•							•
23																			•				
24																					•	•	
25					•					•													
26														•				•					
27								•									•						
28		•		•	•	•	•						•			•							
29		•														•							
30			•							•													
31										•				•							•		•
32																					•		
33																							
34												•				•					•	•	•
35																							
36																			•			•	

Theme Connections

Chapter	Being Me!	Community Involvement	Creative Expression	Creativity	Good Days	Happy Times	Helping Hands	Here and There	Imagine That!	Journeys in Time and Space	Learning and Working	Managing Information	Myself and Others	Neighborhood News	New Friends	New Worlds	Our World	Personal Voice	Problem-Solving	Teamwork	The World Around Us	Traditions	Travel Time	Wishes
1	●												●					●						
2	●				●								●					●						
3	●												●					●						
4	●				●			●					●					●						
5	●							●					●					●						
6	●					●							●					●						
7							●				●									●				
8							●	●		●	●									●			●	
9							●				●							●		●				
10	●						●				●	●						●		●		●		
11							●				●									●				
12					●		●				●			●						●				
13												●					●				●			
14																	●				●			
15																	●				●			
16																	●				●			
17									●			●					●				●			
18					●												●				●			
19			●	●					●															
20			●	●					●															
21			●	●					●															
22			●	●					●															
23			●	●	●				●															●
24			●	●					●															
25		●			●			●					●								●			
26		●						●					●											
27		●		●				●					●											
28		●	●					●					●											
29		●						●					●						●					
30		●						●					●						●					
31										●						●							●	
32										●						●			●				●	
33										●						●				●		●	●	
34	●		●	●				●		●		●				●		●					●	
35								●		●					●	●							●	
36										●		●				●							●	

THEME CONNECTIONS R109

Scope and Sequence

	GR K	GR 1	GR 2	GR 3	GR 4	GR 5
Grammar						
Sentences		•	•	•	•	•
Declarative Sentence		•	•	•	•	•
Interrogative Sentence		•	•	•	•	•
Exclamatory Sentence			•	•	•	•
Imperative Sentence			•	•	•	•
End Punctuation			•	•	•	•
Sentence Structure		•	•	•	•	•
Simple Sentence		•	•	•	•	•
Compound Sentence				•	•	•
Complex Sentence					•	•
Word Order in Sentences		•	•			
Sentence Parts		•	•	•	•	•
Complete Subject				•	•	•
Simple Subject			•	•	•	•
You (understood)				•	•	•
Compound Subject				•	•	•
Complete Predicate				•	•	•
Simple Predicate			•	•	•	•
Compound Predicate			•	•	•	•
Independent Clauses					•	•
Dependent Clauses					•	•
Phrases					•	•
Direct Object						•
Nouns		•	•	•	•	•
Singular Nouns		•	•	•	•	•
Plural Nouns		•	•	•	•	•
Irregular Plural Nouns			•	•	•	•
Possessive Nouns			•	•	•	•
Common and Proper Nouns		•	•	•	•	•
Verbs		•	•	•	•	•
Action Verbs		•	•	•	•	•
Helping Verbs		•	•	•	•	•
Linking Verbs				•	•	•
Regular Verbs		•	•	•	•	•
Irregular Verbs			•	•	•	•
Verb Contractions			•	•	•	•
Verb Tenses		•	•	•	•	•
Present Tense		•	•	•	•	•
Past Tense		•	•	•	•	•
Future Tense				•	•	•
Present-Perfect Tense						•
Past-Perfect Tense						•
Future-Perfect Tense						•

Shaded Area Explicit Instruction/Modeling/Application • Tested

	GR K	GR 1	GR 2	GR 3	GR 4	GR 5
Adjectives		•	•	•	•	•
Common Adjectives		•	•	•	•	•
Proper Adjectives				•	•	•
Articles			•	•	•	•
Comparison with Adjectives			•	•	•	•
Adverbs			•	•	•	•
Adverbs of Place			•	•	•	•
Adverbs of Time			•	•	•	•
Adverbs of Manner			•	•	•	•
Adverbs of Degree			•	•	•	•
Comparison with Adverbs				•	•	•
Pronouns		•	•	•	•	•
Subject Pronouns		•	•	•	•	•
Object Pronouns			•	•	•	•
Possessive Pronouns			•	•	•	•
Reflexive Pronouns						•
Pronouns and Antecedents			•	•	•	•
Prepositions					•	•
Prepositional Phrases					•	•
Negatives				•	•	•
Avoiding Double Negatives				•	•	•
Conjunctions				•	•	•
Coordinating Conjunctions				•	•	•
Subordinating Conjunctions					•	•

Usage and Mechanics

Sentences

	GR K	GR 1	GR 2	GR 3	GR 4	GR 5
Avoid Sentence Fragments and Run-on Sentences				•	•	•
Punctuation and Capitalization	•	•	•	•	•	•
Avoid Run-ons, Fragments			•	•	•	•

Nouns

	GR K	GR 1	GR 2	GR 3	GR 4	GR 5
Abbreviations			•	•	•	•
Plural Forms			•	•	•	•
Appositives					•	•

Verbs

	GR K	GR 1	GR 2	GR 3	GR 4	GR 5
Subject-Verb Agreement			•	•	•	•
Forms of *Be*		•	•	•	•	•
Commonly Misused Verbs			•	•	•	•
Contractions with *Not*			•	•	•	•
Forms of Irregular Verbs			•	•	•	•
Choosing Correct Tense			•	•	•	•

Adjectives

	GR K	GR 1	GR 2	GR 3	GR 4	GR 5
Articles			•	•	•	•
Comparative and Superlative Adjectives		•	•	•	•	•

Adverbs

	GR K	GR 1	GR 2	GR 3	GR 4	GR 5
Comparative and Superlative Adverbs				•	•	•
Distinguish Between Adverbs and Adjectives				•	•	•
Avoiding Double Negatives				•	•	•

Pronouns

	GR K	GR 1	GR 2	GR 3	GR 4	GR 5
Subject Pronouns			•	•	•	•
Object Pronouns			•	•	•	•
Possessive Pronouns			•	•	•	•
Reflexive Pronouns						•
Pronoun-Antecedent Agreement			•	•	•	•

	GR K	GR 1	GR 2	GR 3	GR 4	GR 5
Troublesome Words and Commonly Confused Words			•	•	•	•
Capitalization						
Sentence Beginning	▒	•	•	•	•	•
Pronoun *I*			•	•	•	•
Proper Nouns (Names, Days, Months, Holidays, Titles, Initials)	▒	•	•	•	•	•
Proper Adjectives				•	•	•
Direct Quotations and Dialogue			•	•	•	•
Greetings and Closings of Letters, Addresses			•	•	•	•
Punctuation						
Indentation				•	•	•
Period	▒	•	•	•	•	•
To End Sentences	▒	•	•	•	•	•
In Titles and Abbreviations			•	•	•	•
Question Mark	▒	•	•	•	•	•
Exclamation Point	▒	•	•	•	•	•
Comma			•	•	•	•
In a Series			•	•	•	•
In Letter Parts	▒	▒	•	•	•	•
In Dates and Addresses			•	•	•	•
Compound Sentences				•	•	•
After Introductory Words or Phrases				•	•	•
In Direct Quotations			▒	•	•	•
In Direct Address				•	•	•
With Appositives						•
With Dependent Clauses					•	•
Underlining				•	•	•
Apostrophe			•	•	•	•
In Contractions			•	•	•	•
In Possessive Nouns			•	•	•	•
Quotation Marks		▒	•	•	•	•
Colon				•	•	•
Hyphen					•	•
Writing						
Composition/Writing Process						
Approaches to Writing (Shared, Interactive, Guided; Timed; Writing to Prompts)	▒	▒	▒	▒	▒	▒
Analyze published models		▒	▒	▒	▒	▒
Prewriting	▒	▒	▒	▒	▒	▒
Brainstorming	▒	▒	▒	▒	▒	▒
Gathering Information; Taking Notes		▒	▒	▒	▒	▒
Lists	▒	▒	▒	▒	▒	▒
Graphic Organizers	▒	▒	▒	▒	▒	▒
Logs and Journals		▒	▒	▒	▒	▒
Consider Audience and Purpose	▒	▒	▒	▒	▒	▒
Drafting	▒	▒	▒	▒	▒	▒
Use Graphic Organizers		▒	▒	▒	▒	▒
Organize and Categorize Ideas; Elaboration		▒	▒	▒	▒	▒
Editing/Revising	▒	▒	▒	▒	▒	▒
Add, Delete, Combine, and Rearrange Text	▒	▒	▒	▒	▒	▒
Elaboration		▒	▒	▒	▒	▒
Coherence; Progression; Logical Support		▒	▒	▒	▒	▒

▒ Shaded Area — Explicit Instruction/Modeling/Application   • Tested

	GR K	GR 1	GR 2	GR 3	GR 4	GR 5
Editing/Proofreading	■	■	■	■	■	■
Spelling		■	■	■	■	■
Grammar	■	■	■	■	■	■
Punctuation	■	■	■	■	■	■
Usage	■	■	■	■	■	■
Features of Polished Writing		■	■	■	■	■
Correct Sentence Fragments; Run-ons; Comma Splices			■	■	■	■
Publishing	■	■	■	■	■	■
Refine Selected Pieces			■	■	■	■
Oral Presentation		■	■	■	■	■
Printed	■	■	■	■	■	■
Multimedia			■	■	■	■
Performance/Dramatic Interpretation	■	■	■	■	■	■
Select and Use Reference Materials for Writing, Revising, and Editing			■	■	■	■
Use Technology to Create, Revise, Edit, and Publish Texts		■	■	■	■	■
Writer's Craft/Strategies						
Identify Audience and Purpose		■	■	■	■	■
Personal Voice, Writer's Viewpoint			■	■ •	■ •	■ •
Organizing Information		■	■	■ •	■ •	■ •
Effective Sentences: Opening Sentences, Combining Sentences, Sentence Variety			■ •	■ •	■ •	■ •
Elaboration; Reasons and Details; Developing Ideas; Staying on the Topic			■ •	■ •	■ •	■ •
Paragraphing; Topic Sentence and Details			■	■ •	■ •	■ •
Word Choice: Vivid Words, Sensory Details, Description, Figurative Language	■	■	■ •	■ •	■ •	■ •
Appropriate Language; Tone	■	■	■	■	■	■
Capture Reader's Interest			■	■	■	■
Sequence; Transitions	■	■	■	■	■	■
Writing Purposes						
Informative/Expository Writing	■	■ •	■ •	■ •	■ •	■ •
Expressive/Narrative Writing	■	■ •	■ •	■ •	■ •	■ •
Persuasive Writing			■	■ •	■ •	■ •
Cross-Curricular Writing (Art/Creativity, Health, Science, Social Studies)	■	■	■	■	■	■
Forms of Writing						
Informative/Expository			■ •	■ •	■ •	■ •
Paragraph that Compares				■	■	■
Paragraph that Contrasts				■	■	■
Compare/Contrast Essay; Advantages/Disadvantages Essay				■ •	■ •	■ •
Paragraph of Information				■	■	■
Directions			■	■	■	■
How-to Essay, How-to Paragraph	■	■ •	■ •	■ •	■ •	■ •
Business Letters				■	■	■
News Story			■	■	■	■
Research Report			■ •	■ •	■ •	■ •
Summaries			■	■	■	■
Morning Message	■					
Expressive/Narrative Writing			■ •	■ •	■ •	■ •
Story, Folktale		■ •	■ •	■ •	■ •	■ •
Descriptive Paragraph	■	■ •	■ •	■	■	■
Personal Narrative, Self-Portrait	■	■	■ •	■ •	■ •	■ •
Personal Journal			■	■	■	■
Play			■	■	■	■
Poetry			■	■	■	■
Character Study				■	■	■

	GR K	GR 1	GR 2	GR 3	GR 4	GR 5
Persuasive Writing				•	•	•
Friendly Letter	▓	•	•			
Business Letter						
Letter to the Editor						
Persuasive Essay				•	•	•
Everyday Writing						
Advertisements, Pamphlets, Posters	▓					
Captions, Labels, Titles	▓					
E-mail, Messages	▓					
Forms						
Invitations, Thank-you Notes						
Journals	▓					
Name		▓	▓			
Note Taking	▓	▓				
Recipes						
Surveys						

Reading Comprehension/Strategies

	GR K	GR 1	GR 2	GR 3	GR 4	GR 5
Apply Prior Knowledge; Predict/Preview	▓	▓	▓	▓	▓	▓
Author's Purpose			▓	▓	▓	▓
Cause-Effect			▓	▓	▓	▓
Main Idea and Details: Descriptive, Important, Supporting	▓	▓	▓	▓	▓	▓
Draw Conclusions			▓	▓	▓	▓
Evaluating/Making Judgments			▓	▓	▓	▓
Making Inferences			▓	▓	▓	▓
Sequencing Events/Summarize	▓	▓	▓	▓	▓	▓
Use Text Structure and Format			▓	▓	▓	▓

Vocabulary

	GR K	GR 1	GR 2	GR 3	GR 4	GR 5
Language of School (colors, numbers, position words)	▓	▓				
Synonyms/Antonyms; Connotation/Denotation		▓	▓	▓	▓	▓
Multiple-Meaning Words; Homophones/Homographs		▓	▓	▓	▓	▓
Context Clues		▓	▓	▓	▓	▓
Glossary/Dictionary (for Word Meaning)		▓	▓	▓	▓	▓
Word or Phrase Origins (Acronyms, Brand Names, Clipped and Coined Words, Regionalisms, Etymology, Jargon and Slang, Euphemisms)				▓	▓	▓
Classifying/Categorizing; Comparing/Contrasting	▓	▓	▓	▓	▓	▓
Analogies			▓	▓	▓	▓
Prefixes, Suffixes, Derivatives		▓	▓	▓	▓	▓
Greek and Latin Roots				▓	▓	▓

Listening and Speaking

	GR K	GR 1	GR 2	GR 3	GR 4	GR 5
Respond/React to a Variety of Literature and Spoken Messages	▓	▓	▓	▓	▓	▓
Listen for Purpose (enjoyment, information, vocabulary development, directions, problem solve, main idea and details, fact and opinion, recognize persuasion techniques/bias, plan an activity, take notes)	▓	▓	▓	▓	▓	▓
Interpret Speakers' Verbal and Nonverbal Messages, Purposes, and Perspectives				▓	▓	▓
Eliminate Barriers to Effective Listening				▓	▓	▓
Participate in Conversations, Discussions, Small Groups, Cooperative Groups; Ask and Answer Questions	▓	▓	▓	▓	▓	▓
Listen Critically to Interpret and Evaluate		▓	▓	▓	▓	▓
Develop/Acquire Vocabulary	▓	▓	▓	▓	▓	▓
Identify Rhyme, Repetition, Patterns, Musical Elements of Language	▓	▓	▓	▓	▓	▓
Ask for Repetition, Restatement, or Explanation to Clarify Meaning		▓	▓	▓	▓	▓
Participate in Storytelling, Drama, Music, Poems, Stories	▓	▓	▓	▓	▓	▓
Discuss and Compare/Contrast a Variety of Texts	▓	▓	▓	▓	▓	▓

Shaded Area Explicit Instruction/Modeling/Application • Tested

	GR K	GR 1	GR 2	GR 3	GR 4	GR 5
Reenact, Retell, Dramatize, Role Play Literature Read or Heard	●	●	●	●	●	●
Communicate Experiences, Ideas, Opinions with Others; Clarify or Support Ideas with Evidence	●	●	●	●	●	●
Use Appropriate Rate, Volume, Pitch, Tone	●	●	●	●	●	●
Adapt Spoken Vocabulary to the Purpose, Audience, and Occasion to Describe, Inform, Communicate, Persuade	●	●	●	●	●	●
Read or Retell Stories Orally with Expression, Phrasing, Intonation, Comprehension	●	●	●	●	●	●
Present Oral Reports or Speeches, Conduct Interviews or Surveys		●	●	●	●	●
Clarify/Support Spoken Messages with Props		●	●	●	●	●
Give and Follow Oral Directions		●	●	●	●	●
Viewing and Representing						
Enjoy and Discuss a Variety of Illustrations and Illustrators	●	●	●	●	●	●
Analyze the Purposes and Effects of Illustrations, Visuals, Media	●	●	●	●	●	●
Discuss Illustrator's Choices of Techniques and Media	●	●		●	●	●
Analyze the Way Visual Images, Graphics, and Media Represent, Contribute to, and Support Meaning	●	●	●	●	●	●
Interpret Information from Maps, Charts, Tables, Diagrams, Graphs, Timelines, Media, Illustrations	●	●	●	●	●	●
Select, Organize, Produce Visuals to Complement and Extend Meaning	●	●	●	●	●	●
Use Available Technology or Appropriate Media to Communicate Information and Ideas; to Compare Ideas, Information, Viewpoints	●	●	●	●	●	●
Compare and Contrast Print and Electronic Media	●	●		●	●	●
Research/Study Skills/Inquiry						
Use Study Strategies to Learn and Recall Important Ideas from Text (KWL, SQ3R, Note Taking, Reading Rate, Skim/Scan, Outline)	●	●	●	●	●	●
Follow and Give Directions		●	●	●	●	●
Test-Taking Strategies		●	●	●	●	●
Frame, Identify, Revise Questions for Inquiry		●	●	●	●	●
Select and Use Pictures, Print, People, Media, Multiple Sources, Alphabetical Order to Gather Information and Answer Questions		●	●	●	●	●
Library, Media Center, Card Catalog, Databases, Search Engines, Media		●	●	●	●	●
Almanac, Atlas, Dictionary, Electronic Text, Encyclopedia, Globe, Telephone Directory, Thesaurus, Synonym Finder, Books in Print		●	●	●	●	●
Maps, Charts, Graphs, Diagrams, Timelines, Tables, Schedules, Calendars		●	●	●	●	●
Book Parts and Text Organizers (Title Page, Table of Contents, Indices, Chapter Titles, Headings, Graphic Features, Guide Words, Entry Words, Bibliography, Glossary, Footnotes, Marginal Notes)		●	●	●	●	●
Summarize and Organize Information to Present Findings			●	●	●	●
Outline, Map, Web, Cluster, Venn Diagram, Chart, Table, Time Line		●	●	●	●	●
Displays, Murals, Dramatizations, Oral Reports, Written Reports, Projects, Posters, Speeches			●	●	●	●
Evaluate and Document Information and Research		●	●	●	●	●
Handwriting and Spelling						
Apply Spelling Generalizations and Spelling Strategies	●	●	●	●	●	●
Letter Forms (Manuscript, Cursive)	●	●	●	●	●	●
Elements	●	●	●	●	●	●
Posture, Paper Position	●	●	●	●	●	●
Writing Utensils/Pencil Grip	●	●	●	●	●	●
Directionality/Stroke	●	●	●	●		●

Reviewers

Joan Y. Ashley
Teacher
Salisbury, NC

Pamela J. Beaver
Teacher
Dana, NC

Carolyn Warren Bennett
Lead Teacher
Newton Grove, NC

Pearle B. Collins
Success For All Facilitator
Houston, TX

Barbara Cummings
Teacher
Arlington, TX

Andrea Currier
Teacher
Towson, MD

Brenda D. Ford
Writing Resource Teacher
Chicago, IL

Barbara Haack
Teacher
Des Moines, IA

Deborah S. Hardesty
Teacher
Evansville, IN

Valerie Johse
Teacher
Pearland, TX

Mary Beth Kreml
Instructional Technology Teacher
Klein, TX

Ms. Esther Lauderman
Teacher
Williamstown, WV

Anita Layton
Teacher
Houston, TX

Katherine V. Lee
Teacher
Indianapolis, IN

Frances Martinez
Teacher
El Paso, TX

Majestra McFadden
Language Arts Supervisor
East St. Louis, IL

Gwendolyn D. Mills
Lead Teacher
Houston, TX

Barbara Minnich
Teacher
New Albany, IN

Thelma Muñoz
Teacher
Corpus Christi, TX

Dorothy W. Nolan
Curriculum Specialist
Omaha, NE

Valerie J. Reeves
Teacher
Katy, TX

Betty B. Rickman
Teacher
Horse Shoe, NC

Maureen McLaughlin Scott, Ph.D.
Language Arts Coordinator
Monroe, CT

Cecile Smith
Teacher
Camden, NJ

Linda Smolen
Director of Reading
Buffalo, NY

Amy Tapp
Teacher
Ft. Wayne, IN

Ms. Dominga A. Vela
Principal
Edinburg, TX

Index

KEY
✔ = Tested

Index

adding *s* or *es* to verbs, 172–173

changing verbs that end with *e*, 184–185

changing *y* to *i*, 402–403

commonly misspelled words, R10

contractions, 404–408

plural nouns, 106–114

strategies, R10

Correlation matrices, R108–R109

Critical thinking, 45, 48, 73, 74, 76, 117, 120, 145, 191, 194, 220, 222, 224, 262, 263, 266, 294, 296, 342, 367, 368, 370, 372, 411, 414, 442, 444

Cross-curriculum writing, 92, 164, 238, 310, 386, 458

art connection, 119, 193, 265

health connection, 368

math connection, 47, 146, 220, 370

music connection, 148

science connection, 45, 238, 263, 292, 294, 310, 411, 440, 458

social studies connection, 76, 92, 164, 191, 222, 339, 415

technology connection, 442

Cumulative review

units 1-2, 166–167

units 1-4, 312–315

units 1-6, 460–465

Customizing Instruction, xx–xxi

Daily language practice and proofreading, 24, 26, 28, 30, 32, 34, 36, 38, 40, 42, 44, 46, 48, 50, 51, 52, 54, 56, 58, 60, 62, 64, 66, 68, 70, 72, 82, 84, 86, 88, 96, 98, 100, 102, 104, 106, 108, 110, 112, 114, 116, 118, 120, 122, 123, 124, 126, 128, 130, 132, 134, 136, 138, 140, 144, 154, 156, 158, 160, 170, 172, 174, 176, 178, 180, 182, 184, 186, 188, 190, 192, 194, 196, 197, 198, 200, 202, 204, 206, 208, 210, 212, 214, 216, 218, 228, 230, 232, 234, 242, 244, 246, 248, 250, 252, 254, 256, 258, 260, 262, 264, 266, 268, 269, 270, 272, 274, 276, 278, 280, 282, 284, 286, 288, 290, 300, 302, 304, 306, 318, 320, 322, 324, 326, 328, 330, 332, 334, 336, 338, 340, 342, 344, 345, 346, 348, 350, 352, 354, 356, 358, 360, 362, 364, 366, 376, 378, 380, 382, 390, 392, 394,

396, 398, 400, 402, 404, 406, 408, 410, 412, 414, 416, 417, 418, 420, 422, 424, 426, 428, 430, 432, 434, 436, 438, 448, 450, 452, 454

Description, 205, 245, 255, 423

Details, 59, 116–122

✓**Dialogue,** 190–196

Diary entry, 99

Dictionary, using a, 115, 189

Directions, 69, 338–344, 383

Drafting, 39, 49, 84–85, 121, 156–157, 195, 230–231, 267, 302–303, 343, 378–379, 415, 450–451

Editing *See also* **Revising**

50, 122, 196, 217, 268, 344, 416

Editor's marks, 50, 86–87, 122, 158–159, 232–233, 268, 304–305, 344, 380–381, 416, 452–453

End marks.

See **Punctuation**

Envelope, R8

ESL, 21E, 26, 28, 30, 36, 38, 40, 45, 49, 54, 56, 58, 64, 66, 68, 76, 89, 93E, 98, 100, 102, 108, 110, 112, 117, 118, 126, 128, 130, 136, 138, 140, 148, 161, 167E, 172, 174, 176, 182, 184, 186, 192, 200, 202, 204, 210, 212, 214, 222, 235, 236, 239E, 244, 246, 248, 254, 256, 258, 263, 265, 272, 274, 276, 282, 284, 286, 294, 303, 308, 311, 315E, 320, 322, 324, 330, 332, 334, 348, 350, 352, 358, 360, 362, 370, 376, 378, 387E, 392, 394, 396, 402, 404, 406, 413, 420, 422, 424, 430, 432, 434, 440, 459, 460

Examples, giving, 410–416

✓**Exclamations,** 63–68, 70

Extra practice, R2–R7

adjectives, 248, 258, 276, 286

adverbs, 362

nouns, 40, 102, 112, 130, 140

pronouns, 140, 396

sentences, 30, 58, 424

subject-verb agreement, 406

troublesome words, 434

verbs, 176, 186, 204, 214, 324, 334, 352

Fiction books, 365

Fluency, sentence. *See* **Sentence fluency**

Formal assessment.

See **Assessment, formal**

✓**Friendly letter,** 144–160, 187, R9

Gifted and talented students.

See **Reaching all learners, challenge**

Grammar/mechanics/usage.

See also **Capitalization; Conventions**

adjectives, 242–261, 270–288

adverbs, 356–364

and, 38–39, 174–176, 322–324, 420–421

apostrophe, 100–101, 404–405

capital letters, 28–29, 124–133

commas, 322–323, 332–333, 422–423

end punctuation, 27–31, 54–55, 58, 60, 63–70, 88

nouns, 96–114, 390–398

plural forms of nouns, 106–114

singular forms of regular nouns, 98, 99, 102

pronouns, 134–142, 390–398

he, she, it, they, 136–137

I, me, 138–139, 394–398

pronoun agreement, 136–142, 392, 396

word order for, 394–395

quotation marks, 190–196

sentence composition, 39, 40, 41, 47, 55, 75, 99, 103, 111, 118, 119, 139, 141, 187, 193, 203, 211, 215, 243, 244, 245, 246, 247, 248, 250, 259, 265, 273, 275, 276, 277, 321, 324, 331, 349, 359, 362, 363, 435

sentences, complete, 26, 27, 28, 29, 30, 31, 37, 55, 59, 65, 99, 103, 131, 139, 141, 187, 205, 211, 215, 245, 333, 334, 335, 361, 363, 407, 413, 425, 431, 433, 449

Index

KEY
✔ = Tested

Index

ask relevant questions in small or large group discussions, 25, 89, 210, 383, 455

contribute in small or large group discussions, 24, 25, 29, 33, 46, 52, 54, 56, 58, 62, 63, 67, 68, 71, 72, 77, 78, 96, 100, 103, 106, 107, 108, 110, 113, 115, 120, 124, 126, 134, 135, 136, 138, 140, 176, 180, 182, 184, 186, 192, 198, 199, 200, 202, 203, 204, 207, 210, 212, 214, 242, 243, 244, 245, 246, 248, 252, 254, 255, 256, 257, 258, 261, 264, 270, 271, 272, 273, 274, 275, 276, 279, 322, 324, 330, 332, 334, 335, 337, 338, 346, 348, 350, 353, 357, 366, 371, 390, 391, 393, 399, 400, 401, 402, 404, 406, 407, 409, 412, 418, 419, 420, 422, 424, 425, 427, 428, 432, 434, 438

dramatic interpretations of experiences, stories, poems, or plays, 24, 53, 62, 64, 65, 139, 170, 171, 172, 180, 187, 191, 196, 198, 208, 222, 235, 252, 254, 262, 268, 270, 277, 318, 328, 329, 346, 352, 356, 357, 358, 390, 397, 400, 401, 407, 418, 441

spoken language using appropriate audience and rate, 59, 199, 271, 307, 455

spoken language using appropriate audience and volume, 24, 59, 63, 64, 248, 249, 259, 271, 307, 346, 356, 357, 455

spoken language using appropriate occasion and rate, 64, 66, 89, 199, 212, 455

spoken language using appropriate occasion and volume, 36, 62, 63, 69, 89, 199, 248, 249, 276, 455

spoken language using appropriate purpose and rate, 59, 63, 199, 214, 242, 243, 245, 248, 256, 259, 271, 276, 356, 362, 455

spoken language using appropriate purpose and volume, 24, 34, 59, 62, 63, 64, 69, 103, 140, 182, 199, 208, 210, 214, 248, 249, 258, 259, 272, 276, 346, 356, 455

use nonverbal communication, 69, 76, 161, 307, 360, 370, 377, 383

use verbal communication, 64, 68, 161, 307, 319, 340, 344, 377, 378, 383, 433

Listening/speaking/communicating

clarify spoken messages using appropriate props such as objects, pictures, or charts, 68, 248, 279, 383, 430, 440, 442, 455

retell spoken message by clarifying, 140, 249, 329

retell spoken message by summarizing, 25, 27, 29, 53, 55, 61, 63, 65, 97, 102, 107, 109, 111, 112, 129, 135, 140, 179, 183, 185, 186, 193, 199, 201, 203, 207, 223, 224, 225, 273, 276, 307, 347, 349, 351, 352, 354, 391, 393, 395, 401, 402, 409, 418, 424, 429, 434

support spoken messages using appropriate props such as objects, pictures, or charts, 200, 205, 215, 245, 358, 370, 437, 455

use vocabulary to describe experiences, 34, 35, 72, 91, 97, 111, 139, 141, 144, 146, 172, 215, 252, 253, 319, 331, 366, 424

use vocabulary to describe feelings, 34, 192, 199, 224

use vocabulary to describe ideas clearly, 52, 58, 61, 65, 96, 102, 103, 105, 106, 111, 124, 125, 134, 135, 136, 144, 155, 179, 180, 201, 205, 208, 209, 215, 223, 244, 248, 249, 261, 263, 270, 271, 273, 290, 294, 296, 329, 341, 346, 364, 365, 372, 395, 411, 431, 433, 438, 455

Listening to literature

"Author's Day," 167K–167L

"Dinosaur Babies," 387K–387L

"Night Sounds, Morning Colors," 239K–239L

"The Perfect Spot," 21K–21L

"Wanda's Roses," 93K–93L

"Writing It Down," 315K–315L

Literature model

dialogue, 190–191

friendly letter, 144–150

how-to paragraph, 366–372

paragraph that describes, 290–296

personal story, 72–78

research report, 438–444

story, 218–224

Main idea

paragraphs and, 56–57, 350–351

of research report, 445

Map, using a, 337

Math connection, 47, 146, 220, 370

Mechanics.

See **Grammar/mechanics/usage**

Modified learning.

See **Reaching all learners**

Music connection, 148

Naming part of a sentence, 34–37

combining, 38, 420–421

Newspaper, using a, 327

Nonfiction books, 365

✔**Nouns,** 96–114

definition of, 97

noun-pronoun agreement, 392–393

for people, places, animals, and things, 96–99

plural, 106–114

possessive nouns, 100–102

pronouns, 134–142, 390–398

proper nouns, 124–132

for days, months, and holidays, 128–129

for people, places, and animals, 126–127

that name more than one, 106–111

Oral grammar

complete sentences, 24, 26, 27, 28, 30, 34, 36, 38, 40, 46, 59, 102, 103, 106, 107, 108, 112, 114, 126, 135, 136, 138, 140, 141, 180, 186, 192, 201, 202, 205, 210, 214, 215, 244, 264,

Index

KEY
✔ = Tested

Index

Index

KEY

✔ = Tested

Index

that go together, 56–57
time-order words and, 418–419
word order in, 26–27
Sequence chart, 79, 82–83
Sequencing.
See **Time-order words**
Setting, 225
Social studies connection, 76, 92, 164, 191, 222, 339, 415
Speaking.
See **Listening and speaking; Oral language development**
Spelling
adding *ed* to verbs, 182–183
adding *s* or *es* to verbs, 172–173
changing verbs that end with *e*, 184–185
changing *y* to *i*, 402–403
commonly misspelled words, R10
contractions, 404–405
plural nouns, 106–114
resources
to find correct spelling, 87, 159, 305, 381
to find replacement words, 189, 251
to find synonyms, 245, 251, 256, 257, 264
spell-check, 279
spelling connection, 87, 159, 233, 305, 381, 453
there, their, and *they're,* 430–431, 434–436
tips for, R10
to, too, and *two,* 432–436
words that sound alike, 428–436
Spoken language.
See **Listening/speaking/ audiences/oral grammar; Oral language development**
Standardized test prep, 32, 42, 60, 70, 104, 114, 132, 142, 178, 188, 206, 216, 250, 260, 278, 288, 326, 336, 354, 364, 398, 408, 426, 436
✓**Statements,** 53–55
✓**Story,** 218–234, R9
Strategies, writing, xxvii
Student handbook, R8–R16
Student models
book report, 414
dialogue, 194
envelope, R8
friendly letter, 152–153
how-to paragraph, 374–375
invitation, R8
paragraphs that describe, 298–299

personal story, 80–81
play, R8
poetry, 266
poster that persuades, R8
research report, 446–447
sentences about a picture, 48
story, 226–227
thank-you note, 120
writing directions, 342
Study skills.
See also **Test preparation tips**
ABC order, 43
atlas, 409
dictionary, 115, 189
library, 365
maps, 337
newspaper, 327
parts of your book, 33
pictographs and bar graphs, 289
spell-check, 279
telephone book, 399
test taking, 207
thesaurus, 251
Subject-verb agreement, 400–401
Suffixes, 427
Summarize/reflect
think about it, 45, 78, 117, 150, 191, 224, 263, 296, 339, 372, 411, 444
writing in journal, 25, 27, 29, 35, 37, 39, 47, 49, 51, 53, 55, 57, 63, 65, 67, 83, 85, 87, 97, 99, 101, 107, 109, 111, 117, 119, 121, 123, 125, 127, 129, 135, 137, 139, 155, 157, 161, 171, 173, 175, 181, 183, 185, 191, 193, 195, 196, 197, 199, 201, 203, 209, 213, 229, 231, 233, 243, 245, 247, 253, 255, 257, 263, 265, 267, 269, 271, 273, 281, 283, 285, 301, 303, 305, 319, 321, 323, 329, 331, 333, 339, 341, 343, 347, 349, 351, 357, 359, 361, 377, 379, 381, 391, 393, 395, 401, 403, 405, 411, 413, 415, 419, 421, 423, 429, 431, 433, 449, 451
Synonyms, 179, 251, 256
as adjectives, 256–258
definition of, 256

Technology/computer use
computer graphics, 355
editing on computer, 217

to get information, 437
sending e-mail, 143
spell-check, 279
using, 71
Technology connection, 442
Telephone book, 399
Telling part of sentence, 35–38
combining, 420–421
Test preparation tips
multiple choice, 32, 42, 60, 70, 104, 114, 132, 142, 178, 188, 206, 216, 250, 260, 278, 288, 326, 336, 354, 364, 398, 408, 426, 436
✓**Thank-you note,** 116–122
Thesaurus, 251
Time-order words, 81
sentences and, 418–419
Titles, 133
Topics, 44
Traits of writing,
See **Ideas, Organization, Voice, Word choice, Sentence fluency, Conventions**

Unit opener, 21B, 93B, 167B, 239B, 315B, 387B
Unit planner, 21C–21D, 93C–93D, 167C–167D, 239C–239D, 315C–315D, 387C–387D
Unit Wrap-up, 92, 164, 238, 310, 386, 458
Usage.
See **Grammar/mechanics/usage**

✓**Verbs,** 170–188
adding *ed* to, 182–183
adding *s* or *es* to, 172–173
adverbs, 356–364
am, is, and *are,* 198–201
changing verbs that end with *e*, 184–185
changing *y* to *i*, 402–403
combing sentences with, 174–175
come, run, and *give,* 318–324
contractions, 404–405
definition of, 171
forms of *be,* 198–206

Index

KEY
✔ = Tested

Index

Index

KEY
✔ = Tested

Acknowledgments

For permission to reprint copyrighted material, grateful acknowledgment is made to the following sources:

Caroline House, Boyds Mills Press, Inc.: *Wanda's Roses* by Pat Brisson, cover illustration by Maryann Cocca-Leffler. Text copyright © 1994 by Pat Brisson; illustration copyright © 1994 by Maryann Cocca-Leffler.

Dial Books for Young Readers, a division of Penguin Putnam Inc.: *Night Sounds, Morning Colors* by Rosemary Wells, cover illustration by David McPhail. Text copyright © 1994 by Rosemary Wells; illustration copyright © 1994 by David McPhail.

Marylin Hafner: Cover illustration by Marylin Hafner from *Writing It Down* by Vicki Cobb. Illustration copyright © 1989 by Vicki Cobb.

HarperCollins Publishers: From *Dinosaur Babies* by Kathleen Weidner Zoehfeld, cover illustration by Lucia Washburn. Text copyright © 1999 by Kathleen Weidner Zoehfeld; illustration copyright © 1999 by Lucia Washburn.

Philomel Books, a division of Penguin Putnam Inc.: *The Perfect Spot* by Robert J. Blake. Text and cover illustration copyright © 1992 by Robert J. Blake.

Susan Schulman Agency, on behalf of Vicki Cobb: From *Writing It Down* by Vicki Cobb. Text copyright © 1989 by Vicki Cobb

Simon & Schuster Books for Young Readers, an imprint of Simon & Schuster Children's Publishing Division: From *Author's Day* by Daniel Pinkwater. Copyright © 1993 by Daniel Pinkwater.

The following is the credit list for all photos used in Teacher's Edition Grade 2 Language Arts 2002:

Harcourt Photos by:

21G-H, Ken Kinzie

93G-H, Ron Kunzman

167G-H, Ken Kinzie

239G-H, Greg Leary

315G-H, Ron Kunzman

The following is the credit list for all illustrations used in Teacher's Edition Grade 2 Language Arts 2002:

Ethan Long: Gr 2, TE: 31, 55, 63, 69, 97, 103, 121, 177, 181, 203, 245, 259, 272, 309, 334, 368, 389, 392, 393, 403, 405, 407, 409, 417.

The following is the credit for cover illustrations used in Teacher's Edition Grade 2 Language Arts 2002:

Leland Klanderman